THE SAVE &
RUGBY UNION WHO'S WHO
1996/97

The best of both worlds:
Scotland's Gregor Townsend (below) and New Zealand's Christian Cullen.

PREFACE

MICHAEL LYNAGH and Philippe Sella, two of rugby's greatest names, signing for unfashionable London side Saracens and agreeing to play at a non-league football club; internationals queuing up to leave the front line and play English 2nd-division rugby; Rugby League players being given the red-carpet treatment at Twickenham; League and Union agreeing to share players and facilities; Union selling out to satellite television; and Harlequins, one of the most famous clubs in all the sport, renaming itself NEC Harlequins of London. Welcome to the professional era.

> ### *Rugby Union Who's Who*
> ### survey of international rugby players
>
> **Q:** *Do you really want to be a full-time professional rugby player?*
> **A:** Yes – 49%. No – 41%. Undecided – 10%.
>
> **Q:** *Do you have a duty to entertain now rugby is a professional sport?*
> **A:** Yes – 83%. No – 17%.
>
> **Q:** *Marks out of ten for rugby's handling of the move to professionalism?*
> **A:** Six or more – 35%. Five or less – 65%.

Rugby Union has undergone a metamorphosis since the decision, taken on 26 August 1995 by the International Rugby Football Board, to throw the game open. And if the leading players have not noticed too much difference in terms of the commitment demanded by the sport, then the rewards for that commitment have, not before time, changed out of all recognition. Ben Clarke, the England back-row man, no longer plays amateur rugby for Bath and England. He now receives in the region of £40,000 for his efforts on the international stage, and is to pick up an estimated £150,000 (the first of five annual installments) from newly affluent Richmond.

Not that the players have been altogether impressed with the administrators' handling of the switch from amateur game to professional sport. A *Rugby Union Who's Who* poll found that 65 per cent of players quizzed gave the sport's bosses less than six out of ten for their efforts. Scott Hastings, Scotland's most-capped player, asked if he could give minus figures, while erstwhile England captain Will Carling awarded one out of ten. Harlequins and England team mate Jason Leonard, who gave a big, fat zero, shared the view of many who found fault with the speed of change. 'It should have been a gradual process', he commented. 'Instead the rugby world has been shaken upside down.'

Still, I could not find one top-flight player who yearned for a return to the old ways. And the fact remains that if you don't like it, you are free to drop down the ladder to find a rung commensurate with your ambition or your principles. For all the surgery to the game in the past 12 months, 95 per cent of rugby union remains the same as it ever was.

This is not to say that fears for the future are not well founded, nor to pretend that every player in the uppermost echelon wants to sign his life away to rugby. Indeed, the *Rugby Union Who's Who* reveals this to be far from the case. Of those players questioned as to whether they really want to become full-time professional players, less than 50 per cent replied in the affirmative.

Many felt that breathing rugby day-in, day-out would drive them stark raving mad. Ben Clarke said: 'It's important to have a degree of professionalism for your game to improve, but not full-time rugby. I still want an outside interest in the business world.' Whether he has any choice in the matter, now he is a paid employee, is quite another matter.

The majority seek the best of both worlds – a reflection of the uncertainty pervading the game at present. The rugby, in England certainly, was no better, yet all of a sudden there were sugar daddies coming out of the woodwork to throw money at the sport. By the end of the campaign, English clubs had signed up French, Welsh, Australian, Scottish and Irish internationals. And the other Home Unions were having to offer significant loyalty payments to try and stem the haemorrhage of talent.

For all the riches promised, the players are absolutely right to exercise caution. What if they give up their jobs in favour of rugby, only for the new professional game to bellyflop? What longer-term guarantees do they have? What if the likes of Rupert Murdoch, Sir John Hall, Ashley Levett and Nigel Wray suddenly decide they can get a better return from their investments elsewhere? Where would that leave the sport?

That said, it is incumbent on the players to make the most of this opportunity – to do their utmost to sell the sport to the uncommitted. As Lawrence Dallaglio succinctly put it: 'We are competing for the public's leisure pound, so we absolutely have to provide an attractive product.' For all Jack Rowell's protestations, the truth was that supporting England last season was more an ordeal than a pleasure. Likewise much of the nation's club rugby. And that was before coverage of the all-running, all-handling Super-12 tournament exploded onto our screens and really showed up the Northern Hemisphere game.

Rugby Union in the Southern Hemisphere, for so long an alien game off the park in the way regulations were interpreted, now bears little resemblance on the field of play either. Broadly speaking it is a dynamic entertainment experience which has yet to be replicated in Europe. Anyone doubting this is referred to the management of the Welsh and Scottish tourists, who recently returned, soundly beaten, from Australia and New Zealand respectively. 'We must learn from the lessons on and off the field', said Wales manager Terry Cobner after his side's 2–0 series defeat at the hands of the Wallabies. 'The system that Wales is part of is not challenging the players' ability.' Scott Hastings, Scotland's most-capped player, echoed the sentiments. 'We have got to learn the lessons of what is happening in the Southern Hemisphere, and take it home and make the game change,' he said, after a 2–0 series loss to the All Blacks.

The indications are that Home Union players are ready to take those lessons on board. After a season of often mind-numbing rugby, there is a strong desire to spice up the game. According to our poll, a massive 83 per cent of players questioned acknowledge that they have a duty to entertain – to play enterprising, 15-man rugby. 'It is an attitude of mind which the Southern Hemisphere have long had and which we quickly have to get into', identified Scotland flanker Ian Smith. His skipper Rob Wainwright was amongst those to point out that because spectators have long paid to watch, the duty to entertain has always been there.

Wales captain Jonathan Humphreys observed, 'Our pay is dictated by bums on seats.' And even the goalkickers could not argue with that. 'People do not come to see guys kick penalty goals', admitted Scotland's Mike Dods. 'It is no longer acceptable to win 3–0', added Ireland fly-half David Humphreys, while England wing Jonathan Sleightholme said: 'We must look to win with style, because if we enjoy what we are doing the fans will enjoy it was well.' Will Carling sided with the minority when he expressed the truism that the primary duty of a professional player is 'to win.' But England fly-half Paul Grayson couched it in more diplomatic language: 'The way the game is going, you will have to play an 'entertaining' Super-12 brand of rugby if you want to be successful.'

England failed to entertain in 1995/96 but still retained their Five Nations crown. By contrast, Scotland did entertain, though one suspects because it suited their personnel rather than because they wanted to be aesthetically pleasing on the eye. Wales also decided a more dynamic style suited the players at their disposal. But all in all, with France yet again flattering to deceive, and Ireland once again under-achieving, it was predominantly a championship to forget.

Yet, paradoxically, the season will live long in the memory. Change is never painless, and it was fascinating to compare and contrast how each country responded to the demands of rugby's brave new world. This year's *RUWW* takes an in-depth look at the impact professionalism has had in each of the Big Eight nations (pages 13–131) through the eyes of some of the sport's most respected observers. Dan Retief chronicles the happenings in South Africa, land of the world champions; Greg Campbell and Wynne Gray analyse events in Australia and New Zealand – whilst Ian Borthwick, Mark Jones, Robert Cole and Neil Drysdale report from the Five Nations.

That is only a portion of the fare offered. There is comprehensive statistical coverage of the extraordinary Super-12 tournament (page 139), of Wales' and Scotland's summer tours 'Down Under' (page 132), of the 1995 World Cup (page 193), and of every other major international engagement which took place between May 1995 and June 1996 (page 164). There are profiles of the world's best players (those capped since the start of last summer's World Cup), complete with opinions, between pages 203 and 462; those not to be found there will be residing in the Appendix (page 463). Newcomers to the Test arena are logged, in chronological order, on page 201, while those dismissed during national service are listed in the Hall of Shame on page 200.

As the game grows in stature, so does the list of people to whom I am indebted for their assistance in the compilation of this book. As usual, it is the players to whom I extend the greatest thanks. I had feared that professionalism might have spawned prima donnas not wishing to talk unless their palms were crossed with gold. This most emphatically has not been the case and I am delighted about that. The players have been as generous to me with their time as they have long been to their sport.

Elsewhere, gratitude goes to my team of correspondents – the IRFB and the Big Eight unions: especially Jonathan Goslett and Alex Broun at SARFU, John Davidson at the SRU, Eddie Cripps at the RFU and Jean-Louis Barthes at the FFR; Bill Cotton and *Programme Publications*; Stuart Barnes, Chris Hewitt and Jackie Maitland at *First XV* magazine; *Midi Olympique*, The Sports Business, Westgate Sports: Rob Cole, Terry Godwin, John Kennedy and Howard Evans; Michael Humphrey + Partners, Slattery PR, Julian Yeomans, *The Daily Telegraph*, *Rugby World* and *Rugby News*; and Karen, Tom, Jenny and little Ellie.

Alex Spink, June 1996

FOREWORD

PETER RONEY
Chief Executive, Save & Prosper Group

The 1995/96 season witnessed the true start of professionalism in Rugby Union. The impact of this momentous change will obviously take some time to work through, and this combined with the increasing media attention in the game, will undoubtedly present officials and players with considerable challenges in the months ahead.

The two codes are also coming more in contact. The interchange of players, the entertaining Save & Prosper Challenge between Wigan and Bath, not to mention Wigan's success in the Save & Prosper Middlesex Sevens, are all good signs for the future.

Save & Prosper are delighted to be sponsoring international rugby at Twickenham in 1996/97 for the twelfth year. I am sure we have a great season of rugby ahead at both club and international level. We wish all those involved with the game every success in the 'new world' of rugby.

Emile NTamack (left) and Jim Staples contest a high ball in Paris,
where France trounced Ireland 45–10.

REVIEW OF
THE 1995/96 SEASON

 ## ENGLAND
Alex Spink

'Progress is a nice word. But change is its motivator and change has its enemies' – John F. Kennedy

THIS WAS not a season upon which English rugby should reflect with too much pride. The record books will show that England won the Five Nations Championship for the 22nd time outright, the Triple Crown for the 19th occasion, and along the way pocketed their 57th Calcutta Cup – while away from the park the Rugby Football Union presided over the sport's transition from amateur to professional status and negotiated its richest-ever television rights contract. All true, but the means by which each of these was achieved was, almost without exception, ugly indeed.

The shadow of Jonah Lomu hung over England's campaign. Battered and bruised by their World Cup semi-final thrashing at the hands of Jonah and his All Black pals, Jack Rowell's England struggled to salvage self-confidence. Twelve months after winning the Five Nations with an exciting nine-try campaign, England mustered a miserly three this time round, yet still, somehow, retained their pre-eminence.

If England were rebuilding on the field, the English game seemed intent on self-destructing off it. The IRFB's momentous decision to throw open the game drove a wedge between England's senior clubs and the RFU, and evidently did even greater damage to the internals of the RFU.

Veiled threats had been issued by certain senior players, prior to the IRB announcement on 26 August that were they not permitted by the RFU to cash in on their talents, that they would do so anyway. With the World Rugby Corporation's Kerry Packer and Ross Turnbull circling, cheque books on hand, waiting to swoop for the disenchanted, the establishment had little choice but to acquiesce. The RFU proposed a 'seamless' game, meaning that every club in the land could

13

choose how they interpreted professionalism depending on their ambition, but the Union refused to plunge headlong into open rugby and bought itself additional time by imposing a moratorium until the season's end, during which a status quo had to be preserved.

England's senior clubs could not afford to dally, however, and immediately set about planning for an affluent future. They formed an association – English First Division Rugby Ltd (EFDR) – and issued a manifesto headlining demands for £1 million per club per season. The message basically amounted to 'Accept our demands or we will *run* (off) *with the ball* and play under someone else's jurisdiction.' Unimpressed, the sport's grass roots replied by threatening to re-impose amateurism.

Concerned that the senior minority was imposing its will on the majority, the Union's lower order revolted. A Special General Meeting in Birmingham on 14 January was abandoned amid chaotic scenes, but only after the junior majority had sprung a surprise by electing Cliff Brittle to the chairmanship of the RFU executive.

> '*I thought the word niet had gone out with the end of the Cold War. It hasn't. The RFU have re-invented it and have used it at every turn. You simply cannot carry on negotiations that way. The money required by the game to go professional won't go away*' – Sir John Hall

The RFU's senior officers had confidently anticipated their own unanimous nominee, John Jeavons-Fellows, being swept into office. Instead, by the emphatic margin of 647 votes to 332, they got the representative for Staffordshire, who resides as a tax exile on the Isle of Man. Rather than having a man considered a friend of the elite clubs, the RFU found itself being led by a champion of the county set.

Had Jeavons-Fellows received the nod, it is a fair bet that agreement would have been hastily reached with the senior clubs, rather than a break-up of the Union only narrowly being averted long after the 11th hour on 24 May, after a successful last-ditch mediating job by RFU president Bill Bishop. As it was, all hell broke loose. Brittle, insisting he had a mandate from the grass roots of the game, refused to pander to the senior clubs in any way, shape or form, so infuriating EFDR – soon to become English Professional Rugby Union Clubs Ltd (EPRUC) – that they threatened to break away if amateurism was reimposed at a second SGM on 24 March.

14

That crisis was averted with a 'Yes' vote for professionalism from junior representatives seemingly content at having had their day in the sun. Also, with the England squad having become 'part-time employees' of the RFU by signing 'player-friendly' contracts at Twickenham and agreeing a code of conduct (in return for receiving a basic £24,000 for the season and an additional £2,000 per international), progress seemed to be back on the agenda.

But the power struggle, both between clubs and RFU and within the corridors of power at Twickenham, remained unresolved and would follow the season over the horizon. EPRUC demanded all monies from new competitions (European Cup, Anglo-Welsh league etc), arguing that its clubs had to be able to afford professionalism; but while the RFU were prepared to pay the largest proportion of 'new' money to the participating clubs, they steadfastly refused to yield the whiphand.

EPRUC wanted players to have one contract, to be held by the club with a release clause for internationals, as well as the right to structure, run and administer their own competitions. It wasn't so much that the two sides disagreed, more that meaningful debate was invariably throttled at birth. The clubs accused Brittle, chairman of the RFU's negotiating team, of not being prepared to negotiate. Brittle didn't seem to care what they said, announcing that 'the soul of Rugby Union is not for sale.'

Sir John Hall, whose millions have turned Newcastle United into one of Europe's biggest football clubs and who had taken over Newcastle Gosforth RFC with similar ambitions early in the season, slammed the RFU's intransigence: 'I thought the word *niet* had gone out with the end of the Cold War. It hasn't. The RFU have re-invented it and have used it at every turn. You simply cannot carry on negotiations that way. The money required by the game to go professional won't go away.'

Relations deteriorated to such an extent that on 11 April, after a meeting at which Sir John and Brittle allegedly came close to blows, England's top 24 clubs pulled out of both the Courage League and the Pilkington Cup competitions in a blaze of fury. EPRUC chairman Donald Kerr did not lock and bolt the door to reconciliation but made it quite clear that the RFU would need to find a more dialogue-friendly spokesman than Brittle if there was not to be an 'irreconcilable break'.

Although Bill Bishop agreed to mediate, Brittle, fresh from receiving a rock-solid vote of confidence from the English Rugby Counties Association, rejected concessions offered by EPRUC. That lit the blue touchpaper. Exasperated with the RFU, EPRUC announced they had 'come to the end of the line' and recommended to its members to leave the Union. 'Negotiations have dragged on and we feel we have to bring matters to a conclusion', said Kerr.

As a last throw of the dice, Bishop called an emergency meeting of the full committee to let them, rather than just the negotiating team, hear what EPRUC had to say. It proved a masterstroke, and at 7.30pm on 24 May agreement was reached.

> *A measure of the turmoil that English rugby was in during 1995/96 was that, had Will Carling delayed his 'old farts' comment by 12 months, it might well have passed unnoticed. Moreover, the behaviour of certain figures suggested his infamous evaluation was more right than wrong*

The clubs had won the right to manage much of their own affairs, a seat at the RFU negotiating table and a 12-club League One for 1996/97; the RFU retained overall control of the game. No one would break away from anything. Now could we please get on with playing professional sport? Sadly, no. Just when the players thought the spotlight could return to their efforts, Brittle and the RFU resumed hostilities. In an attempt to sort out their £34 million overdraft and fund the clubs at the same time, the RFU controversially ended their association with the BBC and instead sold the exclusive live television rights for English rugby to British Sky Broadcasting for £87.5 million.

England's Home Union rivals were livid, insisting that through their actions the English had expelled themselves from the Five Nations Championship as from 1997, when the five-year deal commences (only time will tell if they can afford to stick to the principle on this one). Brittle slammed the deal, claiming to have been excluded from all talks relating to the contract. He called on those who had signed the contract to resign or be forced to do so, and added: 'I feel that democracy no longer prevails within the RFU.'

That was too bitter a pill to swallow for the one country to have actually thrown open the debate about professional rugby to its members. And although the RFU executive resolved, behind closed doors, to speak in future with only one voice, the wounds were still gaping as the game headed into summer recess.

A measure of the turmoil that English rugby was in during 1995/96 was that, had Will Carling delayed his 'old farts' comment by 12 months, it might well have passed unnoticed. Moreover, the behaviour of certain figures suggested his infamous evaluation was more right than wrong. Carling remains the most newsworthy rugby player in the sport, however, and probably spent more of 1995/96 on the front pages than the back. His alleged relationship with Princess Diana and the subsequent failure of his marriage provoked such media interest that, on one occasion when he turned out for Harlequins, he received a police escort.

Ironically, his off-field problems coincided with a vintage season on the pitch. While the spotlight was turned on his captaincy and his relations with Rowell as England wrestled with mediocrity, there could be no doubting his personal contribution. And when he decided to relinquish the captaincy, on his terms and at his time of choosing, the tributes poured in from a stunned nation.

England's record under Will Carling:

Opponents	P	W	D	L
France	10	8	0	2
Scotland	9	7	1	1
Wales	8	6	0	2
Ireland	8	6	0	2
Argentina	4	3	0	1
Australia	4	2	0	2
South Africa	4	2	0	2
New Zealand	3	1	0	2
Canada	2	2	0	0
Fiji	2	2	0	0
Western Samoa	2	2	0	0
Italy	1	1	0	0
Romania	1	1	0	0
USA	1	1	0	0
Total	59	44	1	14

Carling led England on 59 occasions, of which England won 44 matches and three Grand Slams, in addition to reaching the 1991 World Cup final and last four in 1995.

Ironically, his farewell match against Ireland at Twickenham was not an altogether glorious finale, as he was stretchered off in the first half after tripping over a blade of grass and landing awkwardly. Still, he ended the match hoisting the Five Nations trophy aloft, after Paul Grayson and Jonathan Sleightholme, two of England's new guard, had stuck 28 points on the Irish.

Grayson, a competent successor to Rob Andrew, contributed 64 of England's 79 points in a predominantly dreary campaign. Never before had the International Championship been won by a side scoring so few tries. Hopefully, it will never happen again either.

England's performances in beating Wales (Twickenham, 3.2.96) and then denying Scotland a Grand Slam at Murrayfield (won 18–9, 2.3.96) were lambasted by the media. 'Scotland trampled by lumbering dinosaur – England have become the most negative side in international rugby', slated *The Guardian* following the try-less Calcutta Cup clash. And that was one of the more considered opinions.

After the Wales game *The Daily Telegraph* carried a mock apology to its readers. 'In previous editions of this newspaper we reported England's intention to play a sharper and more expansive game in keeping with the lessons of the 1995 Rugby World Cup. We acknowledge unreservedly that there was no truth in these suggestions and would like to apologise for any embarrassment or distress caused.'

The youngsters brought in after the World Cup now have a season's experience under their belts, but the evidence given last summer by the performances of Australia and New Zealand, against Wales and Scotland respectively, plus the fare served up in the Super-12 tournament, suggests that for all England's success in the Northern Hemisphere, the game south of the Equator is considerably further advanced.

Will Carling collects the spoils of Five Nations glory and salutes the crowd after his final game as England captain.

ENGLAND (P12 W8 D0 L4 F278 A233)

(–)	v Argentina*	(Durban, 27.5.95)	won24–18
(–)	v Italy*	(Durban, 31.5.95)	won27–20
(–)	v Western Samoa*	(Durban, 4.6.95)	won44–22
(–)	v Australia*	(q/f: Cape Town, 11.6.95)	won25–22
(–)	v New Zealand*	(s/f: Cape Town, 18.6.95)	lost29–45
(–)	v France*	(3/4: Pretoria, 22.6.95)	lost 9–19
(H)	v South Africa	(Twickenham, 18.11.95)	lost14–24
(H)	v Western Samoa	(Twickenham, 16.12.95)	won 27–9
(A)	v France	(Paris, 20.1.96)	lost12–15
(H)	v Wales	(Twickenham, 3.2.96)	won21–15
(A)	v Scotland	(Edinburgh, 2.3.96)	won 18–9
(H)	v Ireland	(Twickenham, 16.3.96)	won28–15

* World Cup

Western Samoa tour in England (P8 W3 D0 L5 F168 A241)

(–)	v Oxford University	(Iffley Road, 21.11.95)	won47–15
(–)	v Cambridge University	(Grange Road, 25.11.95)	lost14–22
(–)	v London/SE Division	(Twickenham, 29.11.95)	won40–32
(–)	v Midlands Division 40	(Leicester, 2.12.95)	lost19–40
(–)	v North Division	(Huddersfield, 5.12.95)	lost 8–34
(–)	v South/SW Division	(Gloucester, 9.12.95)	won31–16

ENGLAND A (P7 W7 D0 L0 F234 A160)

(A)	v Australia XV	(Brisbane, 7.6.95)	won27–19
(A)	v Fiji	(Suva, 10.6.95)	lost25–59
(H)	v Western Samoa	(Gateshead, 12.12.95)	won 55–0
(A)	v France	(Paris, 19.1.96)	won25–15
(H)	v New South Wales	(Leicester, 31.1.96)	won24–22
(A)	v Italy	(L'Aquila, 2.3.96)	won22–19
(H)	v Ireland	(Richmond, 15.3.96)	won56–26

England A to Australia and Fiji (tour record: P7 W3 D0 L4 F263 A186)

(A)	v South Australia	(Adelaide, 20.5.95)	won 66–9
(A)	v Victoria	(Melbourne, 24.5.95)	won76–19
(A)	v Queensland XV	(Brisbane, 28.5.95)	lost15–20
(A)	v Australian Universities	(Sydney, 31.5.95)	lost30–32
(A)	v NSW Country	(Gosford, 4.6.95)	lost24–28

ENGLAND UNDER-21 (P4 W2 D0 L2 F73 A89)

(H)	v Ireland	(Northampton, 15.11.95)	lost10–23
(H)	v Scotland	(Gateshead, 12.12.95)	won21–18
(A)	v Italy	(Pisa, 11.5.96)	won 39–8
(H)	v France	(Bath, 19.4.96)	lost 3–40

ENGLAND STUDENTS (P4 W2 D0 L2 F110 A83)

(A)	v France	(Paris, 19.1.96)	lost14–33
(H)	v Wales	(Roehampton, 2.2.96)	won33–17
(A)	v Scotland	(Inverleith, 1.3.96)	won 44–9
(H)	v Ireland	(Oxford, 15.3.96)	lost19–24

ENGLISH UNIVERSITIES (P3 W1 D0 L2 F65 A75)
(H) v Irish	(Sale, 5.1.96)	lost23–30
(H) v Welsh	(Richmond, 2.2.96)	lost 8–35
(A) v Scottish	(Peffermill, 1.3.96)	won34–10

ENGLAND COLTS (P4 W2 D0 L2 F117 A47)
(A) v Italy	(Brescia, 2.3.96)	won 60–3
(A) v Wales	(Swansea, 24.3.96)	lost 3–9
(H) v Scotland	(Coventry, 13.4.96)	won36–13
(H) v France	(Chester, 20.4.96)	lost18–22

ENGLAND 18 GROUP (P4 W2 D1 L1 F80 A37)
(A) v Scotland	(Hawick, 27.3.96)	won 50–7
(H) v Wales	(Bridgwater & Albion, 30.3.96)	drew 7–7
(A) v France	(Vannes, 6.4.96)	won14–11
(H) v Ireland	(Hull, 10.4.96)	lost 9–12

ENGLAND 18 GROUP A (P1 W1 D0 L0 F34 A12)
(H) v Japan	(Banbury, 24.3.96)	won34–12

ENGLAND 16 GROUP (P2 W2 D0 L0 F65 A8):
(H) v Wales	(Twickenham, 23.3.96)	won 15–3
(H) v Portugal	(Castlecroft, 8.4.96)	won 50–5

ENGLAND 16 GROUP A (P2 W2 D0 L0 F52 A13)
(H) v Wales A	(Imber Court, 22.3.96)	won16–10
(A) v Scotland	(Prestonpans, 12.4.96)	won 36–3

ENGLAND WOMEN (P3 W3 D0 L0 F111 A19):
(H) v Wales	(Leicester, 4.2.96)	won 56–3
(H) v Ireland	(Sunbury, 17.3.96)	won 43–8
(A) v Scotland	(Edinburgh, 3.3.96)	won 12–8

Final standings: (1) England P3 W3 Pts6; (2) Wales P3 W2 Pts4; (3) Scotland P3 W1 Pts2; (4) Ireland P3 W0 Pts0.

Jon Sleightholme celebrates his maiden international try, against Ireland at Twickenham, with Bath and England team mate Mike Catt.

DIVISIONAL CHAMPIONSHIP

	P	W	D	L	F	A	Pts
North	3	3	0	0	101	66	6
Midlands	3	2	0	1	94	90	4
South West	3	1	0	2	52	65	2
London	3	0	0	3	54	80	0

COURAGE CLUB CHAMPIONSHIP

League One	P	W	D	L	F	A	Pts
Bath*	18	15	1	2	575	276	31
Leicester*	18	15	0	3	476	242	30
Harlequins*	18	13	0	5	524	314	26
Wasps*	18	11	0	7	439	322	22
Sale	18	9	1	8	365	371	19
Bristol	18	8	0	10	329	421	16
Orrell	18	7	0	11	323	477	14
Gloucester	18	6	0	12	275	370	12
Saracens	18	5	0	13	284	451	10
West Hartlepool	18	0	0	18	288	634	0

champions: Bath; **relegated:** none; * qualify for European Cup.

League Two	P	W	D	L	F	A	Pts
Northampton	18	18	0	0	867	203	36
London Irish	18	15	0	3	584	405	30
London Scottish	18	10	2	6	361	389	22
Wakefield	18	8	0	10	328	331	16
Waterloo	18	7	2	9	309	483	16
Moseley	18	7	0	11	327	447	14
Blackheath	18	6	1	11	341	469	13
Newcastle Gosforth	18	5	1	12	348	405	11
Nottingham	18	5	1	12	333	433	11
Bedford	18	5	1	12	287	520	11

promoted: Northampton (c), London Irish; **relegated:** none.

League 3 – promoted: Coventry (c), Richmond, Rugby, Rotherham; relegated: none.
League 4 – promoted: Exeter (c), London Welsh, Liverpool St Helens, Walsall, Leeds, Clifton, Redruth, Havant; **relegated:** Plymouth Albion (to 4S), Aspatria (to 4N).
League 5S – promoted (to new 3): Wharfedale (c); relegated: none.
League 5N – promoted (to new 3): Lydney (c); relegated: none.

Women's League One: Champions – Saracens: P14 W13 D0 L1 F410 A110 Pts26

CUP FINALS

Pilkington Cup
Bath 16, Leicester 15 (Twickenham, 4 May 1996)
Bath: J Callard; A Lumsden, P de Glanville (capt), A Adebayo, J Sleightholme; M Catt, A Nicol; D Hilton, G Dawe, J Mallett, M Haag, N Redman, S Ojomoh, A Robinson, E Peters.
   Scorers – Try: Penalty try. *Conversion:* Callard. *Penalty goals:* Callard 2. *Dropped goal:* Catt.

Leicester: J Liley; S Hackney, S Potter, R Robinson, R Underwood; N Malone, A Kardooni; G Rowntree, R Cockerill, D Garforth, M Johnson, M Poole, J Wells, N Back, D Richards (capt).
    Scorers – Tries: Malone, Poole. *Conversion:* Liley. *Penalty goal:* Liley.

Referee: S Lander (Liverpool).

CIS County Championship
Gloucestershire 17, Warwickshire 13 (Twickenham, 20 April 1996)

Pilkington Shield
Helston 6, Medicals 16 (Twickenham, 4 May 1996)

Vaseline BUSA Student Cup
Cardiff Institute 6, Loughborough University 3 (Twickenham, 21.3.96)

Daily Mail U-18 Schools Cup
Colston's Collegiate 20, QEGS Wakefield 0 (Twickenham, 23.3.96)

Women's National Cup:
Saracens 35, Richmond 15 (Staines, 21 April 1996)

Middlesex Sevens:
Wigan RLFC 38, Wasps 15 (Twickenham, 11.5.96)

Cross-code Challenge
Rugby League: Wigan RLFC 82, Bath 6 (Manchester, 8.5.96)
Rugby Union: Bath 44, Wigan RLFC 19 (Twickenham, 25.5.96)

Inter-Services Tournament
Royal Navy 9, Army 6; RAF 14, Navy 12; Army 31, RAF 23 (winners: Army)

114th Varsity Match
Cambridge Univ 21, Oxford Univ 19 (Twickenham 12 December 1995)
Cambridge: M J Singer; D M Casado, T A Q Whitford, S R Cottrell (capt), S P Sexton; R W Ashforth, D M Maslen (B C I Ryan 34); L T Mooney, J Evans, N J Holgate, R Bramley, C R A Simpson, M J Hyde, R D Earnshaw, S D Surridge.
    Scorers – Tries: Penalty try, Jones. *Conversion:* Ashforth. *Penalty goals:* Ashforth 3.
Oxford: S P du Preez; S J Rush, Q A de Bruyn, J M D Riondet (M P Mermagen 48), T G Howe (capt); D G Humphreys, M P Butler; C G B Norton, K F Svoboda, D N Penney, N J Basson, P F Coveney, M P A Reilly, M G P S Orsler, R S Yeabsley.
    Scorer – Try: Humphreys. *Conversion:* Humphreys. *Penalty goals:* Humphreys 3. *Dropped goal:* Humphreys.

Referee: A J Spreadbury (Somerset).

Series score: Played 114, Cambridge 53, Oxford 48, Drawn 13.

Unisys Top Scorers
Points: 445 – **John Liley** (Leicester). 395 – **Mike Corcoran** (London Irish). 376 – **Alex Howarth** (Wharfedale). 354 – **Richard Mills** (Walsall). 347 – **Nick Churchman** (Tabard). 344 – **Jonathan Callard** (Bath). 341 – **Richard Perkins** (Henley). 324 – **Janie Grayshon** (Morley). 323 – **Ralph Zoing** (Harrogate). 317 – **Paul Grayson** (Northampton).
Tries: 33 – **Colin Phillips** (Reading). 25 – **Daren O'Leary** (Harlequins). 23 – **Tom Adams** (Camborne). 22 – **Nick Baxter** (Worcester). 21 – **Jeremy Bennett** (Berry Hill).

1980:

I	W24–9	Twickenham	19 Jan	**t:** Scott, Slemen, SJ Smith
				c: Hare 3
				p: Hare 2
F	W17–13	Paris	2 Feb	**t:** Carleton, Preston
				p: Hare
				dg: Horton 2
W	W 9–8	Twickenham	16 Feb	**p:** Hare 3
S	W30–18	Edinburgh	15 Mar	**t:** Carleton 3, Slemen, Smith
				c: Hare 2
				p: Hare 2

1981:

W	L19–21	Cardiff	17 Jan	**t:** Hare
				p: Hare 5
S	W23–17	Twickenham	21 Feb	**t:** Davies, Slemen, Woodward
				c: Hare
				p: Hare 3
I	W10–9	Dublin	7 Mar	**t:** Dodge, Rose
				c: Rose
F	L12–16	Twickenham	21 Mar	**p:** Rose 4
Arg(1)	D19–19	Buenos Aires	30 May	**t:** Woodward 2, Davies
				c: Hare 2
				p: Hare
Arg(2)	W12–6	Buenos Aires	6 Jun	**t:** Davies
				c: Hare
				p: Hare 2

1982:

A	W15–11	Twickenham	2 Jan	**t:** Jeavons
				c: Dodge
				p: Rose 3
S	D 9–9	Edinburgh	16 Jan	**p:** Dodge 2, Rose
I	L15–16	Twickenham	6 Feb	**t:** Slemen
				c: Rose
				p: Rose 3
F	W27–15	Paris	20 Feb	**t:** Woodward, Carleton
				c: Hare 2
				p: Hare 5
W	W17–7	Twickenham	6 Mar	**t:** Carleton, Slemen
				p: Hare 3
US[+]	W59–0	Hartford	19 Jun	**t:** SJ Smith 2, Swift 2, Scott 2, Carleton, Rendall, Wheeler
				c: Hare 7
				p: Hare 2
				dg: Cusworth
Fj[+]	W60–19	Twickenham	16 Oct	**t:** Trick 3, Swift 2, Gadd 2, Scott, SJ Smith, Cusworth, Dodge, Colclough
				c: Hare 6

1983:

F	L15–19	Twickenham	15 Jan	**p:** Hare 4
				dg: Cusworth
W	D13–13	Cardiff	5 Feb	**t:** Carleton
				p: Hare 2
				dg: Cusworth
S	L12–22	Twickenham	5 Mar	**p:** Hare 3
				dg: Horton
I	L15–25	Dublin	19 Mar	**p:** Hare 5
NZ	W15–9	Twickenham	19 Nov	**t:** Colclough
				c: Hare
				p: Hare 3
C[+]	W27–0	Twickenham	15 Oct	**t:** Youngs, Winterbottom, penalty try
				c: Hare 3
				p: Hare 3

1984:

S	L 6–18	Edinburgh	4 Feb	**p:** Hare 2
I	W12–9	Twickenham	18 Feb	**p:** Hare 3
				dg: Cusworth
F	L18–32	Paris	3 Mar	**t:** R Underwood, Hare
				c: Hare 2
				p: Hare 2
W	L15–24	Twickenham	17 Mar	**p:** Hare 5
SA(1)	L15–33	Port Elizabeth	2 Jun	**p:** Hare 4
				dg: Horton
SA(2)	L 9–35	Johannesburg	9 Jun	**p:** Hare 3
A	L 3–19	Twickenham	3 Nov	**p:** Barnes

1985:

F	D 9–9	Twickenham	2 Feb	**p:** Andrew 2
				dg: Andrew
W	L15–24	Cardiff	20 Apr	**t:** Smith
				c: Andrew
				p: Andrew 2
				dg: Andrew
S	W10–7	Twickenham	16 Mar	**t:** Smith
				p: Andrew 2
I	L10–13	Dublin	30 Mar	**t:** R Underwood
				p: Andrew 2
NZ(1)	L13–18	Christchurch	1 Jun	**t:** Harrison, Teague
				c: Barnes
				p: Barnes
NZ(2)	L15–42	Wellington	8 Jun	**t:** Hall, Harrison
				c: Barnes 2
				dg: Barnes
R	W22–15	Twickenham	5 Jan	**t:** S T Smith
				p: Andrew 4
				dg: Andrew 2

1986:

W	W21–18	Twickenham	17 Jan	**p:** Andrew 6

S	L 6–33	Edinburgh	15 Feb	**dg:** Andrew **p:** Andrew 2
I	W25–20	Twickenham	1 Mar	**t:** Richards 2, penalty try, Davies **c:** Andrew 3 **p:** Andrew
F	L10–29	Paris	15 Mar	**t:** Dooley **p:** Barnes 2
J⁺	W39–12	Twickenham	11 Oct	**t:** R Underwood, Hall, Bailey, Richards, Rees, Salmon **c:** Rose 6 **p:** Rose

1987:

I	L 0–17	Dublin	7 Feb	
F	L15–19	Twickenham	21 Feb	**p:** Rose 4 **dg:** Andrew
W	L12–19	Cardiff	7 Mar	**p:** Rose 4
S	W21–12	Twickenham	4 Apr	**t:** penalty try, Rose **c:** Rose 2 **p:** Rose 3
A*	L 6–19	Sydney	23 May	**t:** Harrison **c:** Webb
J*	W60–7	Sydney	30 May	**t:** R Underwood 2, Rees, Salmon, Richards, Simms, Harrison 3, Redman **c:** Webb 7 **p:** Webb 2
US*	W34–6	Sydney	3 Jun	**t:** Winterbottom 2, Harrison, Dooley **c:** Webb 3 **p:** Webb 4
W*	L 3–16	Brisbane	8 Jun	**p:** Webb

Ben Clarke, the England flanker, waits for the right moment
to feed his line during England's title-winning defeat of Ireland.

1988:

F	L 9–10	Paris	16 Jan	**p:** Webb 2
				dg: Cusworth
W	L 3–11	Twickenham	6 Feb	**p:** Webb
S	W 9–6	Edinburgh	5 Mar	**p:** Webb 2
				dg: Andrew
I(a)	W35–3	Twickenham	19 Mar	**t:** Oti 3, R Underwood 2, Rees
				c: Webb, Andrew 3
				p: Webb
I(b)^	W21–10	Dublin	23 Apr	**t:** R Underwood, Harding
				c: Webb 2
				p: Webb 3
A(a1)	L16–22	Brisbane	29 May	**t:** R Underwood, Bailey
				c: Webb
				p: Webb 2
A(a2)	L 8–28	Sydney	12 Jun	**t:** Richards, R Underwood
Fj	W25–12	Suva	17 Jun	**t:** R Underwood 2, Barley
				c: Barnes 2
				p: Barnes 3
A(b)	W28–19	Twickenham	5 Nov	**t:** R Underwood 2, Morris, Halliday
				c: Webb 3
				p: Webb 2

1989:

S	D12–12	Twickenham	4 Feb	**p:** Andrew 2, Webb 2
I	W16–3	Dublin	18 Feb	**t:** Moore, Richards
				c: Andrew
				p: Andrew 2
F	W11–0	Twickenham	4 Mar	**t:** Carling, Robinson
				p: Andrew
W	L 9–12	Cardiff	18 Mar	**p:** Andrew 2
				dg: Andrew
R	W58–3	Bucharest	13 May	**t:** Oti 4, Guscott 3, Probyn, Richards
				c: Hodgkinson 8
				p: Hodgkinson
				dg: Andrew
Fj	W58–23	Twickenham	4 Nov	**t:** R Underwood 5, Skinner, Bailey, Linnett, Ackford, Guscott
				c: Hodgkinson 5, Andrew
				p: Hodgkinson 2

1990:

I	W23–0	Twickenham	20 Jan	**t:** R Underwood, Probyn, Egerton, Guscott
				c: Hodgkinson 2
				p: Hodgkinson
F	W26–7	Paris	3 Feb	**t:** R Underwood, Guscott, Carling
				c: Hodgkinson
				p: Hodgkinson 4
W	W34–6	Twickenham	17 Feb	**t:** Carling, R Underwood 2, Hill
				c: Hodgkinson 3
				p: Hodgkinson 4

S	L 7–13	Edinburgh	17 Mar	**t:** Guscott
				p: Hodgkinson
It[+]	W33–15	Rovigo	1 May	**t:** Oti, Buckton, Back, Andrew
				c: Hodgkinson 4
				p: Hodgkinson 2
				dg: Andrew
Arg(a1)	W25–12	Buenos Aires	28 Jul	**t:** Ryan, Oti
				c: Hodgkinson
				p: Hodgkinson 5
Arg(a2)	L13–15	Buenos Aires	4 Aug	**t:** Hodgkinson, Heslop
				c: Hodgkinson
				p: Hodgkinson
Ba[+]	W18–16	Twickenham	29 Sep	**t:** Richards, Hodgkinson
				c: Hodgkinson 2
				p: Hodgkinson 2
Arg(b)	W51–0	Twickenham	3 Nov	**t:** R Underwood 3, Guscott 2, Hill, Hall
				c: Hodgkinson 7
				p: Hodgkinson 3

1991:

W	W25–6	Cardiff	19 Jan	**t:** Teague
				p: Hodgkinson 7
S(a)	W21–12	Twickenham	16 Feb	**t:** Heslop
				c: Hodgkinson
				p: Hodgkinson 5
I	W16–7	Dublin	2 Mar	**t:** R Underwood, Teague
				c: Hodgkinson
				p: Hodgkinson 2
F	W21–19	Twickenham	16 Mar	**t:** R Underwood
				c: Hodgkinson
				p: Hodgkinson 4
				dg: Andrew
Fj	W28–12	Suva	20 Jul	**t:** Probyn, R Underwood, Andrew
				c: Webb 2
				p: Webb 2
				dg: Andrew 2
A(a)	L15–40	Sydney	27 Jul	**t:** Guscott
				c: Webb
				p: Webb 3
USSR[+]	W53–0	Twickenham	7 Sep	**t:** Oti 2, Guscott 2, R Underwood 2, Skinner 2, Andrew
				c: Andrew 4, Hodgkinson 3
				p: Hodgkinson
NZ[*]	L12–18	Twickenham	3 Oct	**p:** Webb 3
				dg: Andrew
It[*]	W36–6	Twickenham	8 Oct	**t:** R Underwood, Guscott 2, Webb
				c: Webb 4
				p: Webb 4
US[*]	W37–9	Twickenham	11 Oct	**t:** R Underwood 2, Carling, Skinner, Heslop
				c: Hodgkinson 4
				p: Hodgkinson 3

F*	W19–10	Paris	19 Oct	**t:** R Underwood, Carling **c:** Webb **p:** Webb 3
S(b)*	W 9–6	Edinburgh	26 Oct	**p:** Webb 2 **dg:** Andrew
A(b)*	L 6–12	Twickenham	2 Nov	**p:** Webb 2

1992:

S	W25–7	Edinburgh	18 Jan	**t:** R Underwood, Morris **c:** Webb **p:** Webb 4 **dg:** Guscott
I	W38–9	Twickenham	1 Feb	**t:** Webb 2, Morris, Guscott, R Underwood, Halliday **c:** Webb 4 **p:** Webb 2
F	W31–13	Paris	15 Feb	**t:** Webb, R Underwood, Morris, penalty try **c:** Webb 3 **p:** Webb 3
W	W24–0	Twickenham	7 Mar	**t:** Carling, Skinner, Dooley **c:** Webb 3 **p:** Webb 2
C †	W26–13	Wembley	17 Oct	**t:** Hunter 2, Guscott, Winterbottom **p:** Webb 2
SA	W33–16	Twickenham	14 Nov	**t:** T Underwood, Guscott, Morris, Carling **c:** Webb 2 **p:** Webb 3

1993:

F	W16–15	Twickenham	16 Jan	**t:** Hunter **c:** Webb **p:** Webb 3
W	L 9–10	Cardiff	6 Feb	**p:** Webb 2 **dg:** Guscott
S	W26–12	Twickenham	6 Mar	**t:** Guscott, R Underwood, T Underwood **c:** Webb **p:** Webb 3
I	L 3–17	Dublin	20 Mar	**p:** Webb
NZ	W15–9	Twickenham	27 Nov	**p:** Callard 4 **dg:** Andrew

1994:

S	W15–14	Edinburgh	5 Feb	**p:** Callard 5
I	L12–13	Twickenham	19 Feb	**p:** Callard 4
F	W18–14	Paris	5 Mar	**p:** Andrew 5 **dg:** Andrew
W	W15–8	Twickenham	19 Mar	**t:** R Underwood, Rodber **c:** Andrew **p:** Andrew

SA(1)	W33–15	Pretoria	4 Jun	t: Clarke, Andrew c: Andrew 2 p: Andrew 5
SA(2)	L 9–27	Cape Town	11 Jun	p: Andrew 3
R	W54–3	Twickenham	12 Nov	t: T Underwood 2, Carling, Rodber, R Underwood, penalty try c: Andrew 6 p: Andrew 4
C	W60–19	Twickenham	19 Nov	t: R Underwood 2, Catt 2, Bracken, T Underwood c: Andrew 6 p: Andrew 6

1995:

I	W20–8	Dublin	21 Jan	t: Carling, T Underwood, Clarke c: Andrew p: Andrew
F(a)	W31–10	Twickenham	4 Feb	t: T Underwood 2, Guscott c: Andrew 2 p: Andrew 4
W	W23–9	Cardiff	18 Feb	t: Ubogu, R Underwood 2 c: Andrew p: Andrew 2
S	W24–12	Twickenham	18 Mar	p: Andrew 7 dg: Andrew
Arg*	W24–18	Durban	27 May	p: Andrew 6 dg: Andrew 2
It*	W27–20	Durban	31 May	t: T Underwood, R Underwood c: Andrew p: Andrew 5
WS*	W44–22	Durban	4 Jun	t: R Underwood 2, Back, penalty try c: Callard 3 p: Callard 5 dg: Catt
A*	W25–22	Cape Town	11 Jun	t: T Underwood c: Andrew p: Andrew 5 dg: Andrew
NZ*	L29–45	Cape Town	18 Jun	t: R Underwood 2, Carling 2 c: Andrew 3 p: Andrew
F(b)*	L 9–19	Pretoria	22 Jun	p: Andrew 3
SA	L14–24	Twickenham	18 Nov	t: de Glanville p: Callard 3
WS	W27–9	Twickenham	16 Dec	t: Dallaglio, R Underwood c: Grayson p: Grayson 5

1996:

F	L12–15	Paris	20 Jan	p: Grayson 2 dg: Grayson 2

W	W21–15	Twickenham	3 Feb	t: R Underwood, Guscott
				c: Grayson
				p: Grayson 3
S	W18–9	Edinburgh	2 Mar	p: Grayson 6
I	W28–15	Twickenham	16 Mar	t: Sleightholme
				c: Grayson
				p: Grayson 6
				dg: Grayson

* World Cup
+ Non-cap
† Five-point try introduced from this game onwards
^ Non-championship

*Lawrence Dallaglio, the England flanker, prepares to take on
Scotland centre Scott Hastings in last season's Calcutta Cup clash.*

IRELAND
Mark Jones
Rugby Correspondent, *The Title*

BUFFETED and twisted by the new order, it wasn't too surprising that Ireland's season turned out to be yet another monumental struggle. And that was just off the pitch. In the end, the harassed men of the Irish Rugby Football Union probably needed a summer's rest more than the players, whose holiday reading doubtless included Mark McCormack's *What They Don't Teach You at Harvard Business School*.

At Lansdowne Road's top table, it was the year of the mindshift. The day before the squad left for the World Cup, the IRFU had outlined its position on amateurism. Rugby was 'not a business, but a recreational leisure activity.' Efforts had to be made to limit the number of internationals and to 'reduce both the preparation period before games and the number of squad sessions.'

And then came the bottom line. The concept of pay for play was simply 'not acceptable'. Why? Well, because the 'traditions, ethics and etiquette' of the game – whatever they were – would quickly disappear. In a world of win bonuses and transfer markets, everyone would be threatened by bankruptcy.

The irony of heading out to South Africa, where the IRFU's doomsday scenario was already a burgeoning reality, was not lost on anyone who digested the well-intentioned but hopelessly outmoded ostrichspeak. Little more than three months later, Ireland lamented the passing of amateurism and announced, after all, that it would pay its international players. Mind you, that was all for the moment. Provincial and club players would just have to suck it and see. Little more than three months later, the IRFU backtracked again and agreed to pay its provincial players. It was all happening and fast.

> *The IRFU still regards the interprovincials as a series of trials for the national side. So what now when 12 or 13 of Ireland's first choices are contracted to English clubs?*

Meanwhile, some players were testing the market. There were a fair few decent punts on offer in Ireland, but the real money was across the water. With English scouts at the gates of most Irish First Division clubs, the IRFU reacted by offering improved contracts designed to keep the best players at home.

However, the new deal was too late for Eddie Halvey and David Corkery, and not tempting enough for the likes of Keith Wood, Gabriel Fulcher, Paul Burke, Victor Costello and Niall Woods, who all preferred to earn their money in sterling.

The ramifications of the continuing haemorrhage to the Courage Leagues cannot be ignored. Good for Ireland that the players will be performing at a consistently higher level than the ailing All Ireland League. Maybe. But bad that they are unlikely to be available for important provincial games. The IRFU still regards the inter-provincials as a series of trials for the national side. So what now when 12 or 13 of Ireland's first choices are contracted to English clubs?

The speed of change was such there was hardly time to draw breath. A New Zealander became Ireland's first full-time professional coach, and Nick Popplewell edged out Halvey and Corkery in the race to become the country's first professional player. Murray Kidd wasn't the number one draft pick, but he had a track record at club level and quickly proved himself bloody-minded enough not to worry about having been a Plan C after the unsuccessful courtships of both John Connolly and Bob Dwyer.

Fiji were in town for the opening game of the season in November, and despite favourable reaction from the players to Kidd's early training regime, no one was expecting much from the autumn international, which usually sees Ireland huffing and puffing against the Romanias and the USAs of this world.

But out of nothing here was an Irish side, for once looking purposeful and highly efficient. An utterly convincing win by 44–8 and six tries in the process. Fiji weren't all that hot, but they had run Wales close. So, was it all going to change on the pitch as well? Sadly, no. Another false dawn had risen over Lansdowne Road.

Niall Hogan, appointed captain in mid-championship, is acutely aware that progress will not be made overnight. 'Looking back, the Five Nations was a disappointment. Everything hinged on the Scots game (lost 10–16). We could and should have won. All we had to do was play reasonably well on the day. I still don't think they were a great side. OK, Paris was bad, but we beat Wales well and if we had started off properly then we would have been going to Twickenham with a lot to play for.

'We're really only starting to catch up in the fitness and strength areas. We're only turning the corner to becoming semi-professional. I mean, if you're at a physical disadvantage, you can only go for so long. Eventually fatigue sets in and that's what happened against England. We tackled everything, we ran into brick walls and, in the end, we just got tired.'

> *'We're really only starting to catch up in the fitness and strength areas. If you're at a physical disadvantage, you can only go for so long. Eventually fatigue sets in and that's what happened against England'* – Niall Hogan

'Tired' was a word we heard a lot of during the season. For the players, not naturally attuned to Kidd's fitness factor, January's camp in Atlanta turned out to be one hell of a slog. In search of dry pitches and pleasant temperatures, the squad and management weren't overly impressed with constant rain during the first few days, and when the worst storm in living memory swept through Georgia on the weekend of the Test against the United States, the warm-weather training slot on the calendar had turned into a bad joke.

In the short term, the negatives from Atlanta outweighed the positives. A sharp and focused Scottish side came to Lansdowne Road and ran heavy Irish legs all round the pitch. Mobility quickly became the vogue and Neil Francis, whose early-season form had been inspirational, found himself out in the cold. The halfbacks, Eric Elwood and Christian Saverimutto, were also jettisoned as Kidd prepared for the terrifying prospect of the Parc des Princes.

With all the talk of a big season now banished and confidence levels alarmingly low, Ireland were destroyed by the French. Even though David Humphreys and Victor Costello emerged from the wreckage with some credit, Peter Clohessy stole the show for all the wrong reasons. Adding injury to insult by stamping on Olivier Roumat's head, the recidivist prop was handed a six-month ban and fined his £3,000 match fee, while his international contract was terminated. Harsh, some said. Others, who had called for a life ban, reckoned he got off lightly.

For Niall Hogan, the match was a personal low. Big-hearted and fiercely competitive, the more he tried, the worse he played. Terrible passing, poor kicking, just about everything went wrong. In fact, Hogan's season was a microcosm of an Irish problem that has yet to be resolved. A qualified doctor working around the clock in his intern

Niall Woods, the Ireland wing, scores one of four tries against Wales at Lansdowne Road.

year, the scrum-half was spinning plates rather than passes during the championship and a few were bound to crash to the floor.

Quite simply, hospital hours and international rugby were an impossible mix. Still, the management understood Hogan's predicament and, despite the Paris disaster, he was made captain for the Welsh game where a comprehensive victory saved several reputations.

'It's clear now that the only way to really compete is to give up a job and go virtually full-time. Not all of the Irish guys are going to be able to do that,' Hogan assessed. 'Anyone thinking seriously about the future will have to find something that involves only two or three days work a week and there aren't too many jobs out there like that. It's just not going to be easy to fulfil training commitments and play to the best of our abilities. Quite frankly, it will be difficult for some of our guys to stay in the squad.'

Following a respectable defeat at Twickenham, a positive picture of some of the younger players began to emerge. Fulcher arrived as a championship lock, Humphreys and Costello made further progress, while Paul Wallace also proved he could swim with the big fish. If there had been any doubts over Corkery's qualities, he knocked them on the head with a major performance against England.

Niall Hogan's season was a microcosm of an Irish problem that has yet to be resolved. A qualified doctor working around the clock in his intern year, the scrum-half was spinning plates rather than passes during the championship and a few were bound to crash to the floor

There were still quite a few question marks. A big one over Simon Mason's defence and a smaller one over both Jeremy Davidson and Niall Woods. Frustratingly, Jonathan Bell seemed to fall foul of the second season syndrome, and Wood and Halvey were sorely missed. Ireland needs both players fit and ready by the end of the summer.

With Kidd and manager Pat Whelan now in place until the next World Cup, the push is on to professionalise further. A chance for the Irish to catch up? Or will the rest adapt better to the new order? Last season Ireland only dipped a toe in the real world. Now the players and their masters have to get ready to take the plunge.

IRELAND (P11 W5 D0 L6 F277 A331)

(–)	v New Zealand*	(Johannesburg, 27.5.95)	lost19–42
(–)	v Japan*	(Bloemfontein, 31.5.95)	won50–28
(–)	v Wales*	(Johannesburg, 4.6.95)	won24–23
(–)	v France*	(q/f: Durban, 10.6.95)	lost12–36
(H)	v Fiji	(Dublin, 18.11.95)	won 44–8
(A)	v United States	(Atlanta, 6.1.96)	won25–18
(H)	v Scotland	(Dublin, 20.1.96)	lost10–16
(A)	v France	(Paris, 17.2.96)	lost10–45
(H)	v Wales	(Dublin, 2.3.96)	won30–17
(A)	v England	(Twickenham, 16.3.96)	lost15–28
(H)	v Barbarians +	(Dublin, 18.5.96)	lost38–70

* World Cup; + non-cap.

IRELAND A (P3 W2 D0 L1 F77 A86)

(H)	v Scotland	(Donnybrook, 19.1.96)	won26–19
(H)	v Wales	(Donnybrook, 1.3.96)	won25–11
(A)	v England	(Richmond, 15.3.96)	lost26–56

IRELAND UNDER-21 (P3 W3 D0 L0 F64 A31)

(A)	v England	(Northampton, 15.11.95)	won23–10
(H)	v Scotland	(Blackrock, 19.1.96)	won 21–9
(H)	v Wales	(Wicklow, 1.3.96)	won20–12

IRELAND STUDENTS (P3 W1 D0 L2 F43 A73)

(H)	v Natal	(Cork, 4.11.95)	lost 8–12
(A)	v France	(Clermont Ferrand, 16.2.96)	lost11–42
(A)	v England	(Oxford, 15.3.96)	won24–19

IRISH UNIVERSITIES (P3 W2 D0 L1 F94 A54)

(A)	v English	(Sale, 5.1.96)	won30–23
(H)	v Scottish	(Dublin, 19.1.96)	won 43–9
(H)	v Welsh	(Dublin, 1.3.96)	lost21–22

IRELAND YOUTH (P3 W0 D0 L3 F39 A62)

(A)	v Spain	(Valladolid, 10.3.96)	lost 6–23
(H)	v Scotland	(Galway, 30.3.96)	lost17–18
(A)	v Wales	(Cardiff, 27.4.96)	lost16–21

IRELAND SCHOOLS UNDER-18 (P3 W3 D0 L0 F62 A33)

(H)	v Scotland	(Cork, 6.4.96)	won37–12
(A)	v England	(Hull, 10.4.96)	won 12–9
(H)	v Wales	(Belfast, 17.4.96)	won13–12

IRELAND WOMEN (P3 W0 D0 L3 F17 A86)

(H)	v Scotland	(Blackrock, 21.1.96)	lost 3–21
(H)	v Wales	(Dublin, 3.3.96)	lost 6–22
(A)	v England	(Sunbury, 17.3.96)	lost 8–43

Final standings: (1) England P3 W3 Pts6; (2) Wales P3 W2 Pts4; (3) Scotland P3 W1 Pts2; (4) Ireland P3 W0 Pts0.

SMITHWICKS INTER-PROVINCIAL CHAMPIONSHIP

	P	W	D	L	F	A	Pts
Leinster	4	4	0	0	133	53	8
Ulster	4	3	0	1	73	83	6
Munster	4	2	0	2	91	58	4
Exiles	4	1	0	3	71	113	2
Connacht	4	0	0	4	51	132	0

INSURANCE CORPORATION ALL-IRELAND LEAGUE

League One	P	W	D	L	F	A	Pts
Shannon	10	8	0	2	156	78	16
Garryowen	10	8	0	2	171	165	16
Cork Constitution	10	7	0	3	208	149	14
Young Munster	10	7	0	3	170	127	14
St Mary's College	10	5	1	4	147	119	11
Lansdowne	10	4	1	5	180	172	9
Ballymena	10	4	1	5	157	181	9
Old Wesley	10	3	1	6	156	164	7
Blackrock College	10	3	0	7	160	208	6
Old Belvedere	10	3	0	7	135	189	6
Instonians	10	1	0	9	145	233	2

champions: Shannon; **relegated:** none

League Two	P	W	D	L	F	A	Pts
Old Crescent	10	9	1	0	246	103	19
Dungannon	10	7	1	2	254	171	15
Terenure College	10	7	1	2	191	118	15
Bective Rangers	10	6	0	4	186	147	12
Greystones	10	5	1	4	164	173	11
Sunday's Well	10	4	2	4	223	194	10
Malone	10	5	0	5	205	220	10
Wanderers	10	4	0	6	167	208	8
Clontarf	10	3	0	7	130	212	6
Dolphin	10	1	0	9	165	245	2
N.I.F.C	10	1	0	9	157	299	2

promoted: Old Crescent (c), Dungannon, Terenure; **relegated:** none

League Three – *promoted:* Monkstown (c), City of Derry, Highfield, DLSP, Skerries, UCC; *relegated:* none

League Four – *promoted:* Portadown (c), Collegians, Dublin University, Queen's University; Corinthians; *relegated:* none

Promoted to League Four from junior provincial leagues: Richmond, Suttonians, Ballynahinch, Creggs.

CUP FINALS

Connacht Senior Cup: Galwegians 9, Connemara 6 (Sportsground)

Leinster Senior Cup: Terenure 17, Lansdowne 7 (Lansdowne Road)

Munster Senior Cup: Shannon 15, Cork Constitution 13 (Musgrave Park)

Ulster Senior Cup: Dungannon 22, Malone 10 (Ravenhill)

1980:

E	L 9–24	Twickenham	19 Jan	**p:** Campbell 3
S	W22–15	Dublin	2 Feb	**t:** Keane, Kennedy
				c: Campbell
				p: Campbell 3
				dg: Campbell
F	L18–19	Paris	1 Mar	**t:** McLennan
				c: Campbell
				p: Cambell 3
				dg: Campbell
W	W21–7	Dublin	15 Mar	**t:** Irwin, O'Driscoll, C Fitzgerald
				c: Campbell 3
				p: Campbell
R+	D13–13	Dublin	18 Oct	**t:** F Quinn
				p: Campbell 3

1981:

F	L13–19	Dublin	7 Feb	**t:** MacNeill
				p: Campbell 3
W	L 8–9	Cardiff	21 Feb	**t:** Slattery, MacNeill
E	L 6–10	Dublin	7 Mar	**dg:** Campbell, MacNeill
S	L 9–10	Edinburgh	21 Mar	**t:** Irwin
				c: Campbell
				p: Campbell
SA(1)	L15–23	Cape Town	30 May	**t:** McGrath, McLennan
				c: Campbell 2
				p: Campbell
SA(2)	L10–12	Durban	6 Jun	**t:** O'Brien
				p: Quinn 2
A	L12–16	Dublin	21 Nov	**p:** Ward 4

1982:

W	W20–12	Dublin	23 Jan	**t:** Ringland, Finn 2
				c: Campbell
				p: Campbell 2
E	W16–15	Twickenham	6 Feb	**t:** MacNeill, McLoughlin
				c: Campbell
				p: Campbell 2
S	W21–12	Dublin	20 Feb	**p:** Campbell 6
				dg: Campbell
F	L 9–22	Paris	20 Mar	**p:** Campbell 3

1983:

S	W15–13	Edinburgh	15 Jan	**t:** Kiernan
				c: Campbell
				p: Campbell 3
F	W22–16	Dublin	19 Feb	**t:** Finn 2
				c: Campbell
				p: Campbell 4

W	L 9–23	Cardiff	5 Mar	p: Campbell 2, MacNeill
E	W25–15	Dublin	19 Mar	t: Slattery, Campbell
				c: Campbell
				p: Campbell 5

1984:

F	L12–25	Paris	21 Jan	p: Campbell 4
W	L 9–18	Dublin	4 Feb	p: Campbell 3
E	L 9–12	Twickenham	18 Feb	p: Ward 3
S	L 9–32	Dublin	3 Mar	t: Kiernan
				c: J Murphy
				p: J Murphy
A	L 9–16	Dublin	10 Nov	p: Kiernan 3

1985:

S	W18–15	Edinburgh	2 Feb	t: Ringland 2
				c: Kiernan 2
				p: Kiernan
				dg: Kiernan
F	D15–15	Dublin	2 Mar	p: Kiernan 5
W	W21–9	Cardiff	16 Mar	t: Crossan, Ringland
				c: Kiernan 2
				p: Kiernan 3
E	W13–10	Dublin	30 Mar	t: Mullin
				p: Kiernan 2
				dg: Kiernan

*Ireland No.8 Vincent Costello is halted by Wales
captain Jonathan Humphreys in Dublin.*

J(1)+	W48–13	Osaka	26 May	**t:** Ringland 3, Matthews 2, Kiernan, MacNeill, C Fitzgerald
				c: Kiernan 5
				p: Kiernan 2
J(2)+	W33–15	Tokyo	2 Jun	**t:** Kiernan 2, Mullin, Anderson
				c: Kiernan 4
				p: Kiernan 3
Fj+	W16–15	Dublin	19 Oct	**t:** Bradley
				p: Kiernan 4

1986:

F	L 9–29	Paris	1 Feb	**p:** Kiernan 3
W	L12–19	dublin	15 Feb	**t:** Ringland
				c: Kiernan
				p: Kiernan 2
E	L20–25	Twickenham	1 Mar	**t:** Ringland, Mullin, McCall
				c: Kiernan
				p: Kiernan 2
S	L 9–10	Dublin	15 Mar	**t:** Ringland
				c: Kiernan
				p: Kiernan
R	W60–0	Dublin	1 Nov	**t:** Crossan 3, Mullin 2, Dean 2, Anderson, Bradley, MacNeill
				c: Kiernan 7
				p: Kiernan 2

1987:

E	W17–0	Dublin	7 Feb	**t:** Kiernan, Matthews, Crossan
				c: Kiernan
				p: Kiernan
S	L12–26	Edinburgh	21 Feb	**t:** Lenihan
				c: Kiernan
				p: Kiernan
				dg: Kiernan
F	L13–19	Dublin	21 Mar	**t:** Ringland, Bradley
				c: Kiernan
				p: Kiernan
W(a)	W15–11	Cardiff	4 Apr	**t:** Dean, Mullin
				c: Kiernan 2
				p: Kiernan
W(b)*	L 6–13	Wellington	25 May	**p:** Kiernan 2
C*	W46–19	Dunedin	30 May	**t:** Bradley, Crossan 2, Spillane, Ringland, MacNeill
				c: Kiernan 5
				p: Kiernan 2
				dg: Kiernan, Ward
T*	W32–9	Brisbane	3 Jun	**t:** MacNeill 2, Mullin 3
				c: Ward 3
				p: Ward 2
A*	L15–33	Sydney	7 Jun	**t:** MacNeill, Kiernan
				c: Kiernan 2
				p: Kiernan

1988:

S	W22–18	Dublin	16 Jan	t: Mullin, MacNeill, Bradley
				c: Kiernan 2
				p: Kiernan
				dg: Kiernan
F	L6–25	Paris	20 Feb	p: Kiernan 2
W	L9–12	Dublin	5 Mar	t: Kingston
				c: Kiernan
				p: Kiernan
E(a)	L 3–35	Twickenham	19 Mar	dg: Kiernan
E(b)^	L 10–21	Dublin	23 Apr	t: S Smith, MacNeill
				c: Kiernan
WS	W49–22	Dublin	29 Oct	t: Crossan 2, Kiernan, Matthews,
				Mullin, Francis, McBride, Sexton
				c: Kiernan 4
				p: Kiernan 2
				dg: Sexton
It	W31–15	Dublin	31 Dec	t: Crossan 2, Matthews 2, Aherne
				c: Cunningham
				p: Danaher 2
				dg: Dean

1989:

F	L21–26	Dublin	21 Jan	t: Mullin
				c: Kiernan
				p: Kiernan 5
W	W19–13	Cardiff	4 Feb	t: Mannion, Dean
				c: Kiernan
				p: Kiernan 3
E	L 3–16	Dublin	18 Feb	p: Kiernan
S	L21–37	Dublin	4 Mar	t: Mullin 2, Dunlea
				c: Kiernan 3
				p: Kiernan
C+	W24–21	Victoria	2 Sep	t: Dunlea, Sexton
				c: Kiernan 2
				p: Kiernan 4
US+	W32–7	New York	9 Sep	t: Dunlea, Mannion, Crossan, Bradley
				c: Kiernan 2
				p: Kiernan 3
				dg: B Smith
NZ	L 6–23	Dublin	18 Nov	p: B Smith 2

1990:

E	L 0–23	Twickenham	20 Jan	
S	L10–13	Edinburgh	3 Feb	t: J Fitzgerald
				p: Kiernan 2
F	L12–31	Paris	3 Mar	p: Kiernan 4
W	W14–8	Dublin	24 Mar	t: S Smith, McBride, Kingston
				c: Kiernan
Arg	W20–18	Dublin	27 Oct	t: Hooks, Kiernan
				p: Kiernan 4

1991:

F	L13–21	Dublin	2 Feb	**t:** S Smith
				p: Kiernan 3
W	D21–21	Cardiff	18 Feb	**t:** Clarke, Mullin, Geoghegan, Staples
				c: B Smith
				p: B Smith
E	L 7–16	Dublin	2 Mar	**t:** Geoghegan
				p: B Smith
S	L25–28	Edinburgh	16 Mar	**t:** Crossan, Robinson, Geoghegan, Mullin
				c: B Smith 3
				dg: B Smith
Na(1)	L 6–15	Windhoek	20 Jul	**t:** penalty try
				c: Mullin
Na(2)	L15–26	Windhoek	27 Jul	**t:** Staples, Cunningham
				c: Staples 2
				dg: Curtis
Z*	W55–11	Dublin	6 Oct	**t:** Robinson 4, Geoghegan, Popplewell 2, Curtis
				c: Keyes 4
				p: Keyes 5
J*	W32–16	Dublin	9 Oct	**t:** O'Hara, Mannion 2, Staples
				c: Keyes 2
				p: Keyes 4
S(b)*	L15–24	Edinburgh	12 Oct	**p:** Keyes 4
				dg: Keyes
A*	L18–19	Dublin	20 Oct	**t:** Hamilton
				c: Keyes
				p: Keyes 3
				dg: Keyes

1992:

W	L 15–16	Dublin	18 Jan	**t:** Wallace
				c: Keyes
				p: Keyes 3
E	L 9–38	Twickenham	1 Feb	**t:** Keyes
				c: Keyes
				p: Keyes
S	L10–18	Dublin	15 Feb	**t:** Wallace
				p: Keyes 2
F	L12–44	Paris	21 Mar	**p:** McAleese 4
NZ(1)	L21–24	Dunedin	30 May	**t:** Cunningham 2, Staples
				c: Russell 3
				p: Russell
NZ(2)	L 6–59	Wellington	6 Jun	**t:** Furlong
				c: Russell
A†	L17–42	Dublin	31 Oct	**t:** Wallace
				p: Russell 4

1993:

S	L 3–15	Edinburgh	16 Jan	**p:** Malone
F	L 6–21	Dublin	20 Feb	**p:** Malone 2

W	W19–14	Cardiff	6 Mar	t: Robinson c: Elwood p: Elwood 3 dg: C Clarke
E	W17–3	Dublin	20 Mar	t: Galwey p: Elwood 2 dg: Elwood 2
R	W25–3	Dublin	14 Nov	t: Geoghegan c: Elwood p: Elwood 6

1994:

F	L15–35	Paris	15 Jan	p: Elwood 5
W	L15–17	Dublin	5 Feb	p: Elwood 5
E	W13–12	Twickenham	19 Feb	t: Geoghegan c: Elwood p: Elwood 2
S	D 6–6	Edinburgh	5 Mar	p: Elwood 2
A(1)	L13–31	Brisbane	5 Jun	t: Johns c: Elwood p: Elwood, O'Shea
A(2)	L18–32	Sydney	11 Jun	t: Francis, Clohessy c: O'Shea p: O'Shea dg: O'Shea
US	W26–15	Dublin	5 Nov	t: Geoghegan, Bradley c: McGowan 2 p: McGowan 3, O'Shea

1995:

E	L 8–20	Dublin	21 Jan	t: Foley p: Burke
S	L13–26	Edinburgh	4 Feb	t: Mullin, Bell p: Burke
F(a)	L 7–25	Dublin	4 Mar	t: Geoghegan c: Elwood
W(a)	W16–12	Cardiff	18 Mar	t: Mullin c: Burke p: Burke 2 dg: Burke
It	L12–22	Treviso	8 May	p: Burke 4
NZ*	L19–43	Johannesburg	27 May	t: Halpin, McBride, Corkery c: Elwood 2
J*	W50–28	Bloemfontein	31 May	t: Halvey, Francis, Corkery, Hogan, Geoghegan, penalty tries 2 c: Burke 6 p: Burke
W(b)*	W24–23	Johannesburg	4 Jun	t: Popplewell, McBride, Halvey c: Elwood 3 p: Elwood
F(b)*	L12–36	Durban	10 Jun	p: Elwood 4

| Fj | W 44–8 | Dublin | 18 Nov | **t:** Johns, R Wallace, P Wallace, Staples, Geoghegan, Francis
c: Burke 4
p: Burke 2 |

1996:

US	W25–18	Atlanta	6 Jan	**t:** R Wallace **c:** Elwood **p:** Burke 3, Elwood 3
S	L10–16	Dublin	20 Jan	**t:** Clohessy **c:** Elwood **p:** Elwood
F	L10–45	Paris	17 Feb	**t:** penalty try **c:** Humphreys **p:** Humphreys
W	W30–17	Dublin	2 Mar	**t:** Fulcher, Corkery, Woods Geoghegan **c:** Mason 2 **p:** Mason 2
E	L15–28	Twickenham	16 Mar	**p:** Mason 4 **dg:** Humphreys
Ba +	L38–70	Dublin	18 May	**t:** Costello 2, Burke, Topping Henderson, R Wallace **c:** Mason 4

* World Cup
+ Non-cap
† Five-point try introduced from this game onwards
^ Non-championship

Ireland wing Simon Geoghegan plunges over for one of Ireland's four tries in their 30–17 defeat of Wales in Dublin.

SCOTLAND
Neil Drysdale
Scotland on Sunday

IT WOULD be foolish to believe Scottish rugby embraced professionalism with open arms. Indeed, just four months before the International Rugby Board's historic August meeting in Paris, the chief executive of the Scottish Rugby Union, Bill Hogg, actually wrote in the match programme for the Scotland–Romania game: 'It would seem that, other than for a very few, the majority want rugby to remain amateur. Association with this wonderful game is greatly valued by sponsors of clubs, districts and unions, and many companies have said to me that if it was a professional game they would not wish to be connected with it. Many other people from all levels of rugby would also stop if anyone involved was to be paid.'

But, although the onset of the new era proved a troubling time for the SRU, somehow or other they managed to avoid most of the confrontations and threat of breakaways which pervaded the sport in England.

For sure, there was a regular diet of disagreement for the press to feed upon, with Scotland's international players and Union officials taking an age to draw up match contracts, while the bitter resentment felt at Murrayfield following the Rugby Football Union's decision to negotiate its own TV deal for the Five Nations Championship cast a long shadow over the latter stages of a season which had already seen a new league structure and the inaugural Tennent's Scottish Cup – won respectively by Melrose and Hawick – introduced to the Scottish club scene.

Argument raged over whether clubs or districts should fly the Saltire in Europe, with feelings running sufficiently high that the newly formed limited company of Scotland's professional clubs, led by Melrose, called for a vote on the issue at a Special General Meeting at Murrayfield. Despite recruiting Gavin Hastings to state their case, they were overwhelmingly defeated on a night when the little league outfits exercised their right to stifle ambition, but the First Division clubs' principal fear – that they would lose their best players without recourse to the financial revenue generated by European competition – was a real enough concern, as subsequent events were to demonstrate.

Even before the 1995/96 season had started Gregor Townsend and Michael Dods, two of the leading luminaries of Scotland's unexpectedly successful Five Nations campaign, left Gala to link up with the former

Scotland coach, Ian McGeechan, at Northampton. Then, as the winter progressed, Doddie Weir and Gary Armstrong joined Sir John Hall's Tyneside revolution, Craig Joiner moved to Leicester, and a host of other internationals, including Bryan Redpath, Graham Shiel, Kenny Logan and Tony Stanger, were targetted by Courage League sides.

The threat was recognised, however belatedly, by the SRU's creation of a 'loyalty bonus' – a concept which would have been unthinkable in the very recent past – but the transfer rumours and allegations of player-poaching continued unabated, with most of the dark glances being directed at Melrose, who responded to losing Weir and Joiner by signing a trio of internationals: Peter Wright, Scott Nichol and Derek Stark.

> *'As we rush into the new era it's lift yourself up for this match, lift yourself up for that, and we're going to burn our leading performers out if we simply expect them to play week in, week out without a break ... We're not carthorses' – Rob Wainwright*

Increasingly, the rugby circuit began to resemble the football transfer market, but at least there was one influential player prepared to buck the trend by leaving England and returning to Edinburgh. Rob Wainwright, who enjoyed a particularly impressive first year as Scottish captain, steering his side from the depths of an embarrassing defeat in Italy to three wins out of four in the Five Nations Championship, decided to depart the struggling West Hartlepool club and join Watsonians, and in so doing signalled his determination not to let rugby dictate his life.

So much so, indeed, that Wainwright fears for the future of rugby unless the administrators accept that their most important commodity – the players – are allowed an occasional respite from the sweat and strain of the endless winter scenario in which the game is currently being propelled.

'As we rush into the new era it's lift yourself up for this match, lift yourself up for that, and we're going to burn our leading performers out if we simply expect them to play week in, week out without a break', says Wainwright. 'Since the World Cup finished in South Africa, we've effectively been asked to regard rugby as a full-time occupation, and when you think the leagues got underway at the beginning of September and the Cup didn't finish until the middle of May, two weeks before

Scotland's tour of New Zealand, then you can only guess at how bad the pressure is going to be once you add Europe to the equation.

'Seriously, we need some kind of summer break; we're not cart-horses and the game has to address this question as soon as possible. The fact is that rugby isn't the same as football: it's a far harder contact sport and our bodies can only take so much punishment. I think the various unions know that already, but common sense has gone out of the window in the rush by some authorities to find the television money to pay their players.'

As an army doctor, Wainwright speaks with authority on this subject and he is not the only person to worry about the longterm injury problems which players may be storing up for themselves through being pitched into ever-tougher competitions in an apparently ever-expanding calendar. But, until his message is heeded, there seems little doubt that rugby is bound for a season or two of rampant activity in the market place – a prospect that obviously alarms the normally phlegmatic Wainwright.

> *'We were all aware that professionalism would inevitably change the face of Rugby Union, and not all for good, but it would have been nice to think that representatives of all the Five Nations could have sat down and discussed the best way forward ... but I suppose that's me being naive' – Rob Wainwright*

'We were all aware that professionalism would inevitably change the face of Rugby Union, and not all for good, but it would have been nice to think that representatives of all the Five Nations could have sat down and discussed the best way forward as soon as the IB removed the amateurism regulations from the statute book – but I suppose that's me being naive', added the 31-year-old flanker.

'However, the root of the recent troubles between the clubs and the RFU, and the whole furore over whether England should be permitted to sort out their own broadcasting deal, lies in one basic reality: that no one wants to be left behind in the stampede for TV cash. It's sad, it's greed rearing its ugly head, but then you can't say the governing bodies weren't warned in advance and, frankly, it's they and emphatically not the players who have to sort out the whole mess.'

Not surprisingly, affairs on the field tended to take a back seat to the power struggles, but when granted the chance to exhibit their talents, the Scots recovered well enough from the Italian debacle and a 15–15 home draw with Western Samoa to suggest they are a match for anyone in the Five Nations – except England, who shattered their hopes of a fourth Grand Slam with a clinical if prosaic 18–9 victory at Murrayfield.

'I can't put my finger on it, but the boys simply weren't up for the Samoan game, while we forgot the basics of kicking and tackling against Italy', considered Wainwright. 'Nonetheless, apart from the frustration of losing to the English, there were a lot of positive things to derive from the Five Nations, even though the fact that we failed to reach 20 points in any match underlines our lack of killer instinct and inability to finish off opposition.'

The same could be said of the birth-pangs of professionalism in Scotland. We can be mightily relieved that the SRU have so far avoided a repetition of the very personal feuds which have blighted their English counterparts. But the clubs remain vulnerable and, in the absence of any Scottish businessman to rival Sir John Hall or Ashley Levett, extremely poor. One only hopes that as the likes of Melrose strive to retain their best talents with cobbled-together contracts, they are not spending money they don't have.

*Mike Dods dives over for the first of his two tries in
Scotland's dazzling victory over France at Murrayfield.*

SCOTLAND (P11 W5 D1 L5 F297 A234)

(–)	v Cote d'Ivoire*	Rustenburg, 26.5.95)	won 89–0
(–)	v Tonga*	(Pretoria, 30.5.95)	won 41–5
(–)	v France*	(Pretoria, 3.6.95)	lost19–22
(–)	v New Zealand*	(q/f: Pretoria, 11.6.95)	lost30–48
(H)	v Western Samoa	(Edinburgh, 18.11.95)	drew15–15
(A)	v Ireland	(Dublin, 20.1.96)	won16–10
(H)	v France	(Edinburgh, 3.2.96)	won19–14
(A)	v Wales	(Cardiff, 17.2.96)	won16–14
(H)	v England	(Edinburgh, 2.3.96)	lost 9–18
(A)	v New Zealand (I)	(Dunedin, 15.6.96)	lost31–62
(A)	v New Zealand (ii)	(Auckland, 22.6.96)	lost12–36

* World Cup; + non-cap

Scotland in New Zealand (tour record: P8 W4 D0 L4 F266 A238)

(A)	v Wanganui	Wanganui, 28.5.96)	won49–13
(A)	v Northland	(Whangerei, 31.5.96)	lost10–15
(A)	v Waikato	(Hamilton, 5.6.96)	lost35–39
(A)	v Southland	(Invercargill, 8.6.96)	won31–21
(A)	v South Island Divisional XV	(Blenheim, 11.6.96)	won63–21
(A)	v Bay of Plenty	(Rotorua, 18.6.96)	won35–31

Western Samoa in Scotland (Scottish tour record: P4 W2 D1 L0 F72 A102)

(–)	v Edinburgh Districts	(Inverleith, 8.11.95)	won22–35
(–)	v Scotland A	(Hawick, 12.11.95)	won 26–9
(–)	v North & Midlands	(Perth, 14.11.95)	lost 9–43

SCOTLAND A (P5 W2 D0 L3 F115 A135)

(H)	v Western Samoa	(Hawick, 12.11.95)	lost 9–26
(A)	v Italy	(Rieti, 6.1.96)	lost17–29
(A)	v Ireland	(Donnybrook, 19.1.96)	lost19–26
(H)	v France	(Edinburgh, 2.2.96)	won38–32
(A)	v Wales	(Swansea, 16.2.96)	won32–22

SCOTLAND DEVELOPMENT XV (P1 W0 D0 L1 F11 A48)

(H)	v New South Wales	(Scotland, 11.2.96)	lost11–48

SCOTLAND UNDER-21 (P5 W1 D0 L4 F82 A106)

(A)	v England	(Gateshead, 12.12.95)	lost18–21
(H)	v Italy	(Scotland, 6.1.96)	won31–10
(A)	v Ireland	(Ireland, 19.1.96)	lost 9–21
(H)	v France	(Scotland, 3.2.96)	lost 3–29
(A)	v Wales	(Swansea, 16.2.96)	lost21–25

SCOTLAND STUDENTS (P1 W0 D0 L1 F9 A44)

(H)	v England	(Inverleith, 1.3.96)	lost 9–44

SCOTTISH UNIVERSITIES (P3 W0 D0 L3 F31 A98)

(A)	v Irish	(Dublin, 19.1.96)	lost 9–43
(A)	v Welsh	(Pontypool, 16.2.96)	lost12–21
(H)	v English	(Peffermill, 1.3.96)	lost10–34

SCOTLAND SCHOOLS UNDER-18 (P4 W0 D0 L4 F34 A135)

(H)	v France	(Edinburgh, 22.12.95)	lost 12–18
(A)	v Wales	(Bridgend, 5.1.96)	lost 3–30
(H)	v England	(Hawick, 27.3.96)	lost 7–50
(A)	v Ireland	(Cork, 6.4.96)	lost 12–37

FIRA WORLD YOUTH CUP (Italy: 22 March - 8 April)

(–)	v Chile	(Pool Three, 1.4.96)	drew 17–17
(–)	v South Africa	(Pool Three, 3.4.96)	won 18–15
(–)	v Argentina	(semi-finals, 5.4.96)	lost 20–41
(–)	v Romania	(third-place play-off, 7.4.96)	lost 6–32

SCOTLAND UNDER-19 (P3 W1 D0 L2 F42 A71)

(A)	v Ireland	(Galway, 30.3.96)	won 18–17
(H)	v Wales	(Ayr, 20.4.96)	lost 11–18
(A)	v England	(Coventry, 13.4.96)	lost 13–36

SCOTLAND UNDER-18 (P1 W1 D0 L0 F19 A11)

(H)	v Wales	(Ayr, 20.4.96)	won 19–11

SCOTLAND WOMEN (P3 W1 D0 L2 F35 A26)

(A)	v Wales	(Bridgend, 18.2.96)	lost 6–11
(H)	v Scotland	(Blackrock, 21.1.96)	won 21–3
(H)	v England	(Edinburgh, 3.3.96)	lost 8–12

Final standings: (1) England P3 W3 Pts6; (2) Wales P3 W2 Pts4; (3) Scotland P3 W1 Pts2; (4) Ireland P3 W0 Pts0.

DOMESTIC RUGBY

SRU DISTRICT CHAMPIONSHIP

	P	W	D	L	tries	F	A	Pts
Exiles	4	4	0	0	12	100	50	8
North & Midlands	4	2	0	2	11	95	72	4
Edinburgh	4	2	0	2	10	109	82	4
South	4	2	0	2	4	80	82	4
Glasgow	4	0	0	4	7	63	161	0

Exiles retain title; try-count used to split also-rans.

SRU TENNENTS PREMIERSHIP

League One	P	W	D	L	F	A	Pts
Melrose	14	9	1	4	326	199	19
Stirling County	14	9	1	4	320	215	19
Watsonians	14	8	1	5	393	270	17
Boroughmuir	14	7	2	5	327	301	16
Hawick	14	7	0	7	243	288	14
Heriot's FP	13	5	1	7	278	360	11
Edinburgh Acads	14	4	1	9	243	282	9
Gala	13	2	1	10	179	394	5

champions: Melrose; **relegated:** Gala, Edinburgh Acads

League Two	P	W	D	L	F	A	Pts
Currie	14	11	0	3	357	266	22
Jed-Forest	14	10	0	4	302	185	20
Glasgow H/K	14	8	0	6	377	239	16
West of Scotland	14	7	0	7	268	258	14
Dundee HSFP	14	6	0	8	259	239	12
Kelso	14	6	0	8	275	260	12
Selkirk	14	5	0	9	215	307	10
Stewart's-Melville FP	14	3	0	11	193	492	6

promoted: Currie (c), Jed-Forest; **relegated:** Stewart's-Melville FP, Selkirk

League Three – *promoted:* Glasgow Acads (c), Biggar; *relegated:* Corstorphine, Grangemouth
League Four -- *promoted:* Kilmarnock (c), Glasgow S; *relegated (to National League One):* Wigtownshire, Edinburgh Wanderers

National League One – *promoted:* Glenrothes (c), Hillhead/Jordanhill; *relegated:* Royal High, Dumfries
National League Two – *promoted:* East Kilbride (c), Aberdeen GSFP; *relegated:* Howe of Fife, Perthshire
National League Three – *promoted:* Berwick (c), Allan Glens; *relegated:* North Berwick, Highland
National League Four – *promoted:* Annan (c), Lismore.

Tennent's 1556 Cup final
Hawick 17, Watsonians 15 (Murrayfield, 11.5.96)

Scotland stand-off Gregor Townsend splits the England cover with the one telling break during a tryless Calcutta Cup contest in Edinburgh.

1980:

I	L15–22	Dublin	2 Feb	**t:** Johnston 2
				c: Irvine 2
				p: Irvine
F	W22–14	Edinburgh	16 Feb	**t:** Rutherford, Irvine 2
				c: Irvine, Renwick
				p: Irvine 2
W	L 6–17	Cardiff	1 Mar	**t:** Renwick
				c: Irvine
E	L18–30	Edinburgh	15 Mar	**t:** Tomes, Rutherford
				c: Irvine 2
				p: Irvine 2

1981:

F	L 9–16	Paris	17 Jan	**t:** Rutherford
				c: Renwick
				p: Irvine
W	W15–6	Edinburgh	7 Feb	**t:** Tomes, penalty try
				c: Renwick 2
				p: Renwick
E	L17–23	Twickenham	21 Feb	**t:** Monro 2, J Calder
				c: Irvine
				p: Irvine
I	W10–9	Edinburgh	21 Mar	**t:** Hay
				p: Irvine
				dg: Rutherford
NZ(1)	L 4–11	Dunedin	13 June	**t:** Deans
NZ(2)	L15–40	Auckland	20 Jun	**t:** Hay
				c: Irvine
				p: Irvine 2
				dg: Renwick
R	W12–6	Edinburgh	26 Sep	**p:** Irvine 4
A	W24–15	Edinburgh	19 Dec	**t:** Renwick
				c: Irvine
				p: Irvine 5
				dg: Rutherford

1982:

E	D 9–9	Edinburgh	16 Jan	**p:** Irvine 2
				dg: Rutherford
I	L12–21	Dublin	20 Feb	**t:** Rutherford
				c: Irvine
				p: Renwick 2
F	W16–7	Edinburgh	6 Mar	**t:** Rutherford
				p: Irvine 3
				dg: Renwick
W	W34–18	Cardiff	20 Mar	**t:** J Calder, Renwick, Pollock, White, Johnston
				c: Irvine 4
				dg: Renwick, Rutherford

A(1)	W12–7	Brisbane	3 Jul	t: Robertson
				c: Irvine
				p: Irvine
				dg: Rutherford
A(2)	L 9–33	Sydney	10 Jul	p: Irvine 3
Fj+	W32–12	Edinburgh	25 Sep	t: Dods 2, Johnston, F Calder, Beattie
				c: Dods 3
				p: Dods
				dg: Rutherford

1983:

I	L13–15	Edinburgh	15 Jan	t: Laidlaw
				p: Dods 2
				dg: Renwick
F	L15–19	Paris	5 Feb	t: Robertson
				c: Dods
				p: Dods
				dg: Gossman 2
W	L15–19	Edinburgh	19 Feb	t: Renwick
				c: Dods
				p: Dods 3
E	W22–12	Twickenham	5 Mar	t: Laidlaw, Smith
				c: Dods
				p: Dods 3
				dg: Robertson
NZ	D25–25	Edinburgh	12 Nov	t: Pollock
				p: Dods 5
				dg: Rutherford 2

1984:

W	W15–9	Cardiff	21 Jan	t: Paxton, Aitken
				c: Dods 2
				p: Dods
E	W18–6	Edinburgh	4 Feb	t: Johnston, Kennedy
				c: Dods 2
				p: Dods 2
I	W32–9	Dublin	3 Mar	t: Laidlaw 2, penalty try, Robertson, Dods
				c: Dods 3
				p: Dods 2
F	W21–12	Edinburgh	17 Feb	t: J Calder
				c: Dods
				p: Dods 5
R	L22–28	Bucharest	12 May	t: Leslie, Dods
				c: Dods
				p: Dods 3
				dg: Robertson
A	L12–27	Edinburgh	8 Dec	p: Dods 4

1985:

| I | L15–18 | Edinburgh | 2 Feb | p: Dods 4 |
| | | | | dg: Robertson |

53

F	L 3–11	Paris	16 Feb	p: Dods
W	L21–25	Edinburgh	2 Mar	t: Paxton 2
				c: Dods 2
				p: Dods
				dg: Rutherford 2
E	L 7–10	Twickenham	16 Mar	t: Robertson
				p: Dods

1986:

F	W18–17	Edinburgh	17 Jan	p: G Hastings 6
W	L15–22	Cardiff	1 Feb	t: Duncan, Jeffrey, G Hastings
				p: G Hastings
E	W33–6	Edinburgh	15 Feb	t: Duncan, Rutherford, S Hastings
				c: G Hastings 3
				p: G Hastings 5
I	W10–9	Dublin	12 Mar	t: Laidlaw
				p: G Hastings 2
R	W33–18	Bucharest	30 Mar	t: Jeffrey, S Hastings, Deans
				c: G Hastings 3
				p: G Hastings 5

1987:

I	W16–12	Edinburgh	21 Feb	t: Laidlaw, Tukalo
				c: G Hastings
				dg: Rutherford 2
F(a)	L22–28	Paris	7 Mar	t: Beattie, S Hastings
				c: G Hastings
				p: G Hastings 4
W	W21–14	Edinburgh	21 Mar	t: Beattie, Jeffrey
				c: G Hastings 2
				p: G Hastings 2
				dg: Rutherford
E	L12–21	Twickenham	4 Apr	t: Robertson
				c: G Hastings
				p: G Hastings 2
Sp+	W25–7	Edinburgh	19 Apr	t: Duncan, Tukalo, Deans, Paxton
				c: G Hastings 3
				p: G Hastings
F(b)*	D20–20	Christchurch	23 May	t: White, Duncan
				p: G Hastings 4
Z*	W60–21	Wellington	30 May	t: Tait 2, Duncan 2, Tukalo 2, Paxton 2, Oliver, G Hastings, Jeffrey
				c: G Hastings 8
R*	W55–28	Dunedin	2 Jun	t: G Hastings 2, Tukalo, Duncan Tait 2, Jeffrey 3
				c: G Hastings 8
				p: G Hastings
NZ*	L 3–30	Christchurch	6 Jun	p: G Hastings

1988:

I	L18–22	Dublin	16 Jan	t: Laidlaw, S Hastings
				c: G Hastings 2
				p: G Hastings 2

F	W23–12	Edinburgh	6 Feb	t: G Hastings, Tukalo
				p: G Hastings 4
				dg: Cramb
W	L20–25	Cardiff	20 Feb	t: F Calder, Duncan
				p: G Hastings 4
E	L 6–9	Edinburgh	5 Mar	p: G Hastings 2
A	L13–32	Edinburgh	19 Nov	t: G Hastings, Robertson
				c: G Hastings
				p: G Hastings

1989:

W	W23–7	Edinburgh	21 Jan	t: Armstrong, White, Chalmers
				c: Dods
				p: Dods 2
				dg: Chalmers
E	D12–12	Twickenham	4 Feb	t: Jeffrey
				c: Dods
				p: Dods 2
I	W37–21	Edinurgh	4 Mar	t: Tukalo 3, Jeffrey, Cronin
				c: Dods 4
				p: Dods 3
F	L 3–19	Paris	19 Mar	p: Dods
Fj	W38–17	Edinburgh	28 Oct	t: Stanger 2, K Milne, Gray, G Hastings, Tukalo
				c: G Hastings 4
				p: G Hastings 2
R	W32–0	Edinburgh	9 Dec	t: Stanger 3, White, Sole
				c: G Hastings 3
				p: G Hastings 2

1990:

I	W13–10	Dublin	3 Feb	t: White 2
				c: Chalmers
				p: Chalmers
F	W21–0	Edinburgh	17 Feb	t: F Calder, Tukalo
				c: Chalmers 2
				p: Chalmers 2, G Hastings
W	W13–9	Cardiff	3 Mar	t: Cronin
				p: Chalmers 3
E	W13–7	Edinburgh	17 Mar	t: Stanger
				p: Chalmers 3
NZ(1)	L16–31	Dunedin	16 Jun	t: Lineen, Gray, Sole
				c: G Hastings 2
NZ(2)	L18–21	Auckland	23 Jun	t: Stanger, Moore
				c: G Hastings 2
				p: G Hastings 2
Arg	W49–3	Edinburgh	10 Nov	t: Stanger 2, K Milne 2, Moore, Armstrong, Gray, G Hastings, Chalmers
				c: G Hastings 5
				p: G Hastings

1991:

F	L 9–15	Paris	19 Jan	**p:** Chalmers 2
				dg: Chalmers
W	W32–12	Edinburgh	2 Feb	**t:** Chalmers, White 2, Armstrong
				c: Chalmers, G Hastings
				p: Chalmers, G Hastings 2
				dg: Chalmers
E(a)	L12–21	Twickenham	16 Feb	**p:** Chalmers 4
I(a)	W28–25	Edinburgh	16 Mar	**t:** G Hastings, Stanger, S Hastings
				c: Chalmers 2
				p: Chalmers 3, G Hastings
R	L12–18	Bucharest	31 Aug	**t:** Tukalo
				c: Dods
				p: Dods 2
J*	W47–9	Edinburgh	5 Oct	**t:** S Hastings, Stanger, Chalmers, penalty try, White, Tukalo, G Hastings
				c: G Hastings 5
				p: Chalmers, G Hastings 2
Z*	W51–12	Edinburgh	9 Oct	**t:** Tukalo 3, Turnbull, Stanger, S Hastings, Weir, White
				c: Dods 5
				p: Dods 2
				dg: Wyllie
I(b)*	W24–15	Edinburgh	12 Oct	**t:** Shiel, Armstrong
				c: G Hastings 2
				p: G Hastings 3
				dg: Chalmers
WS*	W28–6	Edinburgh	19 Oct	**t:** Jeffrey 2, Stanger
				c: G Hastings 2
				p: G Hastings 4
E(b)*	L 6–9	Edinburgh	26 Oct	**p:** G Hastings 2
NZ*	L 6–13	Cardiff	30 Oct	**p:** G Hastings 2

1992:

E	L 7–25	Edinburgh	18 Jan	**t:** White
				p: G Hastings
I	W18–10	Dublin	15 Feb	**t:** Stanger, Nicol
				c: G Hastings 2
				p: G Hastings 2
F	W10–6	Edinburgh	7 Mar	**t:** Edwards
				p: G Hastings 2
W	L12–15	Cardiff	21 Mar	**p:** G Hastings, Chalmers 2
				dg: Chalmers
A(1)	L12–27	Sydney	13 Jun	**t:** Wainwright
				c: G Hastings
				p: G Hastings 2
A(2)	L13–37	Brisbane	21 Jun	**t:** Lineen, Sole
				c: Chalmers
				p: Chalmers

1993:

I†	W15–3	Edinburgh	16 Jan	**t:** Stark, Stanger **c:** G Hastings **p:** G Hastings
F	L 3–11	Paris	6 Feb	**p:** G Hastings
W	W20–0	Edinburgh	20 Feb	**t:** Turnbull **p:** G Hastings 5
E	L12–26	Twickenham	6 Mar	**p:** G Hastings 3 **dg:** Chalmers
NZ	L15–51	Edinburgh	20 Nov	**p:** G Hastings 4, Chalmers

1994:

W	L 6–29	Cardiff	15 Jan	**p:** G Hastings 2
E	L14–15	Edinburgh	5 Feb	**t:** Wainwright **p:** G Hastings 2 **dg:** Townsend
I	D 6–6	Dublin	5 Mar	**p:** G Hastings 2
F	L12–20	Edinburgh	19 Mar	**p:** G Hastings 4
Arg(1)	L15–16	Buenos Aires	4 Jun	**p:** M Dods 5
Arg(2)	L17–19	Buenos Aires	11 Jun	**t:** Logan **p:** Shiel 2, M Dods **dg:** Townsend
SA	L10–34	Edinburgh	19 Nov	**t:** Stanger **c:** G Hastings **p:** G Hastings

1995:

C	W22–6	Edinburgh	21 Jan	**t:** Cronin **c:** G Hastings **p:** G Hastings 5
I	W26–13	Edinburgh	4 Feb	**t:** Joiner, Cronin **c:** G Hastings 2 **p:** G Hastings 4
F(a)	W23–21	Paris	18 Feb	**t:** Townsend, G Hastings **c:** G Hastings 2 **p:** G Hastings 3
W	W26–13	Edinburgh	4 Mar	**t:** Peters, Hilton **c:** G Hastings 2 **p:** G Hastings 4
E	L12–24	Twickenham	18 Mar	**p:** G Hastings 4
R	W49–16	Murrayfield	22 Apr	**t:** Stanger 2, G Hastings, Shiel, Logan, Joiner, Peters **c:** G Hastings 4 **p:** G Hastings 2
Sp+	W62–7	Madrid	6 May	**t:** Joiner 3, Wainwright 2, G Hastings 2, Logan, Chalmers, Morrison **c:** G Hastings 6
IC*	W89–0	Rustenburg	26 May	**t:** G Hastings 4, Walton 2, Logan 2, Stanger, Chalmers, Shiel, Burnell, Wright **c:** G Hastings 9 **p:** G Hastings 2

T*	W41–5	Pretoria	30 May	**t:** G Hastings, Peters, S Hastings
				c: G Hastings
				p: G Hastings 8
F(b)*	L19–22	Pretoria	3 Jun	**t:** Wainwright
				c: G Hastings
				p: G Hastings 4
NZ*	L30–48	Pretoria	11 Jun	**t:** Weir 2, S Hastings
				c: G Hastings 3
				p: G Hastings 3
WS	D15–15	Edinburgh	18 Nov	**p:** M Dods 5

1996:

It+	L17–29	Rieti	6 Jan	**t:** Redpath
				p: Shepherd 3, Townsend
I	W16–10	Dublin	20 Jan	**t:** M Dods, McKenzie
				p: M Dods
				dg: Townsend
F	W19–14	Edinburgh	3 Feb	**t:** M Dods 2
				p: M Dods 3
W	W16–14	Cardiff	17 Feb	**t:** Townsend
				c: M Dods
				p: M Dods 3
E	L9–18	Edinburgh	2 Mar	**p:** M Dods 3
NZ(1)	L31–62	Dunedin	15 June	**t:** Joiner, Peters, Townsend
				c: Shepherd 2
				p: Shepherd 3
				dg: Shepherd
NZ(2)	L12–36	Auckland	22 June	**t:** Shepherd, Peters
				c: Shepherd

* World Cup
+ Non-cap
† Five-point try introduced from this game onwards

*Scotland fullback Rowen Shepherd takes the ball despite
the close attentions of France captain Philippe Saint-Andre.*

WALES
Robert Cole

A NEW coach, a new team, new horizons – yet the same old results. Not even the introduction of Terry Cobner as the inaugural Director of Rugby could bring about dramatic changes in fortunes on the field.

With the 1999 World Cup edging ever nearer, the host nation, at least guaranteed qualification, found themselves lifting themselves out of the rut of failure that has dogged them in the nineties. The return to South Africa brought a promising start with a Mark Bennett try within three minutes of the start. But thereafter the world champions progressed to a record win (40–11) for the fixture.

Exit coach Alex Evans, returning to Australia to take up a Cobner-style post ahead of the newly created Welsh position, and enter Kevin Bowring. His honeymoon period as caretaker coach included a 19–15 win over Fiji; his appointment as Wales' first full-time national coach marked by a 31–26 triumph over Italy. Two victories, but little sign of a convincing future for his side.

The Five Nations campaign saw Wales compete vigorously. They went down bravely at Twickenham, 21–15; threw away victory at home to the Scots, losing 14–16; and then collapsed to a record defeat in Ireland, 17–30. That left the final fixture against the French at the Arms Park. Cobner's never-say-die, never-concede-an-inch spirit came shining through in a young team on the day and a famous 16–15 victory was secured.

The statistics showed that Wales had moved off the bottom of the Five Nations table, leaving Ireland clutching the Wooden Spoon, but Bowring, Cobner and captain Jonathan Humphreys knew the road ahead was going to be tougher still.

Yes, Wales had put together the most effective lineout in the Northern Hemisphere – Humphreys the thrower, Gareth Llewellyn and Derwyn Jones the catchers – and in scrum-half Robert Howley uncovered one of the greatest talents in the world game. Leigh Davies, too, had settled in nicely at centre and Gwyn Jones had made a major impact as an old fashioned openside flanker.

There was also the trusty boot of Neil Jenkins to fall back on – the Pontypridd stand-off hoisted his points tally through the 400 barrier during the season, despite missing the first three Five Nations matches – and a renewed sense of style, purpose and pride under Bowring and assistant coach Allan Lewis.

But the familiar story of depressing defeat returned in Australia. A revitalised ACT set the alarm bells ringing on the second match of the eight-game tour with a resounding 69–30 victory. Then the Wallabies ran in seven tries in their 56–25 first Test win and six in a 42–3 second Test victory. It was back to the drawing board for Kevin Bowring.

At least Cobner and Bowring were prepared to view the goings-on in 1996 realistically. Their clear objective is the World Cup, and reaching the final in 1999. The hardest task of all is finding a way – any way – to turn the hopes of a rugby-mad nation into anything approaching reality.

> '*We have discovered a style that suits us. Now we have to make that style instinctive at all levels, to introduce it to schools and clubs. The big danger on the club scene is that I will fail to influence the coaches because they are concerned about winning two league points. I have to convince them that they can still be successful by playing in the new Welsh style*' – *Terry Cobner*

Cobner's view of the victory over France was typical of the man who demanded nothing short of the best from the teams he led at Pontypool, with Wales and the British Lions. His plan to build on the 'feel good' factor created by Wales' first Five Nations win in nine matches was to preach the gospel of the new style adopted by the team to the coaches of the leading clubs and to those in the schools system.

'In terms of progress we have got our feet on the bottom rung of the ladder, at last. Our ultimate aim is to reach the World Cup final in three years time', he said. 'We have discovered a style that suits us. Now we have to make that style instinctive at all levels, to introduce it to schools and clubs. The big danger on the club scene is that I will fail to influence the coaches because they are concerned about winning two league points. I have to convince them that they can still be successful by playing in the new Welsh style.

'I know how difficult it will be, because you wouldn't have convinced me at Pontypool 15 years ago. The more progressive ones are already coming on board, and they know we have to increase the tempo, commitment and skill at all levels of our game.

'Now that we are in a professional era, we have to appreciate that if we want to survive we have to entertain. Referees must be aware of what we are trying to do and be sympathetic.'

Wales may have ended one place off the bottom of the championship table, yet they scored twice as many tries – six – as did Will Carling's title-winning England side. That convinced both the Welsh players and their management team that they were working on the right lines in trying to get back to a more natural Welsh style.

'When we set out on the Five Nations campaign, we wanted to build a team our supporters could be proud of – a team playing with pride and passion and appreciated by the Welsh people', Bowring said. 'We tried to redevelop a style of play that was uniquely Welsh, to revert to a game emphasising speed, speed of hand, speed of thought, playing with guile and cunning. To score tries playing a game that reflected our culture in Wales.'

The joy of victory – and the relief among the Welsh players at not experiencing back-to-back whitewashes in the championship – was evident from the post-match celebrations against the French. Humphreys brought his team back onto the ground from the dressing rooms for a collective back-slapping operation. The players loved the ovation, the crowd loved the players.

> 'Now that we are in a professional era, we have to appreciate that if we want to survive we have to entertain. Referees must be aware of what we are trying to do and be sympathetic' – Cobner

'We don't want to overplay that win, but it was the point when the players realised they could take on, and beat, one of the top sides by playing the style we have been growing into under coach Kevin Bowring', said Humphreys. 'Of course there had been doubts before then, because we were slipping up when we had got into winning positions, so we needed a victory to confirm we were going down the right road. Losing is a bad habit and winning is the habit we want to take on board.

'When we first started playing the more fluid and expansive game, it was alien to the majority of the squad but now most of the Welsh clubs are adopting the same style, where making mistakes is not a hanging offence. Of course there will be mistakes as we develop, but the more we play that way the more comfortable we will be and it will become second nature. That said, what we do need is to up the physical edge. We started that process against the French and now it has to be carried on.

'There is a huge desire in this squad to do well, and a great self-belief that we can become a great side. We have some major individuals playing for Wales now, both in character and ability, who simply won't settle for anything less than being the best. The tour to Australia is bound to play a major part in our development. I would like to see us going into the 1997 championship with a realistic hope of becoming champions.'

Of grave concern to Cobner and Co., not to mention the Welsh rugby public, is why Wales fall to so many humiliating defeats when they travel abroad. Last summer's first Test defeat by the Wallabies was the second-highest defeat suffered by Wales, just behind the 63–6 reverse at the same Ballymore ground in Brisbane in 1991.

> *'There is a huge desire in this squad to do well, and a great self-belief that we can become a great side. We have some major individuals playing for Wales now ... who simply won't settle for anything less than being the best'* – Jonathan Humphreys

So why does it happen? Is it attitude? Is it mentality? Cobner dismisses neither, but has come up with his own idea. 'A lack of preparation has far more to do with Wales' lack of success abroad than attitude or British mentality, call it what you will', he observed. 'Our preparation time for the tour to Australia was appalling and we had to fight like hell for every scrap of that time because of club commitments. With that sort of build-up, we simply have no right to expect to produce winning touring teams. Quite simply, we have not learned the lessons from previous poor tours.'

And it is that fact that really bugs Cobner, who fears that the pattern will be repeated over and over again until it is just too late to learn new tricks. 'Every time we have gone home after getting a stuffing, what happens? Nothing!' he blasted. 'So we go again a year or so later, get another stuffing and again nothing happens.'

'What worries me is that if nothing changes – and it hasn't yet – it will carry on going that way for ever and ever. People at home must be aware of the step-up we are asking our players to take when they come out of our domestic game, which is pedestrian, to take on state and provincial sides who are already playing to a higher standard than the Five Nations. Quite simply, it is unfair. We are not playing on a level field. I felt sorry for the Welsh players against Australia.

> '*I believe we have to react and revamp because the Southern Hemisphere countries are playing a different ball game. The intensity, pace and physical aspects of their game are something else again. In contrast, the quality of our First Division rugby just isn't good enough*' – Cobner

'We have got options. We can stick our heads in the sand – as we have always done previously – or we can change our structure to enable Wales to compete at the highest level. If people want the second option, then we need a structure along the lines adopted by the Southern

Wales scrum-half Rob Howley jumps for joy after scoring a try against England at Twickenham on his full international debut.

Hemisphere countries, where the top players are subjected to high-intensity, high-paced matches on a weekly basis. At the moment, with the different structures between Northern and Southern Hemisphere, our competitive level simply does not measure up.

'I see my role as setting the agenda to discuss change. I have already spoken to the senior players to find out what structure they believe we need in Wales. I think we need something along the lines of the Super-12 with either club teams or provincial sides taking part. That would be a start, at least.

'It is worth pointing out how Australian Capital Territory, who defeated us 69–30, prepared for the game. While we had a weekend camp just before heading 'down under', they had three weekend camps, a full one-week camp and then a three-week tour of Japan. In between, they trained every day from 4pm until 6pm as a team.

'When we met them, we found ourselves facing a side coming into the match on the back of playing an 11-match Super-12 series in which they had beaten both finalists.

'So our cycle simply cannot go on – unless, of course, we are prepared to accept things staying as they are. In which case, so be it.'

But Cobner is no quitter. He has vowed to visit every rugby club in Wales, talk to every club coach, and even move Snowdon if that is what it takes to give the Welsh players the playing structure they need to get back on terms with the best in the world.

'I believe we have to react and revamp because the Southern Hemisphere countries are playing a different ball game', he said. 'The intensity, pace and physical aspects of their game are something else again. In contrast, the quality of our First Division rugby just isn't good enough. It doesn't do anyone any good when sides are winning by 60 or 70 points. And it means the step-up from one-paced club rugby to international rugby is just too big to take. It all goes back to what I said at the beginning. There is always a great level of expectation about a Wales tour, yet there is an appalling lack of preparation. That has to change.'

For the sake of the future of Welsh rugby – will somebody please listen?

WALES (P12 W4 D0 L8 F240 A329)

(–) v Japan*	(Bloemfontein, 27.5.95)	won57–10
(–) v New Zealand*	(Johannesburg, 31.5.95)	lost 9–34
(–) v Ireland*	(Johannesburg, 4.6.95)	lost23–24
(A) v South Africa	(Johannesburg, 2.9.95)	lost11–40
(H) v Fiji	(Cardiff, 11.11.95)	won19–15
(H) v Italy	(Cardiff, 16.1.96)	won31–26
(A) v England	(Twickenham, 3.2.96)	lost15–21
(H) v Scotland	(Cardiff, 17.2.96)	lost14–16
(A) v Ireland	(Dublin, 2.3.96)	lost17–30
(H) v France	(Cardiff, 16.3.96)	won16–15
(A) v Australia (I)	(Brisbane, 8.6.96)	lost25–56
(A) v Australia (ii)	(Sydney, 22.6.96)	lost 3–42

* World Cup

Wales in South Africa (tour record: P2 W0 D0 L2 F17 A87)

(A) v South East Transvaal	(Witbank, 26.9.95)	lost 6–47

Wales in Australia (tour record: P8 W3 D0 L5 F272 A277)

(A) v Western Australia	(Perth, 29.5.96)	won62–20
(A) v ACT	(Canberra, 2.6.96)	lost30–69
(A) v New South Wales	(North Sydney, 5.6.96)	lost20–27
(A) v Australia B	(Brisbane, 12.6.96)	lost41–51
(A) v NSW Country	(Moree, 15.6.96)	won 49–3
(A) v Victoria	(Melbourne, 18.6.96)	won 42–9

Fiji in Wales (tour record: P7 W3 D0 L4 F189 A153)

(A) v Neath	(Neath, 25.10.95)	lost22–30
(A) v Cardiff	(Cardiff, 28.10.95)	lost21–22
(A) v Treorchy	(Treorchy, 1.11.95)	won70–14
(A) v Pontypridd	(Pontypridd, 4.11.95)	lost13–31
(A) v Llanelli	(Llanelli, 7.11.95)	won38–12

WALES A (P4 W0 D0 L4 F56 A116)

(H) v Fiji	(Bridgend, 21.10.95)	lost10–25
(H) v Scotland	(Swansea, 16.2.96)	lost22–32
(A) v Ireland	(Donnybrook, 1.3.96)	lost11–25
(H) v France	(Newport, 15.3.96)	lost13–34

WALES UNDER-21 (P3 W2 D0 L1 F70 A64)

(H) v NZ Rugby News XV	(Pontypridd, 4.11.95)	won33–23
(H) v Scotland	(Swansea, 16.2.96)	won25–21
(A) v Ireland	(Wicklow, 1.3.96)	lost12–20

WALES STUDENTS (P3 W1 D0 L2 F55 A96)

(A) v England	(Roehampton, 2.2.96)	lost17–33
(H) v France	(Aberavon, 15.3.96)	lost15–41
(A) v Italy	(Catania, 18.5.96)	won23–22

Gareth Llewellyn wins lineout ball for Wales against England at Twickenham.

WELSH UNIVERSITIES (P3 W3 D0 L0 F78 A41)

(A) v England	(Richmond, 2.2.96)	won 35–8
(H) v Scotland	(Pontypool, 16.2.96)	won 21–12
(A) v Ireland	(Dublin, 1.3.96)	won 22–21

WALES DISTRICTS (P1 W1 D0 L0 F11 A6)

(A) v Denmark	(Copenhagen, 30.3.96)	won 11–6

WALES SENIOR SCHOOLS (P3 W3 D0 L0 F97 A22)

(H) v Scotland	(Bridgend, 5.1.95)	won 30–3
(H) v Wales Youth+	(Neath, 14.2.96)	won 51–12
(H) v France	(Mountain Ash, 24.2.96)	won 16–7

WALES YOUTH (P5 W5 D0 L0 F103 A46)

(H) v Italy	(Aberavon, 18.2.96)	won 34–8
(A) v France	(Dax, 9.3.96)	won 21–8
(H) v England	(Swansea, 24.3.96)	won 9–3
(A) v Scotland	(Ayr, 20.4.96)	won 18–11
(H) v Ireland	(Cardiff, 27.4.96)	won 21–16

FIRA WORLD YOUTH CUP (Italy: 22 March – 8 April)

(A) v France	(Brescia, 30.3.96)	won 20–11
(A) v Uruguay	(Mantova, 1.4.96)	won 17–3
(A) v Romania	(semi-final, 4.4.96)	won 21–17
(A) v Argentina	(final: Calvasino, 8.4.96)	lost 7–34

WALES YOUTH UNDER-18 (P1 W0 D0 L1 F11 A19)

(A) v Scotland	(Ayr, 20.4.96)	lost 11–19

WALES UNDER-18 (P3 W1 D1 L1 F72 A35)

(A) v England	(Bridgwater, 30, 3.96)	drew 7–7
(A) v Italy	(Sandora, 6.4.96)	won 53–15
(A) v Ireland	(Belfast, 17.4.96)	lost 12–13

WALES UNDER-16 (P2 W1 D0 L1 F40 A22)

(A)	v England	(Twickenham, 23.3.96)	lost 3–15
(H)	v Portugal	(Treherbert, 13.4.96)	won 37–7

WALES UNDER-16 A (P2 W1 D0 L1 F61 A23)

(A)	v England A	(Imber Court, 22.3.96)	lost10–16
(H)	v Portugal	(Llanelli, 11.4.96)	won 51–7

WALES WOMEN (P3 W2 D0 L1 F36 A68)

(A)	v England	(Leicester, 4.2.96)	lost 3–56
(H)	v Scotland	(Bridgend, 18.2.96)	won 11–6
(A)	v Ireland	(Dublin, 3.3.96)	won 22–6

Final standings: (1) England P3 W3 Pts6; (2) Wales P3 W2 Pts4; (3) Scotland P3 W1 Pts2; (4) Ireland P3 W0 Pts0.

DOMESTIC RUGBY

HEINEKEN CLUB CHAMPIONSHIP

League One	P	W	D	L	Bn	Tr	Pts
Neath	22	17	1	4	37	121	72
Cardiff	22	18	1	3	35	119	72
Pontypridd	22	16	1	5	28	98	61
Llanelli	22	15	0	7	29	88	59
Bridgend	22	12	1	9	22	73	47
Swansea	22	11	0	11	22	83	44
Ebbw Vale	22	11	0	11	8	44	30
Newport	22	10	1	11	9	43	30
Newbridge	22	9	0	13	11	47	29
Treorchy	22	5	1	16	10	45	21
Aberavon	22	3	0	19	8	38	14
Abertillery	22	2	0	20	8	43	12

champions: Neath (on try count); **relegated:** Abertillery, Aberavon.

League Two	P	W	D	L	Bn	Tr	Pts
Dunvant	22	18	0	4	24	78	60
Caerphilly	22	18	0	4	14	57	50
Cross Keys	22	11	0	11	18	68	40
Pontypool	22	12	0	10	15	63	39
Bonymaen	22	10	0	12	14	55	34
Llandovery	22	11	2	9	5	37	29
Maesteg	22	10	1	11	7	38	28
Abercynon	22	10	0	12	6	39	26
Ystradgynlais	22	10	1	11	5	38	28
SW Police	22	7	0	15	11	49	25
Llanharan	22	9	0	13	6	41	24
Tenby United	22	4	0	18	4	33	12

promoted: Dunvant (c), Caerphilly; **relegated:** Tenby Utd, Llanharan.

League 3 – promoted: Blackwood (c), Cardiff Institute; **relegated:** Glamorgan Wanderers, Blaina.

League 4 – promoted: Merthyr (c), Rumney; **relegated:** Pontypool Utd, Aberavon Quins.
League 5 – promoted: Kidwelly (c), Oakdale; **relegated:** Hendy, Pontyberem.

SWALEC CUP FINAL:
Neath 22, Pontypridd 29 (Cardiff, 4.5.95)

Neath: Richard Jones; C Higgs, L Davies, J Funnell, G Evans; P Williams, P Horgan; D Morris, B Williams (H Woodland 30), J Davies, Glyn Llewellyn, Gareth Llewellyn (capt), Robin Jones, I Boobyer, S Williams.

Scorers – Tries: Horgan 2, Davies, Richard Jones. *Conversion:* Horgan.

Pontypridd: C Cormack; D Manley, J Lewis, S Lewis, G Evans; N Jenkins, Paul John; N Bezani (capt), Phil John, N Eynon, G Prosser, M Rowley, M Lloyd, R Collins, D McIntosh (M Spiller 75).

Scorers – Tries: Evans 2, Paul John. *Conversion:* Jenkins. *Penalty goals:* Jenkins 3. *Dropped goal:* Jenkins.

Referee: D Bevan (WRU)

*Ecstatic Welsh players celebrate victory over France in Cardiff,
a result which handed Ireland the Five Nations' Wooden Spoon.*

1980:

F	W18–9	Cardiff	19 Jan	**t:** E Rees, Holmes, D S Richards, G Price
				c: G Davies
E	L 8–9	Twickenham	16 Feb	**t:** E Rees, Squire
S	W17–6	Cardiff	1 Mar	**t:** Holmes, Keen, D S Richards
				c: Blyth
				p: Fenwick
I	L 7–21	Dublin	15 Mar	**t:** Blyth
				p: Fenwick
NZ	L 3–23	Cardiff	1 Nov	**p:** Fenwick

1981:

E	W21–19	Cardiff	17 Jan	**t:** G Davies
				c: Fenwick
				p: Fenwick 4
				dg: G Davies
S	L 6–15	Edinburgh	7 Feb	**dg:** Fenwick 2
I	W 9–8	Cardiff	21 Feb	**p:** G Evans 2
				dg: Pearce
F	L15–19	Paris	7 Mar	**t:** D S Richards
				c: G Evans
				p: G Evans 3
A	W18–13	Cardiff	5 Dec	**t:** R Moriarty
				c: G Evans
				p: G Evans 3
				dg: G Davies

1982:

I	L12–20	Dublin	23 Jan	**t:** Holmes
				c: G Evans
				p: G Evans
				dg: Pearce
F	W22–12	Cardiff	6 Feb	**t:** Holmes
				p: G Evans 6
E	L 7–17	Twickenham	6 Mar	**t:** JR Lewis
				dg: G Davies
S	L18–34	Cardiff	20 Mar	**t:** Butler
				c: G Evans
				p: G Evans 4

1983:

E	D13–13	Cardiff	5 Feb	**t:** Squire
				p: Wyatt 2
				dg: Dacey
S	W19–15	Edinburgh	19 Feb	**t:** S Jones, E Rees
				c: Wyatt
				p: Wyatt 3
I	W23–9	Cardiff	5 Mar	**t:** Wyatt, Holmes, E Rees
				c: Wyatt
				p: Wyatt 3

F	L 9–16	Paris	19 Mar	t: Squire
				c: Wyatt
				p: G Evans
J+	W29–24	Cardiff	22 Oct	t: Hadley, Brown, Dacey, Bowen, Giles
				c: Wyatt 3
				p: Wyatt
R	L 6–24	Bucharest	12 Nov	p: G Evans 2

1984:

S	L 9–15	Cardiff	21 Jan	t: Titley
				c: H Davies
				p: H Davies
I	W18–9	Dublin	4 Feb	t: Ackerman
				c: H Davies
				p: H Davies 2, Bowen 2
F	L16–21	Cardiff	18 Feb	t: H Davies, Butler
				c: H Davies
				p: H Davies 2
E	W24–15	Twickenham	17 Mar	t: Hadley
				c: H Davies
				p: H Davies 4
				dg: Dacey 2
A	L 9–28	Cardiff	24 Nov	t: Bishop
				c: Wyatt
				p: Wyatt

1985:

S	W25–21	Edinburgh	2 Mar	t: Pickering 2
				c: Wyatt
				p: Wyatt 4
				dg: G Davies
I	L 9–21	Cardiff	16 Mar	t: P Lewis
				c: G Davies
				p: G Davies
F	L 3–14	Paris	30 Mar	p: Thorburn
E	W24–15	Cardiff	20 Apr	t: J Davies, Roberts
				c: Thorburn 2
				p: Thorburn 3
				dg: J Davies
Fj	W40–3	Cardiff	9 Nov	t: P Davies 2, Titley, Holmes, Hadley, James, Pickering
				c: Thorburn 3
				p: Thorburn 2

1986:

E	L18–21	Twickenham	17 Jan	t: Bowen
				c: Thorburn
				p: Thorburn 3
				dg: J Davies
S	W22–15	Cardiff	1 Feb	t: Hadley
				p: Thorburn 5
				dg: J Davies

I	W19–12	Dublin	15 Feb	**t:** P Lewis, P Davies
				c: Thorburn
				p: Thorburn 3
F	L15–23	Cardiff	1 Mar	**p:** Thorburn 5
Fj	W22–15	Suva	31 May	**t:** J Davies, Bowen
				c: Bowen
				p: Dacey 3
				dg: J Davies
T	W15–7	Nuku'alofa	12 Jun	**t:** P Moriarty
				c: Dacey
				p: Bowen 2, Dacey
WS	W32–14	Apia	14 Jun	**t:** Titley 2, Bowen, R Moriarty
				c: Dacey 2
				p: Dacey 3
				dg: J Davies

1987:

F	L 9–16	Paris	7 Feb	**p:** Thorburn 3
E	W19–12	Cardiff	7 Mar	**t:** S Evans
				p: Wyatt 5
S	L15–21	Edinburgh	21 Mar	**t:** M Jones
				c: Wyatt
				p: Wyatt 2
				dg: J Davies
I	L11–15	Cardiff	4 Apr	**t:** I Evans, Norster
				p: Wyatt
I(b)*	W13–6	Wellington	25 May	**t:** Ring
				p: Thorburn
				dg: J Davies 2
T*	W29–16	Palmerston North	29 May	**t:** Webbe 3, Hadley
				c: Thorburn 2
				p: Thorburn 2
				dg: J Davies
C*	W40–9	Brisbane	3 Jun	**t:** I Evans 4, Bowen, Hadley, Devereux, A Phillips
				c: Thorburn 4
E(b)*	W16–3	Brisbane	8 Jun	**t:** Roberts, Jones, Devereux
				c: Thorburn 2
NZ*	L 6–49	Brisbane	14 Jun	**t:** Devereux
				c: Thorburn
A*	W22–21	Rotorua	18 Jun	**t:** Roberts, P Moriarty, Hadley
				c: Thorburn 2
				p: Thorburn 2
US	W46–0	Cardiff	7 Nov	**t:** Bowen 2, Clement 2, Webbe, Young, P Moriarty, Norster
				c: Thorburn 4
				p: Thorburn 2

1988:

| E | W11–3 | Twickenham | 6 Feb | **t:** Hadley 2 |
| | | | | **dg:** J Davies |

S	W25–20	Cardiff	20 Feb	**t:** J Davies, I Evans, Watkins
				c: Thorburn 2
				p: Thorburn
				dg: J Davies 2
I	W12–9	Dublin	5 Mar	**t:** P Moriarty
				c: Thorburn
				p: Thorburn
				dg: J Davies
F	L 9–10	Cardiff	19 Mar	**t:** I Evans
				c: Thorburn
				p: Thorburn
NZ(1)	L 3–52	Christchurch	28 May	**p:** Ring
NZ(2)	L 9–54	Auckland	11 Jun	**t:** J Davies
				c: Ring
				p: Ring
WS	W24–6	Cardiff	12 Nov	**t:** N Davies 2, J Davies, C Davies
				c: Thorburn 4
R	L 9–15	Cardiff	10 Dec	**t:** Devereux
				c: Thorburn
				p: Thorburn

1989:

S	W23–7	Edinburgh	21 Jan	**t:** Hall
				p: Bowen
I	L13–19	Cardiff	4 Feb	**t:** M Jones
				p: Thorburn 3
F	L12–31	Paris	18 Feb	**p:** Thorburn 4
E	W12–9	Cardiff	18 Mar	**t:** Hall
				c: Thorburn
				p: Thorburn 2
NZ	L 9–34	Cardiff	4 Nov	**p:** Thorburn 3

1990:

F	L19–29	Cardiff	20 Jan	**t:** Titley
				p: Thorburn 4
				dg: D Evans
E	L 6–34	Twickenham	17 Feb	**t:** P Davies
				c: Thorburn
S	L 9–13	Cardiff	3 Mar	**t:** Emyr
				c: Thorburn
				p: Thorburn
I	L 8–14	Dublin	24 Mar	**t:** Ford, G O Llewellyn
Na(1)	W18–9	Windhoek	2 Jun	**t:** Thorburn, Bridges
				c: Thorburn 2
				p: Thorburn 2
Na(2)	W34–30	Windhoek	9 Jun	**t:** Emyr 2, O Williams, penalty try
				c: Thorburn 3
				p: Thorburn 3
				dg: Clement
Ba	L24–31	Cardiff	6 Oct	**t:** Thorburn
				c: Thorburn
				p: Thorburn 5
				dg: D Evans

1991:

E	L 6–25	Cardiff	19 Jan	**p:** Thorburn, N Jenkins
S	L12–32	Edinburgh	2 Feb	**t:** Ford
				c: Thorburn
				p: Thorburn 2
I	D21–21	Cardiff	16 Feb	**t:** Arnold, N Jenkins
				c: Thorburn 2
				p: Thorburn 2
				dg: N Jenkins
F(a)	L 3–36	Paris	2 Mar	**p:** Thorburn
A(a)	L 6–63	Brisbane	21 Jul	**p:** Thorburn
				dg: A Davies
F(b)	L 9–22	Cardiff	4 Sep	**t:** Collins
				c: Ring
				p: Ring
WS*	L13–16	Cardiff	6 Oct	**t:** Emyr, I Evans
				c: Ring
				p: Ring
Arg*	W16–7	Cardiff	9 Oct	**t:** Arnold
				p: Ring 3, Rayer
A(b)*	L 3–38	Cardiff	12 Oct	**p:** Ring

1992:

I	W16–15	Dublin	18 Jan	**t:** S Davies
				p: N Jenkins 3
				dg: C Stephens
F	L 9–12	Cardiff	1 Feb	**p:** N Jenkins 3
E	L 0–24	Twickenham	7 Mar	
S	W15–12	Cardiff	21 Mar	**t:** Webster
				c: N Jenkins
				p: N Jenkins 3
It+	W43–12	Cardiff	7 Oct	**t:** Clement, I Evans, Gibbs, C Stephens, Webster, S Davies, Rayer
				c: C Stephens 4
A	L 6–23	Cardiff	21 Nov	**p:** C Stephens 2

1993:

E	W10–9	Cardiff	6 Feb	**t:** I Evans
				c: N Jenkins
				p: N Jenkins
S	L 0–20	Edinburgh	20 Feb	
I	L14–19	Cardiff	6 Mar	**t:** I Evans
				p: N Jenkins 3
F	L10–26	Paris	20 Mar	**t:** Walker
				c: N Jenkins
				p: N Jenkins
Z(1)	W35–14	Bulawayo	22 May	**t:** Moon, Hill, Proctor, P Davies
				c: N Jenkins 3
				p: N Jenkins 2
				dg: A Davies

Z(2)	W42–13	Harare	29 May	t: G O Llewellyn 2, Bidgood, J Davies, N Jenkins, S Davies
				c: N Jenkins 3
				p: N Jenkins 2
Na	W38–23	Windhoek	5 Jun	t: Lewis 2, Hill, Proctor, Moon
				c: N Jenkins 2
				p: N Jenkins 3
J	W55–5	Cardiff	16 Oct	t: I Evans 2, Gibbs 2, Moon, Clement, Lewis, Rayer, N Jenkins
				c: N Jenkins 5
C	L24–26	Cardiff	10 Nov	p: N Jenkins 8

1994:

S	W29–6	Cardiff	15 Jan	t: Rayer 2, I Evans
				c: N Jenkins
				p: N Jenkins 4
I	W17–15	Dublin	5 Feb	t: N Jenkins
				p: N Jenkins 4
F	W24–15	Cardiff	19 Feb	t: Quinnell, Walker
				c: N Jenkins
				p: N Jenkins 4
E	L 8–15	Twickenham	19 Mar	t: Walker
				p: N Jenkins
P=	W102–11	Lisbon	18 May	t: Walker 4, I Evans 3, Hall 3, R Jones 2, Taylor, Quinnell, Llewelyn, penalty try
				c: N Jenkins 11
S=	W54–0	Madrid	21 May	t: Quinnell, I Evans 3, Walker, G Jenkins, penalty try
				c: N Jenkins 5
				p: N Jenkins 3
C	W33–15	Toronto	11 Jun	t: I Evans, Hall 2
				c: N Jenkins 3
				p: N Jenkins 4
Fj	W23–8	Suva	18 Jun	t: Rayer, Collins
				c: A Davies 2
				p: A Davies 3
T	W 18–9	Nuku'alofa	22 Jun	p: N Jenkins 6
WS	L 9–34	Apia	25 Jun	p: N Jenkins 3
R=	W16–9	Bucharest	17 Sep	t: I Evans
				c: N Jenkins
				p: N Jenkins 3
It=	W29–19	Cardiff	12 Oct	t: N Davies
				p: N Jenkins 7
				dg: N Jenkins
SA	L12–20	Cardiff	26 Nov	p: N Jenkins 4

1995:

F	L 9–21	Paris	21 Jan	p: N Jenkins 3
E	L 9–23	Cardiff	18 Feb	p: N Jenkins 3
S	L13–26	Edinburgh	4 Mar	t: R Jones
				c: N Jenkins
				p: N Jenkins 2

I(a)	L12–16	Cardiff	18 Mar	p: N Jenkins 4
J*	W57–10	Bloemfontein	27 May	t: Thomas 3, I Evans 2, Griffiths, Moore
				c: N Jenkins 5
				p: N Jenkins 4
NZ*	L 9–34	Johannesburg	31 May	p: N Jenkins 2
				dg: N Jenkins
I(b)*	L23–24	Johannesburg	4 Jun	t: Humphreys, Taylor
				c: N Jenkins 2
				p: N Jenkins 2
				dg: A Davies
SA	L11–40	Johannesburg	2 Sep	t: Bennett
				p: N Jenkins 2
Fj	W19–15	Cardiff	11 Nov	t: Moore, N Jenkins
				p: N Jenkins 3

1996:

It	W31–26	Cardiff	16 Jan	t: I Evans 2, J Thomas
				c: A Thomas 2
				p: A Thomas 4
E	L15–21	Twickenham	3 Feb	t: Taylor, Howley
				c: A Thomas
				p: A Thomas
S	L14–16	Cardiff	17 Feb	t: Proctor
				p: A Thomas 3
I	L17–30	Dublin	2 Mar	t: I Evans 2
				c: A Thomas 2
				p: A Thomas
F	W16–15	Cardiff	16 Mar	t: Howley
				c: N Jenkins
				p: N Jenkins 3
A(1)	L25–56	Brisbane	8 June	t: Proctor, Taylor, Llewellyn
				c: N Jenkins 2
				p: N Jenkins 2
A(2)	L3–42	Sydney	22 June	p: N Jenkins

* World Cup
= World Cup qualifier

FRANCE
Ian Borthwick

DESTINY might have chosen Paris as the final burial ground of rugby as an amateur sport, but on and off the field, the first season of transition to the professional era in France was more a period of doubt and uncertainty than of welcoming in a brave new world.

With the stroke of a pen on the balmy summer's day in the French capital that was 26 June 1995, the members of the IRB removed the word 'amateur' from the laws of rugby. But it was clear from the look on the face of the host union's president, Bernard Lapasset (then chairman of the world governing body), that it was a decision made against his better will and judgement.

This impression was confirmed two weeks later when, with the ink barely dry on the IRB's letterhead, the Federation Francaise de Rugby (FFR) announced that it would not follow the rest of the world, and had chosen 'not to become professional.'

It was a puzzling and ironic move – puzzling to the players especially – and the domestic and international season would be a reflection of the reigning uncertainty, resentment and suspicion which characterised their relationship with the FFR.

Ironic, too, as the presence of money in French rugby has long been an open secret, as is attested by the number of foreign internationals who have played in France. Sixty years ago France was expelled from the Five Nations Championship after accusations of professionalism from their British counterparts, and apart from the time-honoured ritual of money in the boots, stories of houses, cars, fictitious jobs and match fees abound in the French championship. In the late sixties, for instance, Beziers was already paying its top players 3,000 francs (£400) per month, not to mention match fees of up to 2,500 francs. One former international confided that in 1972 he earned, under the table through his club, four times his salary as a civil servant.

Incidentally, Beziers, who spent the 1996 season in the second division, won the French championship eight times between 1971 and 1984, and in 1968 were already holding three training sessions a week – something unheard of at the time. 'The payments were a means of getting performance, not an end in themselves', said their coach of the time, Raoul Barriere. 'The money allowed players to train better, longer and more often.' But were they pro, or not?

To return to 1996, however, at the season's end France's rugby establishment was still struggling to come to terms with the advent of the 'open game'. The major clubs were at loggerheads with the FFR; the top players, despite having signed a nebulous 'charter' with their Union, still had no firm contracts worked out; and each major match rekindled a public debate over how France would overcome the professional–amateur dilemma. This debate even overflowed to the national parliament, where a special committee was set up to examine the problem and find a way of 'preserving the specificity of French rugby.'

One of these specifics is *le rugby des villages* – the demographic structure of rugby in France. Many clubs view turning professional as an economic impossibility. Of the 1,754 clubs in France, 1,450 are in towns or villages of less than 5,000 inhabitants. Even a powerful club like Dax, which boasts internationals Richard Dourthe, Olivier Roumat, Thierry Lacroix and Fabien Pelous, represents a town of scarcely 20,000 people.

> *Many clubs view turning professional as an economic impossibility. Of the 1,754 clubs in France, 1,450 are in towns or villages of less than 5,000 inhabitants ...The Mediterranean town of Argeles-sur-Mer (population 5,753), despite having won their long sought-after promotion to Division One, were forced to decline it for economic reasons*

The dilemma was most keenly felt in the Mediterranean town of Argeles-sur-Mer (population 5,753), where despite having won their long sought-after promotion to Division One, the club's officials were forced to decline it for economic reasons, while Nimes, originally relegated to Division Two, was reinstated.

For the time being then, in the hope of preserving *le rugby des villages*, the FFR is still refusing the idea of an elite – a national championship involving only ten or 12 clubs or provincial regions. The first division still consists of 20 clubs, and top players play perhaps more games than in any other major rugby nation. When Toulouse prop Christian Califano turned out against Wales on 16 March, he had already played 37 top-level games. His season's tally, between August 1995 and June 1996, totalled 54 games.

On the field the erratic performances of the French XV were a reflection of their instability – as opposed to the New Zealanders, for instance. Where the All Blacks expressed a feeling of reassurance, of having the total support of their union, France's internationals spent the season floating in a sort of no-man's-land. 'The FFR just doesn't know what it wants', lamented one experienced international after the defeat against Wales in Cardiff. 'One day they decide that we are pro, the next day they change their minds, and we players are kept totally in the dark.'

Pierre Berbizier, despite his fine record as coach, was sacked by Bernard Lapasset in September, and former flanker Jean-Claude Skrela appointed in his place. The French easily won the Latin Cup in Argentina before taking on the All Blacks in two Tests. The first of these was marked by the first-ever 'strike' by French players, in protest at the non-selection of three players – Roumat, Lacroix and Laurent Cabannes – who had spent three months playing for South African provinces after the World Cup and were banned from playing for a month on their return to France. The players' refusal to attend a civic reception two days before the Toulouse Test created a mini-crisis. Team manager Andre Herrero resigned but the players stuck together and, galvanised by the revolt, pulled off a surprise victory (22–15) over New Zealand.

> 'We are losing ground, and if we don't react now we can wave goodbye to the next World Cup. Even Wales and Scotland are working more to the future than we are. French rugby still has a positive image, but we can quickly become a minor sport in France' – Philippe Saint-Andre

The All Blacks easily won the second Test (37–12) at Parc des Princes, and from there onwards the French tottered from match to match, seemingly without design. They beat England (15–12) in Paris, putting an end to an eight-year curse, but then lost to the dynamic Scots (14–19) in Edinburgh. They regained some self-respect against Ireland (45–10), but then again fell away, losing to Wales in Cardiff (15–16) to hand England the Five Nations title.

This was but a shadow of the French team which only three months earlier had finished third in the World Cup, and had come within three inches of beating South Africa in their rain-drenched semi-final in Durban. It appeared that in a few short months the legacy of Berbizier had been entirely frittered away. The *Tricolores* no longer had a game-plan, their skill level was mediocre, and chronic indiscipline, practically eliminated under Berbizier, was once again costing them games.

What with the FFR being rocked by financial scandals, the ongoing power struggle between Lapasset and his detractors, and the players' own expectations in the new professional era, French captain Philippe Saint-Andre decided it was time to sound the alarm.

'We are losing ground, and if we don't react now we can wave goodbye to the next World Cup. Even Wales and Scotland are working more to the future than we are', he warned. 'French rugby still has a positive image, but we can quickly become a minor sport in France. We must hastily move on from this period of transition. Instead of getting lost in petty quarrels for power in the FFR, it is time to think about the best interests of rugby as a whole, and not the personal interests of union officials.'

Saint-Andre clearly feels that professionalism does not mean the end of the large base of amateur rugby. 'I believe the game should be amateur for 95 per cent, with the other five per cent representing a real elite. Professional rugby will never kill *le rugby des villages* – it can only make it stronger.'

Cheeky Thomas Castaignede celebrates his last-gasp winning dropped goal against England in Paris.

FRANCE (P18 W14 D0 L4 F572 A292)

(–)	v Tonga*	(Pretoria, 26.5.95)	won38–10
(–)	v Cote d'Ivoire*	(Rustenburg, 30.5.95)	won54–18
(–)	v Scotland*	(Pretoria, 3.6.95)	won22–19
(–)	v Ireland*	(q/f: Durban, 10.6.95)	won36–12
(–)	v South Africa*	(s/f: Durban, 17.6.95)	lost15–19
(–)	v England*	(3/4: Pretoria, 22.6.95)	won 19–9
(–)	v Italy **	(Buenos Aires, 14.10.95)	won34–22
(–)	v Romania **	(Tucuman, 17.10.95)	won 52–8
(–)	v Argentina **	(Buenos Aires, 21.10.95)	won47–12
(H)	v New Zealand (i)	(Toulouse, 11.11.95)	won22–15
(H)	v New Zealand (ii)	(Paris, 18.11.95)	lost12–37
(H)	v England	(Paris, 20.1.96)	won15–12
(A)	v Scotland	(Edinburgh, 3.2.96)	lost14–19
(H)	v Ireland	(Paris, 17.2.96)	won45–10
(A)	v Wales	(Cardiff, 16.3.96)	lost15–16
(H)	v Romania	(Aurillac, 20.4.96)	won64–12
(A)	v Argentina	(Buenos Aires, 22.6.96)	won34–27
(A)	v Argentina	(Buenos Aires, 29.6.96)	won34–15

* World Cup; ** Latin Cup

New Zealand in France (tour record: P6 W5 D0 L1 F218 A99)

(A)	v French Barbarians	(Toulon, 1.11.95)	won34–19
(A)	v Languedoc-Roussillon	(Beziers, 4.11.95)	won 30–9
(A)	v Basque-Landes	(Bayonne, 7.11.95)	won47–20
(A)	v French Selection	(Nancy, 14.11.95)	won55–17

FRANCE A (P3 W1 D0 L2 F81 A76)

(H)	v England	(Paris, 19.1.96)	lost15–25
(A)	v Wales	(Newport, 15.3.96)	won34–13
(A)	v Scotland	(Scotland, 2.2.96)	lost32–38

FRANCE UNDER-21 (P2 W2 D0 L0 F69 A6)

(A)	v Scotland	(Scotland, 3.2.96)	won 29–3
(A)	v England	(Bath, 19.4.96)	won 40–3

FRANCE STUDENTS (P3 W3 D0 L0 F116 A40)

(A)	v England	(Paris, 19.1.96)	won33–14
(H)	v Ireland	(Clermont Ferrand, 16.2.96)	won42–11
(A)	v Wales	(Aberavon, 15.3.96)	won41–15

FRANCE JUNIORS (P2 W1 D0 L1 F30 A39)

(H)	v Wales	(Dax, 9.3.96)	lost 8–21
(A)	v England	(Chester, 20.4.96)	won22–18

FRANCE 18 GROUP (P2 W0 D0 L2 F18 A30)

(A)	v Wales	(Mountain Ash, 24.2.96)	lost 7–16
(H)	v England	(Vannes, 6.4.96)	lost11–14

FIRA WORLD YOUTH CUP (Italy: 22 March - 8 April)

(–) v Wales	(Pool One)	lost 11–20
(–) v Uruguay	(Pool One)	won 31–0

* Failed to qualify for semi-finals

HEINEKEN EUROPEAN CUP
'Toulouse scoop Euro jackpot at first attempt' – see pages xxx–xxx

DOMESTIC RUGBY

Club Championship
(1) Toulouse, (2) Brive, (3) Pau, (4) Dax

Semi-finals: Toulouse 36, Dax 23 (Bordeaux, 19 May); Brive 23, Pau 21 (Toulouse, 19 May)

Final: Toulouse 20, Brive 13 (Paris, 2 June 1996)

The elusive Emile NTamack breaks through
the English cover at Parc des Princes.

1980:

W	L 9–18	Cardiff	19 Jan	**t:** Marchal **c:** Caussade **dg:** Caussade
E	L13–17	Paris	2 Feb	**t:** Averous, Rives **c:** Caussade **p:** Caussade
S	L14–22	Edinburgh	16 Feb	**t:** Gallion, Gabernet **p:** Gabernet **dg:** Caussade
I	W19–18	Paris	1 Mar	**t:** Gourdon 2 **c:** Aguirre **p:** Aguirre 2 **dg:** Pedeutour
SA	L15–37	Pretoria	8 Nov	**t:** Dintrans **c:** Vivies **p:** Vivies 3
R	L 0–15	Bucharest	23 Nov	

1981:

S	W16–9	Paris	17 Jan	**t:** Blanco, Bertranne **c:** Caussade **p:** Vivies, Gabernet
I	W19–13	Dublin	7 Feb	**t:** Pardo **p:** Laporte 2, Gabernet **dg:** Laporte 2
W	W19–15	Paris	7 Mar	**t:** Gabernet **p:** Laporte 3, Gabernet 2
E	W16–12	Twickenham	21 Mar	**t:** Lacans, Pardo **c:** Laporte **dg:** Laporte 2
A(1)	L15–17	Brisbane	5 Jul	**t:** Mesny **c:** Gabernet **p:** Blanco, Gabernet **dg:** Vivies
A(2)	L14–24	Sydney	11 Jul	**t:** Lacas, Elissalde **dg:** Elissalde, Sallefranque
R	W17–9	Narbonne	1 Nov	**t:** Elissalde 2, Blanco **p:** Gabernet 2 **dg:** Laporte
NZ(1)	L 9–13	Toulouse	14 Nov	**p:** Laporte 2 **dg:** Gabernet
NZ(2)	L 6–18	Paris	21 Nov	**p:** Laporte, Blanco

1982:

W	L12–22	Cardiff	6 Feb	**t:** Blanco **c:** Sallefranque **p:** Sallefranque, Martinez

E	L15–27	Paris	20 Feb	t: Pardo c: Sallefranque p: Sallefranque 2 dg: Lescarboura
S	L 7–16	Edinburgh	6 Mar	t: Rives p: Sallefranque
I	W22–9	Paris	20 Mar	t: Blanco, Mesny c: Gabernet p: Blanco 2, Gabernet 2
R	L 9–13	Bucharest	31 Oct	t: Fabre c: Camberabero dg: Camberabero
Arg(1)	W25–12	Toulouse	14 Nov	t: Sella 2, Esteve, Blanco p: Blanco, Camberabero dg: Camberabero
Arg(2)	W13–6	Paris	20 Nov	t: Begu, Blanco c: Camberabero p: Camberabero

1983:

E	W19–15	Twickenham	15 Jan	t: Esteve, Sella, Paparemborde c: Blanco 2 p: Camberabero
S	W19–15	Paris	5 Feb	t: Esteve 2 c: Blanco p: Blanco 3
I	L16–22	Dublin	19 Feb	t: Blanco, Esteve c: Blanco p: Blanco 2
W	W16–9	Paris	19 Mar	t: Esteve dg: Camberabero p: Blanco 3
A(1)	D15–15	Clermont-Ferrand	13 Nov	p: Lescarboura 3 dg: Lescarboura, Lafond
A(2)	W15–6	Paris	20 Nov	t: Esteve c: Lescarboura p: Gabernet, Lescarboura 2

1984:

I	W25–12	Paris	21 Jan	t: Gallion, Sella c: Lescarboura p: Lescarboura 4 dg: Lescarboura
W	W21–16	Cardiff	18 Feb	t: Sella c: Lescarboura p: Lescarboura 4 dg: Lescarboura
E	W32–18	Paris	3 Mar	t: Cordorniou, Sella, Esteve, Bergu, Gallion c: Lescarboura 3 p: Lescarboura dg: Lescarboura

S	L12–21	Edinburgh	17 Mar	**t:** Gallion
				c: Lescarboura
				p: Lescarboura
				dg: Lescarboura
NZ(1)	L 9–10	Christchurch	16 Jun	**t:** Blanco
				c: Lescarboura
				p: Lescarboura
NZ(2)	L18–31	Auckland	23 Jun	**t:** Lescarboura 2, Bonneval
				p: Lescarboura 2
R	W18–3	Bucharest	11 Nov	**t:** Sella, Lescarboura 2
				c: Lescarboura 2
				p: Lescarboura 2

1985:

E	D 9–9	Twickenham	2 Feb	**dg:** Lescarboura 3
S	W11–3	Paris	16 Feb	**t:** Blanco 2
				p: Lescarboura
I	D15–15	Dublin	2 Mar	**t:** Esteve, Codorniou
				c: Lescarboura 2
				p: Lescarboura
W	W14–3	Paris	30 Mar	**t:** Esteve, Gallion
				p: Lescarboura 2
Arg(1)	L16–24	Buenos Aires	22 Jun	**t:** Blanco, Bonneval
				c: Lescarboura
				p: Lescarboura 2
Arg(2)	W23–15	Buenos Aires	29 Jun	**t:** Codorniou, Erbani, Berbizier, Blanco
				c: Lescarboura 2
				p: Lescarboura
J(1)[+]	W50–0	Dax	19 Oct	**t:** Lafond 4, Fabre, Cassagne, Codorniou, Rodriguez, Detrez, dubroca
				c: Camberabero 5
J(2)[+]	W52–0	Nantes	26 Oct	**t:** Camberabero 2, Lafond 2, Charvet 2, Dintrans 2, Fabre, Rodriguez
				c: Camberabero 6

1986:

S	L17–18	Edinburgh	17 Jan	**t:** Berbizier, Sella
				p: Laporte 2
				dg: Laporte
I	W29–9	Paris	1 Feb	**t:** Berbizier, Marocco, Sella
				c: Laporte
				p: Laporte 3, Blanco
				dg: Lafond
W	W23–15	Cardiff	1 Mar	**t:** Sella, Lafond 2, Blanco
				c: Laporte 2
				dg: Laporte
E	W29–10	Paris	15 Mar	**t:** Sella, Blanco, penalty try, Laporte
				c: Laporte 2
				p: Laporte 3
R(a)	W25–13	Lille	12 Apr	**t:** Charvet, Bonneval, Sella, Erbani, Lagisquet
				c: Laporte
				p: Laporte

Arg(1)	L13–15	Buenos Aires	31 May	**t:** Bonneval
				p: Laporte 3
Arg(2)	W22–9	Buenos Aires	7 Jun	**t:** Lescarboura, Sella, Debroca
				c: Lescarboura 2
				p: Lescarboura 2
A	L14–27	Sydney	21 Jun	**t:** Blanco 2, Sella
				c: Lescarboura
NZ(a)	L 9–18	Christchurch	28 Jun	**dg:** Lescarboura 3
R(b)	W20–3	Bucharest	25 Oct	**t:** Andrieu, Blanco, Berot
				c: Berot
				p: Berot 2
NZ(b1)	L 7–19	Toulouse	8 Nov	**t:** Sella
				p: Berot
NZ(b2)	W16–3	Nantes	15 Nov	**t:** Charvet, Lorieux
				c: Berot
				p: Berot 2

1987:

W	W16–9	Paris	7 Feb	**t:** Mesnel, Bonneval
				c: Berot
				p: Berot 2
E	W19–15	Twickenham	21 Feb	**t:** Bonneval, Sella
				c: Berot
				p: Berot 2
				dg: Mesnel
S(a	W28–22	Paris	7 Mar	**t:** Bonneval 3, Berot
				p: Berot 3
				dg: Mesnel
I	W19–13	Dublin	21 Mar	**t:** Champ 2
				c: Berot
				p: Berot 3
S(b)*	D20–20	Christchurch	23 May	**t:** Sella, Berbizier, Blanco
				c: Blanco
				p: Blanco 2
R(a)*	W55–12	Wellington	28 May	**t:** Charvet 2, Lagisquet 2, Sella, Andrieu, Camberabero, Erbani, Laporte
				c: Laporte 8
				p: Laporte
Z*	W70–12	Auckland	2 Jun	**t:** Modin 3, Camberabero 3, Charvet 2, Dubroca, Rodriguez 2, Esteve, Laporte
				c: Camberabero 9
Fj*	W31–16	Auckland	7 Jun	**t:** Lorieux, Rodriguez 2, Lagisquet
				c: Laporte 3
				p: Laporte 2
				dg: Laporte
A*	W30–24	Sydney	13 Jun	**t:** Lorieux, Sella, Lagisquet, Blanco
				c: Camberabero 4
				p: Camberabero 2
NZ*	L 9–29	Auckland	20 Jun	**t:** Berbizier
				c: Camberabero
				p: Camberabero

S(c)[+]	L12–15	Galashiels	26 Sep	t: Mesnel c: Bianchi p: Bianchi 2
R(b)	W49–3	Agen	11 Nov	t: Berot, Lagisquet 2, Andrieu 2, Ondarts, penalty try c: Berot 6 p: Berot 3

1988:

E	W10–9	Paris	16 Jan	t: Rodriguez p: Berot 2
S	L12–23	Edinburgh	6 Feb	t: Lagisquet c: Berot p: Berot dg: Lescarboura
I	W25–6	Paris	20 Feb	t: Blanco, Lagisquet, Sella, Camberabero, Carminati c: Camberabero dg: Berot
W	W10–9	Cardiff	19 Mar	t: Lescarboura p: Lafond 2
Arg(a1)	W18–15	Buenos Aires	18 Jun	t: Dintrans c: Berot p: Berot 4
Arg(a2)	L 6–18	Buenos Aires	25 Jun	p: Berot 2
Arg(b1)	W29–9	Nantes	5 Nov	t: Blanco 2, Cecillon, Lagisquet, Rodriguez c: Berot 3 p: Berot
Arg(b2)	W28–18	Lille	11 Nov	t: Sanz, Cecillon, Andrieu, Sella c: Berot 3 p: Berot 2
R	W16–12	Bucharest	26 Nov	t: Blanco, Lagisquet c: Berot p: Berot 2

1989:

I	W26–21	Dublin	21 Jan	t: Lagisquet 2, Blanco, Lafond c: Lafond 2 p: Lafond 2
W	W31–12	Paris	18 Feb	t: Blanco 2, Berbizier, Dintrans c: Lafond 3 p: Lafond 2 dg: Mesnel
E	L 0–11	Twickenham	4 Mar	
S	W19–3	Paris	19 Mar	t: Berbizier, Blanco, Lagisquet c: Berot 2 p: Berot
USSR[+]	W18–16	Valence	20 May	t: Roumat c: Lafond p: Lafond 3, Camberabero

86

NZ(1)	L17–25	Christchurch	17 Jun	t: Blanco 2, Cecillon
				c: Berot
				p: Berot
NZ(2)	L20–34	Auckland	1 Jul	t: Rouge-Thomas, Cecillon
				p: Blanco 4
BL	L27–29	Paris	4 Oct	t: Blanco, Benetton, Camberabero
				c: Camberabero 3
				p: Camberabero 3
A(1)	L15–32	Strasbourg	4 Nov	p: Camberabero 4
				dg: Camberabero
A(2)	W25–19	Lille	11 Nov	t: Lagisquet, Andrieu
				c: Lacroix
				p: Lacroix 5

1990:

W	W29–19	Cardiff	20 Jan	t: Lafond, Sella, Camberabero,
				Lagisquet, Rodriguez
				c: Camberabero 3
				p: Camberabero
E	L 7–26	Paris	3 Feb	t: Lagisquet
				p: Charvet
S	L 0–21	Edinburgh	17 Feb	
I	W31–12	Paris	3 Mar	t: Mesnel 2, Lagisquet
				c: Camberabero 2
				p: Camberabero 5
R	L 6–12	Auch	24 May	p: Lescarboura 2
A(1)	L 9–21	Sydney	9 Jun	p: Camberabero 3
A(2)	L31–48	Brisbane	24 Jun	t: Blanco 2, Armary, Lacombe
				c: Camberabero 3
				p: Camberabero 3
A(3)	W28–19	Sydney	30 Jun	t: Camberabero, Mesnel
				c: Camberabero
				p: Camberabero 2, Blanco
				dg: Camberabero 3
NZ(1)	L 3–24	Nantes	3 Nov	p: Camberabero
NZ(2)	L12–30	Paris	10 Nov	p: Camberabero 3
				dg: Camberabero

1991:

S	W15–9	Paris	19 Jan	p: Camberabero 2
				dg: Blanco, Camberabero 2
I	W21–13	Dublin	2 Feb	t: Lagisquet, Cabannes
				c: Camberabero 2
				p: Camberabero 3
W(a)	W36–3	Paris	2 Mar	t: Blanco, Saint-Andre, Mesnel,
				Roumat, Sella, Lafond
				c: Blanco, Camberabero 2
				p: Camberabero 2
E	L19–21	Twickenham	16 Mar	t: Saint-Andre, Camberabero, Mesnel
				c: Camberabero 2
				p: Camberabero

R(a)	W33–21	Bucharest	22 Jun	t: Blanco, Camberabero, Cecillon, Simon
				c: Camberabero
				p: Camberabero 5
US(1)	W41–9	Denver	13 Jul	t: Blanco 2, Lafond, Saint-Andre, Champ, Courtiols, Cecillon, Mesnel
				c: Camberabero 3
				p: Camberabero
US(2)	W10–3	Colorado Springs	20 Jul	t: Mesnel, Blanco
				c: Camberabero
W(b)	W22–9	Cardiff	4 Sep	t: Blanco, Camberabero, Saint-Andre
				c: Camberabero 2
				p: Camberabero 2
R(b)*	W30–3	Beziers	4 Oct	t: penalty try, Saint-Andre, Roumat, Lafond
				c: Camberabero
				p: Camberabero 4
Fj*	W33–9	Grenoble	8 Oct	t: Lafond 3, Sella 2, Camberabero
				c: Camberabero 3
				p: Camberabero
C*	W19–13	Agen	13 Oct	t: Lafond, Saint-Andre
				c: Camberabero
				p: Camberabero, Lacroix 2
E*	L10–19	Paris	19 Oct	t: Lafond
				p: Lacroix 2

1992:

W	W12–9	Cardiff	1 Feb	t: Saint-Andre
				c: Lafond
				p: Viars
				dg: Penaud
E	L13–31	Paris	15 Feb	t: Viars, Penaud
				c: Viars
				p: Viars
S	L 6–10	Edinburgh	7 Mar	p: Lafond 2
I	W44–12	Paris	21 Mar	t: Penaud 2, Viars 2, Cecillon, Cabannes, Sadourny
				c: Viars 5
				p: Viars 2
R	W25–6	Le Havre	28 May	t: Saint-Andre, Cadieu, Galthie, penalty try
				c: Viars, Lacroix 2
				p: Viars
Arg(a1)†	W27–12	Buenos Aires	4 Jul	t: Deylaud, Viars
				c: Deylaud
				p: Viars 4
				dg: Penaud
Arg(a2)	W33–9	Buenos Aires	11 Jul	t: Saint-Andre, Viars, Hueber
				c: Viars 3
				p: Viars 3
				dg: Hueber

SA(1)	L15–20	Lyon	17 Oct	t: Penaud 2
				c: Viars
				p: Viars
SA(2)	W29–16	Paris	24 Oct	t: Penaud, Roumat
				c: Lacroix 2
				p: Lacroix 5
Arg(b)	L20–24	Nantes	14 Nov	t: Gonzalez, Galthie, Sella
				c: Viars
				p: Viars

1993:

E	L15–16	Twickenham	16 Jan	t: Saint-Andre 2
				c: Camberabero
				p: Camberabero
S	W11–3	Paris	6 Feb	t: Lacroix
				p: Camberabero 2
I	W21–6	Dublin	20 Feb	t: Saint-Andre, Sella
				c: Camberabero
				p: Camberabero 2
				dg: Camberabero
W	W26–10	Paris	20 Mar	t: Benetton 2, Lafond
				c: Lafond
				p: Lacroix 3
R(a)	W37–20	Bucharest	20 May	t: Bernat-Salles 3, Cecillon
				c: Viars 4
				p: Viars 3
SA(1)	D20–20	Durban	26 Jun	t: Saint-Andre
				p: Lacroix 5
SA(2)	W18–17	Johannesburg	3 Jul	p: Lacroix 4
				dg: Lacroix, Penaud
R(b)	W51–0	Brive	9 Oct	t: Bernat-Salles 3, Sella, Loppy, Merle
				c: Lacroix 6
				p: Lacroix 3
A(1)	W16–3	Bordeaux	30 Oct	t: Hueber
				c: Lacroix
				p: Lacroix
				dg: Penaud, Sadourny
A(2)	L 3–24	Paris	6 Nov	p: Lacroix

1994:

I	W35–15	Paris	15 Jan	t: Benetton, Saint-Andre, Lacroix, Merle
				c: Lacroix 3
				p: Lacroix 3
W	L15–24	Cardiff	19 Feb	t: Roumat, Sella
				c: Lacroix
				p: Lacroix
E	L14–18	Paris	5 Mar	t: Benazzi
				p: Lacroix 3
S	W20–12	Edinburgh	19 Mar	t: Sadourny, Saint-Andre
				c: Lacroix, Montlaur
				p: Lacroix 2

C(a)	L16–18	Ottawa	5 Jun	t: NTamack
				c: Lacroix
				p: Lacroix 3
NZ(1)	W22–8	Christchurch	26 Jun	t: Benetton
				c: Lacroix
				p: Lacroix 2
				dg: Deylaud 2
NZ(2)	W23–20	Auckland	3 Jul	t: NTamack, Sadourny
				c: Lacroix, Deylaud
				p: Lacroix 2, Deylaud
C(b)	W28–9	Besancon	17 Dec	t: Sadourny, Sella, Benetton
				c: Lacroix 2
				p: Lacroix 2
				dg: Delaigue

1995:

W	W21–9	Paris	21 Jan	t: NTamack, Saint-Andre
				c: Lacroix
				p: Lacroix 3
E(a)	L10–31	Twickenham	4 Feb	t: Viars
				c: Lacroix
				p: Lacroix
S(a)	L21–23	Paris	18 Feb	t: Saint-Andre 2, Sadourny
				p: Lacroix
				dg: Deylaud
I(a)	W25–7	Dublin	4 Mar	t: Delaigue, Cecillon, NTamack, Saint-Andre
				c: NTamack
				p: NTamack
R	W24–15	Bucharest	7 Apr	t: Sadourny, penalty try
				c: Lacroix
				p: Lacroix 4
T*	W38–10	Pretoria	26 May	t: Lacroix 2, Saint-Andre, Hueber
				c: Lacroix 3
				p: Lacroix 3
				dg: Delaigue
IC*	W54–18	Rustenburg	30 May	t: Lacroix 2, Saint-Andre, Accoceberry, Benazzi, Techoueyres, Costes, Viars
				c: Lacroix 4
				p: Lacroix 2
S(b)*	W22–19	Pretoria	3 Jun	t: NTamack
				c: Lacroix
				p: Lacroix 5
I(b)*	W36–12	Durban	10 Jun	t: Saint-Andre, NTamack
				c: Lacroix
				p: Lacroix 8
SA*	L15–19	Durban	17 Jun	p: Lacroix 5
E(b)*	W19–9	Pretoria	22 Jun	t: Roumat, NTamack
				p: Lacroix 3
It **	W34–2	Buenos Aires	4 Oct	t:Sadourny 2, Ntamack, Carminati
				c: Deylaud 4
				p: Deylaud 2

R **	W52–8	Tucuman	17 Oct	**t:** Castaignede, Pelous, Arlettaz 2
				Carminati, Lievremont, Delaigue
				c: Castaignede 4
				p: Castaignede 2
				dg: Castaignede
Arg **	W47–12	Buenos Aires	21 Oct	**t:** NTamack 2, Saint-Andre 2,
				Carbonneau 2, Castaignede
				c: Deylaud 3
				p: Deylaud 2
NZ(1)	W22–15	Toulouse	11 Nov	**t:** Saint-Andre, Dourthe, Sadourny
				c: Castaignede 2
				p: Castaignede
NZ(2)	L12–37	Paris	18 Nov	**t:** Saint-Andre 2
				c: Castaignede

1996:

E	W15–12	Paris	20 Jan	**p:** Lacroix 3
				dg: Lacroix, Castaignede
S	L14–19	Edinburgh	3 Feb	**t:** Benazzi
				p: Lacroix 2, Castaignede
I	W45–10	Paris	17 Feb	**t:** NTamack 2, Castel 2, Campan,
				Saint-Andre, Accoceberry
				c: Castaignede 5
W	L15–16	Cardiff	16 Mar	**t:** NTamack, Castaignede
				c: Castaignede
				p: Castaignede
R	W64–12	Aurillac	20 Apr	**t:** Glas 2, Labrousse 2, Moni,
				Califano 3, Penaud, NTamack
				c: Dourthe 7
Arg(1)	W34–27	Buenos Aires	22 Jun	**t:** NTamack 2, Dourthe, Castaignede,
				Saint-Andre
				c: Dourthe 3
				p: Dourthe
Arg(2)	W34–15	Buenos Aires	29 Jun	**t:** NTamack, Saint-Andre, Benetton,
				Pelous
				c: Castaignede
				p: Castaignede 3, Dourthe

* World Cup
** Latin Cup
+ Non-cap
† Five-point try introduced from this game onwards

AUSTRALIA
Greg Campbell

WHILE the world of rugby was analysing and preparing to entertain the game's professional revolution, Australian rugby spent much of the year counting its victims and attempting to rebuild the bridge between players and officialdom. The war created by the planned rebel World Rugby Championship had ended, but the smell of cordite was still very much in evidence as representatives from both parties brokered a final truce.

And while a settlement was finally signed, it will be some time before the deep wounds are healed and mutual trust is restored. One of the brutal, inescapable ironies resulting from the game's forced and hurried entry into open professionalism is that Australian rugby officials had been genuinely championing the players' cause for a range of financial benefits at the highest international level for over a decade.

The leading Wallaby players knew they were going to win financially from the war, whether they signed for the establishment or with the rebels. However, the doubtful morality surrounding their clandestine WRC operations and their dealings at the negotiation table will never be forgiven by some officials. The willingness by the majority of players to turn their backs on Australian rugby history and tradition by contemplating the rebel route also drew strong criticism from past Wallabies, including a string of former Test captains.

The players formed their own Players' Association and elected the uncapped ex-Wallaby Tony Dempsey as its leader. The Association then used their strong hand and secured 95 per cent of Australian rugby's annual portion of News Corporation's ten-year deal with the Australian, New Zealand and South African Rugby Football Unions. In 1996, this represented over Aus$9 million to be shared by 120 contracted players. This deal has left the senior Sydney and Brisbane clubs, southern state unions, juniors and other parties no better off financially despite their massive injection of money into the game at the top end. On the other hand, leading Wallaby players are on contracts in excess of $400,000 while some Australian Under-21 players are on $100,000-plus contracts.

Many are afraid that the spirit and soul of rugby will now be lost. Dick McGruther, newly elected ARFU chairman and chief architect of the International Rugby Football Board's new professional laws, readily admits the game had to change, but he still remains attached to the game's traditional amateur values. He soberly commented after the historic decision: 'It is somewhat sad we have had to surrender the amateur nature of the game. I just hope officials in the future will judge us kindly.'

Tim Horan, Queensland's new captain, admitted there are still barriers between players and officials despite the peace accord. 'There have been teething problems on both sides and some animosity towards certain players', he said. 'The majority of the administrators are supportive of the players but there are others who are jealous of the amount of money players are now receiving.'

> *'There have been teething problems on both sides and some animosity towards certain players. The majority of the administrators are supportive of the players but there are others who are jealous of the amount of money players are now receiving' – Tim Horan*

One player who remained untouched by the entire controversy was Steve Merrick. Merrick, a strongly built scrum-half from Singleton in country New South Wales, won Wallaby honours for both Tests against the All Blacks after the World Cup. He performed soundly and, if he wished, could have won a sizeable ARFU contract. Instead he chose to turn his back on fame and fortune, and announced his retirement from Test rugby because he didn't like travelling or staying in Sydney.

The revolutionary changes also initiated change within the ARFU, which elected McGruther as its new leader and corporatised its structure, slashing the number of subcommittees from 21 to three and appointing a new chief executive in John O'Neill, a man with a rugby background but who made his mark as Chief Executive of the State Bank.

The World Cup failure and the Bledisloe Cup series loss resulted in Bob Dwyer being replaced as Wallaby coach by New South Wales' Greg Smith, who was surprisingly given a two-year post. Supporting Smith will be the former Wallaby fly-half and centre Lloyd Walker, while Jake Howard makes a welcome return as technical assistant. The appointment of Smith caused justifiable consternation in Queensland, whose own nomination, John Connolly, has performed splendidly since the beginning of the decade. Accusations of state bias were loudly claimed, with Connolly himself saying that Queensland nominees had little chance of winning the coaching ballot because of the unbalanced voting system which gives NSWRU-supported nominees a massive advantage.

Queensland Rugby Union chief executive Terry Doyle resigned, while his NSW Rugby Union counterpart, David Moffett, left the Union to head up SANZAR before abruptly resigning. Moffett's successor, South African Rian Oberholzer, the son-in-law of South African rugby supremo Louis Luyt, served five months in the position before he too quit to return to Johannesburg to take over as chief executive of SARFU.

The introduction of the Super-12 championship saw the pleasing inclusion of a third Australian provincial team, the ACT Brumbies. While ACT has produced a number of Wallabies, its lack of top-grade competition and its poor representative programme saw many leading players, among them David Campese and Michael O'Connor, move to either Sydney or Brisbane to pursue Wallaby careers.

> 'If Australian Rugby Union has ever been given an opportunity to make up ground on Rugby League, now's the time. As in any competitive market you always take advantage of a competitor in trouble. We are about sixth in Australia in terms of popularity. We've got to start appealing to a broader audience' – ARFU chief executive John O'Neill

However, ACT was 'loaned' players from Sydney and Brisbane to strengthen its squad during the Super-12. This system not only saw ACT narrowly miss the 1996 Super-12 semi-finals but also exposed more leading Australian players to top-quality international provincial rugby.

Despite the players' problems with officialdom, they quickly embraced professionalism. Pre-season training started early and there was more intensity in the off-season training programme. Horan explained: 'Players train more often in the summer, there are set times for weights and spring training, and everyone is more punctual when attending training sessions.'

The Super-12 was the first competition under the new SANZAR (South Africa, New Zealand, Australia Rugby) structure. While Queensland was the only Aussie state to win through to the semi-finals, the competition proved to be a hugely popular with the fans. Queensland, ACT and NSW, who recorded crowds in excess of 20,000 for each home game, all broke match attendance records. Prior to the semi-finals, the average Australian home crowd was more than 16,500 – almost 2,000 above the New Zealand average.

The Super-12 has been an exhausting and demanding competition, with each province playing each other once in consecutive weeks, and requiring much travelling time. Horan reflected: 'It has been very tough, as the championship begins very early in our season. It has also required a high level of intensity, as we are playing top-quality provincial teams every week.'

The success of the Super-12, plus the controversy involving the Australian Rugby League–Super League battle, has given Australian rugby union a great opportunity to attract new fans. Judging by the Super-12 attendance figures, Australian rugby has succeeded.

'If Australian Rugby Union has ever been given an opportunity to make up ground on Rugby League, now's the time', said ARFU chief executive O'Neill. 'As in any competitive market you always take advantage of a competitor in trouble. We've got to start appealing to a broader audience. We are about sixth in Australia in terms of popularity. But basketball has gone from number ten to number four in the last ten years,' he added.

But before Australian rugby can hope to achieve a secure position on the public popularity ladder, the WRC hangover involving players and officials must be cured. Anything else may ultimately lead to self-destruction, particularly as those involved in the WRC have not completely given up hope that their vision for rugby will one day be realised.

Wizard of Oz David Campese hands off an admirer.

AUSTRALIA (P10 W6 D0 L4 F329 A176)

(H) v Argentina	(Brisbane, 29.4.95)	won 53–7
(H) v Argentina	(Sydney, 6.5.95)	won 30–13
(–) v South Africa*	(Cape Town, 25.5.95)	lost 18–27
(–) v Canada*	(Port Elizabeth, 31.5.95)	won 27–11
(–) v Romania*	(Stellenbosch, 3.6.95)	won 42–3
(–) v England*	(q/f: Cape Town, 11.6.95)	lost 22–25
(A) v New Zealand **	(Auckland, 22.7.95)	lost 16–28
(H) v New Zealand **	(Sydney, 29.7.95)	lost 23–34
(H) v Wales (I)	(Brisbane, 15.6.96)	won 56–25
(H) v Wales (ii)	(Sydney, 22.6.96)	won 42–3

* World Cup; ** Bledisloe Cup

Wales in Australia (tour record: P8 W3 D0 L5 F272 A277)

(–) v Western Australia	(Perth, 29.5.96)	won 62–20
(–) v ACT	(Canberra, 2.6.96)	lost 30–69
(–) v New South Wales	(Sydney, 5.6.96)	lost 20–27
(–) v Australia B	(Brisbane, 12.6.96)	lost 41–51
(–) v NSW Country	(Moree, 15.6.96)	won 49–3
(–) v Victoria	(Melbourne, 18.6.96)	won 42–9

1996 SUPER-12 TOURNAMENT
'Queensland Reds blow hat-trick bid in semi-final shocker' – see pages 139–163.

Wallaby Jason Little in World Cup action against Canada in Port Elizabeth.

1980:

Fj	W22–9	Suva	24 May	**t:** Martin, Moon
				c: P E McLean
				p: P E McLean 3
				dg: P E McLean
NZ(1)	W13–9	Sydney	21 Jun	**t:** Hawker, Martin
				c: Gould
				dg: M Ella
NZ(2)	L 9–12	Brisbane	28 Jun	**t:** Moon
				c: Gould
				p: Gould
NZ(3)	W26–10	Sydney	12 Jul	**t:** Grigg 2, O'Connor, Carson
				c: Gould 2
				p: Gould
				dg: M Ella

1981:

F(1)	W17–15	Brisbane	5 Jul	**t:** Poidevin, O'Connor, Moon
				c: P McLean
				p: Richards
F(2)	W24–14	Sydney	11 Jul	**t:** Hall, O'Connor
				c: P McLean 2
				p: P McLean 4
I	W16–12	Dublin	21 Nov	**t:** O'Connor
				p: P McLean 3
				dg: Gould
W	L13–18	Cardiff	5 Dec	**t:** Slack, M Cox
				c: P McLean
				p: P McLean
S	L15–24	Edinburgh	19 Dec	**t:** Poidevin, Moon, Slack
				p: P McLean

1982:

E	L11–15	Twickenham	2 Jan	**t:** Moon 2
				p: P McLean
S(1)	L 7–12	Brisbane	3 Jul	**t:** Hawker
				p: Hawker
S(2)	W33–9	Sydney	10 Jul	**t:** Gould 2, O'Connor
				c: P McLean 3
				p: P McLean 5
NZ(1)	L16–23	Christchurch	14 Aug	**t:** Hawker, Campese
				c: Gould
				p: Gould 2
NZ(2)	W19–16	Wellington	28 Aug	**t:** G Ella, Campese
				c: Gould
				p: Gould 3
NZ(3)	L18–33	Auckland	11 Sep	**t:** Gould
				c: Gould
				p: Gould 3
				dg: Hawker

1983:

US	W49–3	Sydney	9 Jul	t: Campese 4, Slack 2, Ross, Roche, Hanley c: Gould 4, Campese dg: M Ella
Arg(1)	L 3–18	Brisbane	31 Jul	dg: Campese
Arg(2)	W29–13	Sydney	8 Aug	t: Moon 2, Roche, Campese, penalty try c: Campese 3 p: Campese
Fj	W16–3	Suva	xx Aug	t: Campese p: Lynagh 4
NZ	L 8–18	Sydney	20 Aug	t: Slack, Poidevin
It	W29–7	Padova	22 Oct	t: Hawker 2, Moon, Williams, M Ella c: M Ella 3 p: M Ella
F(1)	D15–15	Clermont-Ferrand	13 Nov	t: Roche c: Campese p: Campese dg: M Ella, Hawker
F(2)	L 6–15	Paris	20 Nov	p: Campese dg: M Ella

1984:

NZ(1)	W16–9	Sydney	21 Jul	t: Reynolds, Moon c: M Ella p: M Ella dg: Gould
NZ(2)	L15–19	Brisbane	4 Aug	t: M Ella c: M Ella p: M Ella 2, Campese
NZ(3)	L24–25	Sydney	18 Aug	t: Campese c: M Ella p: M Ella 5, Campese
E	W19–3	Twickenham	3 Nov	t: M Ella, Poidevin, Lynagh c: Lynagh 2 p: Lynagh
I	W16–9	Ireland	10 Nov	t: M Ella p: Lynagh dg: M Ella 2, Lynagh
W	W28–9	Cardiff	24 Nov	t: Lawton, Tuynman, M Ella, Lynagh c: Gould 3 p: Gould 2
S	W37–12	Edinburgh	8 Dec	t: Campese 2, Farr-Jones, M Ella c: Lynagh 3 p: Lynagh 5

1985:

C(1)	W59–3	Sydney	15 Jun	t: Burke 2, Lane 2, Grigg 2, Calcraft, Farr-Jones, Kassulke c: Lynagh 7 p: Lynagh 3

C(2)	W43–15	Brisbane	23 Jun	t: Burke 3, Grigg, Cutler, Tuynman, Farr-Jones c: Lynagh 3 p: Lynagh 2 dg: Lynagh
NZ	L 9–10	Auckland	29 Jun	t: Black c: Lynagh p: Lynagh
Fj(1)	W52–28	Brisbane	10 Aug	t: Farr-Jones 2, Reynolds, Cutler, Lawton, Papworth, Grigg c: Knox 3 p: Knox 3 dg: Knox 2, Campese
Fj(2)	W31–9	Sydney	17 Aug	t: Campese 2, Grigg, McIntyre, Cutler c: Knox p: Knox 3

1986:

It	W39–18	Brisbane	1 Jun	t: Campese 2, Tuynman, McIntyre, Moon, Burke c: Lynagh 6 p: Lynagh
F	W27–14	Sydney	21 Jun	t: Campese c: Lynagh p: Lynagh 6 dg: Lynagh
Arg(1)	W39–19	Brisbane	6 Jul	t: Papworth 2, Grigg, Campese c: Lynagh 4 p: Lynagh 5
Arg(2)	W26–0	Sydney	12 Jul	t: Campese 2, Tuynman c: Lynagh p: Lynagh 4
NZ(1)	W13–12	Wellington	9 Aug	t: Campese, Burke c: Lynagh p: Lynagh
NZ(2)	L12–13	Dunedin	23 Aug	p: Lynagh 3 dg: Lynagh
NZ(3)	W22–9	Auckland	6 Sep	t: Leeds, Campese c: Lynagh p: Lynagh 4

1987:

| SK | W65–18 | Brisbane | 17 May | t: Burke 3, Grigg 2, Slack 2, Cook, Gould, B Smith, Miller, James, Farr-Jones
c: Smith 5
p: Smith |
| E* | W19–6 | Sydney | 23 May | t: Campese, Poidevin
c: Lynagh
p: Lynagh 3 |

US*	W47–12	Brisbane	31 May	t: penalty try, Smith, Slack, Leeds 2, Papworth, Campese, Codey c: Lynagh 6 p: Lynagh
J*	W42–23	Sydney	3 Jun	t: Slack 2, Tuynman, Burke 2, Grigg, Hartill, Campese c: Lynagh 5
I*	W33–15	Sydney	7 Jun	t: McIntyre, Smith, Burke 2 c: Lynagh 4 p: Lynagh 3
F*	L24–30	Sydney	13 Jun	t: Campese, Codey c: Lynagh 2 p: Lynagh 3 dg: Lynagh
W*	L21–22	Rotorua	18 Jun	t: Burke, Grigg c: Lynagh 2 p: Lynagh 2 dg: Lynagh
NZ	L16–30	Sydney	25 Jul	t: Papworth p: Leeds 3 dg: Hawker
Arg(1)	D19–19	Buenos Aires	31 Oct	t: Williams, Cutler, Lynagh c: Lynagh 2 p: Lynagh
Arg(2)	L19–27	Buenos Aires	7 Nov	t: Williams 2 c: Lynagh p: Lynagh 3

1988:

E(a1)	W22–16	Brisbane	29 May	t: Williams p: Lynagh 6
E(a2)	W28–8	Sydney	12 Jun	t: Campese, G Ella, Lynagh, Carter c: Lynagh 3 p: Lynagh 2
NZ(1)	L 7–32	Sydney	3 Jul	t: Williams p: Lynagh
NZ(2)	D19–19	Brisbane	16 Jul	t: Grant, Williams c: Leeds p: Leeds 3
NZ(3)	L 9–30	Sydney	30 Jul	t: Walker c: Lynagh p: Leeds
E(b)	L19–28	Twickenham	5 Nov	t: Leeds, Campese, Grant c: Lynagh 2 p: Lynagh
S	W32–13	Edinburgh	19 Nov	t: Lawton 2, Campese 2, Gourley, c: Lynagh 3 p: Lynagh 2
It	W55–6	Milan	3 Dec	t: Campese 3, Niuqila 3, Leeds, Gourley, Lynagh c: Lynagh 8 p: Lynagh

1989:

BL(1)	W30–12	Sydney	1 Jul	**t:** Walker, Gourley, Maguire, Martin
				c: Lynagh 4
				p: Lynagh
				dg: Lynagh
BL(2)	L12–19	Brisbane	8 Jul	**t:** Martin
				c: Lynagh
				p: Lynagh 2
BL(3)	L18–19	Sydney	15 Jul	**t:** Williams
				c: Lynagh
				p: Lynagh 4
NZ	L12–24	Auckland	5 Aug	**t:** Campese
				c: Lynagh
				p: Lynagh 2
F(1)	W32–15	Strasbourg	4 Nov	**t:** Horan 2, Williams, Campese
				c: Lynagh 2
				p: Lynagh 4
F(2)	L19–25	Lille	11 Nov	**t:** Kearns, Farr-Jones
				c: Lynagh
				p: Lynagh 3

1990:

F(1)	W21–9	Sydney	9 Jun	**t:** Martin
				c: Lynagh
				p: Lynagh 5
F(2)	W48–31	Brisbane	24 Jun	**t:** Carozza, Cornish, Gavin, Little, penalty try, Campese
				c: Lynagh 6
				p: Lynagh 4
F(3)	L19–28	Sydney	30 Jun	**t:** Campese, Daly
				c: Lynagh
				p: Lynagh 2
				dg: Lynagh
US	W67–9	Brisbane	8 Jul	**t:** Lynagh 2, Williams 2, Daly, McKenzie, Kearns, Gavin, Little, Farr-Jones, Slattery, Campese
				c: Lynagh 8
				dg: Campese
NZ(1)	L 6–21	Christchurch	21 Jul	**p:** Lynagh 2
NZ(2)	L17–27	Auckland	4 Aug	**t:** Horan, Ofahengaue
				p: Lynagh 2
				dg: Lynagh
NZ(3)	W21–9	Wellington	18 Aug	**t:** Kearns
				c: Lynagh
				p: Lynagh 5

1991:

W(a)	W63–6	Brisbane	21 Jul	**t:** Lynagh 2, Kearns 2, Gavin 2, Ofahengaue, Horan, Roebuck, Campese, Egerton, Little
				c: Lynagh 6
				p: Lynagh

E(a)	W40–15	Sydney	27 Jul	t: Campese 2, Ofahengaue 2, Roebuck c: Lynagh 4 p: Lynagh 4
NZ(a1)	W21–12	Sydney	10 Aug	t: Gavin, Egerton c: Lynagh 2 p: Lynagh 3
NZ(a2)	L 3–6	Auckland	24 Aug	p: Lynagh
Arg*	W32–19	Llanelli	4 Oct	t: Campese 2, Horan 2, Kearns c: Lynagh 3 p: Lynagh 2
WS*	W 9–3	Pontypool	9 Oct	p: Lynagh 3
W(b)*	W38–3	Cardiff	12 Oct	t: Roebuck 2, Slattery, Campese, Horan, Lynagh c: Lynagh 4 p: Lynagh 2
I*	W19–18	Dublin	20 Oct	t: Campese 2, Lynagh c: Lynagh 2 p: Lynagh
NZ(b)*	W16–6	Dublin	27 Oct	t: Campese, Horan c: Lynagh p: Lynagh 2
E*	W12–6	Twickenham	2 Nov	t: Daly c: Lynagh p: Lynagh 2

1992:

S(1)	W27–12	Sydney	13 June	t: Campese 2, Carozza, Lynagh c: Lynagh p: Lynagh 3
S(2)	W37–13	Brisbane	21 Jun	t: Carozza 2, Horan 2, Eales c: Lynagh p: Lynagh 5
NZ(1)†	W16–15	Sydney	14 Jul	t: Campese, Horan p: Lynagh 2
NZ(2)	W19–17	Brisbane	19 Jul	t: Carozza 2 p: Lynagh 3
NZ(3)	L23–26	Sydney	25 Jul	t: Farr-Jones, Herbert c: Lynagh 2 p: Lynagh 3
SA	W26–3	Cape Town	23 Aug	t: Carozza 2, Campese c: Lynagh p: Lynagh 3
I	W42–17	Dublin	31 Oct	t: Campese, McKenzie, Little, Kelaher, Horan c: Roebuck 4 p: Roebuck 3
W	W23–6	Cardiff	21 Nov	t: Wilson, McCall, Campese c: Roebuck p: Roebuck 2

1993:

T	W52–14	Brisbane	3 Jul	**t:** Campese 2, Carozza, Little, Gavin, Morgan, Johnstone **c:** Roebuck 3, Lynagh **p:** Roebuck 3
NZ	L10–25	Dunedin	17 Jul	**t:** Horan **c:** Kelaher **p:** Kelaher
SA(1)	L12–19	Sydney	31 Jul	**p:** Roebuck 4
SA(2)	W28–20	Brisbane	14 Aug	**t:** Little 2, Horan **c:** Roebuck 2 **p:** Roebuck 3
SA(3)	W19–12	Sydney	21 Aug	**t:** Horan **c:** Roebuck **p:** Roebuck 4
US+	W26–22	California	2 Oct	**t:** Wilson, Howard, Tabua, Lea **c:** Lynagh 3
C	W43–16	Calgary	9 Oct	**t:** Campese 3, Horan, Daly, D Smith **c:** Lynagh 2 **p:** Lynagh 3
F(1)	L13–16	Bordeaux	30 Oct	**t:** Gavin **c:** Lynagh **p:** Lynagh 2
F(2)	W24–3	Paris	6 Nov	**t:** Roebuck, Gavin **c:** Roebuck **p:** Roebuck 4

1994:

I(1)	W33–13	Brisbane	5 Jun	**t:** Tabua, Lynagh, Campese, Burke, D Smith **c:** Lynagh **p:** Lynagh 2
I(2)	W32–18	Sydney	11 Jun	**t:** D Herbert, Wilson, Tabua **c:** Lynagh **p:** Lynagh 5
It(1)	W23–20	Brisbane	18 Jun	**t:** Burke, D Herbert **c:** Lynagh, Wallace **p:** Lynagh 2, Wallace
It(2)	W20–7	Melbourne	26 Jun	**t:** Campese **p:** Wallace 5
WS	W73–3	Brisbane	6 Jul	**t:** D Smith 2, Little 2, Campese, Gavin, Pini, Junee, Howard, Ofahengaue, Gregan **c:** Knox 6 **p:** Knox 2
NZ	W20–16	Sydney	17 Aug	**t:** Kearns, Little **c:** Knox 2 **p:** Knox 3

1995:

Arg(1)	W53–7	Brisbane	29 Apr	**t:** Lynagh 2, D Smith, Campese, Pini, Eales, Ofahengaue **c:** Lynagh 3 **p:** Lynagh 4
Arg(2)	W30–13	Sydney	6 May	**t:** Campese 2, Wilson **p:** Lynagh 5
SA*	L18–27	Cape Town	25 May	**t:** Lynagh, Kearns **c:** Lynagh **p:** Lynagh 2
C*	W27–11	Port Elizabeth	31 May	**t:** Tabua, Roff, Lynagh **c:** Lynagh 3 **p:** Lynagh 2
R*	W42–3	Stellenbosch	3 Jun	**t:** Roff 2, D Smith, Wilson, Burke, Foley **c:** Burke 2, Eales 4
E*	L22–25	Cape Town	11 Jun	**t:** D Smith **c:** Lynagh **p:** Lynagh 5
NZ(1)	L16–28	Auckland	22 July	**t:** Ofahengaue **c:** Roff **p:** Roff 2, Burke
NZ(2)	L23–34	Sydney	29 July	**t:** D Smith, Ofahengaue **c:** Burke 2 **p:** Burke 3

1996:

W(1)	W56–25	Brisbane	9 Jun	**t:** Roff, Morgan, Wilson, Howard, Manu, Caputo, Murdoch **c:** Burke 6 **p:** Burke 3
W(2)	W42–3	Sydney	22 Jun	**t:** Burke, Roff, Horan, Finegan, Morgan, Foley **c:** Burke 2, Eales **p:** Burke 2

* World Cup
+ Non-cap
† Five-point try introduced from this game onwards
(TN) Tri-Nation match

NEW ZEALAND
Wynne Gray
New Zealand Herald

THE ARRIVAL of professionalism in rugby was accepted in New Zealand as an inevitable move.

Of course there were reservations, as there always are when significant change occurs. But for almost a decade, since the resounding success of the first World Cup, there had been a feeling in New Zealand that professionalism had to come to rugby and the sooner the better.

The more the International Rugby Board procrastinated, the higher the agitation level became, the greater the frustration about the lack of commercial progress and player benefit to match the excitement on the playing fields.

For too long 'shamateurism' had operated in New Zealand while a heap of players had also gone offshore to tout their rugby skills rather than to offer any other talent to the foreign economies.

The mounting pressure on the NZRFU to push for professionalism in rugby, the IRB's intransigence, the lures of foreign rugby and the threat of Rugby League clearly signalled there was going to be a bust-up after the 1995 World Cup in South Africa.

The All Blacks and leading players wanted to participate in the third global tournament but once that tournament was over it was going to be open slather. Of that there was no doubt in New Zealand.

Rugby League or Super League at that stage was already enticing players with huge offers. Others such as Jamie Joseph, Arran Pene, Graeme Bachop and Ant Strachan chose to play/work in Japan.

> *There was some jealousy over Super-12 payments, with each squad member earning NZ$50,000 for the three-month series regardless of whether he played in every game or none at all*

The rebel Rugby World Corporation was circling, and came within a whisker of having the entire All Blacks squad on their list – the players were sick of earning a huge revenue for the NZRFU and getting very little for their efforts.

So SANZAR secured the NZ$828 million backing of media mogul Rupert Murdoch for a ten-year television deal for a professional rugby series in New Zealand, Australia and South Africa. The war was only just starting though, as the WRC was declaring its stance about the time the Murdoch deal was announced.

Eventually the WRC charge was broken and the new Super-12 tri-series was unveiled, but there were many worries about whether the format would work. Nearly 300 players in New Zealand were contracted to the NZRFU, and the top 125 were then rated and started the Super-12.

The first grumbles came about the teams. In previous international competitions the top four or five provinces in the first division have represented New Zealand. For the Super-12 the organisers decided to dismiss the first-past-the-post rewards and divided the entire country (27 unions) into five regional sides. The five sides could pick players from any of their affiliated unions, and if they were not satisfied with that collection could ask to draft players from other regions.

Initially the premise was that the five sides should be roughly equal, but it was soon apparent that Auckland and Counties together – giving Auckland the services of one Jonah Lomu – would be the best Kiwi side, and so it showed when they won the inaugural Super-12 final from Natal. In contrast, Canterbury and Wellington were near the tail of the competition and clearly in need of some greater player resources for 1997.

Drafted players were supposed to return after the Super-12 to their provincial unions for the national championship, but in practice the new professionals found life enticing and rewarding in their new regions.

There was also some jealousy about the payments, with each player involved in a squad throughout the Super-12, plus each of those on the standby pool of drafted players, earning NZ$50,000 for the three-month series. Thus All Black captain Sean Fitzpatrick, who played all 11 pool matches for the Auckland Blues, then the semi-final and final, earned exactly the same as the squad's reserve hooker, Andrew Roose, who did not take the field – and exactly the same wage as someone like Waikato lock Tiwini Hemi, who was in the standby pool but was never called into a squad.

By the end of the season players were asking how fair the pay scale was. It was obviously not, but it was a bi-product of the battle with WRC that players had to be contracted to the NZRFU and some got much better deals than others. For example, Murdoch insisted that for him to back the Super-12 and the tri-Test series, he wanted the best players in New Zealand. That meant the All Blacks.

Each All Black was guaranteed NZ$250,000 a season for the Super-12, the national championship and the ten-Test programme. All they had to be was fit and available to collect their loot, so someone like Richard Loe, who at 36 was never going to threaten another Test nation, let alone the All Black front row, was laughing. He was fit, available, but never going to be chosen and his wallet was bulging.

That element of professionalism did not sit well, especially when it meant a number of youngsters were missing out, but it was a fact of life if New Zealand wanted Murdoch's money. Arguments will still rage, however, about the worth of individual players.

> *Each All Black was guaranteed NZ$250,000 a season for the Super-12, the national championship and the ten-Test programme. All they had to be was fit and available to collect their loot, so someone like Richard Loe, who at 36 was never going to threaten another Test nation, let alone the All Black front row, was laughing*

Was Jeff Wilson worth more because he flashed over the line? Or should Olo Brown get the reward because he held the tighthead side of the scrum up for the clean possession? Or should it be Josh Kronfeld who recycled the ball from second phase play?

But one thing was for certain: Lomu had a special contract and, with his endorsements pushing his annual income to about NZ$2 million a year, he is the world's highest-paid rugby player. Yet with that went some responsibility, and there were questions about his professional attitude when he was caught speeding without a licence, did not invite his parents to his wedding, broke a photographer's flash in a fit of pique and was then found to be about the most unfit player in his Super-12 squad.

These were yet more growing pains for the latest sport to go pro, while there were groans too from Joe Public that the Super-12 series and the Tests were on Sky pay-television, not free-to-air on state television as All Black internationals had been since Colin Meads was in short pants.

Players started to show their muscle too, with several wearing Nike boots in Tests because they had individual contracts signed at the time the NZRFU wanted to woo all players from WRC. But that Nike deal crossed the NZRFU's deal with Mizuno.

> *'I don't think buying in overseas stars does a lot for rugby – like in England, where Michael Lynagh and Philippe Sella have joined Saracens. I don't think that does the club scene any good' – Sean Fitzpatrick, welcoming the NZRFU's decision to contract New Zealand players*

'Too bad', said the players. 'We want the money to endorse boots, which are specialist equipment like tennis racquets, instead of Mizuno supplying money to the NZRFU and *just* footwear to the players.'

The first chapter in the book on professionalism in New Zealand rugby was only just unfolding but the Super-12 was an enormous success. Crowds were huge, matches became a total entertainment package, often under floodlights in another new move for this country.

The key to the success, though, was the new rugby rules, especially with all eight forwards having to remain bound until scrums were completed. It brought more room, extra attacking avenues and, with lineouts providing more and more swift, clean possession, much of the rugby was spectacularly vibrant. The crowds thought so and filled grounds which had been losing numbers.

For All Black captain Fitzpatrick the new rugby world meant he was getting paid for something he had done all the time – train and play rugby in a very professional manner. 'Now I can justify being away from my job for six months a year and have something in the bank', he said. 'I can also justify the time I have away from my family because I am earning a living.

'I am carrying on because I can earn a useful nest-egg, but also because I still love the sport and at last am being rewarded for it. Why retire as so many have done when you are still enjoying the sport? You don't see many people who leave good jobs, so there is a real incentive to play well, to maintain your position and lift the quality of the sport.'

Fitzpatrick is also glad that the NZRFU has been contracting only New Zealand players. 'I don't think buying in overseas stars does a lot for the rugby – like in England, where Michael Lynagh and Philippe Sella have joined Saracens. I don't think that does the club scene any good.

'Not a lot has changed with the All Blacks because for so long now we have adopted a professional attitude to everything we do about our rugby. Professionalism had to come and now, instead of four or five, there are 125 in New Zealand making an income from rugby.

'There are great pitfalls like some who have overspent or others succumbing to pressures, but that is going to happen anywhere in pro sport', said Fitzpatrick. 'I would also like to see more players taking courses or working round their rugby. I think it is a trap for some who are training, playing, eating and sleeping. I think they will get bored and lose an edge to their play.'

Super-12 was great preparation for the Test series, though it meant clubs never saw their top-line members. It was a very intense competition with tough games every week, though the greatest problem for the new professional athletes was to contend with the mental, rather than any physical fatigue.

'I would also like to see more players taking courses or working round their rugby. I think it is a trap for some who are training, playing, eating and sleeping. I think they will get bored and lose an edge to their play' – Fitzpatrick

Fitzpatrick walked out of his Coca Cola office in Auckland at the end of May with a 'see you in September' message as he prepared for the winter Tests in New Zealand, Australia, then South Africa. Those over, he wants to go back to the office.

The new Test programme is important, as he believed firmly that the 1996 All Blacks were capable of being better than that very good 1987 model which took the first World Cup. 'We let ourselves down in the final of the 1995 World Cup, and we had to show we were capable of playing well and win again', he said. 'Our first Bledisloe Cup win after that against Australia was not so good, but the second was right up there and was probably Jonah's best game for the All Blacks.

'Then we went to France again to tackle Laurie Mains' bogey team. In the first Test we let ourselves down in attitude and lost. That was one thing – I guess we lacked consistency from week to week. The pressure was on for the last Test in Paris, but our minds were on the job and we showed what we were capable of with a 37–12 win.

'Now there is a new regime with John Hart as coach and maybe we will find some more consistency, the only thing we are really lacking is a bit of depth outside the 21-man-strong squad.'

NEW ZEALAND'S INTERNATIONAL SEASON 1995/96

NEW ZEALAND (P14 W12 D0 L2 F682 A248)

(H)	v Canada	(Auckland, 22.4.95)	won 73–7
(–)	v Ireland	(Johannesburg, 27.5.95)	won 43–19
(–)	v Wales*	(Johannesburg, 31.5.95)	won 34–9
(–)	v Japan*	(Bloemfontein, 4.6.95)	won 145–17
(–)	v Scotland*	(q/f: Pretoria, 11.6.95)	won 48–30
(–)	v England*	(s/f: Cape Town, 18.6.95)	won 45–29
(–)	v South Africa*+	(f: Johannesburg, 24.6.95)	lost 12–15
(H)	v Australia **	(Auckland, 22.7.95)	won 28–16
(A)	v Australia **	(Sydney, 29.7.95)	won 34–23
(A)	v Italy	(Bologna, 28.10.95)	won 70–6
(A)	v France (i)	(Toulouse, 11.11.95)	lost 15–22
(A)	v France (ii)	(Paris, 18.11.95)	won 37–12
(H)	v Scotland (i)	(Dunedin, 15.6.96)	won 62–31
(H)	v Scotland (ii)	(Auckland, 22.6.96)	won 36–12

+ (aet); * World Cup; ** Bledisloe Cup

Scotland in New Zealand (P8 W4 D0 L4 F266 A238)

(–)	v Wanganui	(Wanganui, 28.5.96)	won 49–13
(–)	v Northland	(Whangerei, 31.5.96)	lost 10–15
(–)	v Waikato	(Hamilton, 5.6.96)	lost 35–39
(–)	v Southland	(Invercargill, 8.6.96)	won 31–21
(–)	v South Island XV	(Blenheim, 12.6.96)	won 63–21
(–)	v Bay of Plenty	(Rotorua, 18.6.96)	won 35–31

HONG KONG SEVENS
Final: New Zealand 19, Fiji 17

1996 SUPER-12 TOURNAMENT
'Auckland rule the roost' – see pages 139–163.

1995 DOMESTIC RUGBY

AIR NEW ZEALAND NATIONAL PROVINCIAL CHAMPIONSHIP

Division One	P	W	D	L	F	A	B	Pts
Auckland	8	7	0	1	236	118	1	29
Counties	8	6	0	2	233	228	1	25
Otago	8	5	0	3	215	220	2	22
North Harbour	8	4	1	3	247	159	2	20
Canterbury	8	4	1	3	259	232	1	19
Waikato	8	4	0	4	205	206	2	18
Wellington	8	3	0	5	165	230	1	13
King Country	8	2	0	6	150	231	0	8
Southland	8	0	0	8	136	222	6	6

Final: Auckland 23, Otago 19 (Auckland, 15.10.95). **Semi-finals:** Auckland 60, North Harbour 20 (Auckland, 7.10.95); Otago 41, Counties 32 (Pukekohe, 8.10.95).

Division Two	P	W	D	L	F	A	B	Pts
Northland	8	8	0	0	351	101	0	32
Bay of Plenty	8	6	0	2	314	152	1	25
Taranaki	8	6	0	2	342	191	0	24
Hawke's Bay	8	5	0	3	242	196	0	20
Manawatu	8	4	0	4	258	165	3	19
Wairarapa Bush	8	4	0	4	248	239	0	16
South Canterbury	8	2	0	6	135	303	1	9
Nelson Bays	8	1	0	7	115	436	1	5
Mid Canterbury	8	0	0	8	130	352	1	1

Final: Taranaki 22., Northland 18 (Whangarei, 14.10.95). **Semi-finals:** Northland 36, Hawke's Bay 6 (Whangarei, 7.10.95); Taranaki 37, Bay of Plenty 12 (8.10.95).

Division Three
Promoted: Thames Valley. **Final:** Thames Valley 47, Poverty Bay 8 (Paeroa, 17.10.95). **Semi-finals:** Thames Valley 32, Horowhenua 17 (Paeroa, 7.10.95); Poverty Bay 26, Wanganui 19 (Gisborne, 8.10.95).

RANFURLY SHIELD
Holders: Auckland (one defence)
Canterbury 64, Mid Canterbury 19 (Ashburton, 24.6.95); Canterbury 43, Nelson Bays 17 (Christchurch 1.7.95); Canterbury 79, Marlborough 0 (Christchurch, 15.7.95); Canterbury 72, South Canterbury 17 (Christchurch, 29.7.95); Canterbury 27, Southland 22 (Christchurch, 12.8.95); Canterbury 50, Waikato 29 (Christchurch, 19.8.95); Canterbury 66, Wellington 17 (Christchurch, 10.9.95); Canterbury 0, Auckland 35 (Christchurch. 23.9.95); Auckland 26, Waikato 17 (Auckland, 1.10.95).

*All Black wing Jeff Wilson gives Scotland's Kenny Logan the
slip in Dunedin, where New Zealand won the first Test 62–31.*

1980:

A(1)	L 9–13	Sydney	21 Jun	p: Codlin 3
A(2)	W12–9	Brisbane	28 Jun	t: Reid
				c: Codlin
				p: Codlin 2
A(3)	L10–26	Sydney	12 Jul	t: Fraser
				p: Codlin 2
Fj(a)+	W30–6	Suva	23 Jul	t: Fraser 3, Allen, B Robertson
				c: Codlin 2
				p: Codlin 2
Fj(b)+	W33–0	Auckland	30 Sep	t: Osborne 2, K Taylor 2, Wylie, Woodman
				c: Valli 3
				p: Valli
C+	W43–10	Vancouver	11 Oct	t: M Shaw 3, Mourie, Haden, Osborne, S Wilson, Fraser
				c: Rollerson 4
				p: Rollerson
US+	W53–6	San Diego	Oct	t: Woodman 3, Osborne 2, Wilson, Allen, Old
				c: Codlin 6
				p: Codlin 3
W	W23–3	Cardiff	1 Nov	t: Mourie, Fraser, Allen, Reid
				c: Rollerson 2
				p: Rollerson

1981:

S(1)	W11–4	Dunedin	13 Jun	t: Wilson, Loveridge
				p: Hewson
S(2)	W40–15	Auckland	20 Jun	t: Wilson 3, Hewson 2, Robertson, Mourie
				c: Hewson 6
SA(1)	W14–9	Christchurch	15 Aug	t: Rollerson, Wilson, Shaw
				c: Rollerson
SA(2)	L12–24	Wellington	29 Aug	p: Hewson 4
SA(3)	W25–22	Auckland	12 Sep	t: Wilson, Knight
				c: Rollerson
				p: Hewson 3, Rollerson
				dg: Rollerson
R	W14–6	Bucharest	24 Oct	t: Salmon, Dalton
				p: Hewson
				dg: Rollerson
F(1)	W13–9	Toulouse	14 Nov	t: Wilson
				p: Hewson 2
				dg: Hewson
F(2)	W18–6	Paris	21 Nov	t: penalty try, Wilson
				c: Hewson 2
				p: Hewson 2

1982:

A(1)	W23–16	Christchurch	14 Aug	**t:** Mexted, Mourie, Pokere, Fraser
				c: Hewson 2
				p: Hewson
A(2)	L16–19	Wellington	28 Aug	**t:** Shaw, Fraser
				c: Hewson
				p: Hewson 2
A(3)	W33–18	Auckland	11 Sep	**t:** Hewson, Shaw
				c: Hewson 2
				p: Hewson 5
				dg: Hewson, Smith

1983:

BL(1)	W16–12	Christchurch	4 Jun	**t:** Shaw
				p: Hewson 3
				dg: Hewson
BL(2)	W 9–0	Wellington	18 Jun	**t:** Loveridge
				c: Hewson
				p: Hewson
BL(3)	W15–8	Dunedin	2 Jul	**t:** Wilson
				c: Hewson
				p: Hewson 3
BL(4)	W38–6	Auckland	16 Jul	**t:** Wilson 3, Hewson, Hobbs, Haden
				c: Hewson 4
				p: Hewson 2
A	W18–8	Sydney	20 Aug	**t:** Taylor
				c: Hewson
				p: Hewson 4
S	D25–25	Edinburgh	12 Nov	**t:** Fraser 2, Hobbs
				c: Deans 2
				p: Deans 3
E	L 9–15	Twickenham	19 Nov	**t:** Davie
				c: Deans
				p: Deans

1984:

F(1)	W10–9	Christchurch	16 Jun	**t:** Taylor
				p: Hewson 2
F(2)	W31–18	Auckland	23 Jun	**t:** B Smith, Dalton, Taylor
				c: Hewson 2
				p: Hewson 5
A(1)	L 9–16	Sydney	21 Jul	**p:** Hewson 2
				dg: Hewson
A(2)	W19–15	Brisbane	4 Aug	**t:** Pokere
				p: Deans 5
A(3)	W25–24	Sydney	18 Aug	**t:** Clamp, Stone
				c: Deans
				p: Deans 5

1985:

E(1)	W18–13	Christchurch	1 Jun	**p:** Crowley 6

E(2)	W42–15	Wellington	8 Jun	**t:** Green 2, Kirwan, Mexted, Hobbs, Shaw **c:** Crowley 3 **p:** Crowley 3 **dg:** Smith
A	W10–9	Auckland	29 Jun	**t:** Green **p:** Crowley 2
Arg(1)	W33–20	Buenos Aires	26 Oct	**t:** Kirwan 2, Hobbs, Crowley **c:** Crowley **p:** Crowley 4 **dg:** Fox
Arg(2)	D21–21	Buenos Aires	2 Nov	**t:** Kirwan 2, Mexted, Green **c:** Crowley. **p:** Crowley

1986:

F(a)	W18–9	Christchurch	28 Jun	**t:** Brewer **c:** G Cooper **p:** G Cooper **dg:** Botica 2, G Cooper
A(1)	L12–13	Wellington	9 Aug	**t:** Brooke-Cowden **c:** G Cooper **p:** G Cooper 2
A(2)	W13–12	Dunedin	23 Aug	**t:** Kirk **p:** G Cooper 2 **dg:** G Cooper
A(3)	L 9–22	Auckland	6 Sep	**p:** Crowley 3
F(b1)	W19–7	Toulouse	8 Nov	**t:** Shelford **p:** Crowley 3 **dg:** Stone, Crowley
F(b2)	L 3–16	Nantes	15 Nov	**p:** Crowley

1987:

It*	W70–6	Auckland	22 May	**t:** Kirk 2, Kirwan 2, Green 2, M Jones, Taylor, McDowell, Stanley, A Whetton, penalty try **c:** Fox 8 **p:** Fox 2
Fj*	W74–13	Christchurch	27 May	**t:** Green 4, Gallagher 4, Kirk, Kirwan, A Whetton, penalty try **c:** Fox 10 **p:** Fox 2
Arg*	W46–15	Wellington	1 Jun	**t:** Kirk, Z Brooke, Stanley, Earl, Crowley, A Whetton **c:** Fox 2 **p:** Fox 6
S*	W30–3	Christchurch	6 Jun	**t:** Gallagher, A Whetton **c:** Fox 2. **p:** Fox 6
W*	W49–6	Brisbane	14 Jun	**t:** Kirwan 2, Shelford 2, Drake, Brooke-Cowden, Stanley, A Whetton **c:** Fox 7 **p:** Fox

114

F*	W29–9	Auckland	20 Jun	t: Kirk, Kirwan, M Jones
				c: Fox
				p: Fox 4
				dg: Fox
A	W30–16	Sydney	25 Jul	t: Fitzpatrick 2, Kirwan, Green
				c: Fox
				p: Fox 3
				dg: Fox

1988:

W(1)	W52–3	Christchurch	28 May	t: Kirwan 4, Wright 2, Gallagher, Deans, Shelford, G Whetton
				c: Fox 6
W(2)	W54–9	Auckland	11 Jun	t: Kirwan 2, Wright 2, Taylor, Deans, M Jones, McDowell
				c: Fox 8
				p: Fox 2
A(1)	W32–7	Sydney	3 Jul	t: Kirwan 2, McDowell, A Whetton, Schuster
				c: Fox 3
				p: Fox 2
A(2)	D19–19	Brisbane	16 Jul	t: M Jones, Wright, Kirwan
				c: Fox 2
				p: Fox
A(3)	W30–9	Sydney	30 Jul	t: Deans, Gallagher, Kirwan
				c: Fox 3
				p: Fox 4

1989:

F(1)	W25–17	Christchurch	18 Jun	t: Wright 2, A Whetton
				c: Fox 2
				p: Fox 3
F(2)	W34–20	Auckland	1 Jul	t: Stanley, Deans, Fitzpatrick, A Whetton
				c: Fox 3
				p: Fox 4
Arg(1)	W60–9	Dunedin	15 Jul	t: Gallagher 3, Kirwan 2, Wright 2, penalty try, M Jones 2
				c: Fox 7
				p: Fox 2
Arg(2)	W49–12	Wellington	29 Jul	t: Wright 2, Deans 2, Gallagher, Kirwan, A Whetton
				c: Fox 6
				p: Fox 3
A	W24–12	Auckland	5 Aug	t: Gallagher, Loe
				c: Fox 2
				p: Fox 4
W	W34–9	Cardiff	4 Nov	t: Innes 2, Bachop, Wright
				c: Fox 3
				p: Fox 4
I	W23–6	Dublin	18 Nov	t: Gallagher, Wright, Shelford
				c: Fox
				p: Fox 3

1990:

S(1)	W31–16	Dunedin	16 Jun	**t:** Kirwan 2, Crowley, I Jones, Fox
				c: Fox 4
				p: Fox
S(2)	W21–18	Auckland	23 Jun	**t:** Loe
				c: Fox
				p: Fox 5
A(1)	W21–6	Christchurch	21 Jul	**t:** Fitzpatrick, Crowley, Innes, Kirwan
				c: Fox
				p: Fox
A(2)	W27–17	Auckland	4 Aug	**t:** Fitzpatrick, Z Brooke, G Bachop
				c: Fox 3
				p: Fox 2
				dg: Fox
A(3)	L 9–21	Wellington	18 Aug	**p:** Fox 2
				dg: Fox
F(1)	W24–3	Nantes	3 Nov	**t:** Innes, A Whetton
				c: Fox 2
				p: Fox 3
				dg: Fox
F(2)	W30–12	Paris	10 Nov	**t:** Crowley, M Jones
				c: Fox 2
				p: Fox 6

1991:

Arg(1)	W28–14	Buenos Aires	6 Jul	**t:** Wright, Earl
				c: Fox
				p: Fox 5
				dg: Crowley
Arg(2)	W36–6	Buenos Aires	13 Jul	**t:** Z Brooke, M Jones, Kirwan, Wright
				c: Fox 4
				p: Fox 4
A(a1)	L12–21	Sydney	10 Aug	**t:** I Jones
				c: Fox
				p: Fox 2
A(a2)	W 6–3	Auckland	24 Aug	**p:** Fox 2
E*	W18–12	Twickenham	3 Oct	**t:** M Jones
				c: Fox
				p: Fox 4
US*	W46–6	Gloucester	8 Oct	**t:** Wright 3, Timu, Earl, Purvis, Tuigamala, Innes
				c: Preston 4
				p: Preston 2
It*	W31–21	Leicester	13 Oct	**t:** Z Brooke, Tuigamala, Hewitt, Innes
				c: Fox 3
				p: Fox 3
C*	W29–13	Lille	20 Oct	**t:** Timu 2, McCahill, Kirwan, Z Brooke
				c: Fox 3
				p: Fox
A(b)*	L 6–16	Dublin	27 Oct	**p:** Fox 2
S*	W13–6	Cardiff	30 Oct	**t:** Little
				p: Preston 3

1992:

Wd(1)	L14–28	Christchurch	18 Apr	**t:** Turner, Tuigamala **p:** Fox 2
Wd(2)	W54–26	Wellington	22 Apr	**t:** G Cooper 2, Loe 2, Pene, Clarke 2, Tuigamala, Larsen, Strachan **c:** G Cooper 6, Fox
Wd(3)	W26–15	Auckland	25 Apr	**t:** Pene, Kirwan, Loe, Clarke **c:** G Cooper 2 **p:** G Cooper 2
I(1)	W24–21	Dunedin	30 May	**t:** Henderson, Bunce 2, Clarke **c:** G Cooper 4
I(2)	W59–6	Wellington	6 Jun	**t:** Bunce 2, Pene 2, I Jones, Clarke, Timu, M Cooper 2, Kirwan, Strachan **c:** M Cooper 6 **p:** M Cooper
A(1)	L15–16	Sydney	14 Jul	**t:** Tuigamala, Bunce **c:** Fox **p:** Fox
A(2)	L17–19	Brisbane	19 Jul	**t:** Timu, Kirwan **c:** Fox 2 **p:** Fox
A(3)	W26–23	Sydney	25 Jul	**t:** Bunce, Joseph **c:** Fox 2 **p:** Fox 3 **dg:** Fox
SA	W27–24	Johannesburg	15 Aug	**t:** Z Brooke, Kirwan, Timu **c:** Fox 3 **p:** Fox 2

1993:

BL(1)	W20–18	Christchurch	12 Jun	**t:** Bunce **p:** Fox 5
BL(2)	L 7–20	Wellington	26 Jun	**t:** Clarke **c:** Fox
BL(3)	W30–13	Auckland	3 Jul	**t:** Bunce, Fitzpatrick, Preston **c:** Fox 3 **p:** Fox 3
A	W25–10	Dunedin	17 Jul	**t:** Fitzpatrick, Bunce **p:** Fox 5
WS	W35–13	Auckland	31 Jul	**t:** Stensness, Z Brooke **c:** Fox 2 **p:** Fox 7
S	W51–15	Edinburgh	20 Nov	**t:** Wilson 3, Ellis 2, Bunce, Z Brooke **c:** Cooper 4, Wilson **p:** Cooper 2
E	L 9–15	Twickenham	27 Nov	**p:** Wilson 3

1994:

F(1)	L 8–22	Christchurch	26 Jun	**t:** Bunce **p:** M Cooper
F(2)	L20–23	Auckland	3 Jul	**t:** Fitzpatrick **p:** M Cooper 5

SA(1)	W22–14	Dunedin	9 Jul	**t:** Kirwan
				c: Howarth
				p: Howarth 5
SA(2)	W13–9	Wellington	23 Jul	**t:** Timu, Z Brooke
				p: Howarth
SA(3)	D18–18	Auckland	6 Aug	**p:** Howarth 6
A	L16–20	Sydney	17 Aug	**t:** Howarth
				c: Howarth
				p: Howarth 3

1995:

C	W73–7	Auckland	22 Apr	**t:** Osborne 2, Bunce 2, Ellis 2, Wilson, Mehrtens, G Bachop, Brown
				c: Mehrtens 7
				p: Mehrtens 3
I*	W43–19	Johannesburg	27 May	**t:** Lomu 2, Kronfeld, Bunce, Osborne
				c: Mehrtens 3
				p: Mehrtens 4
W*	W34–9	Johannesburg	31 May	**t:** Kronfeld, Little, Ellis
				c: Mehrtens 2
				p: Mehrtens 4
				dg: Mehrtens
J*	W145–17	Bloemfontein	4 Jun	**t:** Ellis 6, Wilson 3, Rush 3, Osborne 2, R Brooke 2, Dowd, Loe, Ieremia, Culhane, Henderson
				c: Culhane 20
S*	W48–30	Pretoria	11 Jun	**t:** Little 2, Lomu, Bunce, Mehrtens, Fitzpatrick
				c: Mehrtens 6
				p: Mehrtens 2
E*	W45–29	Cape Town	18 Jun	**t:** Lomu 4, Kronfeld, G Bachop
				c: Mehrtens 3
				p: Mehrtens
				dg: Mehrtens
SA*	L12–15^	Johannesburg	24 Jun	**p:** Mehrtens 3
				dg: Mehrtens
A(1)	W28–16	Auckland	22 July	**t:** Lomu
				c: Mehrtens
				p: Mehrtens 5
				dg: Mehrtens 2
A(2)	W34–23	Sydney	29 July	**t:** Bunce 2, Wilson, Mehrtens, Lomu
				c: Mehrtens 3
				p: Mehrtens
It	W70–6	Bologna	28 Oct	**t:** Little 2, Lomu 2, Wilson, I Jones Rush, M Jones, Z Brooke, Fitzpatrick
				c: Culhane 7
				p: Culhane 2
F(1)	L15–22	Toulouse	11 Nov	**p:** Culhane 5
F(2)	W37–12	Paris	18 Nov	**t:** Osborne, Lomu, I Jones, Rush
				c: Culhane
				p: Culhane 5

1996:

WS	W51–10	Napier	7 Jun	**t:** Cullen 3, Wilson, Macleod, Brown, Marshall
				c: Mehrtens 5
				p: Mehrtens
				dg: Mehrtens
S(1)	W62–31	Dunedin	15 Jun	**t:** Cullen 4, Lomu, Mehrtens, Marshall, I Jones, Z Brooke
				c: Mehrtens 7
				p: Mehrtens
S(2)	W36–12	Auckland	22 Jun	**t:** Kronfeld 2, M Jones, Z Brooke
				c: Mehrtens 4
				p: Mehrtens

* World Cup matches
^ after extra time
† Five-point try from here onwards
⁺ Non-cap Tests
(TN) Tri-Nation matches

All Black fullback sensation Christian Cullen flies over for the first of his four tries in the first Test against Scotland in Dunedin. New Zealand triumphed 62–31.

119

SOUTH AFRICA

Dan Retief
The Sunday Times (South Africa)

ALTHOUGH the trappings of professionalism are patently evident wherever first-class rugby is played in South Africa, the faceless proletariat just smile cynically at overseas perceptions of the game being awash in money.

South Africa may have led the world in paying match incentives – a euphemism for players being paid to play rugby – but the practice existed only at the top of the pyramid, and then in a meaningful way only among the top four or five provinces. Financial realities dictated that only those who generated sponsorship and gate revenue were able to offer remuneration to players and, while the habit of payment clearly thrived in contravention of IRFB regulations, the big majority of South African players remained pretty much amateur.

The arrival of the official era of professional rugby in August 1995 did not represent the momentous transformation it did in Europe because it postdated the traumatic events shortly after the World Cup which pushed the three big nations of the Southern Hemisphere irretrievably onto a professional footing.

The announcement of the US$555 million SANZAR television rights deal with Rupert Murdoch's News Corporation on the day before the World Cup final meant these three countries had crossed the Rubicon. With that kind of money available and, given the intensity of the programme required to keep the paymaster's television broadcast machines running, officials had no choice but to pay the players.

Thus in the Southern Hemisphere, and especially South Africa, the final battle of the revolution was fought in the weeks after the World Cup as the players found themselves in the powerful bargaining position of being the prize in a battle for control between Murdoch and his SANZAR allies and the World Rugby Corporation, which appeared to have the backing of Kerry Packer.

Francois Pienaar's Springboks, possessing the added status of being world champions, came to hold the balance of control and the upshot was that they were offered enormous payments to remain within the ambit of traditional Rugby Union.

Such action had to be taken to win the battle, but months afterwards South African rugby continued to feel tremors of dissent. The stand-off between SANZAR/Murdoch and WRC/Packer had artificially raised the stakes, and South Africa's dictatorial president, Dr Louis Luyt, was forced to agree to salary scales substantially in excess of the figures he might previously have had in mind.

> *Unions put squads of their leading players ... under a range of contracts, depending on their worth in relation to the performance of the team. Thus an international with age on his side might find himself in the A bracket with the possibility of playing rugby full-time, whereas an ageing candidate required to do little more than provide backup would be offered considerably less and might have to continue plying away at whatever job he might be in*

As it turned out, the 38-month payment structure that Luyt and his lieutenants designed gave rise to almost immediate dissatisfaction, as a mood of resentment on the part of officials, and jealousy on the part of other senior players who had not shared in the bounty, settled on South African rugby.

The terms of the players' professional contracts were clearly designed to provide a longterm buffer against the threat of Super League as well as the WRC (which at that point had not yet collapsed), but did not take into account the realities of players suffering injuries, losing form or being eclipsed by better, younger men.

The South African Rugby Union (SARFU) also came up with a system whereby Murdoch's money would be channelled to provinces, who would then have the responsibility of paying the players affiliated to them. It created an unequal arrangement in a game characterised by its democracy, and left the Springboks feeling isolated, persecuted and unsure of their status.

Luyt, for one, made no effort to disguise his view that the Springboks had been paid too much, and his sentiments were echoed by officials finding themselves having to deal with the wage demands of the next echelon of provincial players.

Slowly, however, a fully fledged professional organisation began to emerge. Unions put squads of their leading players, including those under 21, under a range of contracts, depending on their worth in relation to the performance of the team. Thus an international with age on his side might find himself in the A bracket with the possibility of

121

playing rugby full-time, whereas an ageing candidate required to do little more than provide backup would be offered considerably less and might have to continue plying away at whatever job he might be in.

Younger players were provided with contracts and smaller inducements to prevent others from stripping a province of its assets. This seemed to work well, because after nearly a year of open professionalism no high-profile transfers had taken place. Most leading clubs tried to find ways of compensating their players, but the money available amounted to little more than a good night or weekend away.

Also, with SARFU in effect owning the image and signature of marketable commodities such as Pienaar, Joost van der Westhuizen, Andre Joubert and James Small, the advertising campaigns so prevalent in other sports were not in evidence – a possible reason being Luyt's summary dismissal of SARFU chief executive Edward Griffiths in February.

No reason was given as Griffiths became a victim of a feudal style of administration which showed that nothing much had changed in rugby. His departure brought to a halt not only plans to utilise the Springboks as highly visible agents of South Africa's new democracy but also plans to engage them in recovering some of the funds being expended on their own salaries.

The R50,000 (£9,000) fine handed to Kobus Wiese, in addition to a 30-day suspension, for punching Wales lock Derwyn Jones gave an indication of what the Springboks' salaries might be

One of the most tangible demonstrations of the new order was when Springbok lock Kobus Wiese punched Derwyn Jones in the Test against Wales at Ellis Park in September. Having been cited by Wales, Wiese was sentenced to a 30-day suspension and it was also ruled that R50,000 (approximately £9,000) would be withheld from his forthcoming salary, due to commence in April 1996. Not only did the incident confirm that rugby's goalposts had been moved, but the size of the fine gave an indication of what the Springboks' salaries might be.

The Springboks closed a momentous year by taking on Italy and England during November. They beat Italy 40–21, while their 24–14 victory at Twickenham provided gratifying confirmation of their world champion status. Victory pushed Kitch Christie's tally to 14 straight wins (a record) and set the Springboks up for 1996 – a year in which they will meet the All Blacks five times, and the Wallabies, France and Argentina twice apiece, not to mention one-offs against Fiji and Wales.

It was also the first year of the Super-12 – a competition involving five provincial teams from New Zealand, four from South Africa and three from Australia. Played under the new laws (providing for support in the lineouts with loose forwards staying bound in scrums) the inter-continental tournament was a marked success. It produced rugby with verve and pace, provided a celebration of tries, drew big audiences and finally ended in victory for Auckland over Natal at Eden Park.

South African players complained of jet lag, an onerous fixture list that demanded four games in two weeks away in the Antipodes, and a New Zealand draft system that brought two key Counties men, Jonah Lomu and Joeli Vidiri, into the Auckland side. But they nevertheless gave the Super-12 their full support – something which might not have been the case had a large number of them still been trying to hold down jobs.

Having agreed to coach both Transvaal and South Africa, Kitch Christie took ill while on tour in Australia and was forced to stand down. This brought the man he was meant to groom, former Junior Springbok Andre Markgraaf, to the helm shortly before the start of the SANZAR Tri-Nations series.

Within a year of winning the World Cup, South Africa's 26-man squad had undergone a 43-per-cent change because of injury, loss of form or favour ... but the reality of the professional age was that those discarded were still drawing their salaries and were contractually entitled to do so for another two-and-a-half years

The professional era worked in Markgraaf's favour, as he was able to name a 26-man squad in mid-June for a home Test against Fiji, as well as the first two away games against Australia and New Zealand, and immediately put them on a tour footing even though their first match would not be until July 2. The Springboks gathered for altitude training in Pretoria.

However, although Markgraaf's first effort at selection met with general approval, it was noteworthy that within a year of winning the World Cup, South Africa's 26-man squad had undergone a 43-per-cent change because of injury, loss of form or favour. Men such as

Gavin Johnson, Chester Williams, Brendan Venter, Robbie Brink, Adriaan Richter, Rudolf Straeuli, Hannes Strydom, Kobus Wiese, Garry Pagel, James Dalton and Chris Rossouw were either trying to regain fitness or had been discarded, but the reality of the professional age was that they were still drawing their salaries and were contractually entitled to do so for another two-and-a-half years.

This was not the ideal situation, and there was every indication that there was still some way to go – possibly through a court of law – before rugby in South Africa would reach a fully accepted state of being professional.

Joost van der Westhuizen in inspired form during South Africa's 24–14 victory over England at Twickenham.

SOUTH AFRICA'S INTERNATIONAL SEASON 1995/96

SOUTH AFRICA (P10 W10 D0 L0 F310 A135)

(H) v Western Samoa	(Johannesburg, 12.4.95)	won 60–8
(–) v Australia*	(Cape Town, 25.5.95)	won 27–18
(–) v Romania*	(Cape Town, 30.5.95)	won 21–8
(–) v Canada*	(Port Elizabeth, 3.6.95)	won 20–0
(–) v Western Samoa*	(q/f: Johannesburg, 10.6.95)	won 44–28
(–) v France*	(s/f: Durban, 17.6.95)	won 19–15
(–) v New Zealand* **	(f: Johannesburg, 24.6.95)	won 15–12
(H) v Wales	(Johannesburg, 2.9.95)	won 40–11
(A) v Italy	(Rome, 12.11.95)	won 40–21
(A) v England	(Twickenham, 18.11.95)	won 24–14

* World Cup; ** after extra time

Note: Springbok coach Kitch Christie retired on account of ill health in March 1996 with the immaculate record of 14 wins from 14 games, 452 points scored and 205 conceded. His successor is Andre Markgraaf.

FIRA WORLD YOUTH CUP (Italy: 22 March – 8 April)

(–) v Chile	(Pool Three, 29.3.96)	won 18–9
(–) v South Africa	(Pool Three, 3.4.96)	lost 15–18
(–) v Spain	(5th-8th place play-off)	won 34–12
(–) v France	(5th place play-off)	won 7–8

South Africa Under-17 to France (P7 W7 D0 L0 F397 A3)
South Africa sends out a warning to the rugby world by winning the prestigious Easter Tournament in Marseilles in outstanding style. The young Boks win each of their seven matches, in the process scoring 397 points and conceding just three. They beat Bucharest (Rom) 17–3 in the semi-finals and St-Jean-en-Ryans (Fra) 75–0 in the final.

PROVINCIAL INTERNATIONAL RUGBY
'Natal Sharks speared by Auckland in Super-12 final' – see pages 139–163

DOMESTIC RUGBY

BANKFIN CURRIE CUP

Final
Natal 25, Western Province 17 (Kings Park, Durban, 14.10.95)

	P	W	D	L	F	A	Pts
Natal	10	7	1	2	273	226	15
Western Province	10	7	0	3	256	199	14
Northern Transvaal	10	6	1	3	287	163	13
Transvaal	10	5	0	5	258	229	10
Eastern Province	10	2	1	7	162	302	5
Orange Free State	10	1	1	8	203	320	3

Currie Cup roll of honour (since 1980)

1980 Northern Transvaal	1988 Northern Transvaal
1981 Northern Transvaal	1989 Western Province
1982 Western Province	1990 Natal
1983 Western Province	1991 Northern Transvaal
1984 Western Province	1992 Natal
1985 Western Province	1993 Transvaal
1986 Western Province	1994 Transvaal
1987 Northern Transvaal	1995 Natal

Previous winners: 24 – Western Province (4 draws); 14 – Northern Transvaal (3 draws); 7 – Transvaal (1 draw); 3 – Griquas, Natal, Border; 1 – Orange Free State.

BANKFIN CUP A

	P	W	D	L	F	A	Pts
Griqualand West	10	9	0	1	457	117	18
Border	10	7	1	2	360	207	15
Western Transvaal	10	7	0	3	317	216	14
Northern Free State	10	2	2	6	177	281	6
Eastern Transvaal	10	2	0	8	215	442	4
Namibia XV	10	1	1	8	181	444	3

BANKFIN NITE SERIES
(for non-Super-12 provinces)

Final: Free State 46, Border 34 (Bloemfontein, 24.5.95)
Semi-finals: Free State 52, South Eastern Transvaal 7 (Bloemfontein, 21.5.95); Border 20, Griqualand West 8 (East London, 21.5.95).

Section A

	P	W	D	L	F	A	Tries	Bonus	Pts
Border	12	7	1	4	475	346	66	25	66
SE Transvaal	12	9	0	3	395	234	47	17	65
Eastern Province	12	8	0	4	392	174	49	18	62
Boland	12	6	1	5	480	359	58	21	58
W Transvaal	12	6	0	6	358	395	37	13	49
Namibia	12	1	0	11	138	592	12	4	20

Section B

	P	W	D	L	F	A	Tries	Bonus	Pts
Free State	12	11	0	1	634	218	85	2	84
Griqualand West	12	12	0	0	468	187	70	24	84
E Transvaal	12	3	2	7	333	403	43	17	43
N Free State	12	4	0	8	320	323	30	12	40
SW District	12	2	0	10	217	501	21	8	28
Zimbabwe	12	1	1	11	128	606	11	4	20

Player of the series: Os du Randt (Free State)
Top point scorer: Francois Horne (Boland) 202.

1980:

SAm(a1)	W24–9	Johannesburg	26 Apr	**t:** T du Plessis, Mordt, Germishuys **c:** Botha 3 **p:** Botha **dg:** Botha
SAm(a2)	W18–9	Durban	3 May	**t:** M du Plessis **c:** Botha **p:** Botha **dg:** Botha 3
BL(1)	W26–22	Cape Town	31 May	**t:** Louw, W du Plessis, Van Heerden, Germishuys, Serfontein **c:** Botha 3
BL(2)	W26–19	Bloemfontein	14 Jun	**t:** Louw, Stofberg, Germishuys, Pienaar **c:** Botha 2 **p:** Botha 2
BL(3)	W12–10	Port Elizabeth	28 Jun	**t:** Germishuys **c:** Botha **p:** Botha **dg:** Botha
BL(4)	L13–17	Pretoria	12 Jul	**t:** W du Plessis **p:** Pienaar 2, Botha
SAm(b1)	W22–13	Montevideo	18 Oct	**t:** Stofberg, Gerber, Berger **c:** Botha 2 **p:** Botha **dg:** Botha
SAm(b2)	W30–16	Santiago	26 Oct	**t:** Mordt 2, Germishuys 2, Gerber, M du Plessis **c:** Botha 3
F	W37–15	Pretoria	8 Nov	**t:** Pienaar, Germishuys, Serfontein, Stofberg, Kahts **c:** Botha 4 **p:** Botha 3

1981:

I(1)	W23–15	Cape Town	30 May	**t:** Gerber 2, Louw **c:** Botha **p:** Botha 3
I(2)	W12–10	Durban	6 Jun	**p:** Botha **dg:** Botha 3
NZ(1)	L9–14	Christchurch	15 Aug	**t:** Bekker **c:** Botha **dg:** Botha
NZ(2)	W24–12	Wellington	29 Aug	**t:** Germishuys **c:** Botha **p:** Botha 5 **dg:** Botha
NZ(3)	L22–25	Auckland	12 Sep	**t:** Mordt 3 **c:** Botha 2 **p:** Botha 2

US	W38–7	Glenville		**t:** Mordt 3, Geldenhuys, Germishuys 2, Beck, Berger **c:** Botha 3

1982:

SAm(1)	W50–18	Pretoria	27 Mar	**t:** Gerber 3, Mordt 2, Oosthuizen, C du Plessis, W du Plessis **c:** Botha 6 **p:** Heunis **dg:** Botha
SAm(2)	L12–21	Bloemfontein	3 Apr	**t:** Gerber **c:** Botha **p:** Botha 2

1984:

E(1)	W33–15	Port Elizabeth	2 Jun	**t:** Gerber, C du Plessis, Louw **c:** Heunis 3 **p:** Heunis 5
E(2)	W35–9	Johannesburg	9 Jun	**t:** Gerber 3, Stofberg, Sonnekus, Tobias **c:** Heunis 3, Tobias **p:** Heunis
SAm(1)	W32–15	Pretoria	20 Oct	**t:** Louw, Gerber, Serfontein, Heunis, Mallet **c:** Tobias 2, Gerber **p:** Tobias 2
SAm(2)	W22–13	Cape Town	27 Oct	**t:** C du Plessis, Ferreira, Mordt, Gerber **p:** Tobias 2

1986:

Cv(1)	W21–15	Cape Town	10 May	**t:** C du Plessis **c:** Botha **p:** Botha 3 **dg:** Botha 2
Cv(2)	L18–19	Durban	17 May	**t:** Reinach **c:** Botha **p:** Botha 4
Cv(3)	W33–18	Pretoria	24 May	**t:** Schmidt, Botha, Gerber, Reinach **c:** Botha 4 **p:** Botha 3
Cv(4)	W24–10	Johannesburg	31 May	**t:** Wright **c:** Botha **p:** Botha 5 **dg:** M du Plessis

1989:

Wd(1)	W20–19	Cape Town	26 Aug	**t:** Knoetze, Botha, Smal **c:** Botha **p:** Botha 2
Wd(2)	W22–16	Johannesburg	1 Sep	**t:** Heunis, M du Plessis **c:** Botha **p:** Botha 3 **dg:** Botha

1992:

NZ [†]	L24–27	Johannesburg	15 Aug	**t:** Gerber 2, P Muller **c:** Botha 3 **p:** Botha
A	L3–26	Cape Town	22 Aug	**p:** Botha
F(1)	W20–15	Lyon	17 Oct	**t:** Gerber, Small **c:** Botha 2 **p:** Botha **dg:** Botha
F(2)	L16–29	Paris	24 Oct	**t:** Gerber **c:** Botha **p:** Botha 2 **dg:** Botha
E	L16–33	Twickenham	14 Nov	**t:** Smit **c:** Botha **p:** Botha 2 **dg:** Botha

1993:

F(1)	D20–20	Durban	26 Jun	**t:** Schmidt **p:** van Rensburg 5
F(2)	L17–18	Johannesburg	3 Jul	**t:** Small **p:** van Rensburg 4
A(1)	W19–12	Sydney	31 Jul	**t:** Small 2, Muller **c:** van Rensburg 2
A(2)	L20–28	Brisbane	14 Aug	**t:** Olivier, Stransky **c:** Stransky 2 **p:** Stransky 2
A(3)	L12–19	Sydney	21 Aug	**t:** Small, Pienaar **c:** Stransky
Arg(a1)	W29–26	Buenos Aires	6 Nov	**t:** Small 2, van der Westhuizen, Joubert **c:** Stransky 3 **p:** Stransky
Arg(a2)	W52–23	Buenos Aires	13 Nov	**t:** Strauss 2, Small 2, Williams, van der Westhuizen, Johnson **c:** Johnson 4 **p:** Johnson 3

1994:

E(1)	L15–32	Pretoria	4 Jun	**p:** Joubert 5
E(2)	W27–9	Cape Town	11 Jun	**t:** H le Roux, Joubert **c:** Joubert **p:** Joubert 2, H le Roux 3
NZ(1)	L14–22	Dunedin	9 Jul	**t:** Straeuli **p:** Joubert 3
NZ(2)	L9–13	Wellington	23 Jul	**p:** T van Rensburg
NZ(3)	D18–18	Auckland	6 Aug	**t:** Johnson, Venter **c:** Johnson **p:** Johnson 2
Arg(b1)	W42–22	Port Elizabeth	8 Oct	**t:** Roux 2, Stransky, Strauss, Williams **c:** Stransky 4 **p:** Stransky 3

Arg(b2)	W46–26	Johannesburg	15 Oct	t: Badenhorst 2, Stransky, Andrews, Straeuli, Williams, van der Westhuizen c: Stransky 4 p: Stransky
S	W34–10	Edinburgh	19 Nov	t: van der Westhuizen 2, Williams, Mulder, Straeuli c: Joubert 3 p: Joubert
W	W20–12	Cardiff	26 Nov	t: Straeuli, Williams, Joubert c: H le Roux p: H le Roux

1995:

WS(a)	W60–8	Johannesburg	13 Apr	t: Johnson 3, Williams 2, Small, M Andrews, Rossouw, Stransky c: Johnson 5, Stransky p: Johnson
A*	W27–18	Cape Town	25 May	t: Hendriks, Stransky c: Stransky p: Stransky 4 dg: Stransky
R*	W21–8	Cape Town	30 May	t: Richter 2 c: Johnson p: Johnson 3
C*	W20–0	Port Elizabeth	3 Jun	t: Richter 2 c: Stransky 2 p: Stransky 2
WS(b)*	W42–14	Johannesburg	10 Jun	t: Williams 4, M Andrews, Rossouw c: Johnson 3 p: Johnson 2
F*	W19–15	Durban	17 Jun	t: Kruger c: Stransky p: Stransky 4
NZ*	W15–12^	Johannesburg	24 Jun	p: Stransky 3 dg: Stransky 2
W	W40–11	Johannesburg	2 Sep	t: Small, Mulder, Wiese, Pienaar, Teichmann c: Stransky 3 p: Stransky 3
It	W40–21	Rome	12 Nov	t: Mulder, H le Roux, Pienaar, penalty try c: Stransky 4 p: Stransky 4
E	W24–12	Twickenham	18 Nov	t: Williams 2, van der Westhuisen p: Stransky 3

* World Cup matches
^ after extra time
† Five-point try from here onwards
+ Non-cap Tests
(TN) Tri-Nation matches

Fritz van Heerden gets by with a little help from his friends at Twickenham, where South Africa spanked England 24–14.

SUMMER TOURS

'We must learn from the lessons on and off the field', says manager Terry Cobner after another fruitless Wales visit to Australia. 'The system that Wales is part of is not challenging the players' ability.' Only once, in 1969, have the Dragons beaten the Wallabies 'Down Under', and there is never the slightest chance of the class of 1996 bucking the trend. To be fair, the odds are stacked against them, what with some fairly significant law changes greeting the tourists on arrival – added to the fact that fullback Justin Thomas withdraws from the tour party on the eve of departure after damaging knee ligaments. However, emergency fullback Wayne Proctor proves to be one of the successes of the trip. Wales concede 13 tries in the two Tests but the most devastating result is probably the 69–30 mauling meted out by Australian Capital Territory, which leaves Cobner reflecting: 'Although we had some idea of what we were coming to from watching the Super-12 series, we weren't expecting it to be that tough.'

SQUAD: *Backs* – C Cormack (Pontypridd), I Evans (Llanelli), L Davies (Neath), N Davies (Llanelli), G Thomas (Bridgend), N Jenkins (Pontypridd), R Howley (Bridgend), W Proctor (Llanelli), S Hill (Cardiff), J Funnell (Neath), A Thomas (Swansea), A Moore (Cardiff), D James (Bridgend). *Forwards* – C Loader (Swansea), J Humphreys (Cardiff, capt), J Davies (Neath), G Llewellyn (Neath), D Jones (Cardiff), E Lewis (Cardiff), G Jones (Llanelli), H Taylor (Cardiff), A Lewis (Cardiff), G Jenkins (Swansea), L Mustoe (Cardiff), M Voyle (Newport), P Arnold (Swansea), A Gibbs (Newbridge), B Williams (Neath); S Williams (Neath), K Jones (Ebbw Vale), S Ford (Bridgend).

Results: (1) Western Australia 20, Wales 62 (Perth, 29 May); (2) ACT 69, Wales 30 (Canberra, 2 June); (3) New South Wales 27, Wales 20 (Sydney, 5 June); (4) First Test: **Australia 56, Wales 25** (Brisbane, 8 June); (5) Australia B 51, Wales 41 (Brisbane, 12 June); (6) NSW Country 3, Wales 49 (Moree, 15 June); (7) Victoria 9, Wales 42 (Melbourne, 18 June); (8) Second Test: **Australia 42, Wales 3** (Sydney, 22 June).

Western Australia 20, Wales 62
Perth, 29 May 1996

Western Australia: J Shirkey; D Dunbar, M Skiffington, C Schaumkel, B Hart (S Apaapa 40; C McMullen, A McDonald; D Glenghorn, J O'Callaghan, M Meredith, K Angus (G Thomas 75), T Thomas, M Porter, G Howard, M Brain.
   Scorers – *Tries:* T Thomas, Schaumkel. *Conversions:* Schaumkel 2. *Penalty goals:* Schaumkel 2.

Wales: Cormack; Hill (N Davies 54), G Thomas, Funnell, James; N Jenkins, Moore; A Lewis, G Jenkins, Mustoe, Arnold, D Jones, E Lewis (Voyle 64), K Jones, Taylor.
   Scorers – *Tries:* G Thomas 5, Hill 2, Moore, James, K Jones. *Conversions:* N Jenkins 6.
Referee: P Marshall (Sydney).

ACT Brumbies 69, Wales 30
Canberra, 2 June 1996

ACT: S Larkham; M Hardy, A Magro, P Howard, J Roff; D Knox, G Gregan (P Brown 74); P Noriega, M Caputo (T Tavalea 75), E McKenzie (G Didier 70), J Langford, D Giffin, I Fenukitau, B Robinson (capt), O Finegan.

    Scorers – *Tries:* Roff 4, Howard, Larkham, Gregan, Finegan, Hardy, Robinson. *Conversions:* Knox 8. *Penalty goal:* Knox.

Wales: Cormack; Hill, L Davies (James 67), Funnell, G Thomas; N Jenkins, Howley; Loader, Humphreys (capt), J Davies, Llewellyn, D Jones, Gibbs, Williams, Taylor.

    Scorers – *Tries:* Howley 2, Williams, Hill. *Conversions:* N Jenkins 2. *Penalty goals:* N Jenkins 2.

Referee: W Erickson (Australia).

New South Wales 27, Wales 20
Sydney, 5 June 1996

NSW: T Kelaher (A Apps 13); G Bond, J Madz, R Tombs, M Miller; P Wallace, A Ekert; A Heath, M Bell, A Blades, W Waugh, J Welborn, W Ofahengaue, D Williams (S Domoni 74), T Gavin (capt).

    Scorers – *Tries:* Bond, Ekert. Conversion: Wallace. *Penalty goals:* Wallace 5.

Wales: Cormack; Evans, G Thomas, N Davies, James; A Thomas, Moore; A Lewis (Loader 76), B Williams, Mustoe, Voyle, Llewellyn (capt), E Lewis (Gibbs 70), G Jones (K Jones 62), S Williams.

    Scorers – *Tries:* N Davies, Evans. *Conversions:* A Thomas 2. *Penalty goals:* A Thomas 2.

Referee: B Leask (Australia).

Australia 56, Wales 25
First Test: Brisbane, 8 June 1996

Wales end 266 minutes without a try in Tests against Australia when Wayne Proctor claims the first of three for the tourists at Ballymore. Sadly the Welsh are 42–6 down at the time to a Wallaby side which take the lead through a Joe Roff try after just 54 seconds. Matt Burke, one of the game's most consistent goalkickers, lands nine goals from 11 attempts, including six conversions from a possible seven. Australia, captained for the first time by wonder-lock John Eales and 25/1-on favourites, benefit from poor first-time tackling by Wales.

Australia: M Burke; D Campese (both NSW), J Roff (ACT), T Horan (Queensland), A Murdoch (NSW); P Howard (Queensland), G Gregan (ACT); R Harry (NSW, debut), M Caputo (ACT, debut), E McKenzie (NSW), J Eales (capt), G Morgan (both Queensland), O Finegan (ACT, debut), D Wilson (Queensland), D Manu (NSW). **Replacement:** M Brial (NSW) for Manu, 60 mins.

    Scorers – *Tries:* Roff, Caputo, Wilson, Manu, Howard, Murdoch, Morgan. *Conversions:* Burke 6. *Penalty goals:* Burke 3.

Wales: Proctor; I Evans, L Davies, N Davies, G Thomas; N Jenkins, Howley; Loader, Humphreys (capt), J Davies (Mustoe 69), Llewellyn, D Jones (Voyle 43-46), Taylor, G Jones (Voyle 9-20), S Williams.

    Scorers – *Tries:* Proctor, Taylor, Llewellyn. *Conversions:* N Jenkins 2. *Penalty goals:* N Jenkins 2.

Referee: G Wahlstrom (New Zealand).

Series score: Played 17, Australia 9, Wales 8, Drawn 0.

Australia B 51, Wales 41
Brisbane, 12 June 1996

Australia B: S Larkham; M Hardy, D Herbert, R Tombs, R Constable; S Bowen, S Payne; D Crowley (A Blades 64), M Foley, A Heath, D Giffin, J Welborn, B Robinson, M Brial, T Gavin (capt).

Scorers – *Tries:* Herbert 3, Larkham 2, Payne, Brial, Hardy, Gavin. *Conversions:* Bowen 2, Payne.

Wales: Proctor; Hill, G Thomas, N Davies (capt), James; A Thomas, Moore; A Lewis (J Davies 68), B Williams, Mustoe, Arnold, D Jones, Gibbs, K Jones, E Lewis (H Taylor 53).

Scorers – *Tries:* Proctor, James, G Thomas, Moore, Gibbs, A Thomas. *Conversions:* A Thomas 4. *Penalty goal:* A Thomas.

Referee: S Dickinson (Australia).

NSW Country 3, Wales 49
Melbourne, 16 June 1996

NSW Country: N Lavelle; S Rutledge, D West, A Harding, M Dowling; C Doyle, S Merrick; D Phelps, G Koertz, W Petty, M Harber, G McQueen, B Klasson, P Fox, A McCalman.

Scorer – *Penalty goal:* Lavelle.

Wales: Cormack; I Evans, G Thomas (James 55), N Davies, S Hill; N Jenkins, Moore; Loader, B Williams, J Davies, Voyle (Ford 61), Llewellyn (capt), Gibbs, Taylor (K Jones 71), S Williams (A Lewis 75).

Scorers – *Tries:* Cormack 2, I Evans, S Williams, J Davies, Hill, N Davies. *Conversions:* N Jenkins 4. *Penalty goals:* N Jenkins 2.

Referee: B Fienberg (Australia).

Victoria 9, Wales 42
Melbourne, 18 June 1996

Victoria: S Chrilia (R Bird 42); P Loane, M Nasalio, L Strauss, M Bell; A Hendry, L Daley; A Charles, D Thompson, S Iakovidis, A Scott, B Parsons, C Frater (capt), J Walshe (P McLean 62), P Holstead.

Scorer – *Penalty goals:* Hendry 3.

Wales: Cormack; Proctor, James, Funnell, Hill; A Thomas, Moore; A Lewis, B Williams, J Davies, Ford, Arnold (D Jones 32), Voyle, Gibbs, K Jones.

Scorers – *Tries:* Cormack 3, Gibbs, Moore, Proctor, Voyle. **Conversions:** A Thomas 2. *Penalty goal:* A Thomas.

Referee: M Keogh (Canberra).

Australia 42, Wales 3
Second Test: Sydney, 22 June 1996

Three Wallaby tries in ten second-half minutes seal Wales' fate but cannot disguise a brave and passionate challenge by the tourists under the Sydney lights. Trailing only 13–3 at the midpoint, and that only after Owen Finegan's try on the stroke of half-time, Wales run out of steam in the final half-hour and concede five further touchdowns to lose the series 2–0. But beaten captain Jonathan Humphreys declares: 'We are getting used to the intensity of the rugby out here.' The challenge for Wales now is to maintain the level of performance they show in the first 50 minutes for the duration of a game. If that can be achieved, a rosy future awaits.

Australia: M Burke; D Campese (both NSW), J Roff (ACT), T Horan, B Tune (debut); P Howard (all Queensland), S Payne (debut); R Harry (both NSW), M Caputo (ACT), E McKenzie (NSW), J Eales (capt), G Morgan (both Queensland), O Finegan (ACT), M Brial (NSW), D Wilson (Queensland). **Replacements:** D Crowley (NSW) for McKenzie, 9 mins; M Foley (Queensland) for Caputo, 45 mins; S Larkham (ACT, debut) for Burke, 60 mins; D Manu (NSW) for Foley, 70 mins.

Scorers – *Tries:* Finegan, Burke, Roff, Foley, Morgan, Horan. *Conversions:* Burke 2, Eales. *Penalty goals:* Burke 2.

Wales: Proctor; I Evans, N Davies (D James, debut, 77), G Thomas, Hill; N Jenkins, Howley; Loader (A Lewis 22-34), Humphreys (capt), Mustoe, Llewellyn, D Jones, Gibbs, Taylor, S Williams.

Scorer – *Penalty goal:* N Jenkins.

Referee: C Hawke (New Zealand).

Series score: Played 18, Australia 10, Wales 8, Drawn 0.

SCOTLAND TO NEW ZEALAND
MAY–JUNE 1996: P8 W4 D0 L4 F266 A238

After a season championing the cause of district representation in Europe, Scottish supremo Jim Telfer returns home from New Zealand feeling utterly vindicated. His senior players acknowledge that the playing structure back home has to be overhauled if Scotland, not to mention their Home Union counterparts, are to compete at the top of the international game. Scotland boast fitness, commitment, a positive attitude and no little talent, yet are swept aside by New Zealand in the first Test and fairly comfortably kept at arm's length in the second. 'We have got to learn the lessons of what is happening in the Southern Hemisphere, and take it home and make the game change', insists Scott Hastings, whose 62nd appearance in the second Test at Eden Park makes him Scotland's most-capped player. Notable incidents on a fascinating tour include two nasty flare-ups: the first an unsavoury training skirmish involving four of the Scots forwards; the second a natural eruption – from Mount Ruapehu – which forces the squad to flee a preparatory session in Rotorua.

SQUAD: *Backs* – S Lang (Heriot's), R Shepherd (Melrose), C Joiner (Melrose), K Logan (Stirling Co), A Stanger (Hawick), D Stark (Boroughmuir), R Erikkson (London Scottish), S Hastings (Watsonians), I Jardine (Stirling Co), G Shiel (Melrose), C Chalmers (Melrose), G Townsend (Northampton), G Armstrong (Newcastle), A Nicol (Bath), C Glasgow (Heriot's FP). *Forwards* – D Hilton (Bath), T Smith (Watsonians), B Stewart (Edinburgh Acads), P Wright (Melrose), G Ellis (Currie), K McKenzie (Stirling Co), S Campbell (Dundee HSFP), D Cronin (Bourges), G Weir (Newcastle), S Murray (Edin Acads), N Broughton (Melrose), I Smith (Gloucester), R Wainwright (Watsonians, capt), P Walton (Newcastle), E Peters (Bath), B Renwick (Hawick).

Results: (1) Wanganui 13, Scotland 49 (Wanganui, 28 May); (2) Northland 15, Scotland 10 (Whangerei, 31 May); (3) Waikato 39, Scotland 35 (Hamilton, 5 June); (4) Southland 21, Scotland 31 (Invercargill, 8 June); (5) South Island Divisional XV 21, Scotland 63 (Blenheim, 12 June); (6) First Test: **New Zealand 62, Scotland 31** (Dunedin, 15 June); (7) Bay of Plenty 31, Scotland 35 (Rotorua, 18 June); (8) Second Test: **New Zealand 36, Scotland 12** (Auckland, 22 June).

Justin Marshall, the New Zealand scrum-half, clears from the base of a scrum during his side's 36–12 second Test victory over Scotland in Auckland. Scottish prop David Hilton looks on.

Wanganui (8) 13, Scotland (25) 49
Wanganui, 28 May 1996

Wanganui: J Nahona; R Gedye, J Hamlin, G Lennox, A Nagic; E Hekenui, S Brown; A Bull, A Edwards, V Pomana, G Stantiall, M Ward, A Renata, K Quail, J Gutsell.
    Scorers – Tries: Gutshell, Renata. *Penalty goals:* Nahona.

Scotland: Lang; Joiner, Shiel, Jardine, Stark; Townsend, Nicol; Hilton, McKenzie, Stewart, Cronin, Murray, Walton, Broughton, Peters.
    Scorers – Tries: Stark 2, Cronin, Joiner, Nicol, Peters, Walton. *Conversions:* Lang 4. *Penalty goals:* Lang 2.

Referee: A Riley (Waikato).

Northland (6) 15, Scotland (3) 10
Whangerei, 31 May 1996

Northland: W Johnston; H Taylor, M Going, N Berryman, B Reid; D Holwell, S Moore; L Davies, D Te Puni, T Fukofuka, G Taylor, A Gibbs, N Maxwell, B Waaka, J Campbell (capt).
    Scorer – Penalty goals: Johnston 5.

Scotland: Shepherd; Stanger, Hastings, Logan, Eriksson; Chalmers, Armstrong; T Smith, Ellis, Wright, Campbell, Weir, Wainwright (capt), I Smith, Renwick.
    Scorers – Try: Logan. *Conversion:* Shepherd. *Penalty goal:* Shepherd.

Waikato 39, Scotland 35
Hamilton, 5 June 1996

Waikato: R Reihana; W Jennings (B Meinung 30), W Warlow, M Cooper, J Walters; I Foster, R Duggan; C Stevenson, G Smith, M Driver, T Hemi, S Gordon, D Monkley (B Foote 70), D Muir, D Coleman.

    Scorers – *Tries:* Walters, Warlow, Cooper, Muir, Monkley. *Conversions:* Cooper 4. *Penalty goals:* Cooper 2.

Scotland: Shepherd; Joiner, Hastings, Jardine, Stark; Townsend, Nicol; Hilton, McKenzie, Stewart, Cronin (Walton 40), Weir, Smith, Wainwright, Peters.

    Scorers – *Tries:* Stark, Logan, Shepherd. *Conversions:* Shepherd 3. *Penalty goals:* Shepherd 3.

Referee: C Hawke (NZ).

Southland 21, Scotland 31
Invercargill, 8 June 1996

Southland: E Crossan; P Dynes, J Hedke, M Seymour, H Byars; S Culhane, B McCormack; S Hayes, D Heaps, R Borland, R Newell, M Wilson, P Henderson, J Winders, S Harvey.

    Scorers – *Tries:* Byars, Wilson, penalty try. *Conversions:* Culhane 3.

Scotland: Shepherd; Joiner (Lang 40), Hastings, Eriksson, Logan; Chalmers, Armstrong; Hilton, McKenzie, Stewart, Weir, Campbell, Wainwright (capt), Broughton, Renwick.

    Scorers – *Tries:* Wainwright, Logan, McKenzie. *Conversions:* Shepherd 2. *Penalty goals:* Shepherd 4.

Referee: S Walsh (New Zealand).

South Island 21, Scotland 63
Blenheim, 11 June 1996

South Island: G Dempster; W Havilli, J Connelly, S Tarrant, G Burgess (S Todd 58); L MacDonald, K McDowell; D McRea, W Fletcher, G Cameron, M Kerr, A Gillman, J Mawhinney, J Taeiloa, R Penney (capt).

    Scorers – *Tries:* Connelly, McDowell. *Conversion:* Dempster. *Penalty goals:* Dempster 2. *Dropped goal:* MacDonald.

Scotland: Lang; Stanger, Shiel (Hastings 56, Shepherd 68), Eriksson, Logan; Chalmers (capt), Armstrong; T Smith, Ellis, Wright, Campbell, Murray, Walton, Broughton, Peters.

    Scorers – *Tries:* Logan 2, Stanger 2, Walton 2, Armstrong, Broughton, Chalmers, Shepherd. *Conversions:* Chalmers 5. *Penalty goal:* Chalmers.

Referee: P Honnis (Canterbury).

New Zealand 62, Scotland 31
First Test: Dunedin, 16 June 1996

Scotland become the first country to score more than 30 points against New Zealand, but their feat coincides with conceding more points in one Test than ever before. An extraordinary afternoon at Carisbrook Park is highlighted by the performance of All Black fullback Christian Cullen. A week after marking his debut with a hat-trick of tries against Western Samoa, the 20-year-old sensation grabs four of New Zealand's nine. Even before his seven-try opening salvo, Cullen was the talk of the country as a result of having scored a record 18 tries in six games at the Hong Kong Sevens, for which he was voted player of the tournament in a victorious New Zealand team.

New Zealand: C Cullen (Manawatu); J Wilson (Otago), F Bunce (North Harbour), S MacLeod (Waikato), J Lomu (Counties); A Mehrtens, J Marshall (both Canterbury); C Dowd, S Fitzpatrick (capt), O Brown (all Auckland), I Jones (North Harbour), R Brooke, M Jones (both Auckland), J Kronfeld (Otago), Z Brooke (Auckland). **Replacement:** E Rush (North Harbour) for Lomu, 48 mins.

Scorers – *Tries:* Cullen 4, Z Brooke, I Jones, Lomu, Marshall, Mehrtens. *Conversions:* Mehrtens 7. *Penalty goal:* Mehrtens.

Scotland: Shepherd; Joiner, Eriksson (debut), Jardine, Logan; Townsend, Armstrong; Hilton, McKenzie, Wright, Cronin, Weir, Wainwright (capt), Smith, Peters.

Scorers – *Tries:* Joiner, Peters, Townsend. *Conversions:* Shepherd 2. *Penalty goals:* Shepherd 3. *Dropped goal:* Shepherd.

Referee: W Erickson (Australia).

Series score: Played 19, New Zealand 17, Scotland 0, Drawn 2.

Bay of Plenty 31, Scotland 35
Rotorua, 18 June 1996

Bay of Plenty: D Kaui; G Tamani, J Spanhake, W Clarke, B Daniel; A Miller, J Tauiwi; S Simpkins, J Edwards, P Cook, G Remnant, M Camp, P Tupai, C McMillan, B Sinkinson.

Scorers – *Tries:* Tamani, Spanhake, McMillan, Edwards. *Conversion:* Miller. *Penalty goals:* Miller 3.

Scotland: Lang; Glasgow, Stanger, Eriksson, Stark; Chalmers, Nicol; T Smith, Ellis, Stewart, Campbell, Murray, Walton, Broughton, Renwick.

Scorers – *Tries:* Stark 3, Nicol 2. *Conversions:* Chalmers, Lang. *Penalty goals:* Lang 2.

Referee: P O'Brien (Southland).

New Zealand 36, Scotland 12
Second Test: Auckland, 22 June 1996

Simply hideous weather welcomes Scotland to Eden Park, but the tourists respond with a terrific performance. After letting New Zealand run away with the first Test in Dunedin, Rob Wainwright's charges keep them on a tighter rein this time round, trailing by only ten points at half-time. The All Blacks' greater front-row power and experience is the crucial factor in a game of 44 scrums. Their first four tries come direct from set scrummages.

New Zealand: C Cullen (Manawatu); J Wilson (Otago), F Bunce, W Little, E Rush (all North Harbour); A Mehrtens, J Marshall (both Canterbury); C Dowd, S Fitzpatrick (capt), O Brown (all Auckland), I Jones (North Harbour), R Brooke, M Jones (both Auckland), J Kronfeld (Otago), Z Brooke (Auckland). **Replacements:** A Cashmore (Auckland, debut) for Wilson, 65 mins. Temporary: M Allen for Dowd, 35 mind; B Larsen for M Jones, 60 mins.

Scorers – *Tries:* penalty try, Z Brooke, Kronfeld 2, M Jones. *Conversions:* Mehrtens 4. *Penalty goal:* Mehrtens.

Scotland: Shepherd; Stanger, Hastings, Jardine (Stark 30), Logan; Townsend, Armstrong; Hilton, McKenzie, Stewart (debut), Cronin, Weir, Wainwright (capt), Smith, Peters.

Scorers – *Tries:* Shepherd, Peters. *Conversion:* Shepherd.

Referee: W Erickson (Australia).

Series score: Played 20, New Zealand 18, Scotland 0, Drawn 2.

SUPER-12 1996

Conclusive proof that Rugby Union can be the most exciting sport of all – a three-month festival of glorious open, free-flowing rugby across New Zealand, Australia and South Africa finally culminates in Super-12 glory for the Auckland Blues. But there are no losers in a competition richer in entertainment and colour than any before. The changes to the rulebook – flankers remaining bound to the scrum until the ball emerges, and 'assistance' now being permitted in lineouts – have made for a more exciting product, as the big Super-12 crowds bear testimony. If this is the future for Rugby Union north of the Equator, we have a treat in store. If it is not, then why not?

Auckland – inaugural Super-12 winners
after beating Natal 45–21 in the final.

INTERNATIONAL WATCH
THE TEST STARS PLAYING SUPER-12

Australian Capital Territory Brumbies (Australia unless stated): Marco Caputo, Troy Coker, Ipolito Fenukitau (Tonga), Owen Finegan, George Gregan, Pat Howard, David Knox, Ewen McKenzie, Patricio Noriega (Argentina), Joe Roff, Elisi Vunipola (Tonga).

Auckland Blues (New Zealand unless stated): Robin Brooke, Zinzan Brooke, Olo Brown, Eroni Clarke, Greg Cooper, Craig Dowd, Sean Fitzpatrick, Richard Fromont, Michael Jones, Jonah Lomu, Dylan Mika (Western Samoa), Lee Stensness, Joeli Vidiri (Fiji).

Canterbury Crusaders (New Zealand unless stated): Paula Bale (Fiji), Pat Lam (Western Samoa), Richard Loe, Justin Marshall.

Natal Sharks (South Africa unless stated): John Allan, Mark Andrews, Steve Atherton, Adrian Garvey (Zimbabwe), Henry Honiball, Andre Joubert, Federico Mendez (Argentina), James Small, Gary Teichmann.

New South Wales Waratahs (Australia unless stated): Scott Bowen, Michael Brial, Matt Burke, David Campese, Sam Domoni (Fiji), Tim Gavin, Richard Harry, Mark Hartill, Tim Kelaher, Daniel Manu, Alastair Murdoch, Viliame Ofahengaue, Sam Payne, Richard Tombs, Warwick Waugh.

Northern Transvaal (South Africa): Marius Hurter, Ruben Kruger, Jacques Olivier, Krynauw Otto, Adriaan Richter, Joost van der Westhuizen, Theo Van Rensburg.

Otago Highlanders (New Zealand unless stated): Stephen Bachop, Matt Cooper, Lio Falaniko (Western Samoa), Stu Forster, Paul Henderson, Josh Kronfeld, Rob Lawton (Australia), George Leaupepe (Western Samoa), Brian Lima (Western Samoa), Mike Mika (Western Samoa), To'o Vaega (Western Samoa), Jeff Wilson.

Queensland Reds (Australia): Paul Carozza, Dan Crowley, Tony Daly, John Eales, Michael Foley, Daniel Herbert, Tim Horan, Brett Johnstone, Jason Little, Rod McCall, Garrick Morgan, Damian Smith, David Wilson.

Transvaal (South Africa): James Dalton, Pieter Hendriks, Gavin Johnson, Hennie le Roux, Johan le Roux, Ian MacDonald, Japie Mulder, Francois Pienaar, Chris Rossouw, Johan Roux, Christiaan Scholtz, Philip Schutte, Rudolf Straeuli, Hannes Strydom, Kobus Wiese.

Waikato Chiefs (New Zealand unless stated): Liam Barry, Frank Bunce, Mark Cooksley, Steve Gordon, Ian Jones, Blair Larsen, Walter Little, Glen Osborne, Eric Rush, Richard Turner, Joe Veitayaki (Fiji).

Wellington Hurricanes (New Zealand unless stated): Mark Allen, Marty Berry, Bill Cavubati (Fiji), Norm Hewitt, Alama Ieremia, Simon Mannix, Jon Preston.

Western Province (South Africa): Tommie Laubscher, Garry Pagel, Joel Stransky, Fritz van Heerden, Toks van der Linde, Mornay Visser, Nico Wegner.

Wellington Hurricanes 28, Auckland Blues 36
Palmerston North, 1 March 1996

Auckland make a shaky start to the campaign, falling behind to a third-minute try by Hurricanes' All Black Alama Ieremia, and not taking the lead for the first time until the 77th minute.

Wellington: Cullen; Randle; Ieremia, Berry, Umaga; Cameron, Preston; Allen (capt), Hewitt, Coffin, Waller, Seymour, Davis, Hansen, Tiatia.
    Scorers – *Try:* Ieremia. *Conversion:* Cameron. *Penalty goals:* Cameron 7.

Auckland: Cooper; Sotutu, Clarke, Stensness, Lomu; Spencer, Tonu'u; Dowd, Fitzpatrick, Brown, Fromont, R Brooke (Blowers), Jones, Reichelmann, Z Brooke (capt).
    Scorers – *Tries:* Blowers, Clarke, Tonu'u, Spencer, Dowd. *Conversion:* Cooper. *Penalty goals:* Cooper 3.

NSW Waratahs 32, Transvaal 11
Sydney, 1 March 1996

Transvaal, beaten in the 1995 Super-10 finals, make a wretched start, conceding Alastair Murdoch a try after just 17 seconds, and allowing the Waratahs to gain a four-try bonus point.

NSW: Burke; Murdoch, Madz, Tombs, Campese; Bowen, Ekert; Hartill, Bell, Blades, Waugh, Welborn, Talbot, Manu, Gavin (capt).
    Scorers – *Tries:* Burke 2, Murdoch, Gavin. *Conversions:* Burke 3. *Penalty goals:* Burke 2.

Transvaal: Lawless; Louw, Scholtz, Mulder, Hendriks; Johnson, Roux; Barnard, Dalton, J Le Roux, Wiese, Strydom. Pienaar (capt), Rossouw, Straeuli.
    Scorer – *Try:* Johnson. *Penalty goals:* Johnson 2.

Natal Sharks 28, Western Province 22
Durban, 2 March 1996

Natal, South Africa's Currie Cup champions, make a winning start at Kings Park, with Springbok fullback Andre Joubert leading the way. He bags 18 points, but Western Province not only avoid humiliation, with two late tries, but gain a bonus point for losing by less than seven.

Natal Sharks: Joubert; Small, Thomson, Muir, Van der Westhuizen; Honiball, Putt; Kempson, Allan, Garvey, Andrews, Atherton (Slade), W Van Heerden (Kriese), Fyvie, Teichmann (capt).
    Scorers – *Tries:* Thomson, Joubert, Kriese. *Conversions:* Joubert 2. *Penalty goals:* Joubert 3.

Western Province: Rossouw; Berridge, Linee, Roux, Swart; Cilliers, Scholtz (Kirsten); Pagel, Paterson (Visser), Laubscher, Blom, Wegner (Maree), Krige, F Van Heerden (capt), Brink.
    Scorers – *Tries:* Swart, Rossouw, Blom. *Conversions:* Cilliers 2. *Penalty goal:* Cilliers.

Waikato Chiefs 27, Canterbury Crusaders 26
Hamilton, 3 March 1996

Waikato come from behind to steal a victory through fly-half Ian Foster's fifth penalty goal seconds from time. Consolation for Crusaders comes in the form of a dominant pack performance.

Waikato: Osborne; Woods, Bunce, Little, Rush; Foster, Crabb; Stevenson, McFarland, Veitayaki, Jones, Gordon, Larsen, Barry, Turner.
  Scorers – *Tries:* Osborne, Rush. *Conversion:* Foster. *Penalty goals:* Foster 5.

Canterbury: Forrest; Gibson, Matson (Tukaki), Mayerhofler, Fleming; Miller, Marshall; Loe, Sexton, Barrell, Weedon, Hammett, Coleman, Gardiner, Blackadder.
  Scorers – *Tries:* Tukaki, Fleming. *Conversions:* Miller 2. *Penalty goals:* Miller 3. *Dropped goal:* Miller.

Otago Highlanders 57, Queensland Reds 17
Dunedin, 3 March 1996

Super-10 champions Queensland slump to a catastrophic defeat at Carisbrook, falling behind 35-0 to an Otago side inspired by occasional All Black fly-half Stephen Bachop, who bags two tries. Matt Cooper kicks 22 points.

Otago: Cooper; Lima, Vaega, Leslie (capt), Wilson; Bachop, Forster; Lawton, Latta, Moore, Timmins, Falaniko, Vanisi, Randell, Henderson.
  Scorers – *Tries:* Bachop 2, Randell, Timmins, Falaniko, Vanisi, Lima. *Conversions:* Cooper 5. *Penalty goals:* Cooper 4.

Queensland: Horan; Smith, Herbert, Little, Tune; Flatley, Raulini; Daly, Foley, Crowley, McCall, Morgan, Connors, Wilson, Eales.
  Scorers – *Tries:* Morgan, Tune 2. *Conversion:* Eales.

ACT Brumbies 13, Transvaal 9
Canberra, 5 March 1996

First Queensland are humbled, and now Transvaal lose to a side rated by nobody before the tournament. ACT win a tight encounter courtesy of their Tongan centre Elisi Vunipola's try, but the match is remembered for the appalling behaviour of Johan le Roux. In only his second match back from a 19-month ban for biting Sean Fitzpatrick's ear, Le Roux is red-carded for butting hooker Marco Caputo and handed a seven-week suspension.

ACT: Kafer; Hardy, Larkham, Vunipola, Roff; Knox, Gregan; Noriega, Caputo, McKenzie, Langford, Giffin, Fenukitau, Robinson (capt), Finegan.
  Scorers – *Try:* Vunipola. *Conversion:* Knox. *Penalty goals:* Knox 2.

Transvaal: Lawless; Louw, Mulder, Hoffman, Hendriks; Johnson, Adlam; Barnard, Chris Rossouw, J Le Roux, Schutte, Van Wehting, Luther, Charles Rossouw, Pienaar (capt).
  Scorers – *Penalty goals:* Johnson 2, Lawless.

Otago Highlanders 29, Transvaal 15
Dunedin, 9 March 1996

Transvaal blow it once again, coughing up a 15–0 lead when All Black star Jeff Wilson, playing in his favoured fullback berth, scores two tries to spark an unanswered 29-point burst.

Otago: Wilson; Lima, Vaega, Leslie (capt), Brown; Bachop, Forster; Lawton, Latta, Moore, Timmins, Falaniko, Vanisi, Randell, Henderson.
    Scorers – *Tries:* Wilson 2, Brown, Lima. *Conversions:* Brown 2, Wilson. *Penalty goal:* Wilson.

Transvaal: Johnson; Van der Walt, Mulder, Hoffman, Hendriks; le Roux, Roux; Hattingh, Chris Rossouw, Barnard, Strydom, Schutte, Stewart, Charles Rossouw, Pienaar (capt).
    Scorers – *Tries:* Charles Rossouw, Mulder. *Conversion:* Johnson. *Penalty goal:* Johnson.

ACT Brumbies 35, Wellington Hurricanes 28
Canberra, 9 March 1996

ACT wing Mitch Hardy snatches last-minute victory for surprise-packet Brumbies after a horrendous incident for Hurricanes: an intended touch-finder from fly-half Jamie Cameron ricochets off a team mate into Hardy's grateful hands.

ACT: Kafer; Hardy, Larkham, Vunipola (Friend), Roff; Knox (Williams), Gregan; Noriega, Caputo, McKenzie (capt); Giffin, Sweeny, Langford, Fenukitau, Finegan.
    Scorers – *Tries:* Hardy 2, Fenukitau, Gregan. *Conversions:* Knox 2, Friend. *Penalty goals:* Knox 3.

Wellington: Cullen; Umaga, Ieremia, Berry, Talea; Cameron, Preston (Duggan); Allen (capt), Hewitt, Coffin, Waller, Russell, Davis, Seymour, Tiatia.
    Scorers – *Tries:* Cullen, Duggan, Davis. *Conversions:* Cameron 2. *Penalty goals:* Cameron 3.

Western Province 22, NSW Waratahs 30
Cape Town, 9 March 1996

Not content with his indecently early try against Transvaal, Alistair Murdoch hits Western Province for a 90-second touchdown at Newlands, and NSW don't look back thereafter. Wallaby fullback Matt Burke grabs 20 points.

Western Province: Rossouw; Berridge, Linee, Roux, Swart; Stransky, Scholtz; Pagel, Visser, Laubscher, Blom, Wegner, Krige, Van Heerden (capt), Brink.
    Scorers – *Try:* Swart. *Conversion:* Stransky. *Penalty goals:* Stransky 5.

NSW: Burke; Murdoch, Madz, Tombs, Campese; Bowen, Ekert; Hartill, O'Kane, Blades, Waugh, Welborn, Talbot, Manu, Gavin (capt).
    Scorers – *Tries:* Murdoch, Gavin, Burke. *Conversions:* Burke 3. *Penalty goals:* Burke 3.

Northern Transvaal 30, Natal Sharks 8
Pretoria, 9 March 1996

The Currie Cup holders get a right stuffing at Loftus, with their forwards outclassed and their goalkickers suffering equally at the hands of the Blue Bulls. Jannie Kruger kicks six out of six for the home side, while Natal miss four kicks.

Northern Transvaal: Du Toit; Meiring, Snyman, Van Schalkwyk, Olivier; Jannie Kruger, van der Westhuizen; Bosman, Truscott, Hurter (Proudfoot), Ackerman, Otto, Ruben Kruger (capt), Bekker, Richter.
    Scorers – *Tries:* Olivier, Richter, penalty try. *Conversions:* Kruger 3. *Penalty goals:* Kruger 3.

Natal: Joubert; Small, Thomson, Barnard, Van der Westhuizen; Honiball, du Preez; Kempson (Le Roux), Allan, Garvey, Slade, Andrews, Van Heerden, Fyvie, Teichmann (capt).
    Scorers – *Try:* Small. *Penalty goal:* Joubert.

Canterbury Crusaders 18, Auckland Blues 49
Christchurch, 10 March 1996

Jonah Lomu opens his try account in typically brutal fashion as Canterbury, Super-12 whipping boys-to-be, claim only three of the 11 tries at Lancaster Park.

Canterbury: Forrest; Tukaki, Gibson, Mayerhofler, Fleming; Dempster, Marshall (capt); S Loe, Sexton, Barrell, Weedon, Hammett, Coleman, Gardiner, Blackadder.
  Scorers – *Tries:* Tukaki, Sexton, Fleming. *Dropped goal:* Dempster.

Auckland: Sotutu (G Cooper), Vidiri, Clarke, Stensness, Lomu; Spencer, Tonu'u; Dowd, Fitzpatrick, Brown, Brain, Chandler, Reichelmann, Blowers, Z Brooke (capt).
  Scorers – *Tries:* Stensness, Lomu, Reichelmann, Blowers 2, Sotutu, Brain, penalty try. *Conversions:* Spencer 3. *Penalty goal:* Spencer.

Queensland Reds 26, Waikato Chiefs 22
Brisbane, 10 March 1996

A tight squeak for the Reds, who are outscored 3–2 on the try count, but profit from the goalkicking of versatile lock John Eales. The Wallaby superstar lands 16 points, including converting tries from Ben Tune and Damian Smith.

Queensland: Horan (capt); Smith, Herbert, Little, Tune; Flatley, Raulini; Daly, Foley, Crowley, Eales, Morgan, Kefu (McCall), Wilson, Connors.
  Scorers – *Tries:* Tune, Smith. *Conversions:* Eales 2. *Penalty goals:* Eales 4.

Waikato: Osborne; Berryman, Bunce, Little, Rush; Foster, Gillespie; Stevenson, McFarland, Veitayaki, Jones, Gordon (Anglesey), Larsen, Barry, Turner.
  Scorers – *Tries:* Veitayaki, Little, penalty try. **Conversions:** Foster 2. *Penalty goal:* Foster.

ACT Brumbies 40, Auckland Blues 34
Canberra, 15 March 1996

ACT spring the biggest shock of the competition, beating the mighty Blues with room to spare. Although the margin of victory is six points, the Brumbies lead 40–17 at one point en route to their third straight win.

ACT: Kafer (O'Connor); Hardy, Larkham, Holbeck, Roff; Friend, Gregan; Noriega, Caputo, McKenzie (capt, Didier), Langford, Giffin (Fenukitau), Finegan, Robinson, Coker.
  Scorers – *Tries:* Fenukitau 2, Coker, Finegan, Roff. *Conversions:* Friend 3. *Penalty goals:* Friend 3.

Auckland: Sotutu; Vidiri (Rackham), Clarke, Stensness, Lomu; Spencer, Scott; Nepia, Fitzpatrick, Brown, Chandler, Rose (Mika), Jones, Blowers, Z Brooke (capt).
  Scorers – *Tries:* Vidiri 2, Clarke, Rose, Lomu. *Penalty goals:* Spencer 3.

Wellington Hurricanes 32, Transvaal 16
Napier, 15 March 1996

Transvaal complete their disastrous trip to Australia and New Zealand by taking delivery of their fourth consecutive defeat, after which pneumonia-stricken coach Kitch Christie, bedridden throughout the stay, hands over the reins to Kiwi Alex Wyllie.

Wellington: Cullen; Umaga, Konia, Ieremia (Berry), Talea; Cameron, Duggan; Allen (capt), Hewitt, Coffin, Waller, Russell, Davis, Hansen (Williams), Tiatia.

Scorers – *Tries:* Umaga, Allen, Cullen, Ieremia. *Conversions:* Cameron 3. *Penalty goals:* Cameron 2.

Transvaal: Lawless, Van der Walt, Mulder, Esterhuysen, Hendriks; Van Rensburg (le Roux), Adlam; Campher, Dalton, Van Greuning, Strydom, Niemand, Stewart, Rossouw (Gous), Pienaar (capt).

Scorers – *Try:* Van der Walt. *Conversion:* Lawless. *Penalty goals:* Lawless 3.

Western Province 25, Otago Highlanders 52
Cape Town, 16 March 1996

To'o Vaega scores a first-quarter hat-trick to put unbeaten Otago in the box seat against a winless Western Province. The Chiefs claim eight tries in all – all but one coming from their have-a-go backs.

Western Province: Montgomery; Berridge, Roux, Botha, Swart; Stransky, Viljoen; Pagel, Visser, Laubscher, Blom, Wegner, Krige, Van Heerden (capt), Brink.

Scorers – *Tries:* Berridge, Swart 2. *Conversions:* Stransky 2. *Penalty goals:* Stransky 2.

Otago: Wilson; Lima, Vaega (Brown), Leslie (capt), Cooke; Bachop, Forster; Lawton, Oliver, Moore (Mika), Timmins, Rich (Cullen), Vanisi, Randell, Henderson (England).

Scorers – *Tries:* Vaega 3, Forster, Cooke 2, Timmins, Lima. *Conversions:* Wilson 6.

Northern Transvaal 32, NSW Waratahs 29
Pretoria, 16 March 1996

Two unbeaten sides collide in Pretoria, and there is Afrikaans celebration after the Blue Bulls edge home by virtue of F A Meiring's try, made by Joost van der Westhuizen, two minutes from time.

Northern Transvaal: Du Toit; Meiring, Snyman, Van Schalkwyk, Olivier; Sherrell (J Kruger), van der Westhuizen; Bosman, Truscott, Hurter, Ackerman, Otto, R Kruger (capt), Bekker, Richter.

Scorers – *Tries:* Otto, Meiring. *Conversions:* Sherrell, J Kruger. *Penalty goals:* Sherrell 6.

NSW: Burke; Murdoch (Campese), Madz, Tombs, Kelaher; Bowen, Payne; Harry, Bell, Hartill, Waugh, Welborn, Ofahengaue, Talbot, Gavin.

Scorers – *Tries:* Kelaher, Payne. *Conversions:* Burke 2. *Penalty goals:* Burke 5.

Queensland Reds 52, Canterbury 16
Brisbane, 17 March 1996

Garrick Morgan marks only his third game back from his ill-fated spell in Rugby League with a brace of tries as the formbook holds up at Ballymore. But prop Tony Daly steals the show with a deft chip for Michael Flanagan's try.

Queensland: Horan (capt); Smith, Herbert, Little, Tune; Flatley, Raulini (Johnstone); Daly, Foley, Crowley (Ryan), Eales, Morgan, Flanagan, Wilson, Connors.

Scorers – *Tries:* Morgan 2, Foley, Flanagan, Connors, Tune. *Conversions:* Eales 5. *Penalty goals:* Eales 4.

Canterbury: Rayasi (Bale); Tukaki, Gibson, Mayerhofler, Fleming; Miller (Dempster), Marshall (capt); S Loe, Hammett, R Loe, Kelly, Hammett, Maxwell (Muir), Gardiner, Blackadder.

Scorers – *Try:* Mayerhofler. *Conversion:* Mayerhofler. *Penalty goals:* Miller 3.

Natal Sharks 63, Waikato Chiefs 25
Durban, 17 March 1996

Natal bounce back in some style from their thumping by Northern Transvaal to scalp the visiting Chiefs, with bad boy wing James Small racking up a hat-trick of tries and Springbok team mate pocketing 30 points.

Natal: A Joubert; Small, Thomson, Muir, J Joubert; Honiball, Putt; Le Roux, Allan, Garvey, Slade, Andrews, Van Heerden, Fyvie, Teichmann (capt).

    Scorers – *Tries:* Small 3, Muir, A Joubert, Le Roux, J Joubert. *Conversions:* A Joubert 5. *Penalty goals:* A Joubert 5, Honiball.

Waikato: Osborne; Berryman, Bunce, Little, Rush; Foster, Gillespie; Stevenson, McFarland, Veitayaki, Jones, Larsen, Barry, Monkley, Turner.

    Scorers – *Tries:* Bunce, Turner, Larsen. *Conversions:* Foster 2. **Penalty goal:** Foster. *Dropped goal:* Foster.

Northern Transvaal 59, Otago Highlanders 29
Pretoria, 20 March 1996

Otago's 100-per-cent record goes for a Burton as Blue Bulls run riot at Loftus, inspired by free-scoring fly-half Jannie Kruger, who claims 39 points. Kruger's haul, from five conversions and eight penalty goals, matches a Northern Transvaal record held by Lance Sherrell.

Northern Transvaal: Du Toit (Blauw); Meiring, Snyman, Van Schalkwyk, Olivier; J Kruger, van der Westhuizen; Bosman, Truscott, Hurter, Ackerman, Otto, R Kruger (capt), Bekker, Richter.

    Scorers – *Tries:* Richter, van der Westhuizen, Kruger, Van Schalkwyk, Snyman. *Conversions:* J Kruger 5. *Penalty goals:* J Kruger 8.

Otago: Cooper; Lima, Vaega, Leslie (capt), Wilson (Cooke); Bachop, Forster; Lawton (Mika), Oliver, Moore, Cullen, Falaniko, England, Randell, Henderson (Latta)..

    Scorers – *Tries:* Randell, Cooper. *Conversion:* Cooper 2. *Penalty goals:* Cooper 2, Wilson 3.

Canterbury Crusaders 16, Western Province 16
Christchurch, 22 March 1996

The cellar-dwellers clash at Lancaster Park and finish as they had started – without a win. But Western Province emerge the happier after replacement lock Johan Kapp claims a last-ditch try, converted by Vlok Cilliers.

Canterbury: Forrest; Tukaki, Gibson, Mayerhofler, Bale; Dempster, Hansen; S Loe (Stokes), M Hammett, R Loe (capt), Coleman, C Hammett, Robertson, Gardiner, Blackadder.

    Scorers – *Tries:* Forrest, Dempster 2. *Conversion:* Dempster. *Penalty goals:* Forrest, Dempster 2.

Western Province: Montgomery; Berridge, Botha, Linee, Swart; Stransky (Cilliers), Viljoen; Pagel, Visser, Laubscher, Blom (Kapp), Wegner, Krige, Van Heerden, Brink.

    Scorers – *Try:* Kapp. *Conversion:* Cilliers. *Penalty goals:* Stransky 2. *Dropped goal:* Stransky.

Transvaal 26, Waikato Chiefs 23
Johannesburg, 23 March 1996

Transvaal break their duck at the fifth time of asking, though victory over the mediocre Chiefs is nothing to get too excited about. Two late penalty goals from Transvaal fullback Gavin Lawless provide relief for the Ellis Park faithful.

Transvaal: Lawless, Van der Walt, Mulder, Hoffman, Hendriks; Van Rensburg, Adlam; Barnard, Dalton, Van Greuning (Campher), Strydom, Schutte, Pienaar (capt), MacDonald, Rossouw.

Scorers – *Tries:* Pienaar, Adlam. *Conversions:* Lawless 2. *Penalty goals:* Lawless 4.

Waikato: Osborne; Woods, Bunce, Little, McLeod; Burton, Gillespie; Stevenson, McFarland, Veitayaki, Jones, Cooksley, Larsen, Monkley, Turner.

Scorers – *Tries:* Osborne 2. *Conversions:* Burton 2. *Penalty goals:* Burton 3.

Wellington Hurricanes 25, Queensland Reds 32
Wellington, 24 March 1996

Queensland score five first-half tries to ensure their third straight win, although they have to survive a late onslaught from the aptly named Hurricanes. The star of the show is Reds captain Tim Horan, flourishing in his new fullback berth.

Wellington: Doyle; Umaga, Konia, Ieremia (Mannix), Telea; Cameron, Duggan; Allen (capt, Carubati), Hewitt, Coffin, Waller, Russell, Davis, Simpson, Tiatia.

Scorers – *Tries:* Telea, Davis. *Penalty goals:* Cameron 3, Mannix 2.

Queensland: Horan (capt); Smith, Herbert, Little, Tune; Flatley, Raulini; Daly, Foley, Crowley, Eales, Morgan, Kefu, Wilson, Connors.

Scorers – *Tries:* Horan, Eales, Kefu, Herbert, Tune. *Conversions:* Eales 2. *Penalty goal:* Eales.

NSW Waratahs 44, ACT Brumbies 10
Sydney, 24 March 1996

New South Wales leapfrog ACT at the top of the pile after a comprehensive victory by six tries to two. Jason Madz, the 23-year-old Waratah centre, enhances his already impressive reputation with a try brace as ACT lose their first match on the road.

NSW: Burke; Murdoch, Madz, Tombs, Campese; Bowen, Payne; Harry, O'Kane, Hartill, Waugh, Welborn, Talbot, Manu, Gavin.

Scorers – *Tries:* Madz 2, Burke, Harry, Bowen, Campese. *Conversions:* Burke 4. *Penalty goals:* Burke 2.

ACT: Roff; Hardy, Larkham, Holbeck, Williams; Friend (Howard), Gregan; Noriega, Caputo, McKenzie (capt, Didier), Langford, Sweeny, Finegan, Robinson, Coker (Fenukitau).

Scorers – *Tries:* Roff, Williams.

Auckland Blues 48, Western Province 30
Auckland, 27 March 1996

Western Province belie their dreadful record – winless in four – to make a game of it at Eden Park. But the Auks are never endangered – not with an impressive 23-point display from up-and-coming Kiwi fly-half Carlos Spencer.

Auckland: Cooper; Sotutu (Blowers), Clarke, Stensness, Kerr; Spencer, Tonu'u; Dowd, Fitzpatrick, Brown, Chandler, Fromont, Mika, Jones, Z Brooke (capt).

Scorers – *Tries:* Spencer, Jones, Clarke, Fromont, Blowers, Tonu'u. *Conversions:* Spencer 3. *Penalty goals:* Spencer 3. *Dropped goal:* Spencer.

Western Province: Rossouw; Berridge, Botha, Linee, Swart; Stransky, Viljoen; Van der Linde, Laubscher, Maree, Wegner (Kapp), Krige, Van Heerden (capt), Brink.

Scorers – *Tries:* Linee, Krige, Berridge. *Conversions:* Stransky 3. *Penalty goals:* Stransky 3.

ACT Brumbies 44, Natal Sharks 31
Canberra, 29 March 1996

ACT return to their own patch and pick up the fairytale storyline of their season by recovering a 21–11 half-time deficit to score an emphatic win over crack Bok outfit Natal at the Manuka Oval. Wallaby wing Joe Roff stars with four tries.

ACT: Larkham; Hardy, Holbeck, Howard, Roff; Friend, Gregan; Noriega, Caputo, McKenzie (capt, Didier), Langford, Giffin (Sweeny), Fenikautau, Robinson, Finegan.

Scorers – *Tries:* Roff 4, Holbeck, Larkham. *Conversions:* Friend 4. *Penalty goals:* Friend 2.

Natal: A Joubert; Small, Thomson, Muir (J Joubert), van der Westhuizen; Honiball, Putt; Le Roux, Allan, Garvey, Slade, Andrews (Atherton), Van Heerden, Fyvie, Teichmann (capt).

Scorers – *Tries:* Honiball, Small, Thomson. *Conversions:* Honiball 2. *Penalty goals:* Honiball 4.

*James Small (Natal) brings down Jonah Lomu (Auckland)
in an exciting Super-12 final at Eden Park.*

Canterbury Crusaders 21, NSW Waratahs 16
Christchurch, 29 March 1996

Another serious upset, but a mighty controversial one. Winless Crusaders, who trail 16–7 at the midpoint, topple the league-leading Waratahs, but only after Jason Madz's last–minute try is disallowed after he is adjudged not to have grounded the ball. Ouch!

Canterbury: Forrest (Love); Gibson, Matson, Mayerhofler, Bale; Coffey, Marshall; Loe, M Hammett, Barrell, Maxwell, Weedon, Robertson, Blackadder, Muir.
   Scorers – *Tries:* Mayerhofler, Marshall. *Conversion:* Coffey. *Penalty goals:* Coffey 3.

NSW: Burke (Kelaher); Mostyn, Madz, Tombs, Campese; Bowen, Payne; Harry (Hartill), Bell, Blades, Waugh, Welborn, Manu, Talbot, Gavin.
   Scorers – *Try:* Payne. *Conversion:* Burke. *Penalty goals:* Burke 3.

Queensland Reds 25, Northern Transvaal 18
Brisbane, 29 March 1996

Northern Transvaal suffer their first loss of the season, kicked into submission by the amazing Wallaby second-row John Eales. Big Bad John slots five second-half penalty goals to recover an 18–10 half-time deficit.

Queensland: Horan (capt); Smith, Herbert, Little, Tune; Flatley, Johnston, Daly (Ryan), Foley, Crowley, Morgan, Eales, Kefu, Wilson, Connors.
   Scorers – *Try:* penalty try. *Conversion:* Eales. *Penalty goals:* Eales 6.

Northern Transvaal: Du Toit; Meiring, Snyman, Van Schalkwyk, Olivier; J Kruger, van der Westhuizen; Bosman, Truscott, Hurter, Ackerman, Otto, R Kruger (capt), Bekker, Richter.
   Scorers – *Tries:* Truscott, Van Schalkwyk. *Conversion:* J Kruger. *Penalty goals:* J Kruger 2.

Otago Highlanders 15, Wellington Hurricanes 44
Dunedin, 30 March 1996

Otago drop their second straight match after setting the competition alight with 21 tries in their first four matches. The Highlanders are left high and dry by Wellington's dominant forwards, who hold Otago try-less.

Otago: Wilson; Lima, Vaega (Cooper), Leslie (capt, Bachop), Cooke; Culhane, Forster; Lawton, Oliver, Moore (Mika), Timmins, Cullen, Henderson, Vanisi, Randell.
   Scorers – *Penalty goals:* Culhane 4. *Dropped goal:* Culhane.

Wellington: Doyle; Umaga, Konia, Ieremia, Telea (Berry); Cameron, Duggan; Allen (capt), Hewitt, Coffin, Afeaki, Russell, Davis, Tiatia (Simpson), Williams.
   Scorers – *Tries:* Williams, Doyle, Duggan, Berry, penalty try. *Conversions:* Cameron 5. *Penalty goals:* Cameron 3.

Waikato Chiefs 44, Western Province 17
Hamilton, 30 March 1996

Waikato, stung by Walter Little's one-match suspension for a positive drugs test, claim victory in his absence, though struggling Western Province are less than happy with the display of Kiwi referee Steve Walsh.

Waikato: Johnston; Berryman, Bunce, McLeod, Going; Burton, Gillespie; Stevenson, Mitchell, Veitayaki, Jones, Cooksley, Barry, Monkley, Turner.

Scorers – *Tries:* Going 2, Foster 2, Veitayaki. *Conversions:* Foster 4, Burton. *Penalty goals:* Burton 3.

Western Province: Rossouw; Berridge (Cilliers), Botha, Linee (Roux), Swart; Stransky, Viljoen; Pagel, Visser, Van der Linde (Andrews), Blom, Maree, Krige, Van Heerden (capt), Brink.

Scorers – *Tries:* Swart 2. *Conversions:* Stransky 2. *Penalty goal:* Stransky.

Auckland Blues 51, Otago Highlanders 29
Pukekohe, 2 April 1996

Auckland produce a devastating three-try burst shortly after half-time to inflict on Otago their third consecutive loss. Flanker Andrew Blowers claims two tries to take his competition haul to six.

Auckland: Cunningham; Kerr, Clarke, Stensness, Lomu; Spencer (Rackham), Tonu'u (Scott); Dowd (Nepia), Fitzpatrick (capt), Brown, R Brooke, Riechelmann, Mika, Blowers, Brain.

Scorers – *Tries:* Blowers 2, Cunningham 2, Mika, Kerr, Clarke. *Conversions:* Spencer 4, Cunningham. *Penalty goals:* Spencer 2.

Otago: Cooper; Wilson, Leaupepe, Brown, Cooke (Lima); Culhane, McCormack; Mika, Latta, Moore, England, Rich, Falaniko, Vanisi, Randell.

Scorers – *Tries:* McCormack, Cooper, Leaupepe, penalty try. *Conversions:* Culhane 3. *Dropped goal:* Culhane.

NSW Waratahs 6, Natal Sharks 34
Sydney, 2 April 1996

New South Wales Waratahs' topsy-turvy season takes its biggest jolt yet as the resurgent Sharks take them apart, with five unanswered second-half tries to silence the big Sydney crowd.

NSW: Burke; Mostyn, Madz, Tombs, Campese; Bowen (Wallace), Ekert; Hartill, O'Kane, Blades, Waugh, Welborn, Talbot, Ofahengaue, Gavin.

Scorer – *Penalty goals:* Burke 2.

Natal: A Joubert; Small, Thomson, Muir, J Joubert; Honiball, Putt (Du Preez); Le Roux, Allan, Garvey, Slade, Andrews, Kriese, Fyvie (Van Heerden), Teichmann (capt).

Scorers – *Tries:* Thomson 2, J Joubert, Fyvie, Small. *Conversions:* Honiball 3. *Penalty goal:* Honiball.

Waikato Chiefs 26, ACT Brumbies 18
Whangarei, 3 April 1996

Waikato move alongside ACT on the three-win mark when victory would have put the Brumbies top of the table. Chiefs rally from a 10–5 deficit at the midpoint, with centre McLeod registering the crucial try.

Waikato: Johnston; Berryman, Bunce, McLeod, Rush; Burton, Gillespie; Stevenson, Mitchell, Veitayaki, Jones (capt), Cooksley, Larsen, Monkley, Turner.

Scorers – *Tries:* Monkley, McLeod. *Conversions:* Burton 2. *Penalty goals:* Burton 4.

ACT: Larkham; Hardy, Holbeck (O'Connor), Howard, Roff; Friend, Gregan; Noriega, Caputo, McKenzie (capt), Langford, Giffin, Finegan (Tavalea), Robinson (Fenukitau), Coker.

Scorers – *Tries:* Noriega, Langford. *Conversion:* Friend. *Penalty goals:* Friend 2.

Canterbury Crusaders 18, Northern Transvaal 34
Christchurch, 3 April 1996

Order is restored after an unlikely win for Canterbury and a defeat for Northern in the previous round. The Blue Bulls, inspired by their back-row trio, snatch two tries early doors, but need late tries from David Du Toit and Adriaan Richter to cement the win.

Canterbury: Kaui; Gibson, Matson, Mayerhofler, Bale; Coffey (Miller), Marshall; R Loe (capt, S Loe), Sexton (Kirke), Barrell, Maxwell, Weedon, Robertson, Blackadder (Coleman), Muir.
   Scorers – *Tries:* Kaui 2. *Conversion:* Coffey. *Penalty goals:* Coffey 2.

Northern Transvaal: Du Toit; Olivier, Van Schalkwyk, Snyman, Meiring; Sherrell, van der Westhuizen; Proudfoot, Truscott, Bosman, Ackerman, Otto, R Kruger (capt), Bekker, Richter.
   Scorers – *Tries:* Richter 2, Olivier, Truscott, Du Toit. *Conversions:* Sherrell 3. *Penalty goal:* Sherrell.

Queensland Reds 36, Western Province 26
Brisbane, 3 April 1996

Defending champions Queensland go top with a predictable defeat of Western Province, although the basement side, now winless in seven, give an improved account of themselves. Tim Horan is taken to hospital with an elbow injury.

Queensland: Horan (capt, Mandrusiak); Smith, Herbert, Little, Tune; Flatley, Johnstone; Ryan, Foley, Crowley, Morgan, Eales, Kefu, Wilson, Connors.
   Scorers – *Tries:* Little, Herbert, Johnstone, Horan. *Conversions:* Eales 2. *Penalty goals:* Eales 4.

Western Province: Rossouw; Cilliers, Botha, Roux, Swart; Stransky, Viljoen; Pagel, Visser, Laubscher, Blom, Wegner, Skinstad, Van Heerden (capt), Brink.
   Scorers – *Tries:* Viljoen, Pagel, Kapp. *Conversion:* Stransky. *Penalty goals:* Stransky 3.

Wellington Hurricanes 27, Natal Sharks 43
Wellington, 6 April 1996

Natal win third on the bounce, with Bok stars Andre Joubert and James Small bagging a try hat-trick apiece. Hong Kong Sevens standout Christian Cullen claims try double for an otherwise error-riddled home side in first match back.

Wellington: Cullen; Umaga, Ieremia, Berry, Telea; Cameron, Duggan (Filemu); Allen (capt), Hewitt, Coffin, Waller, Russell, Davis (Cavubati), Simpson (Afeaki), Tiatia.
   Scorers – *Tries:* Cullen 2, Umaga, Berry. *Conversions:* Cameron 2. *Penalty goal:* Cameron.

Natal: A Joubert; Small, Thomson, Muir, J Joubert; Honiball, Putt; Le Roux, Allan, Garvey, Slade, Andrews, Kriese, Fyvie, Teichmann (capt).
   Scorers – *Tries:* A Joubert 3, Small 3. *Conversions:* Honiball 2. *Penalty goals:* Honiball 3.

Auckland Blues 30, Northern Transvaal 26
Auckland, 7 April 1996

A big game calls for big character, and there is no bigger character than jugger-naut Jonah Lomu, who blasts over for two scores, including a 20-metre run through six tackles, to put the Auks 30–16 ahead before the Blue Bulls hit back with two late tries. Crucially, though, Lance Sherrell misses both conversions.

Auckland: Cunningham; Kerr, Clarke, Stensness, Lomu; Spencer, Tonu'u; Nepia, Fitzpatrick (capt), Brown, R Brooke, Riechelmann, Mika, Blowers, Brain.
    Scorers – *Tries:* Lomu 2, Blowers, Stensness. *Conversions:* Spencer 2. *Penalty goals:* Spencer 2.

Northern Transvaal: Du Toit; Olivier, Van Schalkwyk, Snyman, Meiring; Sherrell, van der Westhuizen; Proudfoot, Truscott, Bosman, Ackerman, Otto, R Kruger (capt), Bekker, Richter.
    Scorers – *Tries:* Sherrell, Du Toit, Bosman. *Conversion:* Sherrell. *Penalty goals:* Sherrell 3.

Canterbury Crusaders 7, ACT Brumbies 29
Canterbury, 8 April 1996

No doubt about this one – not with ACT pulling 11–0 clear by half-time through Mitch Hardy's try and two Adam Friend penalties. Richard Loe gives Canterbury some hope with a try after the restart, but not enough to worry ACT, who snap a two-game losing streak.

Canterbury: Kaui; Gibson, Alatini, Mayerhofler, Fleming; Coffey, Marshall; R Loe (capt), Sexton, Barrell, Maxwell, Weedon, Robertson, Coleman, Muir.
    Scorers – *Try:* Loe. *Conversion:* Coffey.

ACT: Larkham; Hardy, Magro, Howard, Roff; Friend, Gregan; Noriega, Caputo, McKenzie (capt), Sweeny, Giffin, Langford, Fenukitau, Coker.
    Scorers – *Tries:* Hardy, Fenukitau, Sweeny. *Conversion:* Friend. *Penalty goals:* Friend 4.

Otago Highlanders 33, Natal Sharks 32
Dunedin, 10 April 1996

Otago, winless in three, rally from 13–32 to beat high-flying Natal in an absolute thriller. Jeff Wilson puts first points on the board by outsprinting Andre Joubert to the line. Joubert replies with two tries to put Natal firmly in the driving seat before Matt Cooper's try and late penalty give Highlanders the final say.

Otago: Wilson (Cooper); Lima, Brown, Leslie (capt), Leaupepe; Bachop, Forster; Lawton, Oliver, Driver, Cullen, Rich, Falaniko, Henderson, Randell.
    Scorers – *Tries:* Wilson, Lima, Cooper, Leslie. *Conversions:* Cooper 2. *Penalty goals:* Wilson, Cooper 2.

Natal: A Joubert; Small, Thomson, Muir, J Joubert; Honiball, Putt; Le Roux, Allan, Garvey, Andrews, Atherton, Van Heerden, Fyvie, Teichmann (capt).
    Scorers – *Tries:* A Joubert 2, Thomson, Van Heerden, Small. *Conversions:* Honiball 2. *Dropped goal:* Small.

Waikato Chiefs 17, Northern Transvaal 9
Hamilton, 11 April 1996

The Blue Bulls lose again as Waikato's defence holds firm against a mighty onslaught. Tries by Norm Berryman and Glen Osborne assure Chiefs of their third straight win, much to the delight of a 19,000 crowd.

Waikato: Osborne; Berryman, Bunce, McLeod, Rush; Burton, Gillespie; Stevenson, Mitchell, Veitayaki, Jones (capt), Cooksley, Larsen, Monkley, Barry.
    Scorers – *Tries:* Berryman, Osborne. *Conversions:* Burton 2. *Penalty goal:* Burton.

Northern Transvaal: Du Toit; Olivier, Van Schalkwyk, Snyman, Meiring; Sherrell, van der Westhuizen; Proudfoot, Truscott, Bosman, Ackerman, Otto, R Kruger (capt), Bekker, Richter.
    Scorers – *Penalty goals:* J Kruger, Du Toit. *Dropped goal:* J Kruger.

Transvaal 23, Western Province 26
Johannesburg, 13 April 1996

Joel Stransky returns to Ellis Park and, much to Western Province's delight, is stirred into a repeat of his World Cup final-winning performance. Seven penalty goals from him lift the Cape side off the foot of the table as the Lions are handed their fifth defeat in six starts.

Transvaal: Lawless, Gillingham, Mulder, H Le Roux, Hendriks; L van Rensburg (Johnson), Adlam; Barnard, Dalton, Van Greuning (Campher), Strydom, Schutte, Pienaar (capt), MacDonald, Rossouw.
    Scorers – *Tries:* Lawless, Dalton. *Conversions:* Lawless 2. *Penalty goals:* Lawless 3.

Western Province: Rossouw; Cilliers, Van Zyl (Botha), Linee, Swart; Stransky, Viljoen; Pagel, Visser, Van der Linde, Blom, Wegner, Brink, Van Heerden (capt), O'Cuinneagain.
    Scorers – *Try:* Swart. *Penalty goals:* Stransky 7.

Wellington Hurricanes 13, Canterbury Crusaders 36
New Plymouth, 14 April 1996

Crusaders fly-half Andy Miller, standing in for injured All Black Andrew Mehrtens, inspires Canterbury's second win of the competition, with 16 points and a generally sound tactical display.

Wellington: Cullen; Umaga, Konia, Berry, Telea; Cameron, Duggan; Allen (capt), Hewitt, Coffin (Cavubati), Waller, Russell, Afeaki (TR Coventry), Simpson, Tiatia.
    Scorers – *Tries:* Cullen, Cameron. *Penalty goals:* Cameron 2.

Canterbury: Kaui; Gibson, Alatini, Mayerhofler (TR Fleming), Tukaki; Miller, Marshall; S Loe, Sexton, Barrell, Maxwell, Weedon, Robertson, Gardiner, Blackadder (capt).
    Scorers – *Tries:* Blackadder, Alatini, Gibson, Kaui. *Conversions:* Coffey 2. *Penalty goals:* Miller 4.

Queensland Reds 15, NSW Waratahs 13
Brisbane, 14 April 1996

The big Aussie clash is decided by the goalkicking of big Aussie John Eales. Queensland's Wallaby lock kicks all 15 of the Reds' points to save Damian Smith's blushes. Queensland play virtially the whole game with 14 men after Smith's seventh-minute dismissal.

Queensland: Mandrusiak; Smith, Herbert, Little, Tune; Flatley, Johnstone; Crowley, Foley, Ryan, Morgan, Eales, Kefu (Carozza), Wilson, Connors. **Sent-off:** Smith (7)
    Scorer – *Penalty goals:* Eales 5.

NSW: Burke; Murdoch, Tombs, Dixon, Campese; Bowen, Payne; Harry, O'Kane, Hartill, Waugh, Welborn, Ofahengaue, Manu, Gavin (capt).
    Scorers – *Try:* O'Kane. *Conversion:* Burke. *Penalty goals:* Burke 2.

Otago Highlanders 5, Waikato Chiefs 22
Invercargill, 16 April 1996

Waikato continue their hot streak after another strong defensive display. Not content with having shut out Northern Transvaal, they allow Otago only one score while themselves claiming three tries.

Otago: Wilson; Lima, Cooper, Leslie (capt), Leaupepe; Bachop, Forster; Mika, Oliver, Driver, Timmins, Rich, Falaniko, Vanisi, Randell.
Scorer – *Try:* Cooper.

Waikato: Osborne; Berryman, Bunce, McLeod, Rush; Burton (Foster), Crabb; Veitayaki, Mitchell, Stevenson, Jones (capt), Cooksley, Larsen, Monkley, Turner (capt).
Scorers – *Tries:* Crabb, Mitchell, Turner. *Conversions:* Foster 2. *Penalty goal:* Foster.

Northern Transvaal 25, Transvaal 15
Pretoria, 19 April 1996

A 50,000 crowd packs Loftus to see further misery heaped on Transvaal by a Blue Bulls side maintaining its 100-per-cent home record. Northern surge 19–0 up in 24 minutes and Transvaal, despite three late tries, pay the price for a too cautious early approach.

Northern Transvaal: Du Toit; Van Rensburg, Van Schalkwyk, Snyman, Venter; J Kruger, van der Westhuizen; Bosman, Truscott, Hurter, Ackerman, Otto, R Kruger (capt, Rossouw), Bekker, Richter.
Scorers – *Penalty goals:* J Kruger, Du Toit. *Dropped goal:* J Kruger.

Transvaal: Lawless, Homan, Mulder, Gillingham, Hendriks; Le Roux, Roux; Hattingh (Barnard), Chris Rossouw, Van Greuning, Strydom, Schutte, Pienaar (capt), Charles Rossouw, Combrink.
Scorers – *Tries:* Hattingh, Lawless, Hendriks.

Auckland Blues 39, Waikato Chiefs 31
Auckland, 20 April 1996

Waikato's four-game winning burst is ended by a five-try Auckland display in front of 35,000 fans. Scores from Jonah Lomu, Zinzan Brooke, Joeli Vidiri, Ofisa Tonu'u and a penalty award give the Blues their sixth win in seven outings.

Auckland: Cashmore: Vidiri, Clarke, Stensness, Lomu; Spencer, Tonu'u; Dowd, Fitzpatrick, Brown, R Brooke, Fromont, Riechelmann, Blowers, Z Brooke (capt, Brain).
Scorers – *Tries:* Z Brooke, Vidiri, Tonu'u, Lomu, penalty try. *Conversions:* Spencer 3, Cashmore. *Penalty goals:* Spencer, Cashmore.

Waikato: Osborne; Berryman, Bunce, McLeod, Rush; Foster, Crabb; Veitayaki, Mitchell, Stevenson, Jones (capt), Cooksley, Larsen, Monkley, Turner (capt).
Scorers – *Tries:* Mitchell, Rush, penalty try. *Conversions:* Foster 2. *Penalty goals:* Foster 4.

ACT Brumbies 21, Queensland Reds 20
Manuka, 20 April 1996

Just when it seems ACT have run out of surprises, they add another amazing chapter to their remarkable season. Having already defeated Transvaal, Wellington, Auckland and Natal at home, they add the name of Queensland –

winners on their previous six starts. The dye is cast when John Eales misses a late penalty for the Reds.

ACT: Larkham; Hardy, Magro, Howard (O'Connor), Roff; Friend, Gregan; Noriega, Caputo, McKenzie (capt), Sweeny, Giffin, Langford, Fenukitau, Finegan.
Scorers – *Tries:* Finegan, Fenukitau. *Conversion:* Friend. *Penalty goals:* Friend 2, Roff.

Queensland: Mandrusiak; Smith, Herbert, Little, Tune; Flatley, Johnstone; Crowley (Daly), Foley, Ryan, Morgan, Eales, Kefu (Carozza), Wilson, Connors.
Scorers – *Tries:* Herbert, Tune. *Conversions:* Eales 2. *Penalty goals:* Eales 2.

NSW Waratahs 29, Otago Highlanders 25
Sydney, 21 April 1996

NSW, after three losses, rediscover the art of winning to keep alive slim hopes of a semi-final place. But it is a close run thing, and late Otago tries by Brian Lima and Kupu Vanisi keep the 25,000 crowd on tenterhooks to the death.

NSW: Burke; Murdoch, Tombs, Dixon, Campese; Wallace, Payne; Harry, O'Kane, Hartill, Domoni, Welborn, Talbot, Brial, Gavin (capt), Manu).
Scorers – *Tries:* Dixon, Wallace, Murdoch, Campese. *Conversions:* Burke 3. *Penalty goal:* Burke.

Otago: Wilson; Lima, Cooper, Leslie (capt), Cooke; Bachop, McCormack; Mika, Oliver, Driver, Falaniko, Timmins, Vanisi, Kronfeld, Randell.
Scorers – *Tries:* Lima 2, Vanisi. *Conversions:* Cooper 2. *Penalty goals:* Cooper 2.

Transvaal 55, Canterbury Crusaders 23
Johannesburg, 23 April 1996

Transvaal vent their frustration at a wretched campaign on hapless Canterbury in front of just 15,000 at Ellis Park. Fullback Gavin Lawless helps himself to one of seven Lions tries en route to a 25-point haul. Controversial hooker James Dalton grabs two.

Transvaal: Lawless, Gillingham, Mulder, Scholtz, Hendriks (Homan); Le Roux, Roux; Barnard (Hattingh), Dalton, Van Greuning, Strydom, Schutte, Pienaar (capt, Chris Rossouw), Charles Rossouw, Combrink.
Scorers – *Tries:* Dalton 2, Lawless, Hendriks, penalty try, Combrink, Roux. *Conversions:* Lawless 4. *Penalty goals:* Lawless 4.

Canterbury: Kaui; Gibson, Alatini, Mayerhofler, Bale; Miller, Marshall; R Loe (capt), Sexton, Barrell, Maxwell, Weedon, Blackadder, Gardiner, Lam.
Scorers – *Tries:* Marshall, Gardiner 2. *Conversion:* Miller. *Penalty goals:* Miller 2.

Western Province 35, Wellington Hurricanes 25
Cape Town, 23 April 1996

Joggie Viljoen, Western province's 20-year-old scrum-half, gives his side their second consecutive win with two late tries at Newlands. Falling behind to a first-minute try, WP look set for defeat before Viljoen's late show.

Western Province: Rossouw; Cilliers, Botha (Prins), Linee (Montgomery), Swart; Stransky, Viljoen; Pagel, Visser, Van der Linde, Blom, Wegner, Brink, Van Heerden (capt, Kapp), O'Cuinneagain.
Scorers – *Tries:* Swart, Viljoen 2. *Conversion:* Stransky. *Penalty goals:* Stransky 6.

Wellington: Cullen; Umaga, Konia, Ieremia, Telea; Mannix, Preston; Allen (capt), Hewitt, Coffin, Waller, Russell, Coventry, Tiatia, Williams (Seymour).

Scorers – *Tries:* Cullen, Konia, Williams. *Conversions:* Preston 2. *Penalty goals:* Preston 2.

Queensland Reds 51, Auckland Blues 13
Brisbane, 26 April 1996

Garrick Morgan claims two tries, the first in the opening minute, to set the Reds on their way to a resounding victory over the Blues at a delirious Ballymore. A record 22,000 crowd delight in Jonah Lomu's inactivity as Queensland hit the half-century.

Queensland: Mandrusiak; Smith (Carozza), Herbert, Little, Tune; Flatley, Johnstone; Daly, Foley, Ryan (Crowley, Cannon), Morgan, Eales, Kefu, Wilson, Connors.

Scorer – *Tries:* Morgan 2, Kefu, Connors, Little, Tune, Smith. *Conversions:* Eales 5. *Penalty goals:* Eales 2.

Auckland: Cashmore; Vidiri, Clarke, Stensness, Lomu; Spencer, Tonu'u; Dowd, Fitzpatrick, Brown, R Brooke (Nepia), Fromont, Riechelmann, Jones (Brain), Z Brooke (capt).

Scorers – *Tries:* Vidiri, Brown. *Penalty goal:* Spencer.

Natal Sharks 58, Canterbury Crusaders 26
Durban, 27 April 1996

The pain continues for Canterbury as Natal run in eight tries before a bumper 38,000 crowd at King's Park, despite only leading by six points at the mid-point. But the second half sees four tries shared equally by Joos Joubert and Cabous van der Westhuizen.

Natal: A Joubert; Small, Thomson (Van der Westhuizen), Muir, J Joubert; Honiball, Putt; Le Roux, Allan, Garvey, Andrews, Atherton, Van Heerden (Kriese), Fyvie, Teichmann (capt).

Scorers – *Tries:* J Joubert 2, Van der Westhuizen 2, Thomson, Le Roux, Small, Allan. *Conversions:* Honiball 5, A Joubert. *Penalty goals:* Honiball 2.

Canterbury: Kaui; Gibson, Alatini, Mayerhofler, Tukaki; Miller, Marshall; R Loe (capt), Sexton, S Loe, Maxwell, Weedon, Robertson, Lam, Blackadder.

Scorers – *Tries:* Tukaki, Maxwell. *Conversions:* Miller 2. *Penalty goals:* Miller 4.

Northern Transvaal 38, Wellington Hurricanes 20
Pretoria, 27 April 1996

Northerns make hard work of slumping Wellington, threatening to blow a 25–10 lead in the second half. Tries by Samoans Tana Umaga and Alex Telea send Afrikaans pulses racing before a try by hooker Andries Truscott steadies the Blue Bulls and gives them a vital bonus point.

Northern Transvaal: Du Toit; Van Rensburg, Van Schalkwyk, Snyman, Venter; J Kruger, Van der Westhuizen; Bosman, Truscott, Hurter, Ackerman, Otto, R Kruger (capt), Bekker, Richter.

Scorers – *Tries:* R Kruger, Van Rensburg 2, Truscott. *Conversions:* J Kruger 3. *Penalty goals:* J Kruger 4.

Wellington: Berry (Preston); Umaga, Ieremia, O'Halloran (Cullen), Telea; Mannix, Duggan; Allen (capt), Hewitt, Coffin, Waller, Russell, Afeaki (Simpson), Seymour (Crowley), Coventry.

Scorers – *Tries:* Cullen, Konia, Williams. *Conversions:* Preston 2. *Penalty goals:* Preston 2.

Waikato Chiefs 39, NSW Waratahs 17
Hamilton, 28 April 1996

First it's John Eales kicking goals, then Garrick Morgan amassing tries in the loose. Now All Black Ian Jones has a try hat-trick to boast about at the next 'second row' convention. Jones is dominant as the Waratahs, trailing 3–29 at half-time, give up any hope of a last-four berth.

Waikato: Osborne; Rush, Going, Bunce, Berryman; Foster, Crabb; Veitayaki, Mitchell, Stevenson, Taylor, Jones (capt), Larsen, Monkley, Turner (capt).
Scorers – *Tries:* Jones 3, Rush 2. *Conversions:* Foster 4. *Penalty goal:* Foster. *Dropped goal:* Foster.

NSW: Burke; Murdoch, Madz, Tombs, Campese; Wallace, Payne; Harry, O'Kane, Hartill (capt), Domoni, Welborn, Talbot, Brial, Manu.
Scorers – *Tries:* Murdoch, Madz. *Conversions:* Burke 2. *Penalty goal:* Burke.

Western Province 25, ACT Brumbies 16
Cape Town, 28 April 1996

After seven winless matches, Western Province have now enjoyed three straight victories, the latest at the expense of an ACT outfit with no rabbits left to pull out of the hat. Vlok Cilliers, Johan Kapp and Rhys Botha touch down for the Cape side.

Western Province: Rossouw; Cilliers, Botha, Prins, Swart; Stransky (capt), Viljoen; Pagel, Visser, Van der Linde, Blom, Wegner, Brink, Kapp, O'Cuinneagain.
Scorers – *Tries:* Cilliers, Kapp, Botha. *Conversions:* Stransky 2. *Penalty goals:* Stransky 2.

ACT: Larkham; Hardy, Magro, Howard, Roff; Friend, Gregan; Noriega, Caputo, McKenzie (capt), Sweeny, Giffin, Langford, Fenukitau, Finegan..
Scorers – *Try:* Noriega. *Conversion:* Knox. *Penalty goals:* Friend, Knox 2.

Auckland Blues 56, NSW Waratahs 44
Auckland, 1 May 1996

There is no Jonah Lomu, and there are precious few fans (9,000), but those who do show at Eden Park are treated to a 100-point thriller. Blues wing Joeli Vidiri claims three of his side's eight tries, while NSW share out their six tries among as many players.

Auckland: Cashmore; Kerr, Clarke, Stensness, Vidiri; Spencer (Cunningham), Tonu'u; Dowd, Fitzpatrick, Brown, R Brooke, Fromont, Reichelmann, Jones, Z Brooke (capt).
Scorers – *Tries:* Vidiri 3, Brown, Tonu'u, Z Brooke, Clarke, penalty try. *Conversions:* Cashmore 5. *Penalty goals:* Cashmore 2.

NSW: Burke; Murdoch, Madz, Tombs, Campese; Bowen, Ekert; Blades (capt), Bell, Harry, Waugh, Domoni, Talbot, Brial, Manu.
Scorers – *Tries:* Murdoch, Manu, Ekert, Waugh, Campese, Blades. *Conversions:* Burke 4. *Penalty goals:* Burke 2.

Natal Sharks 49, Transvaal 13
Durban, 1 May 1996

Henry Honiball piles up 29 points as sorry Transvaal are given a frightful hammering at King's Park. The occasional Bok fly-half claims two of Natal's half-dozen tries, converts five and lands three penalty goals for good measure.

Natal: A Joubert; Small, Muir, J Joubert, Van der Westhuizen; Honiball, Putt; Le Roux, Allan, Garvey, Atherton, Andrews (Slade), Kriese, Fyvie, Teichmann (capt).
    Scorers – Tries: Honiball 2, Fyvie, Small, Garvey, A Joubert. *Conversions:* Honiball 5. *Penalty goals:* Honiball 3.

Transvaal: Lawless, Gillingham, Mulder, Scholtz, Hendriks; le Roux, Roux; Barnard, Dalton, Van Greuning, Strydom, Schutte, Pienaar (capt), Rossouw (MacDonald), Combrinck.
    Scorer – Try: Lawless. *Conversion:* Lawless. *Penalty goals:* Lawless 2.

Waikato Chiefs 15, Wellington Hurricanes 23
Rotorua, 4 May 1996

Waikato's semi-final dream dies at the last as Wellington seize the initiative and run up a 13–0 interval lead. Although Waikato rebound superbly to lead 15–13, a third Jon Preston penalty and a Jason O'Halloran try deny them victory.

Waikato: Osborne (Johnston); Berryman, Bunce, Little, Rush; Foster, Crabb; Stevenson, Mitchell, Veitayaki, Jones, Monkley, Taylor, Larsen, Anglesey.
    Scorers – Tries: Johnston, Anglesey. *Conversion:* Foster. *Penalty goal:* Foster.

Wellington: Cullen; Umaga, Ieremia, O'Halloran, Telea; Mannix, Preston; Allen (capt), Hewitt, Coffin, D Williams, Russell, Coventry, Tiatia (Seymour), K Williams.
    Scorers – Tries: Allen, O'Halloran. *Conversions:* Preston 2. *Penalty goals:* Preston 3.

Northern Transvaal 23, ACT Brumbies 10
Pretoria, 4 May 1996

A crucial match, with both sides battling for a semi-final slot, goes with home advantage as ACT are persistently adjudged offside and Jannie Kruger, with six penalty goals, makes them pay. ACT edge the try count, but so what?

Northern Transvaal: Du Toit; Van Rensburg, Snyman (Breytenbach), Van Schalkwyk, Venter; J Kruger, van der Westhuizen; Bosman, Truscott, Hurter, Ackerman, Otto, R Kruger (capt), Bekker, Richter.
    Scorers – Try: Bosman. *Penalty goals:* J Kruger 6.

ACT: Larkham; Hardy, Magro, Howard, Roff; Knox, Gregan; Noriega, Caputo, McKenzie, Langford, Giffin, Robinson (capt), Fenukitau, Finegan.
    Scorers – Tries: Noriega, Caputo.

Canterbury Crusaders 27, Otago Highlanders 29
Christchurch, 5 May 1996

Canterbury have a match-winning try disallowed after rallying from a 17-point half-time deficit. Two Jeff Wilson tries ultimately allow Otago to celebrate a South Island derby victory and only their second win in seven matches.

Canterbury: Kaui; Gibson, Alatini, Mayerhofler, Tukaki; Miller, Marshall; R Loe (capt), Hammett, Barrell, Maxwell, Weedon, Blackadder, Gardiner, Lam (Coleman).

Scorers – *Tries:* Alatini, Marshall, Loe. *Conversions:* Miller 3. *Penalty goals:* Miller 2.

Otago: Wilson (Cooke); Lima, Cooper (Brown), Leslie (capt), Vaega; Bachop, McCormack; Mika, Latta (Oliver), Moore, Cullen, Falaniko, Henderson, Kronfeld (Maka), Randell.

Scorers – *Tries:* Wilson 2, Vaega. *Conversion:* Cooper. *Penalty goals:* Cooper 4.

Natal Sharks 20, Queensland Reds 21
Durban, 5 May 1996

Wallaby centre Jason Little goes over for an injury-time try to rob Natal of victory and stun a 39,000 crowd at King's Park. Ironically it is Henry Honiball's error that leads to Little's score, as the Natal fly-half had previously put the home side in a winning position with five strikes.

Natal: A Joubert; Small, Muir, J Joubert, Van der Westhuizen; Honiball, Putt; Le Roux, Allan (Mendez), Garvey, Atherton, Andrews, Van Heerden, Fyvie (Kriese), Teichmann (capt).

Scorers – *Try:* A Joubert. *Penalty goals:* Honiball 5.

Queensland: Horan (capt); Carozza, Herbert, Little, Tune; Flatley, Johnstone; Daly, Foley, Crowley, Eales, Morgan, Kefu, Wilson, Connors.

Scorers – *Tries:* Horan, Little. *Conversion:* Eales. *Penalty goals:* Eales 3.

Transvaal 34, Auckland Blues 22
Johannesburg, 7 May 1996

Perhaps it is the prospect of returning to Ellis Park for so many All Blacks in the Auckland side. Whatever, Transvaal's defeat of the Blues is a major kick in the teeth for the formbook. Auckland never recover from conceding three tries in the first half-hour.

Transvaal: Lawless, Johnston, Mulder, Scholtz (Gillingham), Hendriks; H le Roux, Roux; Hattingh, Dalton, J le Roux, Schutte, Strydom, Pienaar (capt), MacDonald, Combrinck.

Scorers – *Tries:* Roux, Pienaar, MacDonald, Gillingham. *Conversions:* Lawless 4. *Penalty goals:* Lawless 2.

Auckland: Cashmore; Vidiri, Clarke, Stensness, Lomu; Spencer, Tonu'u; Nepia, Fitzpatrick, Brown, R Brooke, Fromont, Blowers, Jones, Z Brooke (capt).

Scorers – *Tries:* Vidiri 2, penalty try. *Conversions:* Cashmore 2. *Penalty goal:* Cashmore.

NSW Waratahs 52, Wellington Hurricanes 25
Sydney, 10 May 1996

Alistair Murdoch claims a try hat-trick to take his tally to eight for the tournament and ensure that Waratahs finish on a high. Matt Burke is also in the points, pocketing 22 to end up with 157 in 11 matches. But the match's abiding memory is the brilliant try scored by Wellington's 20-year-old sensation Christian Cullen.

NSW: Burke; Murdoch, Madz, Tombs, Campese (Kelaher); Bowen, Payne; Harry, Bell, Blades (capt), Welborn, Waugh (Domoni), Talbot, Brial, Manu.

Scorers – *Tries:* Murdoch 3, Harry, Madz, Campese, Burke. *Conversions:* Burke 4. *Penalty goals:* Burke 3.

Wellington: Cullen; Umaga, Ieremia, O'Halloran, Telea (Konia); Mannix, Preston; Allen (capt), Hewitt, Coffin, D Williams, Russell, Coventry, Tiatia, K Williams (Seymour).

Scorers – *Tries:* Umaga, Telea, Cullen. *Conversions:* Preston 2. *Penalty goals:* Preston 2.

Western Province 7, Northern Transvaal 35
Cape Town, 10 May 1996

Northern Transvaal imperiously clinch a semi-final berth amid chaotic scenes in Cape Town, where elements among the 43,372 crowd attending Newlands' first floodlit game invade the pitch and force Namibian referee Johan Meuwesen, who is knocked to the ground, to blow prematurely.

Western Province: Rossouw; Cilliers, Botha, Prins, Swart; Stransky, Viljoen; Pagel, Visser, Van der Linde (Laubscher), Blom, Wegner, Brink, Kapp, O'Cuinneagain.
Scorers – *Try:* Wegner. *Conversion:* Cilliers.

Northern Transvaal: Van Rensburg; van der Westhuizen, Van Schalkwyk, Claasens, Venter; J Kruger, Breytenbach; Bosman, Truscott, Hurter, Ackerman, Otto, R Kruger (capt), Bekker, Richter.
Scorers – *Tries:* Van Rensburg 2, Venter 2, Otto. *Conversions:* J Kruger 2. *Penalty goals:* J Kruger 2.

Transvaal 16, Queensland Reds 25
Johannesburg, 11 May 1996

Queensland finish on top of the pile and ensure themselves a home semi-final by ending Transvaal's resurgence four days after the Lions' mauling of Auckland. Transvaal kicker Gavin Lawless has a miserable game. Francois Pienaar and Jason Little are carried off after a sickening collision ten minutes from time.

Transvaal: Lawless, Homan, Mulder, Gillingham, Hendriks; Johnston, Roux; Hattingh, Dalton, J le Roux, Schutte, Strydom, Pienaar (capt, Rossouw), MacDonald, Combrinck.
Scorers – *Tries:* Hendriks, Roux. *Penalty goals:* Lawless 2.

Queensland: Horan (capt); Smith, Herbert, Little (Mandrusiak), Tune; Flatley, Johnstone; Daly, Cannon, Crowley, Eales, Morgan, Kefu, Wilson, Connors.
Scorers – *Tries:* Tune, Johnstone, Horan. *Conversions:* Eales 2. *Penalty goals:* Eales 2.

Natal Sharks 23, Auckland Blues 30
Durban, 11 May 1996

Natal blow their second straight game in the final minute, when Eroni Clarke follows the example of Queensland's Jason Little and scampers over for the winning try to earn Auckland a home semi-final.

Natal: A Joubert (C van der Westhuizen); Small, Thomson, Muir, J Joubert; Honiball, Putt; Le Roux, Allan, Garvey, Atherton, Andrews, Van Heerden, Fyvie, Teichmann (capt).
Scorers – *Tries:* Small, penalty try. *Conversions:* Honiball 2. *Penalty goals:* Honiball 3.

Auckland: Cashmore; Vidiri, Clarke, Ngauamo, Lomu; Spencer (Stensness), Tonu'u; Dowd, Fitzpatrick, Brown, R Brooke, Riechelmann, Jones, Blowers, Z Brooke (capt).
Scorers – *Tries:* Vidiri 2, penalty try. *Conversions:* Cashmore 2. *Penalty goal:* Cashmore.

ACT Brumbies 70, Otago Highlanders 26
Canberra, 12 May 1996

ACT, in many ways the team of the championship, bring the curtain down on the regulation season with the biggest win of the competition.against a disillusioned Otago outfit. The Brumbies run in nine tries, with Mitch Hardy claiming a hat-trick, but finish an agonising one point short of a top-four position.

ACT: Larkham; Hardy, Magro, Howard, Roff; Knox, Gregan; Noriega, Caputo, McKenzie, Langford, Giffin, Fenukitau, Robinson (capt), Finegan.

Scorers – *Tries:* Hardy 3, Giffin, Fenukitau, Finegan, Robinson, Roff, penalty try. *Conversions:* Knox 6, Roff 2. *Penalty goals:* Knox 3.

Otago: Wilson; Cooke; Vaega, Leslie (capt), Lima; Bachop, McCormack; Moore, Oliver, Mika, Cullen, Falaniko, Henderson, Vanisi, Randell.

Scorers – *Tries:* Vanisi, Wilson, England. *Conversion:* Wilson. *Penalty goals:* Wilson 3.

FINAL TABLE	P	W	D	L	F	A	T	Pt
Queensland Reds	11	9	0	2	320	247	35	28
Auckland Blues	11	8	0	3	408	350	53	40
Northern Transvaal	11	8	0	3	329	208	31	23
Natal Sharks	11	6	0	5	389	277	48	31
ACT Brumbies	11	7	0	4	306	273	37	29
Waikato Chiefs	11	6	0	5	291	269	33	28
NSW Waratahs	11	5	0	6	312	290	36	32
Otago Highlanders	11	5	0	6	332	391	38	46
Wellington Hurricanes	11	3	0	8	290	356	30	41
Transvaal	11	3	0	8	233	299	25	32
Western Province	11	3	1	7	251	353	25	42
Canterbury Crusaders	11	2	1	8	234	378	26	44

John Allan, Natal's Scot-turned-Springbok, halts Auckland starlet Andrew Blowers in the Super-12 final.

Queensland Reds (8) 25, Natal Sharks (22) 43
Brisbane, 18 May 1996

Queensland's ambition to achieve three successive Southern Hemisphere titles is shattered by a Natal side dominant in every phase. Unbeaten in 12 matches at Ballymore, Queensland have no answer to the Atherton–Andrews lock partnership, the all-round marshalling of Henry Honiball and the potency of Cobus van der Westhuizen, who scores a try hat-trick.

Queensland: Mandrusiak; Carozza, Herbert, Horan (capt),Tune; Flatley, Johnstone; Daly, Foley, Crowley, Eales, Morgan, Kefu, Wilson, Connors.
    Scorers – *Tries:* Foley, Horan, penalty try. *Conversions:* Eales 2. *Penalty goals:* Eales 2.

Natal: A Joubert; Small, Thomson, Muir, van der Westhuizen (J Joubert); Honiball, Putt; Le Roux, Allan, Garvey, Atherton, Andrews, Van Heerden (Kriese), Fyvie, Teichmann (capt).
    Scorers – *Tries:* Van der Westhuizen 3, A Joubert 2, Van Heerden. *Conversions:* Honiball 2. *Penalty goals:* Honiball 2.

Referee: P O'Brien (New Zealand).

Auckland Blues (15) 48, Northern Transvaal (6) 11
Auckland, 19 May 1996

Auckland score a dazzling victory over the Blue Bulls, with Jonah Lomu in the van of all the best work. A mouthwatering team performance is highlighted by Lomu's two tries. Sean Fitzpatrick, Adrian Cashmore and Johnny Ngauamo all cross to put Auckland 15–6 up at the turnaround before Lomu gets down to some serious work.

Auckland: Cashmore; Vidiri, Clarke, Ngauamo, Lomu; Stensness, Tonu'u; Dowd, Fitzpatrick, Brown, R Brooke, Riechelmann, Mika, Blowers, Z Brooke (capt).
    Scorers – *Tries:* Lomu 2, Fitzpatrick, Cashmore, Vidiri, Ngauamo, R Brooke, Tonu'u. *Conversions:* Cashmore 4.

Northern Transvaal: Van Rensburg; van der Westhuizen, Van Schalkwyk (Van Straaten, Du Toit), Claasens, Venter; J Kruger, Breytenbach; Bosman, Truscott, Hurter, Ackerman, Otto, R Kruger (capt, Reyn), Bekker, Richter.
    Scorers – *Try:* Breytenbach. *Penalty goals:* J Kruger 2.

Referee: W Erickson (Australia).

SUPER-12 FINAL

Auckland Blues (20) 45, Natal Sharks (16) 21
Eden Park, Auckland, 25 May 1996 (att: 45,000)

Auckland continue from where they left off against Northern Transvaal, producing yet another sensational display of 15-man rugby to clinch the Super-12 crown before their jubliant fans. Once again there is no keeping Lomu quiet. He shrugs off Andre Joubert to score the first try, then makes the second for fullback Adrian Cashmore with a 75-metre break. Natal, who prosper in the lineout, reduce the half-time deficit to 20–16, before promising Kiwi flanker Andrew Blowers weighs in with a brace of scores and Natal, South Africa's Currie Cup champions, are left behind.

Auckland: Cashmore; Vidiri, Clarke, Ngauamo, Lomu; Spencer, Tonu'u; Dowd, Fitzpatrick, Brown, R Brooke, Riechelmann (Chandler), Blowers, Jones, Z Brooke (capt).
Scorers – *Tries:* Blowers 2, Lomu, Spencer, Clarke, Riechelmann. *Conversions:* Cashmore 3. *Penalty goals:* Cashmore 3.

Natal: A Joubert; Small (J Joubert), Thomson, Muir, van der Westhuizen; Honiball, Putt (Du Preez); Le Roux, Allan, Garvey, Atherton, Andrews, Van Heerden (Kriese), Fyvie, Teichman (capt).
Scorers – *Tries:* A Joubert, Small. *Conversion:* Honiball. *Penalty goals:* Honiball 3.

Referee: W Erickson (Australia).

SUPER-12 RECORDS

Top points scorers

	tries	cons	pens	drops	total
John Eales (Queensland Reds)	3	25	35	0	160
Matt Burke (NSW Waratahs)	5	27	26	0	157
Jannie Kruger (Northern Transvaal)	1	16	33	0	142
Henry Honiball (Natal Sharks)	3	24	25	0	138
Joel Stransky (Western Province)	0	12	31	1	120
Gavin Lawless (Transvaal)	4	14	21	0	111
Andre Joubert (Natal Sharks)	12	10	9	0	107

Top try scorers (444 tries scored in 69 Super-12 matches)

14	James Small (Natal Sharks)
12	Andre Joubert (Natal Sharks)
10	Joeli Vidiri (Auckland Blues)
9	Andrew Blowers (Auckland Blues)
8	Jonah Lomu (Auckland Blues)
	Alistair Murdoch (NSW Waratahs)
	Justin Swart (Western Province)
	Ben Tune (Queensland Reds)
7	Eroni Clarke (Auckland Blues)
	Christian Cullen (Wellington Hurricane)
	Joe Roff (ACT Brumbies)
	Jeremy Thomson (Natal Sharks)

THE YEAR'S RESULTS

Australia, showing six changes from the side beaten by England in the quarter-finals of the World Cup, blow 16-15 lead in last nine minutes of first Test, and Jonah Lomu rampages through second as New Zealand regain Bledisloe Cup. Lomu claims a late try and Andrew Mehrtens kicks 23 points in an Auckland contest in which Wallaby prop Dan Crowley is suspended for three weeks for kicking All Black flanker Josh Kronfeld. David Campese, dropped from the first match, returns on the bench in Sydney for 100th meeting of the two sides, but Kronfeld, a World Cup star barely five weeks previously, is axed by New Zealand selectors. Lomu, later to be adjudged man of the match, sets the tempo by characteristically bulldozing through four tackles to make the first of five All Black tries after just 85 seconds.

New Zealand 28, Australia 16
First Test: Auckland, 22 July 1995

New Zealand: G Osborne (North Harbour); J Wilson (Otago), F Bunce, W Little (both North Harbour), J Lomu (Counties); A Mehrtens, G Bachop (both Canterbury); C Dowd, S Fitzpatrick (capt), O Brown (all Auckland), I Jones (North Auckland), R Brooke (Auckland), M Brewer, J Kronfeld (both Otago), Z Brooke (Auckland). **Replacement:** M Jones (Auckland) for Z Brooke, 50 mins.

    Scorers – *Try:* Lomu. *Conversion:* Mehrtens. *Penalty goals:* Mehrtens 5. *Dropped goals:* Mehrtens 2.

Australia: M Burke (NSW); D Smith, J Little, T Horan (all Queensland), J Roff (ACT); S Bowen (NSW), S Merrick (debut, NSW Country); D Crowley (Queensland), P Kearns (capt), M Hartill, W Waugh (all NSW), J Eales (Queensland), W Ofahengaue, D Manu, T Gavin (all NSW). **Replacement:** P Howard (Queensland) for Burke, 28 mins.

    Scorers – *Try:* Ofahengaue. *Conversion:* Roff. *Penalty goals:* Roff 2, Burke.

Referee: R Megson (Scotland).

Series score: Played 99, New Zealand 67, Australia 27, Drawn 5.

Australia 23, New Zealand 34
Second Test: Sydney, 29 July 1995

Australia: M Burke (NSW); D Smith (Queensland), J Little, T Horan (both Queensland), J Roff (ACT); S Bowen (NSW), S Merrick (NSW Country); E McKenzie, P Kearns (capt), M Hartill, W Waugh (all NSW), J Eales (Queensland), W Ofahengaue, D Manu, T Gavin (all NSW). **Replacement:** D Campese (NSW) for Smith, 40 mins; T Coker (Queensland) for Gavin.

    Scorers – *Tries:* Smith, Ofahengaue. *Conversions:* Burke 2. *Penalty goals:* Burke 3.

New Zealand: G Osborne (North Harbour); J Wilson (Otago), F Bunce, W Little (both North Harbour), J Lomu (Counties); A Mehrtens, G Bachop (both Canterbury); C Dowd, S Fitzpatrick (capt), O Brown (all Auckland), I Jones (North Auckland), R Brooke (Auckland), M Brewer (Otago), M Jones (Auckland), Z Brooke (Auckland). **Replacement:** J Kronfeld (Otago) for M Jones, 40 mins.

Scorers – *Tries:* Bunce 2, Mehrtens, Lomu, Wilson. *Conversions:* Mehrtens 3. *Penalty goal:* Mehrtens.

Referee: S Hilditch (Ireland).

Series score: Played 100, New Zealand 68, Australia 27, Drawn 5.

1995 LATIN CUP
ARGENTINA: OCTOBER 1995

France, under new coach Jean Claude Skrela, capture the Latin Cup in Buenos Aires with a 47–12 rout of Argentina in the decider. The French, with an eye to the future, travel with ten players new to Test match rugby, including centres Thomas Castaignede and Richard Dourthe, scrum-half Philippe Carbonneau and forwards Franck Tournaire and Fabian Pelous.

	P	W	D	L	F	A	Pts
France	3	3	0	0	134	42	6
Argentina	3	2	0	1	89	69	4
Italy	3	1	0	2	68	64	2
Romania	3	0	0	3	27	143	0

The picture every defence in world rugby fears – Jonah Lomu, who scored tries for New Zealand in both Bledisloe matches.

165

France (16) 34, Italy (10) 22
Buenos Aires, 14 October 1995

France: J-L Sadourny; E NTamack, Hyardet (debut), Y Delaigue, P Saint-Andre (capt); C Deylaud, G Accoceberry; C Califano, J-M Gonzales, F Tournaire (debut), O Merle, O Brouzet, M Lievremont (debut), A Carminati, P Benetton.

    Scorers – *Tries:* Sadourny 2, Ntamack, Carminati. *Conversions:* Deylaud 4. *Penalty goals:* Deylaud 2.

Italy: Vaccari; Roselli, Bordon (Platania 38), Francescato, Mazariol; Bonomi, Troncon; Cuttitta (capt), Orlandi, Dal Sie, Pedroni, Giacheri, Arancio (Giovanelli 67), Checchinato, Sgorlon.

Referee: M Chiciu (Romania).

Series score: Played 18, France 18, Italy 0.

France (25) 52, Romania (0) 8
Tucuman, 17 October 1995

France: J-L Sadourny (Y Delaigue 72); E NTamack, Arlettaz (debut), R Dourthe (debut), P Saint-Andre (capt); T Castaignede (debut), P Carbonneau (debut); L Benezech, Azam (debut), S Graou, O Merle, F Pelous (debut), M Lievremont (P Benetton 63), Juillet (debut), A Carminati.

    Scorers – *Tries:* Carminati, Castaignede, Arlettaz 2, Pelous, Lievremont, Delaigue. *Conversions:* Deylaud 4. *Penalty goals:* Deylaud 3.

Romania: Maftei; Olovasu, Luca, Nedelcu, Solomie; Prospiteanu, Dragnea; Costa, Radoi (Vlad 32), Salageanu, Cojocariu (Girbu 51), Marin (Flutur 52), Guranescu, Draguceanu, Gealapu.

    Scorers – *Try:* Vlad. *Dropped goal:* Maftei.

Referee: M Sklar (Argentina).

Series score: Played 41, France 31, Romania 8, Drawn 2.

Argentina (11) 26, Italy (3) 6
Tucuman, 17 October 1995

Argentina: Jurado; Luna, Cuesta-Silva (Cremaschi 39), Salvat (capt), Teran; Arbizu, Pichot; Mendez, Le Fort, Urbano, Perez, Llanes, Martin, Santamarina, Viel.

    Scorers – *Tries:* Martin, Teran, Salvat. *Conversion:* Luna. *Penalty goals:* Luna 3.

Italy: Pertile (Ravazzolo 60); Vaccari, Bordon, Francescato, Ravazzolo (Mazzariol 60); Bonomi, Troncon; Cuttitta (capt), Orlandi, Dal Sie (Castellani 68), Pedroni, Giacheri, Giovanelli, Sgorlon, Checchinato.

    Scorer – *Penalty goals:* Bonomi 2.

Referee: M Lasaga (France).

Italy (13) 40, Romania (3) 3
Buenos Aires, 21 October 1995

Italy: Vaccari; Bordon, Rosselli, Platania, Francescato, Mazzariol; Bonomi (Filizzola 82), Troncon; Cuttitta (capt), Orlandi (Moscardi 63), Castellani, Pedroni, Giacheri, Giovanelli, Checchinato, Sgorlon (Caione 77).

    Scorers – *Tries:* Checchinato 2, Moscardi, Mazzariol, Rosselli. *Conversions:* Bonomi 3. *Penalty goals:* Bonomi 3.

Romania: Maftei (Rotaru 49); Solomie, Nedelcu, Luca, Fugigi; Bezarau, Flutur; Vlad,

Negraci, Salageanu (Gragos 70), Marin (Draguceanu 55), Cojocariu (capt), Guranescu, Girbu, Gealapu.

    Scorer – *Penalty goal:* Bezarau.

Referee: M Sklar (Argentina).

France (20) 47, Argentina (6) 12
Buenos Aires, 21 October 1995

France: J-L Sadourny; E NTamack, R Dourthe (Hyardet 73), T Castaignede, P Saint-Andre (capt); C Deylaud, P Carbonneau; L Benezech, J-M Gonzales (Azam 49), C Califano, O Merle, F Pelous (O Brouzet 73), P Benetton, Juillet, Carminati (M Lievremont 54).

    Scorers – *Tries:* Saint-Andre 2, Carbonneau 2, Ntamack 2, Castaignede. *Conversions:* Deylaud 3. *Penalty goals:* Deylaud 2.

Argentina: Jurado; Luna, Cuesta-Silva, Salvat (capt), Teran (Albanese 40); Arbizu, Pichot; Mendez, Angelilio, Urbano, Perez, Llanes, Martin, Irazoqui, Viel.

    Scorer – *Penalty goals:* Luna 4.

Referee: M Morandin (Italy).

Series score: Played 27, France 22, Argentina 4, Drawn 1.

FIJI TO WALES AND IRELAND
OCTOBER–NOVEMBER 1995: P9 W3 D0 L6 F217 A209

Not a vintage tour by any means, with Neath, Pontypridd and Connacht each defeating the South Sea Islanders outside the Test arena. The Fijian squad did have one gilt-edged opportunity to make a name for itself, against woeful Wales, but poor defence and poor goalkicking allowed victory to get away. Wales squeezed home 19–15 – a result which Ireland put in context the following week, thrashing the tourists 44–8 at Lansdowne Road.

PARTY: P Bale (Canterbury); M Bari (Tavna); E Batinala (Nadroga); R Bogisa (Nadi); E Bolobolo (Tavna); E Katalau (Poverty Bay); M T Korovou (Nadi); L Little (King Country); W Masirewa (Counties); A Nadolo (Suva); E Natuivau (Suva); F Rayasi (King Country); W Rokotuviwa (Rewa); D Rouse (Nadi); S Sadria (Suva); G Smith (Waikato); S Sorovaki (Wellington); T Tamanivalu (Brothers); I Tawake (Nadroga); O Turuva (Nadi); L Vatureva (Wellington); S Vonalagi (Suva); J Waqa (Nadroga). **Manager:** S Vuetaki. **Coaches:** M Kurisaru, B Johnstone.

Results: (1) Wales A 10, Fiji 25 (Bridgend, 21 October); (2) Neath 30, Fiji 22 (Neath, 25 October; (3) Cardiff 22, Fiji 21 (Cardiff, 28 October); (4) Treorchy 14, Fiji 70 (Treorchy, 1 November); (5) Pontypridd 31, Fiji 13 (Pontypridd, 4 November); (6) Llanelli 12, Fiji 38 (Llanelli, 7 November); (7) *Test:* **Wales 19, Fiji 15** (Cardiff, 11 November); (8) Connacht 27, Fiji 5 (Galway, 14 November); (9) *Test:* **Ireland 44, Fiji 8** (Dublin, 18 November).

Wales A 10, Fiji 25
Bridgend, 21 October 1995

Wales A: J Thomas (Llanelli); A Harris (Swansea), M Taylor (Swansea), G Thomas (Bridgend), W Proctor (Llanelli); A Davies (Cardiff), P John (Pontypridd, capt); A Lewis (Cardiff), R McBryde (Llanelli), S John (Llanelli), G Prosser (Pontypridd), A Moore (Swansea), A Gibbs (Newbridge), O Lloyd (Llanelli), S Williams (Neath). **Replacements:** M Voyle (Newport) for Prosser, 51 mins; L Mustoe (Cardiff) for Lewis, 78 mins.

    Scorers – *Try:* penalty try. *Conversion:* A Davies. *Penalty goal:* A Davies.

Fiji: Rayasi; Bari, Sorovaki, Little, Bale; Bogisi, McLennan; Veitayaki (capt), Batinala, Naituvau, Katalau, Tawake, Tamanivalu, Masirewa, Rouse.

    Scorers – Tries: Bale 2, Bari, Masirewa. *Conversion:* Bogisi. *Penalty goal:* Bogisi.

Referee: P Thomas (France).

Wales 19, Fiji 15
Test: Cardiff, 11 November 1995

Wales: J Thomas (Llanelli); I Evans (Llanelli), G Thomas (Bridgend), N Davies (Llanelli), W Proctor (Llanelli); N Jenkins (Pontypridd), A Moore (Cardiff); C Loader (Swansea), J Humphreys (Cardiff, capt), L Mustoe (Cardiff, debut), A Moore (Swansea), D Jones (Cardiff), C Quinnell (Llanelli, debut), M Bennett (Cardiff), H Taylor (Cardiff). **Replacement:** A Williams (Swansea) for Davies, 23 mins. **Temporary:** G Jenkins (Swansea) for Humphreys.

    Scorers – Tries: Moore, N Jenkins. *Penalty goals:* N Jenkins 3.

Fiji: Rayasi; Bale, Sorovaki, Little, Bari; Waqa (Bogisa 40), Rauluni; Veitayaki (capt), Smith, Natuivau, Katalau, Tawake, Tamanivalu, Masirewa, Rouse.

    Scorers – Tries: Bari, Rayasi. *Conversion:* Waqa. *Penalty goal:* Waqa.

Referee: P O'Brien (New Zealand).

Series score: Played 4, Wales 4, Fiji 0.

Ireland 44, Fiji 8
Test: Dublin, 18 November 1995

Ireland: J Staples (Harlequins, capt); R Wallace (Garryowen), M Field (Malone), J Bell (Northampton), S Geoghegan (Bath); P Burke (Cork Constitution), C Saverimutto (Sale, debut); N Popplewell (Newcastle), T Kingston (Dolphin), P Wallace (Blackrock), G Fulcher (Cork Constitution), N Francis (Old Belvedere), J Davidson (Dungannon, debut), D Corkery (Cork Constitution), P Johns (Dungannon). **Replacements:** A Clarke (Northampton, debut) for Kingston, 45 mins; D McBride (Malone) for Davidson, 75 mins. **Temporary:** S McCahill (Sunday's Well, debut) for Field; H Hurley (Old Wesley, debut) for Popplewell.

    Scorers – Tries: Johns, Francis, Staples, R Wallace, Geoghegan, P Wallace. *Conversions:* Burke 4. *Penalty goals:* Burke 2.

Fiji: Rayasi; Bale, Sorovaki, Little, Bari; Waqa, Rauluni; Veitayaki (capt), Smith, Natuivau, Katalau, Nadolo, Tamanivalu, Masirewa, Tawake.

    Scorers – Try: Masirewa. *Penalty goal:* Waqa.

Referee: P O'Brien (Ireland).

Series score: Played 1, Ireland 1, Fiji 0.

NEW ZEALAND TO ITALY AND FRANCE
OCTOBER–NOVEMBER 1995: P8 W7 D0 L1 F339 A126

New Zealand's French visit breaks all records in terms of spectators and gate receipts. All six matches are sold out, with a total of 114,710 paying spectators bringing £1,920,147 into the coffers of the French Federation. In addition, a monster 30,000 crowd masses in Bologna to see Italy play, and get destroyed, by Jonah Lomu and co. The real business takes place in France, though, against a backdrop of bitterness. New Zealand are angry at France's policy of nucleur testing in the South Pacific, whilst the French are embroiled in something of a rugby civil war. The players are fizzing at the axeing of Thierry Lacroix,

Olivier Roumat and Laurent Cabannes for playing on in South Africa after the World Cup. But that's not all. Livid also over their ticket allocations (reduced from 25 to eight per player) and conditions of payment, they boycott a civic reception on the eve of the first Test in Toulouse. Andre Herrero, the team manager, then announces he will resign. Despite all that, France complete a hat-trick of wins over the All Blacks – remember, they swept the 1994 series in New Zealand – deservedly stealing the opener 22–15 through Philippe Saint-Andre's lateish try, before the Blacks snatch a share of the series with a defiant and altogether impressive 37–12 rout of *Les Tricolores* the following week in Paris.

PARTY: M Allen (Taranaki); L Barry (North Harbour); T Blackadder (Canterbury); R Brooke (Auckland); Z Brooke (Auckland); O Brown (Auckland); F Bunce (North Harbour); S Culhane (Southland); C Dowd (Auckland); S Fitzpatrick (Auckland, capt); S Forster (Otago); R Fromont (Auckland); N Hewitt (Southland); A Ieremia (Wellington); I Jones (North Harbour); M Jones (Auckland); J Kronfeld (Otago); B Larsen (North Harbour); R Loe (Canterbury); J Lomu (Counties); W Little (North Harbour); J Marshall (Canterbury); T Matson (Canterbury); A Mehrtens (Canterbury); G Osborne (North Harbour); T Randell (Otago); E Rush (North Harbour); C Spencer (Auckland); J Wilson (Otago).

Results: (1) Italy A 21, All Blacks 51 (Catania, 26 October); (2) Test: **Italy 6, New Zealand 70** (Bologna, 28 October); (3) French Barbarians 19, All Blacks 34 (Toulon, 1 November); (4) Languedoc-Roussillon 9, All Blacks 30 (Beziers, 4 November); (5) Basque-Landes 20, All Blacks 47 (Bayonne, 7 November); (6) first Test: **France 22, New Zealand 15** (Toulouse, 11 November); (7) French Selection 17, All Blacks 55 (Nancy, 14 November); (8) second Test: **France 12, New Zealand 37** (Paris, 18 November).

Italy A 21, New Zealand 51
Catania, Sicily, 26 October 1995

Italy A: P Dotto; F Roselli, M Piovene, T Visentin, F Donati; G Filizolla, G Guidi; A Castellani, G Decarlo, F Properzi, R Favaro, D Scaglia, C Ciaone, R Saetti, R Piovani.
    Scorers – *Tries:* Castellani, Properzi. *Conversion:* Filizolla. *Penalty goals:* Filizolla 2. *Dropped goal:* Filizolla.

All Blacks: Osborne; Wilson, Bunce, Ieremia, Rush; Mehrtens, Marshall; Allen, Hewitt, Loe, Larsen, Fromont, Randell, Barry, Blackadder.
    Scorers – *Tries:* Ieremia, Bunce, Wilson, Blackadder 2, Osborne. *Conversions:* Mehrtens, Wilson 2. *Penalty goals:* Mehrtens 5.

Italy 6, New Zealand 70
Test: Bologna, 28 October 1995 (att: 30,000)

Italy: M Ravazzolo; P Vaccari, S Bordon, I Francescato, F Mazzariol; M Bonomi, A Troncon; M Cuttitta (capt), C Orlandi, F Properzi, P Pedroni, M Giacheri, M Giovanelli, A Sgorlon, C Checchinato.
    Scorer – *Penalty goals:* Bonomi 2.

New Zealand: Wilson; Rush, Bunce, Little, Lomu; Culhane, Forster, Brown, Fitzpatrick (capt), Dowd, I Jones, R Brooke, Larsen, M Jones, Z Brooke.
    Scorers – *Tries:* Wilson, Rush, Little 2, Lomu 2, Z Brooke, M Jones, I Jones, Fitzpatrick. *Conversions:* Culhane 7. *Penalty goals:* Culhane 2.

Referee: G Gadjovich (Canada).

Series score: Played 3, Italy 0, New Zealand 3.

French Barbarians 19, New Zealand 34
Toulon, 1 November 1995

French Barbarians: O Toulouze; P Bernat-Salles, S Glas, D Charvet, D Venditti; D Camberabero, A Hueber; J-C Crenca, M de Rougemont, J-L Jordana, O Roumat (capt), J Eales, M Lievremont, A Carminati, X Blond.

Scorers – *Tries:* Toulouze 3. *Conversions:* Charvet, Camberabero.

New Zealand: Osborne; Rush, Ieremia, Little, Lomu; Culhane, Marshall; Loe, Hewitt, Allen, I Jones, Fromont, Blackadder, Barry, Z Brooke (capt).

Scorers – *Tries:* Rush 2, Hewitt. *Conversions:* Culhane 2. *Penalty goals:* Culhane 4. *Dropped goal:* Culhane.

Referee: D Davies (Wales).

France 22, New Zealand 15
First Test: Toulouse, 11 November 1995

France: J-L Sadourny (Colomiers); E NTamack (Toulouse), R Dourthe (Dax), T Castaignede (Toulouse), P Saint-Andre (Montferrand, capt); A Penaud (Brive), P Carbonneau (Racing Club); L Benezech (Racing Club), M de Rougemont (Toulon), C Califano (Toulouse), O Merle (Montferrand), F Pelous (Dax), P Benetton (Agen), A Carminati (Brive), A Benazzi (Agen). **Replacement:** D Berty (Toulouse) for Sadourny, 45 mins.

Scorers – *Tries:* Sadourny, Dourthe, Saint-Andre. *Conversions:* Castaignede 2. *Penalty goal:* Castaignede.

New Zealand: Wilson (Osborne 53); Rush, Bunce, Little, Lomu; Culhane, Forster; Dowd, Fitzpatrick (capt), Brown, I Jones, R Brooke, Larsen, M Jones, Z Brooke.

Scorer – *Penalty goals:* Culhane 5.

Referee: P Marshall (Australia).

Series score: Played 31, France 8, New Zealand 23.

France 12, New Zealand 37
Second Test: Paris, 18 November 1995

France: J-L Sadourny (Colomiers); E NTamack (Toulouse), R Dourthe (Dax), T Castaignede (Toulouse), P Saint-Andre (Montferrand, capt); A Penaud (Brive), P Carbonneau (Racing Club); L Benezech (Racing Club), M de Rougemont (Toulon), C Califano (Toulouse), O Merle (Montferrand), F Pelous (Dax), P Benetton (Agen), A Carminati (Brive), A Benazzi (Agen). **Replacements:** S Graou (Colomiers) for Benezech, 40 mins); M Lievremont (Perpignan) for Carminati, 70 mins.

Scorers – *Tries:* Saint-Andre 2. *Conversion:* Castaignede.

New Zealand: Osborne; Rush, Bunce, Little, Lomu; Culhane, Marshall; Dowd (Loe 75), Fitzpatrick (capt), Brown, I Jones, R Brooke, M Jones, Barry, Z Brooke.

Scorers – *Tries:* Rush, Osborne, I Jones, Lomu. *Conversion:* Culhane. *Penalty goals:* Culhane 5.

Referee: P Marshall (Australia).

Series score: Played 32, France 8, New Zealand 24.

South Africa achieve a perfect ten out of ten for a 1995 campaign which features a World Cup triumph and ten wins from ten starts. There is belatedly a measure of controversy, however, as Kobus Wiese commits an act of assault on Derwyn Jones in the opening minutes of South Africa's 40–11 defeat over Wales in Johannesburg, and then World Cup final matchwinner Joel Stransky smacks England No.8 Ben Clarke at Twickenham during the Springboks' 24–14 triumph. Neither incident is spotted by a match official but whilst Stransky escapes censure – 'I was lucky to stay on the field; I feel dreadful about the whole thing; I don't know what got into me' – Wiese is not so lucky. Cited by Welsh team manager Geoff Evans, the Transvaal lock receives a 30-day suspension and is fined £9,000. Jones, who is concussed, later suggests that the punch might have been premeditated. 'There was talk before the match that they were out to get me', says the 6ft 10in Cardiff lighthouse. But the dual controversies cannot overshadow a momentous year for the Boks, highlighted by their World Cup final victory over the previously rampaging All Blacks. Coach Kitch Christie later bows out with a proud record of 14 wins in 14 games.

South Africa 40, Wales 11
Johannesburg, 2 September 1995

Wales restore a semblance of pride after their World Cup nightmare, grabbing a third-minute lead through flanker Mark Bennett's try, yet finish with only 14 men after firebrand hooker Garin Jenkins, a half-time replacement, becomes the sixth forward to be sent off in a Test match when dismissed in injury time by French referee Joel Dume for flattening Springbok scrum-half Joost van der Westhuizen. Despite Wales' improved effort – one not helped by team manager Geoff Evans' decision to drop several players who went on holiday instead of attending a pre-tour training session – South Africa still register a record win in the fixture.

South Africa: A Joubert (Natal); J Small (Natal), H le Roux (Transvaal), J Mulder (Transvaal), J Olivier (Northern Transvaal); J Stransky (Western Province), J van der Westhuizen (Northern Transvaal); B Swart (Transvaal), J Dalton (Transvaal), M Hurter (Northern Transvaal), K Wiese (Transvaal), M Andrews (Natal), F Pienaar (Transvaal, capt), R Kruger (Northern Transvaal), G Teichmann (Natal). **Cited:** Wiese (banned 30 days, fined £9,000).
    Scorers – *Tries:* Wiese, Pienaar, Small, Teichmann, Mulder. *Conversions:* Stransky 3. *Penalty goals:* Stransky 3.

Wales: J Thomas (Llanelli, debut); I Evans (Llanelli), G Thomas (Bridgend), G Jones (Bridgend, debut), S Hill (Cardiff); N Jenkins (Pontypridd), A Moore (Cardiff); C Loader (Swansea, debut), J Humphreys (Cardiff, capt), J Davies (Neath), P Arnold (Swansea), D Jones (Cardiff), A Gibbs (Newbridge), M Bennett (Cardiff), H Taylor (Cardiff). **Replacements:** A Moore (Swansea, debut) for D Jones, 5 mins; G Jenkins (Swansea) for Gibbs, 40 mins; M Taylor (Swansea) for G Thomas, 69 mins. **Sent off:** G Jenkins, 79 mins.
    Scorers – *Try:* Bennett. *Penalty goals:* N Jenkins 2.

Series score: Played 9, South Africa 8, Wales 0, Drawn 1.

ALSO: South East Transvaal 47, Wales 6 (Witbank, 26 August 1995).

Italy (6) 21, South Africa (17) 40
Rome, 12 November 1995

Italy, recently tanned 70–6 by New Zealand, lead the world champions 21–17 in the Olympic Stadium, through tries by Carlo Orlandi and Orazio Arancio, before a degree of order is restored in the fourth quarter.

South Africa: A Joubert (Natal); J Small (Natal), H le Roux (Transvaal), J Mulder (Transvaal), C Williams (Western Province); J Stransky (Western Province), J van der Westhuizen (Northern Transvaal); A van der Linde (Western Province), J Dalton (Transvaal), T Laubscher (Western Province), K Wiese (Transvaal), M Andrews (Natal), R Kruger (Northern Transvaal), F van Heerden (Western Province), F Pienaar (Transvaal, capt).

Scorers – *Tries:* Mulder, le Roux, Pienaar, penalty try. *Conversions:* Stransky 4. *Penalty goals:* Stransky 4.

England 14, South Africa 24
Twickenham, 18 November 1995

Rudderless England are outclassed on their own patch by a Springbok side which cruises to victory without leaving second gear. Joel Stransky missed six kicks at goal and Chester Williams had a perfectly good try disallowed by Scottish whistler Jim Fleming. That was shame, as Williams, the Black Pearl, was so denied a try hat-trick. Then again, as one of the permitted two was gifted to him by Will Carling's errant pass, he will perhaps settle for the brace. It was an altogether sorry day for England's captain who, to much consternation, was stretchered off in a neck brace late on with what appeared to be a serious injury. Thankfully, the diagnosis was nothing more than concussion, requiring a mandatory three-week lay-off.

England: J Callard (Bath); D Hopley (Wasps), W Carling (Harlequins, capt), J Guscott (Bath), R Underwood (Leicester & RAF); M Catt (Bath), K Bracken (Bristol); J Leonard (Harlequins), M Regan (Bristol), V Ubogu (Bath), M Johnson (Leicester), M Bayfield (Northampton), T Rodber (Northampton & Army), A Robinson (Bath), B Clarke (Bath). Replacements: L Dallaglio (Wasps) for Rodber, 67 mins; P de Glanville (Bath) for Carling, 77 mins.

Scorers – *Try:* de Glanville. *Penalty goals:* Callard 3.

South Africa: A Joubert (Natal); J Olivier (Northern Transvaal), H le Roux (Transvaal), J Mulder (Transvaal), C Williams (Western Province); J Stransky (Western Province), J van der Westhuizen (Northern Transvaal); A van der Linde (Western Province), J Dalton (Transvaal), T Laubscher (Western Province), K Wiese (Transvaal), M Andrews (Natal), R Kruger (Northern Transvaal), F van Heerden (Western Province), F Pienaar (Transvaal, capt). *Repl:* J Small (Natal) for Olivier, 47 mins; R Straeuli (Transvaal) for Kruger, 62 mins.

Scorers – *Tries:* Williams 2, van der Westhuizen. *Penalty goals:* Stransky 3.

Referee: J Fleming (Scotland).

Series score: Played 13, England 4, South Africa 8, Drawn 1.

WESTERN SAMOA TO SCOTLAND AND ENGLAND
NOVEMBER–DECEMBER 1995: P12 W5 D1 L6 F253 A330

Western Samoa, deeply upset at having been left out of new Rupert Murdoch-sponsored scheme of things in the Southern Hemisphere, come to Britain with a point to prove. By holding Scotland to a 15–15 draw they make their point well. But sadly they have little else to shout about, as their midweek XV is knocked from pillar to post – Scottish North & Midlands (43–9), England A (55–0), English Midlands (40–19), North of England (34–8) – all winning with plenty to spare. But the Samoans, coached by Bryan Williams and led proudly by Pat Lam, regroup to give England a good enough run for their money at Twickenham, where 17 points from the boot of new cap Paul Grayson basically divides the sides.

PARTY: M Birtwhistle; L Falaniko; P Fatialofa; D Kaleopa; S Kaleta; P Lam (capt); G Latu; P Leavasa; T Leiasamaivao; S Lemamea; T Leota; D Mika; M Mika; J Paramore; B Reidy; S Vaifale; A Autagavaia; C Burnes; T Faamasino; J Filemu; G Harder; D Kellett; S Laeaga; G Leaupepe; B Lima; T Nu'ualitia; V Patu; A Telea; K Tuigamala; T Vaega. **Manager:** Rev Dr F Talapusi. **Coach:** B Williams.

Results: (1) Edinburgh Districts 22, Western Samoans 35 (Inverleith, 8 November); (2) Scotland A 9, Western Samoans 26 (Hawick, 12 November); (3) Scottish North & Midlands 43, Western Samoans 9 (Perth, 14 November); (4) Test: **Scotland 15, Western Samoa 15** (Edinburgh, 18 November); (5) Oxford University 15, Western Samoans 47 (Iffley Road, 21 November); (6) Cambridge University 22, Western Samoans 14 (Grange Road, 25 November); (7) London & SE Division 32, Western Samoans 40 (Twickenham, 29 November); (8) Midland Division 40, Western Samoans 19 (Leicester, 2 December); (9) North 34, Western Samoans 8 (Huddersfield, 5 December); (10) South & South West Division 16, Western Samoans 31 (Gloucester, 9 December); (11) England A 55, Western Samoans 0 (Gateshead, 12 December); (12) Test: **England 27, Western Samoa 9** (Twickenham, 16 December).

Scotland 15, Western Samoa 15
Edinburgh, 18 November 1995

Scotland: R Shepherd (Melrose); M Dods (Northampton), G Townsend (Northampton), G Shiel (Melrose), K Logan (Stirling County); C Chalmers (Melrose), B Redpath (Melrose); D Hilton (Bath), J Hay (Hawick), P Burnell (London Scottish), G Weir (Melrose), D Cronin (Bourges), R Wainwright (West Hartlepool, capt), I Smith (Gloucester), S Reid (Boroughmuir).

    Scorer – *Penalty goals:* Dods 5.

Western Samoa: V Patu (Vaiala); B Lima (Marist), T Vaega (Te Atatu), G Leaupepe (Te Atatu), A Telea (Petone); D Kellett (Marist), J Filemi (Wellington); M Mika (Otago Univ), T Leiasamaivao (Moataa), P Fatialofa (Marist), L Falaniko (Marist), P Leavasa (Apia), S Kaleta (Ponsonby), S Vaifale (Marist), P Lam (Marist, capt).

    Scorers – *Tries:* Leaupepe, Kaleta. *Conversion:* Kellett. *Penalty goal:* Kellett.

Referee: T Henning (South Africa).

Series score: Played 2, Scotland 1, Western Samoa 0, Drawn 1.

England A 55, Western Samoa 0
Gateshead, 12 December 1995

England A: T Stimpson (West Hartlepool); J Sleightholme (Bath), A Blyth (West Hartlepool), W Greenwood (Harlequins), J Naylor (Orrell); A King (Bristol Univ), A Gomarsall (Wasps); K Yates (Bath), P Greening (Gloucester), D Garforth (Leicester), G Archer (Bristol), R West (Gloucester), M Corry (Bristol), R Hill (Saracens), A Diprose (Saracens, capt).

    Scorers – *Tries:* Greenwood 3, Gomarsall 2, Greening, Hill, Garforth. *Conversions:* Stimpson 6. *Penalty goal:* Stimpson.

Western Samoans: A Autagavaia; T Faaiusaso, S Leaega, K Tuigamala, F Fereti; C Burnes, M Vaea; B Reidy, O Matauiau, G Latu, S Lemamea, M Birtwhistle (capt), L Taala, S Smith, M Iupeli.

Referee: K McCartney (Scotland).

England 27, Western Samoa 9

Twickenham, 16 December 1995

England: M Catt (Bath); D Hopley (Wasps), W Carling (Harlequins, capt), J Guscott (Bath), R Underwood (Leicester & RAF); P Grayson (Northampton, debut), M Dawson (Northampton, debut); G Rowntree (Leicester), M Regan (Bristol), J Leonard (Harlequins), M Johnson (Leicester), M Bayfield (Northampton), T Rodber (Northampton), L Dallaglio (Wasps), B Clarke (Bath).

Scorers – *Tries:* Dallaglio, R Underwood. *Conversion:* Grayson. *Penalty goals:* Grayson 5.

Western Samoa: V Patu (Vaiala); B Lima (Marist), T Vaega (Te Atatu), G Leaupepe (Te Atatu), A Telea (Petone); D Kellett (Marist), J Filemi (Wellington); M Mika (Otago Univ), T Leiasamaivao (Moataa), P Fatialofa (Marist), L Falaniko (Marist), P Leavasa (Apia), S Kaleta (Ponsonby), S Vaifale (Marist), P Lam (Marist, capt). **Replacement:** S Smith (Helensville) for Kaleta (26–27); S Smith for Falaniko, 73 mins.

Scorers – *Penalty goals:* Kellett 3.

Referee: I Rogers (South Africa).

Series score: Played 2, England 2, Western Samoa 0.

England wing Damian Hopley is enveloped in the South Africa defence at Twickenham during the home side's 24–14 loss.

No England, but a classy, meaningful competition just the same. English clubs were prevented by the Rugby Football Union from participating, so it was left to Ireland and Wales to carry the flag for the Home Unions. The upshot was a semi-final in Dublin between Irish Inter-Provincial champions Leinster and reigning Welsh champions Cardiff, which went to the visitors 23–14. French kingpins Toulouse prevented an all-Welsh final by demolishing Swansea 30–3 at the Stade des Sept-Deniers, and then proceeded to defeat Cardiff 21–18 in the Welsh capital. A cracking contest climaxed when home fly-half Adrian Davies landed a 45-metre penalty goal with the final kick of injury time to tie the scores up at 18–18 and send the game into extra time, only for French opposite number Christophe Deylaud to win the cup for Toulouse with a straightforward penalty goal. The only real controversy during nine weeks of competition comes from the riotous behaviour of Castres officials after their pool defeat by Swansea. President Pierre-Yves Revol twice invades the pitch to protest against the refereeing of Scotsman Chuck Muir. Apparently he was displeased with an 18–0 penalty count against his side.

FINAL

Cardiff 18, Toulouse 21 (aet)
National Stadium, Cardiff, 7.1.96 (att: 20,000)

Cardiff: M Rayer; S Ford (N Walker 98), M Hall, M Ring (J Davies 40), S Hill; A Davies, A Moore; A Lewis, J Humphreys, L Mustoe, J Wakeford, D Jones, E Lewis, O Williams, H Taylor (capt).
   Scorer – *Penalty goals:* A Davies 6.

Toulouse: S Ougier; E NTamack (capt), P Carbonneau, T Castaignede (O Carbonneau 93), D Berty (U Mola 70); C Deylaud, J Cazalbou; C Califano, P Soula, C Portolan, H Miorin, F Belot, D Lacroix (R Castel 68), H Manent; S Dispagne.
   Scorers – *Tries:* Castaignede, Cazalbou. *Conversion:* Deylaud. *Penalty goals:* Deylaud 2. *Dropped goal:* Castaignede.

Referee: D McHugh (Ireland).

SEMI-FINALS

Leinster (14) 14, Cardiff (20) 23
Lansdowne Road, Dublin, 30.12.95 (att: 7,350)

Leinster: C Clarke (Terenure); P Gavin (Old Belvedere), V Cunningham (St Mary's), K McQuilkin (Bective Rangers), C O'Shea (London Irish); A McGowan, A Rolland (both Blackrock); H Hurley (Old Wesley), S Byrne, P Wallace (both Blackrock), S Jameson (St Mary's), N Francis (Old Belvedere), C Pim (Old Wesley, capt), S Rooney (Lansdowne), V Costello (St Mary's). **Replacement:** R Hennessy (Lansdowne) for Clarke, 55 mins.
   Scorers – *Try:* Pim. *Penalty goals:* McGowan 3.

Cardiff: M Rayer; S Ford, M Hall, M Ring, S Hill; A Davies, A Moore; A Lewis, J Humphreys, L Mustoe, J Wakeford, D Jones, E Lewis, O Williams, H Taylor (capt).
   Scorers – *Tries:* Taylor, Hall. *Conversions:* Davies 2. *Penalty goal:* Davies. *Dropped goals:* Davies, Moore.

Referee: B Campsall (England).

Toulouse (13) 30, Swansea (3) 3
Les Sept-Deniers, Toulouse, 30.12.95 (att: 10,000)

Toulouse: S Ougier; E NTamack (capt), E Artiguste, T Castaignede (P Carbonneau 70), D Berty (U Mola 62); C Deylaud, J Cazalbou; C Califano (P Lasserre 66), P Soula, C Portolan, H Miorin, F Belot, D Lacroix (R Castel 56), H Manent, S Dispagne.
 Scorers – *Tries:* penalty try, Manent, Artiguste. *Conversions:* Deylaud 3. *Penalty goals:* Deylaud 3.

Swansea: R Boobyer; A Harris, D Weatherley, M Taylor, Simon Davies; A Williams, Robert Jones; C Loader, G Jenkins, K Colclough, A Moore (M Thomas 37), S Moore, A Reynolds (M Evans 28), R Appleyard, Stuart Davies (capt).
 Scorer – *Penalty goal:* Williams.

Referee: J Fleming (Scotland).

POOL A

Farul Constanta 10, Toulouse 54
Constanta, 31 October 1995 (att: 3,000)

Farul Constanta: V Brici; C Sasu, A Tinca, N Fulina (capt), E Florea; V Besarau, M Focat; C Pingert, N Lupu (A Secuiu 50), D Manole, N Branescu, N Marin (E Rujada 50), C Florea, A Girbu, T Oroian.
 Scorers – *Try:* Focat. *Conversion:* E Florea. *Penalty goal:* E Florea.

Toulouse: S Ougier; E NTamack (capt), P Carbonneau, T Castaignede (O Carbonneau 48), D Berty; C Deylaud, J Cazalbou (E Artiguste 48); C Califano, P Soula, C Portolan (P Lasserre 70), H Miorin, F Belot, J-L Cester, R Castel, S Dispagne.
 Scorers – *Tries:* NTamack 2, Berty 2, Cester, Castaignede, Ougier, penalty try. *Conversions:* Deylaud 7.

Referee: R G Davies (Wales).

Benetton Treviso 86, Farul Constanta 8
Stadio Comunale di Monigo, 7 November 1995 (att: 3,000)

Benetton Treviso: P Dotto; M Perziano (L Perziano 59), I Francescato, M Visentin, L Manteri; M Lynagh, A Troncon; G Grespan (capt), N Giuliato, G Rossi, D Scaglia, M Giacheri, S Rigo, J Gardner, C Checchinato.
 Scorers – *Tries:* Manteri 2, M Perziano 2, L Perziano 2, Dotto 2, Checchinato, Troncon, Giuliato, Gardner. *Conversions:* Lynagh 10. *Penalty goals:* Lynagh 2.

Farul Constanta: E Florea; C Sasu (V Dragomir 19), A Tinca, N Fulina (capt), D Talaba; V Besarau (D Miron 23), T Coman; C Pingert, N Lupu, D Manole (V Matasaru 74), N Branescu, T Oroian (M Plugaro 70), C Florea (D Chiriac 47), A Girbu, I Ruxanda.
 Scorers – *Try:* Talaba. *Penalty goal:* E Florea.

Referee: B Stirling (Ireland).

Toulouse 18, Benetton Treviso 9
Les Sept-Deniers, 11 December 1995 (att: 6,085)

Toulouse: S Ougier; E NTamack (capt), P Carbonneau, T Castaignede, D Berty (H Mola 77); C Deylaud, J Cazalbou; C Califano, P Soula, C Portolan, H Miorin, F Belot, D Lacroix (N Bacquey 78), H Manent, S Dispagne.
 Scorers – *Penalty goals:* Deylaud 5. *Dropped goal:* Deylaud.

Benetton Treviso: P Dotto; M Perziano, I Francescato, F Mazzariol, L Manteri; M Lynagh,

A Troncon; G Grespan (capt), M Trevisiol, G Rossi, D Scaglia, M Giacheri, S Rigo, J Gardner, C Checchinato (W Cristofoletto 8).

Scorers – *Penalty goals:* Lynagh 2. *Dropped goal:* Lynagh.

Referee: J Bacigalupo (Scotland).

POOL A TABLE

	P	W	D	L	tries	F	A	Pts
Toulouse	2	2	0	0	8	72	19	4
Benetton Treviso	2	1	0	1	12	95	26	2
Farul Constanta	2	0	0	2	2	18	140	0

POOL B

Begles-Bordeaux 14, Cardiff 14
Stade Andre-Moga, 21 November 1995 (att: 10,000)

Begles-Bordeaux: P Fauthoux; P Bernat-Salles, E Darritchon, L Lafforgue, P Tauzin; V Etcheto, G Accoceberry (capt); L Verge, S Morizot, O Sourgens, A Berthozat (S Conchy 65), C Mougeot, M Barrague (P Eyhartz 76), P Farner, J-J Alibert.
Scorers – *Try:* Bernat-Salles. *Penalty goals:* Etcheto 3.

Cardiff: M Rayer; N Walker, M Hall, M Ring, S Hill; A Davies, A Moore; A Lewis, J Humphreys, L Mustoe, J Wakeford, D Jones, E Lewis, M Bennett (C Mills 35), H Taylor (capt).
Scorers – *Try:* Bennett. *Penalty goals:* Davies 3.

Referee: D McHugh (Ireland).

Cardiff 46, Ulster 6
Arms Park, 28 November 1995 (att: 3,600)

Cardiff: M Rayer; S Ford, M Hall, S John, N Walker; A Davies, A Moore; A Lewis, J Humphreys, L Mustoe, J Wakeford, D Jones, E Lewis (Bennett 78), O Williams, H Taylor (capt).
Scorers – *Tries:* Moore 2, John, Taylor, Davies, Hall. *Conversions:* Davies 5. *Penalty goals:* Davies 2.

Ulster: J Bell; J Topping, M Field, W Harbinson (capt), J Cunningham; M McCall, N Doak; R Mackey, A Clarke, G Leslie, J Davidson, G Longwell, S Duncan, D McBride (R Wilson 78), D Erskine.
Scorer – *Penalty goals:* McCall 2.

Referee: G Borreani (France).

Ulster 16, Begles-Bordeaux 29
Belfast, 12 December 1995 (att: 2,500)

Ulster: J Bell; J Topping, W Harbinson (capt), M Field, A Park; M McCall, A Matchett; R Mackey, A Clarke, G Leslie, J Davidson, D Tweed, S Duncan, D McBride, P Johns.
Scorers – *Tries:* Matchett, McBride. *Penalty goals:* McCall 2.

Begles-Bordeaux: P Fauthoux; P Bernat-Salles, S Loubsens, E Darritchon, P Tauzin; J Berthe, X Pierre; L Dehez, S Morizot (V Chambauline 50, F Garcia 56), O Sourgens, A Berthozat (capt), C Mougeot (P Eyhartz 18), S Conchy, P Farner, J-J Alibert.
Scorers – *Tries:* Loubsens 2, Fauthoux, Bernat-Salles, Berthe. *Conversions:* Fauthoux, Berthe.

Referee: W D Bevan (Wales).

POOL B TABLE

	P	W	D	L	tries	F	A	Pts
Cardiff	2	1	1	0	7	60	20	3
Begles-Bordeaux	2	1	1	0	6	43	30	3
Ulster	2	0	0	2	2	22	75	0

POOL C

Milan 21, Leinster 24
Milan, 1 November 1995 (att: 1,200)

Milan: F Williams; R Crotti, M Platania, M Tommasi, M Cuttitta; D Dominguez, M Bonomi; S Cerioni, C Orlandi, F Properzi, F Battista-Croci, F Berni, T Ciccio, D Beretta, T Milano (capt, M Giavonello 52).

Scorers – *Tries:* Crotti, Platania. *Conversion:* Bonomi. *Penalty goals:* Dominguez 3.

Leinster: C O'Shea; P Gavin, V Cunningham, K McQuilkin, N Woods; A McGowan, A Rolland; H Hurley, S Byrne, P Wallace, M O'Kelly, B Rigney, C Pim (capt), D Oswald, V Costello.

Scorers – *Tries:* O'Shea, Woods. *Conversion:* McGowan. *Penalty goals:* McGowan 4.

Referee: F Maciello (France).

Pontypridd 31, Milan 12
Sardis Road, 22 November 1995 (att: 4,500)

Pontypridd: C Cormack; D Manley, S McIntosh, J Lewis, G Jones; N Jenkins, Paul John; N Bezani (capt), Phil John, N Eynon, G Prosser, M Rowley, M Spiller (R Collins 21), P Thomas, M Lloyd.

Scorers – *Try:* Manley. *Conversion:* Jenkins. *Penalty goals:* Jenkins 8.

Milan: F Williams; M Platania, F Gomez, M Tommasi, Marcello Cuttitta; D Dominguez, M Bonomi; Massimo Cuttitta (capt), A Marengoni, F Properzi, P Pedroni, F Berni, D Beretta, M Giovanelli, G Milano.

Scorer – *Penalty goals:* Dominguez 4.

Referee: B Campsall (England).

Leinster 23, Pontypridd 22
Dublin, 4 December 6, 1995 (att: 4,000)

Leinster: C O'Shea; P Gavin, V Cunningham, K McQuilkin, N Woods; A McGowan, A Rolland (P Hogan 32); H Hurley, S Byrne, P Wallace (A McKeen TR), B Rigney, N Francis, C Pim (capt), S Rooney, V Costello (E Millar TR).

Scorers – *Tries:* McGowan, O'Shea. *Conversions:* McGowan 2. *Penalty goals:* McGowan 3.

Pontypridd: C Cormack; D Manley, S McIntosh, J Lewis, S Enoch; L Jarvis, Paul John; N Bezani (capt), Phil John, A Metcalfe, G Prosser, M Rowley, P Thomas, R Collins, M Lloyd.

Scorers – *Try:* Cormack. *Conversion:* Jarvis. *Penalty goals:* Jarvis 5.

Referee: D Gillet (France).

POOL C TABLE

	P	W	D	L	tries	F	A	Pts
Leinster	2	2	0	0	4	47	43	4
Pontypridd	2	1	0	1	2	53	35	2
Milan	2	0	0	2	2	33	55	0

POOL D

Munster 17, Swansea 13
Limerick, 1 November 1995 (att: 6,000)

Munster: P Murray (capt); R Wallace, S McCahill, D Larkin, K Smith; P Burke, D O'Mahoney; J Fitzgerald (M Fitzgerald TR), T Kingston, P Clohessy, M Galwey, G Fulcher, E Halvey (B Toland 32), A Foley, D Corkery.
    Scorers – *Tries:* Wallace, Murray. *Conversions:* Smith 2. *Penalty goal:* Smith.

Swansea: G Thomas; A Harris (L Davies TR), R Boobyer, D Weatherley, Simon Davies; A Williams, Rhodri Jones; C Loader, G Jenkins, C Anthony, S Moore, A Moore, A Reynolds, R Appleyard, Stuart Davies (capt).
    Scorers – *Try:* Harris. *Conversion:* Williams. *Penalty goals:* Williams 2.

Referee: E Morrison (England).

Castres 19, Munster 12
Mazamet, 8 November 1995 (att: 6,500)

Castres: L Labit; C Savy, N Combes, J-M Aue, P Garrigue; F Rui, F Seguier (capt); L Toussaint (S Bristow 70), C Urios, T Lafforgue, T Bourdet, J-F Gourragne, G Pages, N Hallinger, A Cigagna.
    Scorers – *Try:* Combes. *Conversion:* Labit. *Penalty goals:* Labit 4.

Munster: P Murray (capt); R Wallace, S McCahill, D Larkin, K Smith; P Burke (B Walsh 70), D O'Mahoney; J Fitzgerald, T Kingston, P Clohessy, P O'Connor, G Fulcher, M Galwey (D Toland TR), A Foley, D Corkery (B Toland TR).
    Scorer – *Penalty goals:* Smith 4.

Referee: D R Davies (Wales).

Swansea 22, Castres 10
St Helen's, 5 December 1995 (att: 8,000)

Swansea: A Flowers; A Harris, D Weatherley, M Taylor, Simon Davies; A Williams, Robert Jones; K Colclough, G Jenkins, C Anthony, S Moore, A Moore, A Reynolds, R Appleyard, Stuart Davies (capt).
    Scorers – *Tries:* Harris, Jenkins. *Penalty goals:* Williams 4.

Castres: C Savy; J-M Aue, A Hyardet, N Combes, P Garrigue; F Rui, F Seguier (capt); S Bristow, C Urios, T Lafforgue, T Bourdet, J-F Gourragne (G Jeannard 64), G Pages, N Hallinger, A Cigagna. **Sent off:** Jeannard, 66 mins.
    Scorers – *Try:* Aue. *Conversion:* Savy. *Penalty goal:* Savy.

Referee: C B Muir (Scotland).

POOL D TABLE

	P	W	D	L	tries	F	A	Pts
Swansea	2	1	0	1	3	35	27	2
Munster	2	1	0	1	2	29	32	2
Castres	2	1	0	1	2	29	34	2

1996 FIVE NATIONS CHAMPIONSHIP
ENGLAND TRIUMPH IN SPITE OF THEMSELVES

Never, surely, has so much criticism been heaped onto a winner than on England in the course of their improbable title triumph. Their 22nd outright championship (equalling Wales' record) and 19th Triple Crown are accompanied by howls of derision by all and sundry. England are rebuilding, developing a team and strategy for future seasons, argues chief cook and bottle washer Jack Rowell. No excuse, responds seemingly the rest of humanity. In the first season, supposedly, of Rugby Union as a professional game, England manage three tries in the whole championship – the lowest figure ever achieved by winners. Ironically, they receive understanding and sympathy for losing in Paris (for the first time in eight years), yet only dog's abuse for defeating Wales at Twickenham. France blow a championship which has their name written all over it by following victory over *Les Rosbifs* with defeats in Edinburgh and, remarkably, Cardiff, against the previously winless Welsh. Scotland then spurn the chance of a Grand Slam, only their fourth ever, by losing to Dean Richards (sorry England) in a Murrayfield penalty shootout. Wales share the brownie points with the Scots for trying to play open rugby, and even Ireland get a look-in with four tries in their defeat of the Welsh. But it is their only highlight as they suffer a championship record defeat in Paris en route to the Wooden Spoon.

French forwards salute the final whistle in Paris which
brings to an end eight years of English dominance in the fixture.

Best Team Performances: Scotland beating France 19–14; France beating Ireland 45–10; Wales beating France 16–15.

Best Individual performances: Dean Richards (England) vs Scotland; Thomas Castaignede/ Stephane Glas (France) vs Ireland; Abdel Benazzi (France), Gregor Townsend/Bryan Redpath/Rob Wainwright (Scotland) and Robert Howley/Leigh Davies (Wales) vs everyone.

Players to watch: Sleightholme, Dallaglio (England); D Humphreys, Costello (Ireland); Townsend, Redpath (Scotland); Howley, L Davies (Wales); Castaignede, Glas (France).

FINAL TABLE	P	W	D	L	F(t,c,p,dg)	A(t,c,p,dg)	Pts
England (1)	4	3	0	1	79(3,2,17,3)	54(2,1,11,3)	6
Scotland (2)	4	3	0	1	60(5,1,10,1)	56(3,1,13,0)	6
France (3)	4	2	0	2	89(10,6,7,2)	57(4,2,9,2)	4
Wales (5)	4	1	0	3	62(6,4,8,0)	82(9,5,9,0)	2
Ireland (4)	4	1	0	3	65(6,4,8,1)	106(12,8,8,2)	2

England win on points difference (1995 positions given in brackets after each country).

France 15, England 12
Paris, 20 January 1996

England suffer their 100th defeat in Five Nations rugby, but their first in Paris since 1988 in an absorbing though try-less encounter at Parc des Princes. France, taking the pragmatic approach more commonly associated with *Les Rosbifs*, snatch victory with a last-minute drop goal by young centre Thomas Castaignede. England, winners of the last seven championship matches between the two sides, twice come close to scoring tries through Rory Underwood and Mike Catt inside the opening quarter, before the match develops into a shootout. Paul Grayson kicks all 12 points for England on his Five Nations debut, with Thierry Lacroix matching his tally for the home side.

France: J-L Sadourny (Colomiers); E NTamack (Toulouse), R Dourthe (Dax), T Castaignede (Toulouse), P Saint-Andre (Montferrand, capt); T Lacroix (Dax), P Carbonneau (Racing Club); M Perie (Toulon), J-M Gonzales (Bayonne), C Califano (Toulouse), O Merle (Montferrand), O Roumat (Dax), A Benazzi (Agen), L Cabannes (Racing Club), F Pelous (Dax). **Replacement:** P Bernat-Salles (Begles-Bordeaux)) for Sadourny, 55 mins. **Yellow card:** Perie.
    Scorers – *Penalty goals:* Lacroix 3. *Dropped goals:* Lacroix, Castaignede.

England: M Catt (Bath); J Sleightholme (Bath), W Carling (Harlequins, capt), J Guscott (Bath), R Underwood (Leicester & RAF); P Grayson (Northampton), M Dawson (Northampton); G Rowntree (Leicester), M Regan (Bristol), J Leonard (Harlequins), M Johnson (Leicester), M Bayfield (Northampton), S Ojomoh (Bath), L Dallaglio (Wasps), B Clarke (Bath). **Temporary replacement:** D Richards (Leicester) for Clarke (17-25).
    Scorers – *Penalty goals:* Grayson 2. *Dropped goals:* Grayson 2.

Referee: D McHugh (Ireland).

Series score: Played 73, France 26, England 40, Drawn 7.

Ireland 16, Scotland 10
Dublin, 20 January 1996

Scotland extend their unbeaten record against Ireland to nine matches when they upset the odds at Lansdowne Road. Failure to beat either Western Samoa or Italy means little, as the Scots show a greater appetite for the fight against an Irish side previously impressive in beating Fiji and America. Tries by wing Michael Dods and hooker Kevin McKenzie, to one by Irish prop Peter Clohessy, send the visitors into half-time leading 16–10. There then follows only the second scoreless Five Nations second half in 11 years. Ireland assistant coach John Mitchell identifies that 'Scotland won 98% of the 50–50 ball."

Ireland: J Staples (Harlequins, capt); R Wallace (Garryowen), J Bell (Northampton), K McQuilkin (Bective Rangers), S Geoghegan (Bath); E Elwood (Lansdowne), C Saverimutto (Sale); N Popplewell (Newcastle), T Kingston (Dolphin), P Clohessy (Young Munster), G Fulcher (Cork Constitution), N Francis (Old Belvedere), J Davidson (Dungannon), D Corkery (Cork Constitution), P Johns (Dungannon).

    Scorers – *Try:* Clohessy. *Conversion:* Elwood. *Penalty goal:* Elwood.

Scotland: R Shepherd (Melrose); C Joiner (Melrose), S Hastings (Watsonians), I Jardine (Stirling County), M Dods (Northampton); G Townsend (Northampton), B Redpath (Melrose); D Hilton (Bath), K McKenzie (Stirling County), P Wright (Boroughmuir), S Campbell (Dundee HSFP), G Weir (Melrose), R Wainwright (West Hartlepool, capt), I Smith (Gloucester), E Peters (Bath).

    Scorers – *Tries:* McKenzie, Dods. *Penalty goal:* Dods. *Dropped goal:* Townsend.

Referee: B Campsall (England).

Series score: Played 108, Ireland 45, Scotland 57, Drawn 5, Abandoned 1.

Scotland 19, France 14
Edinburgh, 3 February 1996

Scotland again upset the Five Nations applecart with a stirring victory at Murrayfield, even if France have lost on seven of their previous eight visits to Edinburgh. Star of the show on a passionate afternoon is the unheralded Michael Dods, brother of 1984 Grand Slam fullback Peter, who claims all 19 of Scotland's points, through two tries and three penalty goals, to set a new individual record for the fixture. Consolation for France, who had plainly believed the Grand Slam to be theirs after deposing England, is thin on the ground. But the second of Thierry Lacroix's two penalty goals does take him past Didier Camberabero (354) as France's all-time leading points scorer in cap matches (357).

Scotland: R Shepherd (Melrose); C Joiner (Melrose), S Hastings (Watsonians), I Jardine (Stirling County), M Dods (Northampton); G Townsend (Northampton), B Redpath (Melrose); D Hilton (Bath), K McKenzie (Stirling County), P Wright (Boroughmuir), S Campbell (Dundee HSFP), G Weir (Melrose), R Wainwright (West Hartlepool, capt), I Smith (Gloucester), E Peters (Bath).

    Scorers – *Tries:* Dods 2. *Penalty goals:* Dods 3.

France: J-L Sadourny (Colomiers); E NTamack (Toulouse), A Penaud (Brive), T Castaignede (Toulouse), P Saint-Andre (Montferrand, capt); T Lacroix (Dax), P Carbonneau (Racing Club); M Perie (Toulon), J-M Gonzales (Bayonne), C Califano (Toulouse), O Merle (Montferrand), O Roumat (Dax), A Benazzi (Agen), L Cabannes (Racing Club), F Pelous (Dax). **Temporary replacement:** S Glas (Bourgoin) for Lacroix.

    Scorers – *Try:* Benazzi. *Penalty goals:* Lacroix 2, Castaignede.

Referee: C Thomas (Wales).

Series score: Played 68, Scotland 32, France 33, Drawn 3.

England 21, Wales 15
Twickenham, 3 February 1996

Rory Underwood claims his 50th Test try (49 for England, one for Lions) and his sixth against Wales as England consign the Welsh to their fourth successive Twickenham defeat. But an incomplete England performance makes for an inglorious victory, and the new Welsh halfback combination of Robert Howley and Arwel Thomas steals the plaudits.

Thomas cheekily conjures Wales' go-ahead try for Hemi Taylor in the tenth minute, and Howley becomes the first Welsh scrum-half since Chico Hopkins 16 years previously to score a try at Twickenham on his debut. In between, Underwood and Guscott claim touchdowns – Guscott joining Cyril Lowe as England's second-to-top try-scorer on 18.

England: M Catt (Bath); J Sleightholme (Bath), W Carling (Harlequins, capt), J Guscott (Bath), R Underwood (Leicester & RAF); P Grayson (Northampton), M Dawson (Northampton); G Rowntree (Leicester), M Regan (Bristol), J Leonard (Harlequins), M Johnson (Leicester), M Bayfield (Northampton), S Ojomoh (Bath), L Dallaglio (Wasps), B Clarke (Bath). **Temporary replacement:** D Richards (Leicester) for Clarke (17–25).

Scorers – *Tries:* R Underwood, Guscott. *Conversion:* Grayson. *Penalty goals:* Grayson 3.

Wales: J Thomas (Llanelli); I Evans (Llanelli), L Davies (Neath), N Davies (Llanelli), W Proctor (Llanelli); A Thomas (Bristol), R Howley (Bridgend, debut); A Lewis (Cardiff), J Humphreys (Cardiff, capt), J Davies (Neath), G Llewellyn (Neath), D Jones (Cardiff), E Lewis (Cardiff), G Jones (Llanelli), H Taylor (Cardiff). **Replacement:** G Jenkins (Swansea) for Humphreys, 57 mins. **Temporary replacement:** S Williams (Neath) for G Jones and Lewis.

Scorers – *Tries:* Taylor, Howley. *Conversion:* A Thomas. *Penalty goal:* A Thomas.

Referee: K McCartney (Scotland).

Series score: Played 102, England 42, Wales 48, Drawn 12.

France 45, Ireland 10
Paris, 17 February 1996

France take their Murrayfield frustration out on hapless Ireland, scorching to their highest score and biggest winning-points margin in the history of their Five Nations participation. Not surprisingly, the carnage represents Ireland's heaviest-ever defeat in the tournament. To make matters considerably worse, Irish prop Peter Clohessy is adjudged guilty of stamping on Olivier Roumat's head and banned for 26 weeks as Ireland slump to their 12th successive loss to the French, and their 12th in 12 matches at Parc des Princes. The occasion stops just a fraction short of utter humiliation, however, as a last-ditch penalty try gives the Irish their first touchdown in Paris since 1980.

France: J-L Sadourny (Colomiers); E NTamack (Toulouse), O Campan (Agen), T Lacroix (Dax), P Saint-Andre (Montferrand, capt); T Castaignede (Toulouse), G Accoceberry (Begles-Bordeaux); C Califano (Toulouse), J-M Gonzales (Bayonne), F Tournaire (Narbonne), A Benazzi (Agen), O Roumat (Dax), R Castel (Toulouse), L Cabannes (Racing Club), F Pelous (Dax). **Replacements:** S Glas (Bourgoin) for Lacroix, 22 mins; M Perie (Toulon) for Califano, 50 mins; S Dispagne (Toulouse) for Roumat, 55 mins; M de Rougemont (Toulon) for Gonzales, 67 mins.

Scorers – *Tries:* NTamack 2, Castel 2, Saint-Andre, Campan, Accoceberry. *Conversions:* Castaignede 5.

Ireland: J Staples (Harlequins, capt); R Wallace (Garryowen), J Bell (Northampton), K McQuilkin (Bective Rangers), N Woods (Blackrock College); D Humphreys (London Irish, debut), N Hogan (Terenure College); N Popplewell (Newcastle), T Kingston (Dolphin), P Clohessy (Young Munster), P Johns (Dungannon), G Fulcher (Cork Constitution), J Davidson (Dungannon), D Corkery (Cork Constitution), V Costello (St Mary's College). **Replacement:** M Field (Malone) for Staples, 40 mins.

Scorers – *Try:* Penalty try. *Conversion:* Humphreys. *Penalty goal:* Humphreys.

Referee: E Morrison (England).

Series score: Played 70, France 40, Ireland 25, Drawn 5.

Wales 14, Scotland 16
Cardiff, 17 February 1996

Scotland earn themselves a tilt at the Grand Slam, for the second consecutive year, by squeezing past Wales in a desperately tight contest at the Arms Park. Wales, boasting an unchanged side for the first time in three years, watch in horror as Arwel Thomas' last ditch conversion, which would have tied the match, passes six inches wide. If Wales can point to that kick for losing a seventh consecutive championship match for the first time ever, Scotland can point with more justification to Gregor Townsend's brilliance for bringing them victory. Seven minutes from time, he dreams up and executes the try that, despite Wayne Proctor's late retaliatory score, gives the underrated Scots a third successive Five Nations win.

Wales: J Thomas (Llanelli); I Evans (Llanelli), L Davies (Neath), N Davies (Llanelli), W Proctor (Llanelli); A Thomas (Bristol), R Howley (Bridgend); A Lewis (Cardiff), J Humphreys (Cardiff, capt), J Davies (Neath), G Llewellyn (Neath), D Jones (Cardiff), E Lewis (Cardiff), G Jones (Llanelli), H Taylor (Cardiff).

    Scorers – *Try:* Proctor. *Penalty goals:* A Thomas 3.

Scotland: R Shepherd (Melrose); C Joiner (Melrose), S Hastings (Watsonians), I Jardine (Stirling County), M Dods (Northampton); G Townsend (Northampton), B Redpath (Melrose); D Hilton (Bath), K McKenzie (Stirling County), P Wright (Boroughmuir), S Campbell (Dundee HSFP), G Weir (Melrose), R Wainwright (West Hartlepool, capt), I Smith (Gloucester), E Peters (Bath). **Replacement:** K Logan (Stirling County) for Joiner, 39 mins.

    Scorers – *Try:* Townsend. *Conversion:* Dods. *Penalty goals:* Dods 3.

Referee: J Dume (France).

Series score: Played 100, Wales 54, Scotland 44, Drawn 2.

Scotland 9, England 18
Edinburgh, 2 March 1996

Scotland's Grand Slam dreams are extinguished by England for the second consecutive year courtesy of a Herculean display from recalled No.8 Dean Richards. On a day in which Scott Hastings equals brother Gavin's Scottish record by winning his 61st cap, and Rory Underwood breaks the appearance record for the fixture with his 12th appearance, Deano dominates the match and the following day's headlines. A contest widely seen as Beauty versus the Beast goes the Beast's way because Richards wraps Scotland and the ball up in his giant arms, and squeezes the living daylights out of them. Paul Grayson, playing in his first Calcutta Cup match, kicks six penalty goals for England to Michael Dods' three and Scotland are consigned to their seventh straight defeat at the hands of the 'auld enemy'.

Scotland: R Shepherd (Melrose); C Joiner (Melrose), S Hastings (Watsonians), I Jardine (Stirling County), M Dods (Northampton); G Townsend (Northampton), B Redpath (Melrose); D Hilton (Bath), K McKenzie (Stirling County), P Wright (Boroughmuir), S Campbell (Dundee HSFP), G Weir (Melrose), R Wainwright (West Hartlepool, capt), I Smith (Gloucester), E Peters (Bath).

    Scorer – *Penalty goals:* Dods 3.

England: M Catt (Bath); J Sleightholme (Bath), W Carling (Harlequins, capt), J Guscott (Bath), R Underwood (Leicester & RAF); P Grayson (Northampton), M Dawson (Northampton); G Rowntree (Leicester), M Regan (Bristol), J Leonard (Harlequins), M Johnson (Leicester), G Archer (Bristol & Army, debut), B Clarke (Bath), L Dallaglio (Wasps), D Richards (Leicester). **Replacement:** T Rodber (Northampton & Army) for Richards, 78 mins.

    Scorer – *Penalty goals:* Grayson 6.

Referee: D Bevan (Wales).

Series score: Played 113, Scotland 39, England 57, Drawn 17.

Ireland 30, Wales 17
Dublin, 2 March 1996

Pain in Paris gives way to delirium in Dublin as Ireland make the quantum leap from suffering their heaviest championship defeat to achieving their highest-ever championship score after making seven changes to the side destroyed by France. Wales, retaining the same XV in a third consecutive championship game for the first time since 1978, score two tries through the evergreen Ieuan Evans (remarkably, his first away scores in the Five Nations), but concede four to Simon Geoghegan, Niall Woods, Gabriel Fulcher and David Corkery.

Ireland: S Mason (Orrell, debut); S Geoghegan (Bath), J Bell (Northampton), M Field (Malone), N Woods (Blackrock College); D Humphreys (London Irish), N Hogan (Terenure College, capt); N Popplewell (Newcastle), A Clarke (Northampton), P Wallace (Blackrock College), G Fulcher (Cork Constitution), J Davidson (Dungannon), D Corkery (Cork Constitution), D McBride (Malone), V Costello (St Mary's College).

   Scorers – *Tries:* Geoghegan, Woods, Fulcher, Corkery. *Conversions:* Mason 2. *Penalty goals:* Mason 2.

Wales: J Thomas (Llanelli); I Evans (Llanelli), L Davies (Neath), N Davies (Llanelli), W Proctor (Llanelli); A Thomas (Bristol), R Howley (Bridgend); A Lewis (Cardiff), J Humphreys (Cardiff, capt), J Davies (Neath), G Llewellyn (Neath), D Jones (Cardiff), E Lewis (Cardiff), G Jones (Llanelli), H Taylor (Cardiff).

   Scorers – *Tries:* Evans 2. *Conversions:* A Thomas 2. *Penalty goal:* A Thomas.

Referee: D Mene (France).

Series score: Played 100, Ireland 36, Wales 58, Drawn 6.

Wales 16, France 15
Cardiff, 16 March 1996

Wales avoid their second consecutive Five Nations whitewash with a remarkable victory over the infuriatingly enigmatic French in Cardiff. The last championship match to be played at Arms Park before the pitch is swung through 90 degrees as part of a £106 million redevelopment, the game ends in emotional scenes, with Wales captain Jonathan Humphreys leading his side on a mini lap of honour. Wales, buoyed on by faxes of support from Welshmen all over the globe, take the game to the French, beaten only once in this fixture since 1982. Robert Howley caps an outstanding campaign with Wales' solitary try, and the recalled Neil Jenkins kicks the decisive penalty goal – his fourth success – seven minutes from time.

Wales: J Thomas (Llanelli); I Evans (Llanelli), L Davies (Neath), N Davies (Llanelli), G Thomas (Bridgend); N Jenkins (Pontypridd), R Howley (Bridgend); C Loader (Swansea), J Humphreys (Cardiff, capt), J Davies (Neath), G Llewellyn (Neath), D Jones (Cardiff), E Lewis (Cardiff), G Jones (Llanelli), H Taylor (Cardiff).

   Scorers – *Try:* Howley. *Conversion:* Jenkins. *Penalty goals:* Jenkins 3.

France: J-L Sadourny (Colomiers); E NTamack (Toulouse), S Glas (Bourgoin), O Campan (Agen), P Saint-Andre (Montferrand, capt); T Castaignede (Toulouse), G Accoceberry (Begles-Bordeaux); C Califano (Toulouse), J-M Gonzales (Bayonne), F Tournaire (Narbonne), A Benazzi (Agen), O Roumat (Dax), R Castel (Toulouse), L Cabannes (Racing Club), S Dispagne (Toulouse). **Replacements:** O Brouzet (Grenoble) for Dispagne, 63 mins; R Ibanez (Dax) for Castel, 76 mins.

   Scorers – *Tries:* Castaignede, NTamack. *Conversion:* Castaignede. *Penalty goal:* Castaignede.

Referee: B Stirling (Ireland).

Series score: Played 70, Wales 38, France 29, Drawn 3.

England 28, Ireland 15
Twickenham, 16 March 1996

England capitalise upon France's shock defeat in Cardiff to steal the championship title outright for the 17th time. With Paul Grayson setting a record for the fixture with 23 points, to finish his debut campaign with 64 of his country's 79 points, they also capture their 19th Triple Crown. Yet the season will be remembered by many for the fact they only manage three tries. That figure represents the lowest number in the championship and the lowest number ever by a country winning the title. Still, at least Will Carling's farewell as captain ends on a glorious note, if not for him personally. Whilst the celebrity centre is stretchered off injured in the first half, Jon Sleighholme brings the Twickenham crowd to their feet with a belting try two minutes from time.

England: M Catt (Bath); J Sleightholme (Bath), W Carling (Harlequins, capt), J Guscott (Bath), R Underwood (Leicester & RAF); P Grayson (Northampton), M Dawson (Northampton); G Rowntree (Leicester), M Regan (Bristol), J Leonard (Harlequins), M Johnson (Leicester), G Archer (Bristol & Army), B Clarke (Bath), L Dallaglio (Wasps), D Richards (Leicester). **Replacement:** P de Glanville (Bath) for Carling, 35 mins. **Temporary:** T Rodber (Northampton & Army) for Dallaglio, 29–30 mins.

Scorers – *Try:* Sleightholme. *Conversion:* Grayson. *Penalty goals:* Grayson 6. *Dropped goal:* Grayson.

Ireland: S Mason (Orrell); S Geoghegan (Bath), J Bell (Northampton), M Field (Malone), N Woods (Blackrock College); D Humphreys (London Irish), N Hogan (Terenure College, capt); N Popplewell (Newcastle), A Clarke (Northampton), P Wallace (Blackrock College), G Fulcher (Cork Constitution), J Davidson (Dungannon), D Corkery (Cork Constitution), D McBride (Malone), V Costello (St Mary's College). **Replacement:** C McCall (Bangor) for Field, 16 mins.

Scorers – *Penalty goals:* Mason 4. *Dropped goal:* Humphreys.

Referee: E Murray (Scotland).

Series score: Played 109, England 63, Ireland 38, Drawn 8.

OTHER INTERNATIONALS

United States 15, Ireland 25
Atlanta, 6 January 1996

Ireland head to America for warm-weather training, and run into a snowdrift of super-power proportions. Freezing weather and driving rain is the order of the week – what better preparation for the Five Nations Championship? Match day in Atlanta coincides with Georgia being all but washed away, but Ireland keep their heads (and above the water) to win, despite being outscored 2–1 on the try count.

USA: M Williams; V Anitoni, R Green, M Scarrenberg, M Delai; M Alexander, A Bachelet (capt); G McDonald, T Billups, J Rissone, L Gross, A Freeman, R Randell (J Walker 41), D Lyle, R Tardits.

Scorers – *Tries:* Tardits, Walker. *Conversion:* Williams. *Dropped goal:* Alexander.

Ireland: J Staples (Harlequins, capt); R Wallace (Garryowen), J Bell (Northampton), K McQuilkin (Bective Rangers, debut), S Geoghegan (Bath); E Elwood (Lansdowne),

C Saverimutto (Sale); N Popplewell (Newcastle), T Kingston (Dolphin), P Wallace (Blackrock), G Fulcher (Cork Constitution), N Francis (Old Belvedere), V Costello (St Mary's College, debut), D Corkery (Cork Constitution), P Johns (Dungannon). **Replacement:** P Burke (Cork Constitution) for Elwood, 49 mins.

    Scorers – *Try:* R Wallace. *Conversion:* Elwood. *Penalty goals:* Elwood 3, Burke 3.

Referee: G Gadjovich (Canada).

Series score: Played 2, USA 0, Ireland 2.

Wales 31, Italy 26
Cardiff, 16 January 1996 (att: 30,000)

Kevin Bowring, the new Wales coach, uses this Five Nations warm-up, against a country which deserves to be warming up for the same championship, to blood new talent. Five debutants contribute to a victory decidedly more nerve-tingling than it should have been. Wales lead 28–3 and 31–9 before almost blowing it against a side which had previously thumped Scotland's first-choice XV (masquerading as an A team, allegedly to save Murrayfield a few quid). Boy wonder Arwel Thomas impresses, as does Neath centre Leigh Davies.

Wales: J Thomas (Llanelli); I Evans (Llanelli), L Davies (Neath, debut), M Wintle (Llanelli, debut), W Proctor (Llanelli); A Thomas (Bristol, debut), A Moore (Cardiff); A Lewis (Cardiff, debut), J Humphreys (Cardiff, capt), J Davies (Neath), G Llewellyn (Neath), D Jones (Cardiff), E Lewis (Cardiff), G Jones (Llanelli, debut), H Taylor (Cardiff).

    Scorers – *Tries:* Evans 2, J Thomas. *Conversions:* A Thomas 2. *Penalty goals:* A Thomas 4.

Italy: M Ravazzolo; P Vaccari, I Francescato, T Visentin, F Roselli; D Dominguez, A Troncon; M Cuttitta (capt), C Orlandi, F Properzi, M Giacheri, P Pedroni, O Arancio, J Gardner, A Sgorlon.

    Scorers – *Tries:* Gardner, Properzi. *Conversions:* Dominguez 2. *Penalty goals:* Dominguez 4.

Referee: G Black (Ireland).

Series score: Played 2, Wales 2, Italy 0.

France 64, Romania 12
Aurillac, 20 April 1996

The traditional end-of-term jolly to allow the French to top up their old try tallies. But what the front-row union, even the Toulouse branch, will make of a hat-trick by Christian Califano, goodness only knows.

France: R Dourthe (Dax); D Venditti (Bourgoin, debut), O Campan (Agen), S Glas (Bourgoin), P Saint-Andre (Montferrand, capt); A Penaud (Brive), G Accoceberry (Begles-Bordeaux); C Califano (Toulouse), H Guiraud (Nimes, debut), F Tournaire (Narbonne), O Merle (Montferrand), H Miorin (Toulouse, debut), M Lievremont (Perpignan), C Moni (Nice, debut), T Labrousse (Brive, debut). **Replacements:** J-L Jirdana (Pau, debut) for Tournaire, 69 mins; E NTamack (Toulouse) for Venditti, 73 mins; P Carbonneau (Toulouse) for Accoceberry, 74 mins; F Pelous (Dax) for Merle, 74 mins.

    Scorers – *Tries:* Califano 3, Glas 2, Labrousse 2, Moni, Penaud, NTamack. *Conversions:* Dourthe 7.

Series score: Played 42, France 32, Romania 8, Drawn 2.

New Zealand 51, Western Samoa 10
Napier, 7 June 1996

New Zealand: C Cullen (Manawatu, debut); J Wilson (Otago), F Bunce (North Harbour), S MacLeod (Waikato, debut), J Lomu (Counties); A Mehrtens, J Marshall (both Canterbury); C Dowd, S Fitzpatrick (capt), O Brown (all Auckland), I Jones (North Harbour), R Brooke, M Jones (both Auckland), J Kronfeld (Otago), Z Brooke (Auckland).
    Scorers – Tries: Cullen 3, Wilson, Marshall, MacLeod, Brown. *Conversions:* Mehrtens 5. *Penalty goal:* Mehrtens. *Dropped goal:* Mehrtens.

Series score: Played 2, New Zealand 2, Western Samoa 0.

BENEFIT MATCHES

Ieuan Evans Testimonial: British Isles XV 68, International XV 57
Llanelli, 21 November 1995

Jonah Lomu is the star attraction as Ieuan Evans receives a reward for outstanding contribution to Welsh rugby over a long and distinguished career. A 13,000 crowd at Stradey swells Evans' estimated payday to the tune of £70,000. But is he happy? Blissfully, as it happens. By way emphasising that there is still plenty more in the tank, Evans matches Lomu's two-try haul.

British Isles XV: G Hastings (Scotland); I Evans (Wales), V Cunningham (Ireland), S Hastings (Scotland), K Logan (Scotland); C Chalmers (Scotland), R Moon (Wales); C Loader (Wales), G Jenkins (Wales), S John (Wales), P Davies (Wales), G Llewellyn (Wales), A Moore (Wales), R Appleyard (Wales), R Wainwright (Scotland). **Replacements:** R McBryde (Wales), C Quinnell (Wales).
    Scorers – Tries: Evans 2, S Hastings, Logan 2, Appleyard, G Hastings, McBryde, Quinnell. *Conversions:* G Hastings 5, S Hastings, Chalmers, Evans, Logan.

International XV: J Gallagher (New Zealand); D Charvet (France), T Lacroix (France), J Little (Australia), J Lomu (New Zealand); M Catt (England), C Saverimutto (Ireland); R Evans (Wales), S Fitzpatrick (New Zealand), A Skeggs (Queensland), M Tchadjian (Stade Francais), O Roumat (France), L Dallaglio (England), L Cabannes (France), R Straeuli (South Africa).
    Scorers – Tries: Charvet 2, Lomu 2, Gallagher, Little, Straeuli, Lacroix, Dallaglio. *Conversions:* Lacroix 5, Nash.

Referee: D Bevan (Wales).

Peace International: Ireland XV 38, Barbarians 70
Dublin, 18 May 1996

The idea is for Rugby Union to put in a good word for peace in Ireland. The vast majority of people, on both sides of the sectarian divide, do not want a return to violence. Is anyone listening? Well, 33,000 turn up at Lansdowne Road to add their voices to the plea – a number swelled further by the appearance of rugby greats Francois Pienaar, David Campese and Ben Clarke, despite injuries robbing them of their places on the park. Ireland are tanked, but this is no day for critical evaluation. Four youngsters who have lost loved ones in the conflict are presented to the teams on the pitch beforehand. Trevor Ringland, a northern Protestant, who has organised the match with Hugo MacNeill, a southern Catholic, says: 'I do not want them to live through another 27 years of trouble. Rugby in Ireland has always been a vehicle for bringing people together. The kids are our future, and we played the game today in their name."

Ireland XV: S Mason (Orrell); R Wallace (Garryowen), R Henderson (London Irish), J Bell (Northampton), J Topping (Ballymena); D Humphreys (London Irish), N Hogan (Terenure College, capt); H Hurley (Old Wesley), A Clarke (Northampton), A McKeen (Lansdowne), G Fulcher (Cork Constitution), J Davidson (Dungannon), E Halvey (Saracens), D McBride (Malone), V Costello (St Mary's College). **Replacements:** P Johns (Dungannon) for Halvey, 3 mins; M Field (Malone) for Bell, 37 mins; P Flavin (Blackrock College) for Hurley, 38 mins; P Burke (Cork Constitution) for Humphreys, 45 mins; C Saverimutto (Sale) for Hogan, 48 mins; Hogan for Henderson, 65 mins.

    Scorers – *Tries:* Costello 2, Burke, Henderson, Topping, R Wallace. *Conversions:* Mason 4.

Barbarians: J Callard (Bath & England); R Underwood (Leicester & England), P de Glanville (capt, Bath & England), P Sella (Agen & France), E Rush (North Harbour & New Zealand); S Bachop (Otago & New Zealand), J Roux (Transvaal & South Africa); G Rowntree (Leicester & England), R Cockerill (Leicester & England A), D Garforth (Leicester & England A), N Redman (Bath & England), O Brouzet (Grenoble & France), S Ojomoh (Bath & England), L Cabannes (Racing Club & France), D Richards (Leicester & England). **Replacements:** W Greenwood (Harlequins & England A) for de Glanville, 24 mins; M Brewer (Canterbury & New Zealand) for Richards, 54 mins; L Jarvis (Pontypridd) for Rush, 56 mins.

    Scorers – *Tries:* Underwood 2, Cockerill, de Glanville, Greenwood, Jarvis, Redman, Roux, Rush, Sella. *Conversions:* Callard 10.

Referee: D Bevan (Wales).

Auckland's Jonah Lomu 'fells' Natal lock Mark Andrews in the inaugural Super-12 final. Jonah was star attraction in Ieuan Evans' testimonial match.

Italy A 29, Scotland A 17
Rieti, 6 January 1996

Italy A: M Ravazzolo; P Vaccari, I Francescato, T Visentin, F Roselli; D Dominguez, A Troncon; M Dal Sie, C Orlandi, F Properzi, M Giacheri, P Pedroni (R Favaro 56), O Arancio, J Gardner, A Sgorlon (capt).

Scorers – *Tries:* Visentin, Gardner, Arancio, Vaccari. *Conversions:* Dominguez 3. *Penalty goals:* Dominguez.

Scotland A: R Shepherd (Melrose); C Joiner (Melrose), S Hastings (Watsonians), I Jardine (Stirling County), K Logan (Stirling County); G Townsend (Northampton), B Redpath (Melrose); D Hilton (Bath), K McKenzie (Stirling County), P Wright (Boroughmuir), S Campbell (Dundee HSFP), S Murray (Edinburgh Acads), S Reid (Boroughmuir), R Wainwright (West Hartlepool, capt), E Peters (Bath). **Replacement:** G Weir (Melrose) for Reid, 65 mins.

Scorers – *Try:* Redpath. *Penalty goals:* Shepherd 3, Townsend.

Referee: G Simmonds (Wales).

France A 15, England A 25
Paris, 19 January 1996

France A: O Toulouze (Grenoble); S Venditti; S Glas (both Bourgoin), C Lamaison (Bayonne), L Arbo (Perpignan); Y Delaigue (Toulon), F Galthie (Colomiers, capt); J-J Crenca (Agen), H Guiraud (Nimes), F Tournaire (Narbonne), Y Le Meur (Racing), J-P Versailles (Montferrand), L Mallier (Grenoble), C Juillet (Montferrand), P Farner (Begles-Bordeaux). **Replacement:** F Bilot (Toulouse) for Le Meur, 39 mins. **Yellow card:** Tournaire.

Scorer – *Penalty goals:* Lamaison 5.

England A: T Stimpson (West Hartlepool); D Hopley (Wasps), W Greenwood, P Mensah (both Harlequins), A Adebayo (Bath); A King (Bristol Univ), A Gomarsall (Wasps); R Hardwick (Coventry), P Greening (Gloucester), D Garforth (Leicester), G Archer (Bristol), D Sims (Gloucester), M Corry (Bristol), R Jenkins (Harlequins), A Diprose (Saracens, capt). **Yellow cards:** Archer, Greening.

Scorers – *Try:* Stimpson. *Conversion:* Stimpson. *Penalty goals:* Stimpson 5. *Dropped goal:* King.

Referee: B Smith (Ireland).

Ireland A 26, Scotland A 19
Donnybrook, 19 January 1996

Ireland A: C O'Shea (London Irish); S Mason (Orrell), J Gallagher (Blackheath), S McCahill (Sunday's Well), N Woods (Blackrock); D Humphreys (London Irish), A Rolland (Blackrock College, capt); P Flavin, S Byrne, P Wallace (all Blackrock), D Tweed (Ballymena), M O'Kelly (St Mary's), V Costello (St Mary's), E Miller (Leicester), A Foley (Shannon). **Replacement:** L Toland (Old Crescent) for Miller, 51 mins.

Scorers – *Tries:* Wallace, Mason, penalty try. *Conversion:* Mason. *Penalty goals:* Mason 3.

Scotland A: S Lang; C Glasgow (both Heriot's), G Shiel (Melrose), R Eriksson (London Scottish), J Kerr (Watsonians); S Welsh (Hawick), G Armstrong (Newcastle, capt); M Browne (Melrose), D Ellis (Currie), B Stewart (Edinburgh Acads), M Norval (Stirling County), D Cronin (Bourges), P Walton (Newcastle), J Amos (Gala), B Renwick (Hawick).

Scorers – *Tries:* Kerr, Walton. *Penalty goals:* Welsh 3.

Referee: J Pearson (England).

England A 24, New South Wales 22
Leicester, 31 January 1996

England A: T Stimpson (West Hartlepool); P Hull (Bristol), A Blyth (West Hartlepool), W Greenwood (Harlequins), A Adebayo (Bath); A King (Bristol Univ), A Healey (Orrell); R Hardwick (Coventry), R Cockerill (Leicester), D Garforth (Leicester), J Fowler (Sale), G Archer (Bristol), M Corry (Bristol), A Diprose (Saracens, capt), R Hill (Saracens).

Scorers – *Tries:* Greenwood, Blyth. *Conversion:* King. *Penalty goals:* Stimpson 2, King 2.

New South Wales: M Burke; A Murdoch, J Madz, R Tombs, D Campese; S Bowen, S Payne; R Harry (A Blades 54), M Bell, M Hartill, W Waugh, S Domoni, W Ofahengaue, D Manu, T Gavin (capt).

Scorers – *Try:* Manu. **Conversion:** Burke. **Penalty goals:** Burke 5.

Referee: D Davies (Wal).

Ireland A 25, Wales A 11
Dublin, 1 March 1996

Ireland A: C O'Shea (London Irish); R Wallace (Garryowen), R Henderson (London Irish), S McCahill (Sunday's Well), J Topping (Ballymena); E Elwood (Lansdowne), A Rolland (Blackrock College, capt); P Flavin (Blackrock College), P Cunningham (Garryowen), A McKeen (Lansdowne), M O'Kelly (St Mary's College), N Francis (Old Belvedere), A Foley (Shannon), L Toland (Old Crescent), B Walsh (London Irish).

Scorers – *Tries:* Henderson, Walsh, Foley. *Conversions:* Elwood 2. *Penalty goals:* Elwood 2.

Wales A: R Jones (Neath); S Hill (Cardiff), M Taylor (Swansea), M Wintle (Llanelli), G Evans (Llanelli); A Davies (Cardiff), P John (Pontypridd); C Loader (Swansea), R McBryde (Llanelli, capt), S John (Llanelli), M Voyle (Newport), P Jones (Llanelli), A Gibbs (Newbridge), M Williams (Pontypridd), S Davies (Swansea).

Scorers – *Try:* S Davies. *Penalty goals:* A Davies 2.

Referee: D Gillet (France).

Italy A 19, England A 22
L'Aquila, 2 March 1996

Italy: X Pertile; M Perziano, T Visentin, G Filizzola, P Donati, A Scanavacca, A Troncon (capt); A Castellani, G De Carli; D Sie Mauro, P Alessandro, D Scaglia, M Giovanelli, R Rampazzo, J Gardner.

Scorers – *Try:* Perziano. *Conversion:* Scanavacca. *Penalty goals:* Scanavacca 4.

England: P Hull (Bristol); D O'Leary, P Mensaj (both Harlequins), A Blyth (West Hartlepool), A Adebayo (Bath); A King (Bristol Univ), A Gomarsall (Wasps); K Yates (Bath), P Greening (Gloucester), R Hardwick (Coventry), J Fowler (Sale), D Sims (Gloucester), C Sheasby, R Jenkins (both Harlequins), A Diprose (Saracens, capt).
Replacement: W Greenwood (Harlequins) for Blyth.

Scorers – *Try:* Gomarsall. *Conversion:* King. *Penalty goals:* King 5.

Referee: H Rohr (Germany).

England A 56, Ireland A 26
Richmond, 15 March 1996

England A: T Stimpson (West Hartlepool); P Hull (Bristol), W Greenwood (Harlequins), N Greenstock (Wasps), A Adebayo (Bath); A King (Bristol Univ), A Gomarsall (Wasps); R Hardwick (Coventry), R Cockerill (Leicester), D Garforth (Leicester), C Murphy (West Hartlepool), D Sims (Gloucester), M Corry (Bristol), R Jenkins (Harlequins), A Diprose (Saracens, capt).

Scorers – *Tries:* Gomarsall, Adebayo, Stimpson, King, Diprose, Garforth 2. *Conversions:* King 6. *Penalty goals:* King 2. *Dropped goal:* King.

Ireland A: C O'Shea (London Irish); R Wallace (Garryowen), R Henderson (London Irish), S McCahill (Sunday's Well), J Topping (Ballymena); E Elwood (Lansdowne), A Rolland (Blackrock College, capt); P Flavin (Blackrock College), S Byrne (Blackrock Coll), A McKeen (Lansdowne), M O'Kelly (St Mary's College), N Francis (Old Belvedere), A Foley (Shannon), L Toland (Old Crescent), B Walsh (London Irish).

Scorers – *Tries:* O'Shea, Wallace 2, Francis. *Penalty goals:* Elwood 2.

Referee: G Gadjovich (Canada).

Wales A 13, France A 34
Newport, 15 March 1996

Wales A: R Jones (Neath); S Hill (Cardiff), M Taylor (Swansea), J Funnell (Neath), G Evans (Llanelli); S Connor (Abertillery), P John (Pontypridd, capt); A Lewis (Cardiff), B Williams (Neath), S John (Llanelli), M Voyle (Newport), P Arnold (Swansea), A Gibbs (Newbridge), V Davies (Cardiff), M Workman (Newport).

Scorers – *Try:* Penalty try. *Conversion:* Connor. *Penalty goals:* Connor 2.

France A: S Venditti; M Marfaing, C Paille, Y Delaigue, D Berty; L Mazas, P Carbonneau (capt); C Soulette, A Azam, J-L Jordan, H Moirin, L Bonventre, C Moni, T Loppy, T Labrousse.

Scorers – *Tries:* Delaigue, Labrousse, Venditti, Berty. *Conversions:* Mazas 4. *Penalty goals:* Mazas 2.

Referee: A Lewis (Ireland).

FIRA WORLD YOUTH CUP
ITALY: 22 MARCH – 8 APRIL

POOL ONE: France 11, Wales 20; Wales 17, Uruguay 0; France 31, Uruguay 0.

POOL TWO: Argentina 45, Russia 0; Spain 16, Russia 10; Argentina 23, Spain 3.

POOL THREE: South Africa 18, Chile 9; Scotland 17, Chile 17; South Africa 15, Scotland 18.

POOL FOUR: Italy 94, Taiwan 5; Romania 51, Taiwan 0; Italy 5, Romania 27.

SEMI-FINALS: Wales 21, Romania 17; Argentina 41, Scotland 20.

THIRD-PLACE PLAY-OFF: Romania 32, Scotland 6.

FINAL: Argentina 34, Wales 7.

WORLD CUP 1995

ARGENTINA: D Albanase (San Isidro) E; L Arbizu (Belgrano) E(1t,1c,1p),WS,It; N Bossicovich (Gimnasia y Esgrima); P Buabse (Los Tarcos); M Corral (San Isidro) E,WS, It(1t); R Crexell (Jockey Club) E(1p),WS(1t),It; D Cuesta Silva (San Isidro) E,WS,It; F del Castillo (Jockey Club); G del Castillo (Jockey Club); J L Cilley (San Isidro) WS(2c,4p), It(1t,1c,1p); F Garcia (Alumni); S Irazoqui (Palermo Bajo) E(R); E Jurado (Jockey Club) E, WS,It; R Le Fort (Tucuman); G Llanes (La Plata) E,WS,It; R Martin (San Isidro) E,WS, It(1t); F Mendez (Mendoza) E,WS,It; P Noriega (Hindu) E(1t),WS,It; A Pichot (Atletico San Isidro); S Salvat (Alumni) E*,WS*,It*; J Santamarina (Tucuman) E,WS,It; P Sporleder (Curupayti) E,WS,It; M Sugasti (Jockey Club); M Teran (Tucuman) E,WS,It; M Urbano (Buenos Aires C&RC); C Viel (Newman) E,WS,It. *Penalty tries:* 2. **Manager:** L Chaluleu. **Coach:** A Petra. **Summary:** Fourth in Pool B.

AUSTRALIA: S Bowen (NSW) R; M Burke (NSW) C,R(2c,2t),E; D Campese (NSW) SA, C,E; D Crowley (Queensland) SA,E; T Daly (NSW) C,R; J Eales (Queensland) SA,C, R(4c),E; M Foley (Queensland) C(R),R(1t); T Gavin (NSW) SA,C,R,E; G Gregan (ACT) SA,C(R),R,E; M Hartill (NSW) C; D Herbert (Queensland) SA,R; T Horan (Queensland) C,R,E; P Kearns (NSW) SA(1t),C,E; J Little (Queensland) SA,C,E; M Lynagh (Queensland) SA*(1t,1c,2p),C*(1t,3c,2p),E*(1c,5p); R McCall (Queensland) SA,R*,E; E McKenzie (NSW) SA,C(R),R,E; D Manu (NSW) R(TR); W Ofahengaue (NSW) SA,C,E; M Pini (Queensland) SA,R(TR); J Roff (ACT) C(1t),R(2t); P Slattery (Queensland) C, R(R); D Smith (Queensland) SA,R(1t),E(1t); I Tabua (Queensland) C(1t),R; W Waugh (NSW) C; D Wilson (Queensland) SA,R(1t),E. **Manager:** P Falk. **Coach:** R Dwyer. **Summary:** Runners-up in Pool A. **Quarter-final:** lost England 22–25.

CANADA: R Bice (Vancouver); M Cardinal (James Bay) R,SA; A Charron (Ottawa Irish) R(1t),A(1t),SA; G Ennis (Kats) R,A(R),SA; E Evans (UBCOB) R,A,SA; I Gordon (James Bay) R,SA; J Graf (UBCOB) R,A,SA; S Gray (Kats) R,A,SA; J Hutchinson (UBCOB) A, SA(R); M James (Burnaby Lake) R,A; P Leblanc (Kats); D Lougheed (Toronto Welsh) R, A,SA; S Lytton (Meraloma); G MacKinnon (Brittania Lions) A,SA; C McKenzie (UBCOB) R(1t),SA; C Michaluk (Rowing Club) SA(R); G Rees (Oak Bay Castaways) R*(2c,4p,1dg), A*(2p),SA*(off); B Ross (James Bay); G Rowlands (Velox Valhallians) A; R Snow (Dogs) R,A,SA(off); W Stanley (UBC) R,A,SA; C Stewart (Western Province) R,A,SA; S Stewart (UBCOB) R,A,SA(cited); K Svoboda (Ajax Wanderers) A; R Toews (Meraloma); A Tynan (UBC). **Manager:** R Skett. **Coach:** I Birtwell. **Summary:** Third in Pool A.

COTE D'IVOIRE: B Aka (Burotic) F; E Angoran (Rodez) S,F(R),T; G Bado (Cognac) S, T; E Bley (ASPAA) S,F(R),T; P Bouazo (Burotic) S,F(R); M Brito (Biscarosse) S(R),F,T; A Camara (ASPAA) S(R),F(1t),T; F Dago (ASPAA); A Dali (Clamart) S*,T(R:2p); T Djehi (Millau) S,F,T; F Dupont (Nimes) S,F,T; J-P Ezoua (ASPAA) F; A Kone (Soustons) S,F(R),T; S Kone (Burotic); T Kouame (ASPAA) T(R); V Kouassi (Burotic) S,F(1c,2p),T; I Lassissi (Burotic) S,F,T; L Niakou (Niort) S,F,T; L N'Gbala (Cahors) S; A Niamien (Bouake) F; A Okou (Poitiers) S(R),F,T(1t); P Pere (ACBB Paris) S,F,T; D Quansah (ASPAA) T(R); D Sanoko (Biarritz) S,F,T(R); J Sathicq (CASG) S,F*,T*; A Soulama (Burotic) F(1t),T. **Manager:** P Cassagnet. **Coach:** C-A Ezoua. **Summary:** Fourth in Pool D.

ENGLAND: R Andrew (Wasps) Arg(6p,2dg),It(1c,5p),A(1c,5p,1dg),NZ(3c,1p),F(3p); N Back (Leicester) Arg(R),It,WS(1t); M Bayfield (Northampton) Arg,It,A,NZ,F; K Bracken (Bristol) It,WS(R); J Callard (Bath) WS(3c,5p); W Carling (Harlequins) Arg*, WS*,A*,NZ*(2t),F*; M Catt (Bath) Arg,It,WS,A,NZ,F; B Clarke (Bath) Arg,It,A,NZ,F; G Dawe (Bath) WS; P de Glanville (Bath) It,WS; J Guscott (Bath) Arg,It,A,NZ,F; D Hopley (Wasps) WS(R); I Hunter (Northampton) WS,F; M Johnson (Leicester) Arg,It,WSA,NZ,F; J Leonard (Harlequins) Arg,It,A,NZ,F; J Mallett (Bath) WS(R); B Moore (Harlequins) Arg,It,A,NZ,F; D Morris (Orrell) Arg,WS,A,NZ,F; S Ojomoh (Bath) Arg,WS,A(TR),F; D Richards (Leicester) WS,A,NZ; T Rodber (Northampton) Arg,It,WS(R),A,NZ,F; G Rowntree (Leicester) It,WS; V Ubogu (Bath) Arg,WS,A,NZ,F; R Underwood (Leicester) Arg,It(1t),WS(2t),A,NZ(2t),F; T Underwood (Leicester) Arg,It(1t),A(1t),NZ; R West (Gloucester) WS. *Penalty try:* 1. **Manager/Coach:** J Rowell. **Summary:** Fourth. Winners Pool B. **Quarter-final:** beat Australia 25–22. **Semi-final:** lost New Zealand 29–45. **Play-off:** lost France 9–19.

FRANCE: G Accoceberry (Dax) IC(1t),S; L Armary (Lourdes) T,I,SA; A Benazzi (Agen) T,IC(1t),S,I,SA,E; P Benetton (Agen) T,IC(R),S; L Benezech (Racing Club) IC,S,E; O Brouzet (Grenoble) T,IC,E(TR); L Cabannes (Racing Club) T(R),IC,S,I,SA,E; C Califano (Toulouse) IC,S,I,SA,E; M Cecillon (Toulouse) T,S(R),I,SA; A Cigagna (Toulouse) E; A Costes (Montferrand) IC(1t); Y Delaigue (Toulon) T(1dg),IC; M de Rougemont (Toulon) IC; C Deylaud (Toulouse) IC(R),S,I,SA; P Gallart (Beziers) T; F Galthie (Colomiers) SA,E; J-M Gonzales (Bayonne) T,S,I,SA,E; A Hueber (Toulon) T(1t),S(R),I; T Lacroix (Dax) T(2t,3c,3p),IC(2t,4c,2p),S(1c,5p),I(1c,8p),SA(5p),E(3p); O Merle (Grenoble) T,S,I,SA,E; F Mesnel (Racing Club) IC,E; E N'Tamack (Toulouse) T,S(1t),I(1t),SA,E(1t); O Roumat (Dax) IC,S,I,SA,E(1t); J-L Sadourny (Colomiers) T, S,I,SA,E; P Saint-Andre (Montferrand) T*(1t),IC*(1t),S*,I*(1t),SA,E; P Sella (Agen) T,S,I,SA,E; W Techoueyres (Bordeaux University) IC(1t); S Viars (Brive) IC(1t). **Manager:** G Laporte. **Coach:** P Berbizier. **Summary:** Third. Winners Pool D. **Quarter-final:** beat Ireland 36–12. **Semi-finals:** lost South Africa 15–19. **Play-off:** beat England 19–9.

IRELAND: J Bell (Ballymena) NZ,W,F; M Bradley (Cork Constitution) NZ; P Burke (Cork Constitution) J(6c,1p); S Byrne (Blackrock College); D Corkery (Cork Constitution) NZ(1t),J(1t),W,F; P Danaher (Garryowen); E Elwood (Lansdowne) NZ(2c),W(3c,1p), F(4p); M Field (Malone) NZ(R),J; A Foley (Shannon)J(TR); N Francis (Old Belvedere) NZ,J(1t),W,F; G Fulcher (Cork Constitution) J,W,F; S Geoghegan (Bath) NZ,J(1t),W,F; G Halpin (London Irish) NZ(1t),W,F; E Halvey (Shannon) J(1t),W(TR:1t),F(R); N Hogan (Terenure College) J(1t),W,F; H Hurley (Old Wesley); P Johns (Dungannon) NZ,J,W,F; T Kingston (Dolphin) NZ*,J(R),W*,F*; D McBride (Malone) NZ(1t),W(1t),F; B Mullin (Blackrock College) NZ,J,W,F; D O'Mahony (Blackrock College) F; C O'Shea (Lansdowne) J,W,F; N Popplewell (Wasps) NZ,J*,W,F; J Staples (Harlequins) NZ; D Tweed (Ballymena) J; P Wallace (Blackrock College) J; R Wallace (Garryowen) NZ,J,W; K Wood (Garryowen) J. *Penalty tries:* 2. **Manager:** N Murphy. **Coach:** G Murphy. **Summary:** Runners-up in Pool C. **Quarter-final:** lost South Africa 12–36.

ITALY: O Arancio (Amatori Catania) WS,E,Arg; M Bonomi (Milan) WS; S Bordon (Ciabatta Rovigo) E,Arg; M Capuzzoni (Milan); A Castellani (L'Aquila); C Checchinato (Ciabatta Rovigo) WS; Massimo Cuttitta (Milan) WS*,E*(1t),Arg*; Marcello Cuttitta (Milan) WS(1t); M Dal Sie (Lafert San Dona); D Dominguez (Milan) WS(1c,1p,1dg), E(2c,2p),Arg(1t,2c,4p); R Favaro (Benetton Treviso) WS; I Francescato (Benetton Treviso) WS,E,Arg; J Gardner (MDP Roma) WS,E,Arg; M Gerosa (Piacenza) E,Arg(1t); M Giacheri (Benetton Treviso) E,Arg; F Mazzariol (Benetton Treviso); C Orlandi (Lyons Piacenza) WS,E,Arg; P Pedroni (Milan) WS,E,Arg; M Platania (Milan); F Properzi-Curti (Milan) WS,E,Arg; M Ravazzolo (Fly Flot Calvisano) WS; A Sgorlon (Lafert San Dona) E,Arg;

M Trevisiol (Benetton Treviso); L Troiani (L'Aquila) E,Arg; A Troncon (Milan) WS,E,Arg; P Vaccari (Milan) WS(1t),E(1t),Arg(1t). **Manager:** G Dondi. **Coach:** G Coste. **Summary:** Third in Pool B.

JAPAN: T Akatsuka (Meiji University) NZ(R); B Ferguson (Hino Motor) W,I,NZ; K Hamabe (Kinki Nippon Railway); T Haneda (World); S Hirao (Kobe Steel) W,I(1t); K Hirose (Kyoto Sangyo University) NZ; E Hirotsu (Kobe Steel); M Horikoshi (Kobe Steel) W,I; K Imazumi (Suntory); K Izawa (Daito Bunka University) I(R:1t),NZ; H Kajihara (Katsunuma) W,I,NZ; M Kunda (Toshiba Fuchu) W*,I*,NZ*; Sione Latu (Daito Bunka University) W,I; Sinali Latu (Sanyo Electric) W,I(1t),NZ; T Masuho (Kobe Steel) W; T Matsuda (Toshiba Fuchu) W,I,NZ; K Matsuo (World) W,I,NZ; Y Motoki (Kobe Steel) W,I,NZ; W Murata (Toshiba Fuchu) NZ; O Ota (NEC) W,I,NZ; L Oto (Daito Bunka University) W(2t),I,NZ; Y Sakuraba (Nippon Steel Kamaishi) W,I,NZ; K Takahashi (Toyota) W,NZ; M Takura (Mitsubishi Motor Co) I(1t); A Yoshida (Kobe Steel) W,I,NZ; Y Yoshida (Isetan) I(4c),NZ. **Manager:** Z Shirai. **Coach:** O Koyabu. **Summary:** Fourth in Pool C.

NEW ZEALAND: G Bachop (Canterbury) I,W,S,E(1t),SA; M Brewer (Canterbury) I,W, E,SA; R Brooke (Auckland) J(2t),S,E,SA; Z Brooke (Auckland) J,S,E(1dg),SA; O Brown (Auckland) I,W,S,E,SA; F Bunce (North Harbour) I(1t),W,S(1t),E,SA; S Culhane (Southland) J(1t,20c); C Dowd (Auckland) I,W,J(1t),E,SA; M Ellis (Otago) I(R),W(1t),J(6t),S, SA(R); S Fitzpatrick (Auckland) I*,W*,S*(1t),E*,SA*; P Henderson (Southland) J*(1t); N Hewitt (Southland) I(TR),J; A Ieremia (Wellington) J(1t); I Jones (North Harbour) I,W,S,E, SA; J Joseph (Otago) I,W,J(R),S,SA(R); J Kronfeld (Otago) I(1t),W(1t),S,E(1t),SA; B Larsen (North Harbour) I,W,J,E(R); R Loe (Canterbury) J(1t),S,SA(R); J Lomu (Counties) I(2t),W, S(1t),E(4t),SA; W Little (North Harbour) I,W(1t),S(2t),E,SA; A Mehrtens (Canterbury) I(3c,4p),W(2c,4p,1dg),S(1t,6c,2p),E(3c,1p,1dg),SA(3p,1dg); G Osborne (North Harbour) I(1t),W,J(2t),E,SA; E Rush (North Harbour) W(R),J(3t); K Schuler (North Harbour) I(R),J; A Strachan (North Harbour) J,SA(TR); J Wilson (Otago) I,J(3t),S,E,SA. **Manager:** E Kirton. **Coach:** L Mains. **Summary:** Runners-up. Winners Pool C. **Quarter-final:** beat Scotland 48–30. **Semi-final:** beat England 45–29. **Final:** lost South Africa 12–15 (aet).

ROMANIA: V Brici (Farul) SA,A; T Brinza (U.Cluj) SA*,A*; S Ciorascu (Auch) C*,SA,A; C Cojocariu (Bayonne) C,SA,A; L Costea (Steaua) T,F,NZ; C Draguceanu (Steaua); V Flutur (U.Cluj) C(R),SA,A; R Fugigi (CSM Foresta Sibiu); A Gealapu (Steaua) C,SA,A; R Gontineac (U.Cluj) C,SA,A; A Guranescu (Dinamo) SA(1t),A; I Ivanciuc (Suceava) C(R), SA(1p),A(1dg); G Leonte (Vienne) C,SA,A; V Lucaci (Remin Baia Mare); A Lungu (Castres) A(R); D Neaga (Dinamo) C; I Negreci (CFR Constanta) C,SA,A; N Nichitean (U.Cluj) C(1p); D Niculae (Steaua); T Oroian (Steaua) C; N Racean (U.Cluj) C,SA,A; I Rotaru (Dinamo) C; O Slusariuc (Dinamo) C; G Solomie (Timisoara) C,SA,A; G Vlad (Dinamo) C,SA,A; V Tufa (Dinamo) SA(R),A(R). **Manager:** T Radulescu. **Coach:** M Paraschiv. **Summary:** Fourth in Pool A.

SCOTLAND: P Burnell (London Scottish) IC(1t),T; S Campbell (Dundee HSFP) IC,NZ(R); C Chalmers (Melrose) IC(1t),T,F,NZ; D Cronin (Bourges) T,F,NZ; C Glasgow (Heriot's FP); G Hastings (Watsonians) IC(4t,9c,2p),T(1t,1c,8p),F(1c,4p),NZ(3c,3p); S Hastings (Watsonians) T(1t),F,NZ(1t); D Hilton (Bath) T,F,NZ; I Jardine (Stirling County) T,F(R),NZ(R); C Joiner (Melrose) IC,T,F,NZ; K Logan (Stirling County) IC(2t), T,F,NZ; J Manson (Dundee HSFP); K McKenzie (Stirling County) IC; K Milne (Heriot's FP) T,F,NZ; I Morrison (London Scottish) T,F,NZ; D Patterson (West Hartlepool) T; E Peters (Bath) T(1t),F,NZ; B Redpath (Melrose) IC,F,NZ; J Richardson (Edinburgh Academicals); G Shiel (Melrose) IC(1t),F,NZ; I Smith (Gloucester) IC; T Stanger (Hawick) IC(1t); R Wainwright (West Hartlepool) IC,T,F(1t),NZ; P Walton (Northampton) IC(2t); G Weir (Melrose) IC,T,F,NZ(2t); P Wright (Boroughmuir) IC(1t),T,F,NZ. **Manager:** D Paterson. **Coach:** D Morgan. **Summary:** Runners-up in Pool D. **Quarter-final:** lost New Zealand 30–48.

SOUTH AFRICA: M Andrews (Natal) A,WS(1t),F,NZ; R Brink (Western Province) R,C; J Dalton (Transvaal) A,C(off); N Drotske (OFS) WS(R); P du Randt (OFS) A,WS,F,NZ; P Hendriks (Transvaal) A(1t),R,C; M Hurter (Northern Transvaal) R,C; G Johnson (Transvaal) R(1c,3p),C,WS(3c,2p); A Joubert (Natal) A,C,WS,F,NZ; R Kruger (Northern Transvaal) A,R,WS,F(1t),NZ; H le Roux (Transvaal) A,R,C(R),WS,F,NZ; J Mulder (Transvaal) A,WS,F,NZ; K Otto (Northern Transvaal) A(R),R,C(R),WS(R); G Pagel (Western Province) R,C,NZ(R); F Pienaar (Transvaal) A*,C*,WS*,F*,NZ*; A Richter (Northern Transvaal) R*(2t),C(2t),WS(R); C Rossouw (Transvaal) R,WS(1t),F,NZ;J Roux (Transvaal) R,C,F(R); C Schultz (Transvaal) R,C,WS; J Small (Natal) A,R,F,NZ; R Straeuli (Transvaal) A,WS,NZ(R); J Stransky (Western Province) A(1t,1c,4p,1dg),R(TR), C(2c,2p),F(1c,4p),NZ(3p,2dg); H Strydom (Transvaal) A,C,F,NZ; B Swart (Transvaal) A,WS,F,NZ; J van der Westhuizen (Northern Transvaal) A,C(R),WS,F,NZ; K Wiese (Transvaal) R,C,WS,F,NZ; C Williams (Western Province) WS(4t),F,NZ; B Venter (OFS) R,C,WS(R),NZ(R). **Manager:** M du Plessis. **Coach:** K Christie. **Summary:** Champions. Winners Pool A. **Quarter-final:** beat Western Samoa 42–14. **Semi-final:** beat France 19–15. **Final:** beat New Zealand 15–12 (aet).

TONGA: I Afeaki (Wellington) F(R),S,IC; F Fakaongo IC(R); S Fe'ao (Queensland) F,S; I Fenukitau (Queenbeyan & ACT) F,S(1t); T Fukofuka (Grammar OB) F,S,IC; T 'Isitolo (Kolofo'ou) IC(R); P Latu (Vaheloto) F,S,IC; P Latukefu (Canberra Royals & ACT) S,IC(1t); W Lose (North Harbour) F,S,IC; T Lutua (Police RFC) S(R),IC(R); A Mafi (Queenbeyan); F Mafi (Queenbeyan & ACT) F,IC; S Mafile'o IC; F Mahoni (Fasi/ Ma'ufanga) F(off); F Masila (Kolomotu'a) F(R); M 'Otai (Kia-Toa) F*,S*,IC*(1t); E Talakai (Auckland) IC; A Taufa (Wellington Harlequins) F,S; N Tufui (Kolomotu'a) S(R),IC; S Tu'ipuloto (Manly & NSW) F(1c,1p),S,IC(1t,3c,1p); T Va'enuku (Police RFC) F(1t),S, IC; U Va'enuku (Toloa OB) F,S,IC; E Vunipola (Toa-Ko-Ma'afu) F,S,IC; F Vunipola (Toa-Ko-Ma'afu) F(R),S,IC; M Vunipola (Toa-Ko-Ma'afu) F,S. *Penalty try:* 1. **Manager:** H Mailefihi. **Coach:** S Taumoepeau. **Summary:** Third in Pool D.

WALES: M Bennett (Cardiff) NZ; A Clement (Swansea) J,NZ,I; A Davies (Cardiff) J, NZ(1dg); J Davies (Neath) J,NZ,I; S Davies (Swansea) J,I; D Evans (Treorchy) J(R); I Evans (Llanelli) J(2t),NZ,I; R Evans (Llanelli) NZ,I(R); S Ford (Cardiff); M Griffiths (Cardiff) J(1t),I; M Hall (Cardiff) J*,NZ*,I*; J Humphreys (Cardiff) NZ,I(1t); G Jenkins (Swansea) J; N Jenkins (Pontypridd) J(5c,4p),NZ(2p,1dg),I(2c,2p); S John (Llanelli); D Jones (Cardiff) J,NZ,I; R Jones (Swansea) NZ,I; E Lewis (Cardiff) J,I; G Llewellyn (Neath) J,NZ, I; A Moore (Cardiff) J(1t); W Proctor (Llanelli) NZ; G Prosser (Pontypridd) NZ; S Roy (Cardiff) J(R); H Taylor (Cardiff) J,NZ,I(R); G Thomas (Bridgend) J(3t),NZ,I; J Thomas (Cardiff). **Manager:** G Evans. **Coach:** A Evans. **Summary:** Third in Pool C.

WESTERN SAMOA: T Fa'amasino It,Arg,E(2c,1p),SA(2c); L Falaniko (Marist) It,Arg, E,SA; P Fatialofa (Manurewa) It,E(R),SA(R); G Harder It(1t),Arg(1t),SA; M Iupeli (Marist) E(R); S Kaleta (Suburbs); D Kellett (Counties) It(1t,3c,2p),Arg(1c,5p); P Lam (Auckland/Marist) Arg*(1t),E*,SA*; G Latu (Vaimoso) Arg,E,SA; L Leaupepe (Papakura & Counties) Arg(R:1t),E; P Leavasa (Apia) It(R),Arg,E; T Leiasamaivao (Moataa) It,Arg, E,SA; B Lima (Marist) It(3t),Arg,E,SA; S Lemanea (SCOPA) E(R),SA; M Mika (Otago) It, Arg,E,SA; T Nu'uali'itia (Auckland) It,Arg,E,SA(1t); J Paramore (Manurewa) It,Arg,SA; E Puleitu E; B Reidy (Marist) SA(R); F Sini (Marist) A(R),E(R:2t),SA; S Tatupu (Ponsonby & Auckland) It(1t),Arg,E,SA(1t); F Tuilagi (Marist) E(R),SA(R); M Umaga (Wellington) It,Arg,E(1t),SA; T Vaega (Moataa) It,Arg,E,SA; S Vaifale (Marist) It,SA(R); V Vitale (Vaiala) Arg(R); D Williams (Colomiers) It,E. **Manager:** L T Simi. **Coach:** S P Schuster. **Summary:** Runners-up in Pool B. **Quarter-finals:** lost South Africa 14–42.

FINAL

South Africa (6) 15, New Zealand (6) 12
(aet. 12-12 after 80 minutes) Johannesburg, 24 June 1995

South Africa: Joubert; Small (Venter 98), Mulder, le Roux, Williams; Stransky, van der Westhuizen; du Randt, Rossouw, Swart (Pagel 69), Wiese, Strydom, Pienaar (capt), Kruger, Andrews (Straeuli 90).
 Scorer – *Penalty goals:* Stransky 3. *Dropped goals:* Stransky 2.

New Zealand: Osborne; Wilson (Ellis 56), Bunce, Little, Lomu; Mehrtens, Bachop (Strachan TR, 66-71); Dowd (Loe 83), Fitzpatrick (capt), Brown, Jones, R Brooke, Brewer (Joseph 40), Kronfeld, Z Brooke.
 Scorer – *Penalty goals:* Mehrtens 2. *Dropped goal:* Mehrtens.

Referee: E Morrison (England).

THIRD-PLACE PLAY-OFF

France (3) 19, England (3) 9
Pretoria, 22 June 1995

France: Sadourny; NTamack, Sella, Lacroix, Saint-Andre (capt); Mesnel, Galthie; Califano, Gonzales, Benezech, Merle, Roumat, Benazzi, Cabannes, Cigagna.
 Scorers – *Tries:* Roumat, NTamack. *Penalty goals:* Lacroix 3.

England: Catt; Hunter, Carling (capt), Guscott, R Underwood; Andrew, Morris; Leonard, Moore, Ubogu, Johnson, Bayfield, Rodber, Clarke, Ojomoh.
 Scorer – *Penalty goals:* Andrew 3.

Referee: D Bishop (New Zealand).

Ilie Tabua models Australia's alternative kit during the World Cup.

France (6) 15, South Africa (10) 19
Durban, 17 June 1995

France: Sadourny; NTamack, Sella, Lacroix, Saint-Andre (capt); Deylaud, Galthie; Armary, Gonzales, Califano, Merle, Roumat, Benazzi, Cabannes, Cecillon.
  Scorer – *Penalty goals:* Lacroix 5.

South Africa: Joubert; Small, Mulder, le Roux, Williams; Stransky, van der Westhuizen (Roux 51); du Randt, Rossouw, Swart, Wiese, Strydom, Pienaar (capt), Kruger, Andrews.
  Scorers – *Try:* Kruger. *Conversion:* Stransky. *Penalty goals:* Stransky 4.

Referee: D Bevan (Wales).

New Zealand (25) 45, England (3) 29
Cape Town, 18 June 1995

New Zealand: Osborne; Wilson, Bunce, Little, Lomu; Mehrtens, Bachop; Dowd, Fitzpatrick (capt), Brown, Jones, R Brooke, Brewer, Kronfeld, Z Brooke (Larsen 63).
  Scorers – *Tries:* Lomu 4, Kronfeld, Bachop. *Conversions:* Mehrtens 3. *Penalty goal:* Mehrtens. *Dropped goals:* Z Brooke, Mehrtens.

England: Catt; T Underwood, Carling (capt), Guscott, R Underwood; Andrew, Morris; Leonard, Moore, Ubogu, Johnson, Bayfield, Rodber, Clarke, Richards.
  Scorers – *Tries:* R Underwood 2, Carling 2. *Conversions:* Andrew 3. *Penalty goal:* Andrew.

Referee: S Hilditch (Ireland).

France (12) 36, Ireland (12) 12
Durban, 10 June 1995

France: Sadourny; NTamack, Sella, Lacroix, Saint-Andre (capt); Deylaud, Hueber; Armary, Gonzales, Califano, Merle, Roumat, Benazzi, Cabannes, Cecillon.
  Scorers – *Tries:* Saint-Andre, NTamack. *Conversion:* Lacroix. *Penalty goals:* Lacroix 8.

Ireland: O'Shea; D O'Mahony, Mullin, Bell, Geoghegan; Elwood, Hogan; Popplewell, Kingston (capt), Halpin, Fulcher (Halvey 60), Francis, Corkery, McBride, Johns.
  Scorer – *Penalty goals:* Elwood 4.

Referee: E Morrison (England).

South Africa (23) 42, Western Samoa (0) 14
Johannesburg, 10 June 1995

South Africa: Joubert (Venter 19); Johnson, Scholtz, Mulder, Williams; le Roux, van der Westhuizen; du Randt, Rossouw, Swart, Wiese (Drotske 76), Andrews (Otto 70), Pienaar (capt), Kruger (Richter 48), Straeuli.
  Scorers – *Tries:* Williams 4, Rossouw, Andrews. *Conversions:* Johnson 3. *Penalty goal:* Johnson 2.

Western Samoa: Umaga; Lima, Vaega, Fa'amasino, Harder (Tuilagi 40); Sini, Nu'uali'itia; Mika (Reidy 74), Leiasamaivao, Latu (Fatialofa 64), Lemanea, Falaniko, Tatupu, Paramore (Vaifale 71), Lam (capt). *Cited:* Umaga (90-day ban).
  Scorers – *Tries:* Nu'uali'itia, Tatupu. *Conversions:* Fa'amasino 2.

Referee: J Fleming (Scotland).

England (13) 25, Australia (6) 22
Cape Town, 11 June 1995

England: Catt; T Underwood, Carling (capt), Guscott, R Underwood; Andrew, Morris; Leonard, Moore, Ubogu, Johnson, Bayfield, Rodber, Clarke, Richards (Ojomoh TR).

    Scorers – *Try:* T Underwood. *Conversion:* Andrew. *Penalty goals:* Andrew 5. *Dropped goal:* Andrew.

Australia: Burke; Smith, Little, Horan, Campese; Lynagh (capt), Gregan; Crowley, Kearns, McKenzie, McCall, Eales, Ofahengaue, Wilson, Gavin.

    Scorers – *Try:* Smith. *Conversion:* Lynagh. *Penalty goals:* Lynagh 5.

Referee: D Bishop (New Zealand).

New Zealand (17) 48, Scotland (9) 30
Pretoria, 11 June 1995

New Zealand: Wilson; Ellis, Bunce, Little, Lomu; Mehrtens, Bachop; Loe, Fitzpatrick (capt), Brown, Jones, R Brooke, Joseph, Kronfeld, Z Brooke.

    Scorers – *Tries:* Little 2, Lomu, Mehrtens, Bunce, Fitzpatrick. *Conversions:* Mehrtens 6. *Penalty goals:* Mehrtens 2.

Scotland: G Hastings (capt); Joiner, S Hastings, Shiel, Logan; Chalmers (Jardine 40), Redpath; Hilton, Milne, Wright, Cronin (Campbell 62), Weir, Wainwright, Morrison, Peters.

    Scorers – *Tries:* Weir 2, S Hastings. *Conversions:* G Hastings 3. *Penalty goals:* G Hastings 3.

Referee: D Bevan (Wales).

POOL RESULTS

POOL A
Australia 18, South Africa 27 – Canada (11) 34, Romania (3) 3 – South Africa (8) 21, Romania (0) 8 – Australia (20) 27, Canada (6) 11 – Australia (14) 42, Romania (3) 3 – Canada 0, South Africa (17) 20

POOL B
Western Samoa (12) 42, Italy (11) 18 – England (12) 24, Argentina (0) 18 – Western Samoa (10) 32, Argentina (16) 26 – England (16) 27, Italy (10) 20 – Argentina (12) 25, Italy (12) 31 – England (21) 44, Western Samoa (0) 22

POOL C
Wales (34) 57, Japan (0) 10 – New Zealand (20) 43, Ireland (12) 19 – Ireland (19) 50, Japan (14) 28 – New Zealand (20) 34, Wales (6) 9 – New Zealand (84) 145, Japan (3) 17 – Ireland (14) 24, Wales (6) 23

POOL D
Scotland (34) 89, Cote d'Ivoire 0 – France (6) 38, Tonga (0) 10 – France (28) 54, Cote d'Ivoire (3) 18 – Scotland (18) 41, Tonga (5) 5 – Tonga (24) 29, Cote d'Ivoire (0) 11 – Scotland (13) 19, France (3) 22

DISMISSALS

Date	Player	Country	Opposition
Jan 1965	Cyril Brownlie	New Zealand	England
Dec 1967	Colin Meads	New Zealand	Scotland
May 1975	Mike Burton	England	Australia
Jan 1977	Geoff Wheel	Wales	Ireland
	Willie Duggan	Ireland	Wales
Feb 1980	Paul Ringer	Wales	England
Jan 1984	Jean-Paul Garruet	France	Ireland
Jun 1987	Hugh Richards	Wales	New Zealand
	David Codey	Australia	Wales
Jun 1988	M Tagia	Fiji	England
	Alain Lorieux	France	Argentina
Aug 1988	Barry Williams	USA	USSR
	Roman Malikov	USSR	USA
Nov 1989	Tevita Vonslagie	Fiji	England
	Noa Naduku	Fiji	England
Jan 1990	Kevin Moseley	Wales	France
Feb 1990	Alain Carminati	France	Scotland
Jun 1990	Abdelatif Benazzi	France	Australia
	Andre Stoop	Namibia	Wales
Jul 1990	Philippe Gallart	France	Australia
Nov 1990	Federico Mendez	Argentina	England
Jun 1991	Constantin Cojocariu	Romania	France
Oct 1991	Mata'afa Keenan	Western Samoa	Argentina
	Pedro Sporleder	Argentina	Western Samoa
Feb 1992	Vincent Moscate	France	England
	Gregoire Lascube	France	England
Apr 1992	Olivier Roumat	World XV*	New Zealand
Aug 1993	James Small	South Africa	Australia
Oct 1993	Patricio Noriega	Argentina	Uruguay
Jun 1994	Mark Cardinal	Canada	France
	Philippe Sella	France	Canada
Feb 1995	John Davies	Wales	England
Jun 1995	James Dalton	South Africa	Canada
	Gareth Rees	Canada	South Africa
	Rod Snow	Canada	South Africa
Sep 1995	Garin Jenkins	Wales	South Africa

Roll of dishonour by country (total no. of dismissals: 36):
9* – France; 6 – Wales; 3 – Argentina, Canada, Fiji; 2 – New Zealand, South Africa;
1 – Australia, England, Ireland, Namibia, Romania, USA, USSR, Western Samoa

* France lock Olivier Roumat sent off playing for World XV.

DEBUTANTS 1995/96

1995

22 Jul   Steve Merrick (Australia vs New Zealand, Auckland)

29 Sep   Justin Thomas (Wales vs South Africa, Johannesburg)
Andrew Moore (Wales vs South Africa, Johannesburg)
Christian Loader (Wales vs South Africa, Johannesburg)
Gareth Jones (Wales vs South Africa, Johannesburg)

14 Oct   Marc Lievremont (France vs Italy, Buenos Aires)
Franck Tournaire (France vs Italy, Buenos Aires)
Hyardet (France vs Italy, Buenos Aires)

17 Oct   Richard Dourthe (France vs Romania, Tucuman)
Thomas Castaignede (France vs Romania, Tucuman)
Philippe Carbonneau (France vs Romania, Tucuman)
Fabien Pelous (France vs Romania, Tucuman)
Arlettaz (France vs Romania, Tucuman)
Azam (France vs Romania, Tucuman)
Juillet (France vs Romania, Tucuman)

11 Nov   Craig Quinnell (Wales vs Fiji, Cardiff)
Lyndon Mustoe (Wales vs Fiji, Cardiff)

18 Nov   Mark Regan (England vs South Africa, Twickenham)
Lawrence Dallaglio (England vs South Africa, Twickenham)
Toks van der Linde (South Africa vs England, Twickenham)
Christian Saverimutto (Ireland vs Fiji, Dublin)
Jeremy Davidson (Ireland vs Fiji, Dublin)
Allen Clarke (Ireland vs Fiji, Dublin)
Sean McCahill (Ireland vs Fiji, Dublin)
Henry Hurley (Ireland vs Fiji, Dublin)
Rowen Shepherd (Scotland vs Western Samoa, Edinburgh)
Jim Hay (Scotland vs Western Samoa, Edinburgh)
Stuart Reid (Scotland vs Western Samoa, Edinburgh)
Justin Marshall (New Zealand vs France, Paris)
Liam Barry (New Zealand vs France, Paris)

16 Dec   Paul Grayson (England vs Western Samoa, Twickenham)
Matthew Dawson (England vs Western Samoa, Twickenham)

1996

6 Jan   Kurt McQuilkin (Ireland vs US, Atlanta)
          Victor Costello (Ireland vs US, Atlanta)

16 Jan   Leigh Davies (Wales vs Italy, Cardiff)
          Arwel Thomas (Wales vs Italy, Cardiff)
          Matthew Wintle (Wales vs Italy, Cardiff)
          Andrew Lewis (Wales vs Italy, Cardiff)
          Gwyn Jones (Wales vs Italy, Cardiff)

20 Jan   Jonathan Sleightholme (England vs France, Paris)
          Michel Perie (France vs England, Paris)

3 Feb   Robert Howley (Wales vs England, Twickenham)
          Stephane Glas (France vs Scotland, Edinburgh)

17 Feb   David Humphreys (Ireland vs France, Paris)
          Richard Castel (France vs Ireland, Paris)
          Sylvain Despagne (France vs Ireland, Paris)

2 Mar   Garath Archer (England vs Scotland, Edinburgh)
          Simon Mason (Ireland vs Wales, Dublin)

16 Mar   Raphael Ibanez (France vs Wales, Cardiff)

20 Apr   Stephane Venditti (France vs Romania, Aurillac)
          Herve Guiraud (France vs Romania, Aurillac)
          Hugo Miorin (France vs Romania, Aurillac)
          Christophe Moni (France vs Romania, Aurillac)
          Thierry Labrousse (France vs Romania, Aurillac)
          Jean-Luis Jordana (France vs Romania, Aurillac)

7 Jun   Christian Cullen (New Zealand vs Western Samoa)
          Scott MacLeod (New Zealand vs Western Samoa)

8 Jun   Owen Finegan (Australia vs Wales, Brisbane)
          Marco Caputo (Australia vs Wales, Brisbane)
          Richard Harry (Australia vs Wales, Brisbane)

16 Jun   Ron Eriksson (Scotland vs New Zealand)

22 Jun   Barry Stewart (Scotland vs New Zealand)
          Adrian Cashmore (New Zealand vs Scotland)
          Ben Tune (Australia vs Wales)
          Sam Payne (Australia vs Wales)
          Stephen Larkham (Australia vs Wales)
          Dafydd James (Wales vs Australia)

THE PLAYERS A–Z

KEY TO INDIVIDUAL STATISTICS

Take the case of Tom Giles (right) as an example*. Tom was first capped at senior level for England in 1984, won 8 caps last season, and has 35 caps in all, with 60 points to his credit. He played in the 1986 IRB Centenary match in Cardiff (Lions 7, The Rest 15) which has been included as a Lions cap. And in 1993 Tom played two Tests in the series against New Zealand. Each player has his caps listed in order, plus a breakdown of his points tally, again in chronological order. For example, Tom marked his debut against Wales in 1984 with one try. If a nation is

England (1984)		
Last Season	8 caps	18 pts
Career	35 caps	60 pts
Lions (1986)		
Lions (1993)	2 Tests	0 pts

Caps	(35): **1984** W, F, E, S, Fj **1987** S, I, W(a), wc-T, W(b), A **1989** W, S, I, F, Arg(1,2), Fj **1991** F, S, J, W **1993** I, F. Lions–NZ(1,2) **1995** F, S, W, SA(1) **1996** I, F(a), W, S, wc-Arg, NZ, F(b)
Points	(60 – 9t, 4p, 1dg) **1984** W(1t) **1991** F(1t), W(2t) **1993** F(1p) **1995** S(2t, 1p), SA(1:1t) **1996** F(a:1dg), wc-Arg(2t)

played more than once in the same year, the statistic is recorded in one of two ways. For a 3-match series against, say, Australia, the statistic reads: A(1,2,3). If our player has previously turned out against the Aussies in the same year, that statistic reads: A(a), followed by A(b1,b2,b3). This makes identification possible when it comes to points scored, e.g. A(b3:1t) means that our player has scored a try against Australia in the third Test of the second series.

IMPORTANT NOTE

Qualification for inclusion in the *Rugby Union Who's Who* is restricted to those players who appeared in full Test matches between the 1995 World Cup and June 1996. Player statistics do not include the Tri-Nations Tournament, nor Australia vs Canada or South Africa vs Fiji.

ALWAYS ONE TO SPOT A GOOD OPENING, ONCE ARCHIE HEARD ABOUT SAVE & PROSPER UNIT TRUSTS, THERE WAS NO STOPPING HIM

If you'd like to hear more about Save & Prosper Unit Trusts, just ring us on our free Moneyline: 0800 829 100. It could be just the break you need.

© RFU 1990

SAVE & PROSPER
THE INVESTMENT HOUSE
SPONSORS OF ENGLISH RUGBY

Accoceberry, G.   France

Full name: Guy Accoceberry
Club: Begles-Bordeaux
Position: Scrum-half
Height: 5ft 11½ in (1.82m)
Weight: 12st 5lb (76kg)
Occupation: Pharmacist
Born: Vittel, 5.5.67
Family: Married
Former club: Tyrosse
International debut: New Zealand 8, France 22, 1994
Five Nations debut: France 21, Wales 9, 1995
Notable landmarks in rugby career:
Broke his arm at 1995 World Cup, 33 minutes into France's extraordinary 22–19 defeat of Scotland (Pretoria, 3.6.95), but returned to national side for 34–22 defeat of Italy (14.10.95) during France's victorious Latin Cup campaign in Argentina. Thereafter lost out to Toulouse rival Philippe Carbonneau before being reinstated midway through Five Nations Championship and celebrating with a try in the 45–10 defeat of Ireland (Paris,

France (1994)

Last Season	7 caps	10 pts
Career	15 caps	10 pts

Caps (15): **1994** NZ(1,2), C(b) **1995** W, E, S, I, R wc-IC, S. It **1996** I, W, R, Arg(1)

Points (10 – 2t): **1995** wc-IC(1t) **1996** I(1t)

17.2.96). Retained place against Wales and Romania. Rose to prominence as a member of the French side that won the 1992 Students World Cup, but it was not until France toured New Zealand two summers later that he really hit the big time. A visit that has gone down in history as France's most successful ever saw Guy make his debut in the 22–8 shock first Test win and retain it in the heroic 23–20 second Test triumph. The tallest French scrum-half since Jean-Michel Aguirre in 1972, Guy was also a member of the Cote Basque XV which beat the 1990 All Blacks. Tyrosse captain for three seasons before switching to Begles, where he found himself at the heels of a powerful pack, the former French Universities No.9 graduated to the France A side against their English counterparts at Leicester in 1993 as a prelude to a brief tour of duty on the Five Nations bench in place of the unavailable Jerome Cazalbou. No second-best for Guy in 1995, however, as he held his place throughout the championship and the World Cup, where he also appeared, and scored a try, against Cote d'Ivoire.

Andrews, M. G.   South Africa

Full name: Mark Gregory Andrews
Province: Natal
Position: Lock
Height: 6ft 7in (2.0m)
Weight: 17st 5lb (112kg)
Occupation: Student
Born: Elliot, 21.2.72
Former club: Aurillac (Fra)
International debut: South Africa 27, England 9, 1994
Notable landmarks in rugby career:
One of the world's foremost lock forwards, Mark underlined his value with a series of huge Super-12 performances as Natal Sharks reached the final. Equally crucial contribution to South Africa's World Cup winning side, underlining his versatility by moving to No.8 in the semi-final against France (Durban, 17.6.95) to combat Laurent Cabannes at the tail of the lineout. Remained there against All Black Zinzan Brooke as the Boks won a famous final victory in Johannesburg (24.6.95). South Africa's outstanding player on their 1994 tour of New

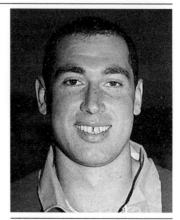

South Africa (1994)

Last Season	8 caps	10 pts
Career	16 caps	15 pts

Caps (16): **1994** E(2), NZ(1,2,3), Arg(1,2), S,W **1995** WS(a) wc-A, WS(b), F, NZ. W, It, E
Points (15 – 3t): **1994** Arg(2:1t) **1995** WS(a:1t) wc-WS(b:1t)

Zealand, former All Black lock Andy Haden opined: 'He is in the top-10 lineout ball winners in the world already and I'm sure he's going to get bigger, stronger and more clever." (A bright lad, that Haden!) Learned much of his trade in France, where cousin Keith Andrews set up the raw 19-year-old to play in Aurillac. He survived 22 bone-crunching games in 25 weeks and returned home a *man*. Really came to the fore in 1994, helping Natal beat England 21–6 and, after England took out their annoyance on the Springboks in a sensationally one-sided first Test, was then summoned to Cape Town to bolster the South African line-up in the second and final Test. England crashed 27–9. However, it was in New Zealand that the former water polo standout left an indelible mark. Targetted by the All Blacks, he shrugged off separate 'assaults' on his head and ankles to build a formidable tour CV, dominating the front of nearly every lineout he graced.
Touchlines: Junior Springbok colours at water polo

Archer, G. S.   England

Full name: Garath Stuart Archer
Nickname: Boulder
Club: Newcastle & Army
Position: Lock
Height: 6ft 6in (1.98m)
Weight: 19st (121kg)
Occupation: Radio telegraphist, Royal Signals
Born: South Shields, 15.12.74
Family: Single
Family links with rugby: Father (Stuart) played for Gosforth, appearing on wing and scoring try in 27–11 John Player Cup final defeat of Waterloo
Former clubs: Westoe, Durham City, Bristol
International debut: Scotland 9, England 18, 1996
Five Nations debut: As above
Best rugby memory: Listening to national anthem before home debut against Ireland
Worst rugby memory: Being sent-off at Bristol when playing for Newcastle.

England (1996)

Last Season	2 caps	0 pts
Career	2 caps	0 pts

Caps (2): 1996 S, I
Points Nil

Toughest opponent: Mark Andrews (Natal & South Africa)
Do you really want to be a full-time professional player? Yes
How well has rugby handled move to professionalism? 6/10. Great that things have moved so fast but I wish it could have been done more amicably. For a long time it appeared that the game would tear itself apart.
Do you have a duty to entertain? Yes, indirectly. Our first responsibility is to become bigger, stronger, fitter and more powerful athletes. But I concede that English rugby concentrates more on defence than attack. I want to see us being more positive.
Notable landmarks in rugby career: One of Rob Andrew's big-money signings when he returned to Newcastle last summer after a season with Bristol, Garath went home with two England caps in his luggage after being summoned by Jack Rowell mid-season. Martin Bayfield's shock demotion after England's unconvincing defeat of Wales (3.2.96) allowed Garath to team up with Bristol hooker Mark Regan in the national side and, despite some fears that discipline might be a problem (he has a collection of yellow cards from club and England A rugby), he contributed fully to wins over Scotland and Ireland that brought England the Calcutta Cup, Triple Crown and Five Nations title. Garath, who

was educated at Durham School, served his apprenticeship in the England A side that enjoyed a successful tour to Australia and Fiji in 1995 before roaming unbeaten through last season. In 1992 he had helped England 18-Group to a Grand Slam before going on to represent England at Colts (whilst with Durham City), Under-21 and Emerging Players levels.

Touchlines: Sea fishing, woodwork

Arnold, P. Wales

Full name: Paul Arnold
Nickname: Arnie
Club: Swansea
Position: Lock
Height: 6ft 5in (1.95m)
Weight: 15st 9lb (99kg)
Occupation: Schools development officer for Swansea RFC
Born: Morriston, 28.4.68
Family: Single
International debut: Namibia 9, Wales 18, 1990
Five Nations debut: Wales 6, England 25, 1991
Best rugby memory: Being named man of the match in Swansea's 1994/95 Swalec Cup final win over Pontypridd
Worst rugby memory: Not being selected for 1995 World Cup
Biggest influence on career: Richard Moriarty (Swansea & Wales)
Serious injuries: Broken shoulder (1995/96)
Toughest opponent: John Eales (Australia)

France (1994)		
Last Season	1 cap	0 pts
Career	13 caps	8 pts

Caps (13): **1990** Na(1,2), Ba **1991** E, S, I, F, A(a) wc-Arg, A(b) **1993** F(R) **1994** wc(q)-Sp **1995** SA
Points (8 – 2t): **1991** I(1t) wc-Arg(1t)

Do you really want to be a full-time professional player? Yes
How well has rugby handled move to professionalism? 5/10. Europe is belatedly heading in the right direction but it needs to get a move on to catch up with the southern hemisphere.
Do you have a duty to entertain? Yes
Do you feel a loyalty to your club in this new era? It's every man for himself.
Notable landmarks in rugby career: Mighty unlucky not to have been picked for the 1995 World Cup, Paul collected his third cap in four years when selected to partner Derwyn Jones in the engine room against the world champion

Springboks (Johannesburg, 2.9.95). Well, that was the idea. Jones was laid out cold by Kobus Wiese early on and Paul played virtually the whole game alongside Swansea team mate and debutant Andrew Moore. That was it for Paul, internationally speaking, as he then broke his shoulder, although he resumed playing in time to win selection for Wales' tour to Australia last summer. Prior to South Africa game, which Wales lost 11–40, he had appeared in the 54–0 World Cup qualifying defeat of Spain (Madrid, 21.5.94) and toured to Zimbabwe and Namibia in 1993. Gained experience playing in New Zealand (summer 1989). Made Wales Under-21 debut in 24–10 defeat of Scotland at Ayr (28.4.90) and within five weeks won his full cap, playing in the 18–9 first Test win over Namibia in Windhoek (2.6.90). Added a B cap in Leiden when helped down Netherlands 34–12 (2.12.90). Made Five Nations debut the following season against Grand Slam 1991 England and scored first Test try later in the Championship in the 21st minute of the 21–21 draw with Ireland in Cardiff (16.2.91). Toured Australia in summer 1991 and played twice in World Cup, scoring the solitary Welsh try in a 16–7 win over Argentina (9.10.91). Helped Swansea beat touring Wallabies 21–6 (4.11.92).

Touchlines: Sunday soccer, indoor 5-a-side, indoor cricket, squash, swimming

---

Back, N. A. England

Full name: Neil Antony Back
Club: Leicester
Position: Openside flanker
Height: 5ft 10in (1.78m)
Weight: 14st 6lb (87kg)
Occupation: Senior pensions supervisor with AXA Equity and Law, Coventry
Born: Coventry, 16.1.69
Family: Single
Former club: Nottingham
International debut: Scotland 14, England 15, 1994
Five Nations debut: As above
Other sporting claims to fame: Cricket for Coventry and Warwickshire Schools
Notable landmarks in rugby career: A season which Neil had begun as a member of England's World Cup squad ended in shame as he was handed a six-month ban for pushing over referee Steve Lander at the end

England (1994)

Last Season	3 caps	0 pts
Career	5 caps	0 pts

Caps (5): **1994** S, I **1995** wc-Arg, It, WS
Points Nil

of the Pilkington Cup final; a match which Leicester lost 16–15 to Bath after Lander had awarded Bath a controversial late penalty try. Neil claimed he had mistaken Lander for Bath rival Andy Robinson. The problem was that while Lander has dark hair and was dressed like a chessboard, Robinson is a blond and was wearing the white and blue/black occasional hoops of Bath. It was the latest blow for a player who always seems to have an obstacle in his way. Hamstring injury ruined his World Cup just when he seemed to be building up a head of steam. And prior to that he was victimised by the 'big is beautiful, small is not' faction among England's selectors. In South Africa, having started out as a 47th-minute replacement for Steve Ojomoh against Argentina (won 24–18), Neil was moved to openside for the next two Pool B games against Italy (won 27–20) and Western Samoa (won 44–22), where he sustained his injury. It was a big shame for the little man, who had waited so long for Test recognition, had then been discarded, and had then fought his way back to prominence. 5 February 1994 was the day when a player told he was too small to grace the international stage did exactly that, against Scotland in Edinburgh. He had won 12 caps in England's second XV dating back to his B debut against the Emerging Wallabies in 1990, a year after he had claimed a hat-trick of tries as England's first-ever under-21 side walloped their Romanian counterparts in sunny Bucharest. He had played, too, for England Under-18s (1985–87) and England Colts (1987/88), had starred for the centenary Barbarians against England (September 1990) and had even scored a try for an England XV in their 33–15 defeat of Italy in 1990. But what he hungered for more than anything was a full cap. Hence the satisfaction when he finally achieved his goal. So disappointed had he been to have missed the All Blacks visit to Twickenham the previous November that he had taken the advice of three fitness advisors and devised a programme that would have him in tiptop shape for 5 February. What a shame after such a long wait that England should turn in such a poor performance, despite Jon Callard's injury-time winner. If anything they were worse on Neil's second outing, when Ireland won at Twickenham for the first time since 1982. The upshot was that Neil was dumped, only to return much later. Don't bet against him doing the same once again.

Touchlines: Training five days a week for rugby, golf, equestrian sports

Bayfield, M. C.   England

Full name: Martin Christopher
Bayfield
Nickname: Bayfs
Club: Northampton
Position: Lock
Height: 6ft 10in (2.08m)
Weight: 18st 2lb (115kg)
Occupation: Full-time rugby player
(on sabbatical from Bedfordshire
Constabulary)
Born: Bedford, 21.12.66
Family: Helena (wife), Rosanna
(daughter) and Polly (daughter)
Former clubs: Metropolitan Police,
Bedford
International debut: Fiji 12, England
28, 1991
Five Nations debut: Scotland 7,
England 25, 1992
Best rugby memory: Lions' second
Test defeat of New Zealand (1993)
Worst rugby memory: Being
dropped by England (1994 & 1996)
Notable landmarks in rugby career:
1995/96 was not a vintage year for
Bayfs, who had been one of
England's few genuinely outstanding
players at the 1995 World Cup.
Ever-present in the side throughout

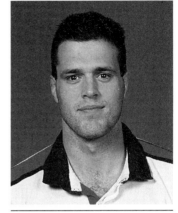

England (1994)		
Last Season	9 caps	0 pts
Career	31 caps	0 pts
Lions (1993)	3 Tests	0 pts

Caps (31): **1991** Fj, A **1992** S, I, F, W, C,
SA **1993** F, W, S, I. Lions-
NZ(1,2,3) **1994** S, I, SA(1,2), R,C
1995 I, F, W, S wc-Arg, It, A, NZ,
F. SA, WS **1996** F, W
Points Nil

1994/95 campaign, save for World Cup tie against Western Samoa (Durban
4.6.95), when Richard West was given his debut, Bayfs then lost his place to
rookie Garath Archer midway through the Five Nations Championship
(blamed for England's lineout failings), thus missing out on the wins over
Scotland and Ireland and the subsequent title-winning celebrations. It was a
shock to the system for the tallest forward ever to have played for England, who
had previously known only praise. Bayfs had graduated to British Lion status
(on the 1993 tour to New Zealand) after just two seasons as his country's first-
choice lock, and he played in all three Tests of a series edged by the hosts. An
injury to his neck and spine, sustained in a fall in New Zealand, kept him out of
the 15–9 autumn defeat of those same All Blacks and, for a period, threatened
his career. Previously made three appearances for England 18-group,
represented Midlands Division and British Police for three seasons, toured with
British Police to Italy (1989) and broke into England's B setup during 1990/91

season, playing against Emerging Australians and Italy. Progressed to England squad for 1991 tour to Fiji and Australia, playing in both Tests after Wade Dooley sustained a hand injury. Missed out on the World Cup squad but, following Paul Ackford's retirement, booked a permanent berth alongside Dooley in England's 1992 Grand Slam XV. Reverted to England B for summer of 1992 tour to New Zealand, where he played in both 'Tests' losses to the All Black XV. Returned to the senior side once back in Blighty, and played the full season before being one of 16 Englishmen measured for Lions blazers.
Touchlines: Weight training

Bell, J. C. Ireland

Full name: Jonathan Charles Bell
Nickname: Dinger
Club: Northampton
Position: Wing, centre
Height: 5ft 11in (1.80m)
Weight: 15st 7lb (98kg)
Occupation: Student, Loughborough University
Born: Belfast, 7.2.74
Family: Single
Former club: Ballymena
International debut: Australia 31, Ireland 13, 1994
Five Nations debut: Scotland 26, Ireland 13, 1995
Best rugby memory: Maiden Ireland try versus Scotland (4.2.95)
Worst rugby memory: Being humiliated by David Campese when Ireland played NSW on 1994 tour
Most embarrassing memory: Needing two hours longer than Neil Jenkins, Emyr Lewis and Paddy Johns to provide a urine sample for a drugs test after the Ireland–Wales World Cup tie in South Africa

Ireland (1994)		
Last Season	6 caps	0 pts
Career	14 caps	5 pts

Caps (14): **1994** A(1,2), US **1995** S, It wc-NZ, W(b), F(b). Fj **1996** US, S, F, W, E
Points (5 – 1t): **1995** S(1t)

Toughest opponent: Frank Bunce (New Zealand)
Do you really want to be a full-time professional player? Yes
How well has rugby handled move to professionalism? 7/10. They got there in the end. Now must ensure that Five Nations Championship remains intact.
Do you have a duty to entertain? Yes. We must seek to emulate the Super-12s. Crowds are now paying more and so are entitled to expect more. The present

'must win' element detracts from the entertainment.

Do you feel a loyalty to your club in this new era? Yes

Other sporting claim to fame: 400 metres for Ulster Schools

Notable landmarks in rugby career: Ever-present for Ireland last season, though did not reach the heights attained in his maiden season at Test level. Try-less as Ireland started well, beating Fiji and USA, but finished poorly, claiming the Five Nations Wooden Spoon after beating only Wales. An Irish Schools cap just four years ago (1992), Jon made swift progress up the representative ladder, appearing at fullback, centre and wing for Schools (three caps), Ireland Under-21s (victory over New Zealand in October 1993) and the national senior side. Toured to Australia in summer 1994, playing against New South Wales, ACT, Queensland and an Australian XV before making his debut in the first Test at Ballymore (5.6.94). Returned home to captain Ireland Under-21s to victory over England and break into the Ulster side for the Inter-Pros. Moved to the left wing for Ireland's 26–15 home defeat of USA (5.11.94) and would have remained in the position for the Five Nations opener against England but for a hamstring injury which forced his withdrawal. Returned in place of Niall Woods a fortnight later, at Murrayfield, and celebrated with his first Test try in a match which Ireland could well have won, but Scotland did. Further injury hampered his international progress thereafter and he did not feature again until the eve of the World Cup, when Ireland went to Treviso (8.5.95) and became the first major nation to lose to Italy (12–22). Fortunately, a place in the World Cup quarter-finals all but erased that memory.

Touchlines: Travelling, downing high-energy drinks with friends at local

---

Benazzi, A.   France

Full name: Abdelatif Benazzi
Club: Agen
Position: No.8, flanker, lock
Height: 6ft 6in (1.98m)
Weight: 17st 6lb (111kg)
Occupation: Sales representative with *Astra-Calve*
Born: Oujda, Morocco, 20.8.68
Family: Single
Former club: Cahors
International debut: Australia 21, France 9, 1990
Five Nations debut: England 21, France 19, 1991
Other sporting claims to fame: Moroccan junior record-holder for discus and shot

Notable landmarks in rugby career:
Preserved superstar status despite being despatched to the second row by new French coach Jean-Claude Skrela midway through the 1996 Five Nations series. Having excelled at the World Cup, inspiring France to the semi-finals, and oh so nearly the final itself, Abdel moved from blindside to No.8 for the shared autumn series with New Zealand. He reverted to blindside for England's visit to Paris, turning in a massive performance as

France (1990)

Last Season	14 caps	10 pts
Career	46 caps	15 pts

Caps (46): **1990** A(1,2,3), NZ(1,2) **1991** E, US(1R,2) wc-Ro, Fj, C **1992** SA(1R,2), Arg(b) **1993** E, S, I, W, A(1,2) **1994** I, W, E, S, NZ(1,2), C(b) **1995** W, E(a), S(a), I(a), R wc-T, IC, S(b), I(b), SA, E(b). NZ(1,2) **1996** E, S, I, W, Arg(1,2)

Points (15 – 3t): **1994** E(1t) **1995** wc-IC(1t) **1996** S(1t)

France ended eight years of English domination at Parc des Princes, scored a try at No.8 as France surprisingly went down in Edinburgh, then moved to the engine room for the remaining matches against Ireland and Wales. Of his 46 caps, 11 have been won at lock, 25 as flanker and 10 as No.8. Just call him Mr Versatility. Bagged his first against England in the 1994 Championship, a Five Nations campaign in which he became the first player for 30 years to wear jerseys 6, 7 and 8. Less glorious had been his Test debut, which lasted 14 minutes before he was sent off for stamping on a Wallaby in Sydney. But modest 14-day ban meant he was able to play in next two Tests of the series at flanker. Came to France by way of Czechoslovakia where, while on tour with Morocco, he met up with a touring fourth-division French club. On learning he wanted to play in France, they advised him to join Cahors. This he did before switching, a year later, to Agen, for whom he appeared in the 1990 French Cup final. Represented Morocco in the African zone of the 1991 World Cup qualifying rounds, against Belgium in Casablanca, and then France in the final stages. Became the first Moroccan to play at Twickenham in his Five Nations debut for France in the 1991 Grand Slam decider. Suspended indefinitely during 1991/92 season by the French Federation after being sent off for fighting with Eric Champ in an Agen–Toulon Cup match. Ban ruled him out of France's summer tour of Argentina. Returned thereafter, but again lost Test place on 1993 summer tour to South Africa after an infected wound required a stay in hospital.

Benetton, P.   France

Full name: Philippe Benetton
Club: Agen
Position: Flanker, No.8
Height: 6ft 3in (1.90m)
Weight: 15st 6lb (98kg)
Occupation: Sports instructor, Agen council
Born: Cahors, 17.5.68
Family: Married with one child
Former club: Cahors
International debut: France 27, British Lions 29, 1989
Five Nations debut: England 16, France 15, 1993
Notable landmarks in rugby career: The World Cup campaign ended prematurely for Philippe, one of the world rugby's most accomplished back-row performers, when he sustained a broken arm 17 minutes into France's thrilling 22–19 defeat of Scotland (Pretoria, 3.6.95). And 1995/96 campaign did not go much better as, having appeared in all three of France's Latin Cup wins in Argentina in October and at blind-side in the shared home series with New Zealand in November, injury ruled out any further involvement. Had marked his senior debut with a try against the 1989 British Lions,

France (1994)

Last Season	10 caps	5 pts
Career	39 caps	34 pts

Caps (39): **1989** BL **1991** US(2) **1992** Arg(a1,a2R), SA(1R,2), Arg(b) **1993** E, S, I, W, SA(1,2), R(b), A(1,2) **1994** I, W, E, S, NZ(1,2), C(b) **1995** W, E, S(a), I wc-T, IC(R), S(b). It, R(R), Arg, NZ(1,2), Arg(1,2)

Points (34 – 7t): **1989** BL(1t) **1993** W(2t) **1994** I(1t), NZ(1:1t) **1995** C(b:1t), Arg (2:1t)

masquerading as a Home Unions XV, in the Paris floodlit international staged to mark the bicentenary of the French Revolution. In common with back-row team mate Abdel Benazzi, he began his playing career with Cahors before switching to Agen in 1988. At international level Philippe graduated through Under-21 and B setups. He missed out on the 1990 and 1991 Five Nations Championships, unable in the latter to displace Xavier Blond from the blindside berth. However, he re-emerged on France's 1991 tour to North America, winning his second cap in the 10–3 second Test win over the US Eagles. Although included in the 1991 World Cup squad, he remained redundant through France's four matches and, at first, continued in the same vein after former club mate Pierre Berbizier succeeded Jacques Fouroux as national coach. However, not only did he return to Test favour in 1992/93, he played in the last nine internationals, as France won the

215

1993 Championship, and he scored two tries in the title-clinching 26–10 defeat of Wales (Paris, 20.3.93). Having found a home at No.8, Philippe toured with France to South Africa (1993) and New Zealand (1994), the latter tour culminating in a historic 2–0 series defeat of the All Blacks. He was the star of the show, scoring the only try in the first Test, and was acclaimed as one of the five players of the year in the *1995 New Zealand Rugby Almanac*.

Benezech, L. — France

Full name: Laurent Benezech
Club: Harlequins
Position: Loosehead prop
Height: 6ft 1in (1.85m)
Weight: 16st 8lb (105kg)
Occupation: Company rep with Agence Audour
Born: Pamiers, 19.12.66
Family: Married
Former clubs: Ariege, Toulouse, Racing Club de France
International debut: France 18, England 14, 1994
Five Nations debut: As above
Notable landmarks in rugby career: Emerged as one of France's most influential players on and off the field, playing a central role in player 'negotiations' with the French Federation during an autumn of discontent in 1995 while cementing his position as the nation's first-choice loosehead – at least until injury intervened following the shared series with New Zealand in November. Laurent, who had also appeared twice in France's Latin Cup-winning campaign the previous month,

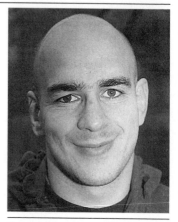

France (1994)
Last Season	7 caps	0 pts
Career	15 caps	0 pts

Caps (15): 1994 E, S, C(a), NZ(1,2), C(b) 1995 W, E(a) wc-IC, S(b), E(b). R, Arg, NZ(1,2)
Points Nil

started life as a second-row forward but was unable to find a place in the Toulouse engine room during his teenage days. So he decided to 'bulk-up' and was rewarded with a place on the loosehead side of the front row. Four years after joining Toulouse from Ariege in 1985, he once again switched allegiances, this time to the capital and the flamboyant Racing Club de France. The move was immediately rewarded as Racing captured the French championship in 1990 and Laurent was selected for France A's tour to Namibia. It was not until 1993 that the senior selectors came calling, including yer man in the tour party for the historic trip to born-again South Africa. But a foot injury meant that the former French Students and French Armed Forces player had to call off, so missing another famous series win. No such rejections in 1993/94, though, when he was called into a French side, reeling after defeat in Cardiff, to pack down against arch-rivals England in Paris. He impressed, not least opposite number Victor Ubogu, and held his place for the Championship finale against Scotland in Edinburgh, before heading to Canada and New Zealand and widespread acclaim as France swept the All Blacks 2–0. Troubled by injury in 1994/95, his World Cup appearances were confined to outings against Cote d'Ivoire, Scotland and England.

Bennett, A. M. Wales

Full name: Anthony Mark Bennett
Nickname: Benny
Club: Cardiff
Position: Flanker
Height: 6ft 1in (1.85m)
Weight: 14st 7lb (92kg)
Occupation: Industrial chemist, Chemviron Speciality Chemicals Ltd
Born: 26.1.69
Family: Single
Former clubs: Swansea University, Ystradgynlais
International debut: Wales 6, New Zealand 34, 1995
Five Nations debut: None
Best rugby memory: First cap against All Blacks and winning 1994 Swalec Cup with Cardiff
Worst rugby memory: Not getting selected to play against Ireland in World Cup
Serious injuries: Shoulder ligaments (1995/96)
Toughest opponent: Jon Hall (Bath & England)

Wales (1995)		
Last Season	3 caps	5 pts
Career	3 caps	5 pts

Caps (3): **1995** wc-NZ. SA, Fj
Points (5 – 1t): **1995** SA(1t)

Do you really want to be a full-time professional player? Yes, but with the proviso that I could return to work in five years' time. I can't afford to give up my career otherwise.
How well has rugby handled move to professionalism? 5/10. There seems to be no great leadership or direction. Administrators seem to be pulling in opposite directions.

Do you have a duty to entertain? Definitely

Do you feel a loyalty to your club in this new era? Definitely, but everyone has their price.

Other sporting claim to fame: Judo black belt

Notable landmarks in rugby career: One for the quiz buffs: name the Welsh player to win his first two caps in Ellis Park, Johannesburg, against two different opponents. Benny shares the distinction with Wales captain Jonathan Humphreys: having made his debut in the World Cup against New Zealand (lost 9–34, 31.5.95), he then returned to the New Republic after the tournament to play against world champion Springboks (lost 11–40, 2.9.95). Despite the results, he richly enjoyed both experiences. In the South Africa game he even managed to silence Ellis Park by scoring a shock go-ahead try, after only three minutes, for the unrated visitors. After winning his third cap on home soil against Fiji (won 19–15, 11.11.95), Benny's luck ran out. After three injury-free years he damaged shoulder ligaments and had an operation in February 1996. First capped by Welsh Schools U-18 in 1986, he played for Welsh Students in 1988 while at Swansea University, playing in the Student World Cup that year.

Touchlines: Surfing

Bernat-Salles, P.   France

Full name: Philippe Bernat-Salles
Club: Begles-Bordeaux
Position: Wing
Height: 5ft 11½ in (1.81m)
Weight: 11st 8lb (74kg)
Occupation: Transport officer, Bordeaux
Born: 17.2.70
Former clubs: Idron, Bizanos, Pau
International debut: France 20, Argentina 24, 1992
Five Nations debut: England 31, France 10, 1995
Notable landmarks in rugby career: Philippe's 1995/96 campaign was confined to 35 minutes as replacement for Jean-Luc Sadourny in France's 15–12 defeat of England in

Paris (20.1.96). Had earned his Five Nations debut against Ireland, also at the Parc (15.1.94), but had to wait a year for his second championship appearance, at Twickenham, as a late call-up for the crocked Emile NTamack. Philippe's third Five Nations cap coincided with Scotland's first-ever win at Parc des Princes, after which NTamack returned. The 'Pau Rocket', Philippe burst explosively onto the

Test scene, scoring six tries in his first five internationals. But don't remind Romania, as both his appearances against them yielded a try hat-trick: in Bucharest (won 37–20, 20.5.93) and Brive (won 51–0, 9.10.93). Established himself as a permanent fixture in the French side until injury curtailed his 1993/94 season, forcing

France (1992)

Last Season	3 caps	0 pts
Career	11 caps	30 pts

Caps (11): **1992** Arg(b) **1993** R(a), SA(1,2), R(b), A(1,2) **1994** I **1995** E, S(a) **1996** E(R)

Points (30 – 6t): **1993** R(a:3t), R(b:3t)

him out of last three championship games. Philippe first earned full international recognition against Argentina, not in South America as he would have initially hoped, having toured there with France in summer 1992 (scoring tries against Cordoba, Buenos Aires and Cuyo), but at Nantes, where the Pumas came, saw and historically conquered on 14 November 1992. France lost 20–24 – their first-ever home loss to the Pumas – and Philippe was one of many who paid the price for team failure. He was dropped down a notch on the representative ladder, and turned out on the right wing for France B at Leicester on 15 January 1993, where England A triumphed 29–17 (11 months on from his B debut against Scotland in its 27–18 win in Albi). Met Scotland again in April 1993 as a member of the French team which contested the World Cup Sevens at Murrayfield.

Berty, D. France

Full name: David Berty
Club: Toulouse
Position: Wing
Height: 5ft 11in (1.80m)
Weight: 13st 5lb (85kg)
Occupation: PR representative
Born: 11.6.70
International debut: France 12, New Zealand 30, 1990
Five Nations debut: None
Notable landmarks in rugby career: Won only his fourth cap in six years last season as a 45th-minute replacement for Jean-Luc Sadourny against New Zealand in his home city of Toulouse (11.11.95). France won the game 22–15. Enjoyed more of a run in the Toulouse side which

won the French club title, beating Brive 20–13 in the final, and captured the inaugural Heineken European Cup, defeating Cardiff in the final. Scored two tries in the 54–10 Pool A defeat of Farul Constanta in Romania (31.10.95).

David's Test debut had come on the left wing against New Zealand on 10 November 1990. The All Blacks triumphed easily in the Parc des Princes, and David subsequently lost his place in the squad for the 1991 Five Nations Championship. But he continued an association with the

France (1990)

Last Season	1 cap	0 pts
Career	4 caps	0 pts

Caps (4): 1990 NZ(2) 1992 R(R) 1993 R(b) 1995 NZ(1R)

Points Nil

national A and B teams which had yielded B caps against Wales and Scotland in the 1989/90 season. It was not until 20 May 1992 that he returned to the senior XV, coming on as a 37th-minute replacement for Sebastien Viars in the 25–6 defeat of Romania at Le Havre. Thereafter, he was overlooked for the two-Test series against South Africa, despite helping France B to a 24–17 win over the Springboks in Bordeaux on 4 October, the visit to Nantes of Argentina and the 1993 Five Nations Championship. However, he did represent France at Murrayfield in the 1993 World Cup Sevens. Added his third cap, again as a replacement, in the 51–0 rout of Romania in Brive in October 1993.

Bowen, S. Australia

Full name: Scott Bowen
State: New South Wales
Club: Southern Districts
Position: Outside-half
Height: 5ft 9in (1.76m)
Weight: 12st 10lb (76kg)
Occupation: Development officer
Born: 20.9.72
Family: Single
International debut: Australia 12, South Africa 19, 1993
Best moment in rugby: Being chosen for first Test against South Africa in 1993
Worst moments in rugby: Being plagued by hamstring injuries in 1992, only playing 10 games; playing only once in 1995 World Cup
Toughest opponent: Hennie le Roux (South Africa)
Serious injuries: Hamstring (1992)
Notable landmarks in rugby career: Emerged from Michael Lynagh's shadow following the great man's

Australia (1993)

Last Season	3 caps	0 pts
Career	6 caps	0 pts

Caps (6): 1993 SA(1,2,3) 1995 wc-R. NZ(1,2)

Points Nil

retirement after the 1995 World Cup – a tournament in which Scott's only appearance came in the 42–3 World Cup win over Romania (Stellenbosch, 3.6.95). Regained the No.10 jersey in the subsequent Bledisloe Cup series, although it was not a particularly happy experience for either him or the Wallabies, swept 2–0 by the All Blacks. Toured England with New South Wales in January 1996 prior to the Super-12s. Scott enjoyed a remarkable rise to prominence in 1993. After playing in a curtain raiser to NSW's Super-10 match against Transvaal, he was asked to come on as an emergency replacement for the injured Tim Wallace after just two minutes. Having impressed, he kept his place and helped the Waratahs defeat South Africa 29–28 (Sydney, 24.7.93) at the same time as Queensland's Pat Howard, who had taken over from an ill Lynagh in the Test side, was off his game. So it came to pass that Scott earned his Wallabies call-up and played throughout the three-Test series against the Springboks. Despite Australia's shock defeat in the first Test (31.7.93), the selectors stood by him and their faith was repaid as the Wallabies bounced back to win the series. The former Aussie Schools international then embarked on Australia's autumn tour of North America and France but, with Lynagh restored to rude health, made only three appearances.

Touchlines: Tennis, golf, beach, spending time with girlfriend

---

Bracken, K. P. P.   England

Full name: Kyran Paul Patrick Bracken
Club: Saracens
Position: Scrum-half
Height: 5ft 11in (1.80m)
Weight: 12st 9lb (80kg)
Occupation: Part-time trainee solicitor with Alsters, College Green, Bristol
Born: Dublin, 22.11.71
Family: Single
Former clubs: Waterloo, Bristol
International debut: England 15, New Zealand 9, 1993
Five Nations debut: Scotland 14, England 15, 1994
Best rugby memory: Final whistle of debut
Worst rugby memory: Getting dropped in 1995 World Cup
Most embarrassing memory: Getting shorts ripped off against Ireland
Serious injuries: Broken nose (at 18); ankle ligaments (vs New Zealand, 1993)
Toughest opponent: Robert Howley (Cardiff & Wales)

Do you really want to be a full-time professional player? I'm really not sure.

How well has rugby handled move to professionalism? 4/10. Too many personalities got in the way during the battle for control. Neither side seemed to appreciate the other's interests, or recognise that it was the players' interests which really mattered.

Do you have a duty to entertain? Yes – at Bristol our sponsorship income was dependent on our scoring tries.

Other sporting claim to fame: Tennis for Jersey Youths

Notable landmarks in rugby career: Heel injury put paid to Kyran's World Cup even though Dewi Morris had already won back the No.9 jersey with combative performances against Argentina and Western Samoa. And if he thought life would get easier once Dewi had retired he was wrong. One game against South Africa, which England lost with plenty to spare (Twickenham, 18.11.95), and Kyran was benched for the remainder of the season (Northampton youngster Matthew Dawson was given his place). Kyran's solitary World Cup start had come in the 27–20 defeat of Italy (Durban, 31.5.95), though he did come on as a replacement eight minutes from the end of the Western Samoa win. Prior to that he had scored his first try in the 60–19 win over Canada (Twickenham, 10.12.94) and then sampled his first Grand Slam as an ever-present through the 1995 campaign. Kyran was thrust into the limelight after the late withdrawal of Morris prior to England's home international with New Zealand (27.11.93), having originally been selected as a first-time bench reserve. Responded with fairytale performance, all the more impressive for the fact that he could hardly walk after Jamie Joseph stamped on his right ankle in an ugly early incident. Kyran, who had played for the South West and England A against the All Blacks earlier in the tour, ignored the obvious pain to celebrate England's 15–9 win before hobbling away on crutches. 'To be honest,' he recalled, 'I thought I was going to have to go off early in the game. Towards the end, I was just living on adrenalin.' Kyran, who graduated through Lancashire, North Schools and England 16-Group as an outside-half, and captained England 18-Group in 1989/90, missed England's 1994 tour to South Africa because of exams.

Touchlines: Cinema, golf, tennis

England (1993)

Last Season	3 caps	0 pts
Career	11 caps	5 pts

Caps (11): **1993** NZ **1994** S, I, C **1995** I, F, W, S wc-It, WS(R). SA

Points (5 – 1t): **1994** C(1t)

Brooke, R. M.   New Zealand

Full name: Robin Brooke
Province: Auckland
Position: Lock
Height: 6ft 5½ in (1.96m)
Weight: 18st 10lb (114kg)
Occupation: Self-employed builder
Born: Warkworth, 10.1.67
Family links with rugby: Zinzan
(brother) plays for Auckland and
New Zealand (40 caps, 53 pts);
Martin (brother) a former New
Zealand triallist.
International debut: New Zealand
59, Ireland 6, 1992
Best moment in rugby: Getting
named to play my first Test while
visiting Zinzan in hospital; winning
1996 Super-12 title.
Worst moment in rugby: Losing
1995 World Cup final
Most embarrassing moment:
Walking into a clear glass door in
front of 500 people at Ellis Park in
1992 while the speeches were on
Notable landmarks in rugby career:
Nine consecutive Tests ranks as
something of a miracle for Robin,

New Zealand (1992)

Last Season	13 caps	10 pts
Career	25 caps	10 pts

Caps (25): **1992** I(2), A(1,2,3), SA **1993**
BL(1,2,3), A, WS **1994** SA(2,3)
1995 C wc-J, S, E, SA. A(1,2), It,
F(1,2) **1996** WS, S(1,2)
Points (10 – 2t): **1995** wc-J(2t)

whose career has been dogged by injury. Not only has he stayed clear of
problems since his World Cup return against Japan (Bloemfontein, 4.6.95), he
has shared in a Bledisloe Cup series win, a shared series in France and savoured
Super-12 glory with the Auckland Blues, who defeated Natal Sharks 45–21 at
Eden Park in the 1996 final. Prior to this happy episode, injury had disrupted
his last three seasons. At the World Cup he sat out the Pool matches against
Ireland and Wales, before returning with a two-try performance against Japan
and being paired with Ian Jones thereafter. In 1994, he played just twice for the
All Blacks, in the second and third Tests against South Africa, and in 1993,
despite touring to England and Scotland, he was unable to take any active part.
His frustration was compounded by the fact that he had become first-choice All
Blacks lock, alongside former North Auckland secondary schools team mate
Jones, during the course of the year, playing all three Tests against the British
Lions, and had helped wrestle the Bledisloe Cup back from world champions
Australia (25–10) in Dunedin. Had settled remarkably easily into the Test side
in 1992, having been given his chance against Ireland in Wellington on 6 June.

223

It might have come earlier for Robin had he not missed the national trials in favour of club commitments in Italy. As one of three All Blacks debutants that June day – along with Auckland prop Olo Brown and Waikato fullback Matthew Cooper – he helped rout the Irish 59–6. His performance earned him a berth on the tour to Australia, where he played alongside Jones in all three matches of the Bledisloe Cup series. But it was in Johannesburg on 15 August that Robin enjoyed his finest hour. With brother Zinzan, he was the star performer as New Zealand beat South Africa for the first time on African soil, 27–24. A member of the New Zealand Maoris since 1988.

Touchlines: Golf, family, travel, basketball

Brooke, Z. V. New Zealand

Full name: Zinzan Valentine Brooke
Club: Marist
Province: Auckland
Position: No.8, flanker
Height: 6ft 3in (1.90m)
Weight: 16st 4lb (99kg)
Occupation: Broadcaster, SKY TV
Born: Waiuku, 14.2.65
Family links with rugby: Martin (brother) is a former New Zealand triallist; Robin (brother) plays for Auckland, Maoris and New Zealand (25 caps, 10 pts)
International debut: New Zealand 46, Argentina 15, 1987
Serious injuries: Broken ankle (1991)
Notable landmarks in rugby career: Captained Auckland Blues to 1996 Super-12 crown after an impressive campaign which culminated with a 45–21 defeat of Natal Sharks before a 45,000 crowd at Eden Park. Zinzan's World Cup had been disrupted by an ankle injury, forcing him to miss two early pool matches. But came back strongly and stunned England with an outrageous 40-metre dropped goal in New Zealand's remarkable 45–29 semi-final win. Despite the disappointment of final defeat, the All Blacks regrouped and swept to Bledisloe Cup glory before splitting a two-Test series in France. Zinzan was No.8 throughout. Had confirmed himself as one of the world's great back rows on New Zealand's tour to England and Scotland in 1993, though only after starting off in the 'dirt trackers' XV as a result of having lost his Test place after the series win over the 1993 British Lions. Only a replacement, albeit it a utilised one, for the third Test win in Auckland, he sat out the Bledisloe Cup victory over Australia before coming on as a replacement against Western Samoa and

scoring a try. On tour in the UK he captained the midweek XV but, after attending the first two Saturday games and then scoring four tries in the 84–5 defeat of South of Scotland, he won a Test place at openside flanker against both Scotland (scored a try) and England. A product of the 1985 New Zealand Colts team, he has represented Auckland since 1986 and the All Blacks since scoring one of their six tries in the 46–15 win over Argentina on his debut in June 1987, at the inaugural World Cup. Came to the fore when he succeeded captain Wayne Shelford at No.8 after the Scotland series in 1990. But although

New Zealand (1987)

Last Season	13 caps	13 pts
Career	40 caps	53 pts

Caps (40): **1987** wc-Arg **1989** Arg(2R) **1990** A(1,2,3), F(1R) **1991** Arg(2), A(a1,a2). wc-E, It, C, A(b), S **1992** A(2,3), SA **1993** BL(1,2,3R), WS(R), S, E **1994** F(2), SA(1,2,3), A **1995** wc-J, S, E, SA. A(1,2), It, F(1,2), **1996** WS, S(1,2)

Points (53 – 11t,1dg): **1987** wc-Arg(1t) **1990** A(2:1t) **1991** Arg(2:1t). wc-It(1t), C(1t) **1992** SA(1t) **1993** WS(R:1t), S(1t) **1994** SA(2:1t) **1995** wc-E(1dg). It(1t), **1996** S(2:1t)

he played in all three Tests against Australia that year, he was injured and replaced in the first Test against France in Nantes. Returned strongly in 1991, after recovering from a broken ankle, and was the All Blacks' first-choice No.8 through the World Cup – a personal campaign that featured tries against Italy and Canada. An impressive Sevens player, he captained New Zealand to victory in the 1989 and 1990 Hong Kong Sevens.

Touchlines: Competing at anything

Auckland captain Zinzan Brooke proudly displays the spoils of victory after a stunning 45– 21 defeat of Natal in the Super-12 final.

Brouzet, O.   France

Full name: Olivier Brouzet
Club: Grenoble
Position: Lock
Height: 6ft 8in (2.03m)
Weight: 18st 7lb (113kg)
Occupation: Student
Born: Beziers, 22.11.72
Family: Single
Former club: Seyssins
International debut: Scotland 12, France 20, 1994
Five Nations debut: As above
Notable landmarks in rugby career:
Just when he thought there were only Oliviers (Roumat and Merle) between him and a place in the French second row, along came a new coach, Jean-Claude Skrela, with a new set of ideas. Consequently, having previously shared the workload down in the engine room with Roumat and Merle, Olivier suddenly found himself fifth in the queue, while Dax's utility forward Fabian Pelous and Agen's versatile Abdel Benazzi were moved ahead of him.

France (1994)

Last Season	6 caps	0 pts
Career	12 caps	0 pts

Caps (12): **1994** S, NZ(2R) **1995** E, S(a), I, R wc-T, IC, E(TR). It, Arg(R) **1996** W(R)

Post-World Cup he was confined to three outings: two as replacement and two in Argentina at the Latin Cup in the absence of Roumat, who was on Currie Cup duty in South Africa. His one other appearance came as 63rd-minute replacement for Sylvain Dispagne in the shock defeat by Wales (Cardiff, 16.3.96). Prior to World Cup the then coach Pierre Berbizier had alternated the three Oliviers throughout the 1994/95 campaign, depending on Roumat's fitness and Merle's disciplinary record. Brouzet played against England and Scotland whilst Merle was suspended, and against Ireland and Romania in the absence of Roumat. Brouzet made his debut against Scotland the previous season in Edinburgh. Olivier hails from a rich sporting lineage: his father Yves is a former French athletics champion, who has held the national shot-put record for 24 years. Olivier plays alongside the former lumberjack in the Grenoble team that reached the 1992/93 French championship final, losing to Castres. He helped France win the 1992 Students World Cup, and as recently as February 1993 in the French Under-21 side which whipped their Scottish counterparts 67–9 in Dijon. Promoted to replacement for the 1994 Championship opener against Ireland in Paris (15.1.94), having been a member of the France A gold medal-winning side at the 1993 Mediterranean Games. Toured with France to New Zealand in 1994 and savoured the glory of the 2–0 series win after coming on as a last-minute substitute in the second Test. In the 60 seconds he was on the field, France ran the length of the pitch for Jean-Luc Sadourny to score the sensational match and series-clinching try.

Brown, O. M.   New Zealand

Full name: Olo Max Brown
Province: Auckland
Position: Tighthead prop
Height: 6ft ½ in (1.85m)
Weight: 15st 11lb (100kg)
Occupation: Chartered accountant, Price Waterhouse
Born: Western Samoa, 24.10.67
International debut: New Zealand 59, Ireland 6, 1992
Most respected player: Colin 'Pine Tree' Meads
Notable landmarks in rugby career: A Polynesian powerhouse who has been a fixture in the All Black front row virtually since his debut in 1992. His one hiccup came in 1993 when he was sidelined by a neck injury. Now settled in at tighthead, he has only missed one game of late – the world-record romp against Japan during last summer's World Cup in South Africa. A member of the Auckland Blues side which won the 1996 Super-12 title, beating Natal 45–21 in the final at a noisy Eden Park. Olo, a Western Samoan, claimed first international try on his 18th appearance, in the

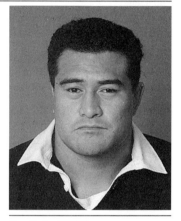

New Zealand (1992)

Last Season	14 caps	10 pts
Career	31 caps	10 pts

Caps (31): **1992** I(2), A(1,2,3), SA **1993** BL(1,2,3), A, S, E **1994** F(1,2), SA(1,2,3), A **1995** C wc-I, W, S, E, SA. A(1,2), It, F(1,2), **1996** WS, S(!,2)
Points (10 – 2t): **1995** C(1t) **1996** WS (1t)

73–7 slaughter of Canada (Auckland, 22.4.95). First represented the All Blacks in 1990 when, having been flown out to join the tour of France as a replacement, he was thrust into the fray and helped the tourists beat France A 22–15. Three months earlier he had helped Auckland beat the touring Australians 16–10 at Eden Park. Although overlooked for the Argentina tour and the World Cup in 1991, a fine display for the Saracens team, which beat a New Zealand XV 20–15 in one of the national trial matches, speeded his return to the big time. Having also helped Auckland destroy Ireland 62–7 at Eden Park (23 May), weighing in with one of his team's 11 tries, his Test debut followed soon after (6 June) when he was selected in place of Richard Loe for the second International against the Irish in Wellington (won 59–6). After that Olo was retained for the tour of Australia and South Africa, and appeared in all four Test matches.

Bunce, F. E.   New Zealand

Full name: Frank Eneri Bunce
Province: North Harbour/ Waikato Chiefs (Super-12)
Position: Centre
Height: 6ft 1in (1.85m)
Weight: 14st 10lb (93kg)
Occupation: Brewery rep, Lion Breweries
Born: Auckland, 4.2.62
Family: Married, three children
Family links with rugby: Steve (brother) plays for Western Australia
Former nation: Western Samoa
Former province: Auckland
Former club: Manukau
International debut (NZ): New Zealand 24, Ireland 21, 1992
Worst moment in rugby: The death of my father before he could see me become an All Black
Most respected opponents: John Kirwan (Auckland & NZ) and Philippe Sella (Saracens & France)
Notable landmarks in rugby career: Among the game's great midfield defenders, Frank also boasts a prolific strike rate, with 17 tries in 36 Tests since switching allegiance from Western Samoa after the 1991 World Cup. Ever-present for the past three years, save for the World Cup romp against Japan. He scored two

Western Samoa (1991)		
Career	4 caps	4 pts
New Zealand (1992)		
Last Season	14 caps	30 pts
Career	36 caps	81 pts

Caps (36): **1992** Wd(1,2,3), I(1,2), A(1,2,3), SA **1993** BL(1,2,3), A, WS, S, E **1994** F(1,2), SA(1,2,3), A **1995** C wc-I, W, S, E, SA. A(1,2), It, F(1,2), **1996** WS, S(1,2)

Points (81 – 17t): **1992** I(1:2t), A(1:1t), A(3:1t) **1993** BL(1:1t), BL(3:1t), A(1t), S(1t) **1994** F(1:1t) **1995** C(2t) wc-I(1t), S(1t). A(2:2t)

crucial tries in Sydney (29.7.95) as New Zealand beat Australia 34–23 to complete a 2–0 Bledisloe Cup series sweep, having previously claimed a brace in the All Blacks' 48–30 World Cup quarter-final victory over Scotland in Pretoria (11.6.95). It is hard to believe that it took six years, after making his debut for Auckland in a Ranfurly Shield game against Horowhenua at Eden

Park, for his All Black Test debut, against a World XV. But it was another two-try show, this time against Ireland, in the following series, which confirmed him as a class act. Mind you, the 30-year-old was no novice that day at Carisbrook. Frustrated at his lack of opportunity in the New Zealand national setup, he had declared his allegiance for Western Samoa in the 1991 World Cup, and featured strongly in each of their four games – against Wales, Australia, Argentina and Scotland – claiming a try in the 35–12 win over the Pumas. Any notion that his heroics in the 24–21 defeat of Ireland at Dunedin were a flash in the pan was dispelled in the second Test, when he weighed in with another try brace.

Burke, M.   *Australia*

Full name: Matthew Burke
State: New South Wales
Club: Eastwood
Position: Fullback, centre
Height: 6ft 1in (1.84m)
Weight: 15st 9lb (95kg)
Occupation: Eastwood rugby
development officer
Born: 26.3.73
Family: Single
International debut: Australia 19,
South Africa 12, 1993
Notable landmarks in rugby career:
Three years ago – to be precise, at the
conclusion of Australia's tour to
North America and France – the
then Wallaby coach Bob Dwyer
described Matt as 'a real investment
for the future'. He was not wrong.
Brave as a lion under the high ball,
Matt has made quite an impression
since – not least at the 1995 World
Cup – though sadly for him the
Wallabies did not, falling to England
in one of three games Matt played.
He also turned out in the wins over
Canada (Port Elizabeth, 31.5.95)
and Romania (Stellenbosch, 3.6.95),
scoring a try and two conversions in

Australia (1993)

Last Season	4 caps	52 pts
Career	13 caps	71 pts

Caps (13): **1993** SA(3R), F(1) **1994**
I(1,2), It(1,2) **1995** wc-C, R, E.
NZ(1,2), **1996** W(1,2)
Points (71 – 4t,12c,9p): **1994:** I(1:1t),
It(1:1t) **1995** wc-R(1t,2c).
NZ(1:1p), NZ(2c,3p), **1996**
W(1:6c,3p), W(2:1t,2c,2p)

the 42–3 defeat of the Romanians. His personal effort was sufficient to cement his berth for the subsequent Bledisloe Cup series against New Zealand, though again, sadly for Matt, who had represented Australia in Schoolboys, Under-21s and Sevens prior to being capped in 1993, the Wallabies crashed again, losing both games (although he contributed 16 points to the gold and green cause). Matt has also appeared at wing and centre, the position he occupied for New South Wales in their thrilling 29–28 defeat of the touring Springboks (24.7.93) – a performance which led to his first cap as a replacement in the decisive third Test victory over South Africa in Sydney (21.8.93). Matt sparked controversy when he displaced Marty Roebuck in the Australia side for the first Test against France in Bordeaux (30.10.93). The Wallabies lost and Roebuck, with his superb goalkicking ability, was recalled to save the series. Returned to favour in 1994, scoring tries in the first Tests of the series against Ireland (Brisbane, 5.6.94) and Italy (Brisbane, 18.6.94).

Burke, P. A. Ireland

Full name: Paul Anthony Burke
Club: Bristol
Position: Fly-half
Height: 5ft 8in (1.73m)
Weight: 12st (76kg)
Occupation: Teacher
Born: London, 1.5.73
Family: Single
Former clubs: London Irish, Cork Constitution
International debut: Ireland 8, England 20, 1995
Five Nations debut: As above
Best rugby memory: Winning first cap against England
Worst rugby memory: Being dropped after second cap
Toughest opponent: Rob Andrew (Newcastle & England)
Do you really want to be a full-time professional player? No, semi-professional. I want to work two days a week.
How well has rugby handled move to professionalism? 6/10. Too much squabbling over personalities rather than issues.

Ireland (1995)

Last Season	2 caps	23 pts
Career	7 caps	67 pts

Caps (7): **1995** E, S, W(a:R), It wc-J. Fj, US(R)
Points (67 – 11c,14p,1dg): **1995** E(1p), S(1p), W(a:1c,2p,1dg), It(4p) wc-

Do you have a duty to entertain? Yes, and I always try to do so.
Do you feel a loyalty to your club in this new era? No, loyalty goes out of the window as soon as a cheque-book is opened.

Other sporting claim to fame: Soccer for British Catholic Schools in 1989. A right back, I also played England 16-Group and almost had trials with Everton.
Notable landmarks in rugby career: An Anglo-Irishman who has been in and out of the Irish side since his debut against England (Dublin, 21.1.95). Post-World Cup, he has started just the one game, the 44–8 defeat of Fiji (Dublin, 18.11.95), as first longtime rival Eric Elwood and then David Humphreys took the reins. Earned his Test call-up on the back of an inter-Provincial title-winning campaign in the colours of Munster, having previously represented England at Schools, Under-18, Colts and Under-21 level. But a Galway-born father and Kildare-born mother meant he could declare for the Emerald Isle in November 1992. Toured with the Irish development squad to Africa in 1993 before working his way through Ireland Under-21 and A teams to the senior side, where he earned his call-up at the expense of Alan McGowan for the 1995 Five Nations opener against England. Despite defeat, he held his place for the Scotland game. However, a poor day's goalkicking contributed to Irish defeat and to his deselection. Elwood, now fit again, returned against France but Ireland looked little different. And the nation seemed on course for the Wooden Spoon when Elwood was clobbered by a late tackle in Cardiff (18.3.95) and Paul was introduced to the fray. The former London Irish mini-player grabbed his chance superbly, dropping a neat goal to settle his nerves, before adding two penalties and the conversion of Brendan Mullin's try as Ireland ran out 16–12 winners. In spite of four penalty goals next time out, Ireland's 'feat' of becoming the first major nation to lose to Italy (Treviso, 6.5.95) counted against Paul in the World Cup reckoning, and although he went to South Africa he lost out to Elwood, playing only against Japan (Bloemfontein, 31.5.95) – a game in which he contributed 15 points to a 50–28 win.
Touchlines: Golf (15 handicap)

*Ireland's Jonathan Bell gets his collar felt by
Scotland wing Michael Dods in Dublin.*

Burnell, A. P.   Scotland

Full name: Andrew Paul Burnell
Nickname: Archie
Club: London Scottish
Position: Prop
Height: 6ft 1in (1.85m)
Weight: 17st 2lb (109kg)
Occupation: Company director, Leisure Enterprises
Born: Edinburgh, 29.9.65
Family: Single
Former clubs: Marlow, Harlequins, Leicester
International debut: England 12, Scotland 12, 1989
Five Nations debut: As above
Best rugby memory: 1990 Grand Slam decider
Worst rugby memory: Being dropped by 1993 Lions
Serious injuries: Ruptured disc in back (1989, required surgery), acute tear in knee medial ligament (1992)
Toughest opponent: David Hilton (Bath & Scotland)
Do you really want to be a full-time professional player? No, part-time. I'm keeping my job.
How well has rugby handled move to professionalism? 7/10. It took far too long to reach agreement but now we have it we must all aspire to Super-12 standards.
Do you have a duty to entertain? Definitely
Do you feel a loyalty to your club in this new era? Yes
Other sporting claim to fame: Golf (20 handicap)

Scotland (1989)		
Last Season	4 caps	5 pts
Career	41 caps	5 pts
Lions (1993)	1 Test	0 pts

Caps (41): **1989** E, I, F, Fj, R **1990** I, F, W, E, Arg **1991** F, W, E, I, R wc-J, Z, I, WS, E, NZ **1992** E, I, F, W **1993** I, F, W, E. Lions-NZ(1). NZ **1994** W, E, I, F, Arg(1,2), SA **1995** wc-IC, T(R), F(R). WS

Points (5 – 1t): **1995** wc-IC(1t)

Notable landmarks in rugby career: Missed out on Scotland's revival in 1995, having lost his place after the 10–34 loss to South Africa (Murrayfield, 19.11.94). Remained on the edge of the team, however, and was rewarded for his continued loyalty with a World Cup appearance and his first-ever Test try, in the 89–0 rout of Cote d'Ivoire (Rustenburg, 26.5.95). Also played the last six minutes of the 41–5 defeat of Tonga (Pretoria, 3.6.95). On his return from South Africa he played the full 80 minutes against Western Samoa (Edinburgh, 18.11.95), but a 15–15 draw did nobody in the Scottish side any good. He was one of six players not to win another cap during the season. Still, he is within

nine appearances of Sandy Carmichael's 50-cap national best for a prop. A British Lion in 1993, Paul played against North Harbour, Canterbury, Otago, Auckland and Waikato, and appeared in the agonising 20–18 first Test defeat in Christchurch against the All Blacks. Missed out on nothing in 1993/94 season except league relegation after sterling end-of-season rally by London Scottish. Scored on first team debut for Leicester and Scotland B debut in 26–3 win over Italy in L'Aquila (1989). Twice helped London Scottish to win promotion – as 1989/90 Third Division and 1991/92 Second Division champions – and featured in their triumphant 1990/91 Middlesex Sevens side. Toured with Scotland to Zimbabwe (1988), New Zealand (1990), having been ever-present in Grand Slam campaign, and Argentina (1994), but missed tours to Japan (1989) and Australia (1992) through injury.
Touchlines: Movies, reading

Cabannes, L. France

Full name: Laurent Cabannes
Club: Harlequins
Position: Flanker
Height: 6ft 2in (1.88m)
Weight: 15st 3lb (92kg)
Occupation: Company manager
Born: Reims, 6.2.64
Family: Married
Former club: Pau, Racing Club de France
International debut: France 12, New Zealand 30, 1990
Five Nations debut: France 15, Scotland 9, 1991
Notable landmarks in rugby career: Dropped through lack of form midway through the 1995 Five Nations Championship, the enigmatic Laurent returned with a vengeance at the World Cup, turning in outstanding displays, both in lineout and loose play. Ever-present in France's impressive run, he was particularly notable against Scotland (Pretoria, 3.6.95), Ireland (Durban, 10.6.95) and South Africa (Durban, 18.6.95). He remained in South Africa to play Currie Cup rugby for

France (1990)

Last Season	10 caps	0 pts
Career	45 caps	8 pts

Caps (45): **1990** NZ(2R) **1991** S, I, W, E, US(2), W wc-Ro, Fj, C,E **1992** W, E, S, I, R, Arg(a2), SA(1,2) **1993** E, S, I, W, R(a), SA(1,2) **1994** E, S, C(a), NZ(1,2) **1995** W, E(a), S(a), R wc-T(R), IC, S(b), I(b), SA, E(b) **1996** E,S,I,W
Points (8 – 2t): **1991** I(1t) **1992** I(1t)

Western Province and was then 'suspended' by the French Federation for the home series against New Zealand before returning for the Five Nations series. Laurent made his senior debut for Pau at the age of just 17. In 1992/93, besides further enhancing his reputation with a hefty contribution to France's Five Nations title triumph, he also turned out for France at Murrayfield in the World Cup Sevens tournament. He has only scored two international tries, but both have been spectacular affairs against Ireland. Scored try in Racing's 1990 French club championship triumph, the Paris club's first success in 31 years. He was also on the side which finished runners-up in 1987 – the year after he had begun playing France B rugby (against Wales B at Pontypridd). However, it was not until November 1990 that he broke into the senior ranks as a replacement for Abdel Benazzi in the second Test against New Zealand in Paris. Laurent played major roles in France's historic series victories in South Africa (1993) and New Zealand (1994).

Califano, C.   France

Full name: Christian Califano
Club: Toulouse
Position: Tighthead Prop
Height: 5ft 11in (1.80m)
Weight: 16st 7lb (100kg)
Occupation: Army (military service)
Born: Toulon, 16.5.72
Family: Single
Former club: Toulon
International debut: New Zealand 8, France 22, 1994
Five Nations debut: France 21, Wales 9, 1995

Notable landmarks in rugby career: A remarkable rise to prominence for Christian, who was voted France's top tighthead prop at the end of the 1993/94 season and celebrated with his international debut on the momentous summer tour of New Zealand. Enjoyed a cracking World Cup and concluded last season by scoring a hat-trick of tries as France hammered Romania 64–12 in Aurillac (20.4.96). Has anchored Toulouse pack in three French Championship wins, in addition to

France (1994)

Last Season	17 caps	15 pts
Career	23 caps	15 pts

Caps (23): **1994** NZ(1,2), C(b) **1995** W, E(a), S(a), I(a) wc-T, IC, S(b), I(b), SA, E(b). It, Arg, NZ(1,2) **1996** E, S, I, W, R, Arg(1,2)
Points (15 – 3t): **1996** R(3t)

the inaugural European Cup, beating Cardiff 21–18 in last season's dramatic final. These days he appears equally at home in loosehead or tighthead berths. Christian's Test bow came in Christchurch (26.6.94) and resulted in a remarkable 22–8 victory for France over the All Blacks. More notable still, France repeated the result on Christian's second appearance, clinching the series by virtue of a last-gasp 23–20 victory in Auckland (3.7.94). Since then he has missed just three games: the pre-World Cup visit to Bucharest, the Cup opener against Tonga and the Latin Cup tie against Romania in October 1995. At first, with Christian around, France could do no wrong. But his run of Test victories came to an end at Twickenham (4.2.95), where England contrived to undo the French challenge. Another defeat followed, this time to Scotland (the first home loss to Ecosse for 26 years), but there was little question of Christian losing his place. Instead it was loosehead prop Laurent Benezech who paid the price, with Pierre Berbizier drafting the experience of Louis Armary into the front row to stave off further Five Nations disaster.

Callard, J. E. B.   England

Full name: Jonathan Edward Brooks Callard
Nickname: J.C.
Club: Bath
Position: Full-back
Height: 5ft 10in (1.78m)
Weight: 12st 7lb (75kg)
Occupation: Student/professional player
Born: Leicester, 1.1.66
Family: Gail (wife), Georgia (daughter)
International debut: England 15, New Zealand 9, 1993
Five Nations debut: Scotland 14, England 15, 1994
Best moment in rugby: Seeing Tony Swift score a superb try at Twickenham in the 1995 Pilkington Cup final in his last game for Bath. It gave the whole team so much pleasure.
Worst moment in rugby: Being dropped after Ireland defeat (1994)
Toughest opponent: All of them
Preferred commitment to rugby: Full-time, I think. I want the rewards

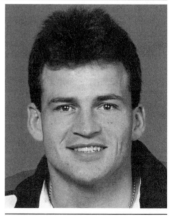

England (1993)

Last Season	2 caps	30 pts
Career	5 caps	69 pts

Caps (5): **1993** NZ **1994** S, I **1995** wc-WS. SA
Points (69 – 3c,18p): **1993** NZ(4p) **1994** S(5p), I(4p) **1995** wc-WS(3c,5p). SA(3p)

that come with being a full-time player, but I still have other interests that I want to pursue.

How well has rugby handled move to professionalism? 8/10 for the clubs' performance, but –2/10 for the RFU. They opened the door to professionalism and then said 'wait a year'. In that time no clear structure for the future was implemented. There should have been more guidelines issued. Instead a series of personality clashes stripped professional rugby of its credibility.

Do you have a duty to entertain? Yes, the product on the field has got to become more exciting. Supporters deserve more for their money. Perhaps competitions to find the best goalkickers, or the hooker with the longest throw. Anything to entertain the paying public.

Do you feel a loyalty to your club in this new era? Yes

Other sporting claim to fame: Junior cricket for Monmouthshire

Notable landmarks in rugby career: After his eventful 1993/94 campaign, the last year has been rather a comedown for Jon internationally speaking. Having lost the England fullback berth to Paul Hull in South Africa (1994), and having almost lost an eye in a vicious stamping incident against Eastern Province that required 25 stitches, he then saw Bath fly-half team mate Mike Catt jump to the head of the queue. But Jon, a persistent matchwinner for Bath on the domestic stage, has sat patiently on the bench, making just the two appearances: in England's impressive 44–22 World Cup defeat of Western Samoa (Durban, 4.6.95) and in their less than impressive 14–24 loss to South Africa (Twickenham, 18.11.95). He marked the occasion against the Samoans with a thoroughly polished 21-point performance (3c,5p) and slotted three penalty goals against the world champion Boks. But there again Jon had already shown England he was a man for the big match, having celebrated his Twickenham debut in 1990 with a try in Bath's Pilkington Cup final triumph, and marked his England debut (Twickenham, 27.11.93) with four penalty goals in the 15–9 defeat of New Zealand. Save for a wayward pass which gifted the Blacks a try against England A, Jon enjoyed their tour, as he landed eight penalty goals against them wearing the colours of South West Division and the national A team. But he saved his finest hour for his Five Nations debut (Edinburgh, 5.2.94), when he pulled the Calcutta Cup out of the fire with a last-gasp penalty goal from 40 metres. 'For a few awful seconds I wanted to run and hide', remembers Jon of the moment when Will Carling turned to him and said, 'Here, it's easy, get on with it.' 'But you can't hide: you have to conquer yourself', added the former Newport player, who had made his debut as an 18-year-old against Bath. Jon's season turned thereafter as he was one of the victims of the purge which followed Ireland's shock Twickenham win. Helped Bath to league and cup double in 1995/96, and so excelled in cross-code challenge against Wigan RLFC that he was offered a RL contract.

Touchlines: Bandit golfer (18-handicap)

Campan, O.   France

Full name: Olivier Campan
Club: Agen
Position: Centre
Height: 5ft 11in (1.80m)
Weight: 13st 7lb (81kg)
Occupation: PE student
Born: 15.3.70
International debut: South Africa 20,
France 20, 1993
Five Nations debut: France 45,
Ireland 10, 1996
Notable landmarks in rugby career:
Injuries delayed Olivier's true
emergence onto the international
stage until February 1996, when he
played his first full match for France,
some three years after making his
Test debut as a replacement in the
20–20 draw with South Africa in
Durban (26.6.93). He also appeared
as a replacement in the second Test,
which France sneaked 18–17
(Johannesburg, 3.7.93) to win the
series. As a teenager in Agen he
played on the wing outside Philippe

France (1993)

Last Season	3 caps	5 pts
Career	6 caps	5 pts

Caps (6): **1993** SA(1R,2R), R(2R) **1996** I, W, R
Points (5 – 1t): **1996** I(1t)

Sella, and appeared for France Juniors. In 1992 he played at fullback in the French Universities side which won the Students World Cup. In fact he had only played at centre four times at club level and once for France A before being handed the midfield berth against Ireland in Paris (17.2.96). France inflicted on the Irish a championship record defeat (45–10) and Olivier claimed one of seven tries. Retained his place for the next engagement, in Cardiff, where France surprisingly lost to surrender the Five Nations title they had in their pocket. Completed his season in Aurillac, helping *Les Tricolores* crush Romania 64–12 (20.4.96).

Campbell, S. J. Scotland

Full name: Stewart Joseph Campbell
Club: Melrose
Position: Lock
Height: 6ft 6in (1.98m)
Weight: 16st 8lb (101kg)
Occupation: Architectural student, Dundee University
Born: Glasgow, 25.4.72
Family: Single
Former clubs: West, Dundee HSFP
International debut: Scotland 22, Canada 6, 1995
Five Nations debut: Scotland 26, Ireland 13, 1995
Best rugby memory: Beating France in Paris (1995)
Worst rugby memory: Two Grand Slam losses to England (1995/96)
Most embarrassing memory: Thinking I had scored a try against France – I was positive until I saw Merle with the ball.
Toughest opponent: Gareth Llewellyn (Harlequins & Wales)
Preferred commitment to rugby: Part-time

Scotland (1995)		
Last Season	6 caps	0 pts
Career	12 caps	0 pts

Caps (12): 1995 C, I, F(a), W, E, R wc-IC, NZ(R) 1996 I, F, W, E
Points Nil

How well has rugby handled move to professionalism? The SRU should be applauded for introducing 'loyalty payments' in Scotland
Do you have a duty to entertain? No, my duty is to win, but there is no reason why we can't do both.
Do you feel a loyalty to your club in this new era? Yes
Notable landmarks in rugby career: Established himself as a regular in the Scotland second row, having appeared in 13 of the 15 Tests prior to the summer tour of New Zealand. His emergence coincided with an upturn in the Scots' fortunes. Prior to Stewart's debut against Canada at a freezing Murrayfield (21.1.95), Scotland had failed to win in nine internationals. Yet his debut ended in a 22–6 triumph, and five of his next seven caps also yielded victories. The sixth member of the Dundee High School Former Pupils club to be capped (following in the bootprints of George Ritchie, J. S. Wilson, Chris Rea, David Leslie and, most recently, Andy Nicol), Stewart represented Scotland in three age groups before stepping out with Scottish Students. There then followed three winning outings for Scotland A: against France, Italy and (most notably) South Africa. The venue was Melrose, the date was 9 November 1994 and the

result was 17–15 in the A-team's favour, thanks to Duncan Hodge's last-gasp dropped goal. It was the Springboks' only defeat other than their tour-ending game against the Barbarians in Dublin. Stewart had also played against another touring side, the 1993 All Blacks, in the Scottish Development XV beaten 31–12 in Edinburgh (16.11.93). He next came across New Zealand in the 1995 World Cup when he came on as a 62nd-minute substitute for Damian Cronin in Scotland's 48–30 quarter-final defeat (Pretoria, 11.6.95). It was his second outing of the tournament, having played all of the opening game against Cote d'Ivoire – a game in which Scotland registered the biggest win in their history, 89–0 (Rustenburg, 26.5.95). Missed Western Samoa's visit to Murrayfield (18.11.95) but returned thereafter to help guide Scots to verge of Grand Slam.
Touchlines: Music, squash

Campese, D. I. Australia

Full name: David Ian Campese
State: New South Wales
Club: Randwick
Position: Wing, fullback
Height: 5ft 10in (1.77m)
Weight: 14st 12lb (90kg)
Occupation: Partner in Campo's Sports Store
Born: 21.10.62
Family: Tony (father), Joan (mother), Mario (brother), Lisa (sister), Corinne (sister)
Former clubs: Queanbeyan (1980–86), Petrarca (Padua, Italy: 1984–87)
International debut: New Zealand 23, Australia 16, 1982
Best moments in rugby: Debut in

first Test against New Zealand in 1982, when I scored a try; 1989 Hong Kong Sevens Player of Tournament; 1991 World Cup.
Worst moment in rugby: Being dropped for first Test vs France in 1990.
Most embarrassing moment: Dropping ball at Cardiff against 1988 Barbarians with try line in sight.
Most respected opponent: Hugo Porta (Argentina)
Serious injuries: Dislocated shoulder (1985), ankle (1987), knee (1992)
Other sporting claims to fame: 1981 ACT Schools Golf Championship
Suggestions to improve rugby: Allow playing the ball on the ground. Stop locks marking wingers under the current maul law. Install professional rugby administrators.

Notable landmarks in rugby career:
The world's leading Test try scorer with 63, 'Campo' is also Australia's most-capped player, with 94 appearances to his name – and he refused to contemplate retirement after Australia's World Cup defence ended in the quarter-finals against England (Cape Town, 11.6.95). That said, his appearances since have been thin on the ground, limited to a replacement cameo in the second Bledisloe Test against New Zealand (29.7.95) before he regained his place for last summer's visit of Wales. Shares with Greg Cornelsen the Aussie record for most tries scored in a single Test, with his four against the US Eagles in 1983. Campo started with Queanbeyan before joining Randwick in 1987. He also switched his State allegiance from Australian Capital Territory to New South Wales. Made his international debut against New Zealand back in 1982 and has been a thorn in opponents' flesh ever since – not least in the 1991 World Cup, when six tries in six appearances helped Australia win the Webb Ellis Cup and led him to be declared both the Player of the Tournament and the Australian Society of Rugby Writers Player of the

Australia (1982)		
Last Season	6 caps	0 pts
Career	94 caps	301 pts

Caps (94): **1982** NZ(1,2,3) **1983** US, Arg(1,2), NZ, It, F(1,2) **1984** Fj, NZ(1,2,3), E, I, W, S **1985** Fj(1,2) **1986** It, F, Arg(1,2), NZ(1,2,3) **1987** wc-E, US, J, I, F, W. NZ **1988** E(1,2), NZ(1,2,3), E, S, It **1989** BL(1,2,3), NZ, F(1,2) **1990** F(2,3), US, NZ(1,2,3) **1991** W, E, NZ(1,2). wc-Arg, WS, W, I, NZ, E **1992** S(1,2), NZ(1,2,3), SA, I, W **1993** T, NZ, SA(1,2,3), C, F(1,2) **1994** I(1,2), It(1,2), WS, NZ **1995** Arg(1,2) wc-SA, C, E. NZ(2R), **1996** W(1,2)

Points (301 – 63t,5c,6p,2dg): **1982** NZ(1:1t), NZ(2:1t) **1983** US(4t, 1c), Arg(1:1p), Arg(2:1t,3c,1p), Fj(1t), F(1:1c,1p), F(2:1p) **1984** NZ(2:1p), NZ(3:1t,1p), S(2t) **1985** Fj(1:1dg), Fj(2:2t) **1986** It(2t), F(1t), Arg(1:1t), Arg(2:2t), NZ(1:1t), NZ(3:1t) **1987** wc-E(1t), US(1t), J(1t), F(1t) **1988** E(a2:1t), E(b:1t), S(2t), It(3t) **1989** NZ(1t), F(1:1t) **1990** F(2:1t), F(3:1t), US(1t,1dg) **1991** W(a:1t), E(a:2t). wc-Arg(2t), W(b:1t), I(2t), NZ(b:1t) **1992** S(1:2t), NZ(1:1t), SA(1t), I(1t), W(1t) **1993** T(2t), C(3t) **1994** I(1:1t), It(2:1t), WS(1t) **1995** Arg(1:1t), Arg(2:2t)

Year, plus a similar accolade from the British Rugby Writers in the form of the Pat Marshall Memorial Award. He was an ever-present throughout Australia's eight-Test campaign in 1992, adding to his try tally against Scotland, New Zealand (first Test), South Africa (No.50), Ireland and Wales. An unbroken run in 1993 included the third try hat-trick of his career, against Canada (having previously claimed two against Tonga). More of the same in 1994, with tries against Ireland, Italy and Western Samoa, before he bagged three in two Tests against Argentina pre-World Cup.

Touchlines: Golf

Carbonneau, P.   France

Full name: Philippe Carbonneau
Club: Toulouse
Positions: Scrum-half, centre
Height: 5ft 9in (1.75m)
Weight: 12st 8lb (75kg)
Occupation: Hypermarket employee
Born: Toulouse, 15.4.71
International debut: France 52, Romania 8, 1995
Five Nations debut: France 15, England 12, 1996
Notable landmarks in rugby career: One of rugby's versatile three-quarters, Philippe has divided his career between centre and scrum-half. The influence of current France coach Jean-Claude Skrela put a No.9 shirt on his back, first in his teenage days at Toulouse, where Skrela coached in 1990. Philippe appeared at scrum-half for France Under-23 in 1993 before being switched to centre after Skrela departed to Colomiers. Philippe met with immediate success, sharing in Toulouse's championship

France (1995)

Last Season	8 caps	10 pts
Career	8 caps	10 pts

Caps (8): **1995** R, Arg, NZ(1,2) **1996** E, S, R(R), Arg(2)
Points (10 – 2t): **1995** Arg(2t)

triumph that year and joining France in New Zealand that summer as a replacement on what turned out to be a historic tour. Although not appearing in either of the Test victories, he scored a try hat-trick on his debut against Nelson Bays, and he continued in midfield for France A on his return. But when Skrela succeeded Pierre Berbizier as France coach in October 1995, he called on Philippe to wear the No.9 shirt again, taking him to the Latin Cup tournament in Argentina. A debut against Romania (Tucuman, 17.10.95) was followed by his first two Test tries on his second outing, in the 47–12 defeat of the Pumas (Buenos Aires, 21.10.95). Held his place throughout the shared home series with New Zealand but lost out to Guy Accoceberry midway through the 1996 Five Nations series. Picked up his seventh cap as a late replacement for Accoceberry against Romania in Aurillac (won 64–12, 20.4.96).

Carling, W. D. C.   England

Full name: William David Charles
Carling
Nickname: Bumface
Club: Harlequins
Position: Centre
Height: 5ft 11lb (1.81m)
Weight: 14st 2lb (89.5kg)
Occupation: Runs own management
training/personal development
company – Insight
Born: Bradford-on-Avon, Wiltshire,
12.12.65
Family links with rugby: Father (Bill)
played for Cardiff
Former club: Durham University
International debut: France 10,
England 9, 1988
Five Nations debut: As above
Best moments in rugby: Three Grand
Slams – beating New Zealand,
Australia and South Africa along the
way.
Worst moment in rugby: 1991
World Cup final; 1995 World Cup
semi-final.
Most embarrassing moment: Being
picked up and carried over dead-ball
line at Middlesex Sevens.
Toughest opponent: Frank Bunce
(North Harbour & New Zealand)
Preferred commitment to rugby: I'm
too old but I would love to have been
a full-time professional player.
**How well has rugby handled move
to professionalism?** 1/10

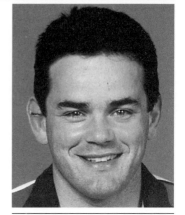

England (1988)		
Last Season	11 caps	10 pts
Career	66 caps	49 pts
Lions (1993)	1 Test	0 pts

Caps (66): **1988** F, W, S, I(1,2), A(a2),
Fj, A(b) **1989** S, I, F, W, Fj **1990** I,
F, W, S, Arg(a1,a2), Arg(b) **1991**
W, S, I, F, Fj, A(a) wc-NZ, It, US,
F, S, A(b) **1992** S, I, F, W, C, SA
1993 F, W, S, I. Lions-NZ(1). NZ
1994 S, I, F, W, SA(1,2), R, C **1995**
I, F(a), W, S wc-Arg, WS, A, NZ,
F(b). SA, WS **1996** F, W, S, I
Points (49 – 11t): **1989** F(1t) **1990** F(1t),
W(1t) **1991** wc-US(1t), F(1t) **1992**
W(1t), SA(1t) **1994** R(1t) **1995**
I(1t) wc-NZ(2t)

Do you have a duty to entertain? The duty is to win.
Do you feel a loyalty to your club in this new era? Yes – far more so.
Other sporting claim to fame: Other? What do you mean other?
Most respected opponent: Denis Charvet (Toulouse & France)
Serious injuries: Fracture of leg (1989)
Suggestions to improve rugby: Where do we start? Greater player involvement
in law changes and in the administration of the game. It seems so logical to me,
yet they continue to ignore it. General level of coaching in English club rugby

must be raised: we're still too stuck in our ways. We must learn from other countries. Better communication is needed, and everyone, regardless of hemisphere, should play by the same rules.

Notable landmarks in rugby career: Stood down as England captain after collecting yet another Five Nations title in 1996, leaving behind a peerless record of 44 victories in the 59 matches he took charge of. Will, who has no plans to give up his England place, produced the best form of his distinguished career last season, at a time when countless observers were pointing him in the direction of the international exit. Among the tributes that followed his decision to relinquish the captaincy, former RFU president Dennis Easby said: 'He is the most successful captain we will ever have. He has been an absolute credit to English rugby and to his country in eight marvellous years.' For the record, Easby was the man who sacked and then reinstated Will as captain on the eve of the 1995 World Cup for his now infamous 'old farts' remark, in which he rather unwisely labelled the RFU's committee as old windbags. England's most-capped centre (66), Will rebounded from the disappointment of being dropped by 1993 Lions (after first Test loss to All Blacks) by leading England to victory over the same opponents (27.11.93). Began playing career as a six-year-old with Terra Nova School Under-11s. First fifth-former (15 years old) to play in Sedbergh's first XV (three years in team – experienced only two defeats), prior to captaining England 18-Group (1984) and moving on to Durham University on an Army scholarship (reading psychology), where he switched to fullback. Northern Division selectors Geoff Cooke and Dave Robinson advised him to play centre, where he has remained ever since. Rates a county performance for Durham against Lancashire as one of the most influential in shaping his future career. Bought himself out of Army (2nd Lt heading towards Royal Regiment of Wales) when told he would not be able to play representative rugby. Helped England B beat France B 22–9 (Bath, 20.2.87). England's youngest captain for 57 years (since P. D. Howard of Old Millhillians, 1931) when handed reins aged 22 years and 11 months for England's 28–19 win over Australia (5.11.88). Captain in three Grand Slams, one World Cup final (1991) and one semi-final (1995). Confessed on Radio 4's 'Desert Island Discs' (May 1992) that, if cast away, he would want with him Tolkein's book *The Hobbit*, Louis Armstrong's record 'What a Wonderful World', and a flotation tank.

Touchlines: Painting (sketching and inks), social golf, filling in questionnaires

A sad end: Will Carling slumps to the turf in agony after injuring his ankle in his final game as England captain against Ireland.

Castaignede, T. France

Full name: Thomas Castaignede
Club: Toulouse
Position: Fly-half, centre
Height: 5ft 9in (1.75m)
Weight: 11st 10lb (70kg)
Occupation: Chemistry student
Born: Mont-de-Marsan, 21.1.75
Family: Single
International debut: France 52, Romania 8, 1995
Five Nations debut: France 15, England 12, 1996
Best rugby memory: Kicking last-minute dropped goal to beat England on Five Nations debut.
Notable landmarks in rugby career: Gained worldwide recognition when he danced a jig with his tongue hanging out after his injury-time dropped goal beat England and ended eight years of dominance by *Les Rosbifs*. That was on his Five Nations debut (20.1.95), some seven hours before he turned 21 years of age. A prodigious talent, Thomas has been a star down Toulouse way since his teenage years. He played lead roles in the club's French championship triumphs of 1994,

France (1995)

Last Season	10 caps	78 pts
Career	10 caps	78 pts

Caps (10): 1995 R, Arg, NZ(1,2) 1996 E, S, I, W, Arg(1,2)
Points (78 – 4t,14c,8p,2dg): 1995 R(1t,4c,2p,1dg), Arg(1t), NZ(1:2c,1p), NZ(2:1c) 1996 E(1dg), S(1p), I(5c), W(1t,1c,1p), Arg(1:1t), Arg(2:1c,3p)

1995 and 1996, and was equally influencial in Toulouse winning the inaugural European Cup, beating Cardiff in the final played in the Welsh capital. His debut was a typically flamboyant affair, as he amassed 22 points including a 'full house' of one try, four conversions, two penalty goals and one dropped goal. Romania did not thank him for it, as they were the opposition in Tucuman, Argentina, where the Latin Cup was being staged. Thomas moved to centre, his regular club position, for the title-clinching victory over Argentina (21.10.95), and claimed a try in the 47–12 result. Remained at centre for the two-Test autumn visit of New Zealand and through the first half of the 1996 Five Nations series, before moving to fly-half after France's shock defeat in Edinburgh. He then produced a magnificent display as Ireland were handed a championship record 45–10 trouncing at Parc des Princes, and took his tally to 62 points in eight appearances with a try, conversion and penalty in the defeat by Wales in Cardiff (16.3.96).

Castel, R.   France

Full name: Richard Castel
Club: Toulouse
Position: Openside flanker
Height: 6ft 2in (1.88m)
Weight: 14st 7lb (87kg)
Occupation: Student
Born: Vendres, 31.12.72
International debut: France 45,
Ireland 10, 1996
Five Nations debut: As above
Notable landmarks in rugby career:
Became the first French forward in
17 years to score two tries on his
debut, bagging a brace in the 45–10
Five Nations defeat of a hapless
Ireland (Paris, 17.2.96). The
previous player to achieve the feat
was Yves Malquier against Scotland
in 1979. Richard deserved the
recognition that accompanied his try
double, as he had spent so much of
his earlier career seemingly nailed to
the replacements bench. A reserve in
Toulouse's 1995 championship win,

France (1996)		
Last Season	2 caps	10 pts
Career	2 caps	10 pts

Caps (2): 1996 I, W
Points (10 – 2t): 1996 I(2t)

he occupied the same berth in both the semi-final (vs Swansea) and final (vs
Cardiff) of the inaugural Heineken European Cup in the autumn of 1995,
though he tasted action in both encounters as Toulouse triumphed. Prone to
injury, Richard's career took off in 1996 as he reached full fitness. After
warming the bench in Edinburgh, where France crashed 14–19 to Scotland
(3.2.96), the French Student international was promoted for the visit of Ireland.
His emergence coincided with France's once compelling performance of the
championship as Ireland were pummelled 45–10 in their biggest ever Five
Nations defeat. Richard moved to blindside for the final round of matches,
which took France to Cardiff, before spending the summer in South Africa,
competing in the Student World Cup.

Catt, M. J.   England

Full name: Michael John Catt
Nickname: Catty
Club: Bath
Position: Centre, outside-half
Height: 5ft 10in (1.78m)
Weight: 13st 2lb (79kg)
Occupation: Professional rugby
player
Born: Port Elizabeth, 17.9.71
Family: Single
International debut: England 15,
Wales 8, 1994
Five Nations debut: As above
**Do you really want to be a full-time
professional?** Yes
Other sporting claims to fame:
Triathlon for Eastern Province
(Under-21 champion)
Notable landmarks in rugby career:
Many people's choice as the best
utility back in England, Mike varies
between fullback, his England
position, and fly-half, his club berth.
In addition, Bath team mate Jeremy
Guscott reckons he has the potential
to become the best centre three-
quarter in world rugby. Grabbed his

England (1994)
Last Season	12 caps	3 pts
Career	18 caps	13 pts

Caps (18): **1994** W(R), C(R) **1995** I,
F(a), W, S wc-Arg, It, WS, A, NZ,
F(b). SA, WS **1996** F, W, S, I
Points (13 – 2t,1dg): **1994** C(R:2t) **1995**
wc-WS(1dg)

England chance with both hands after coming on as a 27th-minute replacement
against Romania (Twickenham, 12.11.94) for Paul Hull, England's outstanding back on the tour to South Africa only months earlier. Mike scored two
tries and has been unchallenged since, although Jack Rowell did move him to
fly-half for one match – against South Africa (lost 14–24, Twickenham,
18.11.95) – before hastily abandoning the experiment and handing him back
the No.15 shirt. Played in all four rounds of England's 1995 Grand Slam and
throughout World Cup campaign, including another one-off game at fly-half
where he dropped a goal in the 44–22 defeat of Western Samoa, and one game
when this Catt was run over, literally, by All Black sensation Jonah Lomu.
Moved to Bath from Eastern Province, South Africa, in 1992, immediately
establishing himself as deputy to Stuart Barnes. Born in Port Elizabeth, he holds
a British passport thanks to his English mother. Toured Australia with
England's Under-21 side in 1993, scoring a try in their 'Test' win. It took him
only nine domestic appearances to get himself nominated for England's
preliminary squad to play 1993 All Blacks, and although he didn't figure in the

final 21, he was drafted into the squad for the 1994 Five Nations Championship, warming the bench in each game before coming on in the 76th minute of the title decider against Wales as a replacement for Rob Andrew. Pivotal in Bath's league and cup double last season.

Chalmers, C. M.   Scotland

Full name: Craig Minto Chalmers
Nickname: Chick
Club: Melrose
Position: Outside-half
Height: 5ft 11in (1.80m)
Weight: 13st 6lb (85kg)
Occupation: Marketing advisor with Scottish Power
Born: Galashiels, 15.10.68
Family: Lucy (wife), Sam (son), Ben (son)
Family links with rugby: Father (Brian) coaches at Melrose
International debut: Scotland 23, Wales 7, 1989
Five Nations debut: As above
Best moments in rugby: Winning 1990 Grand Slam by beating England; all the championship wins with Melrose.
Worst moment in rugby: Being dropped by 1989 Lions after playing in first Test against Australia (lost 12–30); breaking arm at Twickenham (6.3.93) to be ruled out of 1993 Lions selection; being dropped by Scotland (1994).
Toughest opponent: Michael Lynagh (Saracens & Australia)
Do you really want to be a full-time professional? No – not unless I received guarantees of work after my playing days are over.
How well has rugby handled move to professionalism? 6/10. Things have moved too fast. Scotland should field clubs in Europe, not

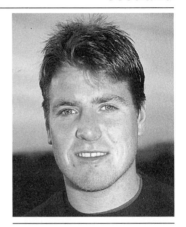

Scotland (1989)		
Last Season	5 caps	0 pts
Career	47 caps	131 pts
Lions (1989)	1 Test	6 pts

Caps (47): **1989** W, E, I, F. Lions-A(1). Fj **1990** I, F, W, E, NZ(1,2), Arg **1991** F, W, E, I, Ro wc-J, Z, I, WS, E, NZ **1992** E, I, F, W, A(1,2) **1993** I, F, W, E, NZ **1994** W, SA **1995** C, I, F(a), W, E, R wc-IC, T, F(b), NZ. WS

Points (131 – 5t,7c,24p,8dg): **1989** W(1t,1dg). Lions-A(1:1p,1dg) **1990** I(1c,1p), F(2c,2p), W(3p), E(3p), Arg(1t) **1991** F(2p,1dg), W(1t,1c,1p,1dg), E(4p), I(2c,3p) wc-J(1t,1p), I(1dg) **1992** W(1dg,2p), A(2:1c,1p) **1993** E(1dg), NZ(1p)

districts, as it is the clubs that have the identity.

Do you have a duty to entertain? Yes

Do you feel a loyalty to your club in this new era? I think ambition will override loyalty.

Serious injuries: Torn knee cartilage, strained groin, dead leg, double fracture of right forearm (1993), partially torn cruciate knee ligament (1994).

Notable landmarks in rugby career: The most experienced bench reserve in the 1996 Five Nations Championship, Craig was not required for front-line national service after making his one appearance of the campaign in Scotland's disappointing 15–15 draw with Western Samoa (Edinburgh, 18.11.95). Succeeded John Rutherford as Scotland's most-capped fly-half when he won his 43rd cap in the 89–0 World Cup rout of Cote d'Ivoire (Rustenburg, 26.5.95). Marked the occasion with a try in Scotland's biggest win of all time. Ever-present in South Africa until he suffered a 'dead thigh' in the quarter-final against New Zealand, limping off at half-time. With him went Scotland's hopes of staying in the tournament. Still, the season was something of a triumph for Craig after an awful 1993/94 campaign, during which he suffered the ignominy of being dropped for first time since his Scotland debut in 1989, and was dogged by injury, which ruled him out of summer tour to Argentina. Paid the price for playing when less than 100% fit against Wales, and was not required thereafter. A far cry from 6 March 1993, when he was considered odds-on to become the British Lions' first-choice stand-off in New Zealand that summer. A double break of his right forearm when playing against England at Twickenham – the last Test hurdle for Scotland before selection was made – put paid to that. Youngest player ever to represent Scotland B – as a 19-year-old in the 18–12 defeat of France B at Chalon-sur-Saone (20.3.88) – having already turned out for Scottish Schools, Under-18, Under-19 and Under-21. Scored a try and dropped goal on full debut against Wales (21.1.89), having marked first XV debut for Melrose with three dropped goals against Harrogate. Earned selection to 1989 Lions tour of Australia and kicked six points in first Test before being replaced by Rob Andrew for remainder of series. Still, played in seven of the 12-match programme. Scotland's Grand Slam No.10 in 1990, kicking three penalty goals in never-to-be-forgotten decider against England. Dropped two goals as England turned the tables in 1995 Grand Slam decider (Twickenham, 18.3.95). Toured with Scotland to New Zealand (1990, 1996), North America (1991) and Australia (1992).

Touchlines: Golf (12 handicap), ten-pin bowling

Clarke, A.   Ireland

Full name: Allen Clarke
Nickname: Sniffer (after Leeds footballer Allan Clarke)
Club: Northampton
Position: Hooker
Height: 5ft 9in (1.75m)
Weight: 14st (89kg)
Occupation: Teacher, Raebourn School, Northampton
Born: Dungannon, 29.7.67
Family: Kerry (wife), Ariane (daughter)
Former club: Dungannon
International debut: Ireland 44, Fiji 8, 1995
Five Nations debut: Ireland 30, Wales 17, 1996
Best rugby memory: Beating Wales on my Five Nations debut
Worst rugby memory: Being relegated with Northampton (1994/95)
Most embarrassing memory: Getting through three pairs of shorts in my first international

Ireland (1995)

Last Season	3 caps	0 pts
Career	3 caps	0 pts

Caps (3): **1995** Fj(R) **1996** W, E
Points Nil

Toughest opponent: The Leicester front-row unit
Do you really want to be a full-time professional? No, I'm in my first year of teaching.
How well has rugby handled move to professionalism? 7/10 for the IRFU, and 9/10 for Northampton, who have been brilliant, putting no pressure on us at all.
Do you have a duty to entertain? Yes, we have a duty to the game.
Do you feel a loyalty to your club in this new era? Yes, without doubt, but the power of the chequebook has got to some people.
Other sporting claim to fame: Soccer for Mid-Ulster, badminton for Ulster.
Notable landmarks in rugby career: A member of Northampton's Second Division championship-winning team last season, Allen also made great progress on the international front in 1995/96. A former Ireland Under-21 cap, he was promoted to the A team towards the end of the 1994/95 season, warming the replacement bench against Wales A in March 1995, a month after winning his first Ulster senior cap against the touring Blue Bulls of South Africa, Northern Transvaal. The former Dungannon player (he moved to Franklins Gardens during the 1991/92 season) continued to impress last season, and was drafted into the full international squad for the early-season visit of Fiji to Lansdowne Road (18.11.95). Ireland roared to a 44–8 win and Allen was given

his debut as a 45th-minute replacement for former captain Terry Kingston. The experienced Dolphin man regained his shirt for the next three Tests before Ireland's Kiwi coach Murray Kidd, under pressure after his side's 10–45 trouncing in Paris, made sweeping changes. In came Allen and he saw the season out, playing against Wales and England.

Touchlines: Golf

Clarke, B. B. England

Full name: Benjamin Bevan Clarke
Club: Richmond
Position: No.8
Height: 6ft 5in (1.95m)
Weight: 16st 13lb (107kg)
Occupation: PR for National Power/professional rugby player
Born: Bishop's Stortford, 15.4.68
Family: Single
Family links with rugby: Father (Bevan) played for Bishop's Stortford and is now club chairman.
Former clubs: Bishop's Stortford, Saracens, Bath
International debut: England 33, South Africa 16, 1992
Five Nations debut: England 16, France 15, 1993
Best moment in rugby: Lions' second Test defeat of All Blacks; England's win over All Blacks (both 1993).
Worst moment in rugby: Being injured and missing climax of 1995/96 season, especially as it was my last with Bath.
Toughest opponent: Dean Richards (Leicester & England)
Do you really want to be a full-time professional? It's important to have a degree of professionalism for your game to improve, but not full-time rugby. I still want an outside interest in the business world.

England (1992)
Last Season	11 caps	5 pts
Career	28 caps	10 pts
Lions (1993)	3 Tests	0 pts

Caps (28): **1992** SA **1993** F, W, S, I. Lions-NZ(1,2,3). NZ **1994** S, F, W, SA(1,2), R, C **1995** I, F, W, S. wc-Arg, It, A, NZ, F. SA, WS **1996** F, W, S, I
Points (10 – 2t): **1994** SA(1:1t) **1995** I(1t)

How well has rugby handled move to professionalism? 3/10. People not speaking to each other was the big problem in England. Very disappointed that English clubs missed out on the European Cup.

Do you have a duty to entertain? Yes, because rugby is now a highly paid sport.

But it would be silly to put entertainment at No.1. It will come naturally if you play the game properly.

Do you feel a loyalty to your club in this new era? It might sound strange given that I've just left Bath, but yes, I do. You've got to believe in your club.

Other sporting claim to fame: Swimming for Hertfordshire

Notable landmarks in rugby career: Big-money signing by Richmond, the newly promoted English Second Division side, last summer ended many weeks of speculation as to Ben's next port of call. No wonder Richmond were so chuffed, as Ben, the cornerstone of England's pack, was also the outstanding British Lion in New Zealand (1993). Stalwart in England's Grand Slam triumph and World Cup campaign in 1995, Ben had previously proved himself one of the most dynamic and dependable of performers on England's 1994 tour to South Africa. Within five caps of his England debut (14.11.92) he had been snapped up by the Lions for their safari in New Zealand – a country he had previously visited in 1992 with England B, though he did not pick up a scalp then, being on the losing side in both Tests. In his formative years with Bishop's Stortford, Ben represented Hertfordshire Colts, Under-21 and full teams. On joining Saracens at start of 1990/91, he was selected for London Division, Public School Wanderers, Penguins, England Students and England B. Toured Australia (1991) with London, and was a member of the 1992 England B 'Grand Slam'-winning side, which accounted for Spain, Ireland B, France B and Italy B (scored tries vs Spain and Ireland). Helped Bath to 1995/96 league and cup double, although injury kept him out of the climax to both competitions.

Touchlines: Golf, squash, hockey

Clohessy, P. M. N. Ireland

Full name: Peter Martin Noel Clohessy

Nickname: The Claw

Club: Garryowen

Position: Tighthead prop

Height: 5ft 11in (1.80m)

Weight: 16st (102kg)

Occupation: Director, Clohessy Couriers, Limerick

Born: Limerick, 22.3.66

Family: Anna (wife), Luke (son)

Family links with rugby: Grandfather (Peter O'Hallaran) won Munster Senior Cup medal with Garryowen

Former club: Young Munster

International debut: Ireland 6, France 21, 1993

Five Nations debut: As above
Best moment in rugby: Beating 1992 Wallabies with Munster
Worst moment in rugby: Being suspended for 26 weeks after trial by video playing for Ireland against France (17.2.96).
Toughest opponent: Louis Armary (Lourdes & France)

Ireland (1993)

Last Season	2 caps	5 pts
Career	16 caps	10 pts

Caps (16): **1993** F, W, E **1994** F, W, E, S, A(1,2), US **1995** E, S, F, W **1996** S, F

Points (10 – 2t): **1994** A(2:1t) **1996** S(1t)

Serious injuries: Slipped disc, broken leg and arm
Do you really want to be a full-time professional? Yes
How well has rugby handled move to professionalism? 5/10. There has not been enough communication between the various sides.
Do you have a duty to entertain? Yes, because we are getting paid.
Do you feel a loyalty to your club in this new era? I do, yes.
Notable landmarks in rugby career: Banned for 26 weeks after what Peter terms 'trial by video' found him guilty of stamping on the head of Olivier Roumat during Ireland's record Five Nations Championship loss to France in Paris (17.2.96). The incident completed a bleak year for 'The Claw', who missed the 1995 World Cup through work commitments, having been regular Ireland tighthead during 1995 Five Nations. Graduated through Irish Under-23 (1989 vs Italy, Ravenhill) and B ranks to full side in 1992/93 season, after helping Munster to beat touring Australians 22–19 at Thomond Park, and Young Munster to win All-Ireland Championship. Debut against France came three years after Ireland B debut in 22–22 draw with Scotland B at Murrayfield (9.12.89). Big breakthrough followed provincial appearances against Ulster, Leinster and Connacht, and came in wake of Ireland's desperately poor defeat by Scotland at Murrayfield. Paul McCarthy was the player to pass over tighthead duties. Peter retained No.3 jersey for the remainder of the Championship, and should have been picked for 1993 British Lions tour to New Zealand. A ten-week suspension (for stamping) ruled him out of Ireland's 1993/94 Test opener against Romania (14.11.93). Regained jersey from Garrett Halpin by time of 1994 Five Nations Championship, after which he toured Australia with Ireland, scoring his first international try in the 32–18 second Test. loss in Sydney.
Touchlines: Waterskiing

Corkery, S. D.   Ireland

Full name: Sean **David** Corkery
Club: Bristol
Position: Flanker
Height: 6ft 4in (1.93m)
Weight: 14st 5lb (86kg)
Occupation: Fitness instructor
Born: Cork, 6.11.72
Former club: Cork Constitution,
Terenure College
International debut: Australia 31,
Ireland 13, 1994
Five Nations debut: Ireland 7,
France 25, 1995
Best memory in rugby: Scoring try vs
All Blacks in 1995 World Cup
Worst moment in rugby: Being
dropped after England match in
1995
Toughest opponent: Tim Rodber
(Northampton & England)
**Do you really want to be a full-time
professional?** Yes
**How well has rugby handled move
to professionalism?** 5/10 the way
England went about it. The speed of
change has been too rapid. There is
big money around now, but in two

Ireland (1994)

Last Season	10 caps	15 pts
Career	14 caps	15 pts

Caps (14): **1994** A(1,2), US **1995** E wc-NZ, J, W(b), F(b). Fj **1996** US, S, F, W, E

Points (15 – 2t): **1995** wc-NZ(1t), J(1t) **1996** W(1t)

or three years it could all be gone. The property speculators in the game might then tear clubhouses down and put houses up.

Do you have a duty to entertain? Now yes – before no, because then we were giving up our time and our money to play rugby.

Do you feel a loyalty to your club in this new era? You have to cash in on what talent you have, because in Ireland rugby goes against you in a job interview, as I discovered to my cost two or three times.

Notable landmarks in rugby career: Surely the biggest mistake Ireland's selectors made in 1994/95 was to drop this man. A cracking tour of Australia (1994) indicated his potential, and a wonderful World Cup in South Africa (1995) confirmed it. In between, the Murphy boys left him on the bench and, save for the face-saver against Wales, Ireland lost the lot. In Oz, David helped the Irish beat Western Australia and ACT, and push Super-10 kings Queensland close (lost 26–29). The former Munster Schools, Under-20 and Ireland Under-21 player then appeared in both Tests against the Wallabies (lost 13–31 and 18–32). But on his return – nothing. His aggression and red-blooded determination was absent from a colourless Five Nations campaign, and he sat on the bench in Treviso while Ireland became the first major nation to lose to Italy (lost 12–20, 8.5.95). The powers that be finally came to their senses in South Africa, and were rewarded with try-scoring displays from David against New Zealand (Johannesburg, 27.5.95) and Japan (Bloemfontein, 31.5.95). He was excellent too in the 24–23 defeat of Wales that booked the Emerald Isle's quarter-final berth. Made his Munster Inter-Provincial debut in 1994/95, and the province ended up kingpins. Ever-present for Ireland in 1995/96, scoring a try in the 30–17 victory over Wales (Dublin, 2.3.96), before switching club allegiances across the Irish Sea to Bristol.

Costello, V. C. P. Ireland

Full name: Victor Carton Patrick Costello
Club: London Irish
Position: No.8/Lock
Height: 6ft 6in (1.98m)
Weight: 18st 3lb (111kg)
Occupation: Company director
Born: Dublin, 23.10.70
Family: Single
Family links with rugby: Father (Patrick) played for Ireland in 6–23 loss to France (Paris, 1960) whilst with Bective Rangers; cousin is Ireland B centre Martin Ridge.
Former club: Blackrock College, St Mary's College
International debut: USA 18, Ireland 25, 1996
Five Nations debut: France 45, Ireland 10, 1996
Best moments in rugby: Scoring try against England Under-21s on 21st birthday (23.10.91); beating Wales in Dublin (2.3.96).

Ireland (1996)		
Last Season	4 caps	0 pts
Career	4 caps	0 pts

Caps (4): **1996** US, F, W, E
Points Nil

Worst moment in rugby: Losing 1995/96 All Ireland League to Shannon
Toughest opponent: Dean Richards (Leicester & England)
Do you really want to be a full-time professional? Professional in attitude, not in occupation.
How well has rugby handled move to professionalism? 7/10. The IRFU have done pretty well.
Do you have a duty to entertain? Yes, to a certain extent, but enjoyment comes

from playing good rugby.

Do you feel a loyalty to your club in this new era? Yes, but loyalty is being diluted by professionalism.

Other sporting claim to fame: Threw shot for Ireland in 1992 Barcelona Olympics. I finished 17th, having put more effort into getting there. Previously held Irish junior (under-21) record with 16.67m.

Notable landmarks in rugby career: Arguably Ireland's outstanding forward in the 1996 Five Nations Championship, Victor realised the potential he had hinted at since making the Ireland Schools team in 1988/89 while at Blackrock College. Broke into Ireland Under-21 side as a 19-year old, playing twice against Italy before sustaining a shoulder injury which ruled out 1990/91 season. Returned in time to play lead role in 19–10 Donnybrook win over England and score decisive try. Athletics took prominence for a while as the outstanding shot-putter was selected to compete for Ireland at the 1992 Olympic Games in Barcelona. Returned to rugby thereafter, and broke into the Ireland A team in February 1994 against England, the nation he had beaten at Under-21 level with a try on his 21st birthday. Toured Australia with the senior squad in 1994, making appearances at No.8, flanker and second row, yet had to wait until 1995 to make his senior Leinster bow. Shortly afterwards Victor was drafted into the full Ireland squad and made his debut, at flanker, against the US Eagles in the Atlanta rain. Moved to No.8 for the Five Nations series, where he particularly impressed in Paris, despite Ireland suffering a record championship hammering.

Touchlines: Athletics

Cronin, D. F. Scotland

Full name: Damian Francis Cronin
Club: Wasps
Position: Lock
Height: 6ft 6in (1.98m)
Weight: 17st 10lb (112.5kg)
Occupation: Self-employed with Bourges reclamation
Born: Wegberg, West Germany, 17.4.63
Family: Annie (wife), Callum (son), Connie (daughter)
Family links with rugby: Father a former president of Ilford Wanderers.
Former clubs: Ilford Wanderers, Bath, Bourges (Fra)
International debut: Ireland 22, Scotland 18, 1988

Five Nations debut: As above

Best moment in rugby: Winning 1990 Grand Slam with Scotland; being selected for the 1993 Lions.

Worst moment in rugby: Being dropped by Scotland during 1991 World Cup

Most embarrassing moment: Getting ball knocked out of my hands as I was going over to score a try against Wellington (1990).

Most respected opponent: Wade Dooley (Preston Grasshoppers & ex-England)

Serious injuries: Ligament damage in both knees (staple put in right knee)

Other sporting achievements: Drove in celebrity race round Brands Hatch; won Victor Ludorum three years in a row at school.

Suggestions to improve rugby: Don't change the lineout. It's a lottery, which is half the fun. Those who survive are technicians who learn to survive. Better off working on keeping the game flowing more. Make people stay on their feet more and referees should be more aware of players, especially flankers, coming over the top.

Notable landmarks in rugby career: A low-profile campaign for French-based 'Del' in 1995/96, having played only against Western Samoa since returning from the World Cup, ended abruptly when he was involved in a training 'brawl' with three team mates while preparing to play Waikato on the summer tour to New Zealand. Earlier in the season he had helped the Exiles retain their Inter District Championship crown. Damian had enjoyed a notable return to the form in 1994/95, scoring tries in his two comeback Tests against Canada (21.1.95) and Ireland (4.2.95) at Murrayfield. Scotland won both to end a nine-game winless period, but a serious arm injury (ruptured tendon in biceps) sustained midway through the Scots' historic win in Paris (18.2.95), required a two-and-a-half-hour operation and four-and-a-half months' recuperation. Returned in the 62–7 non-cap Test victory over Spain in Madrid (6.5.95) – a match staged at altitude to acclimatise the tartan army for South Africa's High Veldt – and held his place in the Pretoria-based World Cup games against Tonga, France and New Zealand. It was all a far cry from the previous season, when Del's only Test outing had been in the record 51–15 loss to New Zealand (Murrayfield, 20.11.93), which, in turn, had followed on from a British Lions tour place in New Zealand, and appearances against North Auckland, NZ Maoris, Southland, Taranaki, Hawke's Bay and Waikato. Had done well to return to rugby after fracturing base of spine aged 22. Built reputation in Scotland with performances for Anglo-Scots, becoming eligible thanks to Lothian-based grandparents. Helped 1987 Anglo's beat French at Cupar, and was included in Scottish XV which achieved a similar feat. Toured with Scotland to Zimbabwe in 1988 (captaining them against Mashonaland District), Japan (1989) and New Zealand (1990). Largely kept out of 1991

Scotland (1988)
Last Season	4 caps	0 pts
Career	36 caps	18 pts

Lions (1993)

Caps (36): **1988** I, F, W, E, A **1989** W, E, I, F, Fj, Ro **1990** I, F, W, E, NZ(1,2) **1991** F, W, E, I, Ro wc-Z **1992** A(2) **1993** I, F, W, E, NZ **1995** C, I, F(a) wc-T, F(b), NZ. WS

Points (18 – 4t): **1989** I(1t) **1990** W(1t) **1995** C(1t), I(1t)

World Cup campaign and 1992 Championship by Doddie Weir and Neil Edwards. Lust for the game returned when he moved from Bath to London Scottish. Helped them win promotion back to Division One in 1991/92 before touring Australia with Scotland in 1992 and recapturing Test place.

Touchlines: Antiques, DIY

Crowley, D. J. Australia

Full name: Daniel (Dan) James Crowley
State: Queensland
Club: Southern Districts
Position: Tighthead prop
Height: 5ft 8in (1.73m)
Weight: 16st 3lb (103kg)
Occupation: Police officer, Queensland Police Service
Born: 28.8.65
Family: Lisa (wife), Jessica (daughter)
International debut: Australia 30, British Lions 12, 1989
Suggestions to improve rugby: No kicking out on the full from anywhere; make the backs do some work.

Notable landmarks in rugby career: Responsible for breaking up one of the great front-row partnerships of all time when selected for first Test vs Argentina (Brisbane, 29.4.95). After a world record of 35 Test appearances together, Tony Daly, Phil Kearns and Ewen McKenzie

Australia (1989)

Last Season	3 caps	0 pts
Career	12 caps	0 pts

Caps (12): **1989** BL(1,2,3) **1991** wc-WS **1992** I, W **1993** C(R) **1995** Arg(1,2) wc-SA. NZ(1), **1996** W(2R)
Points Nil

were split, with Daly making way for Dan in the 53–7 win. He retained his place in the next two games, against Argentina (Sydney, 6.5.95) and in the Wallabies' big World Cup tests (and defeats) against South Africa and England in Cape Town. Added just one cap thereafter, in the Wallabies' Bledisloe Cup defeat by New Zealand in Auckland, before McKenzie returned. Dan had been the man to present HM the Queen with a miniature football prior to Australia's World Cup final win over England in 1991, having made just the one tournament appearance against Western Samoa. Indeed, his links with the UK stretch back to 1989 when he made his debut against the British Lions and retained his place through the three-Test series. That same year he toured Canada and France, but was stood down for the 1990 trip across the Tasman Sea. With Daly and McKenzie pretty much shoring up the Test propping duties, his outings have been restricted to just four appearances since the 1989 Lions left Oz in triumph. He was a reserve in all Tests in 1991. However, he ended 1992 on a high when, with Daly missing the tour to Ireland and Wales, he wore the loosehead's jersey in both internationals. Dan had himself been unavailable for the historic visit to South Africa in August, but once in Britain was one of the busiest players on duty – appearing also against Leinster, Munster, Ulster and Connacht on the Irish leg, and Wales B and Llanelli once the tourists switched their attentions to the Principality. Perhaps his proudest moment came with a try in the 30–20 defeat of the Barbarians at a packed Twickenham.

Culhane, S.   New Zealand

Full name: Simon Culhane
Province: Southland
Position: Fly-half
Height: 5ft 9in (1.75m)
Weight: 12st 7lb (75kg)
Occupation: Self-employed carpenter
Born: 10.3.68
International debut: New Zealand 145, Japan 17
Notable landmarks in rugby career: Modest Test debut in 1995 World Cup. While the world was raving about Canterbury rival Andrew Mehrtens, Simon snuck in for one game against Japan (Bloemfontein, 4.6.95) and went on a record rampage. New Zealand won 145–17 – a best for the World Cup finals – and Simon bagged 45 points. This constituted a world record for a debutant, beating Mehrtens' 28 points against Canada only weeks earlier. It also surpassed Gavin Hastings' 44 points against Cote d'Ivoire – the previous World Cup finals high for an individual. He

New Zealand (1995)

Last Season	4 caps	97 pts
Career	4 caps	97 pts

Caps (4): **1995** wc-J. It, F(1,2)
Points (97 – 1t,28c,12p): **1995** wc-J(1t,20c). It(7c,2p), F(1:5p), F(2:1c,5p)

claimed one of a record 21 tries and his 20 conversions constituted a world record. Only Hong Kong wing Ashley Billington's 50 points (ten tries), in a 164–13 World Cup qualifier romp against hapless Singapore, denied Simon every record in the book. Perhaps we should not have been totally surprised, given the staggeringly prolific form Simon produced for Southland in the New Zealand second division in 1994. He smashed Grant Fox's season-scoring record with 180 points, including 37 against Manawatu. But he is not just about kicking, as he possesses a rare ability to set a back division alight, and is a deceptive runner and fearless tackler. After Mehrtens was injured early in the All Blacks' tour of Italy and France in the autumn of 1995, Simon took his Test tally to 97 points in four games, with 20 points in the 70–6 demolition of Italy, and 32 in the shared two-match series with France.

Touchlines: Hunting and fishing

Dallaglio, L. B. N. England

Full name: Lawrence Bruno Nero Dallaglio
Nickname: Del
Club: Wasps
Position: Flanker
Height: 6ft 4in (1.93m)
Weight: 16st 4lb (99kg)
Occupation: Professional rugby player
Born: London, 10.8.72
Family: Single
International debut: England 14, South Africa 24, 1995
Five Nations debut: France 15, England 12, 1996
Best moment in rugby: Winning 1993 World Cup Sevens with England; England debut vs South Africa.
Worst moment in rugby: Wasps getting hammered 38-3 at Leicester in 1993.
Most embarrassing moment: Having my shorts ripped off against France

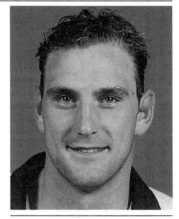

England (1995)

Last Season	6 caps	5 pts
Career	6 caps	5 pts

Caps (6): 1995 SA(R), WS 1996 F, W, S, I
Points (5 – 1t): 1995 WS(1t)

(20.1.96), the cameras panning in on my Y-fronts and the caption under the picture in the Sunday papers reading 'Les Rosbifs!'

Toughest opponent: Andy Robinson (Bath & England)
Do you really want to be a full-time professional rugby player? Yes
How well has rugby handled move to professionalism? 4/10. It took everybody too long to accept that there could be no turning back. It is now a professional game but there is an unwillingness from certain factions to really push on. They want us to do well but won't give us the framework to make that possible.

Do you have a duty to entertain? Yes, of course. We are competing for the public's leisure pound, so we absolutely have to provide an attractive product.
Do you feel a loyalty to your club in this new era? Yes, at least initially. But money is an issue to any player.
Notable landmarks in rugby: In domestic terms, Lawrence was surely 'club man of the season' in England in 1995/96, steering Wasps off the rocks after the main men had upped and flown to Newcastle. He proved an inspirational captain on the domestic stage, and those leadership qualities did him no harm in the international arena where, despite being a rookie, he played with a maturity beyond his years. From the moment he came on as a replacement for Tim Rodber against South Africa at Twickenham (18.11.95), he was earmarked for great things. When Will Carling announced he would be relinquishing the England captaincy, Lawrence was immediately installed as favourite to succeed him. This is a man, a former England 18-Group, Colts, Under-21, Emerging Players, Students and A teams representative, who scored a try on his first senior start for England, in the 27–9 home defeat of Western Samoa (16.12.96), and has a World Cup winner's medal to his name, courtesy of England's shock success in the 1993 World Cup Sevens at Murrayfield. No wonder Italy, the land of his father, regularly try to entice him into their colours. He has suffered great personal tragedy, with the loss of his sister Francesca in the 'Marchioness' Thames riverboat disaster, but that has stiffened his resolve to give his family reason to be proud of his rugby achievements.
Touchlines: Reading

Daly, A. J. Australia

Full name: Anthony (Tony) John Daly
State: New South Wales
Club: Randwick
Position: Loosehead prop
Height: 5ft 10in (1.78m)
Weight: 16st 3lb (103kg)
Occupation: Sales executive with Carmin Office Furniture
Born: 7.3.66
Family: Shannon (wife)
Former clubs: Wests (1985/86), Gordon (1987/90), Easts (1991/92)
International debut: New Zealand 24, Australia 12, 1989
Best moment in rugby: 1991 World Cup victory

Most respected opponent: Olo Brown (Auckland & New Zealand)
Serious injuries: Broken ankle (1988); disc protrusion (1992).
Suggestions to improve rugby: More investments for players; more media for the game.
Notable landmarks in rugby career: Would have become Australia's most-capped had not front-row pal Ewen McKenzie edged him to the honour after Tony lost his place just prior to the World Cup, allowing

Australia (1989)		
Last Season	8 caps	0 pts
Career	41 caps	17 pts

Caps (41): **1989** NZ, F(1,2) **1990** F(1,2,3), US, NZ(1,2,3) **1991** W(a), E(a), NZ(a1,a2) wc-Arg, W(b), I, NZ(b), E(b) **1992** S(1,2), NZ(1,2,3), SA **1993** T, NZ, SA(1,2,3), C, F(1,2) **1994** I(1,2), It(1,2), WS, NZ **1995** wc-C, R
Points (17 – 4t): **1990** F(3:1t), US(1t) **1991** wc-E(b:1t) **1993** C(1t)

McKenzie to move ahead of Andy McIntyre (1982–89: 38). After world-record 35 Test appearances together, the Daly–Phil Kearns–McKenzie front row was broken up, and Dan Crowley was brought in. Having played every international in 1994, Tony was axed from the Argentina series and, though he played in the World Cup-ties against Canada and Romania, he missed the 'big uns' against South Africa and England. Had scored his fourth try in the 43–16 defeat of Canada (Calgary, 9.10.93), though it won't go down as his most notable score. That, without doubt, came in the 1991 World Cup final, when he scored the only try of Australia's 12–6 win. A breakaway wing-forward in his school days at St Joseph's College, he was transformed into a prop when playing under former Wallaby front-rower John Griffiths at Western Suburbs in Sydney. So well did he master the art that he was plucked from the relative obscurity of club rugby in 1989 and asked to prop against Richard Loe in the All Blacks Test at Eden Park. He has since amassed 41 caps despite being unavailable to tour Ireland and Wales in the autumn of 1992. Among his other fond memories are the 1992 Bledisloe Cup series win against New Zealand (though not their one-off loss at Dunedin in 1993) and the defeats of South Africa in 1992 (by a record 26–3 margin) and 1993 (a 2–1 series decision).
Touchlines: Tennis, movies, socialising

*Mike Catt, England's fullback, celebrates
Calcutta Cup victory over Scotland in Edinburgh.*

Dalton, J.   South Africa

Full name: James Dalton
Province: Transvaal
Position: Hooker
Height: 5ft 11in (1.80m)
Weight: 15st 3lb (92kg)
Occupation: Company director
Born: 16.8.72
Family: Single
International debut: South Africa 42, Argentina 22, 1994
Notable landmarks in rugby career: Suspended for two games of 1996 Super-12 tournament after being found guilty of kicking NSW hooker Mark Bell in Sydney, so enhancing his unfortunate reputation as a not altogether clean player. Earned infamy during 1995 World Cup when sent-off in the 'Battle of the Boet' along with Canucks, Gareth Rees and Rod Snow. The match was the Pool A decider between the Springboks and Canada (3.6.95) at the same Port Elizabeth stadium in which England's Tim Rodber had

South Africa (1995)

Last Season	4 caps	0 pts
Career	5 caps	0 pts

Caps (5): **1994** Arg(1R) **1995** wc-A, C. W, E
Points Nil

been dismissed the previous summer playing against Eastern Province. A scuffle quickly broke out following an overzealous tackle by Springbok wing Pieter Hendriks and a provocative late hit on Hendriks by Canadian fullback Scott Stewart (both later cited and banned). From there all hell broke loose, as a result of which Irish referee David McHugh brandished three red cards. 'I have a reputation and I seem to have been hanged for it this time,' said James, 'but I can honestly say that I went in to stop the fighting and not to take part. I've been made a scapegoat. My whole life may be ruined by this decision.' The former Johannesburg nightclub bouncer later broke down in tears at a press conference. Plumbed the depths, having previously reached the highest high on his full Test debut, in the tournament opener at Newlands, Cape Town. After a memorable opening ceremony, the Boks beat world champions Australia in a classic and James played a full part. Post-dismissal, all was not lost, however, as James returned for the Boks against Wales in Johannesburg (won 40–11, 2.9.95) and England at Twickenham (won 24–14, 18.11.95). Toured with South Africa in 1994 to New Zealand (playing against King Country, Wellington, Hanan Shield XV, Taranaki, Waikato, Manawatu, Otago and Bay of Plenty) and Wales, Scotland and Ireland (appearing vs Wales A, Neath,

Scotland A, Scottish Select, Pontypridd and the Barbarians). In between, made his debut as 75th-minute replacement for Uli Schmidt in first Test against Argentina (15.10.94) at – guess where – Port Elizabeth.

Davidson, J. W. Ireland

Full name: Jeremy William Davidson
Club: London Irish
Position: Flanker, lock
Height: 6ft 6in (1.98m)
Weight: 17st 3lb (109kg)
Occupation: Student
Born: Belfast, 28.4.74
Former club: Dungannon
International debut: Ireland 44, Fiji 8, 1995
Five Nations debut: Ireland 10, Scotland 16, 1996
Notable landmarks in rugby career: One of Ireland's band of up-and-coming youngsters, Jeremy needed only three years to bridge the gap between Ireland Schools and the senior side. A member of the Schools XV which turned out against their English counterparts in 1992, he graduated to the Under-21 side in November 1993, again playing against England, and then toured with senior squad in Australia in

Ireland (1995)

Last Season	5 caps	0 pts
Career	5 caps	0 pts

Caps (5): **1995** Fj **1996** S, F, W, E
Points Nil

1994 (playing in four of the eight games). A back injury restricted his progress in 1994/95, but last season he made up for lost time. His debut in the 44–8 rout of Fiji (Dublin, 18.11.95) was followed by a full campaign in the 1996 Five Nations series, though not everything went according to plan. Ireland finished with the Wooden Spoon, and Jeremy was shunted from blindside to second row mid-season after the selectors decided to dispense with Neil Francis.

Davies, J. D.   Wales

Full name: John David Davies
Nickname: Air Wolf
Club: Neath
Position: Tighthead prop
Height: 6ft (1.83m)
Weight: 16st 7lb (100kg)
Occupation: Farmer
Born: Carmarthen, 1.2.69
Family: Veronica (wife)
Former club: Crymych
International debut: Wales 21,
Ireland 21, 1991
Five Nations debut: As above
Best moments in rugby: Beating
France in 1994 and 1996
Worst moment in rugby: Not going
to New Zealand with Wales Under-
19s in 1987/88; losing Swalec Cup
finals to Llanelli (1993) and
Pontypridd (1996).
Most embarrassing moment: Being
given an aerial view of Paris during a
scrum against France
Toughest opponent: Craig Dowd
(Auckland & New Zealand)
**Do you really want to be a full-time
professional rugby player?** Yes, if the
money is right.

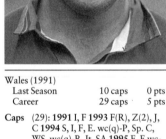

Wales (1991)		
Last Season	10 caps	0 pts
Career	29 caps	5 pts

Caps (29): **1991** I, F **1993** F(R), Z(2), J,
C **1994** S, I, F, E. wc(q)-P, Sp. C,
WS. wc(q)-R, It. SA **1995** F, E wc-
J, NZ, I(b). SA **1996** It, E, S, I, F,
A(1)
Points (5 – 1t): **1993** Z(2:1t)

How well has rugby handled move to professionalism? 4/10. Administrators
took far too long to get to a position which, to us players, seemed obvious from
day one.
Do you have a duty to entertain? Yes
Do you feel a loyalty to your club in this new era? Yes
Other sporting claims to fame: Winning 'Wales' Strongest Man' in 1993
Notable landmarks in rugby career: Ever-present for Wales in 1995/96, save for
the visit to Cardiff of Fiji when, having been selected, JD withdrew injured,
allowing Cardiff's Lyndon Mustoe to make his debut. Enjoyed a fine season
with Neath, beating Fiji at The Gnoll, winning the Welsh league title and
coming closer than he will want to remind himself of adding the Swalec Cup. It
was a distant cry from the previous season when he was sent off by French
referee Didier Mene for clumsy footwork on Ben Clarke 62 minutes into Wales'
9–23 loss to England in Cardiff (18.2.95). It was a wretched enough campaign
for Wales without that. Not only did they take the Wooden Spoon, white-

washed for only the second time ever, they failed to reach the World Cup quarter-finals, despite John's return for all three games in South Africa. Yet in 1994 Wales, with John a permanent fixture, were Five Nations champions. Toured with Wales to Zimbabwe and Namibia in 1993, scoring his first international try in 42–13 second Test win over Zimbabwe (Harare, 29.5.93). Toured to Canada and South Pacific in 1994 after helping Wales qualify for World Cup with wins in Portugal and Spain. Spent last summer in Australia with the national side. First player from Crymych to represent Wales Youth, turning out against Ireland, France and England in 1987, and against the same three opponents the following season. Joined Neath in 1987 and was included in Wales B squad in his first senior season. An Under-21 cap against Scotland in 1989 was followed by B recognition against Holland, in a 34–12 win (1990/91) and against North of England in 1992/93. Graduated to senior side in 1991.
Touchlines: Gardening, renovating houses

Davies, L. B. Wales

Full name: Leigh Barry Davies
Club: Cardiff
Position: Centre
Height: 6ft (1.83m)
Weight: 15st (91kg)
Occupation: Sports Science student at Neath Tertiary College
Born: 20.2.76
Family: Single
Former club: Neath
International debut: Wales 31, Italy 26, 1995
Five Nations debut: England 21, Wales 15, 1996
Notable landmarks in rugby career: Arguably the find of the season in Wales, Leigh helped restore pride in Welsh rugby after the crushing disappointment of the 1995 World Cup failure. His creative midfield partnership with Llanelli's Nigel Davies was one of the features of Wales' improved showing, even if the Dragons did still need to beat

Wales (1996)

Last Season	6 caps	0 pts
Career	6 caps	0 pts

Caps (6): **1996** It, E, S, I, F, A(1)
Points Nil

France (Cardiff, 16.3.96) on the last day of the championship to avoid another Five Nations whitewash. Leigh, who made his first three Test appearances as a teenager, beginning with his debut in the 31–26 win over Italy (Cardiff,

16.1.96), was nearly lost to soccer. A free-scoring striker, he had trials with both Birmingham City and Coventry City. Their loss was Neath's gain; he has represented Neath since August 1994. Down Gnoll way they still talk of the try he scored against the touring Fijians in a 30–22 victory for the Welsh All Blacks. A year after turning out for a Wales Under-21 side comprehensively beaten by France in Rouen (13.5.95), he was being lauded by his midfield rivals in the Five Nations as *the* centre of the future.

Davies, N. G. Wales

Full name: Nigel Gareth Davies
Nickname: Pudding (my father was a baker)
Club: Llanelli
Positions: Centre, wing
Height: 6ft 1in (1.86m)
Weight: 13st 10lb (87kg)
Occupation: Self-employed management consultant
Born: Llanelli, 29.3.65
Family: Maria (wife), Emily (daughter), Samuel (son)
Family links with rugby: Father played for Trimsaran
Former club: Trimsaran
International debut: New Zealand 54, Wales 9, 1988
Five Nations debut: Scotland 23, Wales 7, 1989
Best rugby memory: Beating France in 1996 Five Nations – great pride in having played so well when we simply had to win.
Worst rugby memory: Being dropped from 1995 World Cup squad.
Most embarrassing rugby memory: Playing against Neath (1995/96), I passed to Leigh Davies and he raced 50 metres for a Neath try. My excuse (and I'm sticking to it) was that I am so used to passing to him in a Wales shirt.
Toughest opponent: Philippe Sella (Saracens & France)
Do you really want to be a full-time professional rugby player? No, because I want to hold onto my business. But semi-pro, yes.
How well has rugby handled move to professionalism? 1/10. As soon as the

Wales (1988)

Last Season	7 caps	0 pts
Career	26 caps	13 pts

Caps (26): **1988** NZ(2), WS **1989** S, I **1993** F **1994** S, I, E. wc(q)-P, Sp. C, Fj, T(R), WS. wc(q)-R, It **1995** E, S, I(a), Fj **1996** E, S, I, F, A(1,2)
Points (13 – 3t): **1988** WS(2t) **1994** wc(q)-It(1t)

266

game went pro, the money-making people came in looking to seize control from the amateur unions. A hotchpotch resulted, with the players being treated like pawns, being offered contracts by both club and country.

Do you have a duty to entertain? Yes, but we first need to get fitter. We're a year behind the southern hemisphere in that respect.

Do you feel a loyalty to your club in this new era? No

Other claims to fame: My wife singing on TV on 'Friday Night Live', one of six finalists out of 2,000 contestants; playing in tennis pro-am with Arwel Thomas.

Notable landmarks in rugby career: A key component in Wales' 1994 Five Nations Championship triumph, Nigel experienced the other side of life in 1995, being dropped from the World Cup squad by caretaker coach Alex Evans, before bouncing back in considerable style last season. A hugely intelligent player, his brain combined with young Leigh Davies' brawn to create an impressive midfield combination. Nigel's form in the 1994 title surge had been remarkable in that he had only been rescued from four years in Test wilderness in March 1993 when deployed against France. Thereafter, was forced to pull out of summer tour to Zimbabwe and Namibia before departure. Graduated from Trimsaran Youth to Wales Youth, and passed through national Student and B levels before breaking into Test side in 1988 on disastrous tour to New Zealand. His debut came in second Test – a 54–9 thrashing in Auckland, which clinched one of most convincing 2–0 series results ever. On his return he ran in two tries as Wales defeated Western Samoa 28–6 at Cardiff. Following season made his Five Nations debut against Scotland at Murrayfield in a game that Wales lost 23–7. Lost place after 19–13 home loss to Ireland that same season. Nigel, who toured Italy with Wales B in 1986/87, is very highly regarded on the club scene inside the Principality, and was one of the central figures in Llanelli's League and Cup double and victory over Australia in 1992/93.

Touchlines: Reading, music, motocross

Robert Howley draws an audience of Wales team mates against France in Cardiff.

Dawe, R. G. R.   England

Full name: Richard Graham Reed
Dawe
Nickname: Dawesie
Club: Bath
Position: Hooker
Height: 5ft 11in (1.80m)
Weight: 14st 2lb (85kg)
Occupation: Farmer
Born: Plymouth, 4.9.59
Family: Liz (wife)
Former club: Launceston
International debut: Ireland 17,
England 0, 1987
Five Nations debut: As above
Best rugby memory: Touring South
Africa with England in 1994.
Worst rugby memory: Being told
that I had been banned by England
after 1987 Wales match.
Most embarrassing rugby memory:
Having a pig named after me.
Toughest opponent: Richard
Cockerill (Leicester & England A)
– it's his pig!
**Do you really want to be a full-time
professional rugby?** Yes, it would be interesting.

England (1987)

Last Season	1 cap	0 pts
Career	5 caps	0 pts

Caps (5): 1987 I, F, W wc-US 1995 wc-WS
Points Nil

How well has rugby handled move to professionalism? 6/10. Should have been
introduced after 1991 World Cup. Unions were given no guidance by IRB.
Rugby did not take on board the experiences of other sports.
Do you have a duty to entertain? Yes
Do you feel a loyalty to your club in this new era? Yes, it's instilled in 80% of
players throughout the game.
Suggestions to improve rugby: Anything to speed up the game. Diminish value
of conversion or get rid of it (takes up too much time). Somehow reduce my
travelling.
Notable landmarks in rugby career: Ended eight years in the international
rugby wilderness when recalled to the England side for 1995 World Cup pool
match against Western Samoa (Durban, 4.6.95). It was Graham's first outing
since the first World Cup in 1987, when he turned out against the United States.
That year the Cornwall farmer had played four times for England, but his
suspension after the notorious Wales match (Twickenham, 7.3.87) seemed to
put paid to his longterm senior future. Contented himself instead as a vital
member of England's second string, making 11 appearances, and busied

himself by continuing with his dedicated practice of 300-mile round-trips to get to Bath RFC from his Milton Abbott farm. His reward has been seven cup-winning medals with Bath, the latest coming last season. Took massive pride in Cornwall winning the 1990/91 ADT County Championship (29–20 vs Yorks, 20.4.91) and also reaching Twickenham again the following year. Began career as a scrum-half or fullback at Launceston and reached 26 before making first-class debut for Bath against London Welsh. Holds dubious distinction of being record-holder for most appearances on England bench (34); last season, despite his age, boasted second-best aerobic capacity (running fitness) on Bath roster.

Touchlines: Bell ringing, cycling, sheep shearing

Dawson, M. J. S. England

Full name: Matthew James Sutherland Dawson
Club: Northampton
Position: Scrum-half
Height: 5ft 11in (1.80m)
Weight: 13st (78kg)
Occupation: Teacher at Spratton Hall School, Northampton
Born: Birkenhead, 31.10.72
Family: Single
International debut: England 27, Western Samoa 9, 1995
Five Nations debut: France 15, England 12, 1996
Best rugby memory: Learning of my England selection on car radio.
Worst rugby memory: Tearing hamstring on England A tour to Canada (1993).
Most embarrassing memory: Scoring try vs Wakefield (1995/96): scorched down touchline, gave it the old goosestep, touched down, twisted ankle and crashed into advertising hoarding.

England (1995)

Last Season	5 caps	0 pts
Career	5 caps	0 pts

Caps (5): **1995** WS **1996** F, W, S, I
Points Nil

Do you really want to be a full-time professional player? Yes
How well has rugby handled move to professionalism? 7/10. An average effort.
Do you have a duty to entertain? Yes
Do you feel a loyalty to your club in this new era? Yes
Other sporting claims to fame: Soccer (right-back) for Chelsea Boys; cricket (wicketkeeper) for Buckinghamshire.

Notable landmarks in rugby career: One of Jack Rowell's new kids on the cabbage patch, Matthew was introduced in tandem with Northampton half-back partner Paul Grayson as England moved to rebuild following the 1995 World Cup. The nation's 50th club half-back pairing made their bow in the 27–9 defeat of Western Samoa (Twickenham, 18.11.95), having convinced the selectors of their pedigree in the Midlands' 40–19 victory over the tourists, and having remained untouched throughout the 1995/96 campaign. Given that Northampton were at the time a Second Division outfit, this was no mean feat. Billed as the ideal pivot – a man who could provide fast ball while also possessing the toughness to take on defences – Matthew was let down by the lack of fast ball coming from the forwards. But he still proved a worthy selection, with his fast hands and strong cover tackling. And he had waited long enough for his chance, having been first-choice scrum-half on the 1993 England A tour to Canada, only to pull a hamstring in the opening game; for the next couple of years he had to struggle with some injury or other. Prior to that, he represented England Schools (1990/91) and Under-21s (at centre).

De Glanville, P. R.   England

Full name: Philip Ranulph de Glanville
Nicknames: Too numerous to mention
Club: Bath
Position: Centre
Height: 5ft 11in (1.81m)
Weight: 13st 7lb (81kg)
Occupation: Marketing consultant with Druid Systems Ltd, Chertsey
Born: Loughborough, 1.10.68
Family: Single
Family links with rugby: Father played for Loughborough and Rosslyn Park.
Former clubs: Durham University, Oxford University
International debut: England 33, South Africa 16, 1992
Five Nations debut: Wales 10, England 9, 1993
Best rugby memory: Beating New Zealand (1993)
Worst rugby memory: Someone stamping on my face during South West game against 1993 All Blacks.
Most embarrassing memory: Losing a match for Durham University on their Canadian tour by dropping a goalbound penalty effort beneath the posts: the

University of Victoria team scored a try from the resultant scrum.

Toughest opponent: Philippe Sella (Saracens & France)

Serious injuries: Broken arm; dislocated collarbone; eye gash requiring 15 stitches.

Do you really want to be a full-time professional player? Yes, but in putting rugby first I would not want to exclude myself from doing other things.

England (1992)

Last Season	6 caps	5 pts
Career	16 caps	5 pts

Caps (16): **1992** SA(R) **1993** W(R), NZ **1994** S, I, F, W, SA(1,2), C(R) **1995** wc-Arg(R), It, WS, SA(R) **1996** W(R), I(R)

Points (5 – 1t): **1995** SA(1t)

How well has rugby handled move to professionalism? 2/10. The whole thing has been very poorly managed. Certain sections of the game coped OK, but the IRFB and RFU were not amongst them.

Do you have a duty to entertain? The duty to ourselves is to win, but with admission prices likely to rise, we have to strike the right balance to give the supporters value for money.

Do you feel a loyalty to your club in this new era? Yes, and I think the majority of players still do. But there are now financial considerations which cannot be ignored.

Suggestions to improve rugby: Appoint independent arbitrator to deal with matters of discipline. My eye injury in 1993, caused by a boot, highlighted fact that there is no procedure. We need a neutral body to examine such incidents.

Notable landmarks in rugby career: Captained Bath to league and cup double and, in all the protracted negotiations with the RFU over professionalism, emerged as one of England's most respected voices. A heck of a good player, too: Wigan RLFC declared an interest in 'borrowing' him during the off-season after he impressed their coaches in the two cross-code challenge matches. Despite not being able to shift the Guscott–Carling combination from England's midfield, Phil added three caps to his tally in 1995/96, and bagged his first Test try after coming on as a late replacement for Carling against South Africa (Twickenham, 18.11.95). He also replaced Carling in two other Twickenham internationals, against Wales and Ireland. Prior to last season, the return to full fitness of Jerry Guscott in 1994/95 meant Phil had to make do with 16 minutes against Canada (Twickenham, 10.12.94), and World Cup outings against Italy (Durban, 31.5.95) and Western Samoa (Durban, 4.6.95). It was perhaps no coincidence that England won each game. Having earned his first two caps as a replacement, Phil came into his own in 1993/94. With the season-long injury to Guscott, the former Oxford Blue was given an extended run alongside Carling, growing in confidence as the season progressed. However, he was lucky, not in being selected, but in being fit enough to be considered. Representing South West England against the touring All Blacks (30.10.93), he suffered a horrifying eye injury at the bottom of a ruck. Fifteen stitches were required to keep his left eyelid intact, and there was a deep wound above and below the eye. 'It wasn't an accident', Phil insists. Amazingly, less than a month later he faced up against the tourists again in the colours of England and enjoyed

a sweet victory. Member of original England Under-21 side, scoring two tries against Romania Under-21s (won 54–13, Bucharest 13.5.89). Made England B debut as a 20-year-old in 44–0 defeat of Italy (19.3.89). Helped underdogs Oxford University win 1990 Varsity match (11.12.90).
Touchlines: Golf, cricket

Delaigue, Y.   France

Full name: Yann Delaigue
Club: Toulon
Position: Fly-half, centre
Height: 5ft 11in (1.80m)
Weight: 12st 8lb (75kg)
Occupation: Shopkeeper
Born: Toulon, 5.4.73
Family: Single
International debut: Scotland 12, France 20, 1994
Five Nations debut: As above
Notable landmarks in rugby career: Appeared twice for France in Argentina in October 1995, during the Latin Cup tournament which Jean-Claude Skrela's young team won. Otherwise Yann had little to shout about – a consequence of failing to spark in South Africa – and lost out in the World Cup selection stakes, first to Christophe Deylaud, then to Franck Mesnel. Yet he had been simply outstanding in the 1995 Five Nations match with Ireland in Dublin. Son of Gilles Delaigues, also a centre, who won two caps during

France (1994)		
Last Season	4 caps	8 pts
Career	9 caps	16 pts

Caps (9): **1994** S, NZ(2R), C(b) **1995** I(a), R wc-T, IC. It, R(R)
Points (16 – 1t,2dg): **1994** C(b:1dg) **1995** I(a:1t) wc-T(1dg). R(R:1t)

the 1973 season against Japan and Romania, Yann turned Toulon's back division into one of the most exciting around, and was the guiding light behind the club's championship triumph in 1992. At 22, he was the second youngest member(behind Arnaud Costes) of France's World Cup squad. As a teenager he scored a try against England 18-Group at Franklin Gardens, having gone from school team straight into the Toulon side alongside Aubin Hueber. Played a hefty role in the 67–9 rout of Scotland Under-21s by France Under-21s in Dijon (5.2.93), and helped France A defeat their England second-string counterparts 20–8 in Paris (5.3.94). A fortnight later, with France staring a Five Nations Wooden Spoon square in the face, he was called upon to steer them clear of that

272

unthinkable prospect. Given his debut in Edinburgh, Yann's upright, elusive running was a feature of France's 20–12 win. Indeed, it was his break that made the opening try for Jean-Luc Sadourny. His reward was a place on France's ultra-successful tour to New Zealand, where he appeared as a replacement in the second Test win which clinched a 2–0 series triumph.

De Rougemont, M.   France

Full name: Marc de Rougemont
Club: Toulon
Position: Hooker
Height: 5ft 9in (1.75m)
Weight: 14st 7lb
Occupation: Publican
Born: Marseille, 24.5.72
International debut: England 31, France 10, 1995
Five Nations debut: As above
Notable landmarks in rugby career: A versatile front-row man, and also a tried-and-trusted prop, Marc was handed the French No.2 shirt for the home series against the 1995 All Blacks after first-choice Jean-Michel Gonzales damaged knee ligaments helping France win the Latin Cup in Argentina a month earlier. But having played both Tests in a shared series, Marc again made way for his Bayonne rival, appearing just the once more, as a 70th-minute replacement for Jean-Michel in the 45–10 defeat of Ireland (Paris,

France (1995)

Last Season	6 caps	0 pts
Career	8 caps	0 pts

Caps (8): **1995** E(TR), R(TR) wc-IC. NZ(1,2) **1996** I(R), Arg(1,2)
Points Nil

17.2.96). Prior to 1995/96 Marc had picked up three caps despite only starting and/or finishing one match. Before playing in his first full Test, he picked up two caps as blood-bin replacement in the 10–31 defeat by England (Twickenham, 4.2.95) and France's 24–15 win over Romania (Bucharest, 7.4.95). A member of the 1993/94 France A side that beat their England counterparts in Paris, Marc finally got that first full international start in South Africa. Coach Pierre Berbizier was true to his pledge to give the whole 26-man squad a game, and Marc got his chance against Cote d'Ivoire before an enthusiastic crowd in the rural outpost of Rustenburg (30.5.95). France won 54–18. He remained a valued member of the successful squad thereafter. Impressive performances for Toulon in the French club championship had earned him a place on France's

tour to Canada and New Zealand (1994), but he broke a bone in the quarter-final against Montferrand and had to pull out. His place was taken by friend and rival Christian Califano, who has been the first-choice tighthead prop ever since. Marc recovered from his injury in time to warm the replacements bench against Canada in Besancon (17.12.94) in a match that France won 28–9.
Touchlines: Deep-sea diving

Deylaud, C.   France

Full name: Christophe Deylaud
Club: Toulouse
Position: Centre
Height: 5ft 9½ in (1.76m)
Weight: 11st 11lb (75kg)
Occupation: Sports instructor
Born: Toulouse, 2.10.64
Family: Married with one child
International debut: France 25, Romania 6, 1992
Five Nations debut: France 21, Wales 9, 1995
Notable landmarks in rugby career: Enigmatic player who is magical for Toulouse and, at best, erratic for France. Last season kicked Toulouse to European Cup glory and a third successive French championship title, but played just twice for his country. Both appearances, against Italy and Argentina, came in Argentina during France's Latin Cup winning campaign. Thereafter, the No.10 jersey went to Alain Penaud, then Thierry Lacroix, then Thomas Castaignede. Yet Christophe was the man behind France's finest-ever Test series result – the 2–0 defeat of New Zealand in their own backyard in

France (1992)

Last Season	6 caps	26 pts
Career	16 caps	47 pts

Caps (16): **1992** R, Arg(a1,a2), SA(1) **1994** C, NZ(1,2) **1995** W, E, S(a) wc-IC(R), S(b), I(b), SA. It, Arg

Points (47 – 1t, 9c, 5p, 3dg): **1992** Arg(a1:1t,1c) **1994** NZ(1:2dg), NZ(2:1c,1p) **1995** S(a:1dg), It(4c,2p), Arg(3c,2p)

1994. He had shown genius to dismantle the All Blacks, dropping two goals in the 22–8 first Test triumph (Christchurch, 26.6.94) and landing five points in the 23–20 series clincher at Eden Park (3.7.94). However, he was dreadful in the 1995 Five Nations series and was dropped. Won his place back at the World Cup with a polished display as a replacement against Cote d'Ivoire (Rustenburg, 30.5.95). But his semi-final display against South Africa was abysmal and arguably cost France a spot in the final. Franck Mesnel took over for third place playoff game against England. Christophe had previously ended two years in the cold with a brilliant display in 1994 French Championship final, guiding Toulouse to victory. He was promptly included in France's squad to tour Canada and New Zealand. However, in one-off Test against Canucks, with Christophe at No.10, France crashed 18–16 (Ottawa, 5.6.94). Previously, this highly promising midfielder had failed to sustain his challenge for a Test place in 1992, having initially been blooded in the 25–6 defeat of Romania at Le Havre (28.5.92). He was retained for the summer tour to Argentina, contributing a try and conversion to the 27–12 first Test win in Buenos Aires (4.7.92), although he was later replaced by Christian Courveille, and retained his berth alongside Courveille for the 33–9 second Test win the following week. Returned home with the praise of Robert Paparemborde ringing in his ears. 'Christophe is going to become a magnificent player in our back division.' French fans are still waiting for the potential to be fulfilled.

Dispagne, S. France

Full name: Sylvain Dispagne
Club: Toulouse
Position: No.8
Height: 6ft 5in (1.95m)
Weight: 16st 5lb (99kg)
Occupation: PR executive
Born: 8.2.68
Former clubs: Perpignan, Narbonne
International debut: France 45, Ireland 10, 1996
Five Nations debut: As above
Notable landmarks in rugby career:
Another member of the ultra-successful Toulouse side to break into the international ranks, Sylvain owed his debut to the unlicensed boot of Ireland prop Peter Clohessy, which put Olivier Roumat out of action 52 minutes into France's record 45–10 rout of the boys in green (Paris, 17.2.96). Roumat retired from the fray, allowing the Toulouse back-row man to get his first cap – a tally that he doubled by

France (1996)

Last Season	2 caps	0 pts
Career	2 caps	0 pts

Caps (2): **1996** I(R), W
Points Nil

being selected in his favoured No.8 berth, ahead of Dax's Fabian Pelous, for France's championship finale in Cardiff (16.3.96). Sadly for him, winless Wales chose the occasion to break their duck and clamber off the bottom of the table. Sylvain served his apprenticeship in the wings, waiting for his ticket to the main event. As far back as 1990 he toured Namibia with France A, having started playing senior club rugby for Perpignan as a student. Switched allegiances to Narbonne in 1992, touring New Zealand with the rampant French in 1994, before moving on to Toulouse at the start of 1995/96 to replace the departing Albert Cigagna. Helped Toulouse to European Cup and French championship glory either side of helping himself to his first cap.

Dods, M. Scotland

Full name: Michael Dods
Nickname: Window Ledge
Club: Northampton
Position: Fullback
Height: 5ft 11in (1.81m)
Weight: 11st 9lbs (74kg)
Occupation: Medical sales rep with Merck & Lipha, West Drayton, Middlesex
Born: Galashiels, 30.12.68
Family: Single
Family links with rugby: Brother (Peter) played 23 times for Scotland (1983–91, 210 points: 2t,26c,50p) and British Lions (1989).
Former club: Gala
International debut: Ireland 6, Scotland 6, 1994
Five Nations debut: As above
Best rugby memories: Getting my first cap (vs Ireland): I came on as a replacement for Gavin Hastings, was only on field for eight seconds and didn't even touch the ball. Scoring all 19 points vs France (1996).
Worst rugby memory: Being axed by Scotland for 1996 New Zealand tour
Serious injuries: Broken collarbone (1988), broken nose (1990), broken thumb and hand (1993).
Toughest opponent: John Timu (New Zealand)
Do you really want to be a full-time professional rugby player? No
How well has rugby handled move to professionalism? 3/10. Unions have tried to get it right, but it's been shambolic in England, with the players left in the dark.

Scotland (1994)

Last Season	5 caps	62 pts
Career	8 caps	80 pts

Caps (8): **1994** I(TR), Arg(1,2) **1995** WS **1996** I, F, W, E
Points (80 – 3t, 1c, 21p): **1994** Arg(1:5p), Arg(2:1p) **1995** WS(5p) **1996** I(1t,1p), F(2t,3p), W(1c,3p), E(3p)

Do you have a duty to entertain? Yes, but we always have had. People do not come to see guys kick penalty goals, and I am a goalkicker (supposedly!).

Do you feel a loyalty to your club in this new era? Loyalty is disappearing very quickly now money is in rugby. But you will always find players who are loyal.

Notable landmarks in rugby career: Scotland repaid their debt of gratitude to Mike, leading scorer for them in the 1996 Five Nations Championship and joint leading try scorer with three overall, by omitting him from their squad which toured New Zealand last summer. The reason cited was his poor goalkicking return in a campaign which came so close to yielding only Scotland's fourth Grand Slam but ultimately foundered on Mike's misses against England. But hey, he did an awful lot else for the resurgent team. Not least, grabbing all 19 points, including two tries, in the 19–14 defeat of France (Edinburgh, 3.2.96); a try and penalty in 16–10 victory over Ireland (Dublin, 20.1.96); and 11 points in the 16–14 win against Wales (Cardiff, 17.2.96). Prophetically commented mid-season: 'I never take anything for granted. 'Today's cock, tomorrow's feather duster', as they say, and that could be applied to me if things don't go to plan.' Prior to all this, Mike boasted arguably the briefest Test debut of all time, coming on as a temporary replacement for captain Gavin Hastings during 6–6 draw with Ireland at Lansdowne Road (5.3.94). It is questionable whether the ball was in play at all before he returned to stands. His club form for Gala fully merited the chance, however brief. And he had waited patiently for nearly three years since touring with Scotland to North America in 1991, contributing 44 points in three games, including 28 against Alberta. A chip off the old block, if British Lion and Scotland fullback brother Peter will excuse the 'old' reference, Mike proved he can kick by landing five penalty goals on his first start, against Argentina (lost 15–16, Buenos Aires, 4.6.94) and popping over a touchline penalty goal (his third of the game) to hand a 12–9 victory to Scotland A over France A (Rennes, 20.2.94). He also turned out for A-team against touring All Blacks, kicking a penalty in 9–20 defeat (Glasgow, 13.11.93), and Italy, bagging all 15 points (five penalty goals) in 15–18 loss (Rovigo, 18.12.93). First played for Gala in 1987 when only 17 years old. First represented Scotland at Under-15 and Under-18 Schools grades, going on to win Under-21 honours in 1990.

Touchlines: Golf (12 handicap), shooting, fishing

Dourthe, R.　　　　　　　　　　France

Full name: Richard Dourthe
Club: Dax
Position: Centre, fullback
Height: 6ft 1in (1.85m)
Weight: 13st 6lb (81kg)
Occupation: Physiotherapy student
Born: 13.12.74
Family: Single
Family links with rugby: Father
Claude won 33 caps for France
(1966–75)
International debut: France 52,
Romania 8, 1995
Five Nations debut: France 15,
England 12, 1996
Notable landmarks in rugby career:
Up and down rookie season in Test
match rugby for Richard, who
underlined his class with dazzling
performances in the shared autumn
series with New Zealand, then
blotted his copybook by kicking
England's Ben Clarke in the head on
his Five Nations debut. Richard, like
pal Thomas Castaignede, was seen
as the future of French midfield
rugby when new France coach took

France (1995)
Last Season	8 caps	36 pts
Career	8 caps	36 pts

Caps (8): **1995** R, Arg, NZ(1,2) **1996** E,
R, Arg(1,2)
Points (36 – 2t, 10c, 2p): **1995** NZ(1:1t)
1996 R(7c), Arg(1:1t,3c,1p),
Arg(2:1p)

both youngsters to Argentina in October 1995 and blooded both in the Latin
Cup competition. France won the cup and two 20-year-old stars were born.
However, after each gained further encouraging notices against the All Blacks
– Richard claiming an opportunist try in the 22–15 first Test win in Toulouse
(11.11.95) – their respective careers took different paths in the Five Nations
series. While Castaignede dropped the injury-time goal which beat England and
made him a national hero, Richard misdemeaned, was cited by the English and
then suspended by the French Federation. Although he returned on the bench
for France's final championship engagement against Wales in Cardiff
(16.3.96), he had to wait until mid-April for his next Test match action. Selected
at fullback against Romania in Aurillac (20.4.96), he kicked seven conversions
as France walloped the boys from Bucharest 64–12.

Dowd, C.   New Zealand

Full name: Craig Dowd
Province: Auckland
Club: Suburbs
Position: Loosehead prop
Height: 6ft 4in (1.91m)
Weight: 18st 11lb (115kg)
Occupation: Carpenter, *AIT*
Born: 26.10.69
International debut: New Zealand
20, British Lions 18, 1993
Best moment in rugby: Winning the
Gallagher Shield
Notable landmarks in rugby career:
The outstanding loosehead prop of
the last World Cup and an avid pasta
and potato eater, Craig retained his
place with little difficulty thereafter,
sharing in New Zealand's two-Test
Bledisloe Cup triumph (July 1995)
and then touring to Italy and France.
Such success should come as no
surprise, given that as a youngster he
had announced his Test intentions
by first relieving seasoned All Black
Steve McDowell of his place in the
Auckland scrum, then nicking his
national berth in time for the visit of

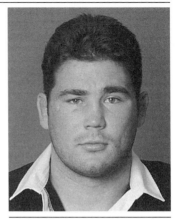

New Zealand (1993)

Last Season	13 caps	5 pts
Career	22 caps	5 pts

Caps (22): **1993** BL(1,2,3), A, WS, S, E
1994 SA(1R) **1995** C wc-I, W, J, E,
SA. A(1,2), It, F(1,2), **1996** WS,
S(1,2)

Points (5 – 1t): 1995 wc-J(1t)

the 1993 British Lions. Lost out the following year, when Richard Loe returned
to favour, but again got his act together in 1995, playing in every game, save for
the World Cup quarter-final defeat of Scotland when he was injured. A
powerfully built, mobile player, Craig came up New Zealand's representative
ladder, playing for both New Zealand Colts (he was a team mate of England
and Lions lock Martin Johnson) and the New Zealand XV; he was also a bench
reserve against England B in 1992. An ever-present in the 2–1 series defeat of
the 1993 Lions (his debut came in Christchurch on 12 June), Craig held his place
for the 25–10 Bledisloe Cup victory over Australia (Dunedin, 17.7.93).
England's 15–9 win over the All Blacks (Twickenham, 27.11.93) ended Craig's
run of never having left the Test arena a loser. Broke his try-duck, along with
most others, in the 145–17 World Cup rout of Japan (Bloemfontein, 4.6.95).
Touchlines: Weight training, bodybuilding

Du Randt, P.   South Africa

Full name: Pieter du Randt
Province: Orange Free State
Position: Prop
Height: 6ft 3in (1.90m)
Weight: 113kg
Occupation: Diesel mechanic,
Barlows Equipment
Born: 8.9.72
International debut: South Africa 42,
Argentina 22, 1994
Notable landmarks in rugby career:
Surfaced internationally in 1995
after an impressive domestic
campaign for Orange Free State that
culminated in a Bankfin Currie Cup
final appearance (Bloemfontein,
1.10.94). Despite losing 56–33 to
defending champions Transvaal,
Pieter's efforts were rewarded almost
immediately with a Test debut the
following weekend vs Argentina in
Port Elizabeth (8.10.94). The Boks
won 42–22 and Pieter – nicknamed
'Ox' or 'Oz' after his wrestling
exploits as a youngster – has scarcely

South Africa (1994)
Last Season	9 caps	0 pts
Career	9 caps	0 pts

Caps (9): **1994** Arg(1,2), S, W **1995**
WS(a) wc-A,WS(b), F, NZ
Points Nil

taken a backward glance since. Retained his place in the 46–26 second Test
defeat of the Pumas, and then toured to Britain, turning out against Wales A,
Neath, Swansea, Scottish Combined Districts and the Barbarians, in addition
to appearing in the victories over Scotland (34–10, Murrayfield 19.11.94) and
Wales (20–12, Cardiff 26.11.94). Continued in the same vein in 1995 – a
campaign of course highlighted by the World Cup, in which Pieter played
against Australia, Western Samoa, France and, particularly notably, New
Zealand in that never-to-be-forgotten final (Johannesburg, 24.6.95). Missed
out, however, on the post-World Cup mini tour to Italy and England.

Eales, J. A.   Australia

Full name: John Anthony Eales
State: Queensland
Club: Brothers
Position: Lock
Height: 6ft 7in (2.00m)
Weight: 17st 8lb (107kg)
Occupation: Promotions manager
with G&E Hotels
Born: 27.6.70
Family: Jack (father), Rosa (mother),
Bernadette (sister), Damian (brother),
Antoinette (sister), Rosaleen (sister)
International debut: Australia 63,
Wales 6, 1991
Toughest opponent: Ian Jones
(North Auckland & New Zealand)
Notable landmarks in rugby career:
We didn't need further confirmation,
but we got it anyway during the
1996 Super-12 tournament when
John proved himself to be the
ultimate forward in world rugby –
peerless along the touchlines, a force
in the engine room and a top-notch
goalkicker. In fact the big man
topped the scoring charts with 160
points in a dozen games, bagging
three tries, 25 conversions and 35
penalty goals. And to think he is only

Australia (1991)

Last Season	12 caps	15 pts
Career	33 caps	19 pts

Caps (33): **1991** W(a), E(a), NZ(a1,a2).
wc-Arg,WS, W(b), I, NZ(b), E(b)
1992 S(1,2), NZ(1,2,3), SA, I **1994**
I(1,2), It(1,2), WS, NZ **1995**
Arg(1,2) wc-SA, C, R, E. NZ(1,2),
1996 W(1,2)
Points (19 – 2t,5c): **1992** S(2:1t) **1995**
Arg(1:1t) wc-R(4c), **1996** W(2:1c)

26 years of age! Queensland Reds suffered semi-final heartbreak this time
round, whereas a year ago John landed two conversions and a penalty goal as
they beat Transvaal 30–16 in the Super-10 final (Johannesburg, 8.4.95). To
prove it was no fluke, he slotted four conversions for Australia in her 42–3
World Cup defeat of Romania (Stellenbosch, 3.6.95). Outstanding in below-
par Wallaby side at World Cup. Ever-present for Wallabies between 1994 and
1996, taking his cap tally to 31. Had announced himself in 1990 when he won
the coveted Rothmans Medal Best-and-Fairest Award in Brisbane club rugby.
His skills were appreciated by a wider audience when he toured Europe with the
Emerging Wallabies, playing in the 12–12 draw with England B at Wasps. From
there he was included in the Aussies' World Cup training squad, and having
made his debut in the record rout of Wales at Ballymore, he played all six
matches in the cup-winning side. His astonishing rise continued in 1992 when
he was selected to play for the World XV in the Centenary Series against New

Zealand. Unfortunately, he damaged a shoulder in the second Test – an injury which forced him to miss the entire 1993 campaign and kept him out until the visit of Ireland in June 1994.

Touchlines: Golf, cricket, reading

Elwood, E. P. Ireland

Full name: Eric Paul Elwood
Club: Lansdowne
Position: Outside-half
Height: 6ft (1.83m)
Weight: 13st 5lb (84kg)
Occupation: Sales representative with Irish Distillers
Born: Galway, 26.2.69
Family: Single
Former club: Galwegians
International debut: Wales 14, Ireland 19, 1993
Five Nations debut: As above
Worst moments in rugby: Lansdowne's relegation from Division One of 1991/92 All Ireland League; losing semi-final of 1993 World Cup Sevens to Australia.
Most respected opponent: Michael Lynagh (Queensland & Australia)
Serious injuries: Chipped vertebrae in neck (1987)
Notable landmarks in rugby career: A second frustrating season in succession for Eric, who was unable to cement his place in the Irish side and maintain the standards he set in his first two international campaigns. Having been dogged by injury in 1994/95, he made the No.10 jersey his own at the World Cup in South

Ireland (1993)

Last Season	5 caps	41 pts
Career	16 caps	135 pts

Caps (16): **1993** W, E, R **1994** F, W, E, S, A(1,2) **1995** F(a), W(a) wc-NZ, W(b), F(b) **1996** US, S
Points (135 – 12c,35p,2dg): **1993** W(1c,3p), E(2p,2dg), R(1c,6p) **1994** F(5p), W(5p), E(1c,2p), S(2p), A(1:1c,1p) **1995** F(a:1c) wc-NZ(2c), W(b:3c,1p), F(b:4p) **1996** US(1c,3p), S(1c,1p)

Africa, his finest hour coming when he slotted four penalties out of four against France in the quarter-final (Durban, 10.6.95). Unfortunately the rest of Ireland's game went to pot. Last season he made just the two appearances, kicking 11 points as Ireland beat the US Eagles 25–18 (Atlanta, 6.1.96) and five points as Scotland upset the formbook in Dublin (20.1.96). Thereafter a player who has twice masterminded wins over England was replaced by rookie David

Humphreys. Eric first wore an Ireland jersey on 30.9.89 when on national Under-21 side beaten 10–9 by Italy in Treviso. Connacht debut came in the same year, vs Ulster. Progressed up international ladder in 1992/93 after a series of impressive displays for Connacht – vs Australia and throughout Inter-Provincial Championship. Missed national trial but was drafted onto Ireland bench for the visit to Dublin of France, and subsequently succeeded Niall Malone as outside-half. Headlined in games vs Wales and England, not least because Ireland won both. He contributed 23 of the 36 points scored by the men in green and was widely acclaimed. His omission from the Lions squad, named 48 hours after England's defeat in Dublin, was contentious, but he put disappointment behind him and enjoyed a fine 1993/94 campaign, scoring 64 of Ireland's 74 points. He also kicked four penalty goals against the touring All Blacks for the Barbarians in a 25–12 loss (Cardiff, 4.12.93).

Touchlines: Gym, walking

Evans, I. C. Wales

Full name: Ieuan Cenydd Evans
Club: Llanelli
Position: Wing
Height: 5ft 10½ in (1.79kg)
Weight: 13st 3lb (84kg)
Occupation: Marketing manager, Forthright Finance Ltd (Cardiff)
Born: Pontardulais, 21.3.64
Family links with rugby: Father (John) played for Aberavon
Former club: Carmarthen Quins
International debut: France 16, Wales 9, 1987
Five Nations' debut: As above
Best rugby memories: Scoring tries that (a) clinched the Test series for 1989 Lions in Australia and (b) beat England in Cardiff (1992).
Worst rugby memory: New South Wales 71, Wales 8, 1991
Toughest opponent: David Campese (NSW & Australia)
Serious injuries: Recurring dislocated shoulder, broken leg
Notable landmarks in rugby career: Wales' record try scorer (27) and most-capped wing (63), Ieuan enjoyed a much-deserved testimonial match last season (21.11.95) when a 13,000 crowd turned out at Stradey Park to see a British Isles XV, featuring Ieuan himself, beat an International XV, featuring Jonah Lomu, 68–57. Ieuan, who has no plans to hang up his boots in the near future, would by now have established even more impressive national records

had his career not been dogged by injury. The early part of his playing career was punctuated by five dislocations and two operations. Most recently, he broke his ankle badly playing for Llanelli and missed three internationals during the 1994/95 campaign. As a consequence of Wales' Five Nations whitewash that season, coach Alan Davies resigned to be replaced by Cardiff supremo Alex Evans, who replaced Ieuan as captain with his club skipper Mike Hall for the ill-fated World Cup campaign. *Rugby World & Post* Player of the Year for 1992/93, Ieuan led Wales to 1994 Five Nations title. Wales' 103rd captain, when he was appointed prior to 1991 World Cup, he became the Principality's longest-serving leader when he took charge of the 1995

Wales (1987)		
Last Season	12 caps	30 pts
Career	63 caps	127 pts
Lions (1989)	3 Tests	4 pts
(1993)	3 Tests	0 pts

Caps (63): **1987** F, E(a), S, I(a) wc-I(b), C, E(b), NZ, A **1988** E, S, I, F, NZ(1,2) **1989** I, F, E. Lions-A(1,2,3) **1991** E, S, I, F(a), A(a), F(b) wc-WS, Arg, A(b) **1992** I, F, E, S, A **1993** E, S, I, F. Lions-NZ(1,2,3). J, C **1994** S, I, F, E. wc(q)-P, S. C, Fj, T, WS. wc(q)-R **1995** E, S, I(a) wc-J, NZ, I(b). SA, Fj **1996** It, E, S, I, F, A(1,2)

Points (127 – 27t): **1987** I(a:1t) wc-C(4t) **1988** S(1t), F(1t) **1989** Lions-A(3:1t) **1991** wc-WS(1t) **1993** E(1t), I(1t), J(2t) **1994** S(1t). wc(q)-P(3t), S(3t). C(1t) wc(q)-R(1t) **1995** wc-J(2t) **1996** It(2t), I(2t)

World Cup qualifier in Portugal (celebrated with try hat-trick). Mission No.19 in charge, a 102–11 win, nudged him past Arthur 'Monkey' Gould. When he was replaced, Ieuan had led Wales 28 times. Played all three Tests in 1989 Lions series win (2–1) in Australia, scoring series-clinching try in final Test in Sydney (won 19–18, 15.7.89), and all three Tests in New Zealand with 1993 Lions. Equalled national single-match try-scoring record with four tries in 40–9 defeat of Canada (1987 World Cup), and contributed one (vs Western Samoa) to Wales' 1991 Cup challenge and two (vs Japan) in 1995. Scored six tries for Wales B in 1985 defeat of Spain (80–9) at Bridgend. National hero when he ran in winning try against England (6.2.93). on the domestic front, scored winning try as Llanelli beat Australia 13–9 (14.11.92) and shared in Scarlets 1992/93 League and Cup double.

Touchlines: Tennis, cricket, squash, golf

Field, M. J. Ireland

Full name: Maurice John Field
Nickname: Flymo
Club: Malone
Position: Centre, wing, fullback
Height: 6ft (1.83m)
Weight: 13st 12lb (88kg)
Occupation: Firefighter with NIFS
Born: Greenisland, 24.2.64
Family: Gillian (wife), Rebekah,
Olivia (daughters), Louis (son)
Former club: NIFC
International debut: England 12,
Ireland 13, 1994
Five Nations debut: As above
Best rugby moment: Beating
England at Twickenham on debut
Worst rugby moment: Not being
picked for 1995 World Cup quarter-
final vs France
Most embarrassing moment: Losing
my rag in 1995/96 Ulster Senior Cup
final when the headmaster of my
daughter's school, Brian Stirling,
was refereeing.
Toughest opponent: Frank Bunce
(North Harbour & New Zealand)

Ireland (1994)

Last Season	6 caps	0 pts
Career	12 caps	0 pts

Caps (12): **1994** E, S,A (1R) **1995**
F(a:R), W(a:R), It(R) wc-NZ(R), J.
Fj **1996** F(R), W, E

Do you really want to be a full-time professional? No, it's not feasible with three young kids and a mortgage. I need to work.
How well has rugby handled move to professionalism? 6/10. The IRFU's big three, Bobby Deacy, Syd Millar and Tom Kiernan, have got their heads screwed on, but it has taken the other committee members too long to get a handle on professionalism.
Do you have a duty to entertain? Yes, but we always have had. Spectators haven't just started paying.
Notable landmarks in rugby career: Won four more caps last season despite being unable to break the Mullin–Danaher midfield stranglehold. And when Jonathan Bell was switched inside from the wing it must have hurt Maurice, who seemed to have done everything that had been asked of him yet had to live off scraps. His one 80-minute stint came at the World Cup in the 50–28 defeat of Japan (Bloemfontein, 31.5.95). Had taken full advantage of his Test opportunity in 1993/94, helping Ireland to a two-match unbeaten run after they had started the 1994 championship campaign with a pair of losses. His promotion to centre berth followed injury to Vinnie Cunningham and the

285

selectors' decision to replace Bangor's Mark McCall after defeat by Wales in Dublin. So Maurice was given his debut at Twickenham (19.2.94), where Ireland had not won since 1982. England were beaten 13–12 and yer man was suitably chuffed. He retained his place for drab 6–6 home draw with Scotland (5.3.94) and was then invited to tour Australia. Started out with NIFC, playing for Ulster at Under-20 level in 1983. The following year he played for Ulster Under-23s but then had to wait six years before senior provincial debut against Irish Exiles. Played in Ulster's defeat by Australia in 1992, and won first international honours in Ireland A side beaten 20–10 by Wales counterparts at Donnybrook (4.2.94).

Touchlines: Golf (17 handicap), rearing kids, cycling

Fitzpatrick, S. B. T.   New Zealand

Full name: Sean Brian Thomas Fitzpatrick
Club: University
Province: Auckland
Position: Hooker
Height: 6ft (1.83m)
Weight: 14st 10lb (93kg)
Occupation: Marketing development manager with Coca-Cola
Born: Auckland, 4.6.63
Family: Bronwyn (wife) and child
Family links with rugby: Brian (father) won three caps as All Black five-eighth (1953 W; 1954 I, F)
International debut: New Zealand 18, France 9, 1986
Best memory in rugby: Beating Australia 30–16 in Sydney (25.7.87) – a great team performance.

Earliest memory in rugby: Being ball-boy for my brother's team when I was 3½. My father was also coach of that team, and no, my brother was not captain!

Notable landmarks in rugby career: Most-capped All Black of all time, his 77 caps putting him 18 clear of Gary Whetton and John Kirwan, the previous co-record holders. All Black Test hooker since 1986 and the world's most-capped player in that position (ahead of England's Brian Moore, 63). Succeeded Whetton as captain prior to the 1992 centenary series. Captaincy has rested well on his shoulders, adding a new dimension to his already immense performances. Sean, who is widely considered to be the world's premier lineout thrower, is the first Auckland hooker to pass the 100-appearance mark for the province – a total amassed since his debut in 1984. And he made his 100th All

Black appearance in 1995 World Cup quarter-final defeat of Scotland (Pretoria, 11.6.95). After losing World Cup final to Boks, Sean and All Black pals took out their annoyance on Australia, sweeping the summer Bledisloe Cup series before flying to Europe and splitting a Test series with France. Sean's Test debut came against France in 1986 in Christchurch, while the Cavaliers were away in South Africa. He was displaced by the returning Hika Reid for the second and third Tests against the Wallabies later in the year, but reversed the roles for the tour of France, and has since resisted each and every pretender to his throne. Equalled NZ record for a hooker when he scored two tries in the 30–16 win over Australia in 1987. He was selected for New Zealand Schools in 1981, progressing to NZ Colts, whom he represented in 1983 (along with John Kirwan, Grant Fox and Murray Mexted) and captained the following year. His 1984 charges included Bernie McCahill, Frano Botica (now Castleford RL) and Paul Henderson.

Touchlines: Golf, fishing, skin diving
Full name: Stuart (Stu) Thomas Forster

New Zealand (1986)		
Last Season	14 caps	10 pts
Career	77 caps	45 pts

Caps (77): **1986** F(a), A(1), F(b1,b2) **1987** wc-It, Fj, Arg, S, W, F. A **1988** W(1,2), A(1,2,3) **1989** F(1,2), Arg(1,2), A, W, I **1990** S(1,2), A(1,2,3), F(1,2) **1991** Arg(1,2), A(a1,a2). wc-E, US, It, C, A(b), S **1992** Wd(1,2,3), I(1,2), A(1,2,3), SA **1993** BL(1,2,3), A, WS, S, E **1994** F(1,2), SA(1,2,3), A **1995** C wc-I, W, J, S, E, SA. A(1,2), It, F(1,2), **1996** WS, S(1,2)

Points (45 – 10t): **1987** A(2t) **1989** F(2:1t) **1990** A(1:1t), A(2:1t) **1993** BL(3:1t), A(1t) **1994** F(2:1t) **1995** wc-S(1t). It(1t)

Ireland centre Maurice Field desperately trying to locate the ball in Paris. It was that sort of a day for the Irish, routed 45–10.

Forster, S. T.   New Zealand

Province: Otago
Club: Southern
Position: Scrum-half
Height: 5ft 7in (1.70m)
Weight: 11st 11lb (75kg)
Born: 12.2.69
Former province: Hawke's Bay
International debut: Scotland 15,
New Zealand 51, 1993
Worst moment in rugby: Getting
thrashed by Waikato in final of 1992
New Zealand Championship
Notable landmarks in rugby career:
Lost his All Black place after France
swept the 1994 series 2–0 in New
Zealand, but returned to favour after
1995 Bledisloe Cup when Graeme
Bachop left New Zealand to live,
work and play in Japan. Toured with
All Blacks to Italy and France in
November, playing in Tests against
both, although Canterbury's Justin
Marshall took over the No.9 jersey
for second Test against France. A
member of the free-flowing Otago

New Zealand (1993)

Last Season	2 caps	0 pts
Career	6 caps	0 pts

Caps (6): **1993** S, E **1994** F(1,2) **1995** It, F(1)
Points Nil

Highlanders side which added such colour to the 1996 Super-12 tournament,
Stu had previously masterminded the province's 37–24 defeat of 1993 British
Lions (Dunedin, 5 June). Five months later the diminutive yet devastating
runner arrived in Britain for the All Blacks' autumn tour as one of the two
selected scrum-halves. A bench reserve (behind Waikato's Simon Crabb) for the
New Zealand XV which swept their 1992 series with England B, Stu's form in
the defeats of London (won 39–12, Twickenham, 23.10.93), North of England
(won 27–21, Liverpool, 2.11.93), England A (won 26–12, Gateshead, 7.11.93)
and Scotland A (won 20–9, Glasgow, 13.11.93) ensured that he displaced
Wellington's Jon Preston (first choice in 1993 against Lions, Australia and
Western Samoa) from the No.9 berth for the two Tests against Scotland
(Edinburgh, 20.11.93) and England (lost 9–15, Twickenham, 27.11.93). He
formed an all-Otago halfback partnership with Marc Ellis. A 1989 New
Zealand Colt, Stu's team mates included Craig Innes (now Leeds RL), Va'iga
Tuigamala (now Wigan RL), John Timu (now Auckland Warriors RL), Blair
Larsen, Craig Dowd and English Lion Martin Johnson.
Touchlines: Boogie boarding, water skiing, mountain biking, skiing, golf
Full name: Neil Patrick John Francis

Francis, N. P. J.   Ireland

Nickname: Franno
Club: Old Belvedere
Position: Lock
Height: 6ft 6in (1.98m)
Weight: 18st 2lb (115kg)
Occupation: Self-employed business consultant to Equity Bank
Born: Dublin, 17.3.64
Family: Single
Former clubs: London Irish, Manly (Australia)
International debut: Ireland 32, Tonga 9, 1987
Five Nations debut: Scotland 37, Ireland 21, 1989
Serious injuries: Broken vertebrae (out for two years)
Best rugby memory: Playing in three World Cups and beating England at Twickenham (1994)
Worst rugby memory: Manner of defeat to Australia in 1991 World Cup quarter-final: we had practically won the match.
Do you really want to be a full-time professional? No
How well has rugby handled move to professionalism? 1.5/10. Unions needed to be *pro*active, but it was as much as some of them could to be *re*active. Why could they not embrace professionalism? Why did they have to hang on grimly to their last vestiges of power rather than have the good grace to accept the inevitable?

Ireland (1987)		
Last Season	7 caps	5 pts
Career	36 caps	19 pts

Caps (36): **1987** wc-T, A **1988** WS, It **1989** S **1990** E, F, W **1991** E, S, Na(1,2) wc-Z, J, S, A **1992** W, E, S **1993** F, R **1994** F, W, E, S, A(1,2), US **1995** E wc-NZ, J, W(b), F(b). Fj **1996** US, S
Points (19 – 4t): **1988** WS(1t) **1994** A(2:1t) **1995** wc-J(1t). Fj(1t)

Do you have a duty to entertain? Yes, but winning must come first.
Do you feel a loyalty to your club in this new era? Absolutely not. It is no longer the game it was five years ago. Rugby had a certain ethos which it has now lost.
Other sporting claims to fame: Javelin for Ireland (national junior and senior champion)
Notable landmarks in rugby career: One of Ireland's star performers in last summer's World Cup, Franno was the catalyst in an exceptional Irish forward effort which accounted for nine of the 13 tries scored in four games. His lineout understanding with Gabriel Fulcher hinted at a bright future, and the present looked pretty good too as he piled into the All Blacks on that unforgettable

evening in Johannesburg (27.5.95). Franno had returned to the front line in 1993/94 after injury had decimated the previous season as far as he was concerned. Sadly for him, the good times did not last, as he was axed after one round of the 1996 Five Nations series following Ireland's surprise loss to Scotland in Dublin. Always an enigmatic player, Franno has been in and out of favour since his debut in the 1987 World Cup. Represented Irish Schools five times (1981/82), but back injury meant no representative rugby for four years from the age of 19, by which time he had already won Leinster Senior Cup medal with Blackrock. Did not represent Leinster until 1986. Scored try for Ireland Under-25s against Canada in 1986. Rejoined Blackrock from London Irish in 1989 and moved on to Old Belvedere in 1994. Sole Irish representative in Home Unions team which played Rest of Europe at Twickenham in 1990 Romania Appeal match. Ever-present in 1991/92 season, including each 1991 World Cup tie, until final Five Nations match in Paris, when Brian Rigney returned, thus breaking Neil's 11-game streak. Missed Ireland's tour to New Zealand in 1992, but visited Namibia (1991) and Australia (1994).
Touchlines: Doing absolutely nothing

Fulcher, G. M. Ireland

Full name: Gabriel Mark Fulcher
Nickname: Fulch
Club: London Irish
Position: Lock
Height: 6ft 5in (1.96m)
Weight: 17st (108kg)
Occupation: Sales representative, Micro-Bio (Ireland) Ltd
Family: Single
Former clubs: UCD, Cork Constitution
Born: England, 27.11.69
International debut: Australia 32, Ireland 18, 1994
Five Nations debut: Ireland 8, England 20, 1995
Best rugby memory: First cap against Australia

Worst rugby memory: Rockwell College losing to Crescent Comp in quarter-finals of 1987 Schools Cup.
Do you really want to be a full-time professional? No, but I might not be able to avoid it eventually.
How well has rugby handled move to professionalism? 0/10. It went OK on first day, but has since gone haywire.

Do you have a duty to entertain? Yes, but we did before.

Do you feel a loyalty to your club in this new era? Yes, but probably not in the old sense of the word.

Notable landmarks in rugby career: Hugely impressive debut season in Test rugby in 1994/95, forming a convincing partnership with Neil

Ireland (1994)

Last Season	10 caps	5 pts
Career	16 caps	5 pts

Caps (16): **1994** A(2),US **1995** E(R), S, F(a), W(a), It wc-NZ, J, W(b), F(b). Fj **1996** US, S, F, W, E

Points (5 – 1t): **1996** W(1t)

Francis in the Irish engine room. Once Gabriel had proved that at 25 he was old enough for the job, the selectors stopped advertising the post. From the moment he came on as a half-time replacement for the injured Mick Galwey against England (Dublin, 21.1.95), he became a permanent fixture thereafter, save for the Japan World Cup tie (Bloemfontein, 31.5.95), when he was given the day off and Davy Tweed had a turn. He carried on in the same fashion in 1995/96, appearing in all six of Ireland's matches and scoring his maiden Test try in the 30–17 defeat of Wales (Dublin, 2.3.96), shortly after he had switched club allegiances from Cork Con to London Irish. Toured Australia with Irish Schools in 1986/87. Helped UC Dublin win the Under-19 McCorry Cup and played for the Munster Under-21s against Italy in Cork. Won two caps for the Ireland Under-21 team in 1990/91, against Netherlands and England, before graduating to Ireland B the following season. Joined Cork Con from UCD and was included in Ireland development squad which toured Zimbabwe, Namibia and South Africa in 1993. Spent the following summer 'down under', making his international debut in the second Test in Sydney (11.6.95), before returning to South Africa for the 1995 World Cup.

Touchlines: Windsurfing

Ireland win the Eurovision song contest – again: (left to right) Paddy Johns, Gary Halpin, Gabriel Fulcher and Eric Elwood.

Gallart, P.   France

Full name: Philippe Gallart
Club: Beziers
Position: Prop
Height: 6ft ½ in (1.85m)
Weight: 17st 5lb (105kg)
Occupation: Commercial agent,
Sarl Usine a Gaz
Born: 18.12.62
Former club: Pezenas
International debut: France 6,
Romania 12, 1990
Five Nations debut: Scotland 10,
France 6, 1992
Notable landmarks in rugby career:
Returned to international favour at
the tail-end of the 1994/95 season,
playing in France's World Cup
warm-up match against Romania in
Bucharest (won 24–15, 7.4.95), and
then going to South Africa with
Pierre Berbizier's side and playing in
the Tricolors' opening engagement
against Tonga (Pretoria, 26.5.95).
But that was that, as Laurent
Benezech and Louis Armary shored
up the loosehead duties thereafter.

France (1990)

Last Season	1 cap	0 pts
Career	17 caps	0 pts

Caps (17): **1990** Ro, A(1,2R,3) **1992** S,
I, R, Arg(a1,a2), SA(1,2), Arg(b)
1994 I, W, E **1995** R wc-T
Points Nil

Recalled in 1992 in place of Philippe Gimbert against Scotland (7.3.92) for the first time since being sent off by Clive Norling for punching Tim Gavin in the 48th minute of the 28–19 third Test win against Australia in Sydney (30.6.90). For that misdemeanour a four-month suspension had been meted out, ensuring that he played no part in the 1991 Five Nations campaign when only England stood between France and a fifth Grand Slam. Despite touring to North America in summer 1991 he was no less redundant, and failed to make the 26-man World Cup squad. However, the Paris debacle which wrote Gimbert and Lascube out of the international script allowed Gallart to restore a representative career which had begun, in Stade Patrice Brocas, Auch, with defeat against Romania (24.5.90). Injury forced him from the field prematurely, to be replaced by Pascal Ondarts, although he returned 'down under' to play in two- and-a-half Tests against the Wallabies. Having been voted 1992 Prop of the Year by French rugby writers, he promptly lost his place to Merignac's Seigne for 1993 Five Nations Championship, but only because of a serious calf injury.

Galthie, F. France

Full name: Fabien Galthie
Club: Colomiers
Position: Scrum-half
Height: 5ft 10½ in (1.80m)
Weight: 12st 4lb (78kg)
Occupation: Executive
Born: Cahors, 20.3.69
International debut: Romania 21, France 33, 1991
Five Nations debut: Wales 9, France 12, 1992
Former club: Tournefeuille
Notable landmarks in rugby career:
Called into France's 1995 World Cup squad as an emergency replacement for Guy Accoceberry, who broke his arm in the Pool D decider against Scotland in Pretoria. Coach Pierre Berbizier courted controversy by picking Fabien ahead of incumbent Aubin Hueber for the semi-final with South Africa, but his decision was vindicated by a strong show from the first Colomiers player ever to be capped. Fabien was similarly impressive in the play-off

France (1990)
Last Season	2 caps	0 pts
Career	16 caps	9 pts

Caps (16): **1991** R, US(1) wc-R, Fj, C, E **1992** W, E, S, R, Arg(b) **1993** I, W, E **1995** wc-SA, E(b)

defeat of England (Pretoria, 22.6.95) but has not played since. Had succeeded Berbizier at No.9 in 1991. Played his debut in Bucharest (22.6.91), and remained intact for eight of the next ten internationals until Hueber took over for Ireland's Championship visit to Paris (21.3.92) following the mounting criticism of Fabien. In the latter's defence, he was unable to settle into a half-back understanding because of the constantly changing identity of his stand-off, with Didier Camberabero, Thierry Lacroix and Alain Penaud all given a shot. He even captained France for part of the Five Nations game against England (15.2.92) when Philippe Sella was injured. Saw little Test action in 1992/93 (Hueber preferred), though Fabien was a try-scorer in both games he did play – against Romania (won 25–6, Le Havre, 28.5.92) and Argentina (lost 20–24, Nantes, 14.11.92). He was one of eight casualties after the Pumas' historic first win on French soil. Bench reserve for both Tests against South Africa in summer of 1993, and was recalled for 1994 Championship before again losing place, for final game against Scotland, to Perpignan's Alain Macabiau. Not seen again in the Test arena until 1995 World Cup.

Gavin, B. T. — Australia

Full name: Bryant Timothy (Tim) Gavin
State: New South Wales
Clubs: Eastern Suburbs (Aus), Mediolanum Milan (It)
Position: No.8, Lock
Height: 6ft 5in (1.96m)
Weight: 16st 12lb (107kg)
Occupation: PR consultant
Born: 20.11.63
Family: Single
International debut: Australia 19, New Zealand 19, 1988
Worst moment in rugby: Sustaining knee injury in club game before 1991 World Cup, which forced me to miss tournament.
Most embarrassing moment: Being sidestepped by a grey-haired Italian at least ten years older than me.
Most respected opponent: Wayne Shelford (New Zealand)
Serious injuries: Knee reconstruction (1991), thigh injury (1992).
Suggestions to improve rugby: Change tackle law, as players are picked because of their ability to kill the ball.
Notable landmarks in rugby career: Australia's most-capped No.8, with 42 of his 44 caps having come at the

Australia (1988)

Last Season	6 caps	0 pts
Career	46 caps	40 pts

Caps (46): **1988** NZ(2,3), S, It(R) **1989** NZ(R), F(1,2) **1990** F(1,2,3), US, NZ(1,2,3) **1991** W(a), E(a), NZ(a1) **1992** S(1,2), SA, I, W **1993** T, NZ, SA(1,2,3), C, F(1,2) **1994** I(1,2), It(1,2), WS, A **1995** Arg(1,2) wc-SA, C, R, E. NZ(1,2)

Points (40 -- 9t): **1990** F(2:1t), US(1t) **1991** W(a:2t), NZ(a1:1t) **1993** T(1t), F(1:1t), F(2:1t) **1994** WS(1t)

back of the scrum (the other two came as replacement lock). Ever-present for Australia in 1994/95, playing in all 14 Tests and contributing a try to the 73–3 defeat of Western Samoa (Sydney, 6.8.94). Debut had come against 1988 All Blacks, but it was a further two years before the second row turned No.8 (with more than a little help from national coach Bob Dwyer) shook off the challenge of Steve Tuynman to secure a regular berth. Once ensconced, he wasted little time attracting a host of admirers, not least the Australian Society of Rugby Writers, who voted him their Player of the Year in 1990. Tim was a racing certainty for the Aussies' 1991 World Cup squad before sustaining a knee injury in club colours and having to watch the crowning glory via satellite from back home in Oz. Injury continued to frustrate him in 1992 when a bruised thigh kept him out of the 2–1 Bledisloe Cup series win. He recovered in time to tour South

Africa and made a wonderful start in the Republic, scoring two tries as the Wallabies downed Western Transvaal 46–13 in Potchefstroom. He did not reappear until the Test match, in Cape Town on 22 August, when the Wallabies handed the Springboks a frightful beating (26–3). From there he toured Ireland and Wales, playing in both internationals in addition to the wins over Leinster, Ulster (two tries), Wales B and the Barbarians, and the losses to Swansea and Llanelli. Stepped up his try-scoring rate in an injury-free 1993, touching down against Tonga, and in both Tests of the shared autumn series against France.
Touchlines: Fishing, skiing

Geoghegan, S. P. Ireland

Full name: Simon Patrick Geoghegan
Club: Bath
Position: Wing
Height: 6ft 1in (1.86m)
Weight: 13st (83kg)
Occupation: Solicitor, Rosling King
Born: Barnet, Herts, 1.9.68
Family: Single
Former clubs: Wasps (Colts), London Irish
International debut: Ireland 13, France 21, 1991
Five Nations debut: As above
Toughest opponent: Patrice Lagisquet (Bayonne & France)
Best rugby memory: Beating England in 1994
Worst rugby memory: Losing to Australia in quarter-finals of 1991 World Cup
Do you really want to be a full-time professional? No
How well has rugby handled move to professionalism? 0/10. RFU imposed a one-year moratorium in order to sort things out and they resolved absolutely nothing. There are so many other professional sports that rugby can learn from. Why isn't it learning? The game is crying out to replace unwieldy unions with boards of directors. We are so far behind the southern hemisphere, and the sooner everyone realises it the better.

Ireland (1991)

Last Season	9 caps	15 pts
Career	37 caps	51 pts

Caps (37): **1991** F, W, E, S, Na(1) wc-Z, S, A **1992** E, S, F, A **1993** S, F, W, E, R **1994** F, W, E, S, A(1,2), US **1995** E, S, F(a), W(a) wc-NZ, J, W(b), F(b). Fj **1996** US, S, W, E
Points (51 – 11t): **1991** W(1t), E(1t), S(1t) wc-Z(1t) **1993** R(1t) **1994** E(1t), US(1t) **1995** F(a:1t) wc-J(1t). Fj(1t) **1996** W(1t)

295

Do you have a duty to entertain? Yes, but we did before too.

Do you feel a loyalty to your club in this new era? Yes. Professionalism doesn't need to change that. Look at someone like Tony Adams at Arsenal FC. There is no more loyal sportsman about.

Notable landmarks in rugby career: Took his try tally to 11, with scores in 1995/96 against Fiji and Wales. Ireland won both games. Unfortunately they only won one other and consequently ended up with Five Nations Wooden Spoon. Groin injury robbed him of an ever-present Test attendance in 1994/95 but at least spared him from any involvement in Italy's first-ever win over one of the Big Eight nations (lost 12–22, Treviso, 8.5.95). That apart, Simon scored tries against USA, France and Japan, and remained influential despite being frustrated by the lack of possession coming his way. Simon's return to form in 1993/94 had been heaven-sent for Ireland. Without him the Irish wouldn't have scored a try all season. With him they managed two – against Romania and England – and you don't need to be Einstein to know which was the best received. Missed Ireland's tour to New Zealand in 1992 but returned to side for visit of world champions Australia to Dublin. Failed to emulate his previous scoring exploits, either in that game or in his subsequent outings in the 1993 Five Nations Championship. Represented Ireland at Under-25, Students, B and full level. Quickly rose to prominence, with try-scoring debuts for Ireland Under-25 (36–17 vs Spain, Limerick, 8.9.90) and Ireland B (27–12 vs Argentina, Limerick, 20.10.90). Quality Inter-Provincial performances for Connacht sped his progress into the senior national XV, for whom he opposed the 'Bayonne Express', Patrice Lagisquet, on his debut against France at Lansdowne Road (2.2.91). Scored tries in next three internationals, against Wales, Ireland and Scotland. Toured Namibia (1991) and Australia (1994), and played in last two World Cups.

Touchlines: Soccer (West Ham fan), cinema, theatre

*Ireland wing Simon Geoghegan outpaces Welsh marker
Wayne Proctor in Dublin, where Ireland won 30–17.*

Gibbs, A.   Wales

Full name: Andrew Gibbs
Club: Llanelli
Position: Flanker
Height: 6ft 3in
Weight: 16st 7lb
Occupation: Police officer, Gwent Constabulary
Born: 20.3.72
Former Club: Newbridge
International debut: Wales 12, Ireland 16, 1995
Five Nations debut: As above
Notable landmarks in rugby career: Became the 922nd player to be capped by Wales when selected by coach Alan Davies for the 1995 Five Nations visit of Ireland to Cardiff (18.3.95), two days before his 23rd birthday. It was a fitting tribute to a player who has overcome serious illness – he required a six-month course of officially sanctioned steroid treatment to cure his reactive arthritis. And his selection was seen

Wales (1995)		
Last Season	2 caps	0 pts
Career	3 caps	0 pts

Caps (3): **1995** I(a). SA **1996** A(2)
Points Nil

as a good omen for the slumping Welsh, as he had never been on the losing side in 15 appearances in a Wales jersey at Youth, Under-19, Under-21 and A levels. But such superstition counted for nought, as Ireland won the match 16–12 to hand Wales their second-ever whitewashed Wooden Spoon. Davies resigned his post, and Andrew was consigned to the ranks of the forgotten men by new coach Alex Evans until after the World Cup. Evans then picked him to return to South Africa to take on the world champion Boks in Ellis Park (2.9.95). Wales lost 11–40, but their showing had much improved on their feeble World Cup effort. The Gwent blindside had represented Newbridge at Under-13 to Under-16 levels before captaining Crumlin Youth for two seasons, during which time he was capped by Wales Youth against Ireland, France, Japan and England in 1991. A member of the brilliant Wales Under-19 side that toured Canada in 1991, Andrew broke into the Newbridge league side in 1994 and represented Wales A (vs Ireland and France) that same year.

Glas, S.   France

Full name: Stephane Glas
Club: Bourgoin-Jallieu
Position: Centre
Height: 5ft 10in (1.78m)
Weight: 12st 4lb (78kg)
Occupation: Student
Born: Bourgoin, 12.11.73
Family: Single
International debut: Scotland 19, France 14, 1996
Five Nations debut: As above
Notable landmarks in rugby career: One of the finds of 1995/96 in Europe, Stephane made such an impression after bursting on the scene midway through the Five Nations Championship that he forced Thierry Lacroix, France's record points scorer, onto the sidelines. A regular in senior club rugby since he was 19, Stephane alerted the national selectors when he destroyed Begles with two tries to send Bourgoin through into the

France (1996)

Last Season	5 caps	10 pts
Career	5 caps	10 pts

Caps (5): **1996** S(TR), I, W, R, Arg(2TR)
Points (10 – 2t): **1996** R(2t)

quarter-finals of the 1994/95 French club championship for the first time in their history. But that was nothing to the impact he had after coming on as a 22nd-minute replacement for Lacroix against Ireland (Paris, 17.2.96). Ten minutes as a temporary replacement against Scotland the previous fortnight might have earned him his first cap, but this was his first real test and he responded by ripping the Irish defence to ribbons with one telling run after another. His partnership with stand-off Thomas Castaignede was the highlight of a record 45–10 victory for France in the fixture. It was no surprise that he started the next game, only that Wales won it (Cardiff, 16.3.96). Normal service was resumed for Stephane and France on the last day of their international campaign as he bagged a brace of tries in the 64–12 defeat of Romania (Aurillac, 20.4.96).

Gonzales, J.-M.   France

Full name: Jean-Michel Gonzales
Club: Bayonne
Position: Hooker, prop
Height: 5ft 9in (1.75m)
Weight: 16st 13lb (103kg)
Occupation: Marketing manager
Born: Bayonne, 10.7.67
Family: Married
International debut: Argentina 12, France 27, 1992
Five Nations debut: France 35, Ireland 15, 1994
Former club: Cambo
Notable landmarks in rugby career: Sustained knee ligament damage playing against Argentina in the Latin Cup (Buenos Aires, 21.10.95) and was sidelined for the November two-Test visit of New Zealand, Marc de Rougemont deputising. However, recaptured place for duration of 1996 Five Nations series. The previous summer Jean-Michel's accurate lineout throwing had been a feature of France's third-place play-off victory over England (Pretoria, 22.6.95) in the World Cup, capping a busy season for the Bayonne hooker – one in which he made the

France (1992)
Last Season	11 caps	0 pts
Career	35 caps	5 pts

Caps (35): **1992** Arg(a1,a2), SA(1,2), Arg(b) **1993** R(a), SA(1,2), R(b), A(1,2) **1994** I, W, E, S, C(a), NZ(1,2), C(b) **1995** W, E(a), S(a), I(a), R wc-T, S(b), I(b), SA, E(b). It, Arg **1996** E, S, I, W
Points (5 – 1t): **1992** Arg(b:1t)

No.2 jersey his own, missing only the 54–18 World Cup romp against Cote d'Ivoire. Yet until Jean-Francois Tordo's switch from flanker prior to the 1993 Five Nations Championship, France had seemed unsure as to who they wanted to perform their hooking duties. Jean-Pierre Genet, the Racing Club de France rake, lost the jersey on tour in Argentina, having done the honours against Romania at Le Havre in May, and coach Pierre Berbizier instead invited Jean-Michel to put in a bid. He played in both Tests in Buenos Aires against a poor Pumas side and kept the job through the two-Test series with South Africa, despite the 15–20 loss which France suffered at Lyon (17.10.92). But his time was nearly up. Had France not allowed Argentina, now themselves on tour, a historic first victory on French soil at Nantes on 14 November, he might have survived. As it was, the Pumas won 24–20 and, in spite of the hooker scoring one of the home side's three tries, he was one of eight dumped. Reappeared at loosehead prop against Romania in Bucharest (20.5.93) where another serious injury to Tordo paved the way for Jean-Michel to reassert himself. He played the next nine Tests and then toured to Canada and New Zealand (1994), contributing fully in France's historic 2–0 series defeat of the All Blacks.

Graou, S. France

Full name: Stephane Graou
Club: Auch
Position: Prop, hooker
Height: 5ft 10in (1.78m)
Weight: 16st 6lb (100kg)
Occupation: Commercial officer
Born: Auch, 1.5.66
International debut: France 20, Argentina 24, 1992
Five Nations debut: None
Notable landmarks in rugby career: As storming starts to Test careers go, Stephane's must rate somewhere down the list – which is a pity, because he worked hard to put himself into the frame. A member of the French squad which won the 1988 Students World Cup, he waited two years before touring Namibia with a French development squad. He finally got his shot at the big time when selected to tour Argentina in 1992 with the senior squad, but rather than exploit the opportunity he had himself sent off against Cuyo, having come on as a replacement in the 30–32 loss in Mendoza (30.6.92). In all, Stephane appeared in four of the

France (1992)

Last Season	3 caps	0 pts
Career	8 caps	0 pts

Caps (8): **1992** Arg(b:R) **1993** SA(1,2), R(b), A(2R) **1995** R,Arg(TR), F(1R)
Points Nil

eight tour games, but remained uncapped until the Pumas visited Nantes on 14 November. At half-time in a Test which was to make history for all the wrong reasons (as far as France was concerned), he entered the fray as replacement for Philippe Gallart. But Argentina won 24–20 to register their first-ever victory on French soil, and Stephane returned from whence he came, while Merignac's Laurent Seigne was presented with the No.3 jersey for the 1993 Five Nations Championship. The Auch skipper had to make do with replacement duties throughout the triumphant campaign to add to those he carried out in South Africa's two-Test visit in October. It was against the 1993 Springboks that he returned, playing in both Tests on the summer tour. However, he lost his place to old foe Seigne after helping trounce Romania 51–0 in Brive (9.10.93). His final appearance of the term came as a 75th-minute replacement for Seigne in the second Test against Australia in Paris (6.11.93). Missed out totally in 1994 before getting only his third start in Argentina, where France beat Romania 52–8 (Tucuman, 17.10.96) en route to Latin Cup glory. Added two more caps without starting either game: as a temporary replacement against Argentina (21.10.95) and as a half-time replacement for Laurent Benezech against New Zealand (Toulouse, 18.11.95).

Grayson, P. J.   England

Full name: Paul James Grayson
Nickname: Grace
Club: Northampton
Position: Fly-half
Height: 6ft (1.83m)
Weight: 12st 7lb (79kg)
Occupation: Insurance broker, Hammon Osborne Ltd, Northampton
Born: Chorley, Lancs, 30.5.71
Family: Emma (wife)
International debut: England 27, Western Samoa 9, 1995
Five Nations debut: France 15, England 12, 1996
Best rugby memory: Winning first cap
Worst rugby memory: Getting relegated with Northampton (1994/95) after missing an important kick at the death against Gloucester
Toughest opponent: Stuart Barnes (ex-Bath & England)
Do you really want to be a full-time professional? No, I'm semi-pro and don't want to go any further.

England (1995)

Last Season	5 caps	81 pts
Career	5 caps	81 pts

Caps (5): 1995 WS 1996 F, W, S, I
Points (81 – 3c,22p,3dg): 1995 WS(1c,5p) 1996 F(2p,2dg), W(1c,3p), S(6p), I(1c,6p,1dg)

How well has rugby handled move to professionalism? 6/10. It all happened a bit too quickly for the northern hemisphere. Unlike the southern hemisphere, we had no infrastructure in place.
Do you have a duty to entertain? The way the game is going, you will have to play an 'entertaining' Super-12 brand of rugby if you want to be successful.
Do you feel a loyalty to your club in this new era? Definitely to Northampton. But money is always going to be a motivating factor for players.
Other sporting claim to fame: Semi-professional soccer for Accrington Stanley

Notable landmarks in rugby career: Had the dubious honour of being successor to record-breaking England fly-half Rob Andrew, after Mike Catt failed his audition. Responded with 64 of England's 79 points in their much-maligned 1996 Five Nations triumph, made up of 12 vs France (lost 12–15, 20.1.96), 11 vs Wales (won 21–15, 3.2.96), 18 vs Scotland (won 18–9, 2.3.96) and 23 vs Ireland (won 28–15, 16.3.96). Having demonstrated a cool head on his debut in the 27–9 defeat of Western Samoa (Twickenham, 16.12.95), accounting for 17 points, Paul performed with equal maturity in the Five Nations, save for a minor blip against the Welsh. Outstanding in Paris on his Five Nations debut, he produced the goods on order in the tension-ridden Calcutta Cup clash at Murrayfield. Earned his Test call-up, alongside Northampton half-back partner Matthew Dawson, with an impressive showing in the Midlands' defeat of the touring Samoans. Previously had been a decent footballer, playing semi-pro with Accrington Stanley, before turning to rugby union with Preston Grasshoppers. Moved to Waterloo and helped them cause the cup upset of all time, beating mighty Bath, before moving onto Northampton and guiding them to the 1995/96 English League Two title with plenty to spare. Toured with England A to Canada (1993), and to Australia and Fiji (1995).

Gregan, G. Australia

Full name: George Gregan
State: Australian Capital Territory
Position: Scrum-half
Height: 5ft 8in (1.72m)
Weight: 12st 1lb (77kg)
Occupation: Marketing trainee
Born: 19.4.73
International debut: Australia 23, Italy 20, 1994
Notable landmarks in rugby career:
Followed in the footsteps of David Campese by winning international recognition whilst playing for the unfashionable Australian Capital Territory – or at least they *were* unfashionable until their super show in the 1996 Super-12 tournament forced a drastic change of perception.

But it was his last-minute tackle on All Black Jeff Wilson that won him worldwide acclaim. The 'hit' came in the Bledisloe Cup match under the Sydney floodlights (17.8.94), and won the Wallabies a match they had threatened to let slip through their hands. Australia had raced into a 17–3 lead, but New Zealand had powered back to 16–17 with just four minutes left. David Knox's penalty for the home side still made it a one-score game, and when Wilson darted past four defenders he appeared to have that score. But wee George arrived from nowhere and put in a shuddering tackle (as he had done previously to stun giant All Black forwards Richard Loe and Mark Cooksley) to dislodge the ball from Golden Boy's grasps. The youngster made his debut in the home series against Italy, and opened his try-scoring account in the 73–3 rout of Manu Samoa (Sydney, 6.8.94). Retained his place in the Wallaby lineup in 1995, but was less effective in the World Cup as the defending champions stuttered their way to the quarter-finals before losing 25–22 to England in a last-minute thriller (Cape Town, 11.6.95).

Australia (1994)		
Last Season	5 caps	5 pts
Career	11 caps	5 pts

Caps (11): 1994 It(1,2), WS, NZ 1995 Arg(1,2) wc-SA, C, R, E 1996 W(1)

Points (5 – 1t): 1994 WS(1t)

Guscott, J. C.   England

Full name: Jeremy Clayton Guscott
Club: Bath
Position: Centre
Height: 6ft 1in (1.86m)
Weight: 13st 5lb (85kg)
Occupation: Marketing co-ordinator with British Gas
Born: Bath, 7.7.65
Family: Jayne (wife), Imogen (daughter)
International debut: Romania 3, England 58, 1989
Five Nations debut: England 23, Ireland 0, 1990
Best rugby memory: Scoring try for 1989 Lions vs Australia in second Test.
Worst rugby memory: Being dropped by Bath for semi-finals of 1989/90 Pilkington Cup.

Suggestions to improve rugby: Reduce the number of offences in lineout: there must be 100-odd, when there should be no more than five or six, and it is such an annoying part of the game.

Notable landmarks in rugby career: Shares with Will Carling the world record for a centre partnership of 43 Tests after a 1995/96 season in which both men were ever-present. Won't go down as one of England's most creative campaigns – no Five Nations champions have ever won the title by scoring as few as three tries – but at least Jeremy claimed one of those, in the 21–15 defeat of Wales

(Twickenham, 3.2.96). That try – his 18th – lifted him into second place alongside Cyril Lowe (1913–23) on England's all-time try-scoring list. In 1995/96 he also helped Bath to English league and cup double before deciding the two-match Cross-code Challenge between Bath and Wigan RLFC was a gimmick he could live without. Still, his season was an improvement on 194/95 when, by his Everest-high standards, he was disappointing. He might have been a member of the England side winning its third Grand Slam in five seasons, but the effects of the long-term groin/pelvic injury which had ruled him out of the entire 1993/94 season perhaps took the edge off his

England (1989)		
Last Season	11 caps	5 pts
Career	45 caps	83 pts
Lions (1989)	2 Tests	4 pts
(1993)	3 Tests	0 pts

Caps (45): **1989** Ro, Fj. Lions-A(2,3) **1990** I, F, W, S, Arg(b) **1991** W, S, I, F, Fj, A(a) wc-NZ, It, F, S, A(b) **1992** S, I, F, W, C, SA **1993** F, W, S, I. Lions-NZ(1,2,3) **1994** R, C **1995** I, F(a), W, S wc-Arg, It, A, NZ, F(b). SA, WS **1996** F, W, S, I

Points (83 – 18t,2dg): **1989** Ro(3t), Fj(1t). Lions-A(2:1t) **1990** I(1t), F(1t), S(1t), Arg(b:2t) **1991** A(a:1t) wc-It(2t) **1992** S(1dg), I(1t), C(1t), SA(1t) **1993** W(1dg), S(1t) **1995** F(a:1t) **1996** W(1t)

performances. Jerry failed to score a try at the World Cup, nor did he dominate the midfield as of old. His only score of the season came in the 31–10 Five Nations defeat of France (Twickenham, 4.2.95). Became an automatic selection for the 1993 Lions (playing in all three Tests) after a super 1992/93 season in which he had bagged tries against Canada, South Africa and Scotland, and dropped a goal in defeat by Wales in Cardiff. For many, though, his most memorable contribution of the campaign was his part in the wonderful move which led to Rory Underwood's try against the Scots (6.3.93). Started out aged seven, with Bath's mini-section as a wing. Meteoric rise in 1989 brought two caps for England B, three tries on full England debut in Bucharest, and one invitation from the British Lions. Scored brilliant crucial try in Brisbane (second Test: won 19–12, 8.7.89) to bring Lions back into the series, which they went on to win 2–1. Ever-present throughout England's back-to-back Grand Slams (1991/92) and wore No.12 jersey in 1991 World Cup final, having previously toured Australia (1991). Toured New Zealand with World XV (April 1992), playing in first two Tests, including famous 28–14 first Test defeat of All Blacks. **Touchlines:** Golf

Halvey, E. O.   Ireland

Full name: Eddie Oliver Halvey
Club: Saracens
Position: Flanker
Height: 6ft 4in (1.93m)
Weight: 15st 8lb (99kg)
Occupation: Full-time player
Born: Limerick, 11.7.70
Former club: Shannon
International debut: Ireland 7,
France 25, 1995
Five Nations debut: As above
Best rugby memory: Scoring World
Cup try against Wales in World Cup
Worst rugby memory: Groin injury
suffered in European Cup against
Swansea (11.11.95), which sidelined
me for four-and-a-half months.
**Do you really want to be a full-time
professional?** Yes
**How well has rugby handled move
to professionalism?** 4/10. No one
really seems to know what is
happening now and what is going to
happen in future.
Do you have a duty to entertain? Yes

Ireland (1995)

Last Season	6 caps	10 pts
Career	6 caps	10 pts

Caps (6): **1995** F(a), W(a), It wc-J,
    W(b:TR), F(b:R)
Points (10 – 2t): **1995** wc-J(1t), W(b:1t)

Do you feel a loyalty to your club in this new era? Yes
Other sporting claims to fame: Played Gaelic football for Limerick (1994), but
majored in rugby as there is no money in Gaelic.
Notable landmarks in rugby career: Assumed national-hero status in Ireland
after coming on as a bloodbin replacement for Denis McBride in the all-or-
nothing World Cup tie against Wales (Johannesburg, 4.6.95). Ireland's early
lead was under severe threat when Eddie's fresh legs were introduced to the
fray, and he responded almost immediately with the try that effectively killed
the contest. He then trotted off, McBride returned bandaged, Ireland advanced
to the quarter-finals and Wales went home. Eddie's performance was typical of
an Ireland pack revitalised after an indifferent Five Nations series. Yet a year
earlier he had only just broken into the Ireland A team, playing against Scotland
and Wales. Named in the Irish Development squad at the start of last season, he
continued in the A side (turning out against England and Scotland) before
getting his senior call-up against France at blindside, after Paddy Johns had
cried off at the eleventh hour and Anthony Foley had switched to No.8. Held
his place against Wales and Italy, in his favoured openside berth, before
marking his World Cup debut with a try in the 50–28 defeat of plucky Japan

(Bloemfontein, 31.5.95). Came on as a replacement for Gabriel Fulcher in the 12–36 quarter-final loss to France (Durban, 10.6.95). Frustrated by longterm groin injury in 1995/96, having joined Saracens, but returned to national setup for the end-of-season Peace match against the Barbarians (18.5.96).

Hartill, M. N.   Australia

Full name: Mark Hartill
Club: Gordon
State: New South Wales
Position: Prop
Height: 6ft (1.83m)
Weight: 17st 11lb (108kg)
Occupation: Accountant
Born: 29.5.64
International debut: New Zealand 12, Australia 13, 1986
Notable landmarks in rugby career: Loyal servant of Wallaby rugby, having first been capped a decade ago against the All Blacks. Remained patient while first-choice NSW front row of Tony Daly, Phil Kearns and Ewen McKenzie strung together a world-record 35 caps together, just appearing now and again. At home on either the loose or tighthead side of the scrum, Mark appeared for Australia Schoolboys in 1981/82 and captained Gordon to premiership wins in 1993 and 1995. Indeed, 1995 was a good year for the player as, in addition to starting in the 27–11 World Cup victory over

Australia (1986)		
Last Season	3 caps	0 pts
Career	20 caps	4 pts

Caps (20): **1986** NZ(1,2,3) **1987** SK wc-J. Arg(1) **1988** NZ(1,2), E, It **1989** BL(1R,2,3), F(1,2) **1995** Arg(1R,2R) wc-C. NZ(1,2)
Points (4 – 1t): **1987** wc-J(1t)

Canada in Port Elizabeth (31.5.95), he won selection for the end-of-term Bledisloe Cup series against New Zealand. Sadly for Mark the outcome was less desirable, as the All Blacks won both the first Test in Auckland (28–16, 22.7.95) and the return in Sydney (34–23, 29.7.95).

Hastings, S.   Scotland

Full name: Scott Hastings
Nickname: Gav's Brother
Club: Watsonians
Positions: Centre, wing, fullback
Height: 6ft 1in (1.86m)
Weight: 14st 4lb (93kg)
Occupation: Director, Barker's, Scotland
Born: Edinburgh, 4.12.64
Family: Jenny (wife), Corey (son), Kerry-Anne (daughter)
Family links with rugby: Clifford (father) played No.8 for Edinburgh XV and Watsonians; Gavin (brother) captained Scotland and British Lions; Graeme (brother) plays centre for Melbourne RFC and Victoria State (Australia); Ewan (brother) plays for Watsonians.
Former club: Newcastle Northern
International debut: Scotland 18, France 17, 1986
Five Nations debut: As above
Best rugby memory: 1989 Lions Test series win; 1990 Grand Slam win with Scotland.
Worst rugby memory: Facial injury on 1993 Lions tour
Most embarrassing moment: Finding out Gavin was my brother
Toughest opponents: Tim Horan, Jason Little (both Australia); Jeremy Guscott (England)
Serious injuries: Torn hamstring; cartilage operation (1985); broken

Scotland (1986)

Last Season	7 caps	0 pts
Career	62 caps	38 pts
Lions (1989)	2 Tests	0 pts
(1993)		

Caps (62): **1986** F, W, E, I, R **1987** I, F, W wc-R **1988** I, F, W, A **1989** W, E, I, F, Fj, R. Lions-A(2,3) **1990** I, F, W, E, NZ(1,2), Arg **1991** F, W, E(a), I(a) wc-J, Z, I(b), WS, E(b), NZ **1992** E, I, F, W, A(1,2) **1993** I, F, W, E, NZ **1994** E, I, F, SA **1995** W, E, R(R) wc-T, F(b), NZ **1996** I, F, W, E, NZ(2)

Points (38 – 9t): **1986** E(1t), R(1t) **1987** F(1t) **1988** I(1t) **1991** I(1t) wc-J(1t), Z(1t) **1995** wc-T(1t), NZ(1t)

cheekbone (1987 vs Wales); fractured jaw and cheekbone (Lions vs Otago, 1993 – 4 ½ hour operation to rebuild face).
Do you really want to be a full-time professional? No, not after ten years at the top: I'm too old now.
How well has rugby handled move to professionalism? Can you give minus figures? The IB messed up by not offering a professional structure to the game, which left Unions in doubt as to the best way forward. The growing pains could all have been averted with a little thought.

Do you have a duty to entertain? Yes, without a doubt. But that's nothing new for Watsonians.

Do you feel a loyalty to your club in this new era? Yes, but the loyalty factor is slowly slipping away as money becomes a greater influence.

Ambition: To get as big an entry as Will Carling in *Rugby Union Who's Who*.

Notable landmarks in rugby career: Scotland's most-capped player, having equalled brother Gavin's 61-cap haul in the 1996 Calcutta Cup clash against England (2.3.96) and then surpassed it in the second Test versus New Zealand (Auckland, 22 June) last summer. Indeed, Scotty had a cracking season as Scotland threatened to make the quantum leap from chumps to champs in the space of four Five Nations matches. Only final defeat by England prevented a side beaten by Italy and held by Western Samoa from claiming the Grand Slam. Still, it was a personal triumph for a player who had been cast into the wilderness after Scotland's 34–10 humping by Springboks (Murrayfield, 19.11.94). Scott watched helplessly as Ian Jardine and Gregor Townsend successfully shored up the midfield duties in the 1995 Five Nations series. Only when Jardine was injured in Paris did Scott return. However, he was again relegated to bench duties, this time behind the new combination of Tony Stanger and Graham Shiel, against Romania, Spain and Cote d'Ivoire, before the selectors drew upon his experience for the remainder of Scotland's World Cup campaign. He responded with tries in Pretoria against Tonga (30.5.95) and New Zealand (11.6.95) – his first Test tries since the 1991 World Cup. Once boasted (with Sean Lineen) the world record for an international centre partnership of 28 games (Lineen retired after 1992 Australia tour). No such fond memories of 1993/94 campaign in which Scotland collected 1994 Five Nations Wooden Spoon and Scott had a nightmare playing out of position as a winger in 51–15 defeat by New Zealand (20.11.93). Captaining Barbarians against same All Black tourists (Cardiff, 4.12.93) was a far more accurate reflection of his international stock. Took his tally of caps to 50 (against France, 19.3.94) on same day as brother Gavin. The pair had become first Scottish brothers to play together in a Lions Test back in 1989. Selected to tour with 1993 Lions to New Zealand, under Gavin's captaincy, but returned early and in agony after sustaining a fractured cheekbone. Former Watsonians captain (1989/90), who helped Edinburgh to three Inter-District Championship 'grand slams' between 1986 and 1988. Also ex-skipper of Scottish Schools. Played three times for Scotland Under-21s and once for Scotland B (at fullback in 9–0 win over Italy B, Glasgow, 7.12.85). Key cog in Scotland's 1990 Grand Slam machine, making famous try-saving tackle on England's Rory Underwood in Murrayfield decider.

Touchlines: Gardening, bandit golfer (18)

Hay, J. A.   Scotland

Full name: James (Jim) Allan Hay
Club: Hawick
Position: Hooker
Height: 5ft 10in (1.78m)
Weight: 13st 5lb (85kg)
Occupation: SRU development officer for South of Scotland
Born: Hawick, 8.8.64
International debut: Scotland 15, Western Samoa 15, 1995
Five Nations debut: None
Notable landmarks in rugby career: The 54th Hawick player to be capped by Scotland, Jim deserved his Test debut against Western Samoa, if only for the loyalty he has accorded Scotland down the years. Four times he has toured abroad with the national team – to Zimbabwe (1988, 1995), Japan (1989) and the South Pacific (1993) – and he has appeared in 13 of the 22 matches played. Yet none carried a cap. Lucky that for Scotland, as Japan had the temerity

Scotland (1995)

Last Season	1 cap	0 pts
Career	1 cap	0 pts

Caps (1): **1995** WS
Points Nil

to beat them in 1989, but not for Jim, as he scored the Scotland try on that otherwise fateful day. That was one of six 'non'-cap Tests in which Jim had worn his national colours before Jim Telfer ended his wait and selected him into a tartan front row, also including Anglos David Hilton and Paul Burnell on 18 November 1995. A player who had also played eight times for Scotland at Under-21 level and for Scotland B (1989) and Scotland A (1995) failed to get a win to celebrate as the plucky Samoans had the better of a 15–15 draw at Murrayfield. Still, he had the consolation of helping Hawick win the inaugural Tennents Cup final in dramatic fashion at Murrayfield (11.5.96), rallying from 15–0 down to beat Watsonians 17–15.

Henderson, P. W.   New Zealand

Full name: Paul William Henderson
Province: Southland
Position: Flanker
Height: 6ft 2in (1.88m)
Weight: 15st (95kg)
Occupation: Farmer
Born: Bluff, South Island, 21.9.64
Former Province: Otago
International debut: Argentina 14,
New Zealand 21, 1991
Serious injuries: Damaged knee
ligaments (vs Neath, 1989)
Notable landmarks in rugby career:
Captained All Blacks to world record
145–17 rout of Japan in World Cup
(Bloemfontein, 4.6.95) and
contributed one of the 21 tries. It
remained his one appearance of the
tournament – indeed his only cap for
three years – but what a memory!
Had announced himself as an 18-
year-old with a stirring performance
for Southland in their 41–3 loss to
the 1983 British Lions at Invercargill.

New Zealand (1991)

Last Season	1 cap	5 pts
Career	7 caps	9 pts

Caps (7): **1991** Arg(1). wc-C **1992** Wd(1,2,3), I(1) **1995** wc-J
Points (9 – 2t): **1992** I(1:1t) **1995** wc-J(1t)

After turning out for the Province for
four seasons he moved to Dunedin in 1987 and played for Otago until reverting
back to Southland at the start of 1992. Paul's international career began when
he represented New Zealand Secondary Schools and, in 1983/84, NZ Colts.
Team mates in 1983 included Sean Fitzpatrick, Grant Fox and Murray Mexted,
while Fitzpatrick captained the 1984 side which featured Bernie McCahill and
Frano Botica. Toured with New Zealand to Wales and Ireland in 1989, but a
knee ligament injury sustained against Neath forced him to return home after
only three games. Luck finally changed in 1991 when, during the All Blacks'
tour of Argentina, he was awarded his first cap in the 28–14 win over the Pumas
in Buenos Aires. Still, he only made the 1991 World Cup squad when Otago's
Mike Brewer was withdrawn through injury. The trip allowed him to collect his
second cap, in the 29–13 quarter-final defeat of Canada in the pouring rain at
Lille's Stade du Nord. Despite missing the final trial in 1992 because of a calf-
muscle strain, Paul made the All Black lineup for the centenary series, retaining
his place in each of the three Tests against the World XV, although he failed to
finish the second and third legs. It was not until Ireland's visit to Dunedin on 30
May that he finally made the scoresheet, crossing for the first of the All Blacks'
four tries as Ireland, 100:1 no-hopers, had their remarkable 12–0 lead pegged

back, eventually losing 24–21. Injury robbed him of further caps when, two games into the tour of Australia and South Africa, he broke his thumb against NSW and was forced to return home.

Hendriks, P. South Africa

Full name: Pieter Hendriks
Club: Roodepoort
Province: Transvaal
Position: Wing
Height: 6ft (1.82m)
Weight: 13st 8lb (86kg)
Occupation: Teacher
Born: Douglas, 13.4.70
International debut: South Africa 24, New Zealand 27, 1992
Other sporting achievements: Former South African junior hurdles champion
Notable landmarks in rugby career: Responsible for two of the most memorable moments of the 1995 World Cup, though for contrasting reasons. Pieter gave the clenched fist in triumph before touching down the first try of the tournament, for the Springboks against reigning champions Australia in the opening match, having left David Campese sprawling in his wake. But he used the same fist (and his boot) for an

South Africa (1992)

Last Season	5 caps	5 pts
Career	7 caps	5 pts

Caps (7): **1992** NZ, A **1994** S, W **1995** wc-A, R, C
Points (5 – 1t): **1995** wc-A(1t)

altogether less acceptable activity in the Battle of the Boet (Port Elizabeth, 3.6.95) during South Africa's 20–0 defeat of Canada. He was cited for his part in a brawl which led to three players being sent off and banned for 90 days for 'kicking and punching', so ending his tournament and allowing back in Chester Williams, whose initial injury had given Pieter his opportunity. Prior to that he had not toured with 1994 Boks to New Zealand, but had made the autumn trip to Scotland and Wales, winning his first caps for two years in the two Tests, and scoring two tries in the 78–7 rout of Swansea (5.11.94). Had set a South African record for tries scored in a season with 33 in the 1992 campaign as Transvaal marched to the Currie Cup final. Picked up his first two caps playing in the New Republic's comeback defeats by New Zealand (24–27, Johannesburg, 15.8.92) and Australia (3–26, Cape Town, 22.8.92). Toured to France and England in 1992, failing to make Test side but turning out against Midlands and North.

Herbert, D.   Australia

Full name: Daniel Herbert
State: Queensland
Club: GPS (Brisbane)
Position: Centre
Height: 6ft 2in (1.87m)
Weight: 15st 7lb (94kg)
Occupation: Student
Born: 6.2.74
Family: Single
Family links with rugby: Brother
Anthony played 10 times for
Australia (1987–93).
International debut: Australia 32,
Ireland 18, 1994
Notable landmarks in rugby career:
Partnered Jason Little in Queensland
midfield en route to the Super-12
semi-finals, but missed out in
Wallaby selection for the opening
Test against Wales (Brisbane,
8.6.96), when Reds team mate Tim
Horan reverted from fullback to
partner ACT star Joe Roff at centre.
Indeed, Horan's return from serious
knee injury cost Danny dear, as he

Australia (1994)		
Last Season	8 caps	10 pts
Career	8 caps	10 pts

Caps (8): **1994** I(2), It(1,2), WS(R) **1995**
Arg(1,2) wc-SA,R
Points (10 – 2t): **1994** I(2:1t), It(1:1t)

found his route to national selection blocked post-World Cup 1995.
Outstanding debut against Ireland (Sydney, 11.6.94) had seen him claim a try
within three minutes of the launch of his international career as the Wallabies
ran out 32–18 winners. Added a second try on his second appearance, in the
23–20 defeat of Italy in Brisbane the following weekend. But that was where his
scoring exploits ended, as in his last six outings he has failed to cross the try line.
Proved a valuable deputy for Horan while the latter was out. Partnered Little in
Wallaby midfield in both pre-World Cup Tests vs Argentina, and got the nod
ahead of Horan in the World Cup opener against South Africa (Cape Town,
25.5.95). Defeat in that game for the defending champions hastened Horan's
return, and Danny's only other outing thereafter in the New Republic came in
the 42–3 win over Romania (Stellenbosch, 3.6.95).

Hill, S. D.   Wales

Full name: Simon David Hill
Club: Cardiff
Position: Wing
Height: 5ft 11in (1.81m)
Weight: 13st 2lb (84kg)
Occupation: Dental student, Cardiff Medical College
Born: Barry, South Glamorgan, 27.5.68
Family: Single
Former club: Headingley
International debut: Zimbabwe 14, Wales 35, 1993
Five Nations debut: Ireland 15, Wales 17, 1994
Best moment in rugby: Scoring try on Wales debut

Notable landmarks in rugby career: Added just the one cap to his tally in 1995/96 when he played on the left wing in the 11–40 post-World Cup defeat to South Africa in Johannesburg (2.9.95). Otherwise divided his time between Welsh replacements bench and helping Cardiff reach the inaugural European Cup final. Had turned out on either wing for Wales in

Wales (1993)

Last Season	2 caps	0 pts
Career	9 caps	10 pts

Caps (9): **1993** Z(1,2), Na **1994** I(R), W, SA **1995** F, SA, **1996** A(2)
Points (10 – 2t): **1993** Z(1:1t), Na(1t)

1994/95, appearing first on the left in the 12–20 loss to South Africa (Cardiff, 26.11.94), then on the right in the 9–21 defeat by France (Paris, 21.1.95). Also helped Cardiff win Heineken league title for first time. Had been a late call-up into the Wales squad for the 1993 summer tour to Zimbabwe and Namibia, but took his opportunity with both hands, playing in all six matches including the three internationals against Zimbabwe (two) and Namibia. To add to his joy, he bagged a try on his Test debut, in Bulawayo on 22 May, and added another in the 38–23 win over Namibia, in Windhoek on 5 June. Wales won all six matches, with Simon also turning out against Zimbabwe B (try in 64–13 win, Harare, 25 May), Namibia B (won 47–10, Windhoek, 2 June) and the South African Barbarians (39th-minute replacement for Wayne Proctor in 56–17 triumph). Played in two legs of Wales' 1994 Five Nations triumph, coming on as a 44th-minute replacement for Proctor in Dublin and playing throughout famous 24–15 defeat of France in Cardiff (19.2.94). Previously represented Glamorgan and Headingley (while studying in Leeds), and included in Wales' preliminary 1991 World Cup squad. Toured Australia with Wales (1996).
Touchlines: Lifeguard in summer

Hilton, D. I. W. Scotland

Full name: David Ivor Walter Hilton
Nickname: Taz (after a couple of shorts I become very like the cartoon character)
Club: Bath
Position: Loosehead prop
Height: 5ft 10in (1.78m)
Weight: 16st 4lb (104kg)
Occupation: Part-time butcher, Broadway Butchers (Bristol)
Born: Bristol, 3.4.70
Family: Annb (fiancee)
Former club: Bristol
International debut: Scotland 22, Canada 6, 1995
Five Nations debut: Scotland 26, Ireland 13, 1995
Best rugby memory: 1995 World Cup
Worst rugby memory: Losing to France in last minute of World Cup tie
Toughest opponent: New Zealand
Do you really want to be a full-time professional? Yes, but on my own terms.
How well has rugby handled move to professionalism? 8/10 for Scotland

Scotland (1995)

Last Season	10 caps	0 pts
Career	16 caps	5 pts

Caps (16): **1995** C, I, F(a), W, E, R wc-T, F(b), NZ. WS **1996** I, F, W, E, NZ(1,2)

but 5/10 for the RFU. It has been a bit of a fiasco down south.
Do you have a duty to entertain? Yes. Bath have always felt the need to entertain, and Scotland, I think, feel much the same.
Do you feel a loyalty to your club in this new era? Yes, loyalty is a very big thing for me.
Notable landmarks in rugby career: Richly enjoyed 1995/96 did David, helping Scotland to three wins in four Five Nations engagements, and Bath to the English league and cup double. Then spent summer touring New Zealand with Scots. It was hard to believe it was only the Bath butcher's second season of international rugby. A part of Scotland's new wave, David was introduced to the national side at a time of some despair. Scotland had failed to win a match in nine attempts when he was called into the lineup to replace injured fellow West Countryman Alan Sharp (that former Scot!) against Canada at a frozen Murrayfield (21.1.95). The Canucks were beaten 22–6 and Scotland went on to enjoy a remarkable 1995, coming within 80 minutes of the Grand Slam and reaching the World Cup quarter-finals, where they became the first side ever to score 30 points against New Zealand and lose (Pretoria, 11.6.95). A member of

the Scotland A side that beat South Africa and Italy in the autumn of 1994, Dave helped the Scottish Exiles win the Inter-District Championship in January 1995, but enjoyed his best moment when he scored a try in the 26–13 defeat of Wales (Edinburgh, 4.3.95). Also helped Bath win successive Pilkington Cups in 1994 (against Leicester) and 1995 (against Wasps). Qualifies for Scotland by virtue of paternal grandfather Walter, who hails from Edinburgh.

Touchlines: Water-skiing, golf

Hogan, N. A. Ireland

Full name: Niall Andrew Hogan
Club: Terenure College
Position: Scrum-half
Height: 5ft 8in (1.73m)
Weight: 12st (76kg)
Occupation: Doctor, Beaumont Hospital
Born: Dublin, 20.4.71
Family: Single
Family links with rugby: Brother (Kevin) captained UC Dublin
International debut: Ireland 8, England 20, 1995
Five Nations debut: As above
Best rugby memory: Being given Ireland captaincy
Notable landmarks in rugby career: Succeeded Jim Staples as Ireland captain midway through 1996 championship after the fullback had been crocked in Paris and ruled out of the subsequent game against Wales in Cardiff (2.3.96). Niall, who had skippered Ireland A in 1993/94, took charge and the green machine

Ireland (1995)

Last Season	6 caps	5 pts
Career	8 caps	5 pts

Caps (8): **1995** E, W(a) wc-J, W(b), F(b) **1996** F, W, E

Points (5 – 1t): **1995** wc-J(1t)

responded by sticking 30 points on the Welsh for the first time ever (won 30–17). That was as good as it got, as Niall, who according to some observers had been a trifle lucky to keep his place ahead of Christian Saverimutto after the Paris trouncing, led his team to a 15–28 defeat to title-clinching England next time out (Twickenham, 16.3.96). Pound for pound, one of the toughest competitors around, Niall took the place of then captain Michael Bradley in 1995, first when the latter was struck with a family tragedy, then purely on selection as Irish bosses looked for new blood to end a winless Five Nations campaign. The tactic worked, as Ireland beat Wales 16–12 in Cardiff (18.3.95)

and left the Wooden Spoon behind in the Principality. Added his third cap in South Africa in the World Cup defeat of Japan, days before enjoying a wonderful weekend – receiving his doctorate in a ceremony at Ireland's Johannesburg hotel on the Saturday, booking a quarter-final place at the expense of the hapless Welsh on the Sunday. Tournament ended in slight disappointment for the Terenure terror as France rolled over the Irish in a one-sided quarter-final under the Durban sun. Captained Leinster at Schools, Under-19 and Under-20 levels, and also represented Irish Colleges and Irish Students. Broke into Ireland Under-21 team in 1990/91 on tour to Netherlands, and was appointed captain in 1991/92 for the games against Wales (lost 15–22) and England (won 19–10).
Touchlines: Golf

Hopley, D. P. England

Full name: Damian Paul Hopley
Club: Wasps
Position: Wing, centre
Height: 6ft 2in (1.88m)
Weight: 15st (95kg)
Occupation: Gilt repro broker, Inter Capital Brokers Ltd
Born: London, 12.4.70
Family links with rugby: Brother Phil plays for Wasps
International debut: England 44, Western Samoa 22, 1995
Five Nations debut: None
Best rugby memory: Winning first cap in 1995 World Cup
Worst rugby memory: Losing England place before 1996 Five Nations

Most embarrassing memory: Being mistaken for Nigel Heslop when on England bench in Cardiff (1991).
Notable landmarks in rugby career: Powerful three-quarter, either in midfield or on wide outside, who let

England (1995)

Last Season	3 caps	0 pts
Career	3 caps	0 pts

Caps (3): **1995** wc-WS(a), SA, WS(b)
Points Nil

nobody down in his three appearances for England in 1995 but was then dropped from the entire squad ahead of the 1996 Five Nations series. Jon Sleightholme's selection ahead of Damian may have been vindicated in that the Bath man turned out to be the find of the season for the Lillywhites, but that did not justify the exclusion of a player first called into the national squad back in

1991. A year before winning his Blue at Cambridge, Damian was selected for bench reserve duties in the match against Wales. Although he did not take to the field it was an eventful day. England won in Cardiff for the first time in 28 years and were then panned for boycotting the post-match press conference. Damian, who had won six caps for England Schools as well as representing England Colts, Scottish Universities (during his time at St Andrews University), England Under-21 and England A (15 caps), finally collected his first cap four years later when coming on as a 71st-minute replacement for Will Carling against Western Samoa at the 1995 World Cup in Durban. On his return home he played in the defeat by South Africa and the Twickenham victory over the touring Samoans before Jack Rowell wielded the axe. Two years before that Damian had picked up a World Cup winner's medal as part of the England VII which won the inaugural World Cup Sevens at Murrayfield.

Touchlines: Piano

Horan, T. J. **Australia**

Full name: Timothy (Tim) James Horan
State: Queensland
Club: Southern Districts
Position: Centre, five-eighth
Height: 6ft (1.83m)
Weight: 14st 8lb (88kg)
Occupation: Commercial leasing consultant
Born: 15.5.70
Family: Katrina (wife), Lucy (daughter)
Former clubs: None: Souths since 1988
International debut: New Zealand 24, Australia 12, 1989
Best moment in rugby: Winning 1991 World Cup

Worst moment in rugby: Losing to New Zealand at Eden Park in second Test of 1991 Bledisloe Cup series.
Most embarrassing moment: Answering just one question on 'Sale of the Century'.
Most respected opponent: Jerry Guscott (Bath & England)
Serious injuries: Knee (1990)
Suggestions to improve rugby: Improve standards of refereeing
Notable landmarks in rugby career: Made a stupendous recovery from knee reconstruction after potentially career-ending injury playing for Queensland in

1994 Super-10 final against Transvaal, and regained midfield position in the 1995 World Cup, playing against Canada, Romania and England. In his two-year absence Danny Herbert, Richard Toombs and Pat Howard had vied for the vacant berth next to Queensland team mate and longterm midfield foil Jason Little. Tim's injury had come as a cruel blow after he'd established himself as the world's premier centre with quite outstanding campaigns for 1992/93. Completed 1995 by playing in both Bledisloe Cup defeats to New Zealand before switching to fullback with great success for Queensland in

Australia (1989)		
Last Season	7 caps	5 pts
Career	40 caps	75 pts

Caps (40): 1989 NZ, F(1,2) 1990 F(1), NZ(1,2,3) 1991 W(a), E(a), NZ(a1,a2). wc-Arg, WS, W(b), I, NZ(b), E(b) 1992 S(1,2), NZ(1,2,3), SA, I, W 1993 T, NZ, SA(1,2,3), C, F(1,2) 1995 wc-C, R, E. NZ(1,2), 1996 W(1,2)

Points (75 – 17t): 1989 F(1:2t) 1990 NZ(2:1t) 1991 W(a:1t). wc-Arg(2t), W(b:1t), NZ(b:1t) 1992 S(2:2t), NZ(1:1t), I(1t) 1993 NZ(1t), SA(2:1t), SA(3:1t), C(1t) 1996 W(2:1t)

the 1996 Super-12. The Reds 'won' the regular season before surprisingly losing at home to Natal in the semi-finals. Tim has proved a highly capable performer since being given his debut as a teenager against the All Blacks in 1989 – two years after helping Australia Under-17s beat their New Zealand counterparts 16–3. A World Cup winner in 1991 and an ever-present since. His glorious 1992 included tries in the 16–15 first Test win over New Zealand, and another in the 42–17 defeat of Ireland. Prior to those, he had represented the World XV against New Zealand in the first and third Tests of the 1992 Centenary Series.

Touchlines: Golf and family

England forward Ben Clarke powers through the French defence during a nailbiting 15–12 victory for the home nation in Paris.

Howard, P. W.

Australia

Full name: Patrick William Howard
Club: Queensland University
State: Queensland
Position: Outside-half, five-eighth, inside-centre
Height: 5ft 10in (1.78m)
Weight: 14st 6lb (87kg)
Occupation: Student pharmacist
Born: 14.11.73
Family: Single
Family links with rugby: Father (Jake) coached Irish club Wanderers
International debut: New Zealand 25, Australia 10, 1993
Best rugby memory: Debut Test against All Blacks (1993)
Worst rugby memory: Getting dropped after above match
Toughest opponent: Grant Fox (ex-Auckland & New Zealand)
Notable landmarks in rugby career: Returned to Wallaby side for Test series vs Wales in June 1996, scoring a try from fly-half in the 56–25 first Test victory at Ballymore (8.6.96). It was a nice way to start 1996, having

Australia (1993)

Last Season	3 caps	5 pts
Career	6 caps	10 pts

Caps (6): **1993** NZ **1994** WS, NZ **1995** NZ(1R), **1996** W(1,2)
Points (10 – 2t): **1994** WS(1t) **1996**

achieved little on the international front in 1995, save for one appearance as a replacement, in the first Test of the Bledisloe Cup series against New Zealand (Auckland, 22.7.95). The son of former Irish club Wanderers coach Jake Howard, Pat delighted Dublin by setting up the winning try for Simon Geoghegan as the Barbarians beat South Africa 23–15 (3.12.94). Such talent earned Pat a place in the Wallaby midfield, during Tim Horan's enforced absence, and he marked his return – a year after his debut – with a try in the extraordinary 73–3 rout of Western Samoa (Sydney, 6.8.94). Retained his place in the thrilling 20–16 Bledisloe Cup victory over New Zealand (Sydney, 17.8.94), but come 1995 he had been usurped by Queenslander Daniel Herbert alongside Jason Little. Had made his debut as a late call-up in the 1993 Bledisloe Cup game against New Zealand in Dunedin (17.7.93). Captain Michael Lynagh withdrew at the eleventh hour through illness, and young Pat was drafted in at fly-half. But New Zealand won 25–10, and the No.10 jersey was taken over by New South Wales' Scott Bowen. Nonetheless, Pat kept himself busy. He represented Queensland in their 17–3 defeat by the touring Springboks at Ballymore (8.8.93) and was then invited on Australia's autumn tour of North America and France. His first outing came as a centre in the non-cap Test against the United States Eagles, and he bagged a try in Australia's 26–22 win, played in severe heat at Riverside, California (2.10.93). After that he made four appearances in France.

Touchlines: Travelling and surfing.

Howley, R. Wales

Full name: Robert Howley
Nickname: Stan (as in Stan Laurel)
Club: Cardiff
Position: Scrum-half
Height: 5ft 10in (1.78m)
Weight: 13st 3lb (84kg)
Occupation: WRU Elite player/full-time marketing officer
Born: Bridgend, 13.10.70
Family: Single
Former clubs: Cardiff, Bridgend
Best moment in rugby: Scoring try against England on Test debut
Worst moments in rugby: (a) A stud coming out of my boot as I walked out of the changing room door prior to my debut at Twickenham – the team had to wait while I replaced it. (b) Tearing knee cartilage playing for Swansea University against Cardiff University in 1991 UAU final at Twickenham (20.3.91, lost 3–14).
Most embarrassing moment: Slicing clearance over my own winger's head for opposition to score during Bridgend–Pontypool game.

Wales (1996)		
Last Season	6 caps	10 pts
Career	6 caps	10 pts

Caps (6): **1996** E, S, I, F, A(1,2)
Points (10 – 2t): **1996** E(1t), F(1t)

Toughest opponent: Niall Hogan (Terenure & Ireland)
Serious injuries: Three cartilage tears, plus one ligament tear (all on left knee)
Do you really want to be a full-time professional? Yes
How well has rugby handled move to professionalism? 3/10. I was not impressed with the way the unions handled it. The players should have been the priority, but there was precious little evidence of that.
Do you have a duty to entertain? Yes
Do you feel a loyalty to your club in this new era? No, players are now looking for quality of rugby.
Other sporting claims to fame: Cricket for Welsh Schools (U-15, U-16 , U-17).
Notable landmarks in rugby career: Welsh find of 1995/96, though Rob, for

some time a considerable domestic talent, was one of rugby's worst kept secrets. Marked his Test debut by becoming the first Wales scrum-half since Chico Hopkins in 1970 to score a try at Twickenham on the occasion of his first cap. Continued to improve throughout remainder of championship, scoring second try of the campaign as Wales defeated France 16–15, amid emotional scenes in Cardiff, to avoid the Wooden Spoon (16.3.96). In between the two scores Rob so impressed playing for Wales at the Hong Kong Sevens that he was selected in the Team of the Tournament alongside the phenomenal likes of All Blacks Jonah Lomu and Christian Cullen. No wonder big-spending English club Saracens tried to prise him away from Bridgend, before Rob elected, post-Australia, to return to Cardiff. Welsh Schools Under-18 captain (1989), playing against Scotland, Ireland, England and France, Rob was called into Wales Under-21 squad two seasons before making his debut against Ireland. Marked the occasion with a try. Added second cap in 28–19 defeat of Scotland Under-21 at Bridgehaugh, Stirling, as Wales maintained their record of never having lost an Under-21 match to the Scots.
Touchlines: Cricket, golf

Humphreys, D. G.   Ireland

Full name: David George Humphreys
Nickname: Humph
Club: London Irish
Position: Fly-half
Height: 5ft 10in (1.78m)
Weight: 11st 10lb (74kg)
Occupation: Apprentice solicitor, Tughan & Co
Born: Belfast, 10.9.71
Family: Single
International debut: France 45, Ireland 10, 1996
Five Nations debut: As above
Best rugby memory: Full Irish debut
Worst rugby memory: Losing 1995 Varsity match in last minute
Do you really want to be a full-time professional? Yes, but once I am qualified.

How well has rugby handled move to professionalism? 6/10. Change has been so sudden that it has been caught unawares. It will take time to iron all the creases out.

Ireland (1996)

Last Season	3 caps	8 pts
Career	3 caps	8 pts

Caps (3): **1996** F, W, E
Points (8 – 1c, 1p, 1dg): **1996** F(1c,1p), E(1dg)

321

Do you have a duty to entertain? Yes, without a doubt. It is no longer acceptable to win 3–0.

Do you feel a loyalty to your club in this new era? Yes, for the forseeable future.

Other sporting claims to fame: Golf (7 handicap)

Notable landmarks in rugby career: Enjoyed a terrific 1995/96 campaign, graduating to full international status on the back of a tremendous display for Oxford University in the 114th Varsity Match (Twickenham, 12.12.95). Although Oxford lost 19–21 in somewhat controversial fashion, David scored all of Oxford's points; in so doing claimed a 'full house' of try (1), conversion (1), penalty goal (3) and dropped goal (1). From there the former Irish Schools captain (won 1990 Triple Crown) joined London Irish and won his fourth Ireland A cap against Scotland before being drafted into the senior side to play France in Paris. Ireland had never previously won at Parc des Princes. They still haven't. Despite an encouraging showing by the new No.10, France handed the Irish a record 45–10 mauling. Still, David, who first represented Munster in 1992 before scoring 19 points on his Ireland A debut against Wales in March 1993, retained his place for the remainder of the campaign. Toured with the Irish Development squad to Zimbabwe, Namibia and South Africa in 1993.

Touchlines: Golf

Humphreys, J. M.   Wales

Full name: Jonathan Matthew Humphreys

Nickname: Humph

Club: Cardiff

Position: Hooker

Height: 6ft (1.83m)

Weight: 16st 4lb (103kg)

Occupation: WRU rugby development officer/ pro rugby player

Born: North Cornelly, 27.2.69

Family: Single

International debut: New Zealand 34, Wales 9, 1995

Five Nations debut: England 21, Wales 15, 1996

Former club: Kenfig Hill

Best rugby memory: First cap against New Zealand

Worst rugby memory: Losing to Ireland in 1995 World Cup

Most embarrassing memory: Being sent off for stamping in my first game for Cardiff (mistaken identity – I was later cleared).

Do you really want to be a full-time professional? Yes

How well has rugby handled move to professionalism? 3/10. I don't think many of the clubs were ready for such a big move. It was inevitable but the structure was not in place to cater for it.

Do you have a duty to entertain? Yes, it is absolutely necessary, as our pay is dictated by bums on seats.

Do you feel a loyalty to your club in this new era? Yes

Wales (1995)

Last Season	11 caps	5 pts
Career	11 caps	5 pts

Caps (11): **1995** wc-NZ, I. SA, Fj **1996** It, E, S, I, F, A(1,2)

Points (5 – 1t): **1995** wc-I(1t)

Notable landmarks in rugby career: The son of an ABA welterweight boxing champion (Colin), Wales have Jonathan's mum Jennifer to thank for his presence on the rugby field rather than in the boxing ring. He has become not any old rugby player either, but the 106th captain of Wales. Not bad for a player who only broke into the Test ranks a year ago at the World Cup. A Welsh Students team member 1991–93, winning four caps and participating in the 1992 Student World Cup, he captained the Wales development tour squad to France in 1993 and made his Wales A debut in January 1995. The arrival of former Aussie assistant coach Alex Evans at Cardiff fast-tracked Jonathan's career to the top. Evans gave him an extended run in the Cardiff side before taking him to South Africa for the 1995 World Cup, where Humph played against New Zealand and Ireland, scoring his maiden Test try in the latter (Johannesburg, 4.6.95). Sadly, Wales lost both matches and returned home prematurely, but that ironically worked in Jonathan's favour, as a disillusioned Mike Hall quit the Wales captaincy and he was handed the reins. In addition to helping Cardiff reach the inaugural European Cup final in 1995/96, Humph captained his country throughout their seven-match campaign and then took the squad to Australia last summer.

Touchlines: Golf (18 handicap)

Ireland captain Niall Hogan fires out a pass against England at Twickenham.

Hurley, H. D.   Ireland

Full name: Henry Denis Hurley
Club: Old Wesley
Position: Prop
Height: 5ft 10in (1.78m)
Weight: 17st 8lb (112kg)
Occupation: Production manager, Alcopo Foil
Born: Doncaster, 28.12.65
International debut: Ireland 44, Fiji 8, 1995
Five Nations debut: None
Notable landmarks in rugby career: A latecomer to rugby, Henry quickly made up for lost time as he broke into the Leinster side in 1992/93, playing against touring Wallabies in the October of that season, before touring Zimbabwe, Namibia and South Africa with Irish Development squad in the summer of 1993. By the next season he was turning out for Ireland A, his debut coming in 9–24 loss to Scotland at Ayr (December 1993), and in 1993/94 he made it

Ireland (1995)

Last Season	1 cap	0 pts
Career	1 cap	0 pts

Caps (1): **1995** Fj(TR)
Points Nil

into the Combined Provinces side which played the touring Springboks at Ravenhill. Although he missed out on the original selection for the 1995 World Cup, he made the plane to South Africa after John Fitzgerald dropped out at the eleventh hour. Not that he was able to break into a side which negotiated the pool stages before being well beaten by France in a lopsided quarter-final at King's Park, Durban. It seemed that he might be set for a frustrating wait for his first full cap until Nick Popplewell needed treatment for a wound sustained in the 69th minute of Ireland's 44–8 season-opening win over Fiji (Lansdowne Road, 18.11.95) and Henry came on briefly for his debut before returning to replacements bench for remainder of 1995/96 season. On the playing front, he also helped Leinster win the Inter-Pros and reach the semi-finals of the inaugural Heineken European Cup, before losing to Cardiff (Dublin, 30.12.95).

Ieremia, A.   New Zealand

Full name: Alama Ieremia
Province: Wellington
Position: Centre
Height: 6ft 1in (1.86m)
Weight: 14st 1lb (85kg)
Occupation: Bank officer, National Bank of New Zealand
Born: 27.10.70
Family: Single
International debut: New Zealand 22, South Africa 14, 1994
Notable landmarks in rugby career: A member of the 1993 Western Samoan side which wrought havoc in New Zealand, winning seven of its nine matches and giving the All Blacks much food for thought in a 13–35 Test loss (Auckland, 31.7.93), Alama threw his hand in with the Kiwis soon after, and was rewarded with a place in the centres, alongside another ex-Samoan Frank Bunce, in the 1994 series defeat of South Africa. His debut came in Dunedin

New Zealand (1994)

Last Season	4 caps	5 pts
Career	4 caps	5 pts

Caps (4): **1994** SA(1,2,3) **1995** wc-J
Points (5 -- 1t): **1995** wc-J(1t)

(9.7.94) and he held his place for the 13–9 second Test win in Wellington, his place of residence (23.7.94), and in the 18–18 third Test draw at Eden Park, Auckland (6.8.94). Walter Little's return to prominence relegated Alama to the replacements bench thereafter, though he did get one outing during last summer's World Cup – and what a day that proved to be! Japan were jettisoned 145–17 (Bloemfontein, 4.6.95) and Alama weighed in with one of the 21 tries. Likens himself to a snake – 'slippery, sly and shy, but lethal.' Regular for outgunned Wellington Hurricanes in 1996 Super-12 tournament.

Jardine, I. C.   Scotland

Full name: Ian Carrick Jardine
Club: Stirling County
Position: Centre
Height: 6ft 1in (1.85m)
Weight: 14st 7lb (93kg)
Occupation: Secondary maths teacher, Larbert High School
Born: Dunfermline, 20.10.64
Family: Ann (wife), Megan (daughter)
Family links with rugby: Four brothers (Stephen, Neil, Colin and Aitken) play at Stirling.
International debut: Scotland 15, New Zealand 51, 1993
Five Nations debut: Wales 29, Scotland 6, 1994
Worst moment in rugby: Scotland's record defeat coinciding with my debut
Most embarrassing moment: Accidentally drinking my wife's contact lenses, which she had left in a glass of water by our bed in hotel room, after a Scotland B game when I was the worse for wear.

Scotland (1993)

Last Season	9 caps	0 pts
Career	17 caps	0 pts

Caps (17): **1993** NZ **1994** W, E(R), Arg (1,2) **1995** C, I, F(a) wc-T, F(b:R), NZ(R) **1996** I, F, W, E, NZ(1,2)
Points Nil

Notable landmarks in rugby career: Missed out on Scotland's season-opener against Western Samoa in 1995/96, but was quickly sent for after the selected XV made a rickets of it, being held 15–15. Although the Scots promptly lost to Italy next time out (Rieti, 6.1.96) the Jardine–Scott Hastings midfield combination was being lauded by the end of a Five Nations campaign in which the Scots upset the formbook to win three matches out of four. Promoted to first-choice centre after Scotland's hammering by South Africa (1994), Ian played a key role in the nation's revival until he fractured his cheekbone in the final seconds of France's historic home burial in Parc des Princes (18.2.95). Returned in time for Scotland's altitude-training trip to Spain, coming on as a 65th-minute replacement in the 62–7 non-cap defeat of the Spaniards (6.5.95), and thereafter appearing in all but one of the Scots' World Cup matches. Helped Stirling win Scottish championship for the first time in their history in 1994/95. Had seemingly waited years for his Test chance only to get the call for Scotland's record defeat (51–15 vs New Zealand). Retained place for 1994 Five Nations opener against Wales, but that result was little better and he was relegated back to the bench to accomodate Doug Wyllie's return. Replacement for Scotland

Under-21s (1986) and Scotland B in Italy (1988/89). Made B debut in 22–22 draw with Ireland B (9.12.89) and, after being only bench reserve in 0–16 loss to Ireland B (22.12.90), made A team's No.12 jersey his own in 1992/93, turning out against Ireland B at Murrayfield (lost 19–29, 28.12.91) and in Albi against France B (3.2.92), where he scored a try in the 18–27 defeat. Helped Glasgow win 1989/90 Inter-District Championship. Toured with Scotland to Canada, the United States (1991), Argentina (1994) and New Zealand (1996).
Touchlines: Hill walking, cycling

Jenkins, G. R. Wales

Full name: Garin Richard Jenkins
Club: Swansea
Position: Hooker
Height: 5ft 10in (1.78m)
Weight: 15st 2lb (96kg)
Occupation: Schools Liaison Officer, Swansea RFC
Born: Ynysybwl, 18.8.67
Family: Helen (wife)
Family links with rugby: Father's uncle played for Wales; Mother's cousin propped for Wales and Lions.
Former clubs: Ynysybwl, Pontypridd, King Country (NZ), Pontypool
Best moment in rugby: Scoring try for Swansea in win over 1992 Wallabies
Other sporting achievements: Marbles champion at Treobart Junior School
Notable landmarks in rugby career: Lost Wales No.2 jersey for the first time in three seasons when displaced by Jonathan Humphreys during last summer's World Cup, and then let himself down by being sent off for punching Joost van der Westhuizen

Wales (1991)

Last Season	4 caps	0 pts
Career	30 caps	5 pts

Caps (30): **1991** F(b) wc-WS(R), Arg, A(b) **1992** I, F, E, S, A **1993** C **1994** S, I, F, E. wc(q)-P, Sp. C, T, WS wc(q)-R, It. SA **1995** F, E, S, I(a) wc-J. SA(R), Fj(TR) **1996** E(R)
Points (5 – 1t): **1994** wc(q)-Sp(1t)

in the final minute of Wales' 40–11 loss to the world champion Springboks back in South Africa (Johannesburg, 2.9.95) – a match which he had only started as a half-time replacement. All things considered, Africa is probably not Garin's favourite continent. Having been ever-present through Wales' dismal Five Nations 1995 campaign, Garin played the World Cup opener vs Japan (won

57–10, Bloemfontein, 27.5.95), but then sat out the defeats by New Zealand and Ireland. It was a far cry from the previous year, when for many he had been the heart and soul of Wales' Five Nations title run. He celebrated his maiden Test try in 54–0 World Cup qualifying win against Spain (Madrid, 21.5.94). Had lost place in Welsh side during 1992/93 after performing hooking duties in 43–12 win over Italy XV at Cardiff (7.10.92) and 6–23 loss to Australia (21.11.92), also in National Stadium. Between those two outings he helped Swansea to a famous win over Wallabies at St Helens, scoring one of the All Whites' two tries in 21–6 victory (4.11.92). But come the 1993 Five Nations Championship Pontypool's Nigel Meek earned the vote, with Llanelli's Andrew Lamerton as his bench deputy. Garin, a former coalminer, represented Boys Clubs of Wales Under-18s and Glamorgan Under-23s. He started his career with Ynysybwl, the birthplace of ex-national coach Alan Davies, and in 1990 toured Kenya with Pontypool, having represented Pooler against 1989 All Blacks. Broke into Wales team at the start of the 1991/92 season when Davies was appointed coach following catastrophic 1991 Australia tour, and played eight games in all, spanning the French 'floodlit' game, the 1991 World Cup and 1992 Five Nations Championship (pack leader). Helped Swansea win 1991/92 and 1993/94 Heineken League titles and 1995 SWALEC Cup.
Touchlines: Soccer, cricket, weightlifting

Jenkins, N. R. Wales

Full name: Neil Roger Jenkins
Club: Pontypridd
Position: Fly-half
Height: 5ft 10in (1.78m)
Weight: 13st 5lb (80kg)
Occupation: PR consultant, Just Rentals Ltd
Born: Pontypridd, 8.7.71
Family: Single
International debut: Wales 6, England 25, 1991
Five Nations debut: As above
Best rugby memory: Winning 1994 Five Nations title
Worst rugby memory: Being sent off in 39th minute of 6–27 1991/92 Schweppes Cup semi-final against Llanelli at Arms Park.

Toughest opponent: Philippe Sella (Saracens & France)
Notable landmarks in rugby career: Wales' record points scorer, Neil broke through the 400 barrier in 1995/96 despite playing just once in the Five Nations

series. But that occasion coincided with Wales' one championship win – a 16–15 defeat of France in Cardiff (16.3.96), in which he kicked 11 crucial points, including the late penalty that gave Wales victory, Ireland the Wooden Spoon and England the title. A broken collarbone meant that he played just one other Test – the 19–15 defeat of Fiji (Cardiff, 11.11.95) – in which he amassed 14 points. As a result of Neil's prolific run, Paul Thorburn's previous national best (304 in 37 matches, 1985–91) has been left back in the dark ages. Neil even picked up a domestic honour, at last, as Pontypridd came from behind to beat Neath 29–22 in a classic Swalec Cup final (4.5.96). It was a far cry from 1994/95 when, for all Neil's 153 points, Wales ended up with zilch,

Wales (1991)

Last Season	8 caps	85 pts
Career	41 caps	443 pts

Caps (41): 1991 E, S, I, F 1992 I, F, E, S 1993 E, S, I, F, Z(1,2), Na, J, C 1994 S, I, F, E. wc(q)-P, Sp. C, T, WS. wc(q)-R, It. SA 1995 F, E, S, I(a) wc-J, NZ, I(b). SA, Fj 1996 F, A(1,2)

Points (443 – 5t,49c,104p,3dg): 1991 E(1p), I(1t,1dg) 1992 I(3p), F(3p), S(1c,3p) 1993 E(1c,1p), I(3p), F(1c,1p), Z(1:3c,2p), Z(2:1t,3c,2p), Na(2c,3p), J(1t,5c), C(8p) 1994 S(1c,4p), I(1t,4p), F(1c,4p), E(1p). wc(q)-P(11c), Sp(5c,3p). C(3c,4p), T(6p),WS(3p). wc(q)-R(1c,3p), It(7p,1dg). SA(4p) 1995 F(3p), E(3p), S(1c,2p), I(a:4p) wc-J(5c,4p), NZ(2p,1dg), I(b:2c,2p). SA(2p), Fj(1t,3p) 1996 F(1c,3p), A(1:2c,2p), A(2:1p)

embarrassed in the Five Nations and the World Cup. Still, for the second year in succession, Neil was named Welsh Player of the Year. Had been central to Wales' 1994 championship win. Buoyed up by his world-record haul of eight penalty goals in 24–26 defeat by Canada (Cardiff, 10.11.93), Neil bagged 14 points against Scotland, all 17 against Ireland, 14 against France and three against England for a 48-point haul. Perhaps yet more significantly, he missed hardly any. Ever-present for Wales in last five Five Nations campaigns, yet, remarkably, until 1993/94 had appeared in no other Tests (including 1991 World Cup). Represented Wales A team in a 21–13 win over North of England at Pontypool (14.10.92) in which he contributed 11 points (1c,3p) and again last season at centre in 61–5 defeat of Japan at Llanelli (claiming 19 points: 2t,3c,1p). Played for East Wales Under-11s vs West Wales, East Glamorgan and Wales Youth (1989/90). Having broken into Wales Under-21s in 1990/91 – playing against New Zealand Under-21 XV (14pts:4c,2p) and Scotland Under-21 (15pts: 1t,1c,3p) – Neil added a second cap and ten points in the 22–15 win over Ireland Under-21 in 1991/92 (2c,2p).

Touchlines: Golf

Johns, P. S.   Ireland

Full name: Patrick Stephen Johns
Nickname: Paddy
Club: Bedford
Position: Lock, No.8
Height: 6ft 6in (1.98m)
Weight: 16st 11lb (102kg)
Occupation: Dentist
Born: Portadown, 19.2.68
Family: Kirsty (wife), Christopher (son)
Former clubs: Newcastle University, Gosforth, Dublin University, Dungannon
International debut: Ireland 20, Argentina 18, 1990
Five Nations debut: Scotland 15, Ireland 3, 1993
Best rugby memory: Winning first cap
Worst moments in rugby: Waiting two years for second cap; being dropped after France defeat in 1995/96.
Most embarrassing memory: Having shorts ripped clean off during World Cup quarter-finals and thinking half the world was probably watching.

Ireland (1990)

Last Season	8 caps	5 pts
Career	28 caps	10 pts

Caps (28): **1990** Arg **1992** NZ(1,2), A **1993** S, F, W, E, R **1994** F, W, E, S, A(1,2), US **1995** E, S, W(a), It wc-NZ, J, W(b), F(b). Fj, US **1996** S, F
Points (10 – 2t): **1994** A(1:1t) **1995** Fj(1t)

Toughest opponent: Dean Richards (Leicester & England)
Serious injuries: Neck injury, broken wrist, knee cartilage (1992) and two operations (1993/94) on left knee.
Do you really want to be a full-time professional? Yes
How well has rugby handled move to professionalism? 7/10. Miraculous how authorities have taken bull by horns whilst also dragging their heels.
Do you have a duty to entertain? Yes, but entertainment should come out of the enjoyment you get yourself.
Do you feel a loyalty to your club in this new era? Yes
Notable landmarks in rugby career: Paddy lasted half-way through 1996 Five Nations series before becoming a victim of coach Murray Kidd's broom following Ireland's hammering in Paris (lost 10–45, 17.2.96). It was a sad and premature end to a Test season which had begun in euphoric style for the big man with a try in Fiji's 44–8 demise at Lansdowne Road (18.11.95). Paddy had also been a revelation in Ireland's vital 24–23 defeat of Wales (Johannesburg, 4.6.95) – a result which booked Ireland's place in the World Cup quarter-finals

and sent Wales home to an uncertain future. Indeed, he appeared in all four of Ireland's matches in South Africa, including the last-eight tie against France – an opponent whom he had missed in the 1995 Five Nations campaign after contracting appendicitis on the eve of combat. Only switched from lock to No.8 midway through 1993/94 season as Ireland moved to change their fortunes for the better, after a 35–15 loss in Paris, where Paddy sustained an eye injury that required an operation and forced him to take a week off work. Impressed in his new position, as England were beaten at Twickenham while Scotland held at Lansdowne Road. Represented Ulster against 1989 All Blacks (lost 3–21, Ravenhill, 21.11.89), and Ireland Schools in 1986, against Japan (twice), Australia, England and Wales. Toured Canada with Dungannon (1989). Played for Ireland at Under-21 and Under-25 level (twice) in 1988/89 season. Also turned out for Irish Students and Universities while at Dublin University. Represented Ireland B in 22–22 draw with Scotland B at Murrayfield (9.12.89) and twice against England B: in 24–10 win at Old Belvedere (scoring try, 1.3.91) and at Richmond (No.8 in 15–47 loss, 31.1.92). First capped by Ireland against touring Argentina Pumas (27.20.90).
Touchlines: Painting, cycling, making wine

Johnson, G. K. South Africa

Full name: Gavin Keith Johnson
Province: Transvaal
Club: Pirates
Position: Fullback
Height: 6ft 1in (1.85m)
Weight: 14st 12lb (90kg)
Occupation: Aircraft parts supplier
Born: Louis Trichardt, 17.10.66
Family: Single
International debut: Argentina 23, South Africa 52, 1993
Notable landmarks in rugby career: Unsung Springbok hero, averaging over 12 points per game for the world champions. Can play equally well in any back position. Made a record-equalling international debut when he scored 22 points in the

Springboks' second Test victory over Argentina (Buenos Aires, 13.11.93). Gavin (nicknamed 'Magic') plundered a try, four conversions and three penalty goals to equal Gerald Bosch's South African single-Test points-scoring record. Moreover, he was within one point of equalling the then world record for points scored on a Test debut (since raised to 45 by All Black Simon Culhane in 145–17 defeat of Japan at Bloemfontein 4.6.95). Gavin had only journeyed to South America as a late call-up, replacing the injured Chris Dirks, who broke his hand in the 'battle of Tucuman' (at which time Gavin was on tour in the UK with the SA Barbarians). From there it was on to Buenos Aires and a tour de force that silenced 30,000 home hopefuls. Recalled to the Bok side for third Test (dead rubber) vs New Zealand (Auckland, 6.8.94) and claimed 13 points in an 18–18 draw. But his most prolific day came at his home Ellis Park, where he plundered 28 points (3t,5c,1p) in the 60–8 defeat of Western Samoa. Collected 12 points against the same opposition at the same Jo'burg venue (10.6.95) in the quarter-finals of a triumphant World Cup campaign in which he also bagged 11 against Romania (Cape Town, 30.5.95). Unused replacement in World Cup final win over Kiwis (Jo'burg, 24.6.95), and has not figured since.

South Africa (1993)

Last Season	3 caps	23 pts
Career	7 caps	86 pts

Caps (7): **1993** Arg(2) **1994** NZ(3), Arg(1) **1995** WS(a) wc-R, C, WS(b)

Points (86 – 5t,14c,11p): **1993** Arg(2:1t,4c,3p) **1994** NZ(3:1t,1c,2p) **1995** WS(a:3t,5c,1p) wc-R(1c,3p), WS(b:3c,2p)

Johnson, M. O. England

Full name: Martin Osborne Johnson
Club: Leicester
Position: Lock
Height: 6ft 7in (2.01m)
Weight: 17st 12lb (109kg)
Occupation: Bank officer, Midland Bank (Market Harborough)
Born: Solihull, 9.3.70
Family: Single
Former clubs: Wigston and College Old Boys (NZ)
International debut: England 16, France 15, 1993
Five Nations debut: As above
Suggestions to improve rugby: Beware of altering too much of the game. If we try to make too many changes, in an attempt to pander to television etc, we stand a good chance of changing the face of the game, and that would be disastrous.

Notable landmarks in rugby career: The subject of big-money domestic transfer speculation, seemingly throughout the 1995/96 season, Martin soon showed why by adding to his collection of master classes at the front of the lineout. By now he is surely the world's premier No.2 jumper. Outstanding against Scotland and Ireland in particular, as England finished strongly to clinch a somewhat improbable 1996 Five Nations title. Save for the 1994 tour to South Africa, when he returned home prematurely after being concussed

England (1993)		
Last Season	12 caps	0 pts
Career	24 caps	0 pts
Lions (1993)	2 Tests	0 pts

Caps (24): **1993** F. Lions-NZ(2,3). NZ **1994** S, I, F, W, R, C **1995** I, F(a), W, S wc-Arg, It, WS(a), A, NZ, F(b). SA, WS(b) **1996** F, W, S, I

Points Nil

during defeat by Transvaal, he has been a regular fixture for the past three seasons. Denied domestic glory by Bath, both in league and cup – the latter being the more galling personally, as he had scored what appeared to be the winning try at Twickenham before Bath were awarded *that* controversial late score. Spent 18 months playing out in New Zealand for College Old Boys (1990/91) and for King Country in Division Two of the Inter-Provincial Championship, during which time he also represented NZ Colts against Australia counterparts on a two-week tour. Team mates included All Blacks Va'aiga Tuigamala, John Timu and Blair Larsen. Planned to remain only 12 months, but niggling shoulder complaint prolonged his stay. Had previously represented England Schools (1987/88) and 1989 England Colts (along with Damien Hopley and Steve Ojomoh) before heading 'down under'. On his return played for England Under-21 – partnering Gloucester's David Sims in 94–0 rout of Belgium (1.9.91), before turning out, again alongside Sims, in England B's away wins against France B (15.2.92) and Italy B (7.3.92). But it was in the 1992/93 season that he really hit the big-time. Expecting to play for England A against France A at Leicester (15.1.93), he was diverted to Twickenham, where Wade Dooley had withdrawn from the senior side with a thigh injury. At less than 24 hours' notice, Martin was thrust into the Five Nations opener against France, and acquitted himself well, especially in the second half. Returned to A team thereafter, playing in wins over Italy A, Spain and Ireland A before touring to Canada and playing in both internationals. So impressive was he that when Dooley returned home early from clashing British Lions tour to New Zealand, Martin was quickly summoned and played in final two Tests.

Joiner, C. A.   Scotland

Full name: Craig Alexander Joiner
Club: Leicester
Position: Wing
Height: 5ft 10in (1.78m)
Weight: 13st 12lb (88kg)
Occupation: Chemical engineering student
Former clubs: Eastern Suburbs (Aus), Melrose
Born: Glasgow, 21.4.74
International debut: Argentina 16, Scotland 15, 1994
Five Nations debut: Scotland 26, Ireland 13, 1995
Notable landmarks in rugby career: In a mirror image of his 1994/95 season, where he was ever-present for Scotland save for the early autumn engagement (vs South Africa), Craig played all Tests in 1995/96 except the autumn draw against Western Samoa (18.11.95). In both cases Scotland recovered from a poor start to the campaign and went on and play Grand Slams against England. Toured New Zealand with national squad in the

Scotland (1994)

Last Season	9 caps	5 pts
Career	17 caps	15 pts

Caps (17): **1994** Arg(1,2) **1995** C, I, F(a), W, E, R wc-IC, T, F(b), NZ **1996** I, F, W, E, NZ(1)
Points (15 – 3t): **1995** I(1t), R(1t) **1996** NZ(1:1t)

summer after switching clubs from Melrose, with whom he shared in four Scottish championship titles, to Leicester. The former Scottish Schools sprint and rugby star had made his debut on the dismal tour of Argentina in 1994, appearing in both Test defeats as well as three of the four other games. But it was his second coming that was of greater note. Son of a national triathlon specialist (Mike) and brother of a Scottish Schools hockey international (Kerry), Craig marked his Five Nations debut with a try in the 26–13 defeat of Ireland (Murrayfield, 4.2.95). He added a second on the same ground in the 49–16 win over Romania (22.4.95), and a fortnight later went try-mad in Spain, bagging one hat-trick against a Spanish XV and another in the 62–7 non-cap Test victory (Madrid, 6.5.95). All of which made his failure to score a try in four World Cup outings rather disappointing, though he did twice run rings around tournament star Jonah Lomu in Scotland's 30–48 quarter-final loss to the All Blacks (Pretoria, 11.6.95).

Jones, D.

Wales

Full name: Derwyn Jones
Club: Cardiff
Position: Lock
Height: 6ft 10in (2.08m)
Weight: 18st 7lb (113kg)
Occupation: WRU national development officer
Born: Pontarddulais, 14.11.70
International debut: Wales 12, South Africa 20, 1994
Five Nations debut: France 21, Wales 9, 1995
Former clubs: Neath, Llanelli, Loughborough University, Northampton
Family links with rugby: Rhodri (brother) plays for Bridgend
Notable landmarks in rugby career: One of only two Welshman (Ieuan Evans being the other) to play in all ten Tests between the start of the World Cup and the end of the 1996 Five Nations series, although he did not last too long in Johannesburg on 2 September before being knocked out by a punch from dirty Springbok

Wales (1994)

Last Season	12 caps	0 pts
Career	16 caps	0 pts

Caps (16): **1994** SA **1995** F, E, S wc-J, NZ, I(b). SA, Fj **1996** It, E, S, I, F, A(1,2)
Points Nil

Kobus Wiese, who was cited, banned and fined for his crime. That apart, Derwyn, who shares with England lock Martin Bayfield the distinction of being the tallest player in international rugby, had a fine season, forming a formidable lineout trio with fellow jumper Gareth Llewellyn and thrower Jonathan Humphreys. Derwyn's route to the top took him via Neath, Llanelli and Loughborough University, with whom he won two UAU Cup victories, to Northampton and then Cardiff, where he shared in the 1994 Swalec Cup triumph and the 1994/95 Heineken League title. His Test debut came against South Africa (Cardiff, 26.11.94) – tourists against whom he had already appeared for both Cardiff and Wales A. Derwyn also earned Wales A honours vs North of England, Ireland and France in 1993/94, having graduated from the Under-21 side with whom he turned out against Ireland (1991) and Scotland (1992). Dropped by the senior side for the 1995 Five Nations finale against Ireland (Cardiff, 18.3.95), which Wales lost to complete only their second-ever whitewash, he was restored by new coach (and Cardiff supremo) Alex Evans for Wales' truncated World Cup campaign, playing in the three games against Japan, New Zealand and Ireland. Helped Cardiff reach inaugural European Cup final in 1995/96.

Jones, R. G.   **Wales**

Full name: Rhodri Gwyn Jones
Club: Llanelli
Position: Flanker
Height: 6ft (1.83m)
Weight: 15st 1lb (95kg)
Occupation: Medical student
Born: 5.10.72
Family: Single
International debut: Wales 31, Italy 26, 1996
Five Nations debut: England 21, Wales 15, 1996
Notable landmarks in rugby career: Gwyn would have received even greater acclaim for his debut season in Test rugby were it not for the fact that Wales had rather a lot of promising rookies to share the praise – Rob Howley and Leigh Davies in particular. One of five youngsters blooded against Italy on the eve of the 1996 Five Nations series (won 31–26, Cardiff, 16.1.96), Gwyn quickly made the No.7 shirt his own

Wales (1996)		
Last Season	6 caps	0 pts
Career	6 caps	0 pts

Caps (6): **1996** It, E, S, I, F, A(1)
Points Nil

with a never-say-die style of rugby that complemented the brand of play being devised for Wales by supremos Terry Cobner and Kevin Bowring. A great-nephew of the legendary Welsh flanker Ivor Jones, Gwyn attended Llandovery College on a Carwyn James scholarship. Captained Wales at Under-15 level against Scotland in 1988 before winning five caps for Wales Under-18s in 1990/91. Toured Canada with Wales Under-19s in 1991, and made his Under-21 bow the following year, one month after making his senior debut in the Scarlets' back row. Two more years elapsed before he broke into the Wales A side against Canada A. Injury then got in the way of further progress: first a dislocated right shoulder, and then a hamstring tear. Medical examinations provided a further distraction from his rugby, but he returned to the fray in 1995/96 and, having played for Llanelli against Fiji, earned his call-up for the Italian job.

Jones, I. D.   New Zealand

Full name: Ian Donald Jones
Province: North Harbour
Club: Kamo
Position: Lock
Height: 6ft 6in (1.98m)
Weight: 16st 8lb (105kg)
Occupation: Sponsorship manager, All Black Club
Family: Single
Born: Whangarei, 17.4.67
International debut: New Zealand 31, Scotland 16, 1990
Notable landmarks in rugby career: Outstanding lineout display in last 1995 World Cup final could not prevent New Zealand suffering a shock extra-time loss to the host nation Springboks (Johannesburg, 24.6.95). Took his disappointment out on Italy and France with try-scoring performances in season-ending Tests in Europe. It completed a satisfying campaign for the Kamo Kid, who had switched clubs from North Auckland to North Harbour after the 1993 autumn tour of England and Scotland. Represented Whangarei Schools (1979) and North Island Under-18s. A teenage Jones broke into both the Kamo first XV and North Auckland Colts side

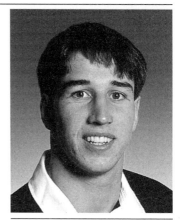

New Zealand (1990)

Last Season	12 caps	5 pts
Career	50 caps	27 pts

Caps (50): **1990** S(1,2), A(1,2,3), F(1,2) **1991** Arg(1,2), A(a1,a2). wc-E, US, It, C, A(b), S **1992** Wd(1,2,3), I(1, 2), A(1,2,3), SA **1993** BL(1,2R,3), WS, S, E **1994** F(1,2), SA(1,3), A **1995** C wc-I, WS, E, SA. A(1,2), It,F(1,2) **1996** WS, S(1,2)

Points (27 – 6t): **1990** S(1:1t) **1991** A(1:1t) **1992** I(2:1t) **1995** It(1t), F(2:1t) **1996** S(1:1t)

in 1986, and two years later made his bow for North Auckland. Having marked his inaugural season of provincial rugby (1988) with four tries in eight matches, he played in the 1989 All Black Trials and was included in the squad for their tour to Wales and Ireland. Failed to make the Test side but did make a lot of friends, and consequently returned to Britain the following year as an invited guest of the centenary Barbarians, playing vs England, Wales and Argentina. By then he had made his Test debut against Scotland at Dunedin, following the retirement of Murray Pierce, and celebrated with a try in the 31–16 win. Ian appeared in all seven All Black Tests in 1990 and toured Argentina the following year, starting both Tests. Scored a try in the 21–12 Bledisloe Cup first Test defeat by Australia. An ever-present in the 1991 World Cup, he maintained his place throughout the nine-Test schedule in 1992, claiming his third international try in the second-Test romp over Ireland. Enjoyed an impressive tour of Australia and South Africa in 1993, edging highly rated Wallaby John Eales in the lineout. Made ten appearances on the tour, including a formidable display as captain against Free State at Bloemfontein. Ended 1995 just 11 caps short of Gary Whetton's New Zealand appearance record for a lock.

Touchlines: Golf, water skiing, swimming

Jones, M. N. New Zealand

Full name: Michael Niko Jones
Province: Auckland
Position: Flanker, No.8
Height: 5ft 11in (1.80m)
Weight: 15st 2lb (96kg)
Born: Auckland, 8.4.65
Former country: Western Samoa
International debut: Western Samoa 14, Wales 32, 1986
International debut (NZ): New Zealand 70, Italy 6, 1987
Serious injuries: Damaged knee (1989)
Notable landmarks in rugby career: Omitted from New Zealand's World Cup squad in 1995 because his religious beliefs prevented him from playing on a Sunday. But Michael still finished the year in the No.7 shirt after Josh Kronfeld, who had earned superstar status in South Africa, lost his place midway through the Bledisloe Cup series. Michael then claimed his tenth Test try in the 70–6 slaughter of Italy in Bologna. Formerly the world's greatest openside flanker, Michael also missed out on much of the 1991 World Cup due to his insistence on keeping Sundays sacred. A potential return to England with the 1993 All Blacks was denied him after he broke his jaw in three places in a training accident shortly before departure. Auckland-born Michael first caught

Western Samoa (1986)		
Career	1 cap	0 pts
New Zealand (1987)		
Last Season	8 caps	10 pts
Career	43 caps	46 pts

Caps (43): **1987** wc-It, Fj, S, F. A **1988** W(1,2), A(2,3) **1989** F(1,2), Arg(1,2) **1990** F(1,2) **1991** Arg(1,2), A(1,2). wc-E, US, S **1992** Wd(1,3), I(2), A(1,3), SA **1993** BL(1,2,3), A, WS **1994** SA(3R), A **1995** A(1R,2), It, F(1,2) **1996** WS, S(1,2)

Points (46 – 11t): **1987** wc-It(1t), F(1t) **1988** W(2:1t), A(2:1t) **1989** Arg(1:2t) **1990** F(2:1t) **1991** Arg(2:1t). wc-E(1t) **1995** It(1t) **1996** S(2:1t)

the eye playing in the colours of Western Samoa against Wales at Suva in 1986. By the following year New Zealand had snapped him up, and he was included in their World Cup-winning squad, scoring a try against Italy at Eden Park 30 minutes into his debut and claiming the All Blacks' first after 17 minutes of their 29–9 World Cup final win over France on the same Auckland field. Had been marked out as something special ever since his provincial debut in 1985, when he scored three tries against South Canterbury. However, his climb to the very pinnacle of the world game was abruptly halted in 1989 when he sustained a serious knee injury playing against Argentina, having scored two tries in the 60–9 first Test defeat of the Pumas at Dunedin. The injury was described by his specialist as 'the equivalent of being hit by a truck doing 60mph.' As a consequence he missed the tour to Wales and Ireland, but returned 18 months later for the 1990 tour of France, during which he crossed for a try in the 30–12 second Test victory in Paris. Scored the only try of the 1991 World Cup opener as England were beaten 18–12 in their own Twickenham backyard, then declined to play in the quarter-final and semi-final ties against Canada and Australia respectively, as the games fell on the traditional day of rest. This refusal to compromise his religious beliefs also caused him to miss the Brisbane Test against Australia in the 1992 Bledisloe Cup series. Prior to that training injury in 1993, Michael had helped the Blacks beat the Lions (over three matches) and the Aussies, and thus to recapture the Bledisloe Cup.

Joseph, J. W. New Zealand

Full name: Jamie Joseph
Province: Otago
Position: Flanker
Height: 6ft 5in (1.96m)
Weight: 16st 8lb (105kg)
Born: Blenheim, 21.11.69
Family links with rugby: Jim (father) played for New Zealand Maoris in 1960s.
International debut: New Zealand 54, World XV 26, 1992
Notable landmarks in rugby career: Controversy has dogged Jamie from the start of his Test career. On his international debut – against the World XV, in the second Test of the 1992 centenary series – he was spotted on the television stamping, and for this he later received a four-week suspension from the Union's judiciary committee. A year on, dateline 27 November 1993 (his sixth tour appearance),

he was again guilty of stamping. Twickenham was the venue, England the opposition, and Kyran Bracken the victim, his ankle crunched by Jamie's studs while the game was still in its infancy. The fact that the All Blacks management failed to make known any punishment prolonged the dissatisfaction over the incident. In between these two unsavoury

New Zealand (1992)
Last Season	5 caps	0 pts
Career	19 caps	5 pts

Caps (19): 1992 Wd(2,3R), I(1), A(1R,3), SA 1993 BL(1,2,3), A, WS, S, E 1995 C wc-I, W, J(R), S, SA(R)

Points (5 – 1t): 1992 A(3:1t)

incidents, Jamie also made news for the right reasons, on the All Blacks tour of Australia and South Africa. He lost out in the selection stakes, first to Mike Brewer, his Provincial skipper, then to Andy Earl, in the first two tests against Australia, although he came on as a 65th-minute replacement for Brewer in Sydney. But he was awarded the start in the 'dead rubber' and scored a wonderful try. Against South Africa, too, he impressed. In all he made nine appearances on the trip, bagging a try in the 80–0 defeat of Western Australia. His other outings were against New South Wales, Victoria, Queensland, Natal, Junior South Africa. A latecomer to top-grade rugby, having completed only two seasons of First Division rugby at Otago, the 1991 national champions. He was acclaimed the Province's most improved player in 1992 and in the same year, excelled in two national trials at Napier, finishing on the winning side for Fitzpatrick's XV and the Saracens team which beat a New Zealand XV 20–15. Completed an excellent campaign by following in his father's studprints and representing the New Zealand Maoris on their tour of the Pacific Islands. Injury sidelined him in 1994, but he returned with a vengeance in 1995, playing in six of New Zealand's seven Tests, including the World Cup final, albeit as a replacement for Mike Brewer.

England's Martin Johnson in characteristic pose – head and shoulders above his rivals.

Joubert, A. J.   South Africa

Full name: Andre Johan Joubert
Province: Natal
Position: Fullback
Height: 6ft 3in (1.90m)
Weight: 14st 6lb (87kg)
Occupation: Money trader, NBS
Born: Ladysmith, 15.4.64
Family: Married
International debut: Australia 19, South Africa 12, 1993
Former province: Orange Free State
Notable landmarks in rugby career:
Arguably the world's premier fullback, Andre played a pivotal role in South Africa's World Cup triumph in 1995, despite having to play in the semi-final and final nursing a broken bone in his hand (sustained in the quarter-final vs Western Samoa). Maintained his form in early 1996 to finish second on the Super-12 try-scoring chart by adding 12 as the Natal Sharks reached the final before losing to the dazzling Auckland Blues. Brilliant on the 1994 Boks' tour of Wales and Ireland, Andre's finest moment came with a national-high 38 points (4t,9c) in the 78–7 rout of Swansea (5.11.94). Had been

South Africa (1993)

Last Season	8 caps	0 pts
Career	19 caps	56 pts

Caps (19): **1989** Wd(1R) **1993** A(3), Arg(1) **1994** E(1,2), NZ(1,2R,3), Arg(2) S, W **1995** wc-A, C, WS(b), F, NZ. W, It, E

Points (56 – 3t,4c,11p): **1993** Arg(1:1t) **1994** E(1:5p), E(2:1t,1c,2p), NZ(1:3p), S(3c,1p), W(1t)

hugely influential in Natal's defeat of England (21.5.94), kicking four penalty goals in the famous 21–6 win, having earlier scored 33 points in a 1994 Super-10 match against Western Samoa. Claimed 28 points in two-Test series against England. Andre had first come to the notice of British audiences when he turned out for centenary Barbarians against Scotland at Murrayfield (7.9.91) and set up the most glorious try in the final minute. From underneath his own posts he broke deep into the Scottish half to set up a spectacular match-saving try. Had to wait a further two years to gain Test recognition by being called up as a replacement for Transvaal's Theo van Rensburg on the Springboks' tour of Australia. Andre scored two tries and two conversions in the 65–5 defeat of Queensland Country (Mackay, 11.8.93), and two conversions and four penalty goals in the 31–20 victory against Sydney (Penrith, 18.8.93). Much to his delight he was then selected to play fullback in the decisive third Test (Sydney, 21.8.93). Unhappily, for him and his compatriots, the Wallabies won 19–12.

Andre then appeared in the Currie Cup final at Kings Park, Durban (16.10.93), where Natal lost 15–21 to Transvaal in front of their own fans. The Sharks from King's Park put matters to rights by triumphing in 1995.

Kearns, P. N. *Australia*

Full name: Philip (Phil) Nicholas Kearns
State: New South Wales
Club: Randwick
Position: Hooker
Height: 6ft (1.83m)
Weight: 17st (108kg)
Occupation: Business development manager, Tooheys Ltd
Born: 27.6.67
International debut: New Zealand 24, Australia 12, 1989
Serious injuries: Not enough room for them in this book
Notable landmarks in rugby career: Most-capped hooker in Australian history, having moved seven caps past previous record-holder, P. G. Johnson (42: 1959–71), in 1995. Succeeded Michael Lynagh as Wallaby captain after 1995 World Cup, leading the side in the ill-fated Bledisloe Cup series. It was a far cry from his 1994 Bledisloe experience, when he scored a crucial try against New Zealand as the Wallabies retained the Cup (Sydney, 6.5.94). Appeared in three of the four World Cup engagements in South Africa, where England ended champions' term in office. Previously skippered Australia during Lynagh's absence in

Australia (1989)

Last Season	5 caps	5 pts
Career	49 caps	34 pts

Caps	(49): **1989** NZ, F(1,2) **1990** F(1,2,3), US, NZ(1,2,3) **1991** W(a), E(a), NZ(a1,a2). wc-Arg, WS, W(b), I, NZ(b), E(b) **1992** S(1,2), NZ(1,2,3), SA, I, W **1993** T, NZ, SA(1,2,3), C, F(1,2) **1994** I(1,2), It(1,2), WS, NZ **1995** Arg(1,2) wc-SA, C, E. NZ(1,2)
Points	(34 – 8t): **1989** F(2:1t) **1990** US(1t), NZ(3:1t) **1991** W(a:2t) wc-Arg(1t) **1994** NZ(1t) **1995** wc-SA(1t)

1994, against Italy, Western Samoa and the All Blacks, as he had done in 1992 vs Wales, just three years after having been a Randwick reserve-grade player. In 1989 he sprang from obscurity to hook against the All Blacks, and has remained in the lineup ever since. Shares with props Tony Daly and Ewen McKenzie the world record for a front-row combination of 36 Tests.
Touchlines: Golf, surfing, reading

Kingston, T. J.   Ireland

Full name: Terence John Kingston
Club: Dolphin
Position: Hooker
Height: 5ft 10in (1.78m)
Weight: 15st (90kg)
Occupation: Director, Computer Accessories & Systems Ltd
Born: Cork, 19.9.63
Family: Single
Former club: Lansdowne
International debut: Ireland 6, Wales 13, 1987
Five Nations debut: Ireland 22, Scotland 18, 1988
Best moment in rugby: Being awarded Ireland captaincy (1995)
Worst moment in rugby: Being dropped from Irish team; Dolphin's failure to qualify for National League in 1989/90 play-off match.
Suggestions to improve rugby: An extra five metres should be added to all penalties as an increased deterrent and to encourage the team benefiting to take a fast, running ball while opposition is retreating.
Notable landmarks in rugby career: Like many Irishmen in 1995/96,

Ireland (1987)

Last Season	8 caps	0 pts
Career	29 caps	8 pts

Caps (29): **1987** wc-W, T, A **1988** S, F, W, E(a) **1990** F, W **1991** wc-J **1993** F, W, E, R **1994** F, W, E, S **1995** F(a), W(a), It wc-NZ, J(R), W(b),F(b). Fj **1996** US, S, F
Points (8 – 2t): **1988** W(1t) **1990** W(1t)

Terry began the season in the national team (albeit having lost the captaincy to Jim Staples), and finished it in the wilderness as Ireland's fortunes plummeted after an encouraging start. His fortunes were in marked contrast to the previous season, which he had started as understudy to Garryowen starlet Keith Wood and ended as the Ireland skipper, guiding his country to the World Cup quarter-finals. Turnaround came midway through 1995 Five Nations campaign, when selectors rested Wood, troubled by a back problem. Terry took over the No.2 jersey against France (Dublin, 4.3.95) and despite a defeat was made captain next time out. Kingston celebrated by leading his side to a 16–12 victory over Wales in the Wooden Spoon decider (Cardiff, 18.3.95), though his next mission ended in embarrassment as Ireland became the first major rugby nation to lose to Italy (Treviso, 8.5.95). Rebounded well in the World Cup. Particularly satisfying for the Munsterman was the performance in South Africa of the forwards – a unit he had led on and off for the previous two seasons. Of Ireland's 13 World Cup tries, the back division accounted for only two. Terry had re-

343

established himself as Ireland's premier hooker in the 1993 Five Nations Championship, having previously been a regular member of the side five years before. Terry's finest hour on the domestic front came when he skippered Munster to a 22–19 victory over the touring Australians (Cork, 21.10.92). Had captained Ireland to a 32–16 World Cup win over Japan (Dublin, 9.10.91) in a 1991/92 season which he otherwise viewed from the bench as Steve Smith monopolised the No.2 jersey. In all, Terry has represented Irish Schools (1982), Ireland Under-21s (1984), Ireland Under-25s (1987, three caps), Ireland B (beat Argentina 27–12, Limerick, 20.10.90) and, on 29 occasions since his debut in the 1987 World Cup (in place of injured Harry Harbison), Ireland Full. Toured with Ireland to Namibia (1991), New Zealand (1992) and Australia (1994). **Touchlines:** Golf

Kronfeld, J. *New Zealand*

Full name: Josh Kronfeld
Province: Otago
Position: Openside flanker
Height: 6ft ½ in (1.84m)
Weight: 16st 6lb (100kg)
Occupation: Teacher, Kings High School
Born: 20.6.71
Family: Single
International debut: New Zealand 73, Canada 7, 1995
Notable landmarks in rugby career: One of the sensations of the 1995 World Cup, Josh sampled the other side of life when he was benched midway through the year-ending Bledisloe Cup series (Michael Jones took over). Nevertheless, the memories of South Africa, where Josh proved that small can be beautiful (albeit in a rugby context), lived on. His scrum-capped shaven head bobbed about all over every pitch he played on – always first to the breakdown, always in the face of oppsion halfbacks. Wales coach

New Zealand (1995)		
Last Season	10 caps	25 pts
Career	11 caps	25 pts

Caps (11): **1995** C wc-I, W, S, E, SA. A(1,2R) **1996** WS, S(1,2)
Points (25 – 5t): **1995** wc-I(1t), W(1t), E(1t) **1996** S(2:2t)

Alex Evans said that but for Jonah Lomu, Josh would have been the All Black superstar and, in all probability, also player of the tournament. Hard to believe he only made his full debut in late April, in the 73–7 rout of Canada (Auckland,

22.4.95), especially as he had so impressed observers during Otago's 37–24 defeat of the 1993 British Lions (Dunedin, 5.6.93) – a match in which Scott Hastings smashed his cheekbone trying to tackle the Kiwi wing-forward. Formerly with Hawke's Bay, Josh made his name in Sevens rugby, and enhanced it tenfold with try-scoring performances against Ireland, Wales and England in South Africa. Bizarrely, if Josh was not Josh, he claims he would like to be English entertainer Michael Barrymore – 'awright?'

Touchlines: Surfing

Kruger, R. J. South Africa

Full name: Ruben Jacobus Kruger
Province: Northern Transvaal
Club: Oostelikes
Position: Flanker
Height: 6ft 2in (1.88m)
Weight: 16st 9lb (101kg)
Occupation: Market agent
Born: Vrede, 30.3.70
Family: Married
Family links with rugby: Brother-in-law is fellow Springbok Drikus Hattingh
International debut: Argentina 26, South Africa 29, 1993
Notable landmarks in rugby career: Ruben, who captained Northern Transvaal to the 1996 Super-12 semi-finals, deserved the Jacques Cousteau award for services to underwater rugby when he splashed over for South Africa's World Cup semi-final-winning try against France in *that* Durban monsoon (17.6.95). It was a deserved reward for a largely unheralded but hugely effective openside flanker. Of his

South Africa (1994)

Last Season	8 caps	5 pts
Career	13 caps	5 pts

Caps (13): **1993** Arg(1,2) **1994** S, W **1995** WS(a) wc-A, R, WS(b), F, NZ. W, It, E
Points (5 – 1t): **1995** wc-F(1t)

display in the final win over New Zealand (Jo'burg, 24.6.95), former England fly-half Stuart Barnes described Ruben as 'the one man who encapsulated Springbok efforts more than any other.' Bok manager Morne du Plessis added: 'He is an exceptional player. He gets the side an extra yard in front of the advantage line.' He missed only one of the Boks' nine matches in 1995 – the 'Battle of the Boet' against Canada in the World Cup pool stages. Ruben represented South Africa at Schools and B levels while playing out of Free State.

In 1993 he toured Australia and Argentina, scoring a try hat-trick against Queensland Country, and making his Test debut in the 29–26 first Test defeat of the Pumas (Buenos Aires, 6.11.93). Toured New Zealand in 1994 (albeit as a replacement) and Britain, appearing in both international wins over Scotland and Wales, and claiming tries against Swansea, Combined Scottish Districts and the Barbarians.

Lacroix, T. France

Full name: Thierry Lacroix
Club: Dax
Position: Outside-half, centre
Height: 5ft 11in (1.80m)
Weight: 13st 2lb (78kg)
Occupation: Physiotherapist
Born: Nogaro, 2.3.67
Family: Married
International debut: France 15, Australia 32, 1989
Five Nations debut: France 36, Wales 3, 1991
Notable landmarks in rugby career: The top scorer in 1995 World Cup, his 116 points from six matches broke down thus: vs Tonga 25; vs Cote d'Ivoire 24; vs Scotland 17; vs Ireland 26; vs South Africa 15; vs

England 9 (average: 19.3). This nudged him ahead of Gavin Hastings, who had shot out of the traps with 75 points in his first two games for Scotland. Overall, Thierry's tally rose to 349, and he extended that to 357 in 1995/96, so usurping Didier Camberabero (354 in 36 matches: 1982–93) as France's all-time leading points scorer. Despite that, it was not a happy campaign for Thierry, who had been omitted from France's early-season campaigns for staying on in South Africa after the World Cup to inspire Natal to Currie Cup glory. Injury, suffered against Ireland three-quarters of the way through the Five Nations series, contributed to his being left out of the team to play Wales, as did the performance of his replacement Stephane Glas in Paris. It had been Thierry's perfect World Cup goalkicking (six out of six) which had allowed France to steal past Scotland in injury time (Pretoria, 3.6.95), and he hardly missed a kick thereafter – a far cry from Paris (18.2.95), where Scotland won at Parc des Princes for the first time, largely because Lacroix couldn't hit his hat. However, he later revealed that his mother had been involved in a life-threatening car smash and that his mind, understandably enough, had not been wholly focused on kicking a pig's bladder through a couple of poles. Goalkicking apart, Thierry enjoyed a magnificent World Cup in the Gallic midfield, and would have had an even better time had his halfbacks been any good. Most observers included him in their teams of the tournament. Thierry proved his versatility when he appeared on the left wing in New Zealand (1994), having also represented France at fly-half on numerous occasions. He had also been a big contributor to the French success in 1993/94, bagging 101 points in nine starts. Was largely responsible for the historic Test series defeat of South Africa (1993) – though he was also responsible for France's first loss to Wales in 12 years. Helped France win 1992 Students World Cup in Italy before turning out for France Espoirs in 24–17 win over touring Springboks in Bordeaux (4.10.92). Scored winning try against Scotland (6.2.93), and three penalty goals against Wales (20.3.93) as France won 1993 Five Nations Championship. Had burst onto international scene with 17 points – five penalty goals and a conversion – on his first start in France's 25–19 defeat of Australia in the second Test in Lille. His debut had come in the first Test as a replacement for Camberabero. In spite of his prolific start, he had to wait until the 1991 Five Nations Championship for his third cap, replacing Philippe Sella in the 36–3 win over Wales (2.3.91).

France (1989)

Last Season	9 caps	134 pts
Career	38 caps	367 pts

Caps (38): **1989** A(1R,2) **1991** W(a:R), W(b:R). wc-R(b), C(R), E(b) **1992** SA(2) **1993** E, S, I, W, SA(1,2), R(b), A(1,2) **1994** I, W, E, S, C(a), NZ(1,2), C(b) **1995** W, E(a), S(a), R wc-T, IC, S(b), I(b), SA, E(b) **1996** E, S, I

Points (367 – 6t,32c,89p,2dg): **1989** A(2:1c,5p) **1991** wc-C(2p), E(2p) **1992** SA(2:2c,5p) **1993** S(1t), W(3p), SA(1:5p), SA(2:4p,1dg), R(b:6c,3p), A(1:1c,1p), A(2:1p) **1994** I(1t,3c,3p), W(1c,1p), E(3p), S(1c,2p), C(a:1c,3p), NZ(1:1c,2p), NZ(2:1c,2p), C(b:2c,2p) **1995** W(1c,3p), E(a:1c,1p), S(a:1p), R(1c,4p) wc-T(2t,3c,3p), IC(2t,4c,2p), S(b:1c,5p), I(b:1c,8p), SA(5p), E(b:3p) **1996** E(3p,1dg), S(2p)

Frenchmen Laurent Cabannes (left) and Thierry Lacroix size up the opposition.

Larsen, B. P.   New Zealand

Full name: Blair Larsen
Province: North Harbour
Position: Lock
Height: 6ft 6in (1.98m)
Weight: 18st 5lb (112kg)
Occupation: Police officer
Born: 20.1.69
Family: Single
International debut: New Zealand 54, World XV 26, 1992
Notable landmarks in rugby career: Switched to blindside flanker after losing his position as a Test lock to Robin Brooke, and picked up two caps in No.6 jersey at tail-end of 1995, against Italy and France. Change for Blair came on 1993 All Blacks' tour of Britain, when he had been called up as a replacement for the aforementioned Brooke. Played so well that he was rewarded with final match against the Barbarians. First-choice New Zealand No.6 throughout 1994, excelling in the 13–9 second Test defeat of South Africa (Wellington, 23.7.94), but

New Zealand (1992)
Last Season	5 caps	0 pts
Career	13 caps	4 pts

Caps (13): **1992** Wd(2,3), I(1) **1994** F(1,2), SA(1,2,3) **1995** wc-I, W, J. It, F(1)

Points (4 – 1t): **1992** Wd(2:1t)

lost out to Jamie Joseph and Mike Brewer in early 1995 and, ironically, had to return to the second row for his three caps in the World Cup. Voted North Harbour's most promising player in 1991, he went on to make a favourable impression in the 1992 national trials (after just 14 Provincial outings), from where a full debut in the second leg of the the centenary series was his next stop. One of six changes to the side beaten 28–14 by the World XV in the first Test, he claimed one of the ten tries scored by the revived All Blacks in a 54–26 win. Blair retained his place for the next two Tests, the victorious centenary decider and New Zealand's decidedly uncomfortable 24-21 first Test win over Ireland. In response to this close squeak, the selectors made widespread alterations to the side for the second Test, Blair being one of the casualties. Nevertheless, he kept his spot in the squad for the tour to Australia and South Africa, and figured in seven of the 16 engagements. His one try came in the second match against South Australia, at Adelaide, where the visitors won 48–18.

Laubscher, T. G.   South Africa

Full name: Tommie Gerbach Laubscher
Province: Western Province
Club: Northerns
Position: Prop
Height: 5ft 9in (1.75m)
Weight: 16st (97kg)
Occupation: Wheat and dairy farmer
Born: Vredenburg, 8.10.63
International debut: South Africa 42, Argentina 22, 1994
Former provinces: Boland, Central Unions
Notable landmarks in rugby career: A Springbok reserve as far back as 1989, Tommie finally broke into the Test side in 1994 when Argentina were the visitors to Port Elizabeth (8.10.94). He came in at loosehead for Transvaal rival Balie Swart, the same player who replaced him 63 minutes into the 46–26 second Test defeat of the Pumas at Ellis Park the following week. Tommie's selection

South Africa (1994)

Last Season	2 caps	0 pts
Career	6 caps	0 pts

Caps (6): **1994** Arg(1,2), S, W **1995** It, E
Points Nil

was remarkable on two counts. It came on his 31st birthday, and at a time when he representing no greater side than Western Province B. He maintained his pre-eminence on the 1994 Springboks' autumn tour of Wales, Scotland and Ireland, turning out in the wins over Wales A, Llanelli, Swansea, Combined Scottish Districts and Irish Provinces XV, in addition to both Test victories. But 1995 proved less fruitful for one of the most awkward props in South Africa, as Swart, Pieter du Randt, Garry Pagel and Marius Hurter shored up the propping duties until after the World Cup. Then, belatedly, Tommie got his chance and played in the defeats of Italy (40–21, Rome, 12.11.95) and England (24-14, Twickenham, 18.11.95).

Leonard, J.   England

Full name: Jason Leonard
Nickname: Golden
Club: Harlequins
Position: Loosehead prop
Height: 5ft 10in (1.78m)
Weight: 17st 2lb (109kg)
Occupation: Sales rep, Gorst Clayton Demolition
Born: Barking, London, 14.8.68
Family: Single
Former clubs: Barking, Saracens
International debut: Argentina 25, England 12, 1990
Five Nations debut: Wales 6, England 25, 1991
Best rugby memories: Grand Slam wins, and New Zealand 7, British Lions 20, 1993
Worst rugby memories: Losing decisive third Test with Lions against 1993 All Blacks; losing 1995 World Cup final and 1995 semi-final.
Most embarrassing memory: Being made songmaster on 1993 Lions tour – I can't sing to save my life!
Toughest opponent: John Davies (Neath & Wales)
Serious injuries: Ruptured disc in neck (1991/92)
Do you really want to be a full-time professional? Yes, for the lifestyle, but I would want to be able to keep hold of an outside job.
How well has rugby handled move to professionalism? 0/10. It should have been a gradual process. Instead the rugby world has been shaken upside down.
Do you have a duty to entertain? Yes, once you are a paid performer the onus is to entertain. If you are not paid, the duty is to yourself and your team mates. Thus criticism of the 1996 Pilkington Cup final was unfair.
Do you feel a loyalty to your club in this new era? Yes, but loyalty is fast becoming an outdated concept.
Biggest influences on career: Mixture of Jeff Probyn, Paul Rendall, Gary Pearce, Brian Moore and John Oliver.
Suggestion to improve rugby: Law-makers must consult players. This is rugby's biggest problem.

England (1990)		
Last Season	11 caps	0 pts
Career	49 caps	0 pts
Lions (1993)	2 Tests	0 pts

Caps (49): **1990** Arg(a1,a2), Arg(b) **1991** W, S(a), I, F(a), Fj, A(a) wc-NZ, It, US, F(b), S(b), A(b) **1992** I, F, W, C, SA **1993** F, W, S, I. Lions-NZ(2,3). NZ **1994** S, I, F, W, SA(1,2), R, C **1995** I, F(a), W, S wc-Arg, It, A, NZ, F(b). SA, WS(b) **1996** F, W, S, I

Points Nil

Notable landmarks in rugby career: England's decision to field a weaker team in last summer's World Cup tie against Western Samoa (4.6.95) brought an end to Jason's amazing run of 40 consecutive international appearances (all at loosehead save for Italy, 31.5.95) – an unbroken run dating back five years to his debut against Argentina (28.7.90). In that period he played on three Grand Slam sides, in a World Cup campaign which culminated in a Final appearance against Australia, and for the 1993 Lions throughout a three-Test series in New Zealand (two at tighthead). The period did not actually feature a try, but it did include an injury which seriously threatened his playing career. After the 1992 Championship a neck injury required delicate surgery, including a muscle graft, and forced him to take three months off work. He had experienced problems at Murrayfield against Scotland (18.1.92) and the disc finally ruptured against Wales (7.3.92). Surgeons replaced the ruptured disc with a piece of bone, then waited for it to bond with existing vertebra. He was off work for three months but, with no England tour, was able to recover in good time before returning for Test against Canada at Wembley (17.10.92). Jason began his career at Barking, helping them win Essex Colts Cup before tasting success at Twickenham, with Eastern Counties winning Under-21 County Championship. Won 1989/90 Courage League division two title with Saracens, and sat on England Under-21 bench in Romania (1989). Broke into England B ranks in 1989/90, winning caps against Fiji and France, and warming bench against USSR before being promoted to senior status on 1990 tour of Argentina, when he made his debut in Buenos Aires. Has since accrued 49 caps, so that he is far and away England's most-capped prop of all time (Probyn comes next with 37).

Le Roux, H. P.   South Africa

Full name: Hendrik (Hennie) Pieter
Le Roux
Province: Transvaal
Club: RAU
Position: Centre, fly-half
Height: 5ft 10in (1.78m)
Weight: 12st 8lb (80kg)
Occupation: Manager, Transvaal
Rugby Academy
Born: Grahamstown, 10.7.67
Family: Single
Former province: Eastern Province
International debut: South Africa 20,
France 20, 1993
Notable landmarks in rugby career:
Mr Versatility, having in 1994/95
been moved from fly-half to centre

mid-season to accomodate South Africa's World Cup winner Joel Stransky in the side. Ever-present for Springboks throughout triumphant 1995 campaign, scoring one try, in the 40–11 defeat of Italy (Rome, 12.11.95). Hennie really made his name in Transvaal's 24–21 defeat of England (28.5.94), with a brilliant running performance. The former Junior Springbok went over in Ellis

South Africa (1993)

Last Season	9 caps	5 pts
Career	20 caps	24 pts

Caps (20): **1993** F(1,2) **1994** E(1,2), NZ(1,2,3), Arg(2), S, W **1995** WS(a) wc-A, R(R), C, WS(b), F, NZ. W, It, E

Points (24 -- 2t,1c,4p): **1994** E(2:1t,3p) W(1c,1p) **1995** It(1t)

Park's left corner for Transvaal's opening try as England were beaten 24–21. A fortnight later he helped beat England again, this time contributing 14 points to the Springboks' 27–9 Newlands rout. Had also played in England the previous season on a Springbok tour which also took in France. He made six appearances and scored five points (one try). However, he had to wait for his Test chance until France visited the Republic in June and July of 1993. Selected to fill the No.10 jersey in the absence of retired legend Naas Botha, Hennie played in both Tests (first: drew 20–20, Durban, 26.6.93; second: lost 17–18, Johannesburg, 3.7.93). But South Africa's failure to even share the series led to changes at outside-half, with Natal's Joel Stransky taking over. Still, Hennie made six appearances on tour in Australia (against South Australia, New South Wales, NSW Country, ACT, Queensland Country and Sydney), and scored 14 points (2t,2c). His tries came against South Australia and NSW. Played four out of the Springboks' six games on their Autumn tour of Argentina – vs Cordoba, Buenos Aires, Tucuman and Rosario – scoring tries against Cordoba and Rosario. Helped Transvaal win 1993 and 1994 Currie Cups, against Natal and Orange Free State respectively.

Mark Andrews wins yet another Super-12 lineout for Natal. Did he ever lose one?

Lewis, A. L. P.   Wales

Full name: Andrew Leighton Paul
Lewis
Nickname: Alp
Club: Cardiff
Position: Loosehead prop
Height: 5ft 10in (1.78m)
Weight: 15st (95kg)
Occupation: Development officer,
Cardiff RFC
Born: Swansea, 13.6.73
Family: Single
International debut: Wales 31, Italy
26, 1996
Five Nations debut: England 21,
Wales 15, 1996
Best rugby memory: Winning my
first cap
Worst rugby memory: Giving away
penalty in extra time, which cost
Cardiff European Cup final victory.
Most embarrassing memory:
Forgetting my boots before my first
league match for Cardiff at Bridgend,
and having to borrow Nigel Walker's.

Wales (1996)

Last Season	5 caps	0 pts
Career	5 caps	0 pts

Caps (5): 1996 It, E, S, I, A(2TR)
Points Nil

Toughest opponent: Paul Wallace (Blackrock & Ireland)
Do you really want to be a full-time professional? Yes, most definitely.
How well has rugby handled move to professionalism? 5/10. There is a lack of
communication between unions and clubs. No one will tell us anything or sit
down and give us a straight answer.
Do you have a duty to entertain? Yes
Do you feel a loyalty to your club in this new era? Yes. Anyone will tell you that
Cardiff is a very hard club to leave.
Notable landmarks in rugby career: One of Wales' new breed last season,
Andrew was introduced to Test rugby by coach Kevin Bowring in the pre-Five
Nations match against Italy (16.1.96). Wales blooded five new boys, won
31–26 and were pretty satisfied – make that relieved, as they at one point
threatened to let slip one of the biggest leads in Test history. Andrew retained
his place for the visit to Twickenham a fortnight later, and indeed for the
Scottish and Irish games before, with Wales staring at a whitewash, Bowring
recalled Swansea's Christian Loader to the No.1 shirt for the finale against
France which Wales sneaked 16–15. Benefited at Test level from his club
partnership with hooker Jonathan Humphreys, with whom he helped Cardiff
reach the inaugural final of the Heineken European Cup, losing to Toulouse in

an exciting final. Andrew, who also turned out for Cardiff (and Wales A) against the touring Fijians, cites former club mate Mike Griffiths, now with Wasps, as being especially influential in his development.

Touchlines: Cricket

Lewis, E. W. Wales

Full name: Emyr Wyn Lewis
Nickname: Tarw (Welsh for 'bull')
Club: Cardiff
Position: Flanker, No 8
Height: 6ft 4in (1.93m)
Weight: 16st 8lb (101kg)
Occupation: Full-time player
Born: Carmarthen, 29.8.68
Family: Single
Former club: Carmarthen Athletic
International debut: Wales 21, Ireland 21, 1991
Five Nations debut: As above
Best rugby memories: Llanelli's defeat of 1992 Wallabies; winning first cap; Wales' 1994 Five Nations triumph.
Worst rugby memories: Losing to England (1994) when Grand Slam and Triple Crown was at stake; Wales' early elimination from 1995 World Cup.
Most embarrassing moment: Having my shorts totally ripped off me by Newbridge. They were 20 yards down the pitch and I had a bare bottom.
Toughest opponent: Dean Richards (Leicester & England)

Wales (1991)

Last Season	7 caps	0 pts
Career	41 caps	15 pts

Caps (41): **1991** I, F(a), A(a), F(b) wc-WS, Arg, A(b) **1992** I, F, S, A **1993** E, S, I, F, Z(1,2), Na, J, C **1994** S, I, F, E wc(q)-P, Sp. Fj, WS wc(q)-R, It. SA **1995** E, S, I(a) wc-J, I(b) **1996** It, E, S, I, F
Points (15 – 3t): **1993** Na(2t), J(1t)

Serious injuries: 1993/94 was a nightmare season – suspected broken back vs Pontypool (lost all feeling in feet and arms); strained knee ligaments vs England; popped rib cartilage.

Do you really want to be a full-time professional? Yes

How well has rugby handled move to professionalism? 4/10. A pretty poor effort by the authorities.

Do you have a duty to entertain? Yes, and referees too – they must weed the cheats out.

Do you feel a loyalty to your club in this new era? Yes – Cardiff somehow commands loyalty. A lot of players have had obscene amounts of money thrown at them by rival clubs, but most have stayed put.

Notable landmarks in rugby career: Joined Cardiff in 1994/95 and helped new team mates to Heineken League title. It was a bright moment in a fairly dismal season, as Wales were humbled in Five Nations and World Cup, and Emyr looked a shadow of his former international self, being dropped for the New Zealand game (Johannesburg, 31.5.95). Last season was better, though, as Cardiff surged to the inaugural European Cup final, and Wales, despite only winning once in the 1996 Five Nations series, were rejuvenated under new coach Kevin Bowring. Emyr discovered the art of Test try-scoring in 1993/94. After 17 internationals without crossing goal line, he bagged a try brace in Wales' 38–23 win against Namibia (Windhoek, 5.6.93) and added a third as Wales crushed Japan 55–5 (Cardiff, 16.10.93). He played at No.8 that day, as he also did against Canada (10.11.93), but was moved to blindside flanker for 1994 Five Nations Championship to accomodate Scott Quinnell at base of pack. Wales' 1991/92 Player-of-the-Year also figured in Llanelli's 13–9 defeat of the touring Wallabies at Stradey (14.11.92) and in their 1992/93 League and Cup double. In the latter case, victory over Neath in the Swalec final was due to him, an improbable hero, as he dropped a late goal to clinch victory. Missed playing for Welsh Schools because he was too old by two days. Could not play for Wales Youth either because still at school, but on leaving represented Wales at Under-20, Under-21 and B before graduating to senior level. Emerged from disastrous 1991 (tour to Australia and World Cup) with reputation enhanced. Shared in a hat-trick of Cup wins with Llanelli in 1990/91 (scoring a try in defeat of Pontypool), 1991/92 and 1992/93.

Touchlines: fishing (river spinning), shooting

A disconsolate Emyr Lewis after Wales had been
pipped to the post by Scotland in Cardiff.

Little, J. S.   Australia

Full name: Jason Sidney Little
State: Queensland
Club: Southern Districts
Position: Centre
Height: 6ft 1in (1.86m)
Weight: 14st 12lb (90kg)
Occupation: Marketing manager, Queensland Cotton Corporation
Born: 26.8.70
International debut: France 15, Australia 32, 1989
Best rugby memory: Test debut vs France
Worst rugby memory: Breaking ankle vs United States prior to 1990 New Zealand tour.
Most embarrassing moment: Accused of enhancing a potential moustache whilst playing in Japan.
Most respected opponent: Frank Bunce (North Harbour & New Zealand)
Other sporting achievements: Limited!
Notable landmarks in rugby career: Having recaptured full fitness and his berth in Wallaby midfield after horrific knee injury in 1994, Jason suffered a freak injury last summer, breaking his collarbone as he tried to put on a shirt. It was obviously one hell of a shirt, as he was ruled out for

Australia (1989)

Last Season	5 caps	0 pts
Career	38 caps	47 pts

Caps (38): 1989 F(1,2) 1990 F(1,2,3), US 1991 W(a), E(a), NZ(a1,a2). wc-Arg, W(b), I, NZ(b), E(b) 1992 NZ(1,2,3), SA, I, W 1993 T, NZ, SA(1,2,3), C, F(1,2) 1994 WS, NZ 1995 Arg(1,2) wc-SA, C, E. NZ(1,2)

Points (47 – 10t): 1990 F(2:1t), US(1t) 1991 W(a:1t) 1992 I(1t) 1993 T(1t), SA(2:2t) 1994 WS(2t), NZ(1t)

five months. Had made three appearances in 1995 World Cup, and then started both the Bledisloe Cup Tests against New Zealand before helping Queensland to the semi-finals of the 1996 Super-12 tournament. It had been in the final of the Super-10s (beat Natal 21–10, 14.5.94) the previous year that he had suffered his knee ligament injury. Returned in time for Western Samoa's trip to Sydney, scoring two tries in 73–3 win (6.8.94), and followed up with a first-minute try in the 20–16 Bledisloe Cup defeat of New Zealand (Sydney, 17.8.94). That got the Rugby League agents back on his tail, and they pestered him thereafter. Partnered Danny Herbert in Wallaby midfield until club and state colleague Tim Horan returned from the same sort of knee injury, suffered similarly in the 1994 Super-10 final. Jason's rise to prominence was helped in no small measure by a strong showing for Australia Under-17s in their 16–3 win over New Zealand in 1987. Two years later he was in Britain with the Emerging Wallabies – playing in the 12–12 draw with England B at Wasps – and the same year he broke into the Test side at Strasbourg in the first match against France during a Wallabies tour which also took in Canada. Featured in the 1991 World Cup final at Twickenham, and played an equally full role in the 1992 Bledisloe Cup triumph over holders New Zealand. Jason, who was reared in the Darling Downs region of Queensland, was an ever-present in the 1992 Wallabies XV, scoring his fourth Test try in the 42–17 rout of Ireland in Dublin, and also fitting in tour appearances against northern Transvaal, Leinster, Ulster (one try), Swansea, Neath (one try), Llanelli and the Barbarians. Retained centre berth throughout 1993, scoring tries against Tonga and South Africa (two in vital second Test at Ballymore).

Touchlines: golf, movies, reading

Little, W. K. New Zealand

Full name: Walter Kenneth Little
Province: North Harbour
Club: Glenfield
Position: Centre, wing, outside-half
Height: 5ft 10 ½ in (1.79m)
Weight: 12st (76kg)
Occupation: Brewery technician, Lion Breweries
Born: Takapuna, 14.10.69
Family: Single, two children
Former province: Auckland
International debut: New Zealand 31, Scotland 16, 1990
Notable landmarks in rugby career: Made brilliant return from medial ligament injury at end of 1994, playing a starring role in New Zealand's narrow Bledisloe Cup loss to Australia (Sydney, 17.8.94). From there Walter lit up the All Black midfield at the World Cup with his straight lines of elusive running. It was his break that set up New Zealand's crucial second try in their stunning semi-final defeat of England (Cape Town, 18.6.95), having dismantled Scotland with two tries in Pretoria the previous weekend. Did much the same to Italy during the All Blacks' 70–6 post-World Cup romp in Bologna, scoring another two tries before having problems with a drug test and not returning to the international arena until the second Test versus Scotland (Auckland, 22.6.96). Walter is the Mr Versatile in the Kiwi setup, having appeared at outside-half, centre and wing

in consecutive Tests in 1993. He was seen as the heir apparent to Grant Fox's No.10 jersey until the Auckland man decided his career was far from over. When Fox was dropped after New Zealand's first test beating at the hands of the World XV, Walter moved from centre into the vacant half-back berth and guided the team to a centenary series win. He retained his job description for the 2–0 series defeat of Ireland before being selected again at centre for the

New Zealand (1990)		
Last Season	11 caps	25 pts
Career	37 caps	34 pts

Caps (37): **1990** S(1,2), A(1,2,3), F(1,2) **1991** Arg(1,2), A(a1). wc-It, S **1992** Wd(1,2,3), I(1,2), A(1,2,3), SA **1993** BL(1), WS(R) **1994** SA(2R), A **1995** C wc-I, W, S, E, SA. A(1,2), It, F(1,2) **1996** S(2)

Points (34 – 7t): **1991** wc-S(1t) **1992** A(3:1t) **1995** wc-W(1t), S(2t). It(2t)

tour of Australia and South Africa as Fox returned to conduct affairs at first-five. His excellent 1992 was sandwiched in between two relatively disappointing years. In 1991 he was replaced in the Test side by Bernie McCahill, following the 21–12 Bledisloe Cup loss to Australia, after a run of ten consecutive Tests. And in 1993 a last-minute injury in the first Test defeat of the British Lions effectively put him out of contention for the rest of the season, including the tour to Britain. Indeed, the UK has not been the happiest of hunting grounds for Walter, who made only two appearances in the 1991 World Cup, scoring the winning try as the All Blacks clinched third place in Cardiff at the expense of Scotland, whom he had come up against on his international debut at Dunedin in 1990. A year earlier, as the youngest member of the touring party to Wales and Ireland, 20-year-old Walter did not make the Test side, though he was picked for bench duties at Cardiff and featured against the Barbarians at Twickenham.

France centre Stephane Glas in dazzling form during the record 45–10 defeat of Ireland in Paris.

Llewellyn, G. O. — Wales

Full name: Gareth Owen Llewellyn
Club: Harlequins
Position: Lock
Height: 6ft 6in (1.98m)
Weight: 16st 8lb (105kg)
Occupation: To be decided
Born: Cardiff, 27.2.69
Family: Mara (wife)
Family links with rugby: Brother (Glyn) plays for Wasps and Wales; father (David), who was in the Army with Will Carling's dad, is a qualified WRU coach.
Former clubs: Llanharan, Neath
International debut: Wales 9, New Zealand 34, 1989
Five Nations debut: England 34, Wales 6, 1990
Best rugby memory: Winning the 1995/96 Heineken League with Neath
Worst rugby memory: Thrice being dropped by Wales
Most embarrassing moment: Almost tripping over when running out at Cardiff for first cap.
Toughest opponent: John Eales (Queensland & Australia)
Do you really want to be a full-time professional? Yes

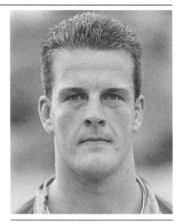

Wales (1989)		
Last Season	10 caps	5 pts
Career	47 caps	24 pts

Caps (47): **1989** NZ **1990** E, S, I **1991** E, S, A(a:R) **1992** I, F, E, S, A **1993** E, S, I, F, Z(1,2), Na, J, C **1994** S, I, F, E. wc(q)-P, Sp. C, T, WS wc-R, It. SA **1995** F, E, S, I(a) wc-J, NZ, I(b) **1996** It, E, S, I, F, A(1,2)
Points (24 – 5t): **1990** I(1t) **1993** Z(2:2t) **1994** wc(q)-P(1t) **1996** A(1:1t)

How well has rugby handled move to professionalism? 7/10. We're going in the right direction and I'm looking forward to a much faster game in 1996/97.
Do you have a duty to entertain? It's not so much a duty as a desire.
Do you feel a loyalty to your club in this new era? Not really. It's every man for himself now.
Notable landmarks in rugby career: Wales' most-capped lock, who left Neath for Harlequins last summer, but not before the Welsh All Blacks had won the most exciting league title race imaginable (by two tries). It was a well-deserved success for Gareth, who has toiled selflessly for club and country with little team reward in recent seasons. Captained Wales three times in 1994/95 (vs Italy, South Africa and France) after Ieuan Evans suffered his horrendous ankle injury. Had previously skippered Wales on 1993 tour to Zimbabwe and Namibia, where he played in all three Tests (scoring two tries in 42–13 second

359

Test defeat of Zimbabwe in Harare). The Neath skipper's performance had been central in the famous 10–9 victory over England (Cardiff, 6.2.93), and his lineout exploits in particular took him to the threshold of Lions selection. To his credit, did not let his standards slip one iota in 1993/94, playing in all eight internationals and captaining side with great distinction in Wales' glorious 24–15 defeat of France (Cardiff, 19.2.94). Added a fourth international try in Wales' 102–11 World Cup qualifying rout of Portugal (Lisbon, 17.5.94). Capped three times by Wales Youth. Toured New Zealand with Welsh Under-19 team (1987), playing at No.8. Also played for Crawshays and Barbarians. Represented Wales against England and Scotland in 1990/91 before losing place to Paul Arnold. Has previously partnered brother Glyn in second row both for Neath and Wales. Toured Australia with Wales in 1991, coming on as a 20th-minute replacement for Phil Davies in 6–63 Test defeat to Wallabies. Omitted from Wales' World Cup squad in 1991, but recalled to side for 1992 Five Nations Championship and has remained there ever since.
Touchlines: Golf, squash, weights

Loader, C. D. — Wales

Full name: Christian David Loader
Club: Swansea
Position: Loosehead prop
Height: 5ft 11in (1.80m)
Weight: 16st 7lb (105kg)
Born: 26.10.73
Family: Single
International debut: South Africa 40, Wales 11, 1995
Five Nations debut: Wales 16, France 15, 1996
Best rugby memory: Beating France in Cardiff on my Five Nations debut
Worst rugby memory: Getting injured and losing my Wales place
Notable landmarks in rugby career: There is nothing quite like a baptism of fire to test a player's mettle, and Christian certainly had that when he was thrown into the Ellis Park cauldron (2.9.95) against the world champion Springboks. Three months earlier Wales had been humiliated in the World Cup while the Boks had won the tournament. Anyway, both

Wales (1995)

Last Season	5 caps	0 pts
Career	5 caps	0 pts

Caps (5): **1995** SA, Fj **1996** F, A(1,2)
Points Nil

Wales and Christian gave good accounts of themselves, and although South Africa ran out emphatic 40–11 winners, Welsh pride was more than partially restored. After he had kept his place for the 19–15 defeat of Fiji at Cardiff (11.11.95), injury robbed Christian of his place for the next Test against Italy. Cardiff rival Andrew Lewis came in, and Christian was unable to dislodge him until the final round of Five Nations matches (16.3.96). The occasion was well worth the wait, however, as winless Wales upset the formbook to beat France 16–15 on a sea of emotion at the National Stadium. A former captain of Wales Schools at Under-16 and Under-18 levels, he made his debut for Swansea in their final match of the 1993/94 season. The following season he helped the All Whites win the Welsh Cup before, in 1995/96, playing a full part in their march to the semi-finals of the inaugural Heineken European Cup – a campaign which ended at Toulouse, the eventual winners. Continued his climb up the representative ladder, taking in the Under-19s, captaining Wales Under-21s on seven occasions and then, last season, graduating to the A-team.

Loe, R. W. New Zealand

Full name: Richard Wyllie Loe
Club: Frazer-Tech
Province: Canterbury
Position: Prop
Height: 6ft 1in (1.85m)
Weight: 17st (108kg)
Occupation: Farmer
Born: Christchurch, 6.4.60
Family: Felicity (wife) and Jessica (daughter)
Family links with rugby: Nephew of former New Zealand coach Alex 'Grizz' Wyllie
Former club/provinces: Lyon (France), Marlborough, Waikato
International debut: New Zealand 70, Italy 6, 1987
Notable landmarks in rugby career:
Returned to international rugby in 1994 after six-month ban, incurred for eye-gouging Otago's New Zealand fullback Greg Cooper. Proved how effective a performer he *can* be by roaming ever-present through New Zealand's 1994 campaign and making three appearances in last summer's World Cup, coming on as replacement for Craig Dowd in the final (Johannesburg, 24.6.95). That outing made him the most-capped All Black prop, surpassing Steve McDowell (46: 1985–92), and he then added number 48 as a replacement in the 37–12 second Test defeat of France (Paris, 18.11.95). Prior to suspension, Richard had

successfully adapted to the loosehead propping role, after more than 50 All Black outings and 34 Tests on the other side, but seriously incurred the wrath of Australia during the 1992 Bledisloe Cup series. During the second Test Richard was seen to break Wallaby match-winning wing Paul Carozza's nose with an elbow smash, having already been accused of inflicting damage to Sam Scott-Young's head in the first Test. A member of the world's most-capped front-row combination (with McDowell and Fitzpatrick), his

New Zealand (1987)		
Last Season	4 caps	5 pts
Career	48 caps	25 pts

Caps (48): **1987** wc-It, Arg **1988** W(1,2), A(1,2,3) **1989** F(1,2), Arg(1,2), A, W, I **1990** S(1,2), A(1,2,3), F(1,2) **1991** Arg(1,2), A(a1,a2). wc-E,It, C, A(b),S **1992** Wd(1,2,3), I(1), A(1,2,3), SA **1994** F(1,2), SA(1,2,3), A **1995** wc-J, S, SA(R). F(2R)

Points (25 – 6t): **1989** A(1t) **1990** S(2:1t) **1992** Wd(2:2t), Wd(3:1t) **1995** wc-J(1t)

international career began out of the blue in 1986 when he was recruited from Lyon, where he was playing club rugby, to bolster an injury-plagued All Blacks touring side in France. His test debut came the following year in the 1987 World Cup rout of Italy, and in the ensuing tour of Japan he succeeded John Drake as regular tighthead. Played for centenary Barbarians against England in 1990, and in eight of New Zealand's nine Tests in 1992, the exception being the second match against Ireland when the calf muscle he had aggravated in the Dunedin opener failed to recover in time to prevent Olo Brown taking over. The highlight of his season was his two-try display in the second Test victory over the World XV.

Wales fullback Justin Thomas tackles Scotland replacement Kenny Logan in Cardiff, where the visitors triumphed 16–14.

Logan, K. M.   Scotland

Full name: Kenneth (Kenny)
McKerrow Logan
Nickname: Serge
Club: Stirling County
Position: Wing, fullback
Height: 6ft 1in (1.85m)
Weight: 13st 9lb (82kg)
Occupation: Farmer, James Logan
and Co.
Born: 3.4.72, Stirling
Family: Single
International debut: Australia 37,
Scotland 13, 1992
Five Nations debut: England 26,
Scotland 12, 1993
Best rugby memory: First cap and
winning 1994/95 Scottish League
title with Stirling
Worst rugby memory: Getting
dropped in 1995/96
Most embarrassing moment: Gregor
Townsend dummying me in the
Gala–Stirling game. Every time he is
shown on TV, that moment is
replayed.
Biggest influence on career: Hamish
Logan (cousin), who played ten
years for West of Scotland.

Scotland (1993)

Last Season	8 caps	10 pts
Career	24 caps	20 pts

Caps (24): **1992** A(2) **1993** E(R),
NZ(TR) **1994** W, E, I, F, Arg(1,2),
SA **1995** C, I, F, W, E, R wc-IC, T,
F, NZ. WS **1996** W(R), NZ(1,2)
Points (20 – 4t): **1994** Arg(2:1t) **1995**
R(1t) wc-IC(2t)

Toughest opponent: Va'aiga Tuigamala (ex-New Zealand)
Do you really want to be a full-time professional? Yes
How well has rugby handled move to professionalism? 1/10. It has been
farcical. Authorities knew professionalism was coming, but had nothing ready.
Consequently, they tried to do in one year what should have taken three years.
Do you have a duty to entertain? Yes – there were 75,000 at the 1996 Pilkington
Cup final picking their noses. If you want fans to pay you must put on a show.
Do you feel a loyalty to your club in this new era? Yes, providing the SRU gets
the loyalty payments sorted out.
Other sporting claims to fame: Turned down soccer trials (goalkeeper) with
Dundee United and Hearts to pursue a rugby career.
Notable landmarks in rugby career: Missed most of the fun in 1995/96 as
unfancied Scotland won three of their four Five Nations matches. Kenny, who
had played against Western Samoa in the season-opener, was dropped after
Scotland's stunning defeat by Italy in Rieti (6.1.96), and did not reappear until

the summer tour of New Zealand, save for the second half against Wales (Cardiff, 17.2.96), when he laid the foundations for Scotland's 16–14 win. Had emerged in 1994/95 as one of Scotland's outstanding players, three years after becoming the first Stirling County player to be capped when selected at fullback in place of the injured Gavin Hastings for 13–37 second Test defeat by Australia (Brisbane, 21.6.92). Kenny had to wait nine internationals for his first try, in the 17–19 loss to Argentina (Buenos Aires, 11.6.94). He added three more in 1995 – two in Scotland's 89–0 World Cup opening romp against Cote d'Ivoire (Rustenburg, 26.5.95) – in addition to helping Stirling win their first Scottish League title. Had played in seven of the eight games (four as wing, three as fullback) on Scotland's 1992 tour of Oz (picked before playing in any national trial), and thoroughly enjoyed the experience, especially the acclaim which followed his try/match-saving tackle on Paul Carozza in the 15–15 draw with Queensland. Cemented his place in Scotland side in 1993/94, playing in all five games, although only as a temporary replacement (again for Gavin) against New Zealand. Represented Scotland Under-18, Under-19 (fullback vs 1991 Aussie Schools) and Under-21 level, and captained Glasgow to 1991/92 Under-21 Championship. Won three Scotland A caps during 1992/93 campaign (scoring try in each game against Spain, Ireland and France), and again in 1993/94. Toured with Scotland to Fiji, Tonga and Western Samoa (1993), Argentina (1994), South Africa (1995) and New Zealand (1996).

Touchlines: Squash, weights, running 400-acre farm, golf (handicap 20)

Lomu, J.   New Zealand

Full name: Jonah Lomu
Province: Counties/Auckland Blues
Position: Wing
Height: 6ft 5in (1.95m)
Weight: 19st (116kg)
Occupation: Bank officer, ASB Bank of New Zealand
Born: Mangere, 12.5.73
Family: Married
International debut: New Zealand 8, France 22, 1994
Notable landmarks in rugby career: A giant of a man, a giant of a rugby player, Jonah is unquestionably the sport's biggest star and, accordingly, its biggest earner. Having resisted the temptation to move to Rugby League or American Football ($6 million bid from Dallas Cowboys) after the 1995

World Cup, in which he finished joint top try-scorer (with seven) and unforgettably smashed four past England in a 45–29 semi-final rout (Cape Town, 18.6.95), Jonah was handed a contract by the NZRFU which, when the endorsements are added, is reckoned to be worth a cool NZ$2 million per annum. His record suggests he is worth it. By the end of 1995 he had played 12 times for New Zealand and scored 12 tries. There isn't a defence in world rugby which doesn't quake at the prospect of him visiting their neighbourhood. At 6ft 5in and 19st (making him the biggest-ever All Black back), having weighed a colossal 11lb at birth, he could have played in just about any position save hooker. But a 100-metres time of 10.7 seconds clinched a wing berth in the New Zealand side in only his second season playing the position. An athlete *par excellence,* he holds athletics records at home in sprint, hurdles, shot and discus, and became the youngest-ever capped All Black when he made his debut in Christchurch against France (26.6.94) aged 19 years and six weeks. Rugby League wanted him, and so too did American Football in the form of the Dallas Cowboys, who were willing to turn him into a $6 million man. A juggernaut presence in attack – first shown in his 70-yard run through four tackles during an awesome two-try display against Ireland (and subsequently vs Scotland and England) – he is not quite so impressive in defence, and was exposed by France during the All Blacks' stunning two-Test whitewash in 1994. Repaired his reputation with a brilliant campaign at the Hong Kong Sevens, where he was player of the tournament in New Zealand's victory. Jonah played Rugby League as a schoolboy, and didn't switch codes until his fourth year at school, when he played at flanker. Helped attract a capacity 13,000 crowd to Llanelli when he played in Ieuan Evans' testimonial (21.11.95) before inspiring Auckland Blues to a dazzling triumph in the 1996 Super-12 tournament, beating Natal in the final at Eden Park.

New Zealand (1994)

Last Season	12 caps	65 pts
Career	14 caps	65 pts

Caps (14): **1994** F(1,2) **1995** wc-I, W, S, SA. A(1,2), It, F(1,2) **1996** WS, S(1)

Points (65 – 13t): **1995** wc-I(2t), S(1t), E(4t). A(1:1t), A(2:1t), It(2t), F(2:1t) **1996** S(1:1t)

McBride, W. D.   Ireland

Full name: William Denis McBride
Club: Malone
Position: Flanker
Height: 5ft 11in (1.80m)
Weight: 13st 10lb (87kg)
Occupation: Mechanical engineer, Ballylumford Power Ltd
Born: Belfast, 9.9.64
Family: Catrina (wife), Stephanie Denise (daughter)
Family links with rugby: Brother also plays
Former club: Queen's University, Belfast
International debut: Ireland 9, Wales 12, 1988
Five Nations debut: As above
Best rugby memories: Beating England in 1993 and 1994
Worst rugby memory: Second half of Ireland's 3–35 defeat by England in 1988, when we conceded 35 points without reply.
Most embarrassing memory: Ireland vs England (1988)
Toughest opponent: David Wilson (Queensland & Australia)
Other sporting claim to fame: Completed 1982 Belfast City Marathon

Ireland (1988)		
Last Season	6 caps	10 pts
Career	25 caps	18 pts

Caps (25): 1988 W, E, WS, It 1989 S 1990 F, W,Arg 1993 S, F, W, E, R 1994 W, E, S, A(1R) 1995 S, F(a) wc-NZ, W(b), F(b). Fj(R) 1996 W, E

Points (18 – 4t): 1988 WS(1t) 1990 W(1t) 1995 wc-NZ(1t), W(b:1t)

Notable landmarks in rugby career: Outstanding World Cup displays against New Zealand and Wales, each featuring tries, rubbished a home-based claim that Denis was an 'irrelevance' to Test rugby. His score against Wales (Jo'burg, 4.6.95) came after a lineout take and a 40-yard burst through the Welsh defence. It knocked Wales out of the tournament. Irrelevant eh?! Took his tally to 25 caps in 1995/96, although he had to wait until the post-Paris clearout to regaining his starting berth. With Jeremy Davidson moving to lock and David Corkery to blindside, Denis came in for the last two engagements against Wales and England. Still recalls with dread his ill-fated tour to New Zealand in 1992, when he returned after just one game – the victim of a freak training accident when he broke a toe after catching a stud in Kelvin Leahy. But Denis is nothing if not a survivor. He returned to the Test arena, after a three-year gap, in the 1993 Five Nations Championship. First representative honours came for Ulster and Irish Schools sides in 1983. Graduated to Ulster Under-20s and Combined

Provinces Under-21s in 1984/85 before making his senior Ulster bow against Connacht in 1987. Having impressed on summer tour to France, which had featured a 19–18 non-cap victory against the French, he was given his Test debut in the 1988 Championship against Wales. Collected his first try third time out against Western Samoa, but lost his place after win over Italy. In and out of favour for the next four years before firmly taking possession of the No.7 jersey in 1992/93.

Touchlines: Athletics (400 metres)

McKenzie, E. J. A. Australia

Full name: Ewen James Andrew McKenzie
State: New South Wales
Clubs: Randwick, Paris University
Position: Tighthead prop
Height: 6ft (1.82m)
Weight: 18st 5lb (112kg)
Occupation: Project manager
Born: 21.6.65
Family: Sally (wife)
Former clubs: Harlequins (Melbourne, 1984),
International debut: France 9, Australia 21, 1990
Best rugby memories: Beating NZ in 1991 World cup semi-final; beating NZ in Wellington (1990); beating South Africa (1992); winning Bledisloe Cup (1992).
Worst rugby memories: Losing Grand Final to Parramatta (1986); missing selection for 1986 Scotland Test; being dropped by NSW selectors in 1989.
Most embarrassing moment: Tony Daly and I doing our fat-percentage tests prior to the 1991 World Cup. (I should also mention that Phil Kearns managed, with Tony Daly alongside, to lose a tighthead in a sixth-grade trial match in 1993 – just in case they forget to mention it!)

Australia (1990)

Last Season	14 caps	0 pts
Career	47 caps	9 pts

Caps (47): **1990** F(1,2,3), US, NZ(1,2,3) **1991** W(a),E (a), NZ(a1,a2). wc-Arg, W(b), I, NZ(b), E(b). **1992** S(1,2), NZ(1,2,3), SA, I, W **1993** T, NZ, SA(1,2,3), C, F(1,2) **1994** I(1,2), It(1,2), WS, NZ **1995** Arg(1,2) wc-SA,C(R), R, E. NZ(2) **1996** W(1,2)

Points (9 -- 2t): **1990** US(1t) **1992** I(1t)

Most respected opponents: Tony Daly (entertainer); Peter Fatialofa (story-telling); Frederico Mendez (scrummaging); Steve McDowell (athleticism);

David Sole (demeanor/ornament to the position); Olo Brown (dancing); Jeff Probyn (drinking games); Pascal Ondarts/Geoff Didier (singing); Jason Leonard (most like to have a drink with).

Serious injuries: Posterior cruciate tear left knee (1987); medial ligament strain (1989); numerous other arthritis-causing ailments that medicine has been unable to cure.

Suggestions to improve rugby: Exotic sevens tournament for tight-five only; more Barbarian-type fixtures; regular Northern vs Southern Hemisphere fixtures; reduce dropped goal value to one point; universal trial by video; standardised elegibility for national teams; improve refereeing standards; more efforts to improve situation for wives and children (they suffer most from the effects of time given up to rugby).

Notable landmarks in rugby career: Australia's most-capped prop (47), having succeeded Andy McIntyre (38 caps: 1982–89) in the 53–7 first Test defeat of Argentina (Brisbane, 29.4.95). Ever-present in Wallaby No.3 jersey through 1995 save for the first Test Bledisloe Cup loss to New Zealand (Auckland, 22.7.95), when Dan Crowley was given a go. The first born-and-bred Victorian since 1932 to represent Australia, Ewen moved to Sydney club Randwick in 1985 to further his rugby career, and five years later was rewarded with his first cap on the tour to France. In the intervening period he built one of the most respected front-row partnerships in world rugby with fellow New South Walians Phil Kearns and Tony Daly. Indeed, the trio hold the record for a front-row combination of 36 Tests together. A measure of the esteem in which he is held is that the World XV included him in their side to play the All Blacks in the 1992 Centenary Series, a year after he had picked up a World Cup winner's medal at Twickenham. Scored his second international try in the 42–17 win over Ireland in Dublin in 1992, and was awarded the captaincy during 1993 in the absence of Michael Lynagh. Ewen skippered the Wallabies in the 25–10 Bledisloe Cup loss to New Zealand and, rather more memorably, throughout home-series win over South Africa. Lynagh (now retired) returned thereafter.

Touchlines: Trying to find ways to spend more time with my wife.

*Hooker Kevin McKenzie does a triumphant jig
after scoring Scotland's first try in Dublin.*

McKenzie, K. D.   Scotland

Full name: Kevin Duncan McKenzie
Club: Stirling County
Position: Hooker
Height: 5ft 6in (1.68m)
Weight: 14st 10lb (93kg)
Occupation: Office manager, Taylor Maxwell Timber Ltd
Born: Stirling, 22.1.68
Family: Fiona (wife)
International debut: Argentina 16, Scotland 15, 1994
Five Nations debut: Ireland 10, Scotland 16, 1996
Best rugby memory: Scoring try on Five Nations debut
Worst rugby memory: Destroying my knee against Melrose last season and missing Western Samoa game.
Most embarrassing memory: Dressing up as William Wallace for *Glasgow Evening Times* photo prior to 1996 Calcutta Cup match – never again!
Toughest opponent: Sean Fitzpatrick (Auckland & New Zealand)

Scotland (1994)

Last Season	7 caps	5 pts
Career	10 caps	5 pts

Caps (10): **1994** Arg(1,2) **1995** R wc-IC **1996** I, F, W, E, NZ(1,2)
Points (5 – 1t): **1996** I(1t)

Do you really want to be a full-time professional? No, unless rugby can improve drastically on its current levels of remuneration.
How well has rugby handled move to professionalism? 4/10. Scottish club rugby is a shambles.
Do you have a duty to entertain? No, because I don't consider myself to be a professional player.
Do you feel a loyalty to your club in this new era? Yes, I've been with Stirling since I was 8. But our careers are short, and I understand others wanting to make of them what they can. I think an SRU loyalty payment would be useful.
Other sporting claim to fame: 12-handicap golfer
Notable landmarks in rugby career: Captain of Scotland A side that inflicted last-gasp 17–15 defeat on touring Springboks (Melrose, 9.11.94) thanks to dropped goal from fly-half Duncan Hodge, Kevin completed a notable double over touring sides in 1995/96 when he led North & Midlands to a 43–9 victory over Western Samoa (Perth, 14.11.95). A dogged competitor, Kevin opened his points-scoring account for Scotland in the 1996 Five Nations opener against Ireland (Dublin, 20.1.96), scoring the first of the visitors' two tries as they upset the formbook. Maintained his place throughout the championship and then

369

toured to New Zealand last summer. Kevin's loyalty and commitment to the sport had been suitably rewarded in 1994/95 – both on the home front, with Stirling County winning its first Scottish League title, and internationally. Five years after making his Scotland B debut in the 22–22 draw with Ireland, he was selected to tour Argentina (1994) and played in both Tests, his debut coming in Buenos Aires on 4 June. Reluctantly surrendered No.2 jersey to Heriot's FP rival Kenny Milne on return, but won it back towards the end of the season, for 49–16 defeat of Romania (Murrayfield, 22.4.95) and for the 89–0 World Cup opener against Cote d'Ivoire (Rustenburg, 26.5.95). In between, he appeared in the 62–7 non-cap defeat of Spain (Madrid, 6.5.95). Has played for Scotland at every level from Schools (1985, captaining the side twice, vs Wales and England), Under-19, Under-21, B and A. Captained Glasgow in 1994/95 Inter-District Championship.

Touchlines: Golf, fitness and more fitness

McQuilkin, K. P. Ireland

Full name: Kurt Peter McQuilkin
Club: Bective Rangers
Position: Centre
Height: 5ft 10in (1.78m)
Weight: 14st (89kg)
Occupation: Development officer, IRFU
Born: Tekuiti, New Zealand, 6.4.66
Former clubs/provinces: Waitete, King Country, North Auckland, Consett
International debut: USA 18, Ireland 25, 1996
Five Nations debut: Ireland 10, Scotland 16, 1996
Notable landmarks in rugby career: Qualified for Ireland through the three-year residency clause after coming to the Emerald Isle in 1992 to visit his father Noel, who was coaching Bective Rangers. Kurt, an All Blacks triallist at out-half, liked what he found and decided to stay. Had previously spent two seasons

Ireland (1995)		
Last Season	3 caps	0 pts
Career	3 caps	0 pts

Caps (3): **1996** US, S, F
Points Nil

across the water in England playing for Consett. A player of considerable representative experience, having played 38 times for North Auckland and having appeared on 58 occasions for King Country, Kurt prospered in his new environment. He helped Leinster win the 1995/96 Inter-Provincial Championship grand slam, scoring a hat-trick of tries in the 42–26 defeat of the Exiles. He then helped Leinster reach the semi-finals of the first Heineken European Cup, before losing to Cardiff in Dublin. Along the way he did enough to get himself invited on Ireland's warm-weather trip to America. As it happened the weather was wet and freezing, but Kurt achieved his goal of gaining Test recognition in the 25–18 win over the US Eagles (Atlanta, 6.1.96). Kept his place for the first two matches of the Five Nations series, but two highly unsatisfactory defeats by Scotland and France led coach Murray Kidd (another Kiwi) to a drastic rethink of personnel: out went Kurt and in came Ulsterman Maurice Field.

Manu, D. Australia

Full name: Daniel Manu
State: New South Wales
Club: Eastwood
Position: Flanker
Height: 6ft 5in (1.96m)
Weight: 18st 2lb (115kg)
Occupation: Trainee, Coopers & Lybrand
Born: Tonga, 4.6.70
Former club/province: Noceto (It), Auckland (NZ)
International debut: Australia 42, Romania 3, 1995
Notable landmarks in rugby career: Like Willie Ofahengaue, Daniel is a Tongan who made a name for himself in New Zealand rugby before going to Australia. His career really took off in 1993 when, having played nine representative games for Kiwi giants Auckland, he moved to Sydney to play with the Eastwood club. His first state match in 1994, for the New South Wales Waratahs against Australian Capital Territory,

Australia (1995)		
Last Season	5 caps	5 pts
Career	5 caps	5 pts

Caps (5): **1995** wc-R(TR). NZ(1,2) **1996** W(1,2R)

Points (5 – 1t): **1996** W(1:1t)

was impressive indeed. Thus, when Troy Coker suffered an injury at the World Cup in South Africa the following year, Daniel was summoned and made his international debut as a temporary replacement for David Wilson at Stellenbosch (3.6.95). Romania were the outclassed opposition as Australia ran out 42–3 winners. On the bench against England in the quarter-finals, Daniel failed to get on and England won, so ending the Wallaby dream of retaining their crown. The big Tongan resumed his Test career in the Bledisloe Cup series the following month, returning to Auckland's Eden Park for his first full start (22.7.95). Sadly for him, New Zealand won 28–16, and whilst he retained his place for the second Test in Sydney (29.7.95), the All Blacks won that too (34–23) to clinch the series win. Began 1996 on tour in England with the Waratahs, scoring the visitors' only try in their 22–24 loss to England A at Leicester (31.1.96), before returning home to gain Wallaby selection against the touring Welsh. A try in the 56–25 first Test victory could not prevent him losing his place to Michael Brial for the second Test.

Mason, S. J. P. Ireland

Full name: Simon John Peter Mason
Club: Richmond
Position: Fullback
Height: 6ft 1in (1.85m)
Weight: 14st 4lb (91kg)
Occupation: Student of building and surveying
Born: Birkenhead, 22.10.73
Family: Single
Former clubs: Liverpool St Helens, Newcastle Gosforth, Orrell
International debut: Ireland 30, Wales 17, 1996
Five Nations debut: As above
Notable landmarks in rugby career: Signed last summer for big-spending Richmond, of English League Two, after his first season of Test rugby yielded 22 points in two Five Nations starts against Wales (2.3.96) and England (16.3.96). Simon, who did his cause considerable good when he starred for Orrell against Saracens in a televised league match on an otherwise blank Saturday,

Ireland (1996)		
Last Season	2 caps	22 pts
Career	2 caps	22 pts

Caps (2): 1996 W, E
Points (2 – 22: 2c, 6p): 1996 W(2c,2p), E(4p)

kicked ten points in the 30–17 defeat of Wales and landed four immaculate penalty goals at Twickenham where Ireland lost 15–28 to collect the Wooden Spoon. Three Irish grandparents had allowed Simon to initiate his representative career with the Irish Exiles, turning out for their Under-21 side in 1992 as a prelude to two seasons in the national age-group XV. Enhanced his reputation as a goalkicker during spells at Liverpool St Helens and Newcastle Gosforth and, having moved on to Orrell, broke into the Irish Students side in

Paris in January 1996. Unable to shift Jim Staples from the Irish Exiles' senior fullback slot yet, ironically, took over from him in the national side after the Irish captain suffered concussion in Paris.

Mehrtens, A.   New Zealand

Full name: Andrew Mehrtens
Province: Canterbury
Position: Fly-half
Height: 5ft 10½ in (1.79m)
Weight: 13st 9lb (82kg)
Occupation: Student
Born: Durban (SA), 28.4.73
Family: Single
Family links with rugby: Father Terry played for Junior All Blacks (1965); grandfather George played for All Blacks (1928).
International debut: New Zealand 73, Canada 7, 1995
Notable landmarks in rugby career: One of the stars of the World Cup, Andrew helped New Zealand sweep the Wallabies in the post-South Africa Bledisloe Cup series before a knee injury sustained in the 51–21 defeat of Italy A in Catania, Sicily, brought a premature end to his end-of-term tour of Italy and France. Still, 1995 was a wonderful year for the youngster, save for the dropped goal he missed two minutes from the end of the World Cup final which proved to be the difference between New Zealand winning and losing.

New Zealand (1995)

Last Season	10 caps	173 pts
Career	11 caps	201 pts

Caps (11): 1995 C wc-I, W, S, E, SA. A(1,2) **1996** WS, S(1,2)
Points (201 – 4t,41c,27p,6dg): **1995** C(1t, 7c,3p) wc-I(3c,4p), W(2c,4p,1dg), S(1t,6c,3p), E(3c,1p,1dg), SA(3p, 1dg). A(1:1c,5p,2dg), A(2:1t,3c, 1p) **1996** WS(5c,1p,1dg), S(1:1t,7c,1p), S(2:4c1p)

Made a record-breaking start to his Test career by bagging 28 points on his debut for the All Blacks against Canada (22.4.95). New Zealand ran out 73–7 winners, and he claimed one try, seven conversions and three penalty goals (previous best for a player making his international bow had been the 23 scored by fellow Kiwi Matthew Cooper against Ireland in 1992, though unfortunately for Andrew another All Black, Simon Culhane, bettered his record inside two months with 45 points on his debut vs Japan, 4.6.95.) Despite Andrew's wonderful start in Auckland (22.4.95), he arrived in South Africa, the country of his birth, virtually unknown. But he quickly rectified that, succeeding with seven kicks at goal (three conversions and four penalties) out of 10 attempts in the 43–19 defeat of Ireland (Johannesburg, 27.5.95). Next up, against Wales, also in Ellis Park, the former New Zealand Colt was the star of the show, turning in a prodigious tactical kicking display. He amassed 19 points, from two conversions, four penalties and a dropped goal, as New Zealand cruised to a 34–9 win. In New Zealand's 48–30 quarter-final defeat of Scotland he unleashed his electrifying pace to claim a try in his 23-point haul, and he added a further 12 in the semi-final win over England – a figure he matched in the final against the Springboks. Returned to the Test side for the 1996 series against Scotland. On the domestic stage Andrew, who had left South Africa for New Zealand aged 18 months, helped Canterbury win and retain the Ranfurly Shield, having made his provincial bow in 1993, and toured Britain with them in 1994/95 (scoring 63 points).

Merle, O. France

Full name: Olivier Merle
Nickname: Massif Central
Club: Grenoble
Position: Lock
Height: 6ft 6in (1.98m)
Weight: 20st (124kg)
Occupation: Rugby development officer with Isere Council
Born: Chamalieres, 14.11.65
Former clubs: Blanzat, Montferrand, Vichy
International debut: South Africa 20, France 20, 1993
Five Nations debut: France 35, Ireland 15, 1994
Notable landmarks in rugby career: A controversial figure, but an increasingly influential one in the French side, despite being ditched by Jean-Claud Skrela midway through the 1996 Five Nations series. Had bounced back from the one-match suspension which followed his head-butt on Wales prop Ricky Evans (Paris, 21.1.95), causing Evans to fall awkwardly and break his leg in two places, to play a full part in France's march to third place in the

France (1993)

Last Season	13 caps	0 pts
Career	29 caps	10 pts

Caps (29): **1993** SA(1,2), R(b), A(1,2)
1994 I, W, E, S, C(a), NZ(1,2), C(b) **1995** W, I(a), R wc-T, S(b), I(b), SA, E(b). It, R, Arg, NZ(1,2) **1996** E, S, R
Points (10 – 2t): **1993** R(b:1t) **1994** I(1t)

World Cup. He then turned in big performances as France won their third straight over the All Blacks (Toulouse, 11.11.95) before settling for a share of the series in Paris the following weekend. An extraordinary athletic specimen, Olivier only took up rugby five years ago, having been one of his country's most promising shot-putters. He boasts being able to achieve an 80cm standing jump in full gear, and is reputedly able to bench-press 180kg. If that's what he says, who are we to argue? Weighing in at an even 20 stones, and the owner of size-17 boots, Olivier's progress up rugby's representative ladder was swift. Joining Grenoble at the start of the 1992/93 season, he powered them to the French Club Championship final, where they lost 14–11 to Castres (Paris, 5.7.92), and he was promptly invited to bolster France's challenge in South Africa during the summer of 1993. The former lumberjack proved invaluable, playing in both Tests as the French won a series in the Republic for the first time since 1958. Thereafter he was a regular, playing in all of France's Test matches in 1993/94 – the shared series with world champions Australia, the 51–0 thrashing of Romania and the 1994 Five Nations Championship – before touring New Zealand and helping France to a historic 2–0 series win.

Moore, A. Pa. Wales

Full name: Andrew Paul Moore
Club: Swansea
Position: Lock
Height: 6ft 7in (2.00m)
Weight: 16st 7lb (105kg)
Born: 25.1.74
Family: Single
Family links with rugby: Brother (Stephen) plays for Swansea/Wales Under-21
International debut: South Africa 40, Wales 11, 1995
Five Nations debut: None
Serious injuries: Knee restructuring (1995/96)
Other sporting claims to fame: Goalkeeper for Wales Under-18
Notable landmarks in rugby career: Arguably Wales' most promising lock forward, Andrew was blooded in the post-World Cup Test against the world champion Springboks in Johannesburg (2.9.95). He initially pulled out of the tour as he had to

Wales (1995)		
Last Season	2 caps	0 pts
Career	2 caps	0 pts

Caps (2): **1995** SA(R), Fj
Points Nil

attend a family funeral, but was later brought back to replace the injured Greg Prosser in the squad. He still did not expect to play, in the same way as Derwyn Jones did not expect to be knocked out by a cowardly punch from behind by Kobus Wiese when the contest was still in its infancy. Thus Andrew entered the fray in only the fifth minute and relished the experience. A North Walian who followed his elder brother south to St Helens, having previously made a name for himself in football as an age-group goalkeeper for Wales, Andrew gained national rugby honours at Under-18, Under-19, Youth and Under-21 grades. Picked up his second full cap at Cardiff in the 19–15 defeat of Fiji (11.11.95), when he partnered a fit-again Derwyn Jones in the engine room. A bright future was delayed as he underwent knee reconstruction, but he is tipped as a man to watch in Wales colours in 1996/97

Touchlines: Football

Moore, A. Ph.   Wales

Full name: Andrew Philip Moore
Nickname: Eric
Club: Richmond
Position: Scrum-half
Height: 5ft 10in (1.78m)
Weight: 12st 10lb (81kg)
Occupation: Professional player
Born: 6.9.68
Family: Alex (wife), Jacob (son)
Former clubs: Oxford University, Bridgend, Cardiff
International debut: Wales 57, Japan 10, 1995
Five Nations debut: None
Best rugby memory: Winning first Welsh cap
Worst rugby memory: Being dropped before 1996 Five Nations
Most embarrassing memory: During my interview for Oxford University, I was taken for lunch by the Fellows and remarked how lovely the new potatoes were – they were water chestnuts.

Wales (1995)		
Last Season	4 caps	10 pts
Career	4 caps	10 pts

Caps (4): **1995** wc-J, SA, Fj **1996** It
Points (10 – 2t): **1995** wc-J(1t). Fj(1t)

Toughest opponent: Joost van der Westhuizen (Northern Transvaal & South Africa)

Do you really want to be a full-time professional? No – ideally part-time. I'd lose my brain just playing rugby. I've got to do something else as well.

How well has rugby handled move to professionalism? –10/10. One day amateur, the next day professional: it has been too black and white. Up until the very end of last season, no one had the first clue what was in store for 1996/97.

Do you have a duty to entertain? Yes, we're being paid to entertain. In business if you are headhunted and you fail to perform, you get the sack, you are out. The same applies to pro sport.

Do you feel a loyalty to your club in this new era? It's more pride than loyalty now. I felt a great pride in playing for Cardiff and it is a big gamble on my part to leave after nine years there.

Notable landmarks in rugby career: Another of Richmond's big-money recruits last summer, Andrew (nicknamed Eric because of his apparent similarity to Monsieur Cantona) is a player for the big occasion: he scored the winning try for Oxford University in the 1990 Varsity Match, gained the man-of-the-match award in Cardiff's Swalec Cup final defeat of Llanelli in 1994, and dropped the goal that beat Leinster in the 1995 European Cup semi-finals. For all that, and despite the fact that he skippered Wales Under-20s and scored Cardiff's only try in their 22–21 defeat of Fiji in 1995/96, the former Bridgend player was unable to stave off the challenge of Brewery Field rival Robert Howley on the international front. Having made his debut at the World Cup scoring a try in the 57–10 defeat of Japan (Bloemfontein, 27.5.95), Andy fitted in two more Tests before the year was out, claiming another try against Fiji (11.11.95). But after winning his fourth cap in the 31–26 defeat of Italy (Cardiff, 16.1.96), he was relegated in favour of Howley, who promptly proved to be the find of the season. It was a significant disappointment for a player who first represented his country at Under-15 and Under-19 levels, touring New Zealand with the latter in 1987. He also turned out on occasion for Welsh Students. Ended his nine-year association with Cardiff when he opted for English League Two rugby at Richmond along with club halfback partner Adrian Davies.

Touchlines: Golf, windsurfing

*England's Will Carling ships the ball as Wales scrum-half
Rob Howley envelops him at Twickenham.*

Mulder, J. C.   South Africa

Full name: Jacobus (Japie) Cornelius
Mulder
Province: Transvaal
Position: Centre
Height: 6ft ½ in (1.84m)
Weight: 14st 11lb (89kg)
Occupation: Self-employed
Born: 18.10.69
Family: Single
International debut: New Zealand
13, South Africa 9, 1994
Family links with rugby: Nephew of
former Springbok Boet Mulder
Notable landmarks in rugby career:
Partnered Hennie le Roux in South
Africa's 1995 World Cup-winning
midfield, turning out in the wins over
Australia (Cape Town, 25.5.95),
Western Samoa (Johannesburg,
10.6.95), France (Durban, 17.6.95)
and the never-to-be-forgotten 15–12
extra-time final vs New Zealand
(Johannesburg, 24.6.95). Completed
a great year, with tries in the wins
over Wales (Johannesburg, 2.9.95)
and Italy (Rome, 12.11.95). Had

South Africa (1994)

Last Season	12 caps	10 pts
Career	12 caps	15 pts

Caps (12): **1994** NZ(2,3), S, W **1995**
WS(a) wc-A, WS(b), F, NZ. W, It, E
Points (15 – 3t): **1994** S(1t) **1995** W(1t),

benefitted from the neck injury suffered by Natal rival Pieter Muller on 1994
tour to New Zealand, being called up as an emergency replacement and going
straight into the second Test. His strong tackling and equally powerful running
ensured his continued presence in the Springbok side, though he had to wait for
the 34–10 defeat of Scotland (Murrayfield, 19.11.94) for his first international
try, during an autumn tour in which he also appeared against Wales A, Llanelli,
Swansea and the Barbarians. Had emerged a player of substance in Britain the
previous year, whilst on tour with the South African Barbarians, for whom he
turned out in five matches, scoring tries vs Northampton and Ulster. Added
further touchdowns in New Zealand against Waikato (Hamilton, 16.7.94) and
Canterbury (2: Christchurch, 30.7.94). Transvaal's continued success (1993/
94 Currie Cup winners) kept Japie in the public eye, and after starting 1995 in
the side against Western Samoa (won 60–8) he was set fair for World Cup glory.

Mustoe, L.   Wales

Full name: Lyndon Mustoe
Club: Cardiff
Position: Tighthead prop
Height: 6ft 1in (1.85m)
Weight: 17st (108kg)
Occupation: Bricklayer
Born: 30.1.69
International debut: Wales 19, Fiji 15, 1995
Five Nations debut: None
Former clubs: Chepstow, Pontypool
Best rugby memory: Winning first cap
Notable landmarks in rugby career: When you have a pillar like John Davies holding up the national scrum, life can get pretty frustrating for wannabee tightheads. Lyndon comes into this category, although he was more fortunate than most, getting a run out against the touring Fijians (Cardiff, 11.11.95) after Davies had been forced to withdraw through injury. JD returned there-

Wales (1995)

Last Season	3 caps	0 pts
Career	3 caps	0 pts

Caps (3): **1995** Fj **1996** A(1R,2)
Points Nil

after, relegating Lyndon to the replacements bench for the duration of the 1996 Five Nations series before he gained his second cap as a 69th-minute replacement for you-know-who in the first Test vs Australia 'down under' last summer. The match was played at Ballymore in Brisbane (8.6.96), and Wales went down 25–56. Lyndon had started life playing for Chepstow, the town in which he was educated, before graduating to Pontypool to study further the art of front-row play. A member of Wales squads at Youth, Under-19 and Under-20 levels, he finally got a game for the Under-21s, against Scotland (1990). That same year he turned out for Wales A vs Holland, and has since taken his A cap tally to nine. Joined Cardiff in 1993 and helped them win both the Swalec Cup (1994) and the Heineken League title (1995).

NTamack, E. France

Full name: Emile NTamack
Club: Toulouse
Position: Fullback, wing
Height: 6ft 2in (1.88m)
Weight: 14st 3lb (90kg)
Occupation: Student
Born: Lyon, 25.6.70
Family: Single
International debut: Wales 24, France 15, 1994
Five Nations debut: As above
Best moment in rugby: Scoring first Test try vs Canada (1994); helping Toulouse win 1994 French championship.
Former clubs: Meyzieu, Lavaur
Notable landmarks in rugby career: A true world star and heart-breaker *par excellence* – Emile it was who muscled over for the try, four minutes into injury time, that earned France a crucial 22–19 World Cup victory over Scotland (Pretoria, 3.6.95). He then repeated the feat in the 36–12 quarter-final defeat of Ireland (Durban, 10.6.95), waiting until stoppage time to run an interception back virtually the length of the field. And very little time remained when the Toulouse star

France (1994)		
Last Season	17 caps	75 pts
Career	25 caps	90 pts

Caps (25): **1994** W, C(a), NZ(1,2), C(b) **1995** W, I(a), R wc-T, S(b), I(b), SA, E(b). It, R, Arg, NZ(1,2) **1996** E, S, I, W, R(R), Arg(1,2)
Points (90 – 17t,1c,1p): **1994** C(a:1t), NZ(2:1t) **1995** W(1t), I(a:1t,1c,1p) wc-S(b:1t), I(b:1t), E(b:1t). It(1t), Arg(2t) **1996** I(2t), W(1t), R(R:1t), Arg(1:2t), Arg(2:1t)

scored the decisive try in the otherwise dreary 19–9 third-place play-off win over England (Pretoria, 22.6.95). But that was only half the story, as Emile, who helped Toulouse complete back-to-back French title wins in 1995, also claimed scores against Ireland, Wales and New Zealand, the latter coming in a 23–20 win (Auckland, 3.7.94) that gave France a historic 2–0 series win. The only disappointment for the ex-Meyzieu and Lavaur player was his clueless goal-kicking vs Ireland (Dublin, 4.3.95). Emile had claimed his first Test try against Canada (Ottawa, 4.6.94), but there was little celebrating as France crashed to a shock 18–16 defeat. His debut had also ended in disappointment in the cauldron of Cardiff Arms Park. A trapped nerve in Philippe Bernat-Salle's neck gave the Toulouse flier his chance, but he didn't receive another once the game got underway, as a marvellous performance handed France their first defeat by Wales in 13 contests. Emile lost his place to Bordeaux University's William

Techoueyres for the 1994 championship closer against Scotland, but was included in France's summer tour squad (while the *garcon* Techoueyres was not). Regarded by many as the new Serge Blanco, Emile enhanced that image after the 1995 World Cup, with seven tries in the next ten Tests. He also powered Toulouse to inaugural European Cup glory (vs Cardiff) and to a third straight French championship crown.

Ofahengaue, V.   Australia

Full name: Viliame Ofahengaue
Nickname: Willie O
State: New South Wales
Club: Manly
Position: Flanker, No.8
Height: 6ft 4in (1.93m)
Weight: 16st 7lb (105kg)
Occupation: Pile driver, Emanon Pty Ltd (Manly, NSW)
Born: 3.5.68
Family: Heleni (wife); Lavinia (mother); Sione (father); Sione Kata (brother); Epalahame (brother); Talia (sister).
International debut: New Zealand 21, Australia 6, 1990
Best moments in rugby: Being picked to play for Wallabies and winning 1991 World Cup.
Worst moment in rugby: Being left in Australia by the New Zealand team when I toured Oz with them in 1988.
Suggestions to improve rugby: Improve discipline.
Notable landmarks in rugby career: 'Willie O' returned strongly from the serious injury which had sidelined him throughout 1993, reclaiming his place in the Test side from Queensland's Ilie Tabua following the

Australia (1990)

Last Season	5 caps	10 pts
Career	26 caps	36 pts

Caps (26): 1990 NZ(1,2,3) 1991 W(a), E(a), NZ(a1,a2). wc-Arg, W(b), I, NZ(b), E(b) 1992 S(1,2), SA, I, W 1994 WS, NZ 1995 Arg(1,2R) wc-SA, C, E. NZ(1,2)

Points (36 – 8t): 1990 NZ(2:1t) 1991 W(a:1t), E(a:2t) 1994 WS(1t) 1995 Arg(1:1t). NZ(1:1t), NZ(2:1t)

winning series against Ireland and Italy in 1994, before turning up the power in 1995. The star of Australia's 1992 tour to Ireland and Wales marked his comeback with a try in the 73–3 rout of Western Samoa (Sydney, 6.8.94) – though, to be fair, most Wallabies *did* score that day. His sixth Test score came in the 53–7 first Test win over Argentina (Brisbane, 29.4.95), and he went on to play in three of the four World Cup matches that constituted Australia's all-too-brief defence of their crown. Thereafter, he scored tries in each of the Bledisloe Cup matches against New Zealand, but Australia still lost them both. Auckland-educated, he toured New Zealand in 1990 as a late inclusion for Jeff Miller. Two years earlier he had been in the New Zealand Schools side, but because of visa difficulties he was refused re-entry into the land of the Kiwi and headed back to Oz to live with his uncle. New Zealand's loss was Australia's gain, as he has quickly amassed 17 caps and developed a fearsome reputation as an explosive runner and bone-crunching defender. Represented the World XV against New Zealand in the 1992 Centenary Series and helped Australia reach the 1993 World Cup Sevens final in Edinburgh.

Touchlines: Music, movies

Ojomoh, S. O. England

Full name: Stephen Oziegbe Ojomoh
Club: Bath
Position: No.8, flanker
Height: 6ft 3in (1.90m)
Weight: 16st 7lb (100kg)
Occupation: Promotions officer, Johnson's News, Bath
Born: Benin City, Nigeria, 25.5.70
Family: Single
International debut: England 12, Ireland 13, 1994
Five Nations debut: As above
Best rugby memory: Walking out onto Parc des Princes pitch in England jersey
Worst rugby memory: Final whistle of 1994 loss to Ireland
Toughest opponent: Chris Sheasby (Harlequins & England A)
Serious injuries: Ankle and knee ligament damage
Other sporting claims to fame: South West decathlon champion (1988); runner-up in 1988 English Schools discus championship; South West long-jump and triple-jump champion; third in All England decathlon championship.

England (1994)		
Last Season	5 caps	0 pts
Career	11 caps	0 pts

Caps	**(11): 1994** I, F, SA(1R,2), R
	1995 S(R) wc-Arg,WS, A(TR), F(b)
	1996 F
Points	Nil

Notable landmarks in rugby career: One of the victims of Jack Rowell's chopping and changing in England's back row in 1995/96, Steve was considered surplus to requirements before Christmas, but was then picked at blindside alongside Lawrence Dallaglio and Ben Clarke for the 1996 Five Nations opener in Paris, which England were mighty unfortunate to lose 12–15 (20.1.96). Thereafter, Rowell had a change of heart and brought in Tim Rodber, although that idea lasted but one game before Clarke was handed a No.6 shirt, which by the season's end had had almost as many different owners as a Moss Bros dinner jacket. Steve had the consolation of helping Bath to the league and cup double, as well as showing favourably in the cross-code challenge against Wigan RFLC – so favourably in fact that London Broncos RLFC approached him about switching to Super League. Steve had built his reputation on an outstanding campaign for England in South Africa (1994), during which he appeared in both Tests. But he was less convincing on his return in the openside berth in the 54–3 defeat of Romania (Twickenham, 12.11.94) and was relegated to bench duties thereafter, as Dean Richards' return for the Five Nations Grand Slam campaign allowed Rowell to move Clarke to No.7. Shared in the last half-hour of the 1995 Grand Slam, coming on as a 51st-minute replacement for Richards in the 24–12 defeat of Scotland (Twickenham, 18.3.95). Further injury to Deano allowed Steve to win three of his four caps at last summer's World Cup, the exception being in the game against Western Samoa when he tried his hand at blindside – England won 44–22. A brilliant natural athlete, Steve has taken the skills that brought him schoolboy honours in the decathlon disciplines and worked them into his rugby to become a very dynamic performer. Previously played for England at 18-Group, Colts and Under-21 levels, and joined Bath from Rosslyn Park in 1989. Toured with England A to New Zealand (1992) and Canada (1993).

Touchlines: Basketball

French youngster Thomas Castaignede shows off his kicking skills in Cardiff.

Osborne, G. M.   New Zealand

Full name: Glen Matthew Osborne
Province: North Harbour
Position: Fullback
Height: 6ft (1.83m)
Weight: 13st 3lb (84kg)
Occupation: Life agent, NZI Life
Born: Wanganui, 27.8.71
Family: Single
Family links with rugby: Brother
Charles plays for Wanganui; uncle
Bill Osborne played for All Blacks
(1975–82).
International debut: New Zealand
73, Canada 7, 1995
Notable landmarks in rugby career:
Scored 15 tries in 19 outings for
North Harbour to earn World Cup
selection by All Blacks, and went on
to make a big impression in South
Africa. Voted player of the tourna-
ment at the 1994 Hong Kong Sevens
(his third visit), Glen proceeded to
represent New Zealand Maoris
(against Mid Canterbury and Fiji)
and the NZ Barbarians before
breaking into the New Zealand side

New Zealand (1995)

Last Season	9 caps	20 pts
Career	10 caps	30 pts

Caps (10): **1995** C wc-I, W, J, E, SA.
A(1,2), F(1R,2)
Points (30 – 6t): **1995** C(2t) wc-I(1t),

against Canada (Auckland, 22.4.95). Two tries in the 73–7 rout of the Canucks
marked Glen out for special attention on reaching the World Cup, but he took
it in his stride, looking both assured and dangerous in the All Blacks' Pool C
matches against Ireland (one try), Wales and Japan (two tries in world-record
hammering). A recurring ankle injury put him out of the quarter-final tie vs
Scotland, with Otago golden boy Jeff Wilson moving to fullback, but Glen was
quickly restored for the England semi-final and looked a million dollars.
Thereafter, helped New Zealand win Bledisloe Cup (2–0) and scored a try as
they won the second Test in Paris to split the end-of-year series 1–1. Glen had
made his first-class debut in 1990 as an 18-year-old, playing at fly-half for
Wanganui vs Wellington. He moved from wing to fullback before representing
the All Black Colts in 1991 and then joining North Harbour in 1992 – the year
in which he represented New Zealand in the World Cup Sevens in Edinburgh.
Won special acclaim in 1994 for his brilliant try-scoring performance in North
Harbour's 27–23 defeat of France (Auckland, 12.6.94). Describes his most
enjoyable tackle as Jonah Lomu – 'Because it's there!'

Patterson, D. W.   Scotland

Full name: Derrick William Patterson
Club: West Hartlepool
Position: Scrum-half
Height: 5ft 9½ in (1.76m)
Weight: 13st 11lb (83kg)
Occupation: Joiner, Heritage Homes, the Yuille Group
Born: Hawick, 6.7.68
Family: Single
International debut: Scotland 10, South Africa 34, 1994
Five Nations debut: None
Former clubs: Hawick, Edinburgh Academicals
Notable landmarks in rugby career: Received a bruising introduction to international rugby, overshadowed by Springbok counterpart Joost van der Westhuizen on his debut (Murrayfield, 19.11.94) – an occasion on which he became Hawick's 53rd player to be capped, and then knocked all over the shop

Scotland (1994)

. Last Season	2 caps	0 pts
Career	2 caps	0 pts

Caps (2): **1994** SA **1995** wc-T
Points Nil

by an over-zealous Tongan side in Scotland's 41–5 World Cup win at the tail end of the season (Pretoria, 30.5.95). However, he proved his worth in the latter game with a combative display on what resembled a battlefield. In between his two Test engagements, Derrick quit Hawick for English first division outfit West Hartlepool (whom he captained in 1995/96), having spent the summer of 1994 on tour in Argentina with Scotland, appearing in the games against Buenos Aires and Rosario. Derrick first played for Hawick in 1987 and went on to represent both South, Edinburgh and Scottish Exiles in the Inter-District Championship. Moved to Edinburgh Accies in 1991, from where he graduated to Scotland B (vs France, 1992), and would have turned out for Scotland A against Spain the same year but for an injury that forced his withdrawal. But played for Scottish Development XV in 12–31 loss to touring All Blacks (Edinburgh, 16.11.93).
Touchlines: Golf

Pelous, F.   France

Full name: Fabien Pelous
Club: Dax
Position: No.8, lock
Height: 6ft 6in (1.98m)
Weight: 16st 12lb (107kg)
Occupation: Physical education student
Born: Toulouse, 7.12.73
Family: Single
Former clubs: Saverdun, Graulhot
International debut: France 52, Romania 8, 1995
Five Nations debut: France 15, England 12, 1996
Notable landmarks in rugby career: Groomed for stardom ever since inspiring France to Student World Cup glory in 1992 with a series of dominant displays in the engine room. Given his Test debut by new French coach Jean-Claude Skrela at the Latin Cup in Argentina in October 1995, scoring a try on his debut in the 52–8 defeat of Romania (Tucuman, 17.10.95). Retained the No.5 shirt for the Cup-clinching

France (1995)

Last Season	10 caps	10 pts
Career	10 caps	10 pts

Caps (10): **1995** R, Arg, NZ(1,2) **1996** E, S, I, R(R) **1996** Arg(1,2)
Points (10 – 2t): **1995** R(1t) **1996**

47–12 win over the host nation (Buenos Aires, 21.1.95) before returning home to be introduced to French fans in the two-Test series against New Zealand. Fabien responded by setting up the opening try in France's stunning 22–15 first Test victory in Toulouse (11.11.95). Come the 1996 Five Nations, he was moved to No.8 to accomodate the return of clubmate Olivier Roumat who, incidentally, had been the star of the 1988 Student World Cup. Fabien retained his place until the final round of the championship, when Sylvain Dispagne, outstanding as replacement for Olivier in the previous mission against Ireland, was given the start at No.8. Fabien picked up his eighth cap as a 74th-minute replacement for Olivier Merle in the 64–12 end-of-term defeat of Romania (Aurillac, 20.4.96).

Penaud, A.   France

Full name: Alain Penaud
Club: Brive
Position: Outside-half
Height: 5ft 11in (1.81m)
Weight: 14st 2lb (90kg)
Born: Juillac, 19.7.69
Former club: Objat
Occupation: Student
International debut: Wales 9, France 12, 1992
Five Nations debut: As above
Notable landmarks in rugby career: Seemingly France's Jacques of all trades, Alain played twice in his favoured fly-half berth in 1995/96, during the split autumn series with New Zealand. He was then dropped for the Five Nations opener against England, then brought in at centre for the visit to Edinburgh in place of Richard Dourthe – suspended for kicking England's Ben Clarke in the head. Alain was then relieved of his duties (again) before being selected at fly-half for the season-ending 64–12 romp against Romania (Aurillac, 20.4.96), in which he contributed a try. Had been axed previously after letting France lose to

France (1992)

Last Season	6 caps	5 pts
Career	25 caps	47 pts

Caps (25): **1992** W, E, S, I, R, Arg(a1, a2), SA(1,2), Arg(b) **1993** R(a), SA(1,2), R(b), A(1,2) **1994** I, W, E **1995** NZ(1,2) **1996** S, R, Arg(1,2)
Points (47 – 7t,5dg): **1992** W(1dg), E(1t), I(2t), Arg(a1:1dg), SA(1:2t), SA(2:1t) **1993** SA(2:1dg), A(1:1dg)

England in Paris (5.3.94), and neither had he been selected to tour Canada and New Zealand that summer. Yet he was the player who had landed the crucial dropped goal in Johannesburg (3.7.93) as France clinched the Test series with a 18–17 defeat of South Africa, and had repeated the feat during France's shock 16–13 defeat of then world champions Australia in Bordeaux (30.10.93). He also drew rave reviews from French team manager Robert Paparemborde for his performances on the 1992 tour of Argentina. 'Penaud confirmed his status as the best fly-half in France," said the team manager. Alain continued to shine in the home series against South Africa, scoring two tries in the 15–20 defeat at Lyon (17.10.92), and another the following week as France gained her revenge by winning 29–16 in Paris. Was then moved to centre for the visit to Nantes of Argentina (14.11.92), and when the Pumas recorded their first-ever win on French soil, Alain was caught in the clearout. Didier Camberabero returned for 1993 Championship, which France won. Alain had made a strong impression after being given his chance out of the blue by new coach Pierre Berbizier in the 1992 Championship. Having dropped a goal in France's three-point defeat of Wales in Cardiff on his debut (1.2.92), he managed a try against England in a 31–13 losing cause next time out (15.2.92), after charging down Will Carling's attempted clearance in the 66th minute. Ended that season with a two-try flourish against Ireland – starting and finishing the seven-try rout with touchdowns in the second and 85th minutes. Originally made a name for himself when he guided French Schools to the 1987 'Triple Crown', with 18 points in wins against Scotland, Wales and England. From there he graduated to France A and the 1989/90 FIRA Championship, in which he tasted triumph when he scored the try that inspired a 22–14 victory over the Soviet Union and gave France A the title on try-difference.

Perie, M. France

Full name: Michel Perie
Club: Toulon
Position: Loosehead Prop
Height: 6ft 1in (1.85m)
Weight: 16st 4lb (104kg)
Occupation: Town council employee
Born: Le Pradet, 20.9.69
International debut: France 15, England 12, 1996
Five Nations debut: As above
Notable landmarks in rugby career: Although Michel only made his Test debut in January, in the much-celebrated 15–12 defeat of England (Paris, 20.1.96), he has been a class act on the Gallic scene for some time. All the way back in 1992, he took the Biarritz scrum to pieces with a superlative scrummaging display that gave unfancied Toulon a 19–14 triumph in the French championship final. Remarkably, that came just a year after his conversion from back row to loosehead. Michel quickly

France (1996)
Last Season	3 caps	0 pts
Career	3 caps	0 pts

Caps (3): **1996** E, S, I(R)
Points Nil

graduated to the France A team, and was a member of the French side which won the gold medal at the 1993 Mediterranean Games. A persistent knee injury then took its toll, hampering further progress until 1995/96 when, with rival Laurent Benezech taking his turn on the treatment table, Michel was given his maiden start against *Les Rosbifs*. He tarnished the occasion by receiving a yellow card from Irish referee David McHugh, but he retained his place for the visit to Edinburgh the following fortnight. However, the Murrayfield jinx struck France again, which lost 14–19 (3.2.96), and Michel was relegated to the replacements bench while Christian Califano moved across from the tighthead side. But injury to the oustanding Toulouse prop 52 minutes into the 45–10 obliteration of Ireland (Paris, 17.2.96) allowed Michel to enter the fray and pick up his third cap.

Peters, E. W. Scotland

Full name: Eric William Peters
Nickname: McNasty
Club: Bath
Position: No.8
Height: 6ft 5½ in (1.95m)
Weight: 16st 10lb (101kg)
Occupation: Chartered surveyor, King Sturge and Co, Bath
Born: Glasgow, 28.1.69
Family: Single
International debut: Scotland 22, Canada 6, 1995
Five Nations debut: Scotland 26, Ireland 13, 1995
Former clubs: Old Brentwoodians, Loughborough University, Cambridge University, Saracens
Best rugby memory: France 21, Scotland 23, 1995
Worst rugby memory: France 22, Scotland 19, 1995 World Cup
Most embarrassing memory: Going along to watch my flatmate play for Old Edwardians and ending up reffing the match.
Toughest opponent: Jamie Joseph (New Zealand)

Scotland (1995)		
Last Season	9 caps	15 pts
Career	15 caps	25 pts

Caps (15): **1995** C, I, F(a), W, E, R wc-T, F(b), NZ **1996** I, F, W, E, NZ(1,2)
Points (25 – 5t): **1995** W(1t), R(1t) wc-T(1t), NZ(1:1t), NZ(2:1t)

Preferred commitment to rugby: Part-time (best of both worlds)
Your blueprint for rugby's future: Unions must cede some power to senior clubs.
Do you have a duty to entertain? Yes, although winning is paramount. But both Bath and Scotland play exciting rugby.
Do you feel a loyalty to your club in this new era? Call me old fashioned but, yes, I do.
Notable landmarks in rugby career? Outstanding newcomer to the international

scene in 1994/95, Eric played in a Scottish back row (alongside Wainwright and Morrison) which bore comparison with the legendary Jeffrey–Calder–White Grand Slam triumvirate five years previously. He scored a brilliant try against Wales, which took the new lid off Murrayfield (4.3.95), and he repeated the five-point trick in the 41–5 World Cup win over Tonga (Pretoria, 30.5.95). After missing out at the start of 1995/96 on selection for the Western Samoa game, Eric was swiftly drafted in for the remainder of the season, and scored his fourth Test try in Scotland's first international against New Zealand on their summer tour, which ended 62–31 at Carisbrook in favour of the All Blacks. Other features of Eric's season were the Scottish Exiles retaining the District Championship and the small matter of Bath's league and cup double. It is hard to believe Eric only broke into Test match rugby in January, such has been his progress. Remember that Scotland had failed to win their nine internationals prior to his debut against Canada (21.1.95). But the Scots won that, and reeled off four straight victories before losing the Grand Slam decider to Eric's former country (Twickenham, 18.3.95). Having captained Cambridge to Varsity glory in 1992, he represented England Under-21s and Students, as well as Barbarians and Penguins. After moving to Bath, and making his first XV debut in October 1993, he quickly progressed further up the representative ladder, helping Scottish Exiles roam unbeaten through 1994/95 Inter-District Championship, playing in a Scottish Select's 10–35 loss to the touring Springboks (Aberdeen, 15.11.94), and turning out in Scotland A's defeat of Italy in January 1995.
Touchlines: Golf

Pienaar, J. F. South Africa

Full name: Jacobus Francois Pienaar
Province: Transvaal
Position: Flanker
Height: 6ft 4in (1.92m)
Weight: 17st 1lb (104kg)
Occupation: Self-employed businessman
Born: Port Elizabeth, 2.1.67
Family: Single
International debut: South Africa 20, France 20, 1993
Notable landmarks in rugby career: A quite remarkable man, having teamed up with South African president Nelson Mandela to give us the enduring memory of the 1995 World Cup. The sight of Mandela in Francois' No.6 Springbok jersey

presenting him with the Webb Ellis trophy on that magical afternoon at Ellis Park, Johannesburg (24.6.95), will surely never be forgotten. He led by splendid example, both on and off the pitch, but especially off the pitch. He not only said the right things at all times, he convinced us that he meant every word of them. He even organised for the cash-strapped Romanians to be given a set of brand-new Adidas kit before they flew home. Francois was a wonderful ambassador for the New Republic, and deserved everything he got. Unhappily, the Transvaal RFU were probaby thinking the same thing when Francois led a walkout of leading players demanding better pay terms, and came close to being sacked by a province whom he had skippered to back-to-back Currie Cup wins (1993–94) and the 1993 Super-10 triumph, not to mention a stunning 24–21 victory over the 1994 England tourists. 1996 was not so clever, however, as Transvaal had a wretched time in the Super-12 tournament. Appointed to skipper South Africa on his Test debut against France (Durban, 26.6.93), so becoming only the third Springbok to be so honoured (after Basil Kenyon and Des van Jaarsveld). The game ended in a 20–20 draw, and France went on to nick the series with an 18–17 win in Johannesburg the following week. Francois toured Argentina and Australia in 1993, his only international try thus far coming in Australia's 19–12 third Test win in Sydney (21.8.93). In 1994, concussion suffered against Wellington forced him to miss the first five matches of a largely unsuccessful New Zealand tour, including the first Test. But he did not miss an international thereafter, save for the midweek World Cup tie vs Romania. Finished the campaign with tries in two of the last three missions, against Wales and Italy.

South Africa (1993)		
Last Season	8 caps	10 pts
Career	24 caps	15 pts

Caps (24): **1993** F(1,2), A(1,2,3), Arg(1,2) **1994** E(1,2), NZ(2,3), Arg(1,2), S, W **1995** WS(a) wc-A, C, WS(b), F, NZ. W, It, E

Points (15 – 3t): **1993** A(3:1t) **1995** W(1t), It(1t)

England's Martin Bayfield tussles for the lineout ball with Springbok rival Fritz van Heerden at Twickenham.

Pini, M.   Australia

Full name: Matthew Pini
State: Queensland
Club: Wests (Brisbane)
Position: Fullback
Height: 5ft 11½ in (1.82m)
Weight: 14st 13lb (90kg)
Occupation: Plumber
Born: 21.3.69
International debut: Australia 33,
Ireland 13, 1994
Notable landmarks in rugby career:
Went to 1995 World Cup as
Australia's first-choice fullback, but
was quickly usurped by Matt Burke
following the Wallabies' opening-
day loss to South Africa (Cape
Town, 25.5.95). Appeared just once
thereafter, and that fleetingly as a
bloodbin replacement for Danny
Herbert during Australia's 42–3 win
over Romania (Stellenbosch,
3.6.95). The former Australia
Under-21 standout had made his
debut in the 33–13 first Test defeat
of Ireland (Brisbane, 5.6.94), only to
strain a hamstring in training for the

Australia (1994)

Last Season	2 caps	0 pts
Career	8 caps	10 pts

Caps (8): **1994** I(1), It(2), WS, NZ **1995**
Arg(1,2) wc-SA, R(TR)
Points (10 – 2t): **1994** WS(1t) **1995**

second Test. Returned against Italy (Melbourne, 26.6.94) after Burke was
crocked, and was a fixture in the next six matches, spanning 11 months. He
claimed his first try in the extraordinary 73–3 rout of Western Samoa (Sydney,
6.8.94), and added a second in the 53–7 first Test defeat of Argentina (Brisbane,
29.4.95).

Popplewell, N. J.   Ireland

Full name: Nicholas James
Popplewell
Nickname: Poppy
Club: Newcastle
Position: Loosehead prop
Height: 5ft 10in (1.78m)
Weight: 17st 3lb (105kg)
Occupation: Broker, Butler Briscoe
Born: Dublin, 6.4.64
Family: Rachel (wife)
Former clubs: Gorey, Greystones,
Wasps
International debut: Ireland 6, New
Zealand 23, 1989
Five Nations debut: Ireland 15,
Wales 16, 1992
Best rugby memory: 1993 Lions
second Test win over New Zealand
Worst rugby memory: Grant Fox's
controversial late penalty winner in
first Test for All Blacks against 1993
Lions.
Toughest opponent: Olo Brown
(Auckland & New Zealand)
Serious injuries: Broken ribs (twice);
cruciate knee ligaments (operation,
May 1994)
Other sporting claims to fame:
Hockey for Irish Schools (three caps)
Suggestions to improve rugby:

Ireland (1989)

Last Season	10 caps	5 pts
Career	39 caps	13 pts

Caps (39): **1989** NZ **1990** Arg **1991**
Na(1,2) wc-Z, S, A **1992** W, E, S,
F, NZ(1,2), A **1993** S, F, W, E, R
1994 F, W, E, S, US **1995** E, S, F(a),
W(a), It wc-NZ, J, W(b), F(b). Fj
1996 US, S, F, W, E
Points (13 – 3t): **1991** wc-Z(2t) **1995** wc-
W(b:1t)

Decrease value of penalty goal to two points; scrap 90-degree scrum wheel law.
Notable landmarks in rugby career: Currently Ireland's most-experienced
forward, Poppy scored the crucial try against Wales (Johannesburg, 4.6.95)
which set Ireland on their way to gaining a place in the World Cup quarter-
finals. Had captained his country in the previous match: a 50–28 win over
Japan (Bloemfontein, 31.5.95) – fitting for a player who in only his second full
season as Ireland's first-choice loosehead prop had gained selection for 1993
British Lions (the Emerald Isle's solitary representative in the Test side) for all
three engagements. Ever-present in 1995/96 – a season in which he left the
Wasps to join Rob Andrew's rugby revolution at Newcastle. Poppy missed
1994 tour to Australia to have an operation on cruciate knee ligaments. Once
repaired, he was an ever-present in 1994/95, sharing with Brendan Mullin the
distinction of starting all 10 internationals. Had taken over the Irish No.1 jersey

during 1991/92 season, following the 1991 tour to Namibia, where he played in both Tests. Made great start to 1991 World Cup when he scored two tries in 55–11 Pool win over Zimbabwe in Dublin (6.10.91). In 1991/92 was one of only three permanent fixtures in the Irish side (along with Vinnie Cunningham and Paddy Johns) throughout seven-Test Irish programme. Previously had been a member of the Irish party which toured France (May 1988) and North America (1989, playing in 24–21 defeat of Canada). Retired injured after 20 minutes of full debut against 1989 All Blacks, and lost place for 1990 Championship. Redundant thereafter, except for 1990 Argentina game (won 20–18). Helped train Presentation Juniors Bray U-15s to two Leinster Junior Cups in three years. Represented Ireland U-25s vs US Eagles (1990). Scored one of Ireland B's four tries in 24–10 win over England B (Old Belvedere, 1.3.91).
Touchlines: Golf (18 handicap), tennis, squash.

Proctor, W. T. Wales

Full name: Wayne Thomas Proctor
Club: Llanelli
Position: Wing, fullback
Height: 6ft (1.83m)
Weight: 13st (78kg)
Occupation: Student, Swansea Institute of Higher Education
Born: Bridgend, 12.6.72
Family: Single
Former club: Cardigan Youth
International debut: Wales 6, Australia 23, 1992
Five Nations debut: Wales 10, England 9, 1993
Best rugby memory: Beating England on Five Nations debut (6.2.93)
Worst rugby memory: Broken jaw suffered against Ireland (1994)
Most embarrassing moment: Being interviewed by the BBC for the first time
Toughest opponent: Tony Underwood (Leicester & England)
Other sporting claims to fame: Represented Wales 11 times at athletics – third in 1988 British Schools 400m hurdles.
Serious injuries: Broken jaw (1994)

Wales (1992)		
Last Season	7 caps	10 pts
Career	24 caps	20 pts

Caps (24): **1992** A **1993** E, S, Z(1,2), Na, C **1994** I, C, Fj, WS, R, It, SA **1995** S, I(a) wc-NZ. Fj **1996** It, E, S, I, A(1,2)
Points (20 – 4t): **1993** Z(1:1t), Na(1t) **1996** S(1t), A(1:1t)

Suggestions to improve rugby: Introduce alternative to the scrum to help speed up the game. Sell the game better. Televise more live games at different levels.

Notable landmarks in rugby career: Wayne's three-year battle with Nigel Walker for the Wales left wing berth was resolved in his favour last summer when he alone was selected in the World Cup squad by caretaker coach Alex Evans – ironically, Walker's club coach at Cardiff. It proved a chastening experience for Wayne, who made just one appearance, and that opposite Jonah Lomu in New Zealand's 34–9 win (Johannesburg, 4.6.95). Much to Wayne's obvious amusement (honest), the All Blacks switched Lomu onto his wing moments before kick-off. Mind you, it was the one and only game Lomu played in which he was anonymous. Wayne's cause was not helped by Gareth Thomas' three-try debut against Japan; Gareth returned for the catastrophic Ireland defeat (Jo'burg, 4.6.95) which condemned Wales to an early flight home. But at least Wayne returned with his health, unlike in 1993/94 when he suffered a broken jaw in Dublin (5.2.94). Ever-present on the left wing for Wales in 1996 Five Nations Championship before moving to fullback on tour in Australia, Justin Thomas having withdrawn from the party injured on eve of departure. Rapidly progressed into Wales senior side in 1992/93, only seven months after having made his debut for Welsh Under-21s in 28–19 win over Scotland (Stirling, 18.4.92). Made his Test debut in the 6–23 loss to Australia (Cardiff, 21.11.92). Wayne, who had previously won four Welsh Youth caps and three Wales Under-19 caps (touring with the latter to Canada), kept his place for the first two matches of the 1993 Five Nations Championship, sharing in the euphoria which surrounded the 10–9 defeat of England at Cardiff, and then in the dejection which followed their 0–20 shutout at Murrayfield. Partook in Llanelli's league and cup double in 1992/93, having turned out in 16–7 cup final defeat of Swansea the previous season.

Touchlines: Athletics, tennis, badminton

Derwyn Jones defies gravity during Wales' stirring defeat of France in Cardiff.

Quinnell, J. C.   Wales

Full name: Jonathan Craig Quinnell
Nickname: Chigley
Club: Richmond
Position: Flanker
Height: 6ft 6in (1.98m)
Weight: 18st 4lb (116kg)
Born: 9.7.75
Family: Single
Former club: Llanelli
Family links with rugby: Father
(Derek) played for Wales (23 caps:
1972–80) and Lions (5 Tests: 1971–
80); brother Scott (Richmond) has
played for Wales (9 caps: 1993–94);
uncle (Barry John) played for Wales
(25 caps: 1966–72) and Lions (5
Tests: 1968–71).
International debut: Wales 19,
Canada 15, 1995
Five Nations debut: None
Best rugby memory: Making Wales
debut vs Fiji
Worst rugby memory: Losing to
Pontypridd in 1994/95 Swalec Cup
semi-final

Wales (1995)		
Last Season	1 cap	0 pts
Career	1 cap	0 pts

Caps (1): 1995 Fj
Points Nil

Do you really want to be a full-time professional player? Yes
How well has rugby handled move to professionalism? 6/10. The powers that
be didn't think it through enough.
Do you have a duty to entertain? No, our duty is to win first and foremost.
Do you feel a loyalty to your club in this new era? No
Other sporting claims to fame: Runner-up in Welsh Schools shot putt aged 18.
Notable landmarks in rugby career: Craig possesses one of the most famous
surnames in Welsh rugby, but one of the newest faces. At the tender age of 20
he followed brother (Scott), father (Derek) and uncle (Barry John) into Wales
senior side when selected for the visit of Fiji to Cardiff (11.11.95). Wales won
19–15, but it was a not altogether convincing team performance, and wholesale
changes were made to the side for the next outing against Italy, among them
Emyr Lewis succeeding Craig at No.6. Craig was not helped by Llanelli leaving
him out for much of the remainder of the season, and he felt sufficiently angry
to follow his brother to Richmond last summer. Nonetheless, he is undoubtedly
one for the future, as was the case with his brother Scott two years earlier. The
second of three sons of 'Big Derek', he was educated at Ysgol y Graig and
Llandovery College, from where he represented Welsh Senior Schools at lock

on four occasions in 1993 before graduating to Wales Youth in 1994/95. He only broke into the Llanelli first team in February 1994, and had to wait until the end of that season for his Heineken League debut. According to those helpful and knowledgeable people in the Welsh Rugby Union press office, Craig is the 922nd player to be capped by Wales and the 150th to be capped whilst with Llanelli.

Touchlines: Weights, running, cinema

Redpath, B. W. Scotland

Full name: Bryan William Redpath
Nickname: Basil
Club: Melrose
Position: Scrum-half
Height: 5ft 7in (1.70m)
Weight: 11st 6lb (73kg)
Occupation: Self-employed joiner
Born: Galashiels, 2.7.71
Family: Single
Family links with rugby: Andrew (brother) has played for Melrose and Scotland Under-21s; Craig (brother) for Melrose, Scotland Under-21s and B; Lynne (sister) for Scotland Women's Under-21s.
International debut: Scotland 15, New Zealand 51, 1993
Five Nations debut: Scotland 14, England 15, 1994
Toughest opponent: Gary Armstrong (Newcastle & Scotland)
Biggest influence on career: Rob Moffat
Other sporting claims to fame: Represented South of Scotland at cricket (also St Boswells) and athletics.

Scotland (1993)		
Last Season	8 caps	0 pts
Career	19 caps	0 pts

Caps (19): **1993** NZ(TR) **1994** E(TR), F, Arg(1,2) **1995** C, I, F(a), W, E, R wc-IC, F(b), NZ. WS **1996** I, F, W, E

Points Nil

Suggestions to improve rugby: Reduce value of penalty goal to make for a more entertaining spectacle.

Notable landmarks in rugby career: Missed last summer's Scotland tour to New Zealand through back injury – which was a tremendous shame, as Bryan had enjoyed a cracking campaign in the 1996 Five Nations alongside Gregor Townsend. The young halfback duo sparked a Scottish side not expected to trouble anyone. In the event, they troubled everyone (although England

ultimately denied them the Grand Slam). Bryan's form was no great surprise, given the quality of performance he had turned in at the World Cup, where he lived up to the standards set by predecessor Gary Armstrong. Ironically, it was the serious injury suffered by Armstrong, and by his understudy Andy Nicol, that gave the opportunity to Bryan, the youngest of three brothers in the Melrose side. Graduated into Scotland side on the back of consistently outstanding displays in Melrose's back-to-back championship winning years (1992/93–1993/94). First two caps came courtesy of temporary replacement ruling. His debut (Murrayfield, 20.11.93) followed an injury to Nicol, which required medical treatment off the field. And Bryan was again required to fill the breach temporarily when Armstrong popped off for attention during Scotland's heartbreaking 14–15 Calcutta Cup loss to England (5.2.94). Finally, the diminutive Borderer won selection in his own right for the 1994 Wooden Spoon decider against France, again in Edinburgh (19.3.94). Scotland lost 12–20, but his services were retained for the summer tour to Argentina, on which he played in both Test defeats. Originally surfaced on the representative scene as a replacement for Scotland Under-18s and Under-19s, and made his Under-21 debut in their loss to Wales at Llanelli (20.4.91). Added a second cap against the Welsh at Bridgehaugh, Stirling (lost 19–28, 18.4.92). First played for Melrose as an 18-year old in October 1989.
Touchlines: Golf, cricket

Regan, M. P. England

Full name: Mark Peter Regan
Nickname: Ronnie
Club: Bristol
Position: Hooker
Height: 5ft 11in (1.80m)
Weight: 16st 2lb (103kg)
Occupation: Work co-ordinator, Avon Crane and Commercial Repairs, Bristol
Born: Bristol, 28.1.72
Family: Single
Family links with rugby: Brother (Paul) plays for Bristol
Former club: St Bernadette's OBs
International debut: England 14, South Africa 24, 1995
Five Nations debut: France 15, England 12, 1996

Best rugby memory: Winning first cap vs South Africa
Worst rugby memory: Losing to France in last minute (1996)

Toughest opponent: James Dalton (Transvaal & South Africa)
Do you really want to be a full-time professional? Yes
How well has rugby handled move to professionalism? 7/10. They have done OK.
Do you have a duty to entertain? Yes
Do you feel a loyalty to your club in this new era? Yes: money talks, but you have to remember where you have come from. Bristol have been everything to me.
Notable landmarks in rugby career: Succeeded England's most-capped hooker Brian Moore in the No.2 jersey at the start of 1995/96 and, despite England's lineout problems early on, retained his place throughout the campaign. Mark, who began his rugby career at Keynsham as an eight-year-old, worked his way up the England representative ladder after first playing for England 16-Group Presidents XV. There followed appearances for the 18-Group, Colts, Students, Under-21s and Emerging Players before his England A debut, against the Irish at Donnybrook in 1994/95. Toured Australia and Fiji with England A while the senior squad were in South Africa at the World Cup, before making his big breakthrough in 1995/96 at the tender age of 23.
Touchlines: Golf, squash, badminton

England (1995)		
Last Season	6 caps	0 pts
Career	6 caps	0 pts

Caps (6): 1995 SA,WS(b) 1996 F, W, S, I
Points Nil

Reid, S. J. Scotland

Full name: Stuart James Reid
Club: Boroughmuir
Position: No.8, flanker
Height: 6ft 3½ in (1.92m)
Weight: 16st 4lb (104kg)
Occupation: Edinburgh police officer
Born: Kendal, 31.1.70
Family: Single
Former club: Vale of Lune
International debut: Scotland 15, Western Samoa 15, 1995
Best rugby memory: Scoring two tries for Scotland XV in 41–12 win over United States.
Worst rugby memory: Loss of form in club rugby during 1991/92 season, which cost me a place in the Scotland trial.
Toughest opponent: Finlay Calder (Stewart's-Melville & Scotland)
Serious injuries: Knee operation to decompress tendons in left knee

Notable landmarks in rugby career:
Waited for what seemed an eternity for his full Scotland debut, having first represented the national team in 1991. That was on a non-cap tour to North America, where he turned in an outstanding two-try display in the

Scotland (1995)

Last Season	1 cap	0 pts
Career	1 cap	0 pts

Caps (1): 1995 WS
Points Nil

41–12 defeat of the US Eagles (Hartford, 18.5.91). Equally impressive next time up against Canada (scoring a try), despite the Scots crashing 19–24. From there the future appeared to be his, but a dip in form cost him a place in the 1991/92 Scotland trial. Nonetheless, he continued to be selected for tours by the senior squad, visiting Australia in 1992, Argentina in 1994 and Zimbabwe in 1995. Out of the 25 games played on his four tours, Stuart has played in 12. Hence the feeling of relief when he finally collected his cap on 18 November 1995, following Scotland's disappointing 15–15 draw with the Samoans. Stuart represented Scotland at Under-19 (1989), Under-21 (1989–91) and B/A levels, although not before he had turned out for England Schools on tour in Australia in 1988 – a result of his being educated down south at St Bees (Whitehaven). Indeed, he was born in England. His parents, however, hail from Hawick.

Touchlines: Fishing

Richards, D.   England

Full name: Dean Richards
Nickname: Deano
Club: Leicester
Position: No.8
Height: 6ft 4in (1.93m)
Weight: 17st 8lb (107kg)
Occupation: Police officer
Born: Nuneaton, 11.7.63
Family: Nicky (wife)
Family links with rugby: Father (Brian) played for Nuneaton
Former club: Roanne (France)
International debut: England 25, Ireland 20, 1986
Five Nations debut: As above
Best rugby memory: Winning decisive third Test with 1989 Lions

Worst rugby memories: Losing four front teeth whilst in action; England losing to Wales in Cardiff (1989).
Toughest opponent: Brian Moore (Richmond & England)

Serious injuries: Recurring dislocated shoulder

Suggestions to improve rugby: Reduce maximum age of committee men to 55.

Notable landmarks in rugby career: One of the Herculean figures of world rugby, Deano is the most-capped No.8 of all time, having exceeded the 46 caps won by the great Mervyn Davies between 1969 and 1976. His 48 England caps, allied to six Lions Tests, give him a grand total of 54. Remarkably, his career has been badly disrupted by injury, not least in 1995 when he had to sit out England's World Cup ties against Argentina, Italy and France. But his reputation has never diminished. Oh yes, some did say he wouldn't be able to play on fast grounds and at altitude, but then he masterminded England's 32–15 rout of South Africa (Pretoria, 4.6.94). They don't say that any more. Then they said he was past it, only to backtrack by selecting him to save England's bacon at Murrayfield (1996). No one says he is past it now, either. Indeed, when Will Carling announced that he was relinquishing the England captaincy, a lot of people thought Deano would be an able successor. Selected to tour with 1993 British Lions despite not figuring in England's plans for 1993 Five Nations Championship, Dean played in all three Tests against New Zealand and then, much to their chagrin, returned to England's side to inspire a 15–9 defeat of the touring All Blacks. An injury spared Scotland, Ireland and France, but he was back for the 1994 championship decider against Wales and, although there had been some concerns as to his match fitness, he typically dominated the game. Joined Leicester in 1982 after a season playing in France. Played for England Schools at lock, before graduating to England Under-23s (against Romania). Has also represented Leicestershire and Midlands Division. Scored two tries on international debut against Ireland, 'but it was one of my worst performances.' Played in 1987 World Cup and returned to Australia with 1989 Lions, playing in all three Tests of the 2–1 series win. Shoulder injury ruled out 1989/90 season. Lynchpin of England's 1991 Grand Slam success. Scored one of England XV's two tries in 18–16 defeat of centenary Barbarians at Twickenham (29.9.90). Voted 1990/91 *Whitbread/Rugby World* Player of Year, and played in three World Cup Pool games in 1991 before Mike Teague took over at No.8 for the knockout stages. His return in time for the 1992 Five Nations series brought predictable results – another England Grand Slam.

Touchlines: Squash, five-a-side soccer

England (1986)		
Last Season	6 caps	0 pts
Career	48 caps	24 pts
Lions (1989)	3 Tests	0 pts
(1993)	3 Tests	0 pts

Caps (48): **1986** I, F **1987** S wc-A, J, US, W **1988** F, W, S, I(1), A(a1,a2), Fj, A(b) **1989** S, I, F, W, R. Lions-A(1,2,3) **1990** Arg **1991** W, S, I, F, Fj, A(a) wc-NZ, It, US **1992** S(R), F, W, C **1993** Lions-NZ(1,2,3). NZ **1994** W, SA(1), C **1995** I, F(a), W, S wc-WS, A, NZ. **1996** F(TR), S, I

Points (24 – 6t): **1986** I(2t) **1987** wc-J(1t) **1988** A(a2:1t) **1989** I(1t), R(1t)

Richter, A.   South Africa

Full name: Adriaan Richter
Club: Harlequins (Pretoria)
Province: Northern Transvaal
Position: No.8
Height: 6ft 4in (1.93m)
Weight: 15st 6lb (98kg)
Occupation: Insurance broker
Born: Roodepoort, 10.5.66
Former province: Transvaal
International debut: France 15,
South Africa 20, 1992
Notable landmarks in rugby career:
Enjoyed a cracking 1995 World
Cup, scoring all four of South
Africa's tries in the two games he
started at No.8, against Romania
(Cape Town, 30.5.95) and Canada
(Port Elizabeth, 3.6.95). To ice the
cake he was made skipper for the
21–8 defeat of Romania. Lost out in
knockout stages of tournament, as
coach Kitch Christie gambled on
playing 6ft 7in lock Mark Andrews
at No.8 to give the Boks greater
height at the tail of the lineout.

South Africa (1992)

Last Season	3 caps	20 pts
Career	10 caps	20 pts

Caps (10): **1992** F(1,2), E **1994** E(2), NZ(1,2,3) **1995** wc-R, C, WS(b:R)
Points (20 – 4t): **1995** wc-R(2t), C(2t)

Adriaan had returned to the South African team for second Test against England in 1994 – a move which contributed to the Springboks turning a 32–15 first Test reversal into a 27–9 win (Cape Town, 11.6.94). Two years previously, he had started the Springboks' tour to France and England as a flanker, played a game at lock, and finished up as No.8 in the Test against England. During the course of the trip he developed into a first-choice player, deposing Transvaal's Ian MacDonald as breakaway wing-forward in the two internationals against France – the 20–15 win in Lyon (17.10.92) and the 16–29 loss in Paris' Parc des Princes the following weekend. Scored a try in the 20–16 defeat of England B (Bristol, 7.11.92). Missed out on selection for the two home Tests against New Zealand and Australia (August 1992), although he did captain Northern Transvaal against the All Blacks (lost 17–24) at Loftus Versfeld (14.8.92), four years after having made his provincial debut for rivals Transvaal, with whom he played 27 times.

Robinson, R. A.   England

Full name: Richard Andrew Robinson
Club: Bath
Position: Openside flanker
Height: 5ft 9in (1.75m)
Weight: 13st 12lb (88kg)
Occupation: Assistant coach, Bath RFC
Born: Taunton, 3.4.64
Family links with rugby: Brother (Sean) played for Saracens
International debut: Australia 28, England 8, 1988
Five Nations debut: England 12, Scotland 12, 1989
Notable landmarks in rugby career: Andy ended six years in the international wilderness when England boss Jack Rowell recalled him for the 1995/96 curtain-raiser against the world champion Springboks at Twickenham (18.11.95). South Africa won 24–14 and the grossly unfortunate Andy was jettisoned back into the wilderness – if you can

England (1988)
Last Season	1 cap	0 pts
Career	8 caps	4 pts

Caps (8): **1988** A(a2), Fj, A(b) **1989** S, I, F, W **1995** SA
Points (4 – 1t): **1989** F(1t)

refer to Bath as a 'wilderness'. While he might not have been a feature on the Test match scene since the late 1980s, Andy has been a dominant figure on the domestic front, as Bath have fairly monopolised the league and cup competitions. In addition, as coach of Colston's Collegiate School, he has turned the Bristol school into the best in the land, winning both the 1994/95 and 1995/96 *Daily Mail* national knockout cup competitions. Andy won the first of his eight caps in Sydney (12.6.88) when England were well beaten by the Wallabies. By the end of the year he had helped England reverse the result, on a famous day at Twickenham (5.11.88), and he then set about European rugby. In 1989 Andy was named European player of the year, and celebrated with a call-up to the British Lions tour of Australia, playing in six matches, though not figuring in a Test series which the Lions won 2–1. Then it all ended for him and he had to make do with captaining England B in 1990. Andy can boast having captained Bath to league and cup double (1992), and the South West in the Divisional Championship.

Rodber, T. A. K. England

Full name: Timothy Andrew Keith Rodber
Clubs: Northampton & Army
Position: Flanker, No.8
Height: 6ft 6in (1.98m)
Weight: 16st 7lb (100kg)
Occupation: Army officer, Green Howards
Born: Richmond, Yorkshire, 2.7.69
Family: Single
Family links with rugby: Father played
Former clubs: Oxford Old Boys, Petersfield
International debut: Scotland 7, England 25, 1992
Five Nations debut: As above
Best rugby memory: Beating South Africa in first Test (1994)
Worst rugby memory: Being sent off against Eastern Province (1994)
Toughest opponent: Dean Richards (Leicester & England) – awesome in every department.
Serious injuries: Popped ribs
Other sporting claims to fame: Hampshire Schools County hockey and cricket

England (1992)

Last Season	11 caps	0 pts
Career	25 caps	10 pts

Caps (25): **1992** S, I **1993** NZ **1994** I, F, W, SA(1,2), R, C **1995** I, F(a), W, S wc-Arg, It, WS(R), A, NZ, F(b). SA, WS(b) **1996** W, S(R), I(TR)
Points (10 – 2t): **1994** W(1t), R(1t)

Suggestions to improve rugby: Anything to take away stagnant play
Notable landmarks in rugby career: What a difference a year appears to make. Tim enjoyed a mighty season for England in 1994/95, being in the vanguard of all their best work, and constantly pestering the gain line with his bullish runs. He appeared in all 12 of England's games, and his whole-hearted displays did much to erase the unhappy memory of his dismissal, for fighting (retaliation), against Eastern Province (Port Elizabeth, 7.6.94) during England's tour to South Africa (the only other player ever to be sent off in an English jersey was Mike Burton back in 1975). Contrast that with 1995/96, when Tim's stock went up and down like a fiddler's elbow. Dropped for the start of the 1996 Five Nations series, Tim was recalled one match later, only to be dumped again after a decent enough performance against Wales (3.2.96). Thankfully he had Northampton's English League Two title charge to distract him from his international frustration, caused more by Jack Rowell's uncertain mind than any failure on his part. Having been selected as a No.8 in his first two international

outings during England's 1992 Grand Slam run, Tim was moved to blindside flanker in 1993/94. Had represented England's inaugural Under-21 side in 54–13 defeat of Romania in Bucharest (13.5.89) and, after helping an England XV beat Italy 33–15 in May 1990 (won 33–15), toured with full England squad to Argentina that summer. In 1990/91 he scored tries for England B against Namibia and Ireland, and represented Northampton in the 1991 Pilkington Cup final, losing to Harlequins in extra time. On a happier note, he helped England win the 1993 World Cup Sevens title in Edinburgh, and scored one of England's paltry two tries (against Wales) in the 1993/94 Five Nations series.

Roff, J. Australia

Full name: Joe Roff
State: Australian Capital Territory
Position: Wing, centre, fullback
Height: 6ft 4in(1.92m)
Weight: 15st 6lb(98kg)
Occupation: Student
Born: 20.9.75
International debut: Australia 27, Canada 11, 1995
Notable landmarks in rugby career: Flagged at the 1995 World Cup as one of Australia's stars in the making, Joe wasted little time in fulfilling his potential. Two appearances in South Africa realised three tries – one on his debut (31.5.95) and two in the 42–3 defeat of Romania (Stellenbosch, 3.6.95) – and also underlined the power of the man. Indeed, it was probably only because Jonah Lomu made such a big impression that Joe escaped the avalanche of hype which descended upon his All Black rival. Returned home to play a full part in Bledisloe Cup series, which New Zealand won 2–0 despite Joe kicking eight points

Australia (1995)		
Last Season	6 caps	33 pts
Career	6 caps	33 pts

Caps (6): **1995** wc-C, R. NZ(1,2) **1996** W(1,2)

Points (33 – 5t,1c,2p): **1995** wc-C(1t), R(2t). NZ(1: 1c, 2p) **1996** W(1:1t), W(2:1t)

in first Test (Auckland, 22.7.95). Against expectation, he got back to winning ways in 1996, wearing colours of Australian Capital Territory in the inaugural Super-12 tournament. ACT, a hitherto unfashionable rugby state, were able to offer a home to disenchanted Reds (Queensland) and Waratahs (New South Wales), and the bulked-up Brumbies made the most of it. They led the standings early in the season, thanks to superb form at their Canberra home, and although they narrowly missed out on the semi-finals, had the satisfaction of beating both finalists, Auckland Blues and Natal Sharks. Buoyed by his Super-12 experience, Joe returned to the Wallaby lair for the home series against Wales, and scored Australia's opening try in their 56–25 first Test victory (Brisbane, 8.6.96).

Roumat, O. France

Full name: Olivier Roumat
Club: Dax
Position: Lock
Height: 6ft 6in (1.98m)
Weight: 17st 5lb (111kg)
Occupation: Master surveyor
Born: Mont-de-Marsan, 16.6.66
Family links with rugby: Father played in Mont-de-Marsan back row.
International debut: New Zealand 34, France 20, 1989
Five Nations debut: Wales 19, France 29, 1990
Notable landmarks in rugby career: Moved alongside Jean Condom as France's most-capped lock of all time (61 apps, 1982–90) and gave us one of the most poignant memories of last summer's World Cup when he collapsed in tears after France's agonising semi-final defeat by South Africa (Durban, 17.6.95). Collapsed for another reason midway through the 1996 Five Nations series, when his head was stamped on by the Irish boot of Peter Clohessy. The cure for his South African ills was the best one imaginable for a Frenchman – the winning try against England, as France ended a run of eight straight defeats at the hands of their long-standing foe with 19–9 victory in a frankly dreadful third-place play-off (Pretoria, 22.6.95). There was no such consolation in 1996 as France blew the championship by losing their final game to Wales. Olivier was 'suspended' by the French Federation from the autumn

France (1989)
Last Season	11 caps	5 pts
Career	61 caps	23 pts

Caps (61): **1989** NZ(2R), BL **1990** W, E, S, I, R, A(1,2,3), NZ(1,2) **1991** S, I, W, F, R, US(1),W wc-R, Fj, C, E **1992** W(R), E(R), S, I, SA(1,2), Arg(b) **1993** E, S, I, W, R(a), SA(1,2), R(b), A(1,2) **1994** I, W, E, C(a), NZ(1,2), C(b) **1995** W, E(a), S(a) wc-IC, S(b), I(b), SA, E(b) **1996** E, S, I, W, Arg(1,2)
Points (23 – 5t): **1991** W(1t) wc-R(1t) **1992** SA(2:1t) **1994** W(1t) **1995** wc-E(b:1t)

1995 Test series against New Zealand as 'punishment' for staying on with Thierry Lacroix in South Africa after the World Cup to help Natal win the Currie Cup. He had previously captained France to their first series win in South Africa since 1958 during the summer of 1993, after 'regular' skipper Jean-Francois Tordo had been stamped out of the tour. France drew first Test 20–20 (Durban, 26.6.93) before winning second Test 18–17 (Johannesburg, 3.7.93). 'Olivier was magnifique, both as a player and a captain,' opined Tordo generously. Olivier retained captaincy on his return home. But his fortunes dipped during 1994 Five Nations Championship when, having scored a try in the defeat by Wales (Cardiff, 19.2.94), he was dropped after England won again in Paris (5.3.94). However, he returned in time to share in France's historic 2–0 series win in New Zealand. Became the first French forward to score a five-point try when he touched down against South Africa (Paris, 24.10.92). This feat partially made up for his dismissal while playing against New Zealand for a World XV in Wellington that summer: Kiwi referee David Bishop dismissed him for illegal use of a shoe after only nine minutes. He was banned for four weeks and missed the tour to Argentina. Formerly a flanker, his position against the British Lions XV in 1989, he built himself an impressive reputation at 1988 Student World Cup.

Roux, J. P.   South Africa

Full name: Johannes (Johan) Petrus Roux
Province: Transvaal
Position: Scrum-half
Height: 5ft 11in (1.80m)
Weight: 13st 5lb (85kg)
Occupation: Stockbroker, Ed Hern Rudolph
Born: Pretoria, 25.2.69
Family: Married
Former clubs/province: Narbonne (Fra), Harlequins (Eng), Northern Transvaal
International debut: South Africa 27, England 9, 1994
Notable landmarks in rugby career: Given his debut after an impressive showing for Transvaal in their 24–21 defeat of England (Johannesburg, 28.5.94), and for South Africa B in their 19–16 defeat of the same tourists (Kimberley, 31.5.94), ex-Harlequin Johan promptly helped turn around the fortunes of the national side. England had recovered from their Transvaal defeat to stun South Africa the following weekend, winning 32–15 in the first Test (Pretoria, 4.6.94). One of the Boks to

pay the price was scrum-half Joost van der Westhuizen – Johan came in and South Africa breezed to a 27–9 victory in the second Test. The Transvaal terror hung onto his place through the tour to New Zealand, operating in all three Tests (none of them wins), and also turning out against Counties (scored two tries), Wellington, Waikato, Otago (as a replacement) and Canterbury. Opened his try-scoring account with a brace in South Africa's 42–22 first Test defeat of Argentina (Port Elizabeth, 8.10.94), but did not then tour to Wales, Scotland and Ireland; Natal's Kevin Putt went along instead as backup to van der Westhuizen. Johan, who had previously captained Northern Transvaal's Under-20 side, re-emerged in the 1995 World Cup, appearing in three games as South Africa surged towards ecstasy.

South Africa (1994)		
Last Season	0 caps	0 pts
Career	8 caps	10 pts

Caps (8): **1994** E(2), NZ(1,2,3), Arg(1) **1995** wc-R, C, F(R)

Points (10 – 2t): **1994** Arg(1:2t)

Rowntree, G. C. England

Full name: Graham Christopher Rowntree
Nickname: Wig (dodgy haircut)
Club: Leicester
Position: Prop
Height: 6ft (1.83m)
Weight: 17st 2lb (104kg)
Occupation: Part-time insurance broker, P&G Bland, Leicester
Born: Stockton-on-Tees, 18.4.71
Family: Single
International debut: England 24, Scotland 12, 1995
Five Nations debut: As above
Best rugby memory: Beating Scotland (1996)
Worst rugby memory: Losing 1996 Pilkington Cup final
Most embarrassing memory: 'Scoring' a try on the five-metre line against London Irish (1992)
Toughest opponent: Jeff Probyn (Wasps & England)
Do you really want to be a full-time professional? Yes, it's the way forward if we are going to keep up with the southern hemisphere.

England (1995)		
Last Season	5 caps	0 pts
Career	8 caps	0 pts

Caps (8): **1995** S(TR) wc-It, WS(a). WS(b) **1996** F, W, S, I

Points Nil

408

How well has rugby handled move to professionalism? 5/10. It has all happened too fast for a lot of people.

Do you have a duty to entertain? Our duty is to perform to the best of our capabilities. If we do our best and become fitter, the game will become more entertaining.

Do you feel a loyalty to your club in this new era? Yes, at Leicester for sure.

Notable landmarks in rugby career: The disappointment of Leicester having both the English league and cup slip through their hands at the death was a sad postscript to an otherwise rewarding 1995/96 for Graham. His first full campaign in full national colours ended with England winning the Five Nations title in a dramatic finale. A part of Leicester's renowned front row (along with Darren Garforth and Richard Cockerill), known as 'The ABC Club', which some believe to be the best in England – the trio even picked up their own sponsorship deal last season. The youngest member of Leicester's 1993 Pilkington Cup-winning side, Graham nonetheless had to exercise patience before gaining his first cap as a temporary replacement for Jason Leonard during the 1995 Grand Slam decider, in which England beat Scotland 24–12 (Twickenham, 18.3.95). An England Colts team mate of Martin Johnson and Steve Ojomoh, he toured with England A to Canada in 1993, playing in both 'Tests', and then traipsed around South Africa with the full England squad in 1994, appearing against Orange Free State (lost 11–22), Western Transvaal (won 26–24), South Africa B (lost 16–19) and Eastern Province (won 31–13), but failing to get a look-in on Test match days. Graham enjoyed better fortune on returning to the New Republic for last summer's World Cup, being awarded starts in the wins against Italy (Durban, 31.5.95) and Western Samoa (Durban, 4.6.95), and making a favourable impression on both occasions. Joined Leicester from Hinckley, where he was educated, in 1990 and three years later broke into the Midlands and England A sides.

Touchlines: Training, golf

Scotland centre Ian Jardine has England forwards Martin Johnson (left) and Graham Rowntree (right) in his clutches.

Rush, E. J. New Zealand

Full name: Eric James Rush
Club: North Harbour
Position: Wing
Height: 6ft (1.83m)
Weight: 13st 5lb (85kg)
Occupation: Solicitor, Copeland Fitzpatrick
Born: 11.2.65
Family: Married, three children
International debut: New Zealand 34, Wales 9, 1995
Notable landmarks in rugby career: An explosive runner, Eric would be the pride of any international team in world rugby – except, it seems, New Zealand. For while he has been a devastating player in both sevens and XVs for many years, Eric has picked up only a handful of caps. That is the problem when you also have Jonah Lomu and Jeff Wilson to accomodate. He finally made his Test debut at the 1995 World Cup, coming on as a 70th-minute replacement for Big Jonah in the 34–9 defeat of Wales (Johannesburg,

New Zealand (1995)
Last Season	6 caps	25 pts
Career	6 caps	25 pts

Caps (6): 1995 wc-W(R), J. It, F(1,2) 1996 S(2)
Points (25 – 5t): 1995 wc-J(3t), It(1t), F(2:1t)

31.5.95). Next time up, he ran in a try hat-trick as New Zealand obliterated Japan 145–17 (Bloemfontein, 4.6.95). But that was that until after the All Blacks had swept Australia in the Bledisloe Cup series in July. He then toured to Italy and France and, with Wilson injured, played in all three Tests, scoring tries in the 70–6 defeat of Italy in Bologna and in the 37–12 series-splitting second Test victory over France (Paris, 18.11.95). Until 1992 Eric had been an openside flanker, and a heck of a good one at that. But that year he became an All Black and a winger, touring Australia and South Africa as a replacement. He remained in the wings until he returned to South Africa three years later for the World Cup, but in the interim made sure that he always remained an option by regularly turning on the style for North Harbour in the National Provincial Championship, along with fellow All Black three-quarters Frank Bunce and Walter Little.

Sadourny, J.-L.   France

Full name: Jean-Luc Sadourny
Club: Colomiers
Position: Wing, fullback
Height: 6ft 1in (1.86m)
Weight: 13st 9lb (86.5kg)
Occupation: Company manager,
Mag Pub L'Espace
Family: Married with two children
Born: Toulouse, 26.8.66
International debut: Wales 9, France
22, 1991
Five Nations debut: France 13,
England 31, 1992
Notable landmarks in rugby career:
Permanent fixture in French fullback
slot in 1995/96, until he was given
the day off against Romania in April.
Before that he had helped France win
the Latin Cup in Argentina, scoring
two tries in the 34–22 defeat of Italy
(14.10.92), and claimed a first Test
try in the 22–15 victory over New
Zealand in Toulouse (11.11.95).
Jean-Luc had been the toast of the
nation after rounding off what
captain Philippe Saint-Andre termed
'the try from the end of the world' in
New Zealand a year earlier. France
had won the first Test 22–8, but
were trailing in the second Test with
seconds to go. From under their own
posts France launched an audacious
counter-attack.

France (1991)

Last Season	16 caps	15 pts
Career	44 caps	50 pts

Caps (44): **1991** W(R) wc-C(R) **1992** E(R), S, I, Arg(a1R,a2), SA(1,2) **1993** R(a), SA(1,2), R(b), A(1,2) **1994** I, W, E, S, C(a), NZ(1,2), C(b) **1995** W, E(a), S(a), I(a), R(a) wc-T, S(b), I(b), SA, E(b). It, R(b), Arg, NZ(1,2) **1996** E, S, I, W, Arg(1,2)

Points (50 – 9t,2dg): **1992** I(1t) **1993** A(1:1dg) **1994** S(1t), NZ(1:1dg), NZ(2:1t), C(b:1t) **1995** S(a:1t), R(a:1t). It(2t), NZ(1:1t)

a touch before Jean-Luc rounded off the match and series-clinching try at the other end of Eden Park (3.7.94). Thereafter he added tries against Canada (17.12.94), Scotland (18.2.95) and Romania (7.4.95), but none came close to giving him the same buzz. One of four fullbacks employed by France during 1992/93, Jean-Luc had to wait until 1993/94 to finally establish himself as the successor to Serge Blanco, playing in all ten Tests (scoring a try against Scotland, 19.3.94, and a dropped goal in the 16–13 defeat of Australia at Bordeaux, 30.10.93). Had deposed Stephane Ougier on the 1992 summer tour of Argentina, after coming on as a 42nd-minute replacement for the Toulouse player in the 27–12 first Test win in Buenos Aires (4.7.92). Jean-Luc retained his place for the second Test the following week, and took his cap tally to nine with appearances in both legs of the drawn series with South Africa back home in October. However, Sebastien Viars was preferred against Argentina in Nantes, and Jean-Baptiste Lafond took over after that humiliating loss. Jean-Luc marked his B debut with a try in 31–10 win over Scotland at Hughenden. He lasted just nine minutes on his Five Nations debut against England in Paris (15.2.92) before running straight into Alain Penaud so that he had to be led groggily out of the arena. His first cap came as a 76th-minute replacement for Blanco in the floodlit international against Wales at the Arms Park (4.9.91).

Saint-Andre, P.   France

Full name: Philippe Saint-Andre
Club: Montferrand
Position: Wing, centre
Height: 5ft 11in (1.80m)
Weight: 13st 6lb (85kg)
Occupation: Publicity officer, Irish pub owner
Family: Married
Born: Romans, 19.4.67
Former clubs: Romans, Clermont-Ferrand
International debut: France 6, Romania 12, 1990
Five Nations debut: Ireland 13, France 21, 1991
Notable landmarks in rugby career: Philippe maintained his prolific strike rate in international rugby

with eight tries in the maximum 12 Tests post-World Cup (giving him 15 in the last 24). If ever a captain led by example it was Philippe, whose tenure as skipper has seen France win in Scotland for the first time in 16 years and inflict the first-ever 2–0 series beating New Zealand (1994). It has also seen Scotland win in France for the first time in 26 years, and France lose to Canada for the first time ever – but enough of that. Philippe was appointed France captain for the 1994 Five Nations finale against Scotland (won 20–12, Murrayfield, 19.3.94) in succession to Olivier Roumat, who had been dropped after the defeat by England a fortnight previously. In being so appointed, Philippe, nicknamed *le goret* ('the piglet'), became the first wing to captain France since Christian Darrouy 27 years ago. He celebrated this with his second try of the championship, his first having come against Ireland (won 35–15, Paris, 15.1.94). Philippe has become one of world rugby's most potent finishers, with 29 Test tries in the past five years. His finest moment came at Twickenham (16.1.91), where he scored 'The Try' against England in a thrilling grand slam decider. The move was initiated by Serge Blanco and fed, via Jean-Baptiste Lafond, Didier Camberabero, Philippe Sella and then Didier Camberabero's boot, to behind enemy lines, where Philippe, who has clocked 10.9sec over 100m, scorched through to apply the *coup de grace*. This feat was bettered only by Jean-Luc Sadourny's try 'from the end of the world', which accounted for the All Blacks on a 1994 tour that saw Philippe play both Tests at centre. Claimed a championship high of three tries – against England (two) and Ireland – as France won 1993 Five Nations Cup. The owner of an Irish pub in Clermont-Ferrand, Philippe first

France (1990)		
Last Season	18 caps	55 pts
Career	62 caps	146 pts

Caps (62): **1990** R, A(3), NZ(1,2) **1991** I(R), W(a), E(a), US(1,2), W(b) wc-R(b), Fj, C, E(b) **1992** W, E, S, I, R, Arg(a1,a2), SA(1,2) **1993** E, S, I, W, SA(1,2), A(1,2) **1994** I, W, E, S, C(a), NZ(1,2), C(b) **1995** W, E(a), S(a), I(a), R(a) wc-T, IC, S(b), I(b), SA, E(b). It, R(b), Arg, NZ(1,2) **1996** E, S, I, W, R, Arg(1,2)

Points (146 – 31t): **1991** W(a:1t), E(a:1t), US(1:1t), W(b:1t) wc-R(b:1t), C(1t) **1992** W(1t), R(2t), Arg(a2:1t) **1993** E(2t), I(1t), SA(1:1t) **1994** I(1t), S(1t) **1995** W(1t), S(a:2t), I(a:1t) wc-T(1t), IC(1t), I(b:1t). Arg(2t), NZ(1:1t), NZ(2:2t) **1996** I(1t), Arg(1:1t), Arg(2:1t)

represented France A and B before stepping into the top flight at Stade Patrice Brocas, Auch (24.5.90) as a centre for the visit of Romania, who triumphed (12–6) on French soil for the first time

Saverimutto, C.   Ireland

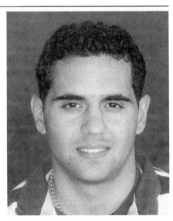

Full name: Christian Saverimutto
Nickname: Savvy
Club: Sale
Position: Scrum-half
Height: 5ft 8in (1.73m)
Weight: 13st (83kg)
Occupation: Chartered surveyor, Hillier Parker
Born: Birkenhead, 8.8.71
Family: Single
Family links with rugby: Brother Robin played for Ireland Under-21
Former clubs: Sheffield University, Waterloo, New Brighton
International debut: Ireland 44, Fiji 8, 1995
Five Nations debut: Ireland 10, Scotland 16, 1996

Serious injuries: Torn cruciate knee ligaments (1996)
Best rugby memories: Helping Waterloo beat Bath 9–8 in 1992/93 Pilkington Cup third round; getting Ireland call-up against Fiji.
Worst rugby memory: Tearing cruciate knee ligaments on eve of professionalism.
Do you really want to be a full-time professional? Yes
How well has rugby handled move to professionalism? 7/10
Do you have a duty to entertain? Yes
Do you feel a loyalty to your club in this new era? Less so
Other sporting claims to fame: Badminton and cricket for Cheshire Schools
Notable landmarks in rugby career: First season of international rugby turned sour for Christian when first he was dropped by Ireland during the 1996 Five Nations series, then he tore cruciate knee ligaments while representing the Irish in the Benidorm Sevens – he will be out for between six and 12 months. How much brighter the season had started for the Cheshire player with Dublin-born grandparents. Having declared for Ireland, after having been a member of both England's Colts and Under-21 squads without getting a game, Christian was selected to represent the Irish Exiles in the Inter-Provincial Championship. That, as well as impressive displays for Sale, persuaded the selectors that he was the man for the No.9 jersey against Fiji (Dublin, 18.11.95). Ireland won 44–8 and he retained his place for the next two games. Sadly for him, after Ireland's win over the US Eagles in Atlanta, they unexpectedly crashed to Scotland in the Five Nations opener. Halfbacks Christian and Eric Elwood paid the price, with Niall Hogan taking over at scrum-half.
Touchlines: Waterskiing

Ireland (1995)		
Last Season	3 caps	0 pts
Career	3 caps	0 pts

Caps (3): **1995** Fj **1996** US, S
Points Nil

Scotland forwards Doddie Weir (below) and Eric Peters prepare for lift-off in a lineout during Scotland's 62–31 first Test loss to New Zealand in Dunedin.

414

Shepherd, R. J. S.   Scotland

Full name: Rowen James Stanley
Shepherd
Nickname: Shep
Club: Melrose
Position: Full-back
Height: 6ft (1.83m)
Weight: 13st 12lb (88kg)
Occupation: District rugby
development officer
Born: Ediburgh, 25.12.70
Family: Girlfriend (Kim)
Family links with rugby: Father
(Gordon) played for Scottish North
& Midlands
Former clubs: Caithness, Edinburgh
Acads
International debut: Scotland 15,
Western Samoa 15, 1995
Five Nations debut: Ireland 10,
Scotland 16, 1996
Best rugby memory: Scotland 19,
France 14, 1996
Worst rugby memory: Italy 29,
Scotland 17, 1996
Most embarrassing memory:

Scotland (1995)		
Last Season	7 caps	23 pts
Career	7 caps	23 pts

Caps (7): **1995** WS **1996** I, F, W, E,
NZ(1,2)
Points (23 – 1t, 3c, 3p, 1dg):
NZ(1:2c,3p,1dg), NZ(1:1t,1c)

Arguing with my dad during a sevens
match in my sixth-form days. Did I give a bad pass or could he not catch?
Toughest opponent: Ian Jardine (Stirling County & Scotland)
Do you really want to be a full-time professional? Yes and no. There is not
enough longterm security/money in Scottish rugby) to put everything into it.
How well has rugby handled move to professionalism: 5/10. Rugby is too
obsessed with the best players. I'd like to see every club make some provision
for youth development, as there will be no future if all the money in rugby is
ploughed into salaries for the top players.
Do you have a duty to entertain? Yes
Do you feel a loyalty to your club in this new era? Yes, I joined Melrose to
further my career in a playing sense.
Notable landmarks in rugby career: The man accorded the dubious honour of
following in the footsteps of one Gavin Hastings, Rowen made a pretty good
fist of it in 1995/96. After a poor goalkicking display in the New Year defeat by
Italy (a full Scotland team masquerading as an A XV), which almost cost him
his place, Rowen bounced back to impress in the 1996 Five Nations series as
unfancied Scotland once again confounded their critics. Had to wait until last

summer's tour to New Zealand to open his points-scoring account, kicking 16 points (2c, 3p, 1dg) in Scotland's 62–31 first Test defeat at the hands of the rampant All Blacks at Carisbrook Park, Dunedin (15.6.96). But it was nothing to his wait to win his first cap. Rowen represented Scotland on three tours, playing in nine of the 16 games in North Africa (1991), Argentina (1994) and Zimbabwe (1995). The SRU's decision not to award caps in Zimbabwe hurt him especially, as he played at fullback in both, scoring a try in the first. Born on Christmas Day in 1970, Rowen has also represented his country at Under-18, Under-19, Under-21 and A grades.

Touchlines: Mixed hockey, golf

Shiel, A. G. Scotland

Full name: Andrew Graham Shiel
Club: Melrose
Position: Outside-half, centre
Height: 5ft 10lb (1.78m)
Weight: 12st 10lb (81kg)
Occupation: Junior site manager, J&R Elliot of Hawick
Born: Galashiels, 13.8.70
Family: Single
Family links with rugby: Father (Andrew) played for Melrose GS
Former club: Manly (Aus)
International debut: Scotland 24, Ireland 15, 1991
Five Nations debut: Scotland 15, Ireland 3, 1993
Best rugby memory: Scoring winning try against Ireland on Scotland debut after coming on as 43rd-minute replacement in 1991 World Cup match at Murrayfield.
Worst rugby memory: Missing most of 1993/94 season through injury.
Most embarrassing memory: Ball toppling over in front of posts before I kicked it during 1990 Hawick Sevens.

Scotland (1991)		
Last Season	1 cap	0 pts
Career	15 caps	14 pts

Caps (15): 1991 wc-I(R),WS 1993 I,F,W,E,NZ 1994 Arg(1,2),SA 1995 R wc-IC,F,NZ. WS
Points (14 – 3t): 1991 wc-I(R:1t) 1994 R(1t) 1995 wc-IC(1t)

Toughest opponent: Sean Lineen (Boroughmuir & Scotland)
Biggest influences on career: Ian McGeechan and Jim Telfer
Serious injuries: Straining inner and exterior quadriceps and adductor muscle (1988/89) and missing over four months of rugby; pelvic strain (November

1990 – three months out); knee ligaments (1993/94 – six months out); flaked bone in ankle, trapping nerve.

Other sporting achievements: Athletics for Borders Schools and Borders AAA

Suggestions to improve Scottish rugby: Playing standards in Scotland need to be improved at club level (inferior to those in England and Wales). Still too forward-orientated in Scotland (lack of running ability).

Notable landmarks in rugby career: The one Scotland centre truly capable of unlocking international midfields, Graham's rugby in 1995/96 was frustrated by injury, which kept him out of the Five Nations campaign and then came back to haunt him on tour in New Zealand, where otherwise he would definitely have played in the Test series. His absence was all the more galling for the form he had shown in the 1995 World Cup – calling the tune against Cote d'Ivoire (and scoring a try), and troubling both France and New Zealand. It was only a shame he had to move to fly-half midway through the quarter-final against the All Blacks (Pretoria, 3.6.95), because the Melrose combination between him and Craig Chalmers (before the latter became dazed) was definitely making the Kiwis think. It was an especially brave performance, as he had sustained a fractured nose cartilage against France (Pretoria, 3.6.95) which, safe to assume, hurt like hell. Injury had also blighted 1993/94 for Graham, who reckons he only played in three-and-a-half out of 12 months due to damaged anterior cruciate ligaments in his left knee (which caused him to miss Scotland's 1992 tour to the South Seas) and a trapped nerve in his ankle caused by a flaked bone. In between injuries, he fitted in one Test cap, as centre in 51–15 loss to New Zealand (Murrayfield, 20.11.93). The run of bad luck started at the end of a season in which he had established himself as heir-apparent to Sean Lineen alongside Scott Hastings in Scottish midfield. He played in all four legs of the 1993 Five Nations Championship after a trial in which he started with the 'possibles' and finished with the 'probables'. Represented Scottish Schools (three times), Scotland Under-19s and Under-21s (twice). Scored six points in 1989/90 defeat (10–24) by Wales Under-21, and played in 15–23 loss to same opposition (1990/91). Toured with Scotland to New Zealand (1990), North America and Canada (1991), Australia (1992) and Argentina (1994), the last trip ending his injury nightmare as he appeared at centre in both Tests. Having been included in Scotland's 1991 World Cup squad, he was given debut against Ireland as a 43rd-minute replacement for outside-half Craig Chalmers. A fairytale scenario saw him score a try as Scotland came from behind to win. Seven days later he won his second cap (as centre) in quarter-final against Western Samoa when knee injury ruled out Lineen. Remained in Australia after 1992 tour to play for Manly.

Touchlines: Social golf, cricket, swimming

Sleightholme, J. M.   England

Full name: Jonathan Mark
Sleightholme
Nickname: Sleights
Club: Bath
Position: Wing
Height: 5ft 10in (1.78m)
Weight: 14st (89kg)
Occupation: Teacher, Culverhay
School, Bath
Born: Malton, North Yorks, 5.8.72
Family: Single
Former clubs: Grimsby, Hull
Ionians, Wakefield
International debut: France 15,
England 12, 1996
Five Nations debut: As above
Best rugby memories: First cap (and
National Anthem) in Paris; scoring
try versus Ireland.
Worst rugby memory: Being
dropped by Bath at start of 1995/96
Most embarrassing memory: Playing
my first game of rugby aged 15,
being put on wing and having the

England (1996)		
Last Season	4 caps	5 pts
Career	4 caps	5 pts

Caps (4): 1996 F, W, S, I
Points (5 – 1t): 1996 I(1t)

ball kicked to me: I had no idea what to do with it so, with three forwards bearing down on me, I just chucked it into touch.
Toughest opponents: Jonah Lomu (New Zealand) and Jason Robinson (Wigan RLFC).
Do you really want to be a full-time professional? Yes – for us to keep up with the Southern Hemisphere and, indeed, Rugby League, we have to have sufficient time to reach our full potential.
How well has rugby handled move to professionalism? 6/10. It was thrust upon the unions, who were caught cold.
Do you have a duty to entertain? Yes, definitely. The desire to win is closely followed by the desire to win with style. We must look to win with style, because if we enjoy what we are doing the fans will enjoy it as well.
Do you feel a loyalty to your club in this new era? Yes, absolutely.
Notable landmarks in rugby career: The find of 1995/96 for England, along with Lawrence Dallaglio, Jon lit up the Five Nations series as much as any player, and did England a huge favour by scoring a magnificent try against Ireland (Twickenham, 16.3.96) which clinched the championship. A refreshing character, Jon only became a Bath regular last season, helping them win the league and cup double and impressing in cross-code challenge against Wigan

RLFC. His try in the union return at Twickenham (25.5.96) was especially memorable, as he scorched past Jason Robinson, who is no slouch himself, en route to the line. Remarkably, Jon only took up rugby as a 15-year-old, having attended a non-rugby school in Grimsby. Made his name at Wakefield, scoring 42 tries in 60 games. A former England representative at Colts, Under-21 and Emerging Players levels, his England A debut came in Dublin (January 1995), and he toured with the A squad to Australia and Fiji later that year. Test debut in Paris (20.1.96) was particularly memorable for the passion with which he sang the National Anthem prior to kickoff.

Touchlines: Being lazy

Small, J. T.   South Africa

Full name: James Terence Small
Province: Natal
Club: Wits
Position: Wing
Height: 6ft (1.82m)
Weight: 13st 3lb (84kg)
Occupation: Self-employed
Born: Cape Town, 10.2.69
Family links with sport: Son of former Springbok soccer player Vernon Small (1956)
Former province: Transvaal
International debut: South Africa 24, New Zealand 27, 1992
Notable landmarks in rugby career: Followed up a tremendous defensive display against Jonah Lomu in the 1995 World Cup final by becoming the leading try-scorer in the 1996 Super-12 tournament (with 14) as Natal reached the final. At last the right sort of headlines for a player of immense talent, who for too long had let himself down. His nadir came in 1994, when he was sent off for verbally abusing English referee Ed Morrison during South Africa's 20–28 second Test defeat against Australia (Brisbane, 14.8.94). He confessed: 'The Springboks blazer means more to me than most things

South Africa (1992)

Last Season	7 caps	5 pts
Career	26 caps	50 pts

Caps (26): 1992 NZ, A, F(1,2), E 1993 F(1,2), Arg(1,2), A(1,2,3) 1994 E(1,2), NZ(1,2,3TR), Arg(1) 1995 WS(a) wc-A, R, F, NZ. W, It, E
Points (50 – 10t): 1992 F(1:1t) 1993 F(2:1t), Arg(1:2t), Arg(2:1t), A(1:2t), A(3:1t) 1995 WS(a:1t). W(1t)

in life, and I let it down. I've also let down my team mates. It will be a while before I can look them in the eye.' But he continued to play over-aggressive rugby, and then started getting himself in trouble away from the pitch. His tour to Australia (1994) was particularly unhappy. It was such a shame, as James had been the most prolific try-scorer in world rugby during 1993, with seven scores in a six-Test spell, and is worshipped by the youth of South Africa. Petulance got the better of him in the first Test against England (4.6.94) and he was fortunate to last the duration. Formerly a superb soccer player – a talent he inherited from his father, a 1956 international – James was included in the first Springbok side selected after the ending of the international boycott. He played not only against New Zealand but also against Australia the following week, before turning out for Transvaal in the 1992 Currie Cup final. Unhappily for the player, victory went to Natal by the odd point in 27 (he then moved to Natal in 1993 and, would you believe, lost to Transvaal in the 1993 final). But his smile was restored when he scored one of South Africa's two tries in their 20–15 victory over France (Lyon, 17.10.92), in addition to retaining his place for the next two Test engagements, against France (lost 16–29, Paris, 24.10.92) and England (lost 16–33, Twickenham, 14.11.92). Ever-present through 1993 campaign, scoring a try against France in the second Test of the home series (lost 17–18, Johannesburg, 3.7.93), and bagging three tries in the two away Test wins over Argentina in the autumn.

Smith, D. P. P.   Australia

Full name: Damien Paul Peter Smith
State: Queensland
Club: Southern Districts
Position: Wing
Height: 6ft 2in (1.88m)
Weight: 14st 9lb (93kg)
Occupation: Property consultant, Colliers Jardine
Born: 1.2.69
International debut: Australia 12, South Africa 19, 1993
Worst moment in rugby: Kicking a ball 20 metres backwards with a gale-force wind behind me against Welsh Students on 1992 Wales/Ireland Tour.
Toughest opponent: James Small (Natal & South Africa)
Serious injuries: Broken wrist and arm (1990)
Notable landmarks in rugby career: Scored a brilliant try in Australia's quarter-

final defeat by England at last summer's World Cup (Cape Town, 11.6.95), leaping high to take an up-and-under then rolling over the line for the score. It capped a prolific year for the strong-running Queenslander, who claimed eight tries in just 13 Tests. Broke into Queensland side in 1992 and quickly graduated into the Wallaby squad which toured Wales and Ireland. Having missed the 1990

Australia (1993)

Last Season	5 caps	15 pts
Career	18 caps	40 pts

Caps (18): **1993** SA(1,2,3), C, F(2) **1994** I(1,2), It(1,2), WS, NZ **1995** Arg(1,2) wc-SA, R, E. NZ(1,2)

Points (40 – 8t): **1993** C(1t) **1994** I(1:1t), WS(2t) **1995** Arg(1:1t) wc-R(1t), E(1t). NZ(2:1t)

season with a broken arm, he was not about to let his chance slip, and he responded with eight starts out of a possible 13, scoring three tries. However, a Test place eluded him until 1993 when he was drafted in for the three-match home series against South Africa – their first visit 'down under' since 1971. Damien occupied the right wing berth in each of the Tests as Australia came from behind to edge a 2–1 decision. Next goal to be fulfilled was his first international try, achieved during Canada's 43–16 beating in Calgary (9.10.93) in the early throes of an autumn tour which also incorporated two Tests against France. Damian lost out to young NSW flier Alistair Murdoch in the first Test selection stakes but, after France triumphed 16–13 in Bordeaux, was recalled for second match, which yielded a 24–3 series-levelling scoreline. He retained his Test place throughout 1994 and in three of the Wallabies' four World Cup engagements in 1995, before scoring a try in the Bledisloe Cup defeat by New Zealand (29.7.95).

Touchlines: Water skiing, mountaineering, surfing and parachuting.

Aussie powerhouse Joe Roff shows Romania that you can't tie a Wallaby down.

Smith, I. R. Scotland

Full name: Ian Richard Smith
Nickname: Smudge
Club: Gloucester
Position: Flanker
Height: 6ft (1.83m)
Weight: 14st (89kg)
Occupation: Civil engineer, Sir William Halcrow Ltd
Born: Gloucester, 16.3.65
Family: Karen (wife), Sam (son) and Matt (son)
Family links with rugby: Father (Dick) was an England triallist who captained Gloucester and the Barbarians.
Former club: Longlevens, Wollongong (Aus, 1988)
International debut (Scotland): Scotland 7, England 25, 1992
Five Nations debut: As above
Best rugby memory: Scotland 19, France 14, 1996
Worst rugby memory: The pure frustration of 1996 Grand Slam game vs England.

Scotland (1992)

Last Season	8 caps	0 pts
Career	18 caps	0 pts

Caps (18): **1992** E, I, W, A(1,2) **1994** E(R), I, F, Arg(1,2) **1995** wc-IC. WS **1996** I, F, W, E, NZ(1,2)
Points Nil

Most embarrassing memory: Being humiliated 48–6 by Gloucester in 1990 Pilkington Cup final.
Toughest opponent: Andy Robinson (Bath & England)
Biggest influences on career: Father and Derek Cook (coach at Longlevens)
Do you really want to be a full-time professional? Yes, but I would still need the mental stimulation of doing something else too. I can only take so many hours of training.
How well has rugby handled move to professionalism? 3/10. It was all too sudden. There seemed to be not nearly enough forethought.
Do you have a duty to entertain? Yes, it is an attitude of mind which the Southern Hemisphere have long had and which we quickly have to get into.
Do you feel a loyalty to your club in this new era? Yes, perhaps because I'm at the older end of the scale. Certain clubs, like Gloucester, promote loyalty.
Suggestions to improve rugby: I'm in favour of setting up refereeing seminars where referees can get together with players and coaches to work things out.
Notable landmarks in rugby career: Arguably the chief beneficiary of Scotland's change to a more expansive game in 1995/96, Ian had a belter of a Five Nations campaign, being rampant in the loose to ensure that Townsend

and Co had quick ball on tap. 'Ian is the first specialist openside I've had', explained SRU supremo Jim Telfer. ' After a long time in the shadow of others his time has come.' What a turnaround from the 1995 World Cup, when the success of the Wainwright–Morrison–Peters back-row combination shut the international door on Smudge, who had to make do with one outing in Scotland's opener against Cote d'Ivoire (won 89–0, Rustenburg, 26.5.95). Had only been recalled to side in 1993/94 after injury forced out Rob Wainwright. Ian replaced him 66 minutes into the 1994 Calcutta Cup clash at Murrayfield (5.2.94) – a match which England won 15–14 with last kick of game – and he held his place for the final two games of the Wooden Spoon campaign, against Ireland and France, before departing for summer tour to Argentina, where he appeared in both Test defeats. Two years previously he had toured Australia, appearing at openside in both Test losses. A former England 18-Group triallist, who played his 200th game for Gloucester in the 1990 Pilkington Cup final (but would rather not be reminded of the occasion), Ian spent 1988 Australian season playing in Wollongong. Toured Spain with England B (1990) and was selected to England's 1991 World Cup squad, having spent 1990 off-season on standby for Argentina tour. But opted to switch allegiance to Scotland (Scottish grandparents on father's side) and played twice for Scotland B in 1990/91 (vs Ireland and France) before leading side in 19–29 home loss to Ireland in 1991/92 – a season in which he also captained Gloucester (as in 1992/93) and broke into the Scotland team for the Five Nations Championship. Captained Scotland vs New South Wales (lost 15–35, Sydney, 6.6.92) on 1992 tour of Australia.
Touchlines: Shooting, squash, trout fishing

Stanger, A. G.   Scotland

Full name: Anthony George Stanger
Club: Hawick
Position: Centre, wing
Height: 6ft 2in (1.88m)
Weight: 15st 2lb (96kg)
Occupation: New Business representative, RoyScot Trust, Edinburgh
Born: Hawick, 14.5.68
Family: Bridget (wife)
Family links with rugby: Peter (brother) plays for Hawick
Former club: Warringah (Aus)
International debut: Scotland 38, Fiji 17, 1989
Five Nations debut: Ireland 10, Scotland 13, 1990

Best rugby memory: Scoring winning try in 1990 Grand Slam decider against England.

Worst rugby memory: Being dropped by Scotland on 1992 Australia tour.

Other sporting claims to fame: Hawick High School athletics champion (three times).

Suggestions to improve rugby: Make everyone play by the same rulebook. So many people are bending the laws at present, and we get upset because we're being made to look stupid.

Notable landmarks in rugby career: Tony's 39-cap haul includes a share

Scotland (1989)

Last Season	2 caps	5 pts
Career	39 caps	81 pts

Caps (39): **1989** Fj, R **1990** I, F, W, E, NZ(1,2), Arg **1991** F, W, E, I, R wc-J, Z, I, WS, E, NZ **1992** E, I, F, W, A(1,2) **1993** I, F, W, E, NZ **1994** W, E, I, F, SA **1995** R wc-IC **1996** NZ(2)

Points (81 – 18t): **1989** Fj(2t), R(3t) **1990** E(1t), NZ(2:1t), Arg(2t) **1991** I(1t) wc-J(1t), Z(1t), WS(1t) **1992** I(1t) **1993** I(1t) **1994** SA(1t) **1995** R(2t) wc-IC(1t)

of the Scottish record for a wing, having won his 37th cap on the wide outside in the second Test vs New Zealand last summer (Auckland, 22 June) to equal the record set by Iwan Tukao (37: 1985–92). Tony's other two caps came in midfield after his decision to switch to centre at the start of 1993/94. An ever-present in Scotland's side for 35 matches since his debut against Fiji in 1989 before missing the 1994 tour to Argentina through unavailability. Left the limelight to hone his skills as a centre, and looked to have emerged as the genuine article when he claimed two tries against Romania (Murrayfield, 22.4.95). But despite another try-scoring display, this time in the 1995 World Cup opener against Cote d'Ivoire, his was not a convincing performance and Scott Hastings was brought back. Still, Tony's 18 Test tries have moved him to within six of Scottish record scorer I. S. Smith (24 in 32 matches: 1924–33). Indeed, the Hawick flier scored six tries in first six internationals (two on debut against Fiji, three against Romania and one against England in 1990 Grand Slam decider). Toured with Scotland to Japan (1989), New Zealand (1990), North America (1991), Australia (1992) and New Zealand (1996). Made debut for Hawick while 17-year-old student. Earned five caps for Scottish Schools at centre in 1985/86, followed by two for Scotland Under-21s. Began 1990/91 season with two tries in 49–3 defeat of Argentina, taking try-tally to nine in as many games. Could not sustain that prolific pace through 1991/92 season's 11-game schedule, but did not do badly, managing four tries – three in World Cup and one against Ireland in Championship for the second consecutive season.

Touchlines: Social golf

Staples, J. E.   Ireland

Full name: James (Jim) Edward Staples
Nickname: Serial – 'it's always the quiet ones!'
Club: Harlequins
Position: Fullback
Height: 6ft 2in (1.88m)
Weight: 14st 4lb (91kg)
Occupation: Bank officer, Societe Generale
Born: London, 20.10.65
Family: Single
Family links with rugby: Younger brother David played for Westcombe Park.
Former clubs: St Mary's, Bromley, Sidcup, London Irish
International debut: Wales 21, Ireland 21, 1991
Five Nations debut: As above
Best rugby memory: Captaining Ireland (1995/96)
Worst rugby memories: Michael Lynagh's last-gasp try for Australia in our World Cup quarter-final; missing out on promotion to English First Division with London Irish in 1988/89 after losing 22–21 to last-minute dropped goal by Blackheath, having led 21–0 at half-time.

Ireland (1991)		
Last Season	4 caps	0 pts
Career	18 caps	25 pts

Caps (18): **1991** W, E, S, Na(1,2) wc-Z, J, S, A **1992** W, E, NZ(1,2), A **1995** F, W, It wc-NZ. Fj **1996** US, S, F
Points (25 – 5t, 2c): **1991** W(1t), Na(2:1t,2c) wc-J(1t) **1992** NZ(1:1t) **1995** Fj(1t)

Most embarrassing memory: Missing flight home from Spain on first county senior trip
Toughest opponent: Jean-Luc Sadourny (Colomiers & France)
Serious injuries: Prolapsed disc in back; broken nose; damaged knee ligaments (missed whole of 1993/94 season); broken hand (1995).
Do you really want to be a full-time professional? No, but the ever-increasing demands are taking the game that way.
How well has rugby handled move to professionalism? 3/10. 1995/96 was pure chaos from start to finish. To have international players being paid but not club players is farcical. Either the game is professional or it is not.
Do you have a duty to entertain? It is a moral duty, yes, but our first obilgation has to be to win.
Do you feel a loyalty to your club in this new era? Yes, but I don't know how

long loyalty will last. For now the game is still dominated by people brought up in the amateur code.

Other sporting claim to fame: Played in the same Greenwich Borough forward line as Arsenal and England striker Ian Wright.

Notable landmarks in rugby career: A real curate's egg of a season was 1995/96 for Jim. Having been handed the national captaincy for the first four games, he was then concussed against France (Paris, 17.2.96) and forced to miss the next game in Wales. In came Simon Mason and in he stayed. So Ireland captain one moment, dumped in the old wilderness the next – a turnaround made all the more remarkable for the fact that he ended the campaign playing some cracking rugby with Harlequins. Jim's Test career has basically been blighted by injury ever since he damaged knee ligaments in the Irish trial preceding the 1993 Five Nations campaign. Prior to that had been first-choice fullback. Missed whole of 1993/94 campaign with damaged knee ligaments, and after returning for 1994 tour of Australia (playing in five of the eight non-Test matches) and switching allegiances from London Irish to neighbouring Harlequins, he got injured again. This time it happened just half an hour into his World Cup campaign, when he collided with All Black wing Jeff Wilson under a high ball (Jo'burg, 27.5.95), suffered a broken hand and his tournament was over. It was a crying shame, as Jim had looked back to near his best in Five Nations outings against France and Wales. Prior to all this Jim had toured to New Zealand in 1992, weighing in with one of the three tries which so nearly proved good enough to beat the All Blacks in the first Test (Dunedin, 30.5.92). Also played in second Test in Wellington and against Australia in Dublin (31.10.92). Took over from former Ireland fullback Hugo MacNeill at No.15 in London Irish team, and followed his footsteps into Ireland side in 1991. He represented Connacht against 1989 All Blacks, but has since switched provincial allegiances to the Exiles, whom he captained in 1995 Inter-Pros. Played twice for Ireland Under-25s before reaching B grade in 1989/90 with appearance in 22–22 draw with Scotland.

Touchlines: Soccer, most other sports

England wing Rory Underwood takes on the Irish green machine.

Straeuli, R. A. W.　　　South Africa

Full name: Rudolph August Wilkens Straeuli
Province: Transvaal
Position: No.8, flanker
Height: 6ft 4in (1.93m)
Weight: 17st (103kg)
Occupation: Attorney clerk
Born: 20.8.63
Family: Married
International debut: New Zealand 22, South Africa 14, 1994
Family links with rugby: Father (Hans) played for Northern Transvaal; brother-in-law is Springbok Johan Roux.
Former club: Penarth (Wales)
Notable landmarks in rugby career: Appeared in three of South Africa's 1995 World Cup victories, including the final (Johannesburg, 24.6.95), when he came on in the tenth minute of extra time for Mark Andrews. Became a more peripheral figure thereafter, touring with the Boks to Europe but appearing only once, as a 62nd-minute replacement for Ruben Kruger. This was in marked contrast

South Africa (1994)		
Last Season	4 caps	20 pts
Career	10 caps	20 pts

Caps (10): **1994** NZ(1), Arg(1,2), S, W **1995** WS(a) wc-A, WS(b), NZ(R). E(R)
Points (20 – 4t): **1994** NZ(1:1t), Arg(2:1t), S(1t), W(1t)

to his entrance onto the international stage in 1994, when he marked his debut against the All Blacks with a try in the first Test (Dunedin, 9.7.94). Had a spell at Welsh club Penarth, helping the Seasiders to some notable results, including a cherished victory over Swansea. Started provincial life with Northern Transvaal (1986). A product of the Tukkies club in Pretoria, he became the 612th player to be capped by South Africa, having previously been involved in the national Schools, University and Defence sides. Switched allegiance to Transvaal in time to help them beat England (Jo'burg, 28.5.94) and to share in the Currie Cup final victory over Orange Free State. Once ensconced, he set about building his international career. His try-scoring debut was matched by repeat performances in three of his next four outings, against Argentina, Scotland and Wales. He also bagged touchdowns on the 1994 British tour against Wales A, Swansea and Combined Scottish Districts, and captained the Boks in the wins over Cardiff and combined Irish Provinces.

Stransky, J. T.   South Africa

Full name: Joel Stransky
Province: Western Province
Club: College Rovers
Position: Fly-half
Height: 5ft 11in (1.80m)
Weight: 13st 5lb (80kg)
Occupation: Co-owner owner of
Cape Town pub 'The Green Man'
Family: Married
Born: Pietermaritzburg, 16.7.67
International debut: Australia 12,
South Africa 19, 1993
Former province: Natal
Notable landmarks in rugby career:
Hero of South Africa after kicking
them to 1995 World Cup final
victory over New Zealand (Jo'burg,
24.6.95). In an absorbing and utterly
memorable game, Joel landed three
penalty kicks and dropped two
goals, the second in the second
period of extra time as the Boks
edged home 15–12. His 15-point
haul highlighted an excellent year's
work, in which he bagged 152 points
in just 11 outings. It was not all
champagne and caviar, however, as
genial Joel shocked himself by
punching Ben Clarke during the
24–14 defeat of England (Twickenham, 18.11.95). 'I have never hit

South Africa (1993)

Last Season	5 caps	103 pts
Career	15 caps	176 pts

Caps (15): **1993** A(1,2,3), Arg(1) **1994**
Arg(1,2) **1995** WS(a) wc-A, R(TR),
C, F, NZ

Points (176 – 5t, 26c, 30p,3dg):
1993 A(2:1t,2c,2p), A(3:1c), Arg
(1:3c,1p) **1994** Arg(1:1t,4c,3p),
Arg(2:1t,4c,1p) **1995** WS(1t,1c)
wc-A(1t,1c,4p,1dg), C(2c,2p),
F(1c,4p), NZ(3p,2dg). W(3c,3p),
It(4c,4p), E(3p)

anyone in my life before', he confessed. 'Ben late tackled me and I reacted. I
don't know what got into me. I was lucky to stay on the field.' It was a minor
blemish on an otherwise outstanding career. Earned Springbok No.10 jersey
after vying with Transvaal's Hennie le Roux throughout 1993. Le Roux got
first shot, but when the Springboks won neither Test against France at which he
was at the helm, Joel was brought in for the country's first tour to Australia in
22 years. His debut (Sydney, 31.7.93) resulted in a famous 19–12 win for the
visitors against shell-shocked world champions. He took over the goalkicking
duties for the second Test (Brisbane, 14.8.93), after Theo van Rensburg had
been forced to return home for emergency surgery on a groin hernia. Joel
responded with 15 points (1t,2c,2p) – yet Australia still won 28–20. One
Stransky conversion in the deciding third Test was insufficient to stop the series

staying in Oz. Still, he finished the tour with 58 points (1t,22c,3p). Lost Test place on subsequent tour to Argentina, but was back in the box seat in 1995, after Le Roux settled into a midfield role.

Strydom, H. South Africa

Full name: Hannes Strydom
Province: Transvaal
Position: Lock
Height: 6ft 6½ in (1.99m)
Weight: 18st 5lb (112kg)
Occupation: Chemist, Roussel Labs
Family: Married with one child
Born: 13.7.65
International debut: South Africa 17, France 18, 1993
Notable landmarks in rugby career: Springbok lock in 1995 World Cup, being enlisted on four missions including the final itself (Jo'burg, 24.6.95), Hannes owed his start in international rugby to France when they sent shockwaves through South Africa by sharing the first Test of their 1993 tour 20–20 (Durban, 26.6.93). Hannes was promptly summoned to the engine room and, although the injection of new brawn made no odds as South Africa crashed 18–17 in Ellis Park, Jo'burg (3.7.93), he was retained, and played

South Africa (1993)

Last Season	4 caps	0 pts
Career	12 caps	0 pts

Caps (12): **1993** F(2), A(1,2,3), Arg(1,2) **1994** E(1) **1995** wc-A, C, F, NZ
Points Nil

the full three-Test complement in Australia over the next two months, on each occasion in second-row partnership with Western Province's Nico Wegner. Hannes remained first-choice lock throughout the tour, turning out in the other 'biggies' against South Australia (won 90–3, Adelaide, 17.7.93), New South Wales (lost 28–29, Sydney, 24.7.93) and Queensland (won 17–3, Brisbane, 8.8.93). Less active in 1994, dropped after England's shock 32–15 win in Pretoria (4.6.94). On a provincial note, 1993 had been a red-letter year for Transvaal, who captured both the prestigious Super-10 trophy (beating Auckland 20–7 in final at Ellis Park, Johannesburg, 22.5.93) and the Currie Cup (as they did again in 1994). After the latter, Hannes departed with the Springboks for Argentina, where he played in four of the six tour missions: both Test wins, the 28–27 loss to Buenos Aires and the 40–12 'battle' of Tucuman. The latter contest (2.11.93) brought shame on the player, as he was one of four dismissed. However, Lady Luck treated him kindly as he, and fellow Springbok Keith Andrews, were handed nothing more than suspended sentences, and so were free to play in the first Test a mere four days later.

Swart, B. South Africa

Full name: Balie Swart
Province: Transvaal
Position: Prop
Height: 6ft ½ in (1.84m)
Weight: 18st 6lb (113kg)
Occupation: Marketing manager, Kohler Corrugated
Family: Single
Born: 18.5.64
International debut: Australia 12, South Africa 19, 1993
Notable landmarks in rugby career: World Cup winner in 1995, Balie performed impressively on the tight-head, especially in the 15–12 final defeat of New Zealand (Jo'burg, 24.6.95) – one of four ties in which he was selected. Beneficiary of Johan le Roux's mega-suspension for disgracefully biting the ear of All Blacks skipper Sean Fitzpatrick in 1994 as it vacated the No.3 jersey. Balie also helped Transvaal complete back-to-back Currie Cup wins at the expense of Free State. Had enjoyed a triumphant debut in Sydney

South Africa (1993)

Last Season	6 caps	0 pts
Career	15 caps	0 pts

Caps (15): **1993** A(1,2,3), Arg(1) **1994** E(1,2), NZ(1,3), Arg(2R) **1995** WS(a) wc-A, WS(b), F, NZ. W
Points Nil

(3.7.93), when South Africa celebrated their return to Australia after a 22-year absence with a 19–12 defeat of the Wallabies. Balie would almost certainly have made his bow earlier, but for an emergency appendectomy which forced him out of the reckoning for the two-Test series with France in June and July of the same year. Still, he made up for lost time in Australia, turning out in eight of the 13 engagements, including each leg of the three-Test series, which the world champions came from behind to win (Sydney, 31.8.93) in a third Test in which Balie departed after 45 minutes with a broken nose. A member of the Transvaal side which won the inaugural Super-10 tournament (beating Auckland 20–7 in final, Johannesburg, 22.5.93), he also toured with the Boks to Argentina in the autumn, but was replaced by Western Province's Keith Andrews at tighthead for the second Test in Buenos Aires – a city in which he had appeared in the first international the previous weekend, and against whom he had played on a Springboks side beaten 28–27 (30.10.93). Despite South American omission, Balie was restored to the Test side for the visit of England (1994), and was superb in the second Test once switched to favoured tighthead berth. Missed out on re-match with England in autumn of 1995 because he did not tour.

Tabua, I. Australia

Full name: Ilie Tabua
State: Queensland
Club: Brothers
Position: Flanker, No.8
Height: 6ft 5in (1.96m)
Weight: 16st 4lb (104kg)
Occupation: Student, marketing rep
Born: Fiji, 30.9.64
Family: single
International debut: Australia 28, South Africa 20, 1993
Best rugby memory: Test debut against South Africa at Ballymore; World Cup Sevens in Edinburgh when I made my Australia debut.
Worst rugby memory: Canterbury verses Old (Christchurch) in 1992 – nearly died of hypothermia.
Notable landmarks in rugby career: Ilie first came to the notice of British audiences when playing for Australia in World Cup Sevens in Edinburgh (16–18.4.93). The Fijian-born Brothers flanker, then uncapped in the XV-man sphere, helped the Wallabies reach the final, where he

Australia (1993)

Last Season	2 caps	5 pts
Career	10 caps	15 pts

Caps (10): **1993** SA(2,3), C, F(1) **1994** I(1,2), It(1,2) **1995** wc-C, R
Points (15 – 3t): **1994** I(1:1t), I(2:1t) **1995** wc-C(1t)

was spared the agony of losing 21–17 to unfancied England. Among his team mates in that tournament were David Campese and Matt Burke, with whom he made his Test debut against South Africa in Brisbane (14.8.93). His call-up was prompted by the Wallabies' shock 12–19 loss in the first Test in Sydney, and his arrival more than redressed the balance. The world champions won the next two Tests. Ilie then embarked on the autumn tour to North America and France, scoring a try in the 26–22 non-cap Test victory over the United States in sweltering California (2.10.93) before appearing against Canada and then France in the surprise 13–16 first Test loss in Bordeaux. It was an especially painful afternoon for Ilie, as he broke his left arm midway through the game and was put out of action for the remainder of the season. Typically positive return in 1994 when he scored a try in each of the two Test wins over Ireland, confirming himself a powerhouse in the 'Willie O' mould. Added his third try at the 1995 World Cup in the Wallabies' 27–11 defeat of Canada (Port Elizabeth, 31.5.95), but has not represented his country.

Touchlines: Relaxing, reading, sleeping

Taylor, H. T. Wales

Full name: Hemi Takatou Taylor
Nickname: The Cuz
Club: Cardiff
Position: Flanker, No.8
Height: 6ft 2in (1.88m)
Weight: 14st 7lb (87.5kg)
Occupation: Rugby development officer, Cardiff RFC
Born: Morrinsville, New Zealand, 17.12.64
Family: Ceri (wife), Jessica (daughter), Ffion (daughter)
Former provinces/clubs: Waikato (NZ), Wairarapa Bush (NZ), Newbridge (Wal), East Brisbane (Aus)
International debut: Portugal 11, Wales 102, 1994
Five Nations debut: Wales 9, England 23, 1995
Toughest opponent: Jamie Joseph (Otago & New Zealand)
Best rugby memory: First time playing on Arms Park in a Wales jersey.
Worst rugby memory: Suffering knee injury on the field at the same time as having appendicitis.

Wales (1994)		
Last Season	12 caps	15 pts
Career	22 caps	20 pts

Caps (22): **1994** wc(q)-P. C, Fj, T, WS(R) wc(q)-R, It. SA **1995** E, S wc-J, NZ, I(b). SA, Fj **1996** It, E, S, I, F, A(1,2)

Points (20 – 4t): **1994** wc(q)-P(1t) **1995** wc-I(b:1t) **1996** E(1t), A(1:1t)

Do you really want to be a full-time professional? No, I've got other interests. There is more to life than rugby.

How well has rugby handled move to professionalism? 7/10. Everyone has been feeling their way, not wanting to make mistakes. I respect that.

Do you have a duty to entertain? My duty is to win, more than to entertain.

Do you feel a loyalty to your club in this new era? There is a certain loyalty towards team members. But loyalty can be bought.

432

Notable landmarks in rugby career: The first New Zealander to represent Wales at Test level, Hemi had further cause for pride when captaining Cardiff to the inaugural Heineken European Cup final in 1995, even if Toulouse did steal the game in extra time. One of only three players (along with Ieuan Evans and Derwyn Jones) to be ever-present for Wales from the start of the World Cup through until the end of the 1995/96 season, he claimed tries in the World Cup loss to Ireland (4.6.95) and the Five Nations defeat at Twickenham (3.2.96). Given his debut in World Cup qualifier against Portugal (Lisbon, 17.5.94), the former New Zealand Colt, whose allegiances in the Land of the Long White Cloud were to Waikato and Wairarapa Bush, marked the occasion with a try in the 102–11 rout. Although he did not play in the second leg of the Iberian trip, against Spain four days later, he was included in the national squad for summer tour of Canada, Fiji, Tonga and Western Samoa. A serious hand injury robbed Wales of his talents midway through 1994/95, and although he returned vs England (making his Five Nations debut on his ninth appearance), he failed to impress at the World Cup – sadly in keeping with most of his team mates. An ever-present in Wales A's 1994 five-match grand slam, he was voted player of the year at Cardiff in 1992/93. Further honours followed at Cardiff as he picked up a Swalec Cup winner's medal in 1993/94 and a league champion's medal the following season.

Touchlines: Scuba diving, basketball, golf

Thomas, A. C. Wales

Full name: Arwel Camber Thomas
Club: Swansea
Position: Fly-half
Height: 5ft 8in (1.73m)
Weight: 10st 10lb (68kg)
Occupation: Student
Born: Trebanos, 8.11.74
Family: Single
Former clubs: Trebanos, Neath, Bristol
International debut: Wales 31, Italy 26, 1996
Five Nations debut: England 21, Wales 15, 1996
Notable landmarks in rugby career: An impish figure who burst onto the international scene in 1996, thanks to the faith shown in him by new

Welsh coach Kevin Bowring and the fact that incumbent Neil Jenkins was nursing a broken collar bone. Arwel responded with 16 points on his full debut against Italy in Cardiff (16.1.96), and then cheekily set up go-ahead try for Hemi Taylor a fortnight later at Twickenham on his Five Nations debut. The season rather went downhill from that point. First, England rallied to win the game, then Arwel missed a last-kick conversion

Wales (1996)		
Last Season	4 caps	37 pts
Career	4 caps	37 pts

Caps (4): **1996** It, E, S, I
Points (37 – 5c, 9p): **1996** It(2c,4p), E(1c,1p), S(3p), I(2c,1p)

which would have given Wales a draw with Scotland in Cardiff (17.2.96), then he had a bit of a mare in Dublin (2.3.96) and was dropped in favour of the fit-again Jenkins for the championship finale against France, which Wales surprisingly won. He then upset Bristol by allegedly reneging on a two-year agreement with the club in order to sign for Swansea on the eve of his departure with the Wales squad for Australia. But all the latter disappointments should not detract from the fact that Arwel is one one of the most gifted and promising prospects in world rugby. From Trebanos, the birthplace of Bleddyn Bowen and Robert Jones, he earned selection for Wales Youth before joining Neath and graduating to Welsh Students. Made his Courage League debut for Bristol just three months before his Test bow.

Thomas, G.   Wales

Full name: Gareth Thomas
Nickname: Alfie
Club: Bridgend
Position: Centre, wing
Height: 6ft 3in (1.90m)
Weight: 15st 3lb (96kg)
Occupation: Trainee manager, Just Rentals
Born: 25.7.64
Family: Single
Former clubs: Pencoed, Pontypridd
International debut: Wales 57, Japan 10, 1995
Five Nations debut: Wales 16, France 15, 1996
Best rugby memory: Scoring three tries on Test debut against Japan.
Worst rugby memory: Injury vs Ebbw Vale that ruled me out of 1996 Five Nations series.
Most embarrassing memory: First game, first touch for Wales, losing my shorts.
Toughest opponent: Walter Little (New Zealand)
Do you really want to be a full-time professional? Yes

How well has rugby handled move to professionalism? 7/10. Definitely going the right way. Whether we get there is another matter.

Do you have a duty to entertain? Yes – no crowd, no money.

Notable landmarks in rugby career: Made quite a splash on entry to Test rugby at 1995 World Cup, scoring a hat-trick of tries from the left wing on his debut against Japan (Bloemfontein, 27.5.95). Moved back into his accustomed centre berth for the challenge of New Zealand before reverting to the outside vs Ireland. Wales lost latter two matches and failed to qualify for knockout stages. However, they returned to the Republic in September when Gareth, a former Youth and Under-21 international, was at centre in the 40–11 defeat (2.9.95). After gaining a fourth cap against Fiji (11.11.95), he sustained an injury against Ebbw Vale which ruled him out of for almost the whole of the 1996 Five Nations campaign. Returned for the finale against France (Cardiff, 16.3.96) – which Wales surprisingly won 16–15 – before switching club allegiance from the Brewery Field to St Helens and then embarking on Wales' summer tour to Australia. Shocked Pontypridd by reverting to Bridgend on return from Oz.

Touchlines: Tennis, music

Wales (1995)		
Last Season	8 caps	15 pts
Career	8 caps	15 pts

Caps (8): 1995 wc-J, NZ, I. SA, Fj 1996 F, A(1,2)

Points (15 – 3t): 1995 wc-J(3t)

Thomas, W. J. L.   Wales

Full name: William Justin Lloyd Thomas

Club: Cardiff

Position: Fullback

Height: 5ft 10in (1.78m)

Weight: 11st 6lb (73kg)

Occupation: WRU development officer

Born: Llansteffan, 1.11.73

Family: Single

Former clubs: Carmarthen Athletic, Cardiff IHE, Llanelli

International debut: South Africa 40, Wales 11, 1995

Five Nations debut: England 21, Wales 15, 1996

Best rugby memory: First cap in South Africa

Worst rugby memory: Having my kick intercepted for a try by Jeremy Guscott on Five Nations debut.

435

Most embarrassing memory: Rooming with Rupert Moon on my first time in Wales squad. He told me we had to get changed into DJs the night before the game and meet in the foyer for a reception with the WRU president. He took a phone call in his

Wales (1995)

Last Season	7 caps	5 pts
Career	7 caps	5 pts

Caps (7): **1995** SA, Fj **1996** It, E, S, I, F
Points (5 – 1t): **1996** It(1t)

DJ and said he would meet me downstairs. I got down, and Rupert and all the others were in tracksuits.

Toughest opponent: Andre Joubert (Natal & South Africa)

Do you really want to be a full-time professional? No, I like the balance between work and training. Full-time rugby would be boring.

How well has rugby handled move to professionalism? 3/10. No one sat down and considered the implications. For example, loss of earnings due to injury. I missed last summer's tour to Australia through injury and would have lost out financially had I not got my own insurance policy.

Do you have a duty to entertain? Yes. If we ask the fans to pay more money, we must give them a good game of rugby.

Do you feel a loyalty to your club in this new era? Yes, but you will see loyalty disappear in the next couple of years. Rugby players have short careers and you have to make hay while the sun shines.

Other sporting claims to fame: Cricket for Camarthen in South Wales League (two centuries).

Notable landmarks in rugby career: Suffered the crushing disappointment of missing summer tour to Australia after suffering partial torn medial ligaments playing in Llanelli's final league game of 1995/96 against Cardiff. Had cemented his place in the Wales squad with a run of impressive performances since making his debut in Johannesburg (2.9.95) in the 11–40 loss to the world champion Springboks. His one blemish came against England (3.2.96), when he delayed his clearance kick a moment too long and it was charged down by Jerry Guscott for the crucial try. Scored his one try to date in the 31–26 defeat of Italy (Cardiff, 16.1.96). First called into Wales squad while at Cardiff Institute of Higher Education to warm replacements bench against Scotland (Edinburgh, 4.3.95). A versatile player in club rugby, having also appeared at fly-half, centre and wing, Justin also represented Wales at Under-18, Under-19, Under-21 and A grades.

Touchlines: Cricket

Tournaire, F.   France

Full name: Franck Tournaire
Club: Narbonne
Position: Tighthead prop
Height: 5ft 11in (1.80m)
Weight: 16st 5lb (104kg)
Occupation: Town council employee
Born: 4.12.72
International debut: France 34, Italy 22, 1995
Five Nations debut: France 45, Ireland 10, 1996
Notable landmarks in rugby career: Benefitted from Christian Califano's switch to the loosehead berth mid-way through the 1996 Five Nations series. Having been given his debut in the Latin Cup in October 1995, when he contributed fully to Italy's 34–22 downfall (14.10.95), he was handed the No.3 jersey as Califano took over from Michel Perie on the other side for the visit of Ireland to Paris (17.2.96). Ireland had never previously won at the Parc des Princes, and Franck and the boys

France (1995)

Last Season	6 caps	0 pts
Career	6 caps	0 pts

Caps (6): **1995** It **1996** I, W, R, Arg(1,2R)
Points Nil

were intent on that record remaining intact. There was never the slightest doubt that would be the case as France rebounded from their shock defeat at Murrayfield two weeks previously to slam the Irish 45–10. Not surprisingly, Franck was retained for the finale in Cardiff. The surprise was that France went down to the previously winless Welsh. However, for one of France's youngest and most promising props, the season ended on a high with the 64–12 defeat of Romania (Aurillac, 20.4.96).

Townsend, G. P. J.   Scotland

Full name: Gregor Peter John Townsend
Nickname: Toony or Tintin
Club: Northampton
Position: Outside-half, centre
Height: 5ft 11in (1.81m)
Weight: 12st 7lb (75kg)
Occupation: Part-time student
Born: Edinburgh, 26.4.73
Family: Single
Family links with rugby: Father Peter played twice for South of Scotland.
Former club: Gala
International debut: England 26, Scotland 12, 1993
Five Nations debut: As above
Best rugby memory: Playing in Australia for Warringah; beating France in Paris (1995).
Worst rugby memory: 1993 World Cup Sevens (I was looking forward to it so much, then played terribly and got dropped); damaging ligaments and missing 1995 World Cup.
Most embarrassing moment: Giving try-scoring 'pass' to French winger Philippe Saint-Andre at Murrayfield (1994).

Scotland (1993)		
Last Season	7 caps	13 pts
Career	19 caps	24 pts

Caps (19): **1993** E(R) **1994** W, E, I, F, Arg(1,2) **1995** C, I, F(a), W, E. WS **1996** I, F, W, E, NZ(1,2)
Points (24 – 3t, 3dg): **1994** E(1dg), Arg(2:1dg) **1995** F(a:1t) **1996** I(1dg), W(1t), NZ(1:1t)

Toughest opponent: David Humphreys (London Irish & Ireland)
Serious injuries: Sprung ribs at 1992 Hong Kong Sevens; damaged knee ligaments in 1993 Scotland trial; broken bone in hand (September 1993 against Boroughmuir – out for 12 weeks).
Do you really want to be a full-time professional? No
How well has rugby handled move to professionalism? 4/10. Everyone's values have changed. Commercial interests are being put ahead of rugby interests.
Do you have a duty to entertain? I don't go out to try and entertain. I go out to play the best rugby. If you win with all 15 men, the crowd will enjoy it.
Do you feel a loyalty to your club in this new era? Yes, but not as much.
Notable landmarks in rugby career: Many people's choice as the outstanding player of the 1996 Five Nations Championship, Gregor got a previously struggling Scotland side playing some sweet rugby with his speed of thought and deed. He dined out on the slick passing of Bryan Redpath, relishing taking a fast and flat delivery and leaving his decision-making until he could see the whites

of the defenders' eyes. Scored a try against Wales in Cardiff (17.2.96) which was as stunning as it was crucial. Still prone to the occasional basic error – usually the product of over-ambition – but maturing by the day, and is undoubtedly one of the jewels in Europe's crown. Directly blamed by then Scotland coach Dougie Morgan for Argentina's 16–15 first Test win over the touring Scots (Buenos Aires, 4.6.94). Nonetheless, Gregor's have-a-go style brightened up a largely tedious international stage in 1994, and in 1995 it inspired the Scots to their first–ever win at Parc des Princes (18.2.95). In a thriller, Gregor scored Scotland's first try and then, after his failure to find touch had gifted Philippe Saint-Andre the go-ahead score, provided the classy inside flick to unlock the French midfield and put Gavin Hastings away for the last-minute winning score. It was a fitting reward for a player who has endured more than his fair share of heartache – in 1994 he had a dropped goal against Wales ruled out by French referee Patrick Robin, who didn't think it had gone over. Then he looked to have won Scotland the Calcutta Cup (Murrayfield, 5.2.94), only for Jon Callard to steal his glory with an injury-time strike from 40 metres. Knee-ligament damage, sustained in the final trial, wrecked his 1993 campaign, and another tear robbed him of a place in Scotland's 1995 World Cup squad. Toured Fiji, Tonga and Western Samoa (1993: playing in latter two Tests and top-scoring on tour with 30 points), Australia (1992) and New Zealand (1996).
Touchlines: Golf (9-handicap), cinema, galleries

Ubogu, V. E. — England

Full name: Victor Eriakpo Ubogu
Club: Bath
Position: Tighthead prop
Height: 5ft 9in (1.76m)
Weight: 16st 2lb (102.5kg)
Occupation: Company director, Cobrawatch (family-owned security firm); owner of London sports bar 'Shoeless Joe's'
Born: Lagos, Nigeria, 8.9.64
Family: Single
Former clubs: Moseley, Richmond
International debut: England 26, Canada 13, 1992
Five Nations debut: Scotland 14, England 15, 1994
Best rugby memories: Being capped by England; Bath beating Toulouse in 1989/90.

Worst rugby memory: England losing 21–6 to Natal in Durban (1994).

Suggestions to improve rugby: Rules must be redefined so we have the same game in both hemispheres. Too many vague interpretations of what is and is not OK, and no consistency in refereeing. The IRB have basically made a hash of the laws.

Notable landmarks in rugby career: Landed a healthy wager when he backed himself to score the first try against Wales (Cardiff, 18.2.95) and then did precisely that. Victor's five-pointer helped England to a 23–9 win en route to their third grand slam in five years, though Shoeless Joe's first. He had high hopes of adding a World Cup winner's medal, but despite five appearances in South Africa, Victor was unable to stir the England pack sufficiently to deal with the All Blacks machine (Cape Town, 18.6.95) on that extraordinary afternoon at Newlands. Held onto his England place for just one more game, the 1995/96 opener against South Africa (Twickenham, 18.11.95), before Jason Leonard switched across to tighthead to make way for Graham Rowntree in the No.1 jersey. Victor's consolation, however, was none too scruffy, as Bath completed another league and cup double (his fourth cup-winner's medal). Wembley debuts are few and far between but Victor, a member of Oxford's beaten Varsity team in 1987, was lucky enough to make his in the shadow of the twin towers when selected ahead of Jeff Probyn against Canada (17.9.92). Twickenham, needless to say, was unavailable due to reconstruction. Although the school wing turned international prop lost his place to Probyn for the 1993 Five Nations campaign, his time came in 1993/94, when he was ever-present throughout.

England (1992)		
Last Season	6 caps	0 pts
Career	21 caps	5 pts

Caps (21): **1992** C, SA **1993** NZ **1994** S, I, F, W, SA(1,2), R, C **1995** I, F(a), W, S wc-Arg, WS, A, NZ, F(b). SA

Points (5 – 1t): **1995** W(1t)

Rory Underwood searches in vain for an opening against France in Paris, where the French won 15–12 to end an eight-year losing run in the fixture.

Underwood, R.   England

Full name: Rory Underwood
Nickname: Rors
Club: Leicester & RAF
Position: Wing
Height: 5ft 9in (1.76m)
Weight: 14st (89kg)
Occupation: RAF pilot
Born: Middlesbrough, 19.6.63
Family: Wendy (wife), Rebecca
(daughter) and Alexandra (daughter)
Family links with rugby: Brother
Tony has played for Leicester,
England and British Lions.
Former club: Middlesbrough
International debut: England 12,
Ireland 9, 1984
Five Nations debut: As above
Best rugby memories: Beating
Australia in 1995 World Cup quarter-finals; winning first (1991) grand slam
with England.

Worst rugby memory: Four days spanning England's 1995 World Cup losses
to New Zealand and France, after the glory of beating Australia.

Most embarrassing moment: Ieuan Evans running past me to score winning try
for Wales in 1993 match against us.

Toughest opponent: Emile NTamack (Toulouse & France)

Biggest influence on career: Geoff Cooke (ex-England manager)

Do you really want to be a full-time professional? Yes, I'd like to be, but I would
need certain guarantees that I can return to work later.

How well has rugby handled move to professionalism? 2/10. Five months of
prevaricating and the RFU comes out with a decision that could have been taken
on day one. They should have grabbed the bull by the horns.

Do you have a duty to entertain? No, not a duty, but with the game becoming
a commercial enterprise, entertainment has to be an important consideration.

Do you feel a loyalty to your club in this new era? Yes

Other sporting claims to fame: Swam and played cricket for the same Barnard
Castle school that England team mate Rob Andrew attended.

Notable landmarks in rugby career: England's most-capped player (85) and
record try-scorer (49), having added another chapter to his glorious career in
1994/95, when he bagged another ten tries in 12 appearances (including braces
versus Canada, Western Samoa and, in an extraordinary World Cup semi-final,
New Zealand). He ignored calls from certain quarters to retire in 1995/96, and
instead took his try tally to within one of an unprecedented half-century. Now
he will not rule out making a challenge for 1997 Lions selection. A remarkable

career had all begun with two tries for Leicester against the 1983 Barbarians. Three months later Rory was in the England team. Missed tour to Argentina in summer of 1990 due to RAF commitments, having already become England's most-capped back and highest try-scorer during 1989/90 season. RAF duties also took precedence over tours to South Africa (1984) and New Zealand (1985). Equalled Dan Lambert's 1907 England record of five tries in an international, against Fiji (won 58–23, Twickenham, 4.11.89). Previously played for England Colts, Under-23 and B teams. Toured Australia with 1989 Lions, playing in all three Tests. Held his Lions place on 1993 tour to New Zealand, where he scored winning try in second Test. Rates his 26th Test try (scored in 16–7 defeat of Ireland during 1991 grand slam run) as most important of career. Also scored in 21–19 win over France (1991 grand slam decider). In 1991/92 he notched a further eight tries: including four en route to World Cup final and three in 1992 grand slam campaign. Retired from international arena once back-to-back grand slams were safely stowed in the bag, but did a Frank Sinatra and returned in 1992/93. Added a third grand slam in 1995. He and Tony are the first brothers to appear in the same England championship side since the Wheatley brothers packed down against Scotland in 1938. Toured South Africa with England (1994).

Touchlines: Crosswords, reading, golf

England (1984)		
Last Season	6 caps	10 pts
Career	85 caps	210 pts
Lions (1986)		
(1989)	3 Tests	0 pts
(1993)	3 Tests	5 pts

Caps (85): 1984 I, F, W, A 1985 R, F, S, I, W 1986 W, I, F 1987 I, F, W, S wc-A, J, W 1988 F, W, S, I(1,2), A(a1,a2), Fj, A(b) 1989 S, I, F, W. Lions-A(1,2,3). R, Fj 1990 I, F, W, S, Arg(b) 1991 W, S, I, F, Fj, A wc-NZ, It, US, F, S, A 1992 S, I, F, W, SA 1993 F, W, S, I. Lions-NZ(1,2,3). NZ 1994 S, I, F, W, SA(1,2), R, C 1995 I, F(a), W, S wc-Arg, It, WS(a), A, NZ, F(b). SA, WS(b) 1996 F, W, S, I

Points (210 – 49t): 1984 F(1t) 1985 I(1t) 1987 wc-J(2t) 1988 I(1:2t), I(2:1t), A(a1:1t), A(a2:1t), Fj(2t), A(b:2t) 1989 Fj(5t) 1990 I(1t), F(1t), W(2t), Arg(b:3t) 1991 I(1t), F(1t), Fj(1t) wc-It(1t), US(2t), F(1t) 1992 S(1t), I(1t), F(1t) 1993 S(1t). Lions-NZ(2:1t) 1994 W(1t), R(1t), C(2t) 1995 W(2t) wc-It(1t), WS(a:2t), NZ(2t). WS(b:1t) 1996 W(1t)

Underwood, T.   England

Full name: Tony Underwood
Club: Newcastle
Position: Wing
Height: 5ft 9in (1.76m)
Weight: 13st 7lb (81kg)
Occupation: Equity broker, Crosby Securities
Born: Ipoh, Malaysia, 17.2.69
Family: Married
Family links with rugby: Brother Rory is England's record try-scorer and most-capped player (85 caps, 49 tries, 210 points).
Former clubs: Cambridge University, Leicester
International debut: England 26, Canada 13, 1992
Five Nations debut: England 26, Scotland 12, 1993
Best rugby memories: 1993 Lions selection; South Africa 15, England 32, 1994
Worst rugby memories: England's 12–13 loss to Ireland (1994); England 29, New Zealand 45, 1995
Most embarrassing memory: Post-try behaviour following my late score in 1991 Varsity match.

England (1992)

Last Season	4 caps	40 pts
Career	20 caps	50 pts

Lions (1993)

Caps (20): **1992** C, SA **1993** S, I, NZ **1994** S, I, W, SA(1,2), R, C **1995** I, F(a), W, S wc-Arg, It, A, NZ
Points (50 – 10t): **1992** SA(1t) **1993** S(1t) **1994** R(2t), C(1t) **1995** I(1t), F(a:2t) wc-It(1t), A(1t)

Toughest opponents: Ian Hunter (Northampton & England B) and David Campese (Randwick & Australia)
Biggest influence on career: My mother (Anne)
Serious injuries: Broken jaw, torn hamstring and damaged knee cartilage – all in second half of 1989/90 season.
Notable landmarks in rugby career: After the drama of 1994/95, Tony had a predominantly miserable time last season. A knee operation kept him out of the England side, allowing Jon Sleightholme to come in and build a major reputation for himself. He used the spare time to give up his job, get married, switch clubs from Leicester to Newcastle and, oh yes, make *those* pizza television adverts. The latter celluloid marvels co-starred Jonah Lomu, the towering All Black, who ruined Tony's World Cup when he run all over him in the Cape Town semi-final between the two nations. Lomu scored four tries. Still, Tony was neither the first nor the last player to find Jonah the Juggernaut hotter to handle than a chili-pepper pizza. The previous weekend (11.6.96), on the same

Newlands pitch, Tony had scored a brilliant try to knock out world champion Wallabies. Ironically, it had been against the All Blacks that Tony had made his name in 1989, uncapped and playing for the Barbarians – and against them that he had celebrated victory with England in 1993. Toured South Africa (1994), having been dropped after England's shock home defeat by Ireland (19.2.94). Replaced by Ian Hunter against France and Wales, but in the latter case he scrambled back in through the back door: injury to Stuart Barnes got Tony onto the bench, from where subsequent injury to David Pears in run-up to game led to Hunter moving to fullback and Tony being reprieved. A midweek British Lion in 1993, Tony had returned home to make the England No.14 jersey his own against All Blacks, Scotland and Ireland. But he shared in the criticism of England's try-scoring failure – ironic, as he has been such a prolific scorer at B and A level. Played for England Schools (18-Group) before graduating to England team for inaugural Student World Cup (1988) and for senior England side in 18–16 non-cap win over Barbarians (1990/91). Went on to represent Combined Students, North of England, England B (13 times) and, latterly, England in traumatic 1990 summer tour of Argentina. Tony's Test debut came against Canada (Wembley, 17.10.92) and his first top-level try arrived in the 33–16 defeat of South Africa (Twickenham, 14.11.92). Helped Leicester win 1992/93 Pilkington Cup and 1993/94 Courage league title.

Touchlines: Cricket, squash, golf, tennis

Van der Heerden, F. J.   South Africa

Full name: Frederick (Fritz) Johannes van der Heerden
Province: Western Province
Position: Lock, flanker
Height: 6ft 7in (1.96m)
Weight: 17st (108kg)
Occupation: Law student
Born: Roodepoort, 29.6.70
Family: Single
Former club: Bologna (It)
International debut: South Africa 32, England 15, 1994
Notable landmarks in rugby career:
Disappointed to miss out on South Africa's World Cup glory, having played for the Boks both beforehand and since. Debut came vs England in Pretoria (4.6.94) in a match which

will live longer in the hearts and minds of the visitors than Fritz. South Africa were toppled 32–15, and yer man was dropped onto replacements bench for the return in Cape Town the following week. But he came off the bench in the 67th minute for Ian Macdonald, and shared in South Africa's 27–9 revenge. Toured with Boks to New Zealand in summer 1994, appearing in third Test at Eden Park, Auckland (6.8.94), where the tourists put

South Africa (1995)

Last Season	5 caps	0 pts
Career	5 caps	0 pts

Caps (5): **1994** E(1,2R), NZ(3) **1995** It, E

Points Nil

behind them the disappointment of defeat in the previous two internationals to hold the All Blacks to an 18–18 draw. Drew a blank in 1995, until excellent provincial form for Western Province forced the selectors' hand post-World Cup. Included in the Springbok party for the mini-tour to Europe, Fritz, who played two seasons with Bologna in Italy, turned out against the Italians in Rome (12.11.95), helping the Boks win 40–21, and then played at Twickenham in the easier-than-it-sounds 24–14 defeat of England (18.11.95).

Van der Westhuizen, J. H.   South Africa

Full name: Joost Heystek van der Westhuizen
Province: Northern Transvaal
Position: Scrum-half
Height: 6ft 1½ in (1.86m)
Weight: 13st 9lb (82kg)
Occupation: Student
Born: Pretoria, 20.2.71
International debut: Argentina 26, South Africa 29, 1993
Other sporting achievements: *Korf bal* (like netball) for South Africa
Notable landmarks in rugby career: Started 1994/95 in contention for a Test place and finished it as arguably the world's premier scrum-half after a marvellous World Cup campaign. A combative, in-your-face sort of No.9 (like Dewi Morris), Joost's finest hour (to date) was probably his display at Murrayfield (19.11.94) where he tore Scotland apart with two magnificent first-half tries, although he claimed another belter in the 24–14 defeat of England at Twickenham a year later (18.11.95).

South Africa (1993)

Last Season	11 caps	15 pts
Career	16 caps	30 pts

Caps (16): **1993** Arg(1,2) **1994** E(1,2R), Arg(2), S, W **1995** WS(a) wc-A, C(R), WS(b), F, NZ. W, It, E

Points (30 – 6t): **1993** Arg(1:1t), Arg(2:1t) **1994** Arg(2:1t), S(2t) **1995** E(1t)

Joost, who resisted offers from Leeds RLFC to switch codes after the World Cup, has a history of prolific try-scoring, mostly for Northern Transvaal. His Springbok debut saw him bag four tries against Western Australia. Granted the opposition was not up to much – they crashed 71–8 (WACA, 14.7.93) – but his remained an outstanding opening effort. He continued in the same prolific vein, crossing New South Wales' line during a 29–28 defeat (Waratah, 24.7.93), repeating the feat against NSW Country (won 41–7, Orange, 31.7.93), and bagging try-braces against Australian Capital Territory (won 57–10, Bruce Stadium, 4.8.93) and Queensland Country (won 63–5, Mackay, 11.8.93). He completed a cracking first tour with a try on his final outing against Sydney (Penrith, 18.8.93), to return home top try-scorer with 11. Little wonder he was promptly redirected to Argentina for the Springboks' autumn visit, and little wonder either that he graduated into the Test XV during the trip. The Pumas could not contain Joost either, as he claimed a try in each Test (first won 29–26, Buenos Aires, 6.11.93; second won 52–23, Buenos Aires, 13.11.93) as South Africa completed a 2–0 series whitewash. He retained his place in 1994 for South Africa's opening mission against England (Pretoria, 2.6.94) and, despite looking lively, was dropped for the Cape Town return as the management changed the gameplan, preferring Johan Roux's more orthodox style. Still, he picked up his cap, as a 30th-minute replacement for injured wing Chester Williams. Toured New Zealand (1994), scoring three tries in five outings, but was unable to shift Roux from the Test berth. But after a try-scoring return in second Test against Argentina (Jo'burg, 15.10.94) he won back first-choice recognition on the autumn tour to Britain.

Wainwright, R. I.   Scotland

Full name: Robert Iain Wainwright
Club: Watsonians
Position: Flanker
Height: 6ft 5in (1.95m)
Weight: 15st 4lb (97kg)
Occupation: Army doctor
Born: Perth, 22.3.65
Family: Romayne (wife), Douglas (son), Natasha (daughter)
Family links with rugby: Father (J. F. Wainwright) was a 1956 Cambridge Blue.
Former clubs: Cambridge University, Edinburgh Acads, West Hartlepool
International debut: Ireland 10, Scotland 18, 1992
Five Nations debut: As above

Toughest opponent: Finlay Calder (Stewart's-Melville FP & Scotland)
Best rugby memory: Scotland beating France in Five Nations in 1995 and 1996
Worst rugby memory: Scotland losing to France in 1995 World Cup
Most embarrassing memory: Getting sent off in 1987
Do you really want to be a full-time professional? No, semi-pro.

Scotland (1992)

Last Season	11 caps	5 pts
Career	24 caps	14 pts

Caps (24): **1992** I(R), F, A(1,2) **1993** NZ **1994** W, E **1995** C, I, F(a), W, E, R wc-IC, T, F(b), NZ. WS **1996** I, F, W, E, NZ(1,2)

Points (14 – 3t): **1992** A(1:1t) **1994** E(1t) **1995** wc-F(b:1t)

How well has rugby handled move to professionalism? 4/10. The game will drift into full professionalism over next few years, but a professional approach is needed by players and administrators now.
Do you have a duty to entertain? Yes, but we probably always have.
Do you feel a loyalty to your club in this new era? Yes
Other sporting claims to fame: Boxing Blue at Cambridge University (1985).
Serious injuries: Broken cheekbone (January 1990), ankle (September 1990).
Notable landmarks in rugby career: Succeeded Gavin Hastings as Scotland captain after 1995 World Cup, and at first this appeared to be a poisoned chalice. Scotland were held by Western Samoa and well beaten by Italy. But then Rob's leadership qualities kicked in, and a well-motivated Scottish side staged a remarkable turnaround in the 1996 Five Nations series, beating all but England. He then took the squad to New Zealand, and although well beaten 62–31 in the first Test, had the satisfaction of his side scoring more points vs New Zealand than any side ever. Injury had prevented him from captaining Scotland on 1994 tour to Argentina, but he underlined his leadership potential during another tartan revival in 1995. Scored only one try, in the heartbreaking World Cup defeat by France (Pretoria, 3.6.95), though he did bag a brace in the 62–7 non-cap Test win over Spain (Madrid, 6.5.95). Ever-present throughout 11 engagements in 1995, combining with Iain Morrison and Eric Peters to form an outstanding back-row combination. Had sustained a broken cheekbone 66 minutes into 15–14 Calcutta Cup defeat by England (5.2.94) – a Murrayfield match in which he scored the solitary try on 28 minutes. One of Scotland's most versatile players, Rob's 22 caps have come at No.8 (four), flanker (17) and replacement lock (one, on debut). His representative career really took off in the 1991/92 season, when he captained Scotland B, broke into senior side and toured Australia in the summer, playing in both Tests and claiming Scotland's only try in 12–27 Sydney loss (13.6.92). First cap had come four months earlier when he replaced Neil Edwards for last two minutes against Ireland in Dublin (15.2.92). Having appeared in three consecutive Varsity matches (1986–88), he made his Scotland B debut in 26–3 win over Italy at L'Aquila.
Touchlines: Fishing, falconry, whisky, wildlife, writing

Wallace, P. S.   Ireland

Full name: Paul Stephen Wallace
Club: Saracens
Position: Prop
Height: 6ft 1in (1.85m)
Weight: 16st (102kg)
Occupation: Employee of First
National Building Society
Born: Cork, 30.12.71
Family: Single
Former clubs: University College,
Cork, Blackrock College
International debut: Ireland 50,
Japan 28, 1995
Five Nations debut: Ireland 30,
Wales 17, 1996
Best rugby memories: First cap vs
Japan; winning Schools 1990 Triple
Crown vs England.
Worst rugby memory: Getting
hammered by New Zealand in 1992
Student World Cup, and only lasting
until half-time.
Most embarrassing memory: In
possession in sevens, I looked inside

Ireland (1995)

Last Season	5 caps	5 pts
Career	5 caps	5 pts

Caps (5): **1995** wc-J. Fj **1996** US, W, E
Points (5 – 1t): **1995** Fj(1t)

for support, and had the ball nicked off me outside by a guy who ran the length
of the pitch for a try.
Do you really want to be a full-time professional? Yes and no – I would like to
give rugby my full attention but I also want to pursue a career.
How well has rugby handled move to professionalism? 5/10. It happened so
suddenly. A momentous change like this shouldn't be rushed, but I appreciate
that with rebel circus hovering they had to move fairly quickly.
Do you have a duty to entertain? Wings have more of a duty than do props.
Winning remains the priority, but I reckon that we must follow the Super-12
example if pro rugby is to work.
Do you feel a loyalty to your club in this new era? Yes
Notable landmarks in rugby career: A former Ireland Under-21 captain who
has also represented his country at Schools, Students, Development XV and A
grades, Paul benefitted from Peter Clohessy's absence in 1995/96. When 'The
Claw' declined to go to the World Cup on account of work commitments, Paul
went along as second-choice tighthead behind Garrett Halpin, and earned his
debut in the 50–28 defeat of Japan (Bloemfontein, 31.5.95). Although that was
the end of his work in South Africa, the former UCC player was retained for the
season curtain-raiser against Fiji (Dublin, 18.11.95) and responded with a try

in Ireland's highly encouraging 44–8 victory. Picked up his third cap in Atlanta (6.1.96) against the US Eagles, where Ireland warmed up for the 1996 Five Nations Championship with a hard-fought 25–18 win. Thereafter he made way for Peter Clohessy, who added two caps to his tally before being cited for foul play after Ireland's drubbing in Paris (17.2.96). Clohessy's resultant six-week suspension allowed Paul to make his Five Nations debut in Dublin against Wales (2.3.96), and then to play at Twickenham (16.3.96) in a defeat which, sadly for him, brought Ireland the Wooden Spoon.

Wallace, R. M.   Ireland

Full name: Richard Michael Wallace
Club: Garryowen
Position: Wing
Height: 5ft 11in (1.80m)
Weight: 13st 7lb (86kg)
Occupation: Financial consultant partner, K. Walshe & Associates
Born: Cork, 16.1.68
Family: Single
Former club: Cork Constitution
International debut: Namibia 15, Ireland 6, 1991
Five Nations debut: Ireland 15, Wales 16, 1992
Best rugby memory: 1993 Lions call-up and defeat of England
Toughest opponent: Philippe Saint-Andre (Montferrand & France)
Serious injuries: Broken right leg (1994)
Other sporting claims to fame: Sailed (Laser class) for Ireland at 1990 European Championships (France).
Notable landmarks in rugby career: After the disappointment of 1994/95, precipitated by a leg-break suffered playing for Garryowen vs Shannon at end of the previous season, Richard returned with a

Ireland (1991)
Last Season	7 caps	10 pts
Career	24 caps	23 pts

Lions (1993)

Caps (24): 1991 Na(1R) 1992 W, E, S, F, A 1993 S, F, W, E, R 1994 F, W, E, S 1995 W(a), It wc-NZ, J, W(b). Fj 1996 US, S, F

Points (23 – 5t): 1991 W(1t), S(1t) 1992 A(1t) 1995 Fj(1t) 1996 US(1t)

bang last season, scoring tries on his first two Test outings of the campaign (vs Fiji and the US Eagles). Made way for the fit-again Simon Geoghegan midway through 1996 Five Nations series, but not before he had made amends for his poor campaign at the 1995 World Cup where, although he played in all three

World Cup pool matches, he was clearly out of form. Was dropped for quarter-final against France, with uncapped Darragh O'Mahony getting the nod. Spent 1992 and 1993 'off'-seasons in New Zealand, each trip providing a tale of the unexpected. In 1992 he had only just overcome jet-lag following the trip out with Ireland when he was punched (playing against Canterbury), sustained a hairline fracture of the jaw, and was flown home. In 1993 he was minding his own business in Moscow when Ian Hunter was injured in the British Lions' first engagement against North Auckland and he was summoned post-haste as a replacement. Once in place he turned out against Canterbury, Taranaki, Southland, Hawke's Bay and Waikato. Richard had taken his first step up the representative ladder when he appeared for Munster Under-18s and Under-21s (1988). A member of 1987/88 Irish Colleges XV, he scored a try in the 20–10 defeat of England B at Old Belvedere on only his second outing for Ireland B (1.3.91). Broke into Ireland senior XV on 1991 tour of Namibia, replacing Simon Geoghegan in 74th minute of first Test (Windhoek, 20.7.91), and scored tour-high five tries in Namibia. Marked Five Nations debut with a try in Dublin loss to Wales (18.1.92). Retained place throughout championship (also crossing vs Scotland) before ill-fated trip to the land of the All Blacks. Helped Ireland reach semi-finals of inaugural World Cup Sevens (Murrayfield, April 1993).
Touchlines: Flying (hold private licence), sailing, reading, music

---

Waugh, W. W.   Australia

Full name: Warwick William Waugh
State: New South Wales
Club: Randwick
Position: Lock
Height: 6ft 7in (2.01m)
Weight: 18st 8lb (118kg)
Occupation: Account executive
Born: 17.9.68
Family: Single
International debut: Australia 12, South Africa 19, 1993
Best rugby memory: Scoring in my first Wallaby game with my first touch of the ball (Western Transvaal vs Australia, 1992).
Worst rugby memory: Breaking my leg (NSW vs Wales, 1991).
Most respected opponent: Ian Jones (North Harbour & New Zealand)

Suggestions to improve rugby: Actively encourage more ex-players to become referees.

Notable landmarks in rugby career:
Finally broke up the John Eales–Rod
McCall second-row combination in
1995, making one appearance
against Canada (Port Elizabeth,
31.5.95) at the World Cup and then
partnering Eales in the two-Test, two-
loss Bledisloe Cup series against New

Australia (1993)		
Last Season	3 caps	0 pts
Career	4 caps	0 pts

Caps (4): **1993** SA(1) **1995** wc-C. NZ(1,2)

Points Nil

Zealand in July 1995. Warwick's debut had actually come two years later than
had been widely anticipated after he had broken his leg playing for New South
Wales against touring Wales in 1991. He had formed a highly successful
partnership with Steve Cutler, soon after making his debut for the state in
Argentina, and was seen as a genuine international contender. However, the leg
break put such thoughts on hold. A powerful scrummager and noted lineout
jumper, he was selected to tour South Africa in the summer of 1992 and marked
his debut with a try against Western Transvaal (won 46–13, Potchefstroom,
11.8.92). He also turned out in the 34–8 victory over Eastern Province in Port
Elizabeth seven days later. On to Wales and Ireland, where he gained further
experience with starts against Munster, Connacht, Swansea, Monmouthshire
and Welsh Students. His apprenticeship complete, Wallaby coach Bob Dwyer
finally gave him his first cap in July 1993 in the first Test against South Africa
in Sydney. Unhappily for Warwick, the Springboks won 19–12 and it was back
to bench duties for the remainder of the series.

Touchlines: Cars, music, skiing, running, golf

Weir, G. W. Scotland

Full name: George Wilson (Doddie)
Weir
Club: Newcastle
Position: No.8, lock
Height: 6ft 6in (1.98m)
Weight: 16st 2lb (98kg)
Occupation: Part-time sales rep,
Carlsberg/Tetley
Born: Edinburgh, 4.7.70
Family: Single
Family links with rugby: Father John
played for Gala; brother Tom plays
for Gala; brother Christopher plays
for Melrose.
Former club: Melrose
International debut: Scotland 49,
Argentina 3, 1990

Five Nations debut: Scotland 7, England 25, 1992
Best rugby memory: Scoring two tries against 1995 All Blacks
Most embarrassing memory: Trying to kick clear and then dive on a loose ball, and missing it both times, in 1991 Melrose Sevens first-round loss to Hawick.
Toughest opponents: John Eales (Queensland & Australia); Ian Jones (North Harbour& New Zealand).
Biggest influence on career: Jim Telfer (as Melrose coach) – told me what to do, when and how.

Scotland (1990)		
Last Season	11 caps	10 pts
Career	39 caps	14 pts

Caps (39): **1990** Arg **1991** Ro wc-J, Z, I, WS, E, NZ **1992** E, I, F, W, A(1,2) **1993** I, F, W, E, NZ **1994** W(R), E, I, F, SA **1995** F(a:R), W, E, R wc-IC, T, F(b), NZ. WS **1996** I, F, W, E, NZ(1,2)

Points (14 – 3t): **1991** wc-Z(1t) **1995** wc-NZ(2t)

Do you really want to be a full-time professional? Yes
How well has rugby handled move to professionalism? 5/10. Floodgates were opened too wide and the authorities have found it difficult to control the flow.
Do you have a duty to entertain? I always try to entertain but to entertain myself not the crowd. More often than not I find that if I'm enjoying myself then it's an enjoyable game for the crowd too.
Do you feel a loyalty to your club in this new era? Yes
Other sporting claims to fame: Stow sprint champion, completing Thirlestone cross-country (horses); 1991 Scottish Horse Trials (intermediate class).
Suggestions to improve rugby: Abolish conversions and instead increase the value of tries.
Notable landmarks in rugby career: Would have assumed national hero status when he scored two tries against New Zealand in 1995 World Cup quarter-final (Pretoria, 11.6.95), had not the All Blacks won 48–30. Nonetheless it was a marvellous effort, and confirmed how far Doddie has come as international force. Last season he was one of only six players to appear in all six games (including non-cap defeat by Italy in Rieti) and still had time to switch club allegiances to Newcastle mid-season. Had moved from No.8 to second row in 1994 after 10–34 home whipping by South Africa (Murrayfield, 19.11.94), but had to wait for Damian Cronin to get injured midway through away win in France to return to favour. Thereafter, he was ever-present in a seven-Test run that culminated in his heroics against the Kiwis. Had not been selected for 1994 Five Nations opener either, but came on against Wales as 18th-minute replacement after Iain Morrison had broken his left leg in two places. Unmoved thereafter. Toured New Zealand with Scottish Schools (1988) and Scotland (1990 and 1996). Represented South of Scotland in Inter-District Championship, Scotland Under-19s, Scotland Under-21s (vs Wales, 1990 and 1991) and Scotland B, becoming youngest forward to represent them (at 19) in 22–22 draw with Ireland B (Murrayfield, 9.12.89). Made full debut against touring Pumas (10.11.90). Toured with Scotland to North America (1991 – playing in all six matches, including two non-cap Tests vs US Eagles and Canada), Australia (1992 – appearing at lock in both Tests), South Pacific (1993 – playing in non-

cap Tests vs Fiji, Tonga and Western Samoa) and Argentina (1994). Helped Melrose win McEwan's Scottish Club Championship for the fourth time in five seasons in 1993/94.

Touchlines: Horseriding (one-day eventing), clay pigeon shooting, golf

Wiese, J. J. South Africa

Full name: Jakobus (Kobus) Johannes Wiese
Province: Transvaal
Position: Lock
Height: 6ft 6in (1.98m)
Weight: 20st 1lb (125kg)
Occupation: Insurance broker
Born: 16.5.64
International debut: South Africa 20, France 20, 1993
Notable landmarks in rugby career: Disgraced himself by punching Derwyn Jones out of the game when world champion Springboks played host to Wales (2.9.95) last season. South Africa won 40–11, but only after Wales had been robbed of their lineout ace, courtesy of Kobus' disgraceful haymaker from behind, in only the third minute. Wales cited bad boy Kobus, who scored a try in the match, and he was banned for 30 days and fined. Earlier in 1995 had made a more legitimate impression when he played a lead role in South

South Africa (1993)

Last Season	8 caps	5 pts
Career	10 caps	5 pts

Caps (10): **1993** F(1) **1995** WS(a) wc-R, C, WS(b), F, NZ. W, It, E

Points (5 – 1t): **1995** W(1t)

Africa's World Cup triumph, having begun tournament as second-choice lock. Toured New Zealand, Britain and Ireland in 1994, but without appearing in Test arena. Ironically, he had troubled England's tourists in 1994 with his bullish runs and immense strength, guiding both Transvaal and South Africa B to accomplished wins. Made such an impact that he was conspicuous by his absence in the two Tests – one of the victims of the selectors' purge after France drew first Test of 1993 series 20–20 in Durban (26.6.93). He and engine-room partner, Natal's Rudie Visagie, were replaced by Hannes Strydom and Nico Wegner for second Test, which France won. Was in 1993 Transvaal side that won inaugural Super–10 tournament (beating Auckland 20–7 in final at Ellis Park, Jo'burg, 22.5.93) and Currie Cup (beating Natal 21–15 in final at Kings Park, Durban, 16.10.93). Between the two he toured Australia with Boks.

Williams, C. M.   South Africa

Full name: Chester Williams
Nickname: Black Pearl
Province: Western Province
Position: Wing
Height: 5ft 8½ in (1.74m)
Weight: 13st 4lb (80kg)
Occupation: Development officer,
Western Province RFU
Born: 9.8.70
Family: Single
International debut: Argentina 23,
South Africa 52, 1993
Notable landmarks in rugby career:
The darling of South African rugby,
Chester was the talk of 1995 World
Cup when he withdrew injured on
eve of competition, returned when
Pieter Hendriks was banned for foul
play and marked his comeback with
a South African record four tries in
the 42–14 quarter-final defeat of
Western Samoa (Jo'burg, 10.6.95).
Organisers used Chester's face to
promote the tournament, with the
slogan 'The Waiting's Over', so it
was something of a relief for them
when his waiting finally ended. A
player who had impressed greatly on

South Africa (1993)
Last Season	5 caps	30 pts
Career	15 caps	65 pts

Caps (15): **1993** Arg(2) **1994** E(1,2),
NZ(1,2,3), Arg(1,2), S, W **1995**
WS(a) wc-WS(b), F, NZ. It, E
Points (65 – 13t): **1993** Arg(2:1t) **1994**
Arg(1:1t), Arg(2:1t), S(1t), W(1t)
1995 WS(a:2t) wc-WS(b:4t). E(2t)

Boks' 1994 tour of Britain, scoring tries in Test defeats of Scotland and Wales,
added a brace of tries vs England when the sides brought the curtain down on
1995 at Twickenham (18.11.95). That gave him 13 tries from 14 starts. How
Western Province could have done with that firepower in the 1996 Super-12
tournament, but Chester missed the competition through injury. First emerged
on 1993 tour of Australia, playing in seven of the 13 matches and contributing
seven tries, including a hat-trick vs Victoria. His services were retained on the
autumn trip to Argentina, where the hosts were handed a 2–0 series whitewash
in the first-ever official Tests between the sides. Chester was deployed in four
out of six games, and responded with three tries. One of these came on his international debut in the second Test against the Pumas in Buenos Aires (13.11.93),
as South Africa ran out convincing 52–23 winners. Collected his second cap
when England won 32–15 in Pretoria (4.6.94), but was stretchered off with a
neck injury 30 minutes into second Test (Cape Town, 11.6.94). Happily, he
returned in time for the tour to New Zealand and played in all three Tests.

Williams, S. M.   Wales

Full name: Steve Michael Williams
Club: Neath
Position: No.8
Height: 6ft 4in (1.93m)
Weight: 17st (108kg)
Occupation: Student
Born: Neath, 3.10.70
Family: Single
Family links with rugby: Mother washes kit, father shouts advice, and brothers laugh when I miss a tackle.
Former clubs: Bryncoch, Swansea
International debut: Tonga 9, Wales 18, 1994
Five Nations debut: England 21, Wales 15, 1996
Best rugby memories: Winning first cap; winning 1995/96 championship with Neath.
Worst rugby memory: Being dropped from Welsh Schools squad; losing 1995/96 Swalec Cup final.
Most embarrassing memory: Opening my bag in the Swansea changing room before my first game and discovering that my brother had put his toys on top of my kit – good for the image!

Wales (1994)

Last Season	4 caps	0 pts
Career	4 caps	0 pts

Caps (4): **1994** T **1996** E(TR), A(1,2)
Points Nil

Suggestions to improve rugby: Change training times from evenings to mornings; simplify rules; improve playing surfaces; stop selling beer in rugby clubs!
Notable landmarks in rugby career: Six years after being voted Most Promising Young Player in Wales, Steve made breakthrough at top level in 1996. Not only did he help Neath win Heineken Welsh Championship in a thrilling finish, and get the Welsh All Blacks to the Swalec Cup final, he made his Five Nations debut and represented Dragons on Test duty 'down under'. A debutant on Wales' tour of South Seas in 1994, playing in 18–9 defeat of Tonga (Nuku'alofa, 22.6.94) – after which a serious knee injury, sustained when playing for Neath vs South Africa (1994), delayed further progress – his entry into the Five Nations history books was a fleeting affair. Twice came on as a temporary replacement vs England as gallant Wales lost 21–15 (Twickenham, 3.2.96). Stayed on bench thereafter, but was selected at No.8 for Wales' first-Test defeat by Australia (56–25, Brisbane, 8.6.96). Won six caps for Wales Schools, U-18s, captained Wales U-21s (1990) and Colleges. Toured as a lock with senior Wales squad to Namibia (1990), and was a non-playing member of the 1991 World Cup squad.
Touchlines: Weightwatchers, break dancing

Wilson, D. J.   Australia

Full name: David John Wilson
State: Queensland
Club: Eastern Districts
Position: Flanker
Height: 6ft 2in (1.88m)
Weight: 14st 11lb (94kg)
Occupation: Area manager, BP Oil
Born: 4.1.67
International debut: Australia 27,
Scotland 12, 1992
Best rugby memory: Second Test win
over All Blacks which secured 1992
Bledisloe Cup series.
Worst rugby memory: Missing 1990
tour to New Zealand due to broken
ankle.
Toughest opponent: Michael Jones
(Auckland & New Zealand)
Serious injuries: Knee reconstruction
(1987); broken ankle (1990);broken
collarbone (1992).
Other sporting claims to fame:
Bettering 105 for a round of golf
Suggestions to improve rugby:
Penalty and dropped goal should be
worth only two points each.
Notable landmarks in rugby career:
Influential performer in 1994 as
Australia impressively lived up to

Australia (1992)

Last Season	5 caps	10 pts
Career	29 caps	25 pts

Caps (29): **1992** S(1,2), NZ(1,2,3), SA, I,
W **1993** T, NZ, SA(1,2,3), C, F(1,2)
1994 I(1,2), It(1,2), WS, E **1996** W(1,2)
Arg(1,2) wc-SA, R, E **1996** W(1,2)
Points (25 – 5t): **1992** W(1t) **1994** I(2:1t)
1995 Arg(2:1t) wc-R(1t) **1996**
W(1:1t)

their billing as world champions with six wins out of six. David played in all
games and retained his place in 1995 in the World Cup warm-up series against
Argentina. Indeed, he scored a try in the 30–13 second Test win (Sydney,
6.5.95). David played in three of the Wallabies' four World Cup ties, which
meant he was on hand when England's Rob Andrew dropped the goal that
ended Australia's tenure as Cup holders (Cape Town, 11.6.95). David had
emerged on the 1989 tour to Canada and France, though his ensuing progress
was slowed by a fractured ankle, which kept him out of the 1990 tour to New
Zealand. However, he had recovered in time to tour Europe with the Emerging
Wallabies later that year. Ever-present in 25 Tests until he sat out the Canada
Cup tie (31.5.95), David was twice winner, in 1989 and 1991, of the
Queensland Rothmans Medal.
Touchlines: Surfing, golf, fishing

Wilson, J. W.   New Zealand

Full name: Jeffrey (Jeff) William
Wilson
Province: Otago
Position: Wing, fullback
Height: 5ft 11in (1.81m)
Weight: 14st 6lb (91kg)
Occupation: Sales and marketing
rep, Nike
Born: 24.10.73
Family: Single
International debut: Scotland 15,
New Zealand 51, 1993
Best rugby memory: Scoring hat-
trick of tries on my Test debut at
Murrayfield.
Worst rugby memory: Result of
1995 World Cup final
Toughest opponent: Serge Blanco
(ex-Biarritz & France) – the greatest
fullback to ever play the game.
Notable landmarks in rugby career:
One of world rugby's most exciting
players, Jeff went from being the All
Blacks' golden boy to their *other*
wing in 1995 as Jonah Lomu hogged
the limelight. But he still had a pretty
good time of it as New Zealand
reached World Cup final, won

New Zealand (1993)

Last Season	12 caps	30 pts
Career	16 caps	61 pts

Caps (16): 1993 S, E 1994 A 1995 C wc-
I, J, S, E, SA. A(1,2), It, F(1) 1996
WS, S(1,2)

Points (61 – 10t,1c,3p): 1993 S(3t,1c),
E(3p) 1995 C(1t) wc-J(3t). A(2:1t),
It(1t) 1996 WS(1t)

Bledisloe Cup and split two-Test series in France. Took try tally to a none-too-
sloppy nine in 13 Tests, with scores against Canada, Japan (3), Australia and
Italy. Started 1996 impressively too, producing some dazzling play for exciting
Otago Highlanders in inaugural Super-12 tournament. Played in five of New
Zealand's six ties at 1995 World Cup. A heavy knock sustained against Ireland
saw him rested against Wales, but he returned vs Japan and scored a hat-trick,
just as he had done on his debut vs Scotland in 1993. Moved to his favoured
position of fullback for quarter-final vs Scotland (Pretoria, 11.6.95), but was
less than awesome (by his own standards) and so was restored to the right wing
thereafter. At the age of 16 Jeff clocked 11 seconds over 100 metres. Played
provincial rugby and cricket while still at High School, and ended 1992 season
as star of New Zealand Secondary Schools rugby side. Let's not forget either
that in June 1992 he scored 66 points (nine tries and 15 conversions) for Cargill
High School, Invercargill – all in the one match. But all that was nothing on
1993. He began year with a call-up to the New Zealand one-day cricket side vs

Australia and, after an impressive bowling performance, stroked the winning runs. Swapped flannels for Black to become All Black at age of 19, scoring two tries on his first start vs London (won 39–12, Twickenham, 23 October). His Test bow vs Scotland yielded a try hat-trick and a touchline conversion for good measure. 'My aim was to get through the game without making a mistake', he said. His bubble deflated a little on second Test outing when, thanks to an injury suffered by first-choice goalkicker Matthew Cooper, he was assigned the duties vs England at Twickenham. Five penalty misses out of eight effectively cost New Zealand the match. But it was a rare off-day for a young man who moved from Invercargill to Dunedin to attend teachers' college and joined Otago.
Touchlines: Cricket, basketball

Wintle, M. E.   Wales

Full name: Matthew Edward Wintle
Club: Llanelli
Position: Centre
Height: 6ft (1.83m)
Weight: 14st 7lb (92kg)
Occupation: Medical student
Born: 12.2.72
Family: Single
Family links with rugby: Brother Richard played for Wales as replacement vs Western Samoa in 1988; cousin Philip plays for Aberavon.
International debut: Wales 31, Italy 26, 1996
Five Nations debut: None
Other sporting claim to fame: Basketball for Wales Under-17s
Notable landmarks in rugby career: One of five rookies blooded by Wales coach Kevin Bowring in the 31–26 defeat of Italy in Cardiff (16.1.96), Matthew was handed his first cap at the same time as midfield partner Leigh Davies (Neath), Arwel

Wales (1996)		
Last Season	1 cap	0 pts
Career	1 cap	0 pts

Caps (1): **1996** It
Points Nil

Thomas (Swansea fly-half), Andrew Lewis (Cardiff prop) and Gwyn Jones (Llanelli flanker). Included in 1996 Five Nations squad but did not figure. Medical student Matthew had previously represented Wales at U-18, U-19, U-21, Youth, Student and A team levels. He captained Wales Students in 1994, the same year that he made his A team debut against Ireland at Donnybrook, having led the ultra-successful Wales Under-19 tour to Canada in 1991.

Wood, K. G. M.   Ireland

Full name: Keith Gerald Mallinson Wood
Club: Harlequins
Position: Hooker
Height: 6ft (1.83m)
Weight: 15st 12lb (101kg)
Occupation: Customer advisor, Irish Permanent PLC
Born: Limerick, 27.1.72
Family links with rugby: Father (Gordon) played for Ireland (29 times: 1954–61) and 1959 British Lions (first and third Tests vs New Zealand).
Former club: Garryowen
International debut: Australia 33, Ireland 13, 1994
Five Nations debut: Ireland 8, England 20, 1995
Notable landmarks in rugby career: Recurring shoulder problem ruined 1994/95 campaign for Keith, who had been Ireland's most valuable player on 1994 tour of Australia, and ruled him out of virtually the

Ireland (1994)

Last Season	1 cap	0 pts
Career	6 caps	0 pts

Caps (6): **1994** A(1,2), US **1995** E, S wc-J

Points Nil

whole of 1995/96 – a season that he ended by switching club allegiances to the Harlequins. Having played in both Tests 'down under' and impressed, despite the defeats, with his pace and mobility, huge things were expected of the Limerick man last term. But nagging injury hampered his form and he was relegated to bench duties midway through the Five Nations Championship. To make matters even worse his replacement, Terry Kingston, was handed the captaincy. Keith returned to the Ireland jersey in South Africa, but his World Cup lasted but nine minutes before his shoulder went again against Japan (Bloemfontein, 31.5.95). A bench replacement since 1992, his path to progress blocked at both provincial (Munster) and national level by Dolphin's Kingston, Keith helped Garryowen win 1991/92 and 1993/94 All-Ireland League titles. As recently as the 1992/93 season he was playing for the Ireland Under-21s. A year previously he had been selected for the senior bench against the 1992 Wallabies, but an injury frustrated him over the remainder of the season. The next time he encountered Australia, in their own backyard, he opposed them on the field, first at Ballymore, then in Brisbane (5.6.94) and then in Sydney (11.6.94), where the Wallabies wrapped up a 2–0 series win with a 32–18 victory. Gerry Murphy, Ireland's coach, said of Keith: 'He has been our outstanding player in both Tests and has the potential to be world class.' His other tour outings came against Western Australia and Queensland; he scored a try in the 29–26 loss to the latter.

Woods, N. K. P. J.   Ireland

Full name: Niall Kevin Patrick John Woods
Club: London Irish
Position: Wing
Height: 5ft 11in (1.80m)
Weight: 12st 4lb (78kg)
Occupation: Trainee chartered accountant, John Woods
Born: Dublin, 21.6.71
Family: Single
Former club: Blackrock College
International debut: Australia 33, Ireland 13, 1994
Five Nations debut: Ireland 8, England 20, 1995
Notable landmarks in rugby career: Finished 1995/96 season strongly, playing in each of Ireland's last three games, although he missed the Peace International against the Barbarians. His maiden Test try came in the middle game as Ireland scored a record 30 points against Wales in winning their Five Nations clash in Dublin 30–17 (2.3.96). Despite

Ireland (1994)

Last Season	3 caps	5 pts
Career	7 caps	5 pts

Caps (7): **1994** A(1,2) **1995** E,F **1996** F,W,E
Points (5 – 1t): **1996** W(1t)

making his Test debut on the 1994 tour to Australia, playing in both matches against the Wallabies, Niall was not required for the 1995 World Cup, where his wing partner in the Ireland A team, Darragh O'Mahony, was preferred. Collected his eighth A cap against Scotland last season before returning to the senior side. As a younger player, he had been selected for the Ireland Under-21 squad after only one season playing with Blackrock College. Played twice for the Under-21s in 1991 before, in 1993, touring Southern Africa with an Irish Development squad, scoring a try hat-trick against South African Provinces. Made two appearances for senior side in 1995 when Jonathan Bell was injured.

Wright, P. H. Scotland

Full name: Peter Hugh Wright
Nickname: Suede (because of my haircut)
Club: Melrose
Position: Prop
Height: 6ft (1.83m)
Weight: 17st 2lb (109kg)
Occupation: Blacksmith, MacDonald & Ross
Born: Bonnyrigg, 30.12.67
Family: Audrey (wife), Eilidh (daughter)
Family links with rugby: Brothers Graham and David play for Lasswade.
Former clubs: Lasswade, Boroughmuir
International debut: Australia 27, Scotland 12, 1992
Five Nations debut: France 11, Scotland 3, 1993
Best rugby memory: Being told I was in the 1993 British Lions squad
Worst rugby memory: Tearing medial and cruciate knee ligaments (1989)
Toughest opponent: Tony Daly (NSW & Australia) and most French props

Scotland (1992)

Last Season	9 caps	5 pts
Career	21 caps	5 pts

Lions (1993)

Caps (21): 1992 A(1,2) 1993 F, W, E 1994 W 1995 C, I, F(a), W, E, R wc-IC, T, F(b), NZ 1996 I, F, W, E, NZ(1)

Biggest influence on career: Bruce Hay (Boroughmuir coach)
Serious injuries: Torn medial and cruciate knee ligaments (October 1989 – out for 18 months)
Do you really want to be a full-time professional? No
How well has rugby handled move to professionalism? 1/10. The game was thrown wide open and the IRFB washed its hands of everything. As governing body they should have put guidelines down to help the unions instead of it being a free-for-all.
Do you have a duty to entertain? We are more accountable now but I am still not sure we have a duty.
Do you feel a loyalty to your club in this new era? Loyalty has gone out of the window (it doesn't pay your mortgage). Eventually rugby will be just like soccer.
Suggestions to improve rugby: Stop chopping and changing rules. It is difficult to keep adapting. When you've decided on them make sure every nation adheres to them.

Notable landmarks in rugby career: Revelled in Scotland's more expansive brand of rugby in 1995/96, his mobility and increased contribution putting an end to the 'teapot' jibes (standing hands on hips, blowing hard) which had stemmed from his less-than-successful campaign with the 1993 Lions. Never a stranger to controversy, however, he was fined by the SRU for foul play against England (Edinburgh, 2.3.96), and was also dismissed (for the third time in his career) while playing for Boroughmuir against Gala for raising his voice in anger. Peter, having switched to tighthead, was ever-present in 1995, helping Scotland to second place in the Five Nations series before claiming his maiden Test try in the 89–0 World Cup rout of Cote d'Ivoire (Rustenburg, 26.5.95). The seventh player from the Boroughmuir club to be capped, Peter appeared on both sides of the Scottish front row in 1992/93 – making his debut on the tour to Australia in the first Test defeat in Sydney (13.6.92). Retained his place the following week at Ballymore when the world champion Wallabies ran out 37–13 winners, but was deposed by Paul Burnell for the 1993 Five Nations Championship. That would have been but for the fact that the Scots were having something of a crisis at loosehead in the wake of David Sole's retirement. Bristol's Alan Sharp was picked but withdrew injured, and after one cap his replacement, GHK's Alan Watt, also pulled out of contention. Peter was offered the job, and did so well against France, Wales and England that he was picked to tour New Zealand with the Lions, playing against North Auckland, NZ Maoris, Southland, Taranaki, Hawke's Bay and Waikato. During previous Lions tour in 1989 he was to be found in Japan with Scotland, where he made appearances against Kanto and Japan Under-23. Indeed, Peter is no stranger to representative rugby, having played for Scotland at Under-15, Under-18, Under-19 and Under-21 levels. He also skippered Edinburgh Under-21s. He played his first senior game for Boroughmuir at the age of 18 and made his Scotland B bow in the 14–12 win over France B at Melrose in 1989.

Touchlines: Golf, cinema

Doddie Weir loses out in an aerial scramble for possession with All Black lock Ian Jones during Scotland's second Test loss to New Zealand last summer.

APPENDIX

ANDREW, Rob. **Country:** England. **Position:** Fly-half. **Club:** Newcastle. **Debut:** England 22, Romania 15, 1985. **Caps:** 70. **Points:** 396 (2t,33c, 86p,21dg). 1995/96: 5. **Born:** 18.2.63. **Height:** 5ft 9in. **Weight:** 12st 8lb. **Occupation:** Director of Rugby, Newcastle RFC. **Notes:** Led England to 1995 World Cup semi-final before becoming highly paid club supremo. **Record** (70–396:2t,33c,86p,21dg): **1985** R(4p,2dg),F(2p,1dg),S(2p),I(2p), W(1c,2p,1dg) **1986** W(6p,1dg),S(2p),I(3c,1p),F **1987** I,F(1dg),W wc-J(R), US **1988**S(1dg),I(1:3c,2),A(a1,a2),Fj,A(b) **1989**S(2p),I(1c,2p),F(1p),W(2p, 1dg),R(1dg),Fj(1c) Lions-A(2:1c,1p,1dg,3) **1990** I,F,W,S,Arg(b) **1991**W,S, I,F(1dg),Fj(1t,2dg),A(a) wc-NZ(1dg),It,US,F,S(1dg),A(b) **1992** S,I,F,W,C, SA **1993**F,W Lions-NZ(1,2:1dg,3). NZ(1dg) **1994** S,I,F(5p,1dg),W(1c,1p), SA(1:1t,2c,5p,1dg,2:3p),R(6c,4p),C(6c,6p) **1995** I(1c,1p),F(2c,4p),W(1c, 2p),S(7p,1dg) wc-Arg(6p,2dg),It(1c,5p),A(1c,5p,1dg),NZ(3c,1p),F(3p)

ARMARY, Louis. **Country:** France. **Position:** Prop. **Club:** Lourdes. **Debut:** France 55, Romania 12, 1987. **Caps:** 47. **Points:** 4 (1t). 1995/96: 1. **Born:** 24.7.63. **Height:** 6ft. **Weight:** 16st 2lb. **Occupation:** Business executive. **Notes:** Legendary prop who departed Test fray after helping France reach semi-finals of 1995 World Cup. **Record** (47 – 4: 1t): **1987** wc-R(a). R(b) **1988** S, I, W, Arg(b1,b2), R **1989** W, S, A(1,2) **1990** W,E,S,I,A(1, 2:1t, 3), NZ(1) **1991** W(b) **1992** S, I, R, Arg(a1,a2), SA(1,2), Arg(b) **1993** E, S, I, W, SA(1,2), R(b), A(1,2) **1994** I, W, NZ(1R,2R) **1995** I, R wc-T, I, SA

ARMSTRONG, Gary. **Country:** Scotland. **Position:** Scrum-half. **Club:** Newcastle. **Debut:** Scotland 13, Australia 32, 1988. **Caps:** 32. **Points:** 16 (4t). 1995/96: 2 (0). **Born:** 30.9.66. **Height:** 5ft 8in. **Weight:** 13st 10lb. **Occupation:** Rugby player. **Notes:** Recent career blighted by injury but, having switched to Newcastle in 1995/96, returned to Test arena in New Zealand, replacing injured incumbent Bryan Redpath. **Record** (32 – 16: 4t): **1988** A **1989** W(1t),E,I,F,Fj,R **1990** I,F,W,E,NZ(1,2),Arg(1t) **1991** F, W(1t),E,I(a),R wc-J,I(b:1t),WS,E,NZ **1993** I,F,W,E **1994** E,I **1996** NZ(1,2)

BACHOP, Graeme. **Country:** New Zealand. **Position:** Scrum-half. **Club:** Canterbury. **Debut:** Wales 9, New Zealand 34, 1989. **Caps:** 31. **Points:** 18 (4t). 1995/96: 5. **Born:** 11.6.67. **Height:** 5ft 10in. **Weight:** 13st. **Occupation:** Sports trainer. **Notes:** Most-capped All Black scrum-half (best passer in game), who departed Test scene after 1995 Bledisloe Cup to work/play in Japan. **Record** (31 – 18: 4t): **1989** W(1t), I **1990** S(1,2), A(1, 2:1t, 3), F(1,2) **1991** Arg(1,2), A(a1,a2). wc-E, US, C, A(b), S **1992** Wd(1) **1994** SA(1,2,3), A **1995** C(1t) wc-I, W, S, E(1t), SA. A(1,2)

BARRY, Liam. **Country:** New Zealand. **Position:** Openside flanker. **Province:** North Harbour. **Debut:** France 12, New Zealand 37, 1995. **Caps:** 1. **Points:** 0. 1995/96: 1. **Born:** 15.3.71. **Height:** 6ft 4½in. **Weight:** 14st 13lb. **Notes:** Toured to Britain with 1993 All Blacks but forced to wait two more years for debut in Paris (18.11.95). Third-generation All Black. **Record** (1): **1995** F(2)

BRADLEY, Michael. **Country:** Ireland. **Position:** Scrum-half. **Club:** Cork Constitution. **Debut:** Ireland 9, Australia 16, 1984. **Caps:** 40. **Points:** 21 (5t). 1995/96: 1 (0). **Born:** 17.11.62. **Height:** 5ft 10in. **Weight:** 13st 2lb. **Occupation:** Security manager. **Notes:** Ireland's most-capped scrum-half and a former captain, who retired after 1995 World Cup. **Record** (40 – 21: 5t): **1984** A **1985** S, F, W, E **1986** F, W, E, S, R(1t) **1987** E, S, F(1t), W(a) wc-W(b), C(1t), T, A **1988** S(1t), F, W, E(a) **1990** W **1992** NZ(1,2) **1993** S, F, W, E, R **1994** F, W, E, S, A(1,2), US(1t) **1995** S, F wc-NZ

BREWER, Michael. **Country:** New Zealand. **Position:** Flanker, No.8. **Province:** Otago. **Debut:** New Zealand 18, France 9, 1986. **Caps:** 30. **Points:** 4 (1t). 1995/96: 4. **Born:** 6.11.64. **Height:** 6ft 5in. **Weight:** 16st 9lb. **Occupation:** Marketing manager. **Notes:** Retired from Test rugby after 1995 World Cup, but played in Peace International for Barbarians against Ireland (18.5.95). **Record** (30 – 4: 1t): **1986** F(a:1t), A(1,2,3), F(b1,b2) **1988** A(1) **1989** A, W, I **1990** S(1,2), A(1,2,3), F(1,2) **1992** I(2), A(1) **1994** F(1,2), SA(1,2,3), A **1995** C wc-I, W, E, SA

BRINK, Robbie. **Country:** South Africa. **Position:** Flanker. **Province:** Western Province. **Debut:** South Africa 21, Romania 8, 1995. **Caps:** 2. **Points:** 0. 1995/96: 2. **Born:** 21.7.71. **Height:** 6ft 5in. **Weight:** 17st 10lb. **Occupation:** Student. **Notes:** One of three uncapped Boks in the World Cup-winning squad, he played in wins over Romania and Canada. **Record** (2): **1995** wc-R, C

CAPUTO, Marco. **Country:** Australia. **Position:** Prop. **State:** Australian Capital Territory. **Debut:** Australia 56, Wales 25, 1996. **Caps:** 2. **Points:** 5 (1t). 1995/96: 2 (5). **Notes:** Won his Test selection on back of a superb campaign with surprise packets ACT Brumbies in 1996 Super-12 tournament. Marked debut with try (Ballymore, 15.6.96) but lasted only 44 minutes of Sydney return. **Record** (2 – 5: 1t): **1996** W(1:1t), W(2)

CARMINATI, Alain. **Country:** France. **Position:** Openside flanker. **Club:** Brive. **Debut:** France 20, Romania 3, 1986. **Caps:** 20. **Points:** 14 (3t). 1995/96: 5 (10). **Born:** 17.8.66. **Notes:** Defected to RL in 1990 after being banned for stamping on Scot John Jeffrey's head at Murrayfield. Returned to RU with Brive, and represented France in Latin Cup and vs All Blacks (November 1995). **Record** (20 – 14: 3t): **1986** R(2), NZ(2) **1987** wc-R, Z **1988** I(1t), W, Arg(1,2) **1989** I, W, S, NZ(1R,2), A(2) **1990** S **1995** It(1t), R(1t), Arg, NZ(1,2)

CECILLON, Marc. **Country:** France. **Position:** No.8, flanker, lock. **Club:** Bourgoin. **Debut:** France 25, Ireland 6, 1988. **Caps:** 46. **Points:** 38 (9t). 1995/96: 4. **Born:** 30.7.59. **Height:** 6ft 3in. **Weight:** 15st 2lb. **Occupation:** Schoolmaster. **Notes:** An ultra-loyal servant of French rugby, who finally bowed out of the Test arena after he had helped France to the 1995 World Cup semi-finals. **Record** (46 – 38: 9t): **1988** I, W, Arg(a2), Arg(b1:1t, b2:1t), R **1989** R, I, E, NZ(1:1t, 2:1t), A(1) **1990** S, I, E(R) **1991** R(1t), US(1:1t), W wc-E **1992** W, E, S, I(1t), R, Arg(a1,a2), SA(1,2) **1993** E, S, I, W, R(a:1t), SA(1,2), R(b), A(1,2) **1994** I, W **1995** I(a:1t), R wc-T, S(b), I(b), SA

CIGAGNA, Albert. **Country:** France. **Position:** No.8. **Club:** Toulouse. **Debut:** France 19, England 9, 1995. **Caps:** 1. **Points:** 0. 1995/96: 1. **Born:** 25.9.60. **Height:** 6ft 1½in. **Weight:** 16st 6lb. **Notes:** Was called up as an emergency replacement after Philippe Benetton broke his arm in 1995 World Cup. Made his debut in third-place play-off defeat of England (22.6.95). **Record (1): 1995** wc-E(b)

CLEMENT, Anthony. **Country:** Wales. **Position:** Fullback. **Club:** Swansea. **Debut:** Wales 46, US Eagles 0, 1987. **Caps:** 37. **Points:** 16 (3t,1dg). 1995/96: 3 (0). **Born:** 8.2.67. **Height:** 5ft 9in. **Weight:** 13st 8lb. **Notes:** A member of the 1989 and 1993 Lions parties, Tony missed 1995/96 season with shoulder injury. **Record (37 – 16:** 3t, 1dg): **1987** US(R:2t) **1988** E, NZ, WS(R), Ro **1989** NZ **1990** S(R), I(R), Na(1, 2:1dg) **1991** S(R), A(a:R), F(b) wc-WS, A(b) **1992** I, F, E, S **1993** I(R), F, J(1t), C **1994** S, I, F. wc(q)-Sp. C(R), T, WS. wc(q)-It. SA **1995** F, E wc-J, NZ,I(b)

COKER, Troy. **Country:** Australia. **Position:** Lock/back row. **State:** ACT. **Debut:** Australia 19, England 6, 1987. **Caps:** 17. **Points:** 0. 1995/96: 1. **Born:** 30.5.63. **Height:** 6ft 6in. **Weight:** 17st 13lb. **Occupation:** Industrial relations advocate. **Notes:** Moved from Queensland to ACT for Super-12 tournament, having played in second leg of 1995 Bledisloe Cup series. **Record (17): 1987** wc-E, US, F, W **1991** NZ(a2). wc-Arg, WS, NZ(b), E(b) **1992** NZ(1,2,3), W(R) **1993** T, NZ **1995** Arg(2), NZ(1R)

COSTES, Arnaud. **Country:** France. **Position:** Flanker. **Club:** Montferrand. **Debut:** France 28, Canada 9, 1994. **Caps:** 3. **Points:** 5 (1t). 1995/96: 1 (5). **Born:** 16.6.73. **Height:** 6ft 1in. **Weight:** 16st. **Occupation:** Student. **Notes:** Represented France in 1995 World Cup, scoring try against Cote d'Ivoire, having made his debut the previous December vs Canada in Besancon. **Record (3 – 5:** 1t): **1994** C(b) **1995** R wc-IC(1t)

CULLEN, Christian. **Country:** New Zealand. **Position:** Fullback. **Province:** Manawatu. **Debut:** New Zealand 51, Western Samoa 10, 1996. **Caps:** 3. **Points:** 35 (7t). 1995/96: 3 (35). **Born:** 12.2.76. **Height:** 5ft 10½in. **Weight:** 13st 3lb. **Occupation:** Marketing student. **Notes:** Player of the tournament at the Hong Kong Sevens, scoring a record 18 tries in six games. He carried that form into the Test arena, claiming seven tries on his first two starts. If 1995 was about Lomu, 1996 is about this man – a 1995 NZ Colt. **Record (3 – 35:** 7t): **1996** WS(3t), S(1:4t), S(2)

DAVIES, Adrian. **Country:** Wales. **Position:** Fly-half. **Club:** Richmond. **Debut:** Wales 24, Barbarians 31, 1990. **Caps:** 9. **Points:** 22 (2c,3p,3dg). 1995/96: 2. **Born:** 9.2.69. **Height:** 5ft 10in. **Weight:** 12st 10lb. **Occupation:** Surveyor. **Notes:** Kicked Cardiff into European Cup final extra time before losing to Toulouse, then kicked Cardiff into touch and joined Richmond. **Record (9 – 22:** 2c, 3p, 3dg): **1991** Ba(R), A(1dg) **1993** Z(1:1dg), Z(2), J, C **1994** Fj(2c,3p) **1995** wc-J, I(b:1dg)

DAVIES, Stuart. **Country:** Wales. **Position:** Flanker. **Club:** Swansea. **Debut:** Ireland 15, Wales 16, 1992. **Caps:** 15. **Points:** 9 (2t). 1995/96: 2. **Born:** 2.9.65. **Height:** 6ft 3in. **Weight:** 17st 4lb. **Occupation:** Environmental health officer. **Notes:** Captained Swansea to 1995 Welsh Cup and played twice in 1995 World Cup, but then absent from international stage. **Record (15 – 9:** 2t): **1992** I(1t),F,E,S,A **1993** F,S,I,Z(1R,2:1t),Na,J **1995** F wc-J,I(b)

ELLIS, Marc. Country: New Zealand. **Position:** Centre, wing, fly-half. **Province:** Otago. **Debut:** Scotland 15, New Zealand 51, 1993. **Caps:** 8. **Points:** 33 (11t). 1995/96: 5. **Born:** 8.10.71. **Height:** 5ft 11in. **Weight:** 13st 10lb. **Notes:** Fly-half turned wing cum centre, who switched codes after impressive World Cup campaign, highlighted by six tries vs hapless Japan. **Record** (8 – 33: 11t): **1993** S(2t),E **1995** C(2t) wc-I(R),W(1t),J(6t),S,SA(R)

ERICKSSON, Ronnie. Country: Scotland. **Position:** Centre. **Club:** London Scottish. **Debut:** New Zealand 62, Scotland 31, 1996. **Caps:** 1. **Points:** 0. 1995/96: 2 (0). **Born:** 22.4.72. **Height:** 6ft 1in. **Weight:** 15st 6lb. **Notes:** Big midfielder paired with Ian Jardine to do a defensive job in first Test vs New Zealand last summer in the absence of injured Scott Hastings and Graham Shiel. The All Blacks still scored 62 points. **Record** (1): **1996** NZ(1)

EVANS, David. Country: Wales. **Position:** Utility back. **Club:** Treorchy. **Debut:** France 31, Wales 12, 1989. **Caps:** 12. **Points:** 6 (2dg). 1995/96: 1 (0). **Born:** 1.11.65. **Height:** 5ft 9in. **Weight:** 12st 11lb. **Occupation:** Sports Council officer. **Notes:** Dogged by injury since 1991, but played once in 1995 World Cup vs Japan (27.5.95). **Record** (12 – 6: 2dg): **1989** F,E,NZ **1990** F(1dg),E,S,I,Ba(1dg) **1991** A(a:R),F(b:R) wc-A(b:R) **1995** wc-J(R)

EVANS, Ricky. Country: Wales. **Position:** Prop. **Club:** Wales. **Debut:** Wales 10, England 9, 1993. **Caps:** 19. **Points:** 0. 1995/96: 2. **Born:** 23.6.61. **Height:** 6ft 2in. **Weight:** 17st 3lb. **Occupation:** Fireman. **Notes:** Butted by France's lock Merle (21.1.95) and fell awkwardly, breaking a leg in two places. Returned for World Cup and played twice. **Record** (19): **1993** E, S,I,F **1994** S,I,F,E. wc(q)-P,Sp. C,Fj,WS. wc(q)-R,It. SA **1995** F wc-NZ, I(b)

FINEGAN, Owen. Country: Australia. **Position:** Flanker, No.8. **State:** ACT. **Debut:** Australia 56, Wales 25, 1996. **Caps:** 2. **Points:** 5 (1t). 1995/96: 2 (5). **Height:** 6ft 5in. **Weight:** 18st. **Notes:** One of several ACT players to enter Wallabies from previously unfashionable state because of Brumbies' dazzling Super-12 campaign. Scored first Australian try in second Test vs Wales (won 42–3, Sydney, 22.6.96). **Record** (2 – 5: 1t): **1996** W(1,2:1t)

FOLEY, Anthony. Country: Ireland. **Position:** Flanker. **Club:** Shannon. **Debut:** Ireland 8, England 20, 1995. **Caps:** 6. **Points:** 5 (1t). 1995/96: 1. **Born:** 30.10.73. **Height:** 6ft 3in. **Weight:** 16st 8lb. **Occupation:** Student. **Notes:** Marked debut with try vs England (Dublin, 21.1.95); needs five caps to match the 11 won by dad Brendan (1976–81). **Record** (6 – 5: 1t): **1995** E(1t), S, F, W, It wc-J(TR)

FOLEY, Michael. Country: Australia. **Position:** Hooker. **State:** Queensland. **Debut:** Australia 27, Canada 11, 1995. **Caps:** 3. **Points:** 10 (2t). 1994/95: 2. **Born:** 7.6.67. **Height:** 6ft. **Weight:** 17st 2lb. **Occupation:** Student. **Notes:** Made debut at World Cup as 70th-minute replacement for Phil Kearns (Port Elizabeth, 31.5.95). Scored try vs Romania on first start. **Record** (3 – 10: 2t): **1995** wc-C(R), R (1t) **1996** W(2R:1t)

GRIFFITHS, Mike. Country: Wales. **Position:** Prop. **Club:** Wasps. **Debut:** Scotland 23, Wales 7, 1989. **Caps:** 34. **Points:** 5 (1t). 1995/96: 2. **Born:** 18.3.62. **Height:** 5ft 11in. **Weight:** 16st 10lb. **Occupation:** Pro rugby player. **Notes:** One of world rugby's most experienced props, Mike left Cardiff in big-money move to Wasps at end of this season. **Record** (34 – 5: 1t): **1988** WS,R **1989** S,I,F,E,NZ **1990** F,E,Na(1,2),Ba **1991** I,F(a),F(b) wc-WS,Arg, A(b) **1992** I,F,E,S,A **1993** Z(1,2),Na,J,C **1995** F(R),E,S,I(a) wc-J(1t), I(b)

GUIRAUD, Herve. **Country:** France. **Position:** Hooker. **Club:** Nimes. **Debut:** France 64, Romania 12, 1996. **Caps:** 1. **Points:** 0. 1995/96: 1. **Notes:** One of six players given their full debut by France in the 64–12 end-of-term romp against Romania (Aurillac, 20.4.96) in a front row in which Christian Califano scored with a try-hat trick. Represented France A in 15–25 loss to England (Paris, 19.1.96). **Record** (1): **1996** R

HALL, Mike. **Country:** Wales. **Position:** Centre. **Club:** Cardiff. **Debut:** New Zealand 52, Wales 3, 1988. **Caps:** 42. **Points:** 33 (7t). 1995/96: 3. **Born:** 13.10.65. **Height:** 6ft 1in. **Weight:** 15st 3lb. **Occupation:** Chartered surveyor. **Notes:** World Cup captain who retired from Test rugby after Wales' hugely disappointing showing. **Record** (42 – 33: 7t): **1988** NZ(R1,2), WS, R **1989** S(1t), I, F, E(1t), NZ. Lions-A(1) **1990** F, E, S **1991** A(a), F(b) wc-WS, Arg, A(b) **1992** I, F, E, S, A **1993** E, S, I **1994** S, I, F, E wc(q)-P(3t), Sp. C(2t), T wc(q)-R, It. SA **1995** F, S, I(a) wc-J, NZ, I(b)

HALPIN, Garrett. **Country:** Ireland. **Position:** Prop. **Club:** London Irish. **Debut:** England 23, Ireland 0, 1990. **Caps:** 11. **Points:** 5 (1t). 1995/96: 3 (5). **Born:** 14.2.66. **Height:** 6ft. **Weight:** 17st 6lb. **Occupation:** Teacher. **Notes:** Scored cracking World Cup try against All Blacks (27.5.95) before putting Test ambitions on hold to captain club to English League Two promotion. **Record** (11 – 5: 1t): **1990** E **1991** wc-J **1992** E, S, F **1993** R **1994** F(R) **1995** It wc-NZ(1t), W(b), F(b)

HARRY, Richard. **Country:** Australia. **Position:** Prop. **Club:** Sydney University. **State:** New South Wales. **Debut:** Australia 56, Wales 25, 1996. **Caps:** 2. **Points:** 0. 1995/96: 1. **Born:** 30.11.67. **Height:** 6ft 1in. **Weight:** 18st 8lb. **Occupation:** Sales rep. **Notes:** Flanker turned prop who toured Africa with Emerging Wallabies in 1994 before succeeding Tony Daly as the Waratahs' first-choice loosehead. Possesses great mobility for such a big man. **Record** (2): **1996** W(1,2)

HASTINGS, Gavin. **Country:** Scotland. **Position:** Fullback. **Club:** Watsoni ans. **Debut:** Scotland 18, France 17, 1986. **Caps:** 61. **Points:** 667 (17t,86c, 140p). 1995/96: 4 (104). **Born:** 3.1.62. **Height:** 6ft 2in. **Weight:** 14st 7lb. **Notes:** Multi-record-breaker who retired after World Cup to join Scottish Claymores in World League of American football. **Record** (61 – 667: 17t, 86c,140p): **1986** F(6p),W(1t,1p),E(3c,5p),I(2p),R(3c,5p) **1987** I(1c),F(1c, 4p),W(2c,2p),E(1c,2p) wc-F(4p),Z(1t,8c),R(2t,8c,1p),NZ (1p) **1988** I(2c, 2p),F(1t,4p),W(4p),E(2p),A(1t,1c,1p) **1989** Fj(1t,4c,2p), R(3c,2p) Lions-A(1:2p,2:1t,1p,3:5p) **1990** I,F(1p),W,E,NZ(1:2c,2:2c, 2p),Arg(1t,5c,1p) **1991** F,W(1c,2p),E(a),I(a:1t,1p) wc-J(1t,5c,2p),I(b:2c, 3p),WS(2c,4p),E (b:2p),NZ(2p) **1992** E(1p),I(2c,2p),F(2p),W(1p),A(1:1c, 2p) **1993** I(1c,1p), F(1p),W(5p),E(3p). Lions-NZ(1:6p,2:4p,3:1c,1p). NZ (4p) **1994** W(2p),E(2p),I(2p),F(4p),SA(1c,1p) **1995** C(1c,5p),I(2c,4p),F(a: 1t,2c,3p),W(2c,4p),E(2p),R(1t,4c,2p) wc-IC(4t,9c,2p),T(1t,1c,8p),F(b: 1c,4p),NZ(3c,3p)

HEWITT, Norm. **Country:** New Zealand. **Position:** Hooker. **Province:** Southland. **Caps:** 2. **Points:** 0. 1995/96: 2. **Born:** 11.11.68. **Height:** 5ft 10in. **Weight:** 17st 10lb. **Occupation:** Marketing director. **Notes:** Played outstandingly for NZ Maoris and Hawke's Bay against 1993 Lions, but had to wait for Test debut until 1995 World Cup, against Ireland and Japan. **Record** (2): **1995** wc-I(TR), J

HUEBER, Aubin. **Country:** France. **Position:** Scrum-half. **Club:** Toulon. **Debut:** Australia 19, France 28, 1990. **Caps:** 22. **Points:** 18 (3t,1dg). 1995/96: 3. **Born:** 5.4.67. **Height:** 5ft 8in. **Weight:** 12st 12lb. **Occupation:** PR officer. **Notes:** Lost No.9 jersey to Fabien Galthie during 1995 World Cup, after which Philippe Carbonneau and Guy Accoceberry took over. **Record** (22 – 18: 3t, 1dg): **1990** A(3), NZ(1) **1991** US(2) **1992** I, Arg(a1, a2:1t,1dg), SA(1,2), Arg(b) **1993** E, S, I, W, R(a), SA(1,2), R(b), A(1, 2:1t) **1995** wc-T(1t), S(b:R), I(b)

HUNTER, Ian. **Country:** England. **Position:** Fullback, wing, centre. **Club:** Northampton. **Debut:** England 26, Canada 13, 1992. **Caps:** 7. **Points:** 15 (3t). 1995/96: 2 (0). **Born:** 15.2.69. **Height:** 6ft 4in. **Weight:** 14st 2lb. **Occupation:** Commercial artist. **Notes:** 1993 Lion whose career has been plagued by injury. Managed to stay fit long enough to appear twice in the 1995 World Cup. **Record** (5 – 15: 3t): **1992** C(2t) **1993** F(1t), W **1994** F, W **1995** wc-WS(a), F(b)

HURTER, Marius. **Country:** South Africa. **Position:** Prop. **Province:** Northern Transvaal. **Debut:** South Africa 21, Romania 8, 1995. **Caps:** 3. **Points:** 0. 1995/96: 3 (0). **Born:** 8.10.70. **Height:** 6ft 2in. **Weight:** 18st 1lb. **Occupation:** Student. **Notes:** One of three uncapped Boks in World Cup-winning squad, playing against Romania and Canada; third cap against Wales (2.9.95). **Record** (3): **1995** wc-R, C. W

IBANEZ, Raphael. **Country:** France. **Position:** Hooker. **Club:** Dax. **Debut:** Wales 16, France 15, 1996. **Caps:** 1. **Points:** 0. 1995/96: 1 (0). **Born:** 17.12.73. **Height:** 5ft 11in. **Weight:** 14st 9lb. **Occupation:** Student. **Notes:** 76th-minute replacement for Richard Castel in Cardiff (16.3.96); plays in the Dax XV coached by his father Jacques; mainstay of French Universities front row. **Record** (1): **1996** W(R)

JAMES, Dafydd. **Country:** Wales. **Position:** Centre, wing. **Club:** Bridgend. **Debut:** Australia 42, Wales 3, 1996. **Caps:** 1. **Points:** 0. 1995/96: 1 (0). **Born:** 24.7.75. **Height:** 6ft 3in. **Weight:** 14st 7lb. **Occupation:** Student. **Notes:** Graduated from Under-21 to full honours in 1995/96, making his senior debut as an injury-time replacement for Nigel Davies in second Test defeat by Australia in Sydney (22.6.96). **Record** (1): **1996** A(2R)

JIRDANA, Jean-Louis. **Country:** France. **Position:** Prop. **Club:** Pau. **Debut:** France 64, Romania 12, 1996. **Caps:** 1. **Points:** 0. 1995/96: 1 (0). **Notes:** One of six players blooded by France coach Jean-Claude Skrela in end-of-term Test against Romania (won 64–12, Aurillac, 20.4.96), as a 69th-minute replacement for Narbonne tighthead Franck Tournaire. **Record** (3): **1996** R(R), Arg(1TR,2)

JONES, Gareth. **Country:** Wales. **Position:** Centre. **Club:** Cardiff. **Debut:** South Africa 40, Wales 11, 1995. **Caps:** 1. **Points:** 0. 1995/96: 1. **Born:** 31.5.75. **Height:** 6ft. **Weight:** 14st 2lb. **Notes:** Son of Cardiff legend P. L. Jones, Gareth moved to Cardiff from Bridgend in a season in which he made his Test breakthrough (Jo'burg, 2.9.95). Injury and slight loss of form thereafter curtailed his progress, though he played for Wales Under-21s. **Record** (1): **1995** SA

JONES, Robert. Country: Wales. **Position:** Scrum-half. **Club:** Bristol **Debut:** England 21, Wales 18, 1986. **Caps:** 54. **Points:** 14 (3t). 1995/96: 2. **Born:** 10.11.65. **Height:** 5ft 8in. **Weight:** 11st 8lb. **Occupation:** Development consultant. **Notes:** Succeeded the great Gareth Edwards as Wales' most-capped scrum-half when he won his 54th cap in the disastrous World Cup loss to Ireland (Jo'burg, 4.6.95). **Record** (54 – 14: 3t): **1986** E, S, I, F, Fj, T, WS **1987** F, E(a), S, I(a), US wc-I(b), T, E(b:1t), NZ, A **1988** E, S, I, F, NZ(1), WS, R **1989** I, F, E, NZ. Lions-A(1,2,3) **1990** F, E, S, I **1991** E, S, F(b) wc-WS, Arg, A(b) **1992** I, F, E, S, A **1993** E, S, I **1994** I(R). wc(q)-P(1t) **1995** F, E, S(1t), I(a) wc-NZ, I(b)

LABROUSSE, Thierry. Country: France. **Position:** No.8. **Club:** Brive. **Debut:** France 64, Romania 12, 1996. **Caps:** 1. **Points:** 10 (2t). 1995/96: 1. **Notes:** Try-scorer for France A in 34–13 defeat of Wales A (Newport, 15.3.96) before impressing on his full debut. One of six new caps vs Romania (Aurillac, 20.4.96), Thierry scored two tries in the rout. **Record** (1 – 10: 2t): **1996** R

LIEVREMONT, Marc. Country: France. **Position:** Flanker, No.8. **Club:** Perpignan. **Debut:** France 34, Italy 22, 1995. **Caps:** 4. **Points:** 5 (1t). 1995/96: 4 (5). **Notes:** One of a number of youngsters blooded by French coach Jean-Claude Skrela in Argentina at the 1995 Latin Cup, which France won. Marc played in three matches, scoring in the 52–8 defeat of Romania, before heaping further misery on the Romanians in Aurillac (won 64–12, 20.4.96). **Record** (5 – 1t): **1995** It, R(1t), Arg(R), NZ(2R) **1996** R, Arg(1R)

LYNAGH, Michael. Country: Australia. **Position:** Fly-half. **Club:** Saracens. **Debut:** Fiji 3, Australia 16, 1984. **Caps:** 72. **Points:** 911 (17t,140c, 176p,9dg). 1995/96: 3 (47). **Born:** 25.10.63. **Height:** 5ft 10in. **Weight:** 12st 8lb. **Notes:** Bowed out of international rugby after 1995 World Cup as Australia's captain and the world's all-time leading scorer. Signed to play for English League One side Saracens in 1996/97. **Record** (72 – 911: 17t,140c,176p,9dg): **1984** Fj(3p),E(1t,2c,1p),I(1p,1dg),W(1t),S(3c,5p) **1985** C(1:7c,3p,2:3c,2p,1dg),NZ(1c,1p) **1986** It(6c,1p),F(1c,6p,1dg), Arg(1:4c,5p,2:1c,4p),NZ(1:1c,1p,2:3p,1dg,3:1c,4p) **1987** wc-E(1c,3p), US(6c,1p),J(5c),I(4c,3p),F(2c,3p,1dg),W(2c,2p,1dg). Arg(1:1t,2c,1p,2: 1c,3p) **1988** E(a1:6p,a2:1t,3c,2p),NZ(1:1p,3R:1c),E(b:2c,1p),S(3c,2p), It(1t,8c,1p) **1989** BL(1:4c,1p,1dg,2:1c,2p,3:1c,4p),NZ(1c,2p),F (1:2c, 4p,2:1c,3p) **1990** F(1:1c,5p,2:6c,4p,3:1c,2p,1dg),US(2t,8c),NZ(1:2p,2: 2p,1dg,3:1c,5p) **1991** W(a:2t,6c,1p),E(a:4c,4p),NZ(a1:2c,3p,a2:1p) wc-Arg (3c,2p),WS(3p),W(b:1t,4c,2p),I(1t,2c,1p),NZ(b:1c,2p),E(b:1c,2p) **1992** S(1:1t,1c,3p,2:1c,5p),NZ(1:2p,2:3p,3:2c,3p),SA(1c,3p),I **1993** T(1c),C(2c,3p),F(1:1c,2p,2) **1994** I(1:1t,1c,1p,2:1c,5p),It(1:1c,2p) **1995** Arg(1:2t,3c,4p,2:5p) wc-SA(1t,1c,2p),C(1t,3c,2p),E(1c,5p)

McCAHILL, Sean. Country: Ireland. **Position:** Centre. **Club:** Sunday's Well. **Debut:** Ireland 44, Fiji 8, 1995. **Caps:** 1. **Points:** 0. 1995/96: 1. **Born:** Auckland, 23.10.68. **Height:** 5ft 10in. **Weight:** 13st. **Occupation:** Electrician. **Notes:** Younger brother of All Black centre Bernie. Played for Munster in European Cup after making Irish debut as temporary replacement (18.11.95). **Record** (1): **1995** Fj(TR)

McCALL, Mark. **Country:** Ireland. **Position:** Centre, fly-half. **Club:** Bangor. **Debut:** New Zealand 24, Ireland 21, 1992. **Caps:** 4. **Points:** 0. 1995/96: 1. **Born:** 29.11.67. **Height:** 5ft 9in. **Weight:** 12st 7lb. **Occupation:** Public servant. **Notes:** 16th-minute replacement for fellow Ulsterman Maurice Field in 15–28 loss to England (Twickenham, 16.3.96). **Record (4): 1992** NZ(1R,2) **1994** W **1996** E(R)

McCALL, Rod. **Country:** Australia. **Position:** Lock. **State:** Queensland. **Debut:** France 15, Australia 32, 1989. **Caps:** 40. **Points:** 5 (1t). 1995/96: 3 (0). **Born:** 20.9.63. **Height:** 6ft 6in. **Weight:** 17st 5lb. **Occupation:** Sales director. **Notes:** Retired from Test rugby in 1995, having joined Steve Cutler as Australia's most-capped lock when he won his 40th cap in the Wallabies' 22–25 World Cup quarter-final loss to England (Cape Town, 11.6.95). **Record (40 – 5: 1t): 1989** F(1,2) **1990** F(1,2,3),US,NZ(1,2,3) **1991** W(a),E(a),NZ(a1,a2). wc-Arg,W(b),I,NZ(b),E(b) **1992** S(1,2),NZ (1,2,3),SA,I, W(1t) **1993** T,NZ,SA(1,2,3),C,F(1,2) **1994** It(2) **1995** Arg (1,2) wc-SA,R,E

McLEOD, Scott. **Country:** New Zealand. **Position:** Centre. **Province:** Waikato. **Debut:** New Zealand 51, Western Samoa 10, 1996. **Caps:** 2. **Points:** 5 (1t). 1995/96: 2 (5). **Born:** 28.2.73. **Height:** 6ft 3in. **Weight:** 15st 10lb. **Notes:** Made his reputation with 15 tries for Waiakto in 1995. Broke into All Black midfield early in 1996 in absence of Walter Little; marked debut with try (Napier, 7.6.96). **Record (2 – 5:1t): 1996** WS(1t), S(1)

MALLETT, John. **Country:** England. **Position:** Prop. **Club:** Bath. **Debut:** England 44, Western Samoa 22, 1995. **Caps:** 1. **Points:** 0. 1995/96: 1. **Born:** 28.5.70. **Height:** 6ft 2in. **Weight:** 17st 6lb. **Occupation:** Student teacher. **Notes:** Ex-England Colts captain (1989), who made senior debut at 1995 World Cup as 24th-minute replacement for Graham Rowntree (Durban, 4.6.95). **Record (1): 1995** wc-WS(a:R)

MARSHALL, Justin. **Country:** New Zealand. **Position:** Scrum-half. **Province:** Canterbury. **Debut:** France 12, New Zealand 37, 1995. **Caps:** 4. **Points:** 10 (2t). 1995/96: 4 (10). **Born:** 5.8.73. **Height:** 5ft 10½in. **Weight:** 13st 9lb. **Notes:** Succeeded Graeme Bachop post-1995 Bledisloe Cup, touring France and making debut in second Test (Paris, 18.11.95). Scored tries in first two starts. **Record (4 – 10:2t): 1995** F(2) **1996** WS(1t),S(1:1t,2)

MESNEL, Franck. **Country:** France. **Position:** Centre, fly-half. **Club:** Racing Club. **Debut:** France 7, New Zealand 19, 1986. **Caps:** 56. **Points:** 41 (8t, 3dg). 1995/96: 2. **Born:** 30.6.61. **Height:** 5ft 11in. **Weight:** 14st 2lb. **Occupation:** Architect. **Notes:** One of rugby's most stylish players, who ended two years in Test wilderness when he steered France to World Cup wins over Cote d'Ivoire and England in South Africa. **Record (56 – 41: 8t, 3dg): 1986** NZ(1R,2) **1987** W(1t),E(1dg),S(a:1dg),I wc-S(b),Z,Fj,A,NZ. R(b) **1988** E,Arg(a1,a2),Arg(b1,b2),R **1989** I,W(1dg),E,S,NZ(1),A(1,2) **1990** E,S,I(2t), A(2,3:1t),NZ(1,2) **1991** S,I,W(a),E(a:1t),R(a),US(1:1t, 2:1t),W(b) wc-R(b),Fj,C,E(b) **1992** W,E,S,I,SA(1,2) **1993** E(R),W **1995** I,R wc-IC,E(b)

470

MILNE, Kenneth. **Country:** Scotland. **Position:** Hooker. **Club:** Heriot's FP. **Debut:** Scotland 23, Wales 7, 1989. **Caps:** 39. **Points:** 12 (3t). 1995/96: 3(0). **Born:** 1.12.61. **Height:** 6ft. **Weight:** 15st 2lb. **Occupation:** Sales manager. **Notes:** Scotland's most-capped hooker after Hawick legend Colin Deans (52), Kenny retired from Test rugby after Scotland's 1995 World Cup run ended in quarter-finals. **Record** (39 – 12: 3t): **1989** W,E,I,F,Fj(1t),R **1990** I, F,W,E,NZ(2),Arg(2t) **1991** F,W,E wc-Z **1992** E,I,F,W,A(1) **1993** I,F,W,E. Lions-NZ(1). NZ **1994** W,E,I,F,SA **1995** C,I,F(a),W,E wc-T,F(b),NZ

MOORE, Brian. **Country:** England. **Position:** Hooker. **Club:** Richmond. **Debut:** England 21, Scotland 12, 1987. **Caps:** 64. **Points:** 4 (1t). 1995/96: 5 (0). **Born:** 11.1.62. **Height:** 5ft 9in. **Weight:** 14st 3lb. **Occupation:** Commercial litigations solicitor. **Notes:** England's most-capped hooker, who came out of retirement to join Richmond as an amateur in 1996/97. **Record** (64 – 4: 1t): **1987** S wc-A, J, W(b) **1988** F, W, S, I(1,2), A(a1,a2), Fj, A(b) **1989** S, I(1t), F, W, Ro, Fj. Lions-A(1,2,3) **1990** I, F, W, S, Arg(a1,a2) **1991** W, S(a), I, F(a), Fj, A(a) wc-NZ, It, F(b), S(b), A(b) **1992** S, I, F, W, SA **1993** F, W, S, I. Lions-NZ(2,3). NZ **1994** S, I, F, W, SA(1,2), R, C **1995** I, F(a), W, S wc-Arg, It, WS(R), A, NZ, F

MORRIS, Dewi. **Country:** England. **Position:** Scrum-half. **Club:** Orrell. **Debut:** England 28, Australia 19, 1988. **Caps:** 26. **Points:** 21 (5t). 1995/96: 5 (0). **Born:** 9.2.64. **Height:** 6ft. **Weight:** 13st 7lb. **Occupation:** Leisurewear sales executive. **Notes:** Star of England's 1995 World Cup campaign, Dewi then retired, three caps short of Richard Hill's English record for a No.9. **Record** (26 – 21: 5t): **1988** A(1t) **1989:** S, I, F, W **1992** S(1t), I(1t), F(1t), W, C, SA(1t) **1993** F, W, S, I. Lions-NZ(1,2,3) **1994** F, W, SA(1,2), R **1995** S(TR) wc-Arg, WS(a), A, NZ, F(b)

MORRISON, Iain. **Country:** Scotland. **Position:** Flanker. **Club:** London Scottish. **Debut:** Scotland 15, Ireland 3, 1993. **Caps:** 15. **Points:** 0. 1995/96: 3. **Born:** 14.12.62. **Height:** 6ft 1in. **Weight:** 15st 7lb. **Occupation:** Money broker. **Notes:** An integral part of Scotland's outstanding back row in 1995, Iain produced arguably his best ever rugby in his final season before retiring after 1995 World Cup. **Record** (15): **1993** I, F, W, E **1994** W, SA **1995** C, I, F(a), W, E, R wc-T, F(b), NZ

MULLIN, Brendan. **Country:** Ireland. **Position:** Centre. **Club:** Blackrock College. **Debut:** Ireland 9, Australia 16, 1984. **Caps:** 55. **Points:** 72 (17t,1c). 1995/96: 4 (0). **Born:** 31.10.63. **Height:** 6ft 1in. **Weight:** 13st 3lb. **Occupation:** Stockbroker. **Notes:** Came out of 33 months retirement in 1994/95 to extend Irish try-scoring record to 17. Hung up boots a second time after 1995 World Cup. **Record** (55 – 72: 17t,1c): **1984** A **1985** S,W, E(1t) **1986** F,W,E(1t),S,R(2t) **1987** E,S,F,W(a:1t) wc-W(b),C,T(3t),A **1988** S(1t),F,W,E(a,b)WS(1t),It **1989** F(1t),W,E,S(2t),NZ. Lions-A(1) **1990** E,S,W,Arg **1991** F,W(1t),E,S(a:1t),Na(1:1c,2) wc-J,S(b),A **1992** W, E,S **1994** US **1995** E,S(1t),F(a),W(a:1t),It wc-NZ,J,W(b),F(b)

OLIVIER, Jacques. **Country:** South Africa. **Position:** Wing. **Club:** Tukkies. **Province:** Northern Transvaal. **Debut:** France 15, South Africa 20, 1992. **Caps:** 6. **Points:** 0. 1995/96: 3. **Born:** Pretoria, 13.11.68. **Height:** 5ft 10in. **Weight:** 13st 3lb. **Notes:** Quit codes for Rugby League 'down under' after reviving Test career with appearances in each of South Africa's last three internationals of 1995. **Record** (6): **1992** F(1,2), E **1995** W, It(R), E

O'MAHONY, Darragh. Country: Ireland. **Position:** Wing. **Club:** Black rock. **Debut:** Ireland 12, France 36, 1995. **Caps:** 1. **Points:** 0. 1995/96: 1. **Born:** 18.8.72. **Height:** 5ft 10in. **Weight:** 13st 11lb. **Occupation:** Student. **Notes:** Handed debut in World Cup quarter-final (Durban, 10.6.95) after selectors dropped off-form Richard Wallace. One of two uncapped in squad. **Record (1): 1995** F(b)

O'SHEA, Conor. Country: Ireland. **Position:** Fullback. **Club:** London Irish. **Debut:** Ireland 25, Romania 3, 1993. **Caps:** 13. **Points:** 14 (1c,3p, 1dg). 1995/96: 3. **Born:** 21.10.70. **Height:** 6ft 2in. **Weight:** 14st 6lb. **Occupation:** Bank executive. **Notes:** Lost Ireland place in 1995/96 after three appearances in 1995 World Cup. **Record (13 – 14:1c,3p, 1dg): 1993** R **1994** F,W,E,S,A(1:1p,2:1c,1p,1dg),US(1p) **1995** E,S wc-J,W(b),F(b)

PAYNE, Sam. Country: Australia. **Position:** Scrum-half. **Club:** Eastern Suburbs. **State:** NSW. **Debut:** Australia 42, Wales 3, 1996. **Caps:** 1. **Points:** 0. 1995/96: 1. **Born:** 11.11.71. **Height:** 5ft 9in. **Weight:** 11st 11lb. **Occupation:** Sales rep. **Notes:** Ousted Gregan from Wallaby No.9 jersey for second Test vs Wales last summer after series of impressive displays for Waratahs and Australia B in 51–41 defeat of Wales (12.6.96). **Record (1): 1996** W(2)

PROSSER, Greg. Country: Wales. **Position:** Lock. **Club:** Pontypridd. **Debut:** Wales 9, New Zealand 34, 1995. **Caps:** 1. **Points:** 0. 1995/96: 1. **Born:** 21.5.66. **Height:** 6ft 6in. **Weight:** 17st 4lb. **Occupation:** South Wales Police officer. **Notes:** Made debut in Johannesburg (31.5.95), having risen to prominence with Wales A and in Pontypridd's impressive 1994/95 campaign. **Record (1): 1995** wc-NZ

ROSSOUW, Chris. Country: South Africa. **Position:** Hooker. **Province:** Transvaal. **Debut:** South Africa 60, Western Samoa 8, 1995. **Caps:** 5. **Points:** 10 (2t). 1995/96: 5. **Born:** 14.9.68. **Height:** 5ft 11½in. **Weight:** 17st 5lb. **Occupation:** Importer/exporter. **Notes:** Came into Bok World Cup team after James Dalton had been sent off. Try on debut (Jo'burg, 13.4.95). **Record (5 – 10: 2t): 1995** WS(a:1t) wc-R, WS(b:1t), F, NZ

ROY, Stuart. Country: Wales. **Position:** Lock. **Club:** Cardiff. **Debut:** Wales 57, Japan 10, 1995. **Caps:** 1. **Points:** 0. 1995/96: 1. **Born:** 25.12.68. **Height:** 6ft 6in. **Weight:** 17st 8lb. **Occupation:** Medical practitioner. **Notes:** Given debut as 72nd-minute replacement for Derwyn Jones (Bloemfontein, 27.5.95), having helped Cardiff win 1994/95 Heineken League title. **Record (1): 1995** wc-J(R)

SCHOLTZ, Christiaan. Country: South Africa. **Position:** Centre. **Province:** Transvaal. **Debut:** South Africa 42, Argentina 22, 1994. **Caps:** 4. **Points:** 0. 1994/95: 4. **Born:** 22.10.70. **Height:** 6ft 1½in. **Weight:** 15st 5lb. **Occupation:** Antique dealer. **Notes:** Helped Transvaal beat England (28.5.94). Bok debut in Port Elizabeth (8.10.94). Started three games in World Cup. **Record (4): 1994** Arg(1) **1995** wc-R, C, WS(b)

SCHULER, Kevin. Country: New Zealand. **Position:** No.8, flanker. **Province:** North Harbour. **Debut:** New Zealand 27, Australia 17, 1990. **Caps:** 4. **Points:** 0. 1994/95: 2. **Born:** 21.3.67. **Height:** 6ft 3in. **Weight:** 16st 6lb. **Occupation:** Japan-based. **Notes:** Made first Test start in 145–17 rout of Japan (Bloemfontein, 4.6.95), almost five years after winning first cap. **Record (4): 1990** A(2R) **1992** A(R) **1995** wc-I(R), J

SELLA, Philippe. **Country:** France. **Position:** Centre. **Club:** Saracens.
Debut: Romania 13, France 9, 1982. **Caps:** 111. **Points:** 125 (30t).
1995/96: 5 (0). **Born:** 14.2.62. **Height:** 5ft 11in. **Weight:** 13st 4lb. **Notes:**
The world's most-capped player, Philippe finally declared on 111 and
came to England in search of a new challenge: teaming up with the world's
top Test points scorer, Aussie Michael Lynagh, at wealthy Saracens.
Record (111 – 125: 30t): **1982** R,Arg(1:2t,2) **1983** E(1t),S,I,W,A(1,2),R
1984 I(1t),W(1t),E(1t),S,NZ(1,2),R(1t) **1985** E,S,I,W,Arg(1,2) **1986**
S(1t),I(1t),W(1t),E(1t),R(a:1t),Arg(1,2:1t),A(1t),NZ,R(b),NZ(1:1t,2)
1987 W,E(1t),S,I wc-S(1t),R(1t),Z(R),Fj,A(1t),NZ **1988** E,S,I(1t),W,Arg
(a1,a2),Arg(b1,b2:1t),R **1989** I,W,E,S,NZ(1,2),BL,A(1,2) **1990** W(1t),E,
S,I,A(1,2,3) **1991** W(1t),E,R,US(1,2),W,Fj(2t),C,E **1992** W,E,S,I,Arg
(b:1t) **1993** E,S,I(1t),W,R(a),SA(1,2),R(b:1t),A(1,2) **1994** I,W(1t),E,S,
C(a),NZ(1,2),C(b:1t) **1995** W,E(a),S(a),I(a) wc-T,S(b),I(b),SA,E(b)

SLATTERY, Peter. **Country:** Australia. **Position:** Scrum-half. **State:**
Queensland. **Debut:** Australia 67, USA 9, 1990. **Caps:** 17. **Points:** 8 (2t).
1995/96: 2 (0). **Born:** 6.6.65. **Height:** 5ft 9in. **Weight:** 12st 4lb. **Occupation:** Sports administrator. **Notes:** Halfback partner of Michael Lynagh
for state and country, Peter retired from Test rugby after making two
appearances in the 1995 World Cup. **Record** (17 – 8: 2t): **1990** US(R:1t)
1991 W(a:R), E(a:R). wc-WS(1t), W(b:1t), I(R) **1992** I, W **1993** T, C,
F(1,2) **1994** I(1,2), It(1R) **1995** wc-C, R(R)

STARK, Derek. **Country:** Scotland. **Position:** Wing. **Club:** Melrose.
Debut: Scotland 15, Ireland 3, 1993. **Caps:** 5. **Points:** 5 (1t). 1995/96: 1 (0).
Born: 13.4.66. **Height:** 6ft 2in. **Weight:** 13st 12lb. **Occupaton:** Chef.
Notes: Ended three years in the international wilderness when he came on
as 25th-minute replacement for Ian Jardine in Scotland's 12–36 second
Test defeat by New Zealand (Auckland, 22.6.96). **Record** (5 – 5: 1t): **1993**
I(1t), F, W, E **1996** NZ(2R)

STEWART, Barry. **Country:** Scotland. **Position:** Prop. **Club:** Edinburgh
Academicals. **Debut:** New Zealand 36, Scotland 12, 1996. **Caps:** 1. **Points:**
0. 1995/96: 1 (0). **Born:** 3.6.75. **Height:** 6 ft 1½in. **Weight:** 16st 3lb.
Occupation: Student. **Notes:** Former Scottish Schools player who made
his Test bow in New Zealand last summer, coming in for Peter Wright in
the second Test (Auckland, 22.6.96). **Record** (1): **1996** NZ(2)

STRACHAN, Ant. **Country:** New Zealand. **Position:** Scrum-half.
Province: North Harbour. **Debut:** New Zealand 54, World XV 26, 1992.
Caps: 11. **Points:** 8 (2t). 1995/96: 2 (0). **Born:** 7.6.66. **Height:** 5ft 9in.
Weight: 13st. **Notes:** Ended two years out in the cold when he was recalled
for the 1995 World Cup, where he played in the 145–17 defeat of hapless
Japan (4.6.95), then came on as temporary replacement for Graeme
Bachop in World Cup final (24.6.95). **Record** (11 – 8: 2t): **1992** Wd(2:1t,
3), I(1, 2:1t), A(1,2,3), SA **1993** BL(1) **1995** wc-J, SA(TR)

TAYLOR, Mark. **Country:** Wales. **Position:** Centre. **Club:** Pontypool.
Debut: Wales 12, South Africa 20, 1994. **Caps:** 4. **Points:** 0. 1995/96: 1.
Born: 27.2.73. **Height:** 6ft 1in. **Weight:** 13st 10lb. **Occupation:** Trainee
accountant. **Notes:** Blooded in Test arena while playing for a Pontypool
side that was being regularly trounced; added fourth cap as replacement
for Gareth Thomas vs Boks (2.9.95). **Record** (4): **1994** SA **1995** F, E. SA

TECHOUEYRES, William. **Country:** France. **Position:** Wing. **Club:** Bordeaux University. **Debut:** France 14, England 18, 1994. **Caps:** 3. **Points:** 5 (1t). 1995/96: 1 (5). **Born:** 12.2.66. **Height:** 6ft. **Weight:** 13st 6lb. **Occupation:** Cafe owner. **Notes:** Celebrated his third cap with a try in 54–18 defeat of Cote d'Ivoire at World Cup in South Africa (30.5.95). **Record** (3 – 5: 1t): **1994** E, S **1995** wc-IC(1t)

TUNE, Ben. **Country:** Australia. **Position:** Wing. **State:** Queensland. **Debut:** Australia 42, Wales 3, 1996. **Caps:** 1. **Points:** 0. 1995/96: 1 (0). **Born:** 1976. **Notes:** Wallaby starlet who earned Test recognition with eight-try Super-12 campaign for Queensland Reds. Unavailable for first Test vs Wales because of a shoulder injury, but drafted into the side at the expense of Alistair Murdoch for second Test. **Record** (1): **1996** W(2)

TWEED, Davy. **Country:** Ireland. **Position:** Lock. **Club:** Ballymena. **Debut:** Ireland 7, France 25, 1995. **Caps:** 4. **Points:** 0. 1995/96: 1. **Born:** 13.11.59. **Height:** 6ft 5in. **Weight:** 18st 2lb. **Occupation:** Machine operator. **Notes:** Became oldest-ever Irish debutant (aged 35) when called up at the 11th hour for Ireland's 7–25 loss to France (Dublin, 4.3.95). Retained for World Cup, where he played in 50–28 win over Japan (Bloemfontein, 31.5.95). **Record** (4): **1995** F, W, E wc-J

VAN DER LINDE, Toks **Country:** South Africa. **Position:** Loosehead Prop. **Province:** Western Province. **Debut:** Italy 21, South Africa 40, 1995. **Caps:** 2. **Points:** 0. 1995/96: 2. **Born:** 30.12.69. **Height:** 6ft 3in. **Weight:** 19st 5lb. **Occupation:** Sales rep. **Notes:** Former Natal and Free State player who broke into Springbok side on post-World Cup mini-tour to Italy and England, wearing the No.1 jersey in both Tests. **Record** (2): **1995** It, E

VENTER, Brendan. **Country:** South Africa. **Position:** Centre. **Province:** Orange Free State. **Debut:** South Africa 15, England 32, 1994. **Caps:** 11. **Points:** 5 (1t). 1995/96: 4 (0). **Born:** 29.12.69. **Height:** 6ft ½in. **Weight:** 14st 4lb. **Occupaton:** Doctor. **Notes:** Emerged on the back of Free State's run to 1994 Currie Cup final. Replaced James Small in 1995 World Cup final. **Record** (11 – 5: 1t): **1994** E(1,2), NZ(1,2,3:1t), Arg(1,2) **1995** wc-R, C, WS(b:R), NZ(R)

VIARS, Sebastien. **Country:** France. **Position:** Wing, fullback. **Club:** Brive. **Debut:** Wales 9, France 12, 1992. **Caps:** 14. **Points:** 115 (7t,16c,17p). 1995/96: 1 (5). **Born:** 24.6.71. **Height:** 6ft ½in. **Weight:** 13st 5lb. **Notes:** Prolific points-scorer for France, but lacks the consistency of performance to break the Saint-Andre–NTamack monopoly in the wing slots. **Record** (14 – 115: 7t, 16c, 17p): **1992** W(1p), E(1t,1c,1p), I(2t,5c,2p), R(1c,1p), Arg(a1:1t,4p, a2:1t,3c,3p), SA(1:1c,1p), Arg(b:1c,1p) **1993** R(a:4c,3p) **1994** C(a:R), NZ(1TR) **1995** E(aR:1t) wc-IC(1t)

VOYLE, Michael. **Country:** Wales. **Position:** Lock, flanker. **Club:** Llanelli **Debut:** Australia 56, Wales 25, 1996. **Caps:** 1. **Points:** 0. 1995/96: 1 (0). **Born:** 3.1.70. **Height:** 6ft 6in. **Weight:** 16st 12lb. **Occupation:** Production worker. **Notes:** Capped on tour 'down under' last summer, coming on as an early bloodbin replacement for Gwyn Jones in the first Test (Brisbane, 8.6.96) before later doing likewise for Derwyn Jones. **Record** (1): **1996** A(1)

WALTON, Peter. Country: Scotland. **Position:** Flanker. **Club:** Newcastle. **Debut:** Scotland 14, England 15, 1994. **Caps:** 6. **Points:** 10 (2t). 1995/96: 1 (10). **Born:** 3.6.69. **Height:** 6ft 3in. **Weight:** 18st. **Occupation:** Livestock fieldsman. **Notes:** A former Scottish Schools captain who has had to struggle for Test exposure, what with Rob Wainwright competing for the No.6 jersey. Marked his one outing in 1995/96 with two tries in 89–0 World Cup rout of Cote d'Ivoire. **Record** (6 – 10: 2t): **1994** E, I, F, Arg(1,2) **1995** wc-IC(2t)

WEST, Richard. Country: England. **Position:** Lock. **Club:** Richmond. **Debut:** England 44, Western Samoa 22, 1995. **Caps:** 1. **Points:** 0. 1995/96: 1. **Born:** 28.3.71. **Height:** 6ft 11in. **Weight:** 20st. **Occupation:** Business/property manager, Hartpury Agricultural College. **Notes:** Surprise World Cup pick ahead of Nigel Redman, but impressed on debut (Durban, 4.6.95). **Record** (1): **1995** wc-WS

WILLIAMS, Aled. Country: Wales. **Position:** Fly-half. **Club:** Swansea. **Debut:** Namibia 30, Wales 34, 1990. **Caps:** 2. **Points:** 0. 1995/96: 1. **Born:** 26.1.64. **Height:** 5ft 5in. **Weight:** 12st 2lb. **Occupation:** Groundwork surveyor. **Notes:** Made debut as last-minute replacement in Windhoek (9.6.90), but had to wait more than five years for second cap, as 23rd-minute replacement for centre Nigel Davies in the 19–15 defeat of Fiji (Cardiff, 11.11.95). **Record** (2): **1990** Na(2R) **1995** Fj(R)

*England wing Jon Sleightholme carves his way through
the Irish defence on his angled try-scoring run.*

MAJOR FIXTURES 1996/97

August 1996
17	Scotland vs Barbarians	Edinburgh
24	Wales vs Barbarians	Cardiff

October 1996
5	ITALY vs WALES	Rome
30	Scotland A vs Australia	Galashiels

November 1996
2	Comb Scot Districts vs Australia	Glasgow
5	Scottish District XV vs Australia	Perth
9	SCOTLAND vs AUSTRALIA	Edinburgh
	ARGENTINA vs SOUTH AFRICA (i)	Buenos Aires
13	Leinster vs Australia	Dublin
16	ARGENTINA vs SOUTH AFRICA (ii)	Buenos Aires
	Ulster vs Australia	Belfast
20	Connacht vs Australia	Galway
21/22	World Cup Sevens (qualifying)	Dubai
23	ENGLAND vs ITALY	Twickenham
	Munster vs Australia	Limerick
26	Ireland A vs Australia	Belfast
30	IRELAND vs AUSTRALIA	Dublin
	FRANCE vs SOUTH AFRICA (i)	TBA
	England vs NZ Barbarians	Twickenham

December 1996
7	FRANCE vs SOUTH AFRICA (ii)	Paris
	Barbarians vs Australia	Twickenham
14	ENGLAND vs ARGENTINA	Twickenham
15	WALES vs SOUTH AFRICA	Cardiff

January 1997
4	European Club Cup final	TBC
18	SCOTLAND vs WALES	Edinburgh
	IRELAND vs FRANCE	Dublin

February 1997
1	ENGLAND vs SCOTLAND	Twickenham
	WALES vs IRELAND	Cardiff
15	IRELAND vs ENGLAND	Dublin
	FRANCE vs WALES	Paris

March 1997

1	ENGLAND vs FRANCE	Twickenham
	SCOTLAND vs IRELAND	Edinburgh
15	WALES vs ENGLAND	Cardiff
	FRANCE vs SCOTLAND	Paris

May 1997

24	Eastern Province XI vs British Lions	Port Elizabeth
28	Western Province vs British Lions	Cape Town
31	Free State vs British Lions	Bloemfontein

June 1997

4	Transvaal vs British Lions	Johannesburg
7	Northern Transvaal vs British Lions	Pretoria
11	SE Transvaal vs British Lions	Witbank
14	Natal vs British Lions	Durban
17	Emerging Springboks vs British Lions	Wellington
21	South Africa vs British Lions (i)	Cape Town
24	Border vs British Lions	East London
28	South Africa vs British Lions (ii)	Durban

July 1997

1	SA Barbarians vs British Lions	Welkom
5	South Africa vs British Lions (iii)	Johannesburg

Springbok scrum-half Joost van der Westhuizen evades England captain Will Carling at Twickenham. South Africa won 24–14.

INDEX

Accoceberry, Guy (France)
Andrew, Rob (England)
Andrews, Mark (South Africa)
Archer, Garath (England)
Armary, Louis (France)
Armstrong, Gary (Scotland)
Arnold, Paul (Wales)

Bachop, Graeme (New Zealand)
Back, Neil (England)
Barry, Liam (New Zealand)
Bayfield, Martin (England)
Bell, Jonathan (Ireland)
Benazzi, Abdelatif (France)
Benetton, Philippe (France)
Benezech, Laurent (France)
Bennett, M (Wales)
Bernat-Salles, Philippe (France)
Berty, David (France)
Bowen, Scott (Australia)
Bracken, Kyran (England)
Bradley, Michael (Ireland)
Brewer, Michael (New Zealand)
Brink, Robbie (South Africa)
Brooke, Robin (New Zealand)
Brooke, Zinzan (New Zealand)
Brouzet, Olivier (France)
Brown, Olo (New Zealand)
Bunce, Frank (New Zealand)
Burke, Matthew (Australia)
Burke, Paul (Ireland)
Burnell, Paul (Scotland)

Cabannes, Laurent (France)
Califano, Christian (France)
Callard, Jonathan (England)
Campan, Olivier (France)
Campbell, Stewart (Scotland)
Campese, David (Australia)
Caputo, Marco (Australia)
Carbonneau, Philippe (France)
Carling, Will (England)
Carminati, Alain (France)
Castaignede, Thomas (France)
Castel, Richard (France)
Catt, Michael (England)
Cecillon, Marc (France)

Chalmers, Craig (Scotland)
Cigagna, Albert (France)
Clarke, Allen (Ireland)
Clarke, Ben (England)
Clement, Anthony (Wales)
Clohessy, Peter (Ireland)
Coker, Troy (Australia)
Corkery, David (Ireland)
Costello, Victor (Ireland)
Costes, Arnaud (France)
Cronin, Damian (Scotland)
Crowley, Dan (Australia)
Culhane, Simon (New Zealand)
Cullen, Christian (New Zealand)

Dalton, James (South Africa)
Daly, Tony (Australia)
Davidson, Jeremy (Ireland)
Davies, Adrian (Wales)
Davies, John (Wales)
Davies, Leigh (Wales)
Davies, Nigel (Wales)
Davies, Stuart (Wales)
Dawe, Graham (England)
Dawson, Matthew (England)
De Glanville, Philip (England)
Delaigue, Yann (France)
De Rougemont, Marc (France)
Deylaud, Christophe (France)
Dispagne, Sylvain (France)
Dods, Michael (Scotland)
Dourthe, Richard (France)
Dowd, Craig (New Zealand)
Du Randt, Pieter (South Africa)

Eales, John (Australia)
Ellis, Marc (New Zealand)
Elwood, Eric (Ireland)
Ericksson, Ronnie (Scotland)
Evans, David (Wales)
Evans, Ieuan (Wales)
Evans, Ricky (Wales)

Field, Maurice (Ireland)
Finegan, Owen (Australia)
Fitzpatrick, Sean (New Zealand)
Foley, Anthony (Ireland)

Foley, Michael (Australia)
Forster, Stuart (New Zealand)
Francis, Neil (Ireland)
Fulcher, Gabriel (Ireland)

Gallart, Philippe (France)
Galthie, Fabien (France)
Gavin, Tim (Australia)
Geoghegan, Simon (Ireland)
Gibbs, Andrew (Wales)
Glas, Stephane (France)
Gonzales, Jean-Michel (France)
Graou, Stephane (France)
Grayson, Paul (England)
Gregan, George (Australia)
Griffiths, Mike (Wales)
Guiraud, Herve (France)
Guscott, Jerry (England)

Hall, Mike (Wales)
Halpin, Garrett (Ireland)
Halvey, Eddie (Ireland)
Harry, Richard (Australia)
Harthill, Mark (Australia)
Hastings, Gavin (Scotland)
Hastings, Scott (Scotland)
Hay, Jim (Scotland)
Henderson, Paul (New Zealand)
Hendriks, Pieter (South Africa)
Herbert, Danny (Australia)
Hewitt, Norm (New Zealand)
Hill, Simon (Wales)
Hilton, David (Scotland)
Hogan, Niall (Ireland)
Hopley, Damian (England)
Horan, Tim (Australia)
Howard, Pat (Australia)
Howley, Robert (Wales)
Hueber, Aubin (France)
Humphreys, David (Ireland)
Humphreys, Jonathan (Wales)
Hunter, Ian (England)
Hurley, Henry (Ireland)
Hurter, Marius (South Africa)

Ibanez, Raphael (France)
Ieremia, Alama (New Zealand)

James, Dafydd (Wales)
Jardine, Ian (Scotland)
Jenkins, Garin (Wales)
Jenkins, Neil (Wales)
Jirdana, Jean-Louis (France)
Johns, Paddy (Ireland)

Johnson, Gavin (South Africa)
Johnson, Martin (England)
Joiner, Craig (Scotland)
Jones, Derwyn (Wales)
Jones, Gareth (Wales)
Jones, Gwyn (Wales)
Jones, Ian (New Zealand)
Jones, Michael (New Zealand)
Jones, Robert (Wales)
Joseph, Jamie (New Zealand)
Joubert, Andre (South Africa)

Kearns, Phil (Australia)
Kingston, Terry (Ireland)
Kronfeld, Josh (New Zealand)
Kruger, Ruben (South Africa)

Labrousse, Thierry (France)
Lacroix, Thierry (France)
Larsen, Blair (New Zealand)
Laubscher, Tommie (South Africa)
Leonard, Jason (England)
Le Roux, Hennie (South Africa)
Lewis, Andrew (Wales)
Lewis, Emyr (Wales)
Lievremont, Marc (France)
Little, Jason (Australia)
Little, Walter (New Zealand)
Llewellyn, Gareth (Wales)
Loader, Christian (Wales)
Loe, Richard (New Zealand)
Logan, Kenny (Scotland)
Lomu, Jonah, (New Zealand)
Lynagh, Michael (Australia)

McBride, Denis (Ireland)
McCahill, Sean (Ireland)
McCall, Mark (Ireland)
McCall, Rod (Australia)
McKenzie, Ewen (Australia)
McKenzie, Kevin (Scotland)
McLeod, Scott (New Zealand)
McQuilkin, Kurt (Ireland)
Mallett, John (England)
Manu, Daniel (Australia)
Marshall, Justin (New Zealand)
Mason, Simon (Ireland)
Mehrtens, Andrew (New Zealand)
Merle, Olivier (France)
Mesnel, Franck (France)
Milne, Kenny (Scotland)
Moore, Andrew Paul (Wales)
Moore, Andrew Philip (Wales)

Moore, Brian (England)
Morris, Dewi (England)
Morrison, Iain (Scotland)
Mulder, Japie (South Africa)
Mullin, Brendan (Ireland)
Mustoe, Lyndon (Wales)

NTamack, Emile (France)

Ofahengaue, Willie (Australia)
Ojomoh, Steve (England)
Olivier, Jacques (South Africa)
O'Mahony, Darragh (Ireland)
Osborne, Glen (New Zealand)
O'Shea, Conor (Ireland)

Patterson, Derrick (Scotland)
Payne, Sam (Australia)
Pelous, Fabien (France)
Penaud, Alain (France)
Perie, Michel (France)
Peters, Eric (Scotland)
Pienaar, Francois (South Africa)
Pini, Matt (Australia)
Popplewell, Nick (Ireland)
Proctor, Wayne (Wales)
Prosser, Greg (Wales)

Quinnell, Craig (Wales)

Redpath, Bryan (Scotland)
Regan, Mark (England)
Reid, Stuart (Scotland)
Richards, Dean (England)
Richter, Adriaan (South Africa)
Robinson, Andrew (England)
Rodber, Tim (England)
Roff, Joe (Australia)
Rolland, Alain (Ireland)
Rossouw, Chris (South Africa)
Roumat, Olivier (France)
Roux, Johan (South Africa)
Rowntree, Graham (England)
Roy, Stuart (Wales)
Rush, Eric (New Zealand)

Sadourny, Jean-Luc (France)
Saint-Andre, Philippe (France)
Saverimutto, Christian (Ireland)
Scholtz, Christiaan (South Africa)
Schuler, Kevin (New Zealand)
Sella, Philippe (France)
Shepherd, Rowen (Scotland)
Shiel, Graham (Scotland)
Slattery, Peter (Australia)

Sleightholme, Jonathan (England)
Small, James (South Africa)
Smith, Damien (Australia)
Smith, Ian (Scotland)
Stanger, Tony (Scotland)
Staples, Jim (Ireland)
Stark, Derek (Scotland)
Stewart, Barry (Scotland)
Strachen, Ant (New Zealand)
Straeuli, Rudi (South Africa)
Stransky, Joel (South Africa)
Strydom, Hannes (South Africa)
Swart, Balie (South Africa)

Tabua, Ilie (Australia)
Taylor, Hemi (Wales)
Taylor, Mark (Wales)
Techoueyres, William (France)
Thomas, Arwel (Wales)
Thomas, Gareth (Wales)
Thomas, William (Wales)
Tournaire, Franck (France)
Townsend, Gregor (Scotland)
Tune, Ben (Australia)
Tweed, Davy (Ireland)

Ubogu, Victor (England)
Underwood, Rory (England)
Underwood, Tony (England)

Van der Heerden, Fritz (South Africa)
Van der Linde, Toks (South Africa)
Van der Westhuizen, Joost (South Africa)
Venter, Brendan (South Africa)
Viars, Sebastien (France)
Voyle, Michael (Wales)

Wainwright, Rob (Scotland)
Wallace, Paul (Ireland)
Wallace, Richard (Ireland)
Walton, Peter (Scotland)
Waugh, Warwick (Australia)
Weir, George (Scotland)
West, Richard (England)
Wiese, Kobus (South Africa)
Williams, Chester (South Africa)
Williams, Aled (Wales)
Williams, Steve (Wales)
Wilson, David (Australia)
Wilson, Jeff (New Zealand)
Wintle, Matthew (Wales)
Wood, Keith (Ireland)
Woods, Niall (Ireland)
Wright, Peter (Scotland)